615.5 ODO

Accession no.
00949593

MCHT

Promoting TREATMENT ADHERENCE

ET Library
Educ.. & Training Li

D1387754

WITHDRAWN
FROM
STOCK

JET LIBRARY

To my wife, Jane, for all her support.

W. T. O.

*To my wife, Elizabeth, from whom I have learned
a great deal about self-management.*

E. R. L.

Promoting TREATMENT ADHERENCE

A Practical Handbook for Health Care Providers

William T. O'Donohue
University of Nevada, Reno

Eric R. Levensky
University of New Mexico

Editors

SAGE Publications
Thousand Oaks ▪ London ▪ New Delhi

Copyright © 2006 by Sage Publications, Inc.

All rights reserved. No part of this book may be reproduced or utilized in any form or by any means, electronic or mechanical, including photocopying, recording, or by any information storage and retrieval system, without permission in writing from the publisher.

For information:

Sage Publications, Inc.
2455 Teller Road
Thousand Oaks, California 91320
E-mail: order@sagepub.com

SAGE Publications Ltd
1 Oliver's Yard
55 City Road
London EC1Y 1SP
United Kingdom

Sage Publications India Pvt. Ltd.
B-42, Panchsheel Enclave
Post Box 4109
New Delhi 110 017 India

Printed in the United States of America

Library of Congress Cataloging-in-Publication Data

O'Donohue, William T.
Promoting treatment adherence : a practical handbook for health care providers / William T. O'Donohue,
Eric R. Levensky.
       p. cm.
Includes bibliographical references and index.
ISBN 1-4129-4482-1 (pbk)
   1. Patient compliance. I. Levensky, Eric R. II. Title.
R727.43.O36 2006
615.5—dc22

                                                2006004937

This book is printed on acid-free paper.

06   07   08   09   10   10 9 8 7 6 5 4 3 2 1

Acquisitions Editor:	Kassie Graves
Editorial Assistant:	Veronica Novak
Production Editor:	Kristen Gibson
Typesetter:	C&M Digitals (P) Ltd.
Cover Designer:	Candice Harman

Contents

Acknowledgments

We would like to thank several individuals who made significant contributions to this volume. First, much thanks to Arthur Pomponio, Senior Acquisitions Editor at Sage Publications, for making this volume possible and for his valuable guidance and support. Second, we have a great deal of gratitude for Veronica Novak, Editorial Assistant at Sage, for her enormous assistance in getting this text to press. Finally, we would like to thank Lauren Woodward for her extremely careful and diligent work in organizing the editorial process.

PART I

Introduction

1

Patient Adherence and Nonadherence to Treatments

An Overview for Health Care Providers

Eric R. Levensky

William T. O'Donohue

Advancements in health care have yielded numerous effective medical and behavioral health treatments which, if administered correctly, can help patients live healthier, happier, and longer lives. However, all too often the benefits of these treatments are not fully realized because of patient nonadherence. Virtually all medical and behavioral health treatments require at least some degree of behavior change on the part of the patient (e.g., coming to appointments, picking up medications, agreeing to have assessments and procedures performed), and many treatments require significant behavior change (e.g., following demanding and complex medication regimens; making dietary, activity, or other lifestyle changes; enduring sometimes aversive behavioral interventions such as self-monitoring or exposure). Unfortunately, many

patients fail to make these behavior changes fully. In the medical treatment literature, rates of nonadherence to treatment have generally been found to be 20 to 40% for acute illness regimens, 30 to 60% for chronic illness regimens, and 50 to 80% for preventative regimens (Christensen, 2004). Nonadherence to treatment has also been found to be high in the psychotherapy and behavior therapy literature, with premature treatment dropout rates ranging from 30 to 60% (Garfield, 1994; Reis & Brown, 1999; Wierzbicki & Pekarik, 1993) and average rates of failing to complete assigned homework of roughly 50% (Detweiler & Whisman, 1999; Spiegler & Guevremont, 2003).

The consequence of this nonadherence to medical and behavioral health treatments is often that the beneficial impact of potentially effective treatments is reduced, and substantial and unnecessary health, social, and financial costs are incurred (Bryant, Simons, & Thase, 1999; Christensen, 2004; Cleemput, Kesteloot, & DeGeest, 2002; Reis & Brown, 1999; Rogers & Bullman, 1995). Health consequences can include no change or worsening of the health problem, the development of collateral health problems, the provider being unable to evaluate the effectiveness of the treatment (and potentially prematurely terminating or over-prescribing the treatment), and death of the patient.

Financial consequences of patient nonadherence can include the cost of additional services and treatment (e.g., additional visits, medications, and tests; emergency room visits, and hospitalizations), as well as decreases in the quality of life and work productivity of the patient. Poor adherence to prescribed medications, for example, is estimated to cost over $100 billion each year in the United States through increasing health care use and decreasing patient productivity (Grahl, 1994).

Given that patient nonadherence is such a significant barrier to effective and efficient health care delivery, better understanding and addressing this problem is a crucial step toward improving patient care, outcomes, and treatment costs (e.g., Haynes, McDonald, Garg, & Montague, 2002). The purpose of this chapter is to provide a primer of the clinically relevant issues in the area of patient adherence, which are greatly expanded on in the subsequent chapters of this text. Specifically, this chapter will review definitions and types of adherence and nonadherence, methods of assessing adherence in clinical practice, factors associated with patient adherence and nonadherence, interventions to facilitate adherence, and conceptual issues and directions for future research in this area.

Definitions of Adherence and Nonadherence

Although there is much variability in the definition of the term *adherence*, it generally refers to the "*extent to which patients follow the instructions*

they are given for prescribed treatments" (Haynes et al., 2002, p. 2). In recent years, the term adherence has begun to be used in place of the more traditionally used term, *compliance*. This shift in terminology has occurred because many researchers and clinicians have believed that the term compliance suggests passivity and obedience on the part of patients, whereas the term adherence implies patient-provider collaboration and an active role of patients in their treatment (Rogers & Bullman, 1995). Nonadherence to treatments can take a number of forms:

- Not attending or coming late to appointments
- Not initiating a recommended treatment
- Not completing behavioral recommendations or homework (e.g., increases in physical activity, changes in diet, self-monitoring, in vivo exposure, relaxation exercises)
- Not taking medication as prescribed (e.g., taking too many or too few pills, taking medication at incorrect times, not following special dietary restrictions)
- Terminating the treatment prematurely

Clinical Assessment of Adherence

Clearly, an important component to addressing patient nonadherence to treatment is identifying its occurrence. With some aspects of treatment, the extent of patients' adherence can be directly observed by providers, such as with appointment attendance, in-session participation, or receiving provider-observed or -administered medication or procedures. However, most often providers do not have direct access to patients' adherence to treatment (e.g., following prescribed medication regimens, completing homework assignments, making changes in diet or exercise). In these cases, other methods of assessing patient adherence must be used.

There are a number of methods for measuring patients' adherence to treatment when it is not directly observable to the provider. These include obtaining patient report, conducting pill counts and assessing pharmacy records, using medication event monitoring system (MEMS) caps and other electronic measures (e.g., pedometers), and assessing biological indicators (e.g., blood levels) and health outcomes. Each of these methods has its relative strengths and weaknesses in terms of reliability, validity, utility, and practicality, and there is no clear gold standard for measuring adherence across settings.

Patient report is the most commonly used method of assessing adherence in clinical practice because this method is relatively quick, easy, and inexpensive. Common methods of obtaining patient report data include questionnaires, daily self-monitoring diaries, and interviews. Although patient report is the most practical method of adherence assessment, the accuracy of this method is often reduced by patients' hesitancy to report nonadherence and by limitations in patients' ability to recall past adherence-related behavior, often resulting in under-reporting of nonadherence (e.g., Rand & Weeks, 1998).

Despite these limitations, patient report can be a valuable clinical tool and has been found to be a predictor of adherence and clinical outcomes (Rand & Weeks, 1998; Stone, 2001). Additionally, an important advantage of the patient report method is that it can provide information about the patterns and timing of treatment-related behavior as well as information about barriers to adherence. This can be particularly the case when patients use daily self-monitoring diaries to record the time of day of their treatment-related behaviors (e.g., medication taking, diet, behavioral activation, homework) as well as reasons for nonadherence. Methods that can increase the accuracy of patient self-report of adherence include the following: using brief, structured questionnaires; asking patients to report on levels of nonadherence rather than on levels of adherence; specifying a specific time frame; assessing a recent time frame (e.g., the last 4 days); using cues to facilitate recall; having patients use a daily diary to record treatment-related behavior; and

reassuring patients that problems with adherence are normal, they will not be punished for non-adherence, and that accurate reporting of adherence problems is crucial for effective treatment (Andrews & Friedland, 2000; Dunbar-Jacob, Burke, & Puczynski, 1995; Rabkin & Chesney, 1999; Stone, 2001; Vitolins, Rand, Rapp, Ribisl, & Sevick, 2000). Chapter 2 of this volume provides further discussion of the use of patient self-report and other methods of assessing adherence in clinical settings, and also reviews in detail commonly used methods of assessing adherence in research settings.

Factors Related to Patient Nonadherence to Treatments

Because patient nonadherence has been found to be a significant barrier to effective health care delivery, there has been great interest in understanding the causes of this problem. Over the last several decades, hundreds of studies have been conducted in this area, and a wide range of factors have been found to be associated with adherence and nonadherence to treatments. This work has been an important step toward helping clinicians and researchers begin to better understand the nature of adherence and develop interventions to improve it. Table 1.1 summarizes clinically relevant factors that have empirical support for their association to nonadherence to treatments. In this table, factors have been organized into those related to (1) the patient, (2) the treatment, (3) the patient-provider relationship, (4) the clinical setting, and (5) the target problem or disease, because this can be a useful way of conceptualizing barriers to treatment adherence (Ickovicks & Meisler, 1997).

Although progress has been made in better understanding the nature and causes of nonadherence, much work remains to be done. To date, it has been difficult to make clear conclusions from the literature as to the specific factors or sets of factors that are the most significant determinants of patient nonadherence as well as

Table 1.1   Factors Related to Nonadherence to Treatments

Factors related to the patient

Lack of knowledge of treatment requirements

Cognitive, language, or literacy deficits

Lack of self-management and coping skills (e.g., self-control, problems solving)

Lack of tangible resources (e.g., financial, housing, transportation, time)

Stressful life events (e.g., death of loved one, ending of important relationship)

Problematic health and treatment-related beliefs (e.g., regarding need for treatment, seriousness of the health problem, efficacy of the treatment, relative costs and benefits of adhering, and adherence self-efficacy)

Mental health problems (e.g., depression, substance abuse, and psychotic symptoms)

Inadequate social support (e.g., emotional and instrumental support; reminder and encouragement of adherence)

Low motivation, apathy, or pessimism about health and future

Problematic past experiences with adherence (e.g., adverse effects, difficulty with adherence)

Fear of stigma for health problem

Treatment is an unwelcome reminder of illness

Problematic responses to slips in adherence

Factors related to the treatment regimen

High complexity and demands of the treatment (e.g., large number of pills to take, complex time-consuming homework assignments, substantial change in daily activities or diet)

Poor fit between treatment requirements and patient's lifestyle and daily activities (e.g., eating and sleeping patterns, work schedule, social life, other daily activities)

Long duration of the treatment

Frequent and severe side effects

High cost of treatment

Factors related to features of the disease or target problem

Health problem not serious or threatening to health

Long-term duration of health problem

Lack of symptoms or related problems experienced by patient

Symptoms of health problem interfere with adherence (e.g., problems with memory, mobility, or vision)

Factors related to the patient-provider relationship

Poor communication between patient and provider

Provider does not adequately assess problems with treatment and/or adherence

Patient has difficulty discussing problems with treatment and/or adherence

Patient uncertain about provider's ability to help

Patient lacks trust and/or comfort with provider

Patient and provider have differing conceptualizations or expectations of problem and/or treatment

Factors related to the clinical setting

Poor accessibility of services (e.g., availability of appointments/staff, hours of operation, waits for services)

Lack of continuity or cohesiveness of care

Unfriendly or unhelpful staff

NOTE: For recent detailed discussions of these factors and their empirical support see the following: Christensen (2004); DiMatteo (2004); Myers and Midence (1998); Roter et al. (1998); Scheel, Hanson, and Razzhavaikina (2004); Shumaker, Schron, Ockene, and McBee (1998); Vermeire, Hearnshaw, and Van Royen (2001); World Health Organization (2003).

the way in which factors interact to affect adherence. This has been partly because there have been wide variations across studies in definitions and measurements of examined factors as well as in the definitions and measurements of adherence. Additionally, factors that have been identified as related to adherence have generally accounted for small to moderate proportions of the variance in adherence and are not consistently related to adherence across comparable studies. For these reasons, using commonly identified barriers to predict whether any one patient will adhere has been, generally, unsuccessful (for reviews see Burke & Ockene, 2001; Christensen, 2004; Dunbar-Jacob & Mortimer-Stephens, 2001; Fincham, 1995; Ickovics & Meisler, 1997; Meichenbaum & Turk, 1987; Morris & Schulz, 1992; Myers & Midence, 1998; Pampallona, Bollini, Tibaldi, Kupelnick, & Munizza, 2002; Reis & Brown, 1999; Scheel, Hanson, & Razzhavaikina, 2004; Shumaker, Schron, Ockene, & McBee, 1998; Vermeire, Hearnshaw, & Van Royen, 2001; World Health Organization, 2003). A number of theoretical models have been developed to aid in the understanding and prediction of adherence- and nonadherence-related behaviors. However, to date these models have been relatively unsuccessful at meeting these goals (see Christensen, 2004).

Several important themes do emerge from this literature. First, as pointed out by Meichenbaum and Turk (1987), although these factors are listed in Table 1.1 as though each is a discrete construct, many are likely to be somewhat overlapping and should not be thought of as completely independent. Second, despite these overlaps, treatment adherence appears to be complex and multidetermined. Many different types of factors likely affect patients' adherence, including factors relating to the patient, disease/target problem, treatment, provider, and clinical setting/health care system. This is important to note because the common practice of focusing solely on the patient-related factors when considering barriers to adherence and interventions to improve it can neglect the often significant impact of other determinants. Third,

patients appear to be quite heterogeneous in terms of if and how any of these factors affect their adherence. Specific barriers are present for some patients and not for others (e.g., organizational problems, depression, problematic treatment-related beliefs), and for patients who do encounter specific barriers, some have adherence problems as a result of the barriers and some do not. Fourth, barriers to patients' adherence do not tend to be static. Rather, patients' adherence barriers will likely change over time. As will be discussed later in this chapter, the important implication of this is that adherence and adherence barriers need to be assessed regularly. And finally, given the high rate of patient nonadherence, and given the fact that a reliable method of predicting whether or not any one patient will adhere is yet to be developed, it is best to assume that *every* patient is at risk for nonadherence.

Putting these themes together suggests that improving patient adherence should involve conducting thorough and regular assessments of potential barriers to adherence for each patient and then developing tailored interventions that address these identified barriers. This will require an understanding of the potential barriers to patient adherence as well as the development of methods for reliably assessing these for a given patient. Despite the limitations of the barriers-to-adherence literature discussed above, it can serve to facilitate this process by orienting clinicians to potential barriers to patients' adherence as well as to potentially effective interventions. See Chapter 4 of this volume for further discussion of how this can be done systematically.

Interventions for Increasing Patient Adherence to Treatments

The problem of patient nonadherence to treatments has also produced a great deal of interest in the development and evaluation of methods for improving adherence. However, as is the case with the literature on factors relating to nonadherence, the literature on the effectiveness of interventions is somewhat unclear. This is partly because a relatively small number of studies have been conducted examining adherence interventions (for reviews of this literature, see Burke & Ockene, 2001; Christensen, 2004; Dunbar-Jacob & Mortimer-Stephens, 2001; Dunbar-Jacob & Schlenk, 1996; Falvo, 2004; Fincham, 1995; Haynes et al., 2002; Ickovics & Meisler, 1997; McDonald, Garg, & Haynes, 2002; Meichenbaum & Turk, 1987; Mullen, Green, & Persinger, 1985; Myers & Midence, 1998; Pampallona et al., 2002; Roter et al., 1998; Scheel et al., 2004; Shumaker et al., 1998; Vermeire et al., 2001). Additionally, many of these studies have been limited by methodological and other problems that have made interpreting their results difficult, including the use of measures of adherence that have problematic validity; a lack of random assignment or control groups; confounding variables; small sample sizes; short follow-up periods; a lack of detailed descriptions of the interventions; and differing definitions of adherence across studies. Matters have been complicated further because many studies have evaluated interventions that have consisted of multiple components as opposed to stand-alone techniques or strategies, making it difficult to identify specific strategies that may be most effective, and methodologically sound studies of similar interventions have produced different outcomes (e.g., Haynes, Wang, & Da Mota Gomes, 1987).

Despite the limitations of this research, the literature has produced some useful guidelines and information regarding the effects of adherence interventions. A detailed description of all the strategies included in adherence interventions that have support for their efficacy is well beyond the scope of this brief chapter. However, the primary strategies that have garnered empirical support as stand-alone interventions or as part of multicomponent interventions are summarized in Table 1.2.

Several considerations in interpreting this literature should be noted. First, the majority of

research in this area has focused on improving adherence to medical treatments, particularly focusing on medication regimens and keeping appointments. Second, as discussed earlier, strong conclusions regarding the extent and relative efficacy of any one of these interventions or strategies are limited by the problems in the literature described above. Third, a number of these interventions and strategies are somewhat overlapping and, therefore, any one should not necessarily be considered as discrete and independent from another.

In summarizing this literature, a number of important observations can be made. First, effective interventions have been delivered through a range of modes (e.g., face to face contact, phone, and mail), by a range of providers (e.g., physicians, nurses, adherence counselors, mental health providers, and computers), with a range of adherence targets (e.g., medication regimen adherence, appointment keeping, treatment retention, and behavioral assignments), and with a range of patient populations (e.g., patients with chronic and acute medical and mental illness, patients in need of preventative health treatment). Second, no single adherence-promoting strategy appears to be clearly most effective across patients, conditions, and clinical settings. However, interventions found to significantly improve adherence generally include educational, social support, cognitive-behavioral, and/or behavioral components. Third, multicomponent interventions are generally more effective than single-strategy interventions, and interventions that involve multiple sessions or follow-ups tend to be more effective in sustaining adherence over time than one-time interventions. Fourth, the impact of these interventions has been generally modest, with effect sizes rarely exceeding more than .34. These findings taken together are consistent with the notion that adherence involves a complex, multidetermined, and dynamic set of behaviors and circumstances that are not easily changed (for reviews of this literature, see Haynes et al., 2002; Malouff & Schutte, 2004; Morris & Schulz, 1992;

Table 1.2   Strategies for Increasing Patient Adherence to Treatments

Assessing readiness to begin treatment

Assessing past adherence patterns and current beliefs and concerns about the treatment
Discussing pros and cons of initiating treatment
Asking patient to rate confidence in carrying out treatment
Identifying potential barriers to treatment

Increasing treatment-related knowledge

Educating patient
　　–Nature of health problem and action of the treatment
　　–Specific behavioral requirements of the treatment (what, where, when, and how)
　　–Importance of adherence
　　–Nature and management of likely aversive effects of treatment (e.g., side effects)
Using simple, understandable language
Using visual aids
Providing all information in written form
Assessing comprehension
Having patient demonstrate proficiency

Increasing adherence skills

Providing information on treatment-related aids and training in their use
　　–Using cues for engaging in treatment behaviors (e.g., alarms, notes, and stickers)
　　–Linking treatment behaviors to daily activities such as morning and bedtime routines, meals,
　　　television shows, etc.
　　–Self-monitoring (e.g., tracking treatment-related behaviors)
　　–Using medication organizers (e.g., pill boxes), special medication packaging (e.g., blister
　　　packaging)
Teaching how to integrate treatment into routines
Teaching skills in anticipating, avoiding, and managing slips in adherence
Teaching problem-solving skills
Teaching skills for communicating with providers (e.g., asking questions, reporting problems)
Using role-playing behavioral rehearsal

Increasing resources and support

Referring to social services or social worker for assistance with accessing resources (e.g., financial,
　　housing, transportation, child care)
Reminder calls and letters
Increasing social support, including
　　–Increased support and help with adherence from friends or family
　　–Increased contact with staff (additional appointments, telephone "check-ins," home visits)
　　–Support groups or individual counseling

Increasing motivation

Maintaining warm, empathetic, genuine, collaborative, nonconfrontational stance
Having patient take an active role in treatment planning and decisions
Making treatment recommendations as behaviorally specific as possible
Simplifying treatment as much as possible to match patient capabilities
Tailoring treatment to fit patient's lifestyle, therapy goals, natural reinforcements
Helping patient reduce or manage identified barriers and aversive effects of treatment (e.g., side effects)

(Continued)

Table 1.2 (Continued)

Enhancing patient's self-efficacy (e.g., pointing out past successes and successes of similar patients; affirming patient's ability to adhere)

Helping patient to reframe problematic health beliefs and beliefs about the treatment

Getting firm commitments from patient regarding specific treatment-related behaviors

Having patient self-monitor adherence and treatment progress

Establishing a reinforcement system for adherent behavior (e.g., self-reinforcement; praise from staff, friends, or family; financial or other tangible reinforcements such as vouchers)

Orienting patient to benefits of adherence and costs of nonadherence (e.g., on health, treatment goals, future goals), using adherence- and health-related feedback

Treating mental health problems (e.g., depression, substance abuse)

Minimizing barriers at clinic (e.g., long waits, limited appointment times)

Having continuity of patient care at clinic

Using therapy and behavior change preparatory techniques such as treatment contracting, role induction, vicarious therapy retraining, experimental pretraining, and motivational interviewing (see Lash and Burden, in press; Walitzer, Dermen, & Connors, 1999; Zweben & Zuckoff, 2004)

Maintenance

Having regular follow-up visits with patient

Regularly assessing adherence

Regularly assessing barriers to adherence helping patient to reduce, manage, or otherwise overcome these barriers

NOTE: For more detailed discussions of these strategies as well as their empirical support see the following sources: Burke and Okene (2001); Christensen (2004); Dunbar-Jacob and Mortimer-Stephens (2001); Dunbar-Jacob and Schlenk (1996); Falvo (2004); Fincham (1995); Haynes, McDonald, and Garg (2002); Heiby and Lukens (Chapter 4, this volume); Helmus, Saules, Schoener, and Roll (2003); Ickovics and Meisler (1997); Kirschenbaum and Flanery (1983); Lash and Burden (Chapter 19, this volume) Malouff and Schutte (2004); McDonald, Garg, and Haynes (2002); Meichenbaum and Turk (1987); Mullen, Green, and Persinger, (1985); Myers and Midence (1998); Pampallona et al. (2002); Roter et al. (1998); Scheel, Hanson, and Razzhavaikina (2004); Shumaker, Schron, Ockene, and McBee (1998); and Vermeire, Hearnshaw, and Van Royen (2001).

Pampallona et al., 2002; Roter et al., 1998; Scheel et al., 2004; Walitzer, Dermen, & Connors, 1999; World Health Organization, 2003).

A number of other important themes emerge from this literature that map on well to the topics discussed in the chapters of this volume. First, "patient readiness" and motivation to adhere to a treatment appear to be important considerations when beginning a treatment or attempting to improve patient adherence and should be addressed (see Chapters 3 and 5 for discussions of these issues). Second, it appears that adherence interventions may be most effective if tailored to the specific demands of each treatment and the identified barriers and needs of each patient (see Chapter 4 for guidelines on how to do assessment-based tailored adherence interventions, and see Chapters 12 to 29 for discussions of special considerations in facilitating adherence to specific treatments and with specific patient populations). Third, patient adherence is affected by specific behaviors (or lack of behaviors) of providers as well as the structure and contingencies of the health care system, including the continuity of the care within the system. This is an important theme in that it can orient providers and administrators to making behavioral and systemic changes to promote adherence rather than assuming that it is only patients that need to change. In each chapter of this text are examples of how this can be done in different clinical settings with a variety of different treatments and patient populations. Fourth, providing treatment and adherence-related information to patients effectively is often important, but not typically sufficient, to facilitate adherence (see Chapter 6), as is the case with increasing patients' adherence-related resources and social support (see Chapter 8). Fifth, much of adherence interventions involve adherence-related skill building. It can be very useful to think about adherence as a "skill to be learned." Taking this perspective reduces patient and provider judgments about nonadherence and also orients both to approach nonadherence as a problem to be solved rather that an unmalleable trait of the patient (see Chapters 7, 9, and 10). Sixth, regularly following up with patients on their adherence (and barriers to adherence) is critical to improving it.

Conceptual Issues in Understanding and Facilitating Treatment Adherence

One of the problems associated with understanding and making progress in treatment adherence is that it is a very complex construct. Some philosophers of science such as Laudan (1977) have recognized that science has both conceptual and empirical problems. Psychologists can easily recognize the latter but at times have more difficulty recognizing the former. Conceptual problems are important to recognize because progress on these may be necessary before substantial empirical progress can be made. There are clear examples of conceptual problems in science, such as definitions of species in biology or mass in physics. In psychology, certainly, some conceptual problems are recognized, such as what "abnormal behavior" or a "mental disorder" is and is not (Szasz, 1960), or more specifically, what the criteria of certain diagnostic categories should be (O'Donohue & Elliot, 1992).

The construct of treatment adherence is complex for a number of reasons. First, it denotes a wide variety of actual behaviors. It can involve a single discrete episode of behavior, such as coming for a one-time procedure on Friday at 9:00 a.m., or behaviors that occur over a lifetime, such as exercising three times a week for 45 minutes or taking medication three times a day for the rest of a patient's life. Second, the behaviors involved in adherence can range from simple and discrete and of the same response class, such as taking one pill each day, to complex and involving multiple kinds of behavior, such as taking one pill, pricking the finger and performing a glucose test, checking the feet, limiting sugar intake, and exercising each day. Third, the behaviors involved in adherence can involve increasing behavior, such as eating more fiber, or reducing behaviors, such as eating less fat. Fourth, the behaviors can involve contrary motivational systems, such as quitting smoking or taking a medication which brings about adverse side effects such as nausea, or consistent motivational systems, such as taking medications that reduce symptoms of illness and have no side effects. Fifth, the behaviors can be relatively easy to understand and perform, such as simple pill taking; or very complex and demanding, such as with HIV medication, which often involves taking multiple medications at different times of the day as well as other special instructions (e.g., dietary restrictions). Sixth, the patient can be ideally suited to comply (e.g., adult, cognitively sound, motivated, good organizational skills, and self-control), or not ideally constituted for adherence (e.g., cognitive or motivational limitations). Seventh, the psychological meaning of the treatment can be complex, such as in the case when the patient is embarrassed about the health problem or the patient has a poor relationship with the provider and/or caregiver.

This heterogeneity will likely produce heterogeneous responses to the problem of treatment adherence. Because treatment adherence covers so much ground, empirical strategies to understand and improve specific regimens will necessarily cover a lot of ground also. It would be useful to determine if a principle-based subtype can be discovered to deal with this complexity and heterogeneity. There are two possibilities concerning this: (1) that a few principles, such as self-control, organizational skills, education, and so on, will be so powerful that they will have a large, wide effect across all or most facets of treatment adherence or (2) that there will be different principles, albeit with some overlap across different domains. For example, organizational skills may be most important for complex medication dosages, whereas social support may be more important with an oppositional adolescent. More modeling and research is needed to determine what sort of personality characteristics and mental disorders (even common low level problems such as depression) affect the probabilities of adherence to different adherence tasks. These are important empirical questions, but empirical questions best answered with these sorts of distinctions in mind.

Directions for Future Research

Patient nonadherence to treatment continues to be a significant barrier to effective health care delivery, and the literature on the effectiveness of interventions to improve adherence is fairly inconclusive. More work is certainly needed in this area. First, continued efforts are needed in the development and testing of models of adherence and nonadherence that will facilitate understanding and prediction of adherence as well as guide the development of effective interventions. It is likely that researchers will need to start thinking more "outside the box" to accomplish this. It might also be the case as alluded to above that adherence is not one single problem but a variety of problems. It might mirror Gordon Paul's question of psychotherapy outcome research, "What intervention, delivered by what kind of professional, to what kind of patient, with what kind of problem, produces what kind of effects, under what circumstances?" This kind of question might suggest that adherence is actually a multitude of somewhat related problems rather than a single problem as the single noun "adherence" denotes. Second, further work is needed in developing and testing valid and reliable methods of assessing adherence to treatments. This should include the development of technologies for assessing adherence as well as methods for integrating these into clinical practice. Cost and convenience are key parameters, but unfortunately these usually involve trade-offs with validity. In addition, it might be that treatment nonadherence should be assumed rather than detected later and become part of the standard treatment. Third, existing interventions, as well as new and innovative interventions, need to be tested using sound methodology that will enable the determination of what interventions are effective. Specifically, more outcome studies need to be conducted that use valid and reliable measures of adherence, use random assignment to a control group, lack significant confounding variables, have adequate sample sizes (e.g., >60 subjects per group), have longer follow-up periods (e.g., >6 months), provide detailed descriptions of the interventions, and use standardized operational definitions of adherence (so outcomes can be compared across studies). These studies should also report titration results in which levels of treatment outcome are shown as a function of levels of adherence. This will allow determination of the degree of adherence that is necessary. Fourth, as this line of adherence research develops, conducting outcome studies on what interventions and combinations of interventions are best for specific populations and treatments could be extremely clinically useful as well as potentially cost-effective. Finally, for nonadherence assessments and interventions that are found to be effective, provider training and dissemination methods need to be developed and evaluated.

References

Andrews, L., & Friedland, G. (2000). Progress in HIV therapeutics and the challenges of adherence to antiretroviral therapy. *Infectious Disease Clinics of North America, 14*(4), 901–928.

Bryant, M. J., Simons, A. D., & Thase, M. E. (1999). Therapist skill and patient variables in homework compliance: Controlling an uncontrolled variable in cognitive therapy outcome research. *Cognitive Therapy and Research, 23,* 381–399.

Burke, L. E., & Ockene, I. S. (Eds.). (2001). *Compliance in healthcare and research.* Armonk, NY: Futura.

Christensen, A. J. (2004). *Patient adherence to medical treatment regimens: Bridging the gap between behavioral science and biomedicine.* New Haven, CT: Yale University Press.

Cleemput, I., Kesteloot, K., & DeGeest, S. (2002). A review of the literature on the economics of noncompliance. Room for methodological improvement. *Health Policy, 59,* 65–94.

Detweiler, J. B., & Whisman, M. A. (1999). The role of homework assignments in cognitive therapy for depression: Potential methods for enhancing adherence. *Clinical Psychology: Science and Practice, 6,* 267–282.

DiMatteo, M. R. (2004). Variations in patients' adherence to medical recommendations: A quantitative review of 50 years of research. *Medical Care, 42,* 200–209.

Dunbar-Jacob, J., Burke, L. E., & Puczynski, S. (1995). Clinical assessment and management of adherence to medical regimens. In P. M. Nicassio & T. W. Smith (Eds.), *Managing chronic illness: A biopsychosocial perspective* (pp. 313–349). Washington, DC: American Psychological Association.

Dunbar-Jacob, J., & Mortimer-Stephens, M. (2001). Treatment adherence in chronic disease. *Journal of Clinical Epidemiology, 54,* S57–S60.

Dunbar-Jacob, J., & Schlenk, E. (1996). Treatment adherence and clinical outcome: Can we make a difference? In R. J. Resnick & R. H. Rozensky (Eds.), *Health psychology through the life span: Practice and research opportunities* (pp. 323–343). Washington, DC: American Psychological Association.

Falvo, D. R. (2004). *Effective patient education: A guide to increased compliance.* Boston: Jones & Bartlett.

Fincham, J. (Ed.). (1995). *Advancing prescription medicine compliance: New paradigms, new practices.* Binghamton, NY: Pharmaceutical Products Press.

Garfield, S. L. (1994). Research on client variables in psychotherapy. In A. E. Bergin & S. L. Garfield (Eds.), *Handbook of psychotherapy and behavior change* (4th ed., pp. 190–228). New York: Wiley.

Grahl, C. (1994, June). Improving compliance: Solving a $100 billion problem. *Managed Health Care,* pp. 11–13.

Haynes, B., McDonald, H., Garg, A. X., & Montague, P. (2002). Interventions for helping patients to follow prescriptions for medications (Cochrane Review). In *The Cochrane library* (Issue 4). Oxford: Update Software.

Haynes, B., Wang, E., & Da Mota Gomes, M. (1987). A critical review of interventions to improve compliance with prescribed medications. *Patient Education and Counseling, 10,* 155–166.

Heiby, E. M., & Lukens, C. (2006). Identifying and addressing barriers to treatment adherence using behavioral analysis and modification techniques. In W. T. O'Donohue & E. R. Levensky (Eds.), *Promoting treatment adherence: A practical handbook for health care providers.* Thousand Oaks, CA: Sage.

Helmus, T. C., Saules, K. K., Schoener, E. P., & Roll, J. M. (2003). Reinforcement of counseling attendance and alcohol abstinence in a community-based dual-diagnosis treatment program: A feasibility study. *Psychology of Addictive Behaviors, 17*(3), 249–251

Ickovics, J. R., & Meisler, A. (1997). Adherence in AIDS clinical trials: A framework clinical research and clinical care. *Journal of Clinical Epidemiology, 50,* 385–391.

Kirschenbaum, D. S., & Flanery, R. C. (1983). Behavioral contracting: Outcomes and elements. In M. Hersen, R. M. Eisler, & P. M. Miller (Eds.), *Progress in behavior modification* (Vol. 15, pp. 217–275). New York: Academic Press.

Lash, S. J., & Burden, J. L. (2006). Adherence to treatment of substance use disorders. In W. T. O'Donohue & E. R. Levensky (Eds.), *Promoting treatment adherence: A practical handbook for health care providers.* Thousand Oaks, CA: Sage.

Laudan, L. (1977). *Progress and its problems.* Berkeley: University of California Press.

Malouff, J. M., & Schutte, N. S. (2004). Strategies for increasing client completion of treatment assignments. *The Behavior Therapist, 27*(6), 118–121.

McDonald, H. P., Garg, A. X., & Haynes, R. B. (2002). Interventions to enhance patient adherence to medication prescriptions. *Journal of the American Medical Association, 288,* 2868–2879.

Meichenbaum, D., & Turk, D. (1987). *Facilitating treatment adherence: A practitioner's guidebook.* New York: Plenum Press.

Morris, L., & Schulz, R. (1992). Patient compliance: An overview. *Journal of Clinical Pharmacy and Therapeutics, 17,* 283–295.

Mullen, P., Green, L., & Persinger, G. (1985). Clinical trials of patient education for chronic conditions: A comparative meta-analysis of intervention types. *Preventative Medicine, 14,* 753–781.

Myers, L., & Midence, K. (Eds.). (1998). *Adherence to treatment in medical conditions.* London, UK: Harwood Academic.

O'Donohue, W. T., & Elliot, A. (1992). The current status of post-traumatic stress disorder: Problems and proposals. *Journal of Traumatic Stress, 5*(3), 421–439.

Pampallona, S., Bollini, P., Tibaldi, G., Kupelnick, B., Munizza, C. (2002). Patient adherence in the treatment of depression. *British Journal of Psychiatry, 180,* 184–189.

Rabkin, J. G., & Chesney, M. (1999). Treatment adherence to HIV medications: The achilles heal of new therapeutics. In D. G. Ostrow & S. C. Kalichman (Eds.), *Psychosocial and public health impacts of new HIV therapies. AIDS prevention and mental health* (pp. 61–82). New York: Kluwer Academic.

Rand, C. S., & Weeks, K. (1998). Measuring adherence with medication regimens in clinical care and research. In S. Shumaker, E. Schron, J. Ockene, & W. McBee (Eds.), *The handbook of health behavior change* (pp. 114–132). New York: Springer.

Reis, B. F., & Brown, L. G. (1999). Reducing psychotherapy dropouts: Maximizing perspective convergence in the psychotherapy dyad. *Psychotherapy, 36,* 123–136.

Rogers, H., & Bullman, W. (1995). Prescription medication compliance: A review of the baseline knowledge (A report of the National Council of Patient Information and Education). *Journal of Pharmacoepidemiology, 3*(2), 3–36.

Roter, D., Hall, J., Merisca, R., Nordstrom, B., Cretin, D., & Svarstad, B. (1998). Effectiveness of interventions to improve patient compliance: A meta-analysis. *Medial Care, 36*(8), 1138–1161.

Scheel, M. J., Hanson, W. E., & Razzhavaikina, T. L. (2004). The process of recommending homework in psychotherapy: A review of the therapist delivery methods, client acceptability, and factors that affect compliance. *Psychotherapy: Theory, Research, Practice, Training, 41*(1), 38–55.

Shumaker, S., Schron, E., Ockene, J., McBee, W. (Eds.). (1998). *The handbook of health behavior change.* New York: Springer.

Spiegler, M. D., & Guevremont, D. C. (2003). *Contemporary behavior therapy* (4th ed.). Melbourne: Thomas Nelson.

Stone, V. E. (2001). Strategies for optimizing adherence for highly active antiretroviral therapy: Lessons from research and clinical practice. *Clinical Infectious Diseases, 33,* 865–872.

Szasz, T. S. (1960). The myth of mental illness. *American Psychologist, 15,* 113–118.

Vermeire, E., Hearnshaw, H., & Van Royen, P. (2001). Patient adherence to treatment: Three decades of research. A comprehensive review. *Journal of Clinical Pharmacy and Therapeutics, 26,* 331–342.

Vitolins, M. Z., Rand, C. S., Rapp, S. R., Ribisl, P. M., & Sevick, M. A. (2000). Measuring adherence to behavioral and medical interventions. *Controlled Clinical Trials, 21,* 188S–194S.

Walitzer, K. S., Dermen, K. H., & Connors, G. J. (1999). Strategies for preparing clients for treatment. *Behavior Modification, 23,* 129–151.

Wierzbicki, M., & Pekarik, G. (1993). A meta-analysis of psychotherapy dropout. *Professional Psychology Research and Practice, 24,* 190–195.

World Health Organization. (2003). Adherence to long-term therapies: Evidence for action. Geneva: Author. Available from www.who.int/chronic_conditions/adherencereport/en

Zweben, A., & Zuckoff, A. (2004). Motivational interviewing and treatment adherence. In W. R. Miller & S. Rollnick (Eds.), *Motivational interviewing: Preparing people for change* (2nd ed.). New York: Guilford Press.

PART II

Assessment Strategies in Promoting Adherence

2

Integrating Regimen Adherence Assessment Into Clinical Practice

Kristin A. Riekert

If a clinician feels it is important to recommend a regimen, be it diet, exercise, or medication, to a patient, it should be just as important to the clinician to know the extent to which the patient followed that recommendation. Unfortunately, few clinicians routinely incorporate a standardized and valid protocol for assessing regimen adherence into their daily practice. This is despite a well-developed body of literature demonstrating that about half of all medical patients in the United States do not adhere to physicians' advice (Haynes et al., 2000). Nonadherence can lead to misdiagnoses and unnecessary treatment (Joshi & Milfred, 1995) and significantly contributes to patient outcomes including laboratory values (e.g., cholesterol levels, blood pressure, and glycosolated hemoglobin levels), disease exacerbations and relapses, and mortality (DiMatteo, Giordani, Lepper, & Croghan, 2002). Thus, nonadherence is highly prevalent and is associated with negative health outcomes. Moreover, nonadherence has been associated with increased health care use and health care costs and decreased cost-effectiveness of interventions (Anis et al., 2001; Cleemput, Kesteloot, & DeGeest, 2002; Hepke, Martus, & Share, 2004; McCombs, Nichol, Newman, & Sclar, 1994; Patrick et al., 2001; Svarstad, Shireman, & Sweeney, 2001). Sullivan, Kreling, and Hazlet (1990) estimated that 5.3% of all hospital admissions were due to poor medication adherence and the cost of hospital expenditures, lost productivity, and premature deaths due to nonadherence was $25 to $33 billion annually.

From a clinician's perspective, an accurate assessment of regimen adherence can have a significant influence on clinical decision making. If a patient has not adhered "enough" to a prescribed first-line medication and remains symptomatic, it may not be in the patient's best interest or cost-effective to increase the dose, switch to a more expensive medication, or recommend additional costly or invasive medical procedures. In contrast, identifying patients who are nonadherent, their patterns of nonadherence and the unique set of circumstances leading up to it, can help clinicians tailor their educational message or suggest cognitive-behavioral interventions that will support patients' efforts to increase their level of regimen adherence.

How Can I Assess Adherence?

Many articles and chapters have been written highlighting the pros and cons of using the various different methodologies for assessing regimen adherence (e.g., Haskell & Kiernan, 2000; Quittner, Espelage, Ievers-Landis, & Drotar, 2000; Rand & Wise, 1994; Rapoff, 1999; Vitolins, Rand, Rapp, Ribisl, & Sevick, 2000). Thus, the purpose of this section is to briefly introduce the reader to the wide variety of adherence measurement options and not provide a detailed scholarly evaluation of the validity of such measures. Table 2.1 provides additional strengths and limitations of each approach.

Objective Measures

Objective measures of adherence are viewed as superior to subjective measures. This is because they are perceived to be less vulnerable to patient falsification or manipulation. Objective measures also put less day-to-day burden on patients than subjective measures. The downside of objective measures, however, is that they are costly and are often not feasible or available for many behaviors of interest, particularly diet and exercise.

Directly Observed Therapy

Directly observed therapy (DOT) requires that a patient attend a clinic to perform the prescribed behavior under the supervision of a clinician. This approach provides complete certainty of timing of the behavior, but it is cost and labor intensive. DOT is widely used to ensure tuberculosis medication adherence (Davies, 2003; Mukherjee et al., 2004) and has been used with antiretroviral therapy adherence in some HIV treatment settings (Lucas, Flexner, & Moore, 2002; Mitty, Macalino, Taylor, Harwell, & Flanigan, 2003). Although not called DOT, the principles of DOT are in place when a patient attends a weight loss program, such as a weeklong camp or spa, where all food is provided at the prescribed amount and access to other food is limited and/or there is required attendance to exercise classes.

Biochemical Measures

Biochemical measures are obtained from bodily fluid samples such as blood serum, urine, and saliva or measuring byproducts of breathing. They can assess drug levels (e.g., theophylline levels, Weinstein & Cuskey, 1985), markers or tracers added to the drug and food (e.g., riboflavin, Dubbert et al., 1985; doubly labeled water, Schoeller et al., 1986), or metabolic products of behavior (e.g., vitamin levels). Although biochemical measures can verify a behavior occurred and allow for the calculation of a dose response, they can be invasive, have high interperson variability, and only serve as a short-term approximation of patient behavior.

Electronic Monitoring

Electronic monitoring of behavior (e.g., electronic caps that affix to pill containers, accelerometers, and blood glucose monitors) are often considered the "gold standard" for assessing patient adherence. There are many advantages; the behavior is automatically date and time stamped, so a great deal of information is obtained about patterns of behavior with little additional burden to the patient. There are also, unfortunately, many disadvantages including cost of the devices and the time it takes to analyze the data obtained. See Riekert and Rand (2002) for a comprehensive discussion of using electronic monitoring to assess medication adherence.

Table 2.1   Summary of Adherence Measurement Methods

Method	Examples	Strengths	Limitations
Objective approaches			
Directly observed therapy (DOT)	Medication taking for tuberculosis treatment Participation in exercise classes where attendance is taken Diet programs where food is provided and access to other food is limited	Verifies behavior occurred Can identify dose-response characteristics Could be used for any prescribed behavior	Cost Labor-intensive Unlikely to reflect patients' typical behavioral patterns in their natural environment Intrusive on patients' lives
Biochemical measures	Drug levels (theophylline) Metabolic products of behavior Inert markers or tracers (e.g., riboflavin for medications, doubly labeled water for physical activity)	Verifies behavior occurred Allows for titration of dose	Not available for most prescribed regimens Cost Invasive procedure Short-term approximation of patient behavior; influenced by "white coat" compliance (becoming more adherent immediately before a doctor's visit) Pharmacokinetic variations
Electronic monitoring	Medication Event Monitors (MEMS) caps Blood glucose monitors Pedometers Heart rate monitors Accelerometers	Can identify behavioral patterns Can identify dose-response characteristics Not affected by social desirability reporting Recorded regardless of who administers the therapy	Cost Malfunctions May need to be calibrated for each individual patient May interfere with established adherence patterns Reactivity Not available for many prescribed regimens Time-consuming for staff to maintain devices and calculate scores (particularly if software is not available) Recorded regardless of who administers the therapy

(Continued)

Table 2.1 (Continued)

Method	Examples	Strengths	Limitations
Objective approaches			
Medical/pharmacy/ insurance claims records	Appointment attendance Medication refill records Chart documentation of nonadherence	Confirms an event occurred Provides information on the maximum dose that could have been consumed	Cannot confirm content of visit or ingestion of medication Not available for many prescribed regimens Not standard practice for most clinicians to document nonadherence Is a global estimate; cannot identify patterns of behavior during the interval Requires patient consent for release of records Will be inaccurate if patient pays out of pocket (insurance claim) or if doesn't accurately report which clinics or pharmacies used
Medication measurement	Pill counts Canister weights	Provides information on the maximum dose that could have been consumed Easy to calculate Inexpensive	Cannot confirm ingestion Is a global estimate; cannot identify patterns of behavior during the interval Not available for many prescribed regimens Dependent on patient bringing all medications to each visit If patient knows medications will be measured, increased chance of "dumping" (dispensing medication from container before a visit)
Subjective approaches			
Daily patient logs/diaries	Paper or computer (PDA)-based log of behavior Food diaries Medication use	Can identify behavioral patterns Can be used for any prescribed behavior	Influenced by social desirability responding ("faking good") Time-consuming for patient to complete Reactivity

Method	Examples	Strengths	Limitations
Subjective approaches			
Daily patient logs/diaries		Can concurrently obtain data on barriers to adherence Can link adherence to health outcomes if patient also records health outcomes (e.g., symptoms, weight loss)	Logs are often retrospectively completed by a patient or have significant missing data Time-consuming for clinician to review and calculate an adherence score (less of an issue for computer-based logs) Technology-based logs subject to availability to patients and patient's comfort in using them
Retrospective patient report	Can be patient completed surveys or structured interviews Food frequency questionnaires Seven-day physical activity recall	Quick, inexpensive, and easy to obtain Can be used for any prescribed behavior Patients who *say* they are nonadherent *are* nonadherent	Highly influenced by social desirability responding ("faking good") Memory limitations affect accuracy of results Often a global estimate; cannot identify patterns of behavior Depending on length of survey, may be time-consuming for clinician to calculate an adherence score (if software not available)
Twenty-four-hour recall interview	Diet Diabetes management	Most patients can accurately recall activities over the past 24 hr Can be used for any prescribed behavior Can concurrently obtain data on barriers to adherence Can limit social desirability responding by asking about all activities during	Cost Time-consuming for clinician to obtain data, review them, and calculate an adherence score Short-term approximation of patient behavior If behavior naturally varies from day-to-day, may not obtain representative assessment Can be influenced by "white coat" compliance (patient briefly modifies behavior if knows will soon be asked about it)

(Continued)

Table 2.1 (Continued)

Method	Examples	Strengths	Limitations
Subjective approaches			
Twenty-four-hour recall interview		the past 24 hr not just health activities	Influenced by social desirability responding ("faking good")
Clinician impression	Informal (or nonexistent) assessment during a clinical encounter	Quick, inexpensive, and easy to obtain during a clinical interaction Can be used for any prescribed behavior	Often based on whether or not patient fits clinician's stereotype of what an adherent patient looks like Estimations often no better than chance Global estimate; cannot identify patterns of behavior

Medical, Pharmacy, and Insurance Claims Records

Medical, pharmacy, and insurance claims records are beneficial means of tracking behaviors that are contained within the health care system, such as prescription medication dispensations, screening procedures (e.g., mammograms), and doctor's visits. The accuracy of this approach depends on a well-documented, current, and integrated database from which it is easy to obtain needed data to calculate adherence and requires that the patient stay "in-network" when receiving the services of interest. See Steiner and Prochazka (1997) for a detailed review of the validity of using pharmacy records to assess medication adherence.

Medication Measurement

As the name implies, this approach involves counting or weighting medication at one visit, counting or weighting medication at a subsequent visit, and assuming the difference is the amount the patient consumed during the interval. Although seemingly simple, this calculation is potentially complicated if the patient (1) obtains a refill during the interval, (2) has unused medication from a previous prescription at home that was not included in the initial count, or (3) forgets to bring the medication in to be measured.

Subjective Measures

Subjective measures of adherence are the most commonly used in both research and clinical practice. They tend to be used because of their face validity, ease of administration, low cost, and applicability to any behavior of interest. Research has shown, however, that within the same patient, adherence assessed by subjective measures, such as self-report, is higher than when compared with objective adherence measures (DiMatteo, 2004; Riekert & Rand, 2002). Thus, subjective measures tend to overreport adherence.

Daily Patient Logs or Diaries

Logs or diaries can track any prescribed behavior including medication taking, exercise (type, frequency, duration, and intensity), and diet (type and quantity of food consumed) and are intended to be completed on a daily basis, preferably soon after the behavior occurred. They can track multiple behaviors and can identify behavioral patterns and barriers. Self-monitoring, in the form of keeping a log, is often a strategy recommended to improve adherence. Unfortunately, diaries are burdensome for patients to complete and, as a result, there are often significant missing data or they are completed just prior to a clinic visit.

Retrospective Patient Report

Retrospective patient report (self-report) requires patients to think back over some period of time (e.g., 1 week, 2 months, 1 year, or lifetime) and report on their regimen adherence. Sometimes they are asked to give a global estimate (e.g., "In general would you say your adherence has been poor, adequate, good, excellent?") or a precise number (e.g., "How many doses of medicine did you miss in the past week?"). Although quick and inexpensive to obtain, self-reports of behavior are highly influenced by social desirability responding ("faking good") and memory limitations. See Stone et al. (2000) for a comprehensive review of the benefits and limitations of using patient self-report.

Twenty-Four-Hour Recall Interview

To minimize the time burden of patient diaries and the memory problems of retrospective patient reports, many clinicians and researchers recommend the use of 24-hour recall interviews. In this procedure, the clinician reviews the previous 24 hours with the patient to comprehensively assess his or her adherence to the prescribed behavior(s). In some 24-hour recall interviews, the focus is only the prescribed behaviors (Johnson, Freund, Silverstein, Hansen, & Malone, 1990); in others, all activities performed that day are assessed, which is thought to minimize social desirable responding and help identify barriers to adherence (Wiener, Riekert, Ryder, & Wood, 2004). A critique of this approach

is that it is unlikely that 24 hours represents typical behavior, particularly if the patient knows he or she will be assessed. In response, many researchers recommend conducting three 24-hour recall interviews, including one weekend day (Quittner & Opipari, 1994; Reynolds, Johnson, & Silverstein, 1990), but it is unclear if this improves the validity.

Clinician Impression

On the whole, clinicians are typically no better than chance in determining a patient's level of adherence. More specifically, clinicians have the greatest difficulty identifying patients who are nonadherent (Finney, Hook, Friman, Rapoff, & Christophersen, 1993; Mushlin & Appel, 1977; Steele, Jackson, & Gutmann, 1990). Part of the problem stems from an incomplete assessment of adherence during a clinic visit (Steele et al., 1990), but error is also added when clinicians use additional factors to form their impression. These factors can include (1) the patient's health outcome (see following section), (2) patient characteristics such as race, socioeconomic status, and level of education, and (3) patient's level of participation and perceived motivation during the visit (Rand and Wise, 1994; Rapoff, 1999).

Health Outcomes

A recent meta-analysis found that the difference in risk of a null (or poor) health outcome after adhering to a regimen versus not adhering was 26% (DiMatteo et al., 2002). That is, for every 100 adherent patients, on average, 63 can be expected to have a good outcome and 37 a null or poor outcome compared with the 50/50 split that would be expected if there were no relationship between adherence and outcome. These results suggest that although adherence is significantly associated with positive patient health outcomes, there is not a one-to-one relationship. Some patients who do not follow the regimen will get better, whereas others who religiously follow recommendations will deteriorate. The relationship between regimen adherence and health outcome is affected by many factors including the efficacy of the regimen and individual variation in metabolism. Assuming a patient with worsening health is nonadherent can be detrimental as it may negatively affect the clinician-patient relationship, or worse, lead to withholding potentially beneficial treatment alternatives. As such, patient health outcomes should *never* serve as a proxy measure for adherence (DiMatteo, 2004).

What Are the Most Commonly Used Patient-Reported Measures?

The "gold standard" adherence assessment tools used by researchers (e.g., electronic medication monitors, doubly labeled water) are often too expensive or time-consuming for practicing clinicians to incorporate into clinical encounters. Unfortunately, there are no widely accepted, standardized patient-report adherence instruments validated for clinical practice. Given below is a discussion of self-report measures for assessing adherence to medications, diet, and physical activity that could potentially be integrated into clinical practice.

Medication

Hundreds of different scales have been developed to assess medication adherence. The simplest approach is to ask the patient, "How many doses of medicine did you miss over the past [insert time frame]?" and then divide the number of doses taken by the number of doses prescribed during that interval. The most widely known medication adherence scale is the Morisky score (Morisky, Green, & Levine, 1986). This scale consists of four "yes"/"no" items ("Do you ever forget to take your medicine?" "Are you careless at times about taking your medicine?" "When you feel better, do you sometimes stop taking

your medicine?" and "Sometimes if you feel worse when you take the medicine, do you stop taking it?"). It is easily scored by summing the number of "yes" answers, and scores can range from 0 to 4. Some researchers (Erickson, Coombs, Kirking, & Azimi, 2001) have used a modified 5-point scale for each item ranging from most of the time to none of the time. The Morisky score has been used to assess medication adherence across a wide variety of health conditions, including cardiovascular disease (Shalansky, Levy, & Ignaszewski, 2004), asthma (Erickson et al., 2001), diabetes (Krapek et al., 2004), HIV (Fairley et al., 2003; Gao & Nau, 2000; Pratt et al., 2001), osteoporosis (Turbi et al., 2004), and depression (George, Peveler, Heiliger, & Thompson, 2000) and has been shown to be generally associated with other measures of adherence (Erickson et al., 2001; George et al., 2000; Shalansky et al., 2004). However, the Morisky score may be of limited clinical utility, because it is not accurate at predicting whether a specific individual is adherent or not. That is, the false-positive rate (scoring in the nonadherent range when an objective measure suggests that the patient is adherent) is high, ranging from 15% to 83%, and the false-negative rate (scoring in the adherent range when an objective measure suggests that the patient is nonadherent) is also high, ranging from 15% to 27% (Erickson et al., 2001; George et al., 2000; Shalansky et al., 2004). Most adherence scales, even the single straightforward question suggested at the start of this section, do not accurately classify patients, but in contrast to the Morisky score, most errors on adherence scales tend to be false negatives rather than false positives (Rand, 2000).

Physical Activity

There are multiple dimensions of physical activity, including caloric expenditure, aerobic intensity, weight bearing, flexibility, and strength, and each dimension influences various health outcomes (e.g., cardiovascular risk, osteoporosis risk) differently (Kriska & Caspersen, 1997).

Therefore, no one measure can accurately assess all these dimensions while remaining brief and easy to administer. Most physical activity surveys focus on energy expenditure, but there is no gold-standard measure (Kriska et al., 1997). The journal *Medicine and Science in Sports and Exercise* published a special issue in 1997 that described 28 commonly used physical activity questionnaires and provided samples of the surveys, data on their reliability and validity, and administration and scoring rules (Pereira et al., 1997). To illustrate the issues in measuring physical activity, the 7-day Physical Activity Recall survey (PAR; Blair et al., 1985) will be discussed here. The PAR provides details regarding the duration, intensity, and volume of physical activity. The respondent is asked to report the amount of moderate, hard, and very hard activities that they performed for longer than 10 minutes. They are also asked to report the number of hours spent sleeping, and all other times in the day is assumed to be light activity. At the group level, results from the PAR are significantly correlated with activity monitors (Rauh, Hovell, Hofstetter, Sallis, & Gleghorn, 1992) and daily activity logs (Dishman & Steinhardt, 1988). Recall of very hard activities tend to be accurate; however, recall of moderate and light activity tends to be poor (Richardson, Ainsworth, Jacobs, & Leon, 2001; Sallis et al., 1985). When compared with objective measures, individuals completing the PAR tend to overestimate their energy expenditure (Conway, Seale, Jacobs, Irwin, & Ainsworth, 2002). Furthermore, there is high individual variability in the ability to accurately report activity level on the PAR (Washburn, Jacobsen, Sonko, Hill, & Donnelly, 2003). Therefore, the PAR, and other measures like it, may be of limited clinical utility because they are not accurate at predicting a specific individual's level of physical activity.

Diet

As with physical activity, there are many dimensions of nutrition that can affect health outcomes such as total calories, total fat, saturated fat, cholesterol, fiber, fruits and vegetables, calcium, alcohol, sugar, and sodium consumption. Given these many dimensions, it is understandable that a comprehensive assessment of dietary patterns is complicated. For this reason, dietary researchers and dieticians tend to consider 24-hour recall interviews or food frequency questionnaires (FFQ) to be the gold standard in self-reported diet adherence (O'Neil, 2001; Schatzkin et al., 2003). These methods require highly trained personnel to accurately administer and score them. Therefore, without a dietician available, these approaches are unlikely to be feasible for regular clinical practice. Unfortunately, there have been few surveys developed that could practically be integrated into clinical practice (Calfas, Zabinski, & Rupp, 2000). Those that have been developed tend to focus on the assessment of fat intake (Calfas et al., 2000), have little published data on their validity or reliability, tend to be compared with other self-report measures (e.g., food frequency questionnaires) rather than objective outcomes, and lack replication of results with independent samples, including those of various ethnic backgrounds. The Brief Food Screener (Block, Gillespie, Rosenbaum, & Jenson, 2000) is a recent example of a measure developed for clinical use. It consists of two screener scores: Fat Screener (15 items about meats, dairy, spreads, snacks) and the Fruit/ Vegetable Screener (7 items about fruits, vegetables, juices). With cut points determined from the same sample, the false-positive rate (e.g., eating 5+ servings of fruits and vegetables or having <30% energy from fat on the FFQ but screening positive for poor eating habits) was low for both screeners (around 11–12%). False-negative rates (e.g., screening negative for poor eating habits when actually had poor habits) were quite high for both screeners: 69% for fruits and vegetables and 50% for percent energy from fat. Therefore, as with the Morisky score and the PAR, the Brief Food Screener is limited in its ability to accurately classify individuals.

How Do I Maximize the Usefulness of Patient-Provided Information?

The most essential component of an adherence assessment is asking a question pertaining to adherence and then *listening* to the answer with every patient during every encounter. Even a cursory, poorly worded question such as, "You've been taking your medicine, right?" will result in some patients saying, "Well . . . actually . . . uhmmm . . ." Regardless of the behavior of interest or how it is assessed, research has shown that people are more likely to answer in a socially desirable manner that makes them appear to be healthier or more adherent than they actually are. Only rarely will someone who actually is adherent say that he or she is not. If a patient reports that he or she is 100% adherent to recommendations, it's about 50-50 that this is an accurate report. However, if a patient reports any level of nonadherence (e.g., not taking medicine, not exercising, not eating healthy), a clinician can be reasonably sure that this is his or her maximum possible level of adherence. That is, if a patient said he or she took 80% of a medication, it is almost certain that he or she took no more than 80% and possibly less.

Ask Questions That Will Minimize Socially Desirable Responding

Asking questions about patient behavior in a supportive, nonjudgmental, and nonassuming manner will help limit, but not remove, the bias toward responding in a socially desirable manner. Saying, "You didn't stop taking your medicine did you?" will result in few patients confessing nonadherence (Steele et al., 1990). Prefacing adherence questions with a permissive statement is thought to help improve patients' candor. An example of a permissive introductory statement is this:

> I know it is hard to follow a regimen day-in and day-out, particularly when you have so many other things going on with your life.

I am going to ask you some questions about what you have been able to do. I'm not here to judge you on whether you did right or wrong. It is ultimately up to you to decide how to care for your health. Accurate answers to my questions, however, will help me know if this is the right treatment for you or if I should recommend changes.

A good introductory adherence assessment question does not assume that any level of adherence has occurred. Examples of *less effective questions* include, "Have you noticed any changes since you've started taking that medication?" "You've been taking your medications?" (Steele et al., 1990), and "How's the diet going?" Examples of *more effective questions* include, "Were you able to take the medication I prescribed last visit? [patient says yes] . . . How have you been using it?" and "Last visit you said you were interested in losing weight. Have you been able to make any changes? [patient says yes] . . . What have you tried? . . . How has that been working for you?"

Ask Questions That Will Limit Memory Errors

For a person to provide an accurate answer about adherence, he or she must understand the question being asked, recall information from memory, place the behavior in the referenced time period, make decisions about the accuracy of the recalled information, and format an answer (Jobe, 2000). Many factors can affect the effort required to retrieve the needed information and the accuracy of that information. For example, if a person is not aware that he or she will be asked about a behavior and that behavior is simple to perform and highly routine (e.g., taking a pill everyday), the behavior may not be sufficiently coded into memory for subsequent recall. Similarly, as the time frame for recalling the event becomes longer or the number of performances of the behavior increases (or both), people switch from counting the events to providing a general estimate of the frequency

(Burton & Blair, 1991). To minimize these influences on the accuracy of self-report, research suggests several interviewing strategies. First, use the shortest time frame that will give meaningful information and anchor it to temporal boundaries or landmarks (e.g., holidays, meaningful events) rather than dates. For example, instead of saying "in the past 3 months . . ." ask "Since New Years Eve . . .." Second, it is sometimes helpful to ask respondents to recall events in reverse chronological order. For example, instead of saying. "In the past 7 days . . ." ask "What did you eat yesterday? . . . What did you eat Wednesday? . . . What did you eat Tuesday?" Third, use decomposition, a strategy that breaks a class of event down into subclasses or cues. To be useful, the subclasses or cues used in the question should match how the respondent would naturally classify the event. For example, instead of asking about eating habits in general, ask about eating habits for breakfast, lunch, dinner, snacks at work, snacks after dinner, and so on. Finally, providing individuals with more time to answer the question may increase the accuracy of the response. If a patient feels rushed, he or she may not feel there is enough time to "count" the number of events and instead will provide an estimate that may be more prone to biases.

Assess That the Patient Knows What He or She Was Recommended to Do

For a non-inconsequential number of patients, nonadherence can result from not understanding what they were prescribed to do. Research has shown that patients and clinicians often disagree whether a medication has been prescribed (Riekert, Butz, Eggleston, Winkelstein, & Rand, 2003) and how it should be taken (Hulka, Cassel, Kupper, & Burdette, 1976). Schillinger and colleagues (2003) have shown that physicians of patients with diabetes rarely assess patient comprehension of medical instructions. However, they found that patients whose physicians did assess recall and understanding of health information or

treatment recommendations were 15 times more likely to have good glycemic control. Thus, minimizing misunderstandings about the regimen is an important first step in ensuring that the prescribed regimen is followed. Appropriate assessment of understanding includes the following: (1) what does the patient think was prescribed? (e.g., "What have you been doing to manage your high blood pressure?"). (2) How much should be done? (e.g., "What dose do you take?" "What size portion of chicken do you eat?"). (3) How often should it be done? (e.g., "How often do you take your medicine?" "How many times a week do you exercise?").

Assess That the Patient Has the Skills and Knowledge to Perform the Behavior(s)

In addition to knowing what to do, it is important to assess if a patient has the skills and knowledge to carry out the recommendation. People will become frustrated if they think they are strictly following a regimen but not seeing results, which can lead to the belief that the regimen is ineffective and reluctance to continue following it. Unintentionally or intentionally implementing the regimen inappropriately may be a factor in the lack of a treatment effect. For example, if an elderly patient cannot open a pill container, it may decrease the likelihood that the medication will be taken (Nikolaus et al., 1996). Similarly, cognitive deficits, often prevalent among the elderly or certain illnesses, such as HIV or severe mental illnesses, are predictive of nonadherence (Hinkin et al., 2004; Jeste et al., 2003; Salas et al., 2001). Some regimens may involve a complex set of behaviors, which can lead to nonadherence. For example, individuals with asthma must follow a series of steps to appropriately deliver inhaled medications to their lungs. Research has shown that 24% to 79% of patients make at least one inhaler technique error that could affect the efficacy of the treatment (Hesselink, Penninx, Wijnhoven, Kriegsman, & van Eijk, 2001; Scarfone, Capraro, Zorc, & Zhao,

2002; Shrestha et al., 1996). Furthermore, it is one thing to know that one should lose weight; it is another to understand how this should be achieved. Does the patient know how to read and interpret food labels and then determine if the food is "allowed" for the particular diet he or she is attempting to follow? Research has shown that about half of consumers have poor comprehension and understanding of food labels (Fullmer, Geiger, & Parent, 1991; Miller, Probart, & Achterberg, 1997; Montgomery & Amos, 1991). Similarly, does the patient know the frequency, duration, and level of intensity of exercise required to achieve physical fitness goals?

Assess Patterns of Adherence

It is much easier to obtain a global estimate of regimen adherence than a detailed assessment of patterns of behavior over time. However, asking about patterns of adherence can help a clinician understand the different circumstances that lead to nonadherence and help guide the appropriate selection of an intervention approach. Greater clinician focus on adherence can increase the patient's perception of the importance of adhering. Moreover, inquiring about a patient's life outside of managing a health condition can make a patient feel cared about and understood by the physician and result in greater patient motivation to accurately answer questions.

So what patterns should one look for?

1. *Never initiating the regimen*—the patient did not take a single dose of the regimen. It has been documented that nearly one third of medications prescribed are not filled within 1 year of the medical encounter (Bronstein, Santer, & Johnson, 2000; Watts, McLennan, Bassham, & el Saadi, 1997).

2. *Discontinuing the regimen*—the patient started the regimen, followed it for a while, but then stopped it and never resumed it. Among adults treated with antihypertensive drugs, the odds of experiencing intracerebral hemorrhage were significantly higher in those who had discontinued therapy than those continuing treatment (Thrift, McNeil, Forbes, & Donnan, 1998). Similarly, discontinuation of medication resulted in a fivefold increase in the risk of relapse among individuals with schizophrenia or schizoaffective disorder (Robinson et al., 1999).

3. *Regimen holidays*—stopping the regimen for some period of time and then resuming it. Depending on the regimen, the frequency and duration of regimen holiday(s) may significantly affect the efficacy of the regimen. For example, in HIV, one study found that a history of two or more drug holidays (≥48 hours unplanned stoppage of nonnucleoside reverse transcriptase inhibitor [NNRTI] medication) was more highly related to viral load than a Morisky score (relative risk of 4.4 compared with 1.7) and was associated with developing resistance to the whole class of NNRTI medications (Parienti et al., 2004). Wilbur, Chandler, & Miller (2001) conducted a 24-week exercise program for women where they were prescribed to take four walks a week. Results showed that there were significant improvements in VO_2 (a measure of cardiorespiratory endurance) for all women, even those who took <80% of prescribed walks, as long as they had no more than one instance of ≥3 weeks of no walks taken.

4. *Adherence tracking with symptoms experience*—a patient adheres differently based on whether he or she feels better or worse. For example, two studies (Erickson et al., 2001; Shalansky et al., 2004) found that two questions from the Morisky score, "When you feel better, do you sometimes stop taking your medicine?," and "Sometimes if you feel worse when you take the medicine, do you stop taking it?," were each strongly predictive of actual medication nonadherence in asthmatic and cardiac populations.

5. *Nonadherence with no apparent pattern*—the pattern of doses taken is erratic and unpredictable. Although discussing appropriate interventions associated with each of these outcomes is beyond the scope of this chapter, Table 2.2 outlines some possible causes of the nonadherence pattern as a way to illustrate the value of assessing adherence patterns.

Table 2.2   Patterns of Nonadherence and Possible Causes

Pattern	Possible Cause(s)
Never initiating the regimen	Rejection of the diagnosis Perception that regimen will not improve one's health Lack of confidence in ability to initiate or sustain the regimen Lack of resources (e.g., no health insurance, no place to exercise) Social or cultural barrier to performing the regimen Misunderstanding about how to follow regimen
Discontinuing the regimen	Loss of social support Experience-based perception that regimen did not improve one's health Lack of confidence in ability to sustain the regimen Resistant to making regimen permanent part of life Change in access to resources Social or cultural barrier to performing the regimen Misunderstanding about how to follow regimen Concerns about addiction, tolerance, or side-effects
Regimen holidays	Changing schedule Life event (e.g., vacation, illness, injury, family crisis, deadline at work) Lack of confidence in ability to sustain the regimen Sporadic resources available to support regimen Social or cultural barrier to performing the regimen Misunderstanding about how to follow regimen Concerns about addiction, tolerance, or side effects
Adherence tracking with symptom experience	Perception that no symptoms mean no disease and therefore don't need regimen when asymptomatic Perception that one should only follow regimen when one does not feel well or weighs above a certain amount Memory problems; symptoms serve as cue to follow regimen Social or cultural barrier to performing the regimen Misunderstanding about how to follow regimen Concerns about addiction, tolerance, or side-effects
Nonadherence with no apparent pattern	Misunderstanding about how to follow regimen Lack of stable daily routine Busy schedule Memory problems

Use the Data Obtained From Questioning as the Sole Basis for Determining a Patient's Adherence Level

As noted in the section on using clinician impression to assess adherence, many clinicians use outside factors to form an estimation of a patient's level of adherence. Unfortunately, data do not consistently support a relationship between patient characteristics, including gender, race, income, education level, and level of adherence. Adolescents on the whole, however, tend to be less adherent than children or adults

(Brownlee-Duffeck et al., 1987; Fotheringham & Sawyer, 1995), but this does not imply that all adolescents are nonadherent. Health outcomes and illness severity are also not predictive of the level of adherence. At a population level, motivation to follow a regimen is associated with a greater likelihood that the patient will be adherent (Courneya & McAuley, 1995; Flynn, Lyman, & Prentice-Dunn, 1995). Intending to follow a regimen, however, is no guarantee that a specific patient will follow it at a sufficient level. Thus, a clinician's best bet is to ask specific questions about adherence and use that data, and only that data, to form an estimation of the patient's adherence status.

So How Do I Select the Right Assessment Tools for Me?

The magnitude of the association between adherence and health outcome is moderated by how adherence is measured. In a recent meta-analysis, the association between adherence and outcome was stronger when adherence was measured on a continuum (vs. dichotomized), more than one method for assessing adherence was used and a measure of patient-reported adherence was included (DiMatteo et al., 2002). Recently, the World Health Organization (2003) determined that a multimethod approach combining self-report and reasonable objective measures was the current state-of-the-art method for the assessment of adherence. It is clear that despite its limitations, patient self-report is one of the most cost-effective means of assessing regimen adherence. If while using the adherence interviewing strategies discussed in this chapter, a patient reports nonadherence, implementing a second assessment approach is probably unnecessary, unless there is need to know the exact magnitude of nonadherence. If a patient reports he or she is highly adherent, however, a clinician needs to consider the costs and benefits of further assessment. Most important, how will

knowing a patient's level of regimen adherence affect clinical decision making for this patient?

If knowing whether a patient is nonadherent will not result in a change in diagnostic or treatment recommendations, additional adherence assessment may not be worth the expense, effort, and possible detrimental effect on the clinician-patient relationship (e.g., "I told the doctor I take my medicine so why does he want to check my refill records? Does he think I'm a liar?"). If, however, knowing whether a patient is nonadherent will result in a change in diagnostic or treatment recommendations, additional adherence assessment may be as valuable as any laboratory test. Which follow-up assessment tool to choose depends on many factors including (1) availability for a particular behavior, (2) financial, staff, and technical resources to support the assessment approach, (3) the implications of not adhering to a particular regimen, (4) the patient's current health status, (5) the degree of intrusiveness the patient is willing to accept, and (6) the importance of knowing a precise level of adherence. In populations where nonadherence is highly linked to negative outcomes (e.g., transplant, HIV, tuberculosis), some clinics have integrated objective assessment of adherence, such as electronic monitoring or DOT, into standard care for all patients. Making adherence assessment standard practice ensures the data are available for a clinician to use if needed and no patient feels unfairly singled out. Moreover, a clinician may find it easier to advocate for additional adherence assessment, and a patient may be more willing to allow it, if the patient is frustrated by his or her poor health outcome. In research, greater measurement precision will help increase the statistical power of a study. In clinical practice, there are few instances where precise measurement of adherence is crucial.

Instead of immediately implementing a different assessment approach, which may or may not affect clinical decision making, it may be more therapeutic to emphasize the importance of adherence, empathize with the difficulties of sticking to a regimen day after day, suggest strategies (e.g., keeping a diary) to reduce barriers to adherence, and then reassess regimen adherence at the next visit. This brief intervention, particularly if provided at every visit and in a supportive, nonconfrontational manner, may help a patient recognize and report nonadherence at a subsequent visit.

References

Anis, A. H., Lynd, L. D., Wang, X. H., King, G., Spinelli, J. J., Fitzgerald, M., et al. (2001). Double trouble: Impact of inappropriate use of asthma medication on the use of health care resources. *CMAJ: Canadian Medical Association Journal, 164,* 625–631.

Blair, S. N., Haskell, W. L., Ho, P., Paffenbarger, R. S., Jr., Vranizan, K. M., Farquhar, J. W., et al. (1985). Assessment of habitual physical activity by a seven-day recall in a community survey and controlled experiments. *American Journal of Epidemiology, 122,* 794–804.

Block, G., Gillespie, C., Rosenbaum, E. H., & Jenson, C. (2000). A rapid food screener to assess fat and fruit and vegetable intake. *American Journal of Preventive Medicine, 18,* 284–288.

Bronstein, J. M., Santer, L., & Johnson, V. (2000). The use of Medicaid claims as a supplementary source of information on quality of asthma care. *Journal for Healthcare Quality, 22,* 13–18.

Brownlee-Duffeck, M., Peterson, L., Simonds, J. F., Goldstein, D., Kilo, C., & Hoette, S. (1987). The role of health beliefs in the regimen adherence and metabolic control of adolescents and adults with diabetes mellitus. *Journal of Consulting and Clinical Psychology, 55,* 139–144.

Burton, S., & Blair, E. (1991). Task conditions, response formulation processes, and response accuracy for behavioral frequency questions in surveys. *Public Opinion Quarterly, 33,* 50–79.

Calfas, K. J., Zabinski, M. F., & Rupp, J. (2000). Practical nutrition assessment in primary care settings: A review. *American Journal of Preventive Medicine, 18,* 289–299.

Cleemput, I., Kesteloot, K., & DeGeest, S. (2002). A review of the literature on the economics of noncompliance. Room for methodological improvement. *Health Policy, 59,* 65–94.

Conway, J. M., Seale, J. L., Jacobs, D. R., Jr., Irwin, M. L., & Ainsworth, B. E. (2002). Comparison of energy expenditure estimates from doubly labeled water, a physical activity questionnaire, and physical activity records. *American Journal of Clinical Nutrition, 75,* 519–525.

Courneya, K. S., & McAuley, E. (1995). Cognitive mediators of the social influence-exercise adherence relationship: A test of the theory of planned behavior. *Journal of Behavioral Medicine, 18,* 499–515.

Davies, P. D. (2003). The role of DOTS in tuberculosis treatment and control. *American Journal of Respiratory Medicine, 2,* 203–209.

DiMatteo, M. R. (2004). Variations in patients' adherence to medical recommendations: A quantitative review of 50 years of research. *Medical Care, 42,* 200–209.

DiMatteo, M. R., Giordani, P. J., Lepper, H. S., & Croghan, T. W. (2002). Patient adherence and medical treatment outcomes: A meta-analysis. *Medical Care, 40,* 794–811.

Dishman, R. K., & Steinhardt, M. (1988). Reliability and concurrent validity for a 7-day recall of physical activity in college students. *Medicine and Science in Sports and Exercise, 20,* 14–25.

Dubbert, P. M., King, A., Rapp, S. R., Brief, D., Martin, J. E., & Lake, M. (1985). Riboflavin as a tracer of medication compliance. *Journal of Behavioral Medicine, 8,* 287–299.

Erickson, S. R., Coombs, J. H., Kirking, D. M., & Azimi, A. R. (2001). Compliance from self-reported versus pharmacy claims data with metered-dose inhalers. *Annals of Pharmacotherapy, 35,* 997–1003.

Fairley, C. K., Levy, R., Rayner, C. R., Allardice, K., Costello, K., Thomas, C., et al. (2003). Randomized trial of an adherence programme for clients with HIV. *International Journal of STD & AIDS, 14,* 805–809.

Finney, J. W., Hook, R. J., Friman, P. C., Rapoff, M. A., & Christophersen, E. R. (1993). The overestimation of adherence to pediatric medical regimens. *Child Health Care, 22,* 297–304.

Flynn, M. F., Lyman, R. D., & Prentice-Dunn, S. (1995). Protection motivation theory and adherence to medical treatment regimens for muscular dystrophy. *Journal of Social and Clinical Psychology, 14,* 61–75.

Fotheringham, M. J., & Sawyer, M. G. (1995). Adherence to recommended medical regimens in childhood and adolescence. *Journal of Paediatrics and Child Health, 31,* 72–78.

Fullmer, S., Geiger, C. J., & Parent, C. R. (1991). Consumers' knowledge, understanding, and attitudes toward health claims on food labels. *Journal of the American Dietetic Association, 91,* 166–171.

Gao, X., & Nau, D. P. (2000). Congruence of three self-report measures of medication adherence among HIV patients. *Annals of Pharmacotherapy, 34,* 1117–1122.

George, C. F., Peveler, R. C., Heiliger, S., & Thompson, C. (2000). Compliance with tricyclic antidepressants: The value of four different methods of assessment. *British Journal of Clinical Pharmacology, 50,* 166–171.

Haskell, W. L., & Kiernan, M. (2000). Methodologic issues in measuring physical activity and physical fitness when evaluating the role of dietary supplements for physically active people. *American Journal of Clinical Nutrition, 72,* 541S–550S.

Haynes, R. B., Montague, P., Oliver, T., McKibbon, K. A., Brouwers, M. C., & Kanani, R. (2000). Interventions for helping patients to follow prescriptions for medications. *Cochrane Database of Systematic Review, CD000011.*

Hepke, K. L., Martus, M. T., & Share, D. A. (2004). Costs and utilization associated with pharmaceutical adherence in a diabetic population. *American Journal of Managed Care, 10,* 144–151.

Hesselink, A. E., Penninx, B. W., Wijnhoven, H. A., Kriegsman, D. M., & van Eijk, J. T. (2001). Determinants of an incorrect inhalation technique in patients with asthma or COPD. *Scandinavian Journal of Primary Health Care, 19,* 255–260.

Hinkin, C. H., Hardy, D. J., Mason, K. I., Castellon, S. A., Durvasula, R. S., Lam, M. N., et al. (2004). Medication adherence in HIV-infected adults: Effect of patient age, cognitive status, and substance abuse. *AIDS, 18*(Suppl. 1), S19–S25.

Hulka, B. S., Cassel, J. C., Kupper, L. L., & Burdette, J. A. (1976). Communication, compliance, and concordance between physicians and patients with prescribed medications. *American Journal of Public Health, 66,* 847–853.

Jeste, S. D., Patterson, T. L., Palmer, B. W., Dolder, C. R., Goldman, S., & Jeste, D. V. (2003). Cognitive predictors of medication adherence among middle-aged and older outpatients with schizophrenia. *Schizophrenia Research, 63,* 49–58.

Jobe, J. B. (2000). Cognitive processes in self-report. In A. A. Stone, J. S. Turkkan, C. A. Bachrach, J. B. Jobe, H. S. Kurtzman, & V. S. Cain (Eds.), *The science of self-report: Implications for research and practice* (pp. 25–28). Mahwah, NJ: Erlbaum.

Johnson, S. B., Freund, A., Silverstein, J., Hansen, C. A., & Malone, J. (1990). Adherence-health status relationships in childhood diabetes. *Health Psychology, 9,* 606–631.

Joshi, N., & Milfred, D. (1995). The use and misuse of new antibiotics. A perspective. *Archives of Internal Medicine, 155,* 569–577.

Krapek, K., King, K., Warren, S. S., George, K. G., Caputo, D. A., Mihelich, K., et al. (2004). Medication adherence and associated hemoglobin A1c in type 2 diabetes. *Annals of Pharmacotherapy, 38,* 1357–1362.

Kriska, A. M., & Caspersen, C. J. (1997). Introduction to a collection of physical activity questionnaires. *Medicine and Science in Sports and Exercise, 29,* S5–S9.

Lucas, G. M., Flexner, C. W., & Moore, R. D. (2002). Directly administered antiretroviral therapy in the treatment of HIV infection: Benefit or burden? *AIDS Patient Care and STDs, 16,* 527–535.

McCombs, J. S., Nichol, M. B., Newman, C. M., & Sclar, D. A. (1994). The costs of interrupting antihypertensive drug therapy in a Medicaid population. *Medical Care, 32,* 214–226.

Miller, C. K., Probart, C. K., & Achterberg, C. L. (1997). Knowledge and misconceptions about the food label among women with non-insulin-dependent diabetes mellitus. *Diabetes Educator, 23,* 425–432.

Mitty, J. A., Macalino, G., Taylor, L., Harwell, J. I., & Flanigan, T. P. (2003). Directly observed therapy (DOT) for individuals with HIV: Successes and challenges. *Medscape General Medicine, 5,* 30.

Montgomery, D. A., & Amos, R. J. (1991). Nutrition information needs during cardiac rehabilitation: Perceptions of the cardiac patient and spouse. *Journal of the American Dietetic Association, 91,* 1078–1083.

Morisky, D. E., Green, L. W., & Levine, D. M. (1986). Concurrent and predictive validity of a self-reported measure of medication adherence. *Medical Care, 24,* 67–74.

Mukherjee, J. S., Rich, M. L., Socci, A. R., Joseph, J. K., Viru, F. A., Shin, S. S., et al. (2004). Programmes and principles in treatment of multidrug-resistant tuberculosis. *Lancet, 363,* 474–481.

Mushlin, A. I., & Appel, F. A. (1977). Diagnosing potential noncompliance. Physicians' ability in a behavioral dimension of medical care. *Archives of Internal Medicine, 137,* 318–321.

Nikolaus, T., Kruse, W., Bach, M., Specht-Leible, N., Oster, P., & Schlierf, G. (1996). Elderly patients' problems with medication. An in-hospital and follow-up study. *European Journal of Clinical Pharmacology, 49,* 255–259.

O'Neil, P. M. (2001). Assessing dietary intake in the management of obesity. *Obesity Research, 9* (Suppl. 5), 361S–366S.

Parienti, J. J., Massari, V., Descamps, D., Vabret, A., Bouvet, E., Larouze, B., et al. (2004). Predictors of virologic failure and resistance in HIV-infected patients treated with nevirapine- or efavirenz-based antiretroviral therapy. *Clinical Infectious Diseases, 38,* 1311–1316.

Patrick, D. L., Ramsey, S. D., Spencer, A. C., Kinne, S., Belza, B., & Topolski, T. D. (2001). Economic evaluation of aquatic exercise for persons with osteoarthritis. *Medical Care, 39,* 413–424.

Pereira, M. A., FitzerGerald, S. J., Gregg, E. W., Joswiak, M. L., Ryan, W. J., Suminski, R. R., et al. (1997). A collection of physical activity questionnaires for health-related research. *Medicine and Science in Sports and Exercise, 29,* S1–205.

Pratt, R. J., Robinson, N., Loveday, H. P., Pellowe, C. M., Franks, P. J., Hankins, M., et al. (2001). Adherence to antiretroviral therapy: Appropriate use of self-reporting in clinical practice. *HIV Clinical Trials, 2,* 146–159.

Quittner, A. L., Espelage, D. L., Ievers-Landis, C., & Drotar, D. (2000). Measuring adherence to medical treatments in childhood chronic illness: Considering multiple methods and sources of information. *Journal of Clinical Psychology in Medical Settings, 7,* 41–54.

Quittner, A. L., & Opipari, L. C. (1994). Differential treatment of siblings: Interview and diary analyses comparing two family contexts. *Child Development, 65,* 800–814.

Rand, C. S. (2000). "I took the medicine like you told me, doctor": Self-report of adherence with medical regimens. In A. A. Stone, J. S. Turkkan, C. A. Bachrach, J. B. Jobe, H. S. Kurtzman, & V. S. Cain (Eds.), *The science of self-report: Implications for research and practice* (pp. 257–276). Mahwah, NJ: Erlbaum.

Rand, C. S., & Wise, R. A. (1994). Measuring adherence to asthma medication regimens. *American Journal of Respiratory and Critical Care Medicine, 149,* S69–S76.

Rapoff, M. A. (1999). *Adherence to pediatric medical regimens.* New York: Kluwer Academic.

Rauh, M. J., Hovell, M. F., Hofstetter, C. R., Sallis, J. F., & Gleghorn, A. (1992). Reliability and validity of self-reported physical activity in Latinos. *International Journal of Epidemiology, 21,* 966–971.

Reynolds, L. A., Johnson, S. B., & Silverstein, J. (1990). Assessing daily diabetes management by 24-hour recall interview: The validity of children's reports. *Journal of Pediatric Psychology, 15,* 493–509.

Richardson, M. T., Ainsworth, B. E., Jacobs, D. R., & Leon, A. S. (2001). Validation of the Stanford 7-day recall to assess habitual physical activity. *Annals of Epidemiology, 11,* 145–153.

Riekert, K. A., Butz, A. M., Eggleston, P. A., Winkelstein, M., & Rand, C. S. (2003). Caregiver-physician medication concordance and under-treatment of asthma among inner-city children. *Pediatrics, 111,* e214–e220.

Riekert, K. A., & Rand, C. S. (2002). Electronic monitoring of adherence: When is high-tech best? *Journal of Clinical Psychology in Medical Settings, 9,* 25–34.

Robinson, D., Woerner, M. G., Alvir, J. M., Bilder, R., Goldman, R., Geisler, S., et al. (1999). Predictors of relapse following response from a first episode of schizophrenia or schizoaffective disorder. *Archives of General Psychiatry, 56,* 241–247.

Salas, M., In't Veld, B. A., van der Linden, P. D., Hofman, A., Breteler, M., & Stricker, B. H. (2001). Impaired cognitive function and compliance with antihypertensive drugs in elderly: The Rotterdam Study. *Clinical Pharmacology and Therapeutics, 70,* 561–566.

Sallis, J. F., Haskell, W. L., Wood, P. D., Fortmann, S. P., Rogers, T., Blair, S. N., et al. (1985). Physical activity assessment methodology in the Five-City Project. *American Journal of Epidemiology, 121,* 91–106.

Scarfone, R. J., Capraro, G. A., Zorc, J. J., & Zhao, H. (2002). Demonstrated use of metered-dose inhalers and peak flow meters by children and adolescents with acute asthma exacerbations. *Archives of Pediatrics and Adolescent Medicine, 156,* 378–383.

Schatzkin, A., Kipnis, V., Carroll, R. J., Midthune, D., Subar, A. F., Bingham, S., et al. (2003). A comparison of a food frequency questionnaire with a 24-hour recall for use in an epidemiological cohort study: Results from the biomarker-based Observing Protein and Energy Nutrition (OPEN) study. *International Journal of Epidemiology, 32,* 1054–1062.

Schillinger, D., Piette, J., Grumbach, K., Wang, F., Wilson, C., Daher, C., et al. (2003). Closing the loop: Physician communication with diabetic patients who have low health literacy. *Archives of Internal Medicine, 163,* 83–90.

Schoeller, D. A., Ravussin, E., Schutz, Y., Acheson, K. J., Baertschi, P., & Jequier, E. (1986). Energy expenditure by doubly labeled water: Validation in humans and proposed calculation. *American Journal of Physiology, 250,* R823–R830.

Shalansky, S. J., Levy, A. R., & Ignaszewski, A. P. (2004). Self-reported Morisky score for identifying nonadherence with cardiovascular medications. *Annals of Pharmacotherapy, 38,* 1363–1368.

Shrestha, M., Parupia, H., Andrews, B., Kim, S. W., Martin, M. S., Park, D. I., et al. (1996). Metered-dose inhaler technique of patients in an urban ED: Prevalence of incorrect technique and attempt at education. *American Journal of Emergency Medicine, 14,* 380–384.

Steele, D. J., Jackson, T. C., & Gutmann, M. C. (1990). Have you been taking your pills? The adherence-monitoring sequence in the medical interview. *Journal of Family Practice, 30,* 294–299.

Steiner, J. F., & Prochazka, A. V. (1997). The assessment of refill compliance using pharmacy records: Methods, validity, and applications. *Journal of Clinical Epidemiology, 50,* 105–116.

Stone, A. A., Turkkan, J. S., Bachrach, C. A., Jobe, J. B., Kurtzman, H. S., & Cain, V. S. (2000). *The science of self-report: Implications for research and practice.* Mahwah, NJ: Erlbaum.

Sullivan S. D., Kreling D. H., & Hazlet T. K. (1990). Noncompliance with medication regimens and subsequent hospitalisations: A literature analysis and cost of hospitalisation estimate. *Journal of Research in Pharmaco-Economics, 2,* 19–33.

Svarstad, D. L., Shireman, T. I., & Sweeney, J. K. (2001). Using drug claims data to assess the relationship of medication adherence with hospitalization and costs. *Psychiatric Services, 52,* 805–811.

Thrift, A. G., McNeil, J. J., Forbes, A., & Donnan, G. A. (1998). Three important subgroups of hypertensive persons at greater risk of intracerebral hemorrhage. Melbourne Risk Factor Study Group. *Hypertension, 31,* 1223–1229.

Turbi, C., Herrero-Beaumont, G., Acebes, J. C., Torrijos, A., Grana, J., Miguelez, R., et al. (2004). Compliance and satisfaction with raloxifene versus alendronate for the treatment of postmenopausal osteoporosis in clinical practice: An open-label, prospective, nonrandomized, observational study. *Clinical Therapeutics, 26,* 245–256.

Vitolins, M. Z., Rand, C. S., Rapp, S. R., Ribisl, P. M., & Sevick, M. A. (2000). Measuring adherence to behavioral and medical interventions. *Controlled Clinical Trials, 21,* 188S–194S.

Washburn, R. A., Jacobsen, D. J., Sonko, B. J., Hill, J. O., & Donnelly, J. E. (2003). The validity of the Stanford seven-day physical activity recall in young adults. *Medicine and Science in Sports and Exercise, 35,* 1374–1380.

Watts, R. W., McLennan, G., Bassham, I., & el Saadi, O. (1997). Do patients with asthma fill their prescriptions? A primary compliance study. *Australian Family Physician, 26*(Suppl. 1), S4–S6.

Weinstein, A. G., & Cuskey, W. (1985). Theophylline compliance in asthmatic children. *Annals of Allergy, 54,* 19–24.

Wiener, L., Riekert, K., Ryder, C., & Wood, L. V. (2004). Assessing medication adherence in adolescents with HIV when electronic monitoring is not feasible. *AIDS Patient Care and STDs, 18,* 31–42.

Wilbur, J., Chandler, P., & Miller, A. M. (2001). Measuring adherence to a women's walking program. *Western Journal of Nursing Research, 23,* 8–24.

World Health Organization. (2003). *Adherence to long-term therapies: Evidence for action* (Rep. No. 11500526). Geneva: Author.

3

Assessing Readiness for Adherence to Treatment

Janice M. Prochaska

James O. Prochaska

Sara S. Johnson

To date, existing interventions designed to improve adherence have had limited success. According to a recent review of randomized clinical trials of adherence interventions (McDonald, Garg, & Haynes, 2002), theoretical, multifaceted interventions in clinic settings are common. Based on a review of 33 trials, including 39 interventions, less than half (19) were associated with statistically significant improvements in adherence.

The most effective interventions were multifaceted, combining several of the following common strategies: increased patient education and counseling, convenience of care, and patient involvement in care; use of reminders; and rewards or reinforcements for adherence (McDonald et al., 2002). Although these complex interventions

may produce greater success in many cases, there are several limitations. Such interventions are not typically based on an empirically supported theoretical model, and thus combine various strategies in a "hit or miss" fashion. This makes it difficult to determine which strategies were most effective with which patients. Moreover, interventions that adopt a one-size-fits-all approach are not tailored to an individual's unique needs (Miller, 1997) and assume readiness to be adherent. Finally, using a wide variety of strategies with all patients is expensive and impractical to deliver.

The transtheoretical model (TTM) has been suggested as an approach to overcome these limitations by delivering individualized, theoretically delivered interventions for entire populations of individuals (Willey, 1999; Willey et al., 2000), including those individuals who may not be ready to be adherent. The TTM systematically integrates four theoretical constructs central to change:

1. *Stages of change*: Readiness for treatment adherence

2. *Decisional balance*: Pros and cons associated with treatment adherence

3. *Self-efficacy*: Confidence to practice and sustain treatment adherence

4. *Processes of change*: Ten cognitive, affective, and behavioral activities that facilitate progress through the stages of treatment adherence

The TTM construes change as progress over time, through a series of stages: precontemplation, contemplation, preparation, action, and maintenance. Over 25 years of research on a variety of health behaviors have identified processes of change that work best in each stage to facilitate progress.

The Stages of Change

Stage of change is the TTM's central organizing construct. Longitudinal studies of change have found that people move through a series of five stages when modifying behavior on their own or with the help of formal interventions (DiClemente & Prochaska, 1982; Prochaska & DiClemente, 1983). In the first stage, *precontemplation*, individuals may deny they have a problem and thus are resistant to change their behavior, are unaware of the negative consequences of their behavior, believe the consequences are insignificant, or have given up the thought of changing because they are demoralized. They are not intending to take action in the next 6 months. Individuals in the *contemplation* stage are more likely to recognize the benefits of changing their behavior. However, they continue to overestimate the costs of changing and,

therefore, are ambivalent and not ready to change. Those in the *preparation* stage are seriously intending to make a change within the next 30 days and have already begun to take small steps toward the goal. Individuals in the action stage are overtly engaged in modifying their problem behaviors or acquiring new, healthy behaviors. Individuals in the *maintenance* stage have been able to sustain action for at least 6 months and are actively striving to prevent relapse. The stages form a simplex pattern in which adjacent stages are more highly correlated with each other than with more distant stages (Prochaska, DiClemente, Velicer, Ginpil, & Norcross, 1985). For most people, the change process is not linear, but spiral, with several relapses to earlier stages before they attain permanent behavior change (Prochaska & DiClemente, 1983, 1986).

Research comparing stage distributions across behaviors and populations finds that only a minority are in preparation with a majority in precontemplation and contemplation (Laforge, Velicer, Richmond, & Owen, 1999; Velicer et al., 1995). These data suggest that if we offered all individuals action-oriented interventions that assume readiness to participate in treatment adherence, we would be mis-serving the majority who are not prepared to take action.

Stage-matched interventions can have a greater impact than action-oriented, one-size-fits-all programs by increasing participation and increasing the likelihood that individuals will take action. Stage-matched interventions for smokers more than doubled the smoking cessation rates of the best action-oriented interventions available (Prochaska, DiClemente, Velicer, & Rossi, 1993). Stage-matched interventions have also outperformed one-size-fits-all interventions for exercise acquisition (Marcus et al., 1998), dietary behavior (Campbell et al., 1994), and mammography screening (Rakowski et al., 1998).

Assessing Stages

Stage of change is generally assessed using a staging algorithm, a set of decision rules that places an individuals in one of the five mutually exclusive stage categories based on their responses to a few questions about their intentions, past behavior, and present behavior. This approach to staging is robust across behaviors and populations (e.g., DiClemente et al., 1991; Prochaska et al., 1994). In the staging measure used in a recent study of a TTM-based intervention to improve adherence to antihypertensive medication funded through the Small Business Intervention Research Grant mechanism from the National Institutes of Health (NIH), participants were given a definition of "taking high blood pressure pills as directed," which included taking the entire dose prescribed by a physician on time every day. A staging item asked, "Do you consistently take all your high blood pressure pills as directed by your doctor?" (Johnson, Driskell, Johnson, Prochaska, Zwick, & Prochaska, in press).

Participants who responded "No" to the staging item were asked if they intended to do so in the next 6 months or 30 days and were staged in precontemplation, contemplation, or preparation based on their responses. Participants who responded "Yes" to the staging items were asked how long they had been taking their pills as directed and were initially in action (6 months or less) or maintenance (more than 6 months). Participants who self-staged in action or maintenance were also asked additional items to verify stage—if they take their medication at the same time every day, in the same place every day, and if they use a pill organizer or case. Participants responding "No" to any of these questions were asked if they intended to change the way they took their medications so they could do all these things. Participants' responses to these questions were only used when participants exceeded thresholds on a series of questions regarding missed, forgotten, or intentionally skipped pills in the previous week, month, and 3 months. For example, if participants self-staged in maintenance but reported that they intentionally skipped pills, the answers to the stage questions were examined to reclassify them into the appropriate stage.

Decisional Balance

Change requires the consideration of the potential gains (pros) and losses (cons) associated with a behavior's consequences. The Decisional Balance Inventory (Velicer, DiClemente, Prochaska, & Brandenburg, 1985) consists of two scales, the pros of change and the cons of change. Longitudinal studies have found those measures to be among the best available predictors of future change (e.g., Velicer et al., 1985). In an integrative report of 12 studies, Prochaska et al. (1994) found that the balance of pros and cons was systematically related to stage of change in all 12 behaviors examined. The cons of changing to a health-promoting behavior outweighed the pros in the precontemplation stage, the pros surpassed the cons in the middle stages, and the pros outweighed the cons in the action stage. From these 12 studies, Prochaska et al. (1994) discovered the degree of change in pros and cons needed to progress across the stages of change: Progression from precontemplation to action involved approximately a 1 standard deviation increase in the pros of making the healthy behavior change, and progression from contemplation to action involved a one-half standard deviation decrease in the cons. The pros of adherence could include the following: makes me feel more in control of my health, can help me live longer, makes me feel more responsible, will help me participate in my health care, and could make my loved ones worry less about my health. Among individuals not adhering to a treatment regimen, increasing the salience and enhancing the decisional weight of the pros of treatment adherence, and decreasing the cons, can help increase readiness to adhere.

Self-Efficacy

Self-efficacy, or the degree to which an individual believes he or she has the capacity to attain a desired goal, can influence motivation and persistence (Bandura, 1977). Self-efficacy in the TTM has two components that are distinct but related: (1) confidence to make and sustain changes and (2) temptation to relapse. Like decisional balance, levels of self-efficacy differ systematically across the stages of change, with subjects further along in the stages of change generally experiencing greater confidence and less temptation. Self-efficacy for treatment adherence means having the confidence to practice adherence in a variety of difficult situations (e.g., when one is stressed, has financial difficulties, or has side effects).

Processes of Change

In a comparative analysis of 24 major systems of psychotherapy, Prochaska (1979) distilled a set of 10 fundamental processes by which people change. The set was refined following further theoretical analyses (Prochaska & DiClemente, 1984) and empirical studies (Prochaska & DiClemente, 1985, 1986). These 10 processes describe the basic strategies that can be used to change problem behaviors, affects, cognitions, or interpersonal relationships. The 10 processes most often applied to treatment adherence are defined below with examples of interventions:

Consciousness-raising: Increasing awareness and information about treatment adherence (bibliotherapy, Internet resources, diary of behavior)

Dramatic relief: Experiencing strong negative emotions that go along with not practicing treatment adherence (grieving losses, personal testimonials)

Environmental reevaluation: Realizing the impact that one's effective treatment adherence has on other people (empathy training, asking others about their feelings about the patient's behavior)

Self-reevaluation: Emotional and cognitive reappraisal of values and self-image related to treatment adherence (value clarification, self-narratives)

Self-liberation: Making and demonstrating a firm commitment to adhere to a treatment regimen (New Year's resolutions, contracts)

Reinforcement management: Increasing intrinsic and extrinsic rewards for treatment adherence (self-rewards, overt and covert reinforcement)

Helping relationships: Seeking and using social support to encourage or help with treatment adherence (help lines, self-help groups, buddy systems)

Counterconditioning: Substituting new behaviors and cognitions for old responses to treatment adherence (positive statements, relaxation, exercise)

Stimulus control: Adding cues or reminders to adhere to the treatment regimen (avoiding high-risk cues, posting notes)

Social liberation: Realizing that society is changing to support treatment adherence (noticing policy, others becoming empowered)

An 11th process, health care provider helping relationships, can also be important in the adherence area. This process involves relying on medical professionals for assistance with adherence.

The data from our research show that self-changers in different stages rely on different processes of change, naturally integrating change strategies and processes often considered incompatible. Individuals in the early stages rely more on cognitive, affective, and evaluative processes of change; individuals in the later stages rely more on social support, commitments, and behavior management techniques. Table 3.1 summarizes the current understanding of self-changers' patterns of emphasizing particular processes as they progress through the stages (see Prochaska, DiClemente, & Norcross, 1992).

Table 3.1   Integration of the Stages, Processes, and Principles of Change

Precontemplation	Contemplation	Preparation	Action	Maintenance
Consciousness raising				
Dramatic relief				
Environmental reevaluation				
	Self-reevaluation			
		Self-liberation		
Reinforcement management				
Helping relationships				
Counterconditioning				
Stimulus control				
	Pros of changing increasing			
		Cons of changing decreasing		
			Self-efficacy increasing	

NOTE: Social Liberation has been found to not have differentiated emphasis across all five stages.

Continuum of Adherence

We have found that it is important to create interventions that are appropriate for the specific adherence behavior that a patient confronts. The intervention for a patient who has not even been screened for a possible risk factor like hypertension would be quite different from a patient with hypertension who has discontinued using antihypertensives. Table 3.2 outlines a continuum of adherence that we use in developing such interventions.

Screening

Screening is the first phase of intervention that is needed to determine if patients have risk factors that need to be treated. If patients have not been screened for risk factors like hypertension, hyperlipidemia, depression, stress, or a high-fat diet, then that is the first challenge. A big question is who is not being adherent, the patient or the professional? If clinical guidelines call for population-based screening, and particular practices are not following the guidelines, then these practices would be having problems with adherence. Medical practices tend to be much more proactive in following such screening guidelines when the risk factors are seen as more biological in nature, such as hypertension and hyperlipidemia. Practices tend to have more problems in being proactive in screening behaviors like alcohol abuse, depression, diet,

Table 3.2   Continuum of Adherence

Behavior	Appropriate Intervention
Screening	Promote screening so individuals with risk can be identified and treated appropriately
Acquisition	Prepare those in early stages, provide action plans for those in preparation, and provide relapse prevention for those in action
Adherence (continuation/ persistence)	Provide action-oriented advice and relapse prevention
Nonadherence	Prepare those in early stages to become more adherent (raise pros, reduce cons, etc.)
Discontinuation	Increase readiness for reacquisition

smoking, or stress. The difference is due in large part to physicians having more confidence in prescribing medications, like antihypertensives or statins, than in providing counseling for more behavioral risk factors.

In general, patients tend to be passive when it comes to screening. They tend to take their lead from their physician. If the practitioner does not take the time and make the effort to screen for particular risks, then patients are likely to conclude that such screening is not particularly important.

Acquisition

Once screened, the second phase is the patient's acquisition of the prescribed intervention. Here problems can arise if clinicians have not assessed the patient's readiness to acquire a prescribed intervention. Patients diagnosed with hyperlipidemia, for example, are very likely to be prescribed a medication like a statin. Clinicians take care to match the appropriate biological treatment to the patient's biological condition that has been assessed. But clinicians are not likely to recognize that they are prescribing behavior as well as biology. Are patients ready to start on the prescribed medication? Just because the clinicians are ready to prescribe doesn't mean that all patients are ready to follow the biological

prescription of taking the medication. Patients may have entered the office with no intention of starting to take a medication each day for the rest of their lives. Patients in precontemplation are likely to weigh the cons of taking the medication (e.g., costs, side effects, hassles) as clearly outweighing the pros. Their decisional balance is likely to lead them to not even fill their prescription. The clinician has prescribed the correct biological medicine but not the appropriate behavioral medicine.

Continuation

In this phase patients have started the acquisition process, but the question is will they continue with the prescription. Patients in the contemplation stage may be very ambivalent about taking a particular pill every day for the rest of their lives. Their clinicians may convince them that the prescription is correct for them. Wanting to be cooperative patients, they may go along with their physician's recommendation initially. So they fill the prescription, take it daily as prescribed but begin to experience some cons, such as costs, side effects, or doubts about their real risk. An ambivalent decisional balance can now shift in a negative direction with the cons outweighing the pros. These patients are at increased risk of discontinuation. Here again, the clinicians may have provided the appropriate biological medicine but an inappropriately matched behavioral medicine. An excellent adherence opportunity can be lost.

Nonadherence

In this phase, the patients are continuing with the prescription but are not taking it as prescribed. They may be cutting their pills in half, taking drug holidays, or missing pills on a repeated basis. Here, the assessment needs to be whether the problem is more of a memory problem, confidence problem, or a decision problem. If lapses are due mainly to memory, then a particular process like stimulus control technique can be used to help cure the patient. Pill containers can be of help as can computerized calls to high-cost patients who need more intensive help. If the problem is due to lowered self-efficacy under tempting situations, like times of stress or depression, then help may be needed on coping with such conditions. A stress management or mood management program may be prescribed.

If the problem is more decisional in origin such as cutting the pills in half as a way to cope with the price, then different help may be needed. Patients may need to be informed of lower cost options, like generic medications, if comparable ones exist.

Discontinuation

Once patients discontinue the prescribed biological and/or behavioral medications, then the major challenge is to help them recycle back through the stages to take more effective action. With behavioral discontinuation, such as relapse from a smoking cessation or exercise prescription, clinicians can be more optimistic or ambitious. The vast majority (about 85%) will regress only back to the contemplation or preparation stage. There, patients are ready to start contemplating or preparing for another serious action attempt. These patients can be helped to process

what they did right and what they need to do next time to be better prepared to sustain the action.

Patients in precontemplation need to be helped to not give up on their abilities to change or to not give up on their prescribed medicine. With behavioral medicine like smoking cessation or exercise, this challenge holds only for about 15% of patients. With medication, on the other hand, we have found that a much larger percentage of patients may regress all the way back to precontemplation. If these initial results continue to hold, then the implication would be that patients may give a particular prescription only one chance in the foreseeable future. If this chance fails, then an important opportunity may be lost. These results would suggest that taking the time and making the effort to prepare patients for the behavioral requirements of their biological medication may be particularly important. Recycling patients who discontinue medications may be much more challenging than recycling patients who discontinue behavioral treatments.

Stage-Matched Interventions Based on the TTM

In addition to providing an assessment framework, the TTM provides a scheme for tailoring programs by matching them to the needs of patients at each stage of change for treatment adherence. The degree of tailoring possible depends directly on the extent of the assessment. The following are descriptions of how one could use TTM for increasing treatment adherence through manuals, provider interventions, or Internet-based programs.

Stage-Based Manuals

When only the staging algorithm is administered, tailoring can occur at the stage level. Stage-based manuals describe how self-changers progress through each stage of change, and how they recycle if they relapse. The manuals teach users about general principles of behavior change, about their particular stage of change, and the processes they can use to progress to the next stage. Appropriate sections of the manuals are matched to each stage of change, and they provide details on change processes and stage-matched exercises. There are several ways to use the manuals. First, they could be read through to get the big picture of how people change. Second, readers could turn to the section for the stage they are in and study that stage for a while. This is a good way to be sure they are heading in the right direction. Finally, users could look ahead to the next stage to learn more about how to move forward.

For example, if a patient in the precontemplation stage for adherence to statins is underestimating the pros of adhering to their medication regimen, that patient could use the section of the manual that describes dozens of documented pros of adhering to one's lipid-lowering medication regimen. The patient would be also encouraged to seek more information about the importance of adherence from the media, their health care provider, and their pharmacist.

Because each manual contains sections relevant to each stage of change, readers can refer to the appropriate chapters as they advance or regress through the stages. In addition, the manual underscores that the principles the patient is using to change his or her behavior relating to statin adherence can also be applied to other behavior changes. Individuals are taught that they can systematically use the 15 principles and processes of change to make progress on multiple behaviors simultaneously rather than focusing on only one. Given the generalizability of TTM's principles and the importance of diet and exercise to the treatment of hyperlipidemia, for example, stage-matched guidance of these behaviors is included in the manual to assist patients in making dietary modification and exercise essential parts of their treatment regimen (Johnson et al., in press).

Stage-Based Provider Guidance

Health care providers could also tailor interventions to the patient's stage of change for adherence by administering the staging algorithm (e.g., in the waiting room). Providers could then base brief interventions on processes that are most helpful to a particular stage. For example, precontemplators come in denying or minimizing their problems. They may be unaware of the negative consequences of their unhealthy behavior or they may be demoralized because of repeated failures in changing their behavior.

The goal for the provider is to engage precontemplators in the change process. Lecture and confrontation won't work. Providers can help precontemplators raise consciousness by teaching them about the stages of change, asking them to name as many benefits of treatment adherence as they can (precontemplators can typically name three to five), and providing more information about the treatment regimen to dispel any misconceptions the patient may have.

During the first appointment with precontemplators, providers can ask if they are willing to do any of the following before the next time they meet:

- Read about treatment adherence (e.g., the importance of depression management)
- Double or triple their list of the pros of treatment adherence
- Talk with someone who is currently adhering to a similar treatment

Providers should reinforce the notion that their patients have the capacity to be adherent. They should remind their patients that any forward movement (e.g., becoming more open to considering alternatives, becoming more aware) is progress; change does not equal action—change means progressing to the contemplation stage.

Contemplators are thinking about changing but are not yet committed to do so. They are more likely to acknowledge that their behavior needs to be changed, but they substitute thinking about it for acting on it. They recognize the benefits of changing but overestimate the cons. Contemplators are ambivalent about changing and are often waiting for the magic moment. Providers can assist by acknowledging the ambivalence and work to resolve it by encouraging contemplators to weigh the pros of treatment adherence against the cons. Patients are asked to shrink cons by comparing them to the growing list of pros, by asking how important they are relative to the pros, and by challenging themselves to counter the cons. Interventions in these appointments can be more intensive including taking small steps toward treatment adherence. Providers can help by using motivational interviewing strategies like reflective listening to assist contemplators to resolve their ambivalence by working with them to identify the negative consequences on others of continuing not to be adherent, and by providing case examples of people who have been able to change to adhere to the treatment regimen. Helping patients create a new self-image is important in contemplation. Providers can encourage patients to ask themselves about their self-image. For example, "How do you think and feel about yourself as someone who doesn't adhere to your treatment regimen? What might it be like if you changed that behavior?"

Patients in preparation assess the pros as more important than the cons, are more confident and less tempted, are developing a plan, and are ideal patients most likely to participate in programs. With those in preparation, providers need to be experienced coaches to provide encouragement. They need to coach, not lecture, and give praise, support, and recognition for taking small steps; keep interventions short, focused, and action oriented; be available for phone support; focus on developing a plan for treatment adherence; and problem solve.

Providers can enhance progress by ensuring that patients choose steps that are realistic, concrete, and measurable. Those in preparation should be asked to put treatment adherence plans in writing and to role-play how they will tell others about their commitment to adhere. It is important to help patients identify sources of support for their new behaviors—family members, coworkers, or friends. Providers should encourage the patients in preparation to be as specific as possible about the type and amount of support they need as well as role-play with their requests for support and identify additional sources of support. Providers can also help the patients to think about how they will feel about themselves after they have started making changes.

Patients in action have recently begun adhering to the treatment regimen. They are using behavioral processes of change. Their confidence is building but temptation and risk of relapse is a concern. Providers with patients in action need to be facilitators for the behavior change. The focus is on the behavioral processes of change—counterconditioning, stimulus control, and reinforcement management. It is important to also offer guidance for patients to plan ahead to prevent lapses and relapses.

Providers can help by getting patients to identify problematic beliefs and behaviors that inhibit treatment adherence and then by problem solving on positive alternatives that they believe will work for them. People, places, and things that increase the likelihood of not adhering need to be avoided (tempting cues). Reminders in both familiar and unexpected places that support treatment adherence need to be left around, like a gym bag filled and ready to use, a picture on the desk of relaxing with friends, or pill taking scheduled on the calendar. Those in action also need to notice the intrinsic rewards of their treatment adherence—better health, more energy, more control of life. Patients need to reward themselves with positive statements; providers can praise achievements and help patients recognize the benefits of their efforts.

Patients in maintenance have high confidence, and temptations are low. They are at risk primarily in times of distress or atypical temptations.

With those in maintenance, the provider needs to be a consultant to provide advice regarding relapse prevention. Providers can do this by helping patients to cope with distress (the major cause of relapse), continuing to refine a relapse prevention plan, being available to provide support, and establishing a support system in the community. For many people, maintenance can be a lifelong struggle—it is a dynamic, not a static stage. This may be particularly true in the area of adherence, where the regimen requires daily action and may be associated with ongoing cons. There needs to be work to consolidate gains and increase self-efficacy through increasing coping skills. Remember, a majority of individuals relapse to earlier stages before reaching permanent maintenance.

Intranet and Internet Expert System Program

Lengthier assessments that include each of the constructs of the TTM permit significantly more tailoring but may be impractical in a clinic setting where competing demands limit time. We have developed computerized tailored treatment adherence programs that are designed to be easy and engaging for patients to use and can be delivered over Intranet or Internet platforms which offer a cost-effective, easily disseminated alternative. The technical basis for these systems relies on the integration of statistical, word processing, multimedia, and database software. A system resides either on the Internet or on a web server and can be accessed by anyone who has the appropriate address and password. Once a patient logs onto the program, he or she is asked to complete a TTM treatment adherence assessment that evaluates stage, decisional balance, self-efficacy, and the processes of change.

In developing our treatment adherence programs, a series of multivariate statistical analyses are used to verify empirically the hypothesized relations between the constructs of the TTM (stage, decisional balance, self-efficacy, processes of change) and to determine the programs'

empirical decision rules. For each stage, the goal of the analysis is to empirically determine levels of construct use to optimize movement to the next stage. To generate individualized expert system feedback, an individual is assessed on all relevant TTM constructs. The assessment provides the input for the expert system (i.e., the basis for the tailoring and individualization of the intervention materials each participant receives). After a patient completes the assessment for each construct, his or her responses are analyzed by the expert system. The expert system then produces individualized feedback reports that are provided to the patient through text and graphical feedback on his or her computer screen.

People could use processes too little or too much, depending on their stage of change. If they are not using a process enough they would receive negative feedback. An example of the environmental reevaluation process is, "You're not paying enough attention to how your decision not to adhere to your medication regimen affects other people. Remind yourself that you could set a good example for others if you were to take your medication as directed." The decision rules depend on stage of change. The same process may be involved in more than one stage. For example, increasing an individual's knowledge may be important for those in both precontemplation and contemplation. How much of an increase is necessary for progress may, however, differ at different stages. In a similar manner, the decisional balance and self-efficacy scales represent sensitive change principles for facilitating progress. An example of positive feedback for someone in precontemplation is as follows:

> Great! You seem to be well aware of the pros (benefits) of taking your high blood pressure medication each day. This is a good sign that you're ready to think more seriously about taking them as prescribed. If you want to make more progress, continue to think about the many pros.

The feedback also includes exercises for the participant to complete (e.g., set a start date, list who can support your efforts and how they can help) and recommended strategies (e.g., how to deal with unexpected temptations, how to make a commitment to change behavior, strategies for building confidence) to help participants move forward. The feedback report (typically two to three printed pages) can be printed out at the end of the session.

During a patient's first use of the program, feedback is based on a comparison of the responses of the individual to a larger comparative sample of successful and unsuccessful individuals making the behavior change to treatment adherence. This feedback relies only on normative comparisons that differ by stages. The initial norms were derived from a naturalistic sample of individuals at risk for treatment adherence. Evaluation of the expert system provides updated norms at periodic intervals. The second and subsequent interactions compare the individual with both the normative group and his or her own previous responses and provide both ipsative (i.e., self-comparisons) and normative comparisons. The ipsative comparisons require access to the database for the results of the previous contact. The program makes individualized recommendations of change and guides the participants through the behavior change process that meets their individual needs.

The computer-generated feedback also links or refers participants to sections of a stage-matched self-help interactive resource workbook. Like the stage-matched manual described above, the online integrated workbook teaches users about general principles of behavior change as well as their particular stage of change and the processes they can use to progress to the next stage. The individualized feedback reports refer participants (via links) to appropriate sections of the workbook to provide more details on change processes and stage-matched exercises. For example, a participant can link to the online workbook where there are testimonials about the effects of stress from people who are now effectively managing their stress, an exercise to learn about what controls one's behavior, a bulletin board listing rewards people give

themselves for effectively managing stress, and substitutes for unhealthy stress management that don't involve food, smoking, or alcohol. For a demo of this program designed for stress management, please go to www.prochange.com/stressdemo

Conclusion

From a transtheoretical perspective, assessing and increasing treatment adherence is a complex challenge involving multiple variables for multiple behaviors. Fortunately, the same variables are assessed and applied to each behavior on the continuum of adherence. These variables are the stages of change, pros and cons of changing, self-efficacy about changing, and the processes of change. Depending on the depth of the assessment, varying degrees of tailoring are available to intervene on adherence. Once all variables are assessed for a specific adherence behavior (e.g., screening, acquisition, or discontinuation), the assessments can then drive an intervention designed to increase the specific adherence behavior. The intervention can vary from expert provider interventions to expert computers or some combination of each.

The literature to date indicates that the most promising approaches to increasing adherence will be multifaceted interventions on multiple variables for multiple behaviors. The TTM measures and intervention modalities can provide a framework that can systematically, empirically, and practically tailor these complex approaches to enhance adherence for populations at each point of the adherence continuum.

References

Bandura, A. (1977). Self-efficacy: Toward a unifying theory of behavior change. *Psychological Review, 84,* 191–215.

Campbell, M. K., DeVellis, B. M., Strecher, V. J., Ammerman, A. S., Devellis, R. F., & Sandler, R. S. (1994). Improving dietary behavior: The

JET LIBRARY

effectiveness of tailored messages in primary care settings. *American Journal of Public Health, 84,* 783–787.

DiClemente, C. C., & Prochaska, J. O. (1982). Self-change and therapy change of smoking behavior: A comparison of processes of change in cessation and maintenance. *Addictive Behaviors, 7,* 133–142.

DiClemente, C. C., Prochaska, J. O., Fairhurst, S. K., Velicer, W. F., Velasquez, M. M., & Rossi, J. S. (1991). The process of smoking cessation: An analysis of precontemplation, contemplation, and preparation stages of change. *Journal of Consulting and Clinical Psychology, 59,* 295–304.

Johnson, S. S., Driskell, M. M., Johnson, J. L., Dyment, S. J., Prochaska, J. O., Prochaska, J. M., & Bourne, L. (2006). Transtheoretical model intervention for adherence to lipid-lowering drugs. *Disease Management, 9,* 102–114.

Johnson, S. S., Driskell, M. M., Johnson, J. L., Prochaska, J. M., Zwick, W., & Prochaska, J. O. (in press). Efficacy of a transtheoretical model-based expert system for antihypertensive adherence. *Disease Management.*

Laforge, R. G., Velicer, W. F., Richmond, R. L., & Owen, N. (1999). Stage distributions for five health behaviors in the United States and Australia. *Preventive Medicine, 28,* 61–74.

Marcus, B. H., Bock, B. C., Pinto, B. M., Forsyth, L. H., Roberts, M. B., & Traficante, R. M. (1998). Efficacy of an individualized, motivationally-tailored physical activity intervention. *Annals of Behavioral Medicine, 20,* 174–180.

McDonald, H. P., Garg, A. X., & Haynes, R. B. (2002). Interventions to enhance patient adherence to medication prescriptions. *Journal of the American Medical Association, 288*(22), 2868–2883.

Miller, N. H. (1997). Compliance with treatment regimens in chronic asymptomatic diseases. *The American Journal of Medicine, 102*(2A), 43–49.

Prochaska, J.O. (1979). *Systems of psychotherapy: A transtheoretical analysis.* Homewood, IL: The Dorsey Press.

Prochaska, J. O., & DiClemente, C. C. (1983). Stages and processes of self-change of smoking: Toward an integrative model of change. *Journal of Consulting and Clinical Psychology, 51,* 390–395.

Prochaska, J. O., & DiClemente, C. C. (1984*).* The *transtheoretical approach: Crossing traditional boundaries of change.* Homewood, IL: Dorsey Press.

Prochaska, J. O., & DiClemente, C. C. (1985). Common processes of change in smoking, weight control, and psychological distress. In S. Shiffman & T. Wills (Eds.), *Coping and substance use: A conceptual framework* (pp. 345–363). New York: Academic Press.

Prochaska, J. O., & DiClemente, C. C. (1986). Toward a comprehensive model of behavior change. In W. R. Miller & N. Heather (Eds.), *Treating addictive behaviors: Processes of change.* New York: Plenum Press.

Prochaska, J. O., DiClemente, C. C., & Norcross, J. C. (1992). In search of how people change: Application to addictive behaviors. *American Psychologist, 47,* 1102–1114.

Prochaska, J. O., DiClemente, C. C., Velicer, W. F., Ginpil, S., & Norcross, J. (1985). Predicting change in smoking status for self-changers. *Addictive Behavior, 10,* 395–406.

Prochaska, J. O., DiClemente, C. C., Velicer, W. F., & Rossi, J. S. (1993). Standardized, individualized, interactive, and personalized self-help programs for smoking cessation. *Health Psychology, 12,* 399–405.

Prochaska, J. O., Velicer, W. F., Rossi, J. S., Goldstein, M. G., Marcus, B. H., Rakowski, W., et al. (1994). Stages of change and decisional balance for twelve problem behaviors. *Health Psychology, 13,* 39–46.

Rakowski, W., Ehrich, B., Goldstein, M. G., Rimer, B. K., Pearlman, D. N., Clark, M., et al. (1998). Increasing mammography screening among women aged 40–74 by use of a stage-matched tailored intervention. *Preventive Medicine, 27,* 748–756.

Velicer, W. F., DiClemente, C. C., Prochaska, J. O., & Brandenburg, N. (1985). Decisional balance measure for assessing and predicting smoking status. *Journal of Personality and Social Psychology, 48,* 1279–1289.

Velicer, W. F., Fava, J. L., Prochaska, J. O., Abrams, D. B., Emmons, K. M., & Pierce, J. P. (1995). Distribution of smokers by stage in three representative samples. *Preventive Medicine, 24,* 401–411.

Willey, C. (1999). Behavior-changing methods for improving adherence to medication. *Current Hypertension Reports, 1,* 477–481.

Willey, C., Redding, C., Stafford, J., Garfield, F., Geletko, S., Flanigan, T., et al. (2000). Stages of change for adherence with medication regimens for chronic disease: Development and validation of a measure. *Clinical Therapeutics, 22*(7), 858–871.

4

Identifying and Addressing Barriers to Treatment Adherence Using Behavioral Analysis and Modification Techniques

Elaine M. Heiby

Carrie Lukens

Rationale for Importance of Behavioral Analysis and Modification

Behavioral approaches are readily applicable to the development and maintenance of adherence to health regimens. Well over a dozen forms of behaviorism have been identified (O'Donohue & Kitchener, 1999). Common among behavioral approaches to causal modeling, assessment, and treatment is a focus on low inference constructs that are conducive to time-series measurements (Haynes & O'Brien, 2000). Health regimens generally involve such behaviors (e.g., taking a pill daily).

Early behavioral approaches to the enhancement of adherence to health prescriptions employed operant techniques that included repeated assessment of directly observable behaviors and manipulation of environmental discriminative stimuli and consequences (e.g., Melamed & Siegel, 1975). Such methods proved to be effective in maintaining adherence for children and other individuals whose health behaviors often are exhibited in controlled situations where discriminative stimuli can be engineered and contrived contingent environmental reinforcement can be administered (e.g., daCosta, Rapoff, Lemanek, & Goldstein, 1997).

Under most circumstances external control of environmental discriminative stimuli and consequences is not feasible. To enhance adherence to health regimens in the general population, there proved to be a need to focus also on individual difference variables that generalize across a person's environments. Some behavioral approaches began to include cognitive variables such as health beliefs, attributions concerning health behavior outcome contingencies, and self-efficacy for exhibiting the health behavior (Horne & Weinman, 1998). These cognitive variables are amenable to empirically supported treatments (e.g., O'Donohue, Fisher, & Hayes, 2003). Nevertheless, none of the cognitive-behavioral approaches has accounted sufficiently for variance in adherence or led to the development of widely accepted adherence assessment devices or enhancement strategies (Frank, 2000; Weinstein, 1993).

More recently, a psychological behaviorism (Staats, 1996) approach to the understanding of adherence has been proposed in the Health Compliance Model-II (HCM-II; Frank, 2000; Frank, Heiby, & Lee, in press; Heiby & Frank, 2003). The HCM-II includes the environmental conditions, operant behaviors, and cognitive variables proposed by earlier behavioral models. In addition, the HCM-II emphasizes individual differences in emotional factors deemed critical for motivation to adhere to medical regimens.

The HCM-II posits that the acquisition and maintenance of prescribed health behaviors involve consideration of individual difference variables in four basic behavioral repertoires (BBRs) as follows: language-cognitive, verbal-emotional, emotional-motivational, and sensory-motor. The language-cognitive BBR refers to health imagery, knowledge, words, beliefs, and information processing. The verbal-emotional BBR refers to affect-eliciting health imagery, knowledge, words, beliefs, and information processing. The emotional-motivational BBR is characterized by conditioned affective responses to stimuli inherent to the health regimen (i.e., without intervening cognitive mediation involved

in the verbal-emotional BBR). The emotional-motivational BBR represents affective, reinforcing and directive stimuli capable of controlling future occurrences of adherence-related behavior. The sensory-motor BBR involves all instrumental and operant skills that are necessary for the execution of a given health behavior. The four BBRs are proposed to interact with facilitating conditions/discriminative stimuli and consequences.

The HCM-II proposes that the types of predictors of adherence are expected to vary somewhat across health behaviors depending on the BBRs involved in the regimen and the context in which the regimen is exhibited. Some health behaviors may not require the acquisition of sensory-motor or language-cognitive skills because the instrumental behaviors and knowledge about the regimen are prevalent, such as with seatbelt use whenever in a moving automobile. In contrast, the HCM-II posits that the verbal-emotional and emotional-motivational repertoires are essential for compliance to health behavior prescriptions. These two BBRs are deemed essential because they refer to which health situations, sensory-motor behaviors, and language-cognitions elicit positive affect, direct approach to the health behavior, and function as reinforcement when the health behavior is exhibited. The HCM-II posits that sensory-motor and language-cognitive skills inherent to a health regimen will not be exhibited without concomitant health behavior specific verbal-emotional and emotional-motivational characteristics.

The HCM-II has implications for adherence enhancement strategies derived from earlier behavioral models. The operant approach's environmental engineering designed to shape the sensory-motor BBR involved in the health behavior is expected to be ineffective unless the environmental stimuli involved are consistent with the verbal-emotional and emotional-motivational repertoires. In addition, cognitive-behavioral approaches are expected to be ineffective if they do not target emotion-eliciting aspects of the health regimen.

Specific BBR, facilitating condition/discriminative stimuli, and consequence variables posited in the HCM-II are presented in Table 4.1. Supporting citations for each of the model variables are provided. Treatment implications for components of the HCM-II are indicated later.

Table 4.1 Component Constructs of the Health Compliance Model-II (HCM-II) and Selective Citations

HCM-II Domain	Component Constructs	Selective Citations
Language-cognitive	Instrumental knowledge needed to perform specific health regimen	Heiby and Carlson (1986)
	Self-goal to comply with specific health regimen	Conner and Sparks (1996)
	Knowledge relevant to specific health regimen	Frank (2000) and Heiby and Frank (2003)
Verbal-emotional	Behavior-specific self-efficacy	Bandura (1991)
	Outcome efficacy of specific health regimen	Bandura (1991)
	Susceptibility of adverse outcome if noncompliant to specific regimen	Van der Pligt (1996)
	Severity of adverse outcome if noncompliant to specific regimen	Van der Pligt (1996)
	Health locus of control (regimen specific)	Wallston (1992)
	Self-reinforcement for compliance to specific regimen	Heiby and Carlson (1986)
	Perceived ease of performing the task	Frank (2000) and Heiby and Frank (2003)
	Worry about behavior-relevant health outcomes (e.g., AIDS)	McCaul, Schroeder, and Reid (1996) and Sheeran and Abraham (1996)
	Health care satisfaction	Horne (1998)
	Positive evaluation of health care provider	Frank (2000) and Heiby and Frank (2003)
	Personal goal to comply with health regimen	Frank (2000) and Heiby and Frank (2003)
	Feels health regimen disrupts daily schedule	Dubbert, Rappoport, and Martin (1987)
Emotional-motivational	Global health value	Wallston (1992)
	Motivation and commitment to comply with health regimen	Heiby and Carlson (1986)
	Emotional states incompatible with compliance	Heiby and Carlson (1986)
	Pleasure gained during health behavior	Heiby, Gafarian, and McCann (1989)
	Pleasure following health behavior	Heiby and Carlson (1986) and Heiby et al. (1989)
	Discomfort during health behavior (e.g., embarrassment, pain)	Heiby and Carlson (1986) and Heiby et al. (1989)
	Discomfort following health behavior	Heiby and Carlson (1986) and Heiby et al. (1989)

(Continued)

Table 4.1 (Continued)

HCM-II Domain	Component Constructs	Selective Citations
	New health information elicits anxiety, anger, or depression	Heiby and Carlson (1986) and Murray and McMillan (1993)
Sensory-motor	Successful past compliance to a health regimen	Heiby and Carlson (1986) and Prochaska, Redding, Harlow, Rossi, and Velicer (1994)
	Time-management skills	Heiby and Carlson (1986) and Gafarian, Heiby, Blair, Gallagan, and Singer (1995)
	Active lifestyle	Heiby and Carlson (1986) and Heiby et al. (1989)
	General self-care skills	Heiby and Carlson (1986) and Gafarian, Heiby, Blair, and Singer (1999)
	Use of prompts and reminders	Heiby and Carlson (1986)
	Instrumental skills needed to engage in behavioral regimen	Heiby and Carlson (1986)
Facilitating conditions/ discriminative stimuli	**Physician variables**	
	Explicitly recommends compliance	Heiby and Carlson (1986) and Rimer, Denmark-Wahnefried, and Egert (1997)
	Provides instructions with appropriate language and print size	Heiby and Carlson (1986) and DiMatteo (1997)
	Having a regular physician	Gochman (1997)
	Physician-patient interaction variables	
	Solicits and answers patient's questions	Heiby and Carlson (1986), Gafarian et al. (1995), Rimer et al. (1997), and O'Brien, Petrie, and Raeburn (1992)
	Includes patient in treatment planning decisions	Heiby and Carlson (1986), Rimer et al. (1997), Gochman (1997), and O'Brien et al. (1992)
	Assesses patient's understanding and expectations	Heiby and Carlson (1986), Rimer et al. (1997), Gochman (1997), and O'Brien et al. (1992)
	Assesses previous health behavior changes	Heiby and Carlson (1986)
	Continuity of health prescriptions	Frank (2000) and Heiby and Frank (2003)
	Compliance promotion variables	
	Availability of time needed to engage in health regimen	Heiby and Carlson (1986)

HCM-II Domain	Component Constructs	Selective Citations
	Social support	Heiby and Carlson (1986) and O'Brien et al. (1992)
	Optimal quantity and frequency of prompts	Heiby and Carlson (1986)
	Medical environment variables	
	Time waiting to see physician	Heiby and Carlson (1986) and Wallston (1992)
	Convenience of location of health care facility	Heiby and Carlson (1986), Wallston (1992), and Meichenbaum and Turk (1987)
	Friendliness of medical staff	Heiby and Carlson (1986), DiMatteo (1997), Gochman (1997), and O'Brien et al. (1992)
Consequences	Compliance results in symptom relief	Heiby and Carlson (1986) and Wallston (1992)
	Compliance results in contracted material reinforcement	Heiby and Carlson (1986) and Wallston (1992)
	Compliance results in naturally occurring social reinforcement	Heiby and Carlson (1986) and Wallston (1992)
	Compliance results in engineered social reinforcement	Frank (2000) and Heiby and Frank (2003)
	Compliance aggravates symptoms	Heiby and Carlson (1986) and Wallston (1992)
	Financial costs associated with behavioral health regimen	Heiby and Carlson (1986) and Wallston (1992)
	Interference with daily schedule and social activities (inconvenient)	Heiby and Carlson (1986) and Prochaska et al. (1994)

SOURCE: Adapted and modified from Frank (2000).

NOTE: All variables should be assessed in as health behavior-specific a manner as possible.

Empirical Evidence for the Effectiveness of the HCM-II

Many of the variables in the HCM-II are conducive to assessment by self-report and have been measured with a model-generated questionnaire, the Health Behavior Schedule-II (HBS-II; Frank et al., in press). The HBS-II includes 45 HCM-II derived predictor items, most of which are rated on a 4-point Likert scale. The items have been evaluated in the

prediction of compliance to the following 12 commonly recommended health practices: (1) performing breast self-exams once per month (for women only); (2) obtaining pap smear screen once every 3 years (for women only); (3) taking medication as prescribed; (4) not smoking cigarettes; (5) wearing a bike safety helmet (if applicable); (6) protecting skin from sun (i.e., use sunscreen, avoid direct exposure to the sun); (7) flossing teeth daily; (8) wearing a seat belt when in a moving vehicle; (9) limiting alcohol consumption (i.e., consume no more than one drink per day); (10) practicing safe sex (i.e., sexual abstinence, monogamy, use of condom); (11) exercising regularly (i.e., 20 minutes of exercise, three times per week); and (12) eating a healthy diet (i.e., a low-fat, high-fiber diet).

In one study, Frank et al. (in press) reported that the HBS-II showed acceptable content validity evaluations and internal consistency and stability reliability estimates when administered to a multiethnic sample of 461 college students. However, convergent validity estimates justified the retention of only 22 of the 45 predictor items. Therefore, the HBS-II fails to adequately assess all the variables posited in the HCM-II, and the model itself may omit predictors relevant to the 12 health behaviors investigated. The model's hypothesis that the verbal-emotional and emotional-motivational BBRs are critical to adherence was supported for each of the 12 health behaviors. The 45 predictor items version of the HBS-II is available from authors either in English or in German languages. Both language versions are currently undergoing self-monitoring criterion and additional construct validity evaluations by the second author. In addition, a version of the HBS-II designed to assess predictors of blood glucose monitoring by people with diabetes is undergoing evaluation and is available from the first author. Meanwhile, use of the HCM-II to guide adherence assessment and enhancement strategies should be done with caution.

Table 4.2 provides the HBS-II Reduced (HBS-IIR), which consists of the 22 HBS-II predictor items that have empirical support currently (Frank et al., in press) and the compliance rating item that can be repeated for the 12 health behaviors. Scoring less than a 3 on any items rated on a 4-point scale indicates a deficit in facilitating conditions/discriminative stimuli, BBRs, or consequences (Frank, 2000).

Table 4.3 presents the percentage of the variance of 12 health behaviors accounted for by particular HBS-IIR items (Frank et al., in press). Depending on the health behavior of interest, the number of predictor items ranges from two to eight, making assessment for prevention and treatment planning feasible in most health care settings.

Items on the HBS-IIR correspond to variables that can be manipulated by empirically supported treatments (Heiby & Frank, 2003). Table 4.4 posits behavior modification techniques that may be suggested by each of the items on the HBS-IIR. Table 4.4 also indicates the HCM-II variables and components that the items are designed to measure. A guide to the implementation of each treatment listed in Table 4.4 is provided in O'Donohue et al. (2003). Treatments with empirical support for the commonly prescribed health behaviors measured on the HBS-IIR are listed in Table 4.5.

Brief Discussion of Theoretical Underpinnings of the HCM-II

The psychological behaviorism theory (Staats, 1996), which underlies the HCM-II and the HBS-II questionnaire, has been shown to be a useful framework for integrating the literatures for a range of other complex human behaviors. The theory has promoted the synthesis of research concerning anxiety disorders, depression, self-regulation, mental retardation, severe disabilities (Eifert & Evans, 1990), bipolar disorder (Reidel, Heiby, & Kopetskie, 2001), and pain (Staats, Hekmat, & Staats, 1996). The theory also has guided the development of a structured interview designed to assess the situational factors, BBRs, and organic conditions relevant to prevention and treatment of depression among elders (Dubanoski, Kameoka, Heiby, & Wong, 1996).

Indications and Counterindications of the HCM-II Approach

The evidence supporting the use of the HCM-II (Frank, 2000; Frank et al., in press; Heiby & Frank, 2003; see Table 4.1) as a fairly comprehensive behavioral approach to the understanding and enhancement of adherence to health regimens thus far is limited to 22 predictors measured on a self-report questionnaire, the HBS-IIR (see Tables 4.2 and 4.3). Most of the predictors involve BBRs rather than facilitating conditions/discriminative stimuli and consequences. The HBS-II has been evaluated with a multiethnic college population for 12 health behaviors only and generalizability to other populations and health behaviors is unknown. Completion of the HBS-II requires at least an eighth grade reading level in English or German and an accurate response style, which can be evaluated by a separate instrument such as an indicator of social desirability or malingering (e.g., having a raw score lower than 10 [a z-score below 78] on the Minnesota Multiphasic Personality Inventory (MMPI) Lie scale (Dahlstrom, Welsh, & Dahlstrom, 1972). The treatment suggestions listed in Table 4.4 are empirically supported interventions but they have not been evaluated for the range of health behaviors or their theoretical determinants proposed in the HCM-II. For some of the health behaviors, however, the effectiveness of some treatments to increase compliance has been tested and these are listed in Table 4.5. Therefore, the usefulness of the application of the HCM-II to any population and health regimen requires empirical evaluation.

Step-by-Step Description of How to Implement the HCM-II

An HCM-II-guided behavioral analysis, assessment, and modification of adherence to a health regimen would consider the dynamic effects of the potential causal variables listed in Table 4.1. Idiographic causal analysis or case formulation would involve person- and context-specific variables that direct selection of assessment targets and treatments. Repeated assessment is necessary to evaluate the effects of treatments on targeted causal variables and health behavior outcomes as well as the adequacy of the case formulation. When feasible, multimodal assessment is encouraged to reduce measurement error (Haynes & O'Brien, 2000).

Step 1: Define the Health Regimen and Its Context

Identify the specific behaviors involved in exhibiting a particular regimen. Some health prescriptions may be vague, such as "exercise regularly," and need to be operationalized (e.g., walk 20 minutes three times per week). Some regimens are to be exhibited in a circumscribed context (e.g., protecting skin from the sun) whereas others are to be exhibited in a range of environments (e.g., eating low-fat, high-fiber foods). Operationalizing the health behaviors and the situations in which they are to be exhibited will assist in proposing a causal analysis.

Step 2: Posit a Causal Analysis or Case Formulation

Considering the nature and context of the health regimen, identify potentially relevant causal variables including those in Table 4.1. First, posit which BBRs would facilitate execution of the regimen. Second, posit the facilitating conditions/discriminative stimuli and consequences that may affect exhibiting the relevant BBRs and health behaviors defining the regimen. The causal analysis will guide assessment and treatment selection. Examples of how different regimens can involve different causal variables are provided below.

The language-cognitive BBRs regarding health knowledge needed to exhibit prescribed health behaviors would be more extensive for some regimens than others. For example, understanding the prescription of taking an antibiotic pill daily for a week following the diagnosis of a bacterial infection can be fairly simple. In contrast, understanding the prescription to modify the amount and frequency of insulin injections as a function of blood glucose level, diet, and exercise following a diagnosis of diabetes can be fairly complex.

The verbal-emotional and emotional-motivational BBRs are deemed critical for adherence to all health regimens. Some emotional characteristics may be essential to exhibiting most health behaviors, such as self-efficacy and motivation to comply. Other emotional characteristics may be more relevant to health behaviors with delayed positive consequences, such as self-reinforcement and pleasure gained during the health behavior.

The sensory-motor BBRs needed to exhibit prescribed health behaviors vary across regimens. Some instrumental health behaviors, such as swallowing a pill, involve a few simple sensory-motor skills that are fairly easy for most people to acquire. Other instrumental health behaviors, such as walking 20 minutes three times per week, are more complex. Walking as an exercise involves the sensory-motor skills of stretching, foot placement, posture, breathing, pacing, and vigilance for danger and obstructions.

Facilitating conditions/discriminative stimuli that are under the control of the health care provider and medical environment (e.g., physician-patient interactions and waiting time to see a physician) are more likely to be deemed relevant for regimens prescribed by the provider for a specific condition, such as in the treatment of a muscle injury, than for regimens encouraged for most people by public health efforts, such as use of a seat belt in a moving vehicle. Social support may be more important for regimens exhibited around other people (e.g., eating a particular diet) than for regimens often exhibited when one is alone (e.g., flossing one's teeth). The provision of prompts may be more important for health regimens that are preventive given there is no pain and discomfort to serve that function.

Consequences of adhering to a regimen may be inherent or contrived. Some regimens are in part maintained by inherent symptom relief and social reinforcement, such as a reduction in coughing and an increase in acceptance by others following cessation of cigarette smoking. When regimens result in punishing consequences, such as the expense, pain, and inconvenience involved in blood glucose monitoring, adherence may be better maintained by an introduction of contrived reinforcement.

Step 3: Assessment

Adherence to health regimens can be measured by self-report (interview, self-monitoring, and questionnaire), direct observation, and in some cases biological indicators. Repeated multimodal assessment of the specific prescribed health behaviors across contexts is necessary to evaluate adherence maintenance. Such assessment also permits an evaluation of the causal analysis or case formulation developed in Step 2 and the treatments developed in Step 4. The causal analysis guides the selection of BBRs, facilitating conditions/discriminative stimuli, and consequences to target for assessment and modification.

Most of the potential causal variables listed in Table 4.1 are conducive to assessment by interview, self-monitoring, and self-report questionnaire (e.g., HBS-IIR in Table 4.2). Assessment of some of the sensory-motor BBRs, facilitating conditions/discriminative stimuli, and consequences are also conducive to measurement by direct observation. If the targeted health behavior is 1 of the 12 that have been investigated using the HBS-II (Frank et al., in press), then Table 4.3 provides a guide of which items may be useful.

Step 4: Treatment Selection and Implementation

Deficits in behavioral competencies and situational conditions identified in Step 3 provide a guideline for selection of treatments designed to enhance adherence. Empirically supported treatments whose effects may generalize to the deficits posited in the HCM-II (Frank, 2000; Heiby & Frank, 2003) can be found in O'Donohue et al. (2003). Table 4.4 illustrates how deficit scores on HBS-IIR items can direct the selection of adherence enhancement interventions. Table 4.5 indicates which of the treatments have been evaluated for the health behaviors assessed on the HBS-IIR. As indicated in Step 3, periodic assessment of targeted deficits and adherence provides corrective feedback for causal analysis or case formulation and treatment selection.

Table 4.2   Health Behavior Schedule-II Reduced (HBS-IIR)

1. It is inconvenient for me to get to my doctor's office. *Reverse scored*.
   (not true)1   2   3   4 (very true)

2. I lead an active lifestyle (i.e., I'm engaged in many daily activities)
   (not true)1   2   3   4 (very true)

3. I worry about contracting the AIDS virus.
   (not true)1   2   3   4 (very true)

4. Of all things important to me, my health is most important.
   (not true)1   2   3   4 (very true)

5. I worry about how much I have been drinking.
   (not true)1   2   3   4 (very true)

6. I am concerned that I might develop lung cancer.
   (not true)1   2   3   4 (very true)

7. Compared with other people, I'd say that I'm pretty good at taking care of myself.
   (not true)1   2   3   4 (very true)

8. I am good at reminding myself to stay on track with my daily responsibilities.
   (not true)1   2   3   4 (very true)

9. I get nervous before receiving any new information about my health. *Reverse scored*.
   (not true)1   2   3   4 (very true)

10. (For women only) It's embarrassing to get a gynecological exam. *Reverse scored*.
    (not true)1   2   3   4 (very true)

11. Is it your *goal* to adopt or maintain this behavior?
    (yes) 1 (no) 0

12. How fully do you *understand* why you should do this?
    (don't understand)1   2   3   4 (fully understand)

13. Have you specifically *promised* anyone else that you'll do this?
    (yes) 1 (no) 0

14. How certain are you of your *ability* to maintain this behavior in the future?
    (not certain)1   2   3   4 (very certain)

15. How *seriously* would your health be at risk if you *never* practiced this behavior?
    (not seriously)1   2   3   4 (very seriously)

16. If you passed up an opportunity to do this, would you *feel* bad about it later?
    (yes) 1 (no) 0

17. How fully do you *intend* to practice this behavior in the future?
    (don't intend)1   2   3   4 (fully intend)

18. Has a health care professional *told* you to do this?
    (yes) 1 (no) 0

19. How *motivated* are you to practice this behavior in the future?
    (not motivated)1   2   3   4 (very motivated)

20. This behavior makes me *feel good*.
    (not true)1   2   3   4 (very true)

(Continued)

Table 4.2 (Continued)

21. Do you experience any *discomfort* from this behavior?*Reverse scored.*
    (yes) 1 (no) 0

22. How *inconvenient* is this behavior?
    (not inconvenient)1   2   3   4 (very inconvenient)

23. How *successful* have you been at making this health behavior a habit?
    (not at all)1   2   3   4 (very successful)

Items 11–23 are repeated for the following 12 health behaviors:
   Performing breast self-exams once per month (for women only)
   Obtaining pap smear screen once every 3 years (for women only)
   Taking medication as prescribed
   Not smoking cigarettes
   Wearing a bike safety helmet (if applicable)
   Protecting your skin from sun (i.e., use sunscreen, avoid direct exposure to the sun)
   Flossing your teeth daily
   Wearing your seat belt when you ride in a car
   Limiting alcohol consumption (i.e., consume no more than one drink per day)
   Practicing safe sex (i.e., sexual abstinence, monogamy, condom use)
   Exercising regularly (i.e., 20 min of exercise, three times per week)
   Eating a healthy diet (i.e., a low-fat, high-fiber diet)

Reprinted from Frank, M. & Heiby, E., Health Behavior Schedule II, copyright © 1999. Reprinted with permission.

Several behavioral and cognitive-behavioral treatments to improve adherence have empirical support in the literature (see Table 4.5 for treatment citations by health behavior). These include behavioral contracting, multimodal behavior therapy, contingency management, generalization promotion, harm reduction, self-management, shaping, bibliotherapy, modeling, self- monitoring, and problem solving.

Brief Case Study

The following case is designed to illustrate how to implement the HCM-II. A male dentist has an adult female patient who has several cavities and is at high risk of gum disease. The patient has failed to adhere to the dentist's repeated instruction that she should floss her teeth. He wants the patient to start flossing daily to decrease this risk and wants to help ensure compliance to his request. The dentist begins by administering the HBS-IIR. After inspecting the results, the dentist finds his patient has obtained a deficient score on several items. He then collaborates with a male behavioral health specialist to help her increase her compliance.

Step 1

The behavioral health specialist begins by operationalizing the health behavior. Daily flossing is vague and so in accordance with the dentist, the behavior is operationalized as flossing twice daily, once in the morning after breakfast and once in the evening before bedtime.

Step 2

The behavioral health specialist posits a case formulation. He starts by deciding which BBRs would facilitate execution of the behavior. In this case, the language-cognitive BBR is important because the patient may have little knowledge of the benefits of daily flossing. The emotional-motivational BBR is also important for motivation to perform the behavior. Finally, the sensory-motor BBR may be important if the patient doesn't have the instrumental skills to perform flossing. The behavioral health specialist then decides which facilitating conditions/discriminative stimuli would be important. The provision of prompts may be important if the patient has difficulty remembering to perform the new behavior as they introduce it into her daily routine.

Step 3

Now the behavioral health specialist proceeds to the third step, which is assessment. He begins by readministering the HBS-IIR (see Table 4.2), to gauge the level of compliance (Item 23) and deficits in compliance enhancement conditions (Items 1–22) for this patient and a second assessment device, the MMPI Lie scale (Dahlstrom et al., 1972), to gauge response style to aid in interpretation of HBS-IIR scores. For this patient, response style score was in the normal range (i.e., raw score less than 10 on the MMPI Lie scale), suggesting the responses to the HBS-IIR and other self-reports may be fairly reliable. The HBS-IIR scores indicate a low level of compliance and of some compliance enhancement skills. She reported a score of 1 (not at all successful) on Item 23 concerning degree of compliance to daily flossing. In terms of compliance enhancement skills, she reported a score of 2 on Item 14 regarding her appraisal of her own ability to floss daily, a score of 1 on Question 17 regarding the intention to perform this behavior, and a score of 2 on Question 19 regarding the motivation to perform this behavior. These scores indicate deficient knowledge about and sense of ability to floss daily, as well as a low intention and low motivation for flossing teeth. Items 14, 17, and 19 are the three items that have accounted for significant variance with teeth flossing (see Table 4.3).

Table 4.3   Percentage of the Variance Accounted for by Health Behavior Schedule-II Reduced (HBS-IIR) Items for 12 Health Behaviors

Health Behavior	Items	Variance* (%)
Breast self-exam	12, 13, 14, 19, 20, 22	38
Pap smear	10, 12, 14, 15, 16, 18, 22	65
Medication	1, 8, 11, 14, 16	42
Not smoking	6, 14, 20, 22	62
Bike safety helmet	14, 19	51
Sun protection	8, 11, 14, 17, 19	52
Flossing teeth	14, 17, 19	56
Seatbelt	11, 14, 19, 22	60
Moderate alcohol	5,11,14,17,22	47
Safe sex practices	3, 9, 11, 14, 18, 20, 21, 22	47
Exercise	2, 4, 7, 11, 14, 17, 20, 22	57
Healthy diet	2, 7, 14, 17, 19, 22	52

*$p < .00001$.

The HCM-II posits that verbal-emotional and emotional motivational skills are necessary for the compliance of the daily flossing behavior. The behavioral health specialist looks at the items that had a deficient score on the HBS-II to see which component is represented. Self-efficacy is verbal-emotional, intention is language-cognitive, and motivation is emotional-motivational. This case, therefore, illustrates this aspect of the model.

After scoring the HBS-IIR, the behavioral health specialist conducts an interview with the patient, asking how often she currently flosses her teeth, what barriers prevent her from doing this behavior on a more regular basis, and her appraisal of her ability to perform teeth flossing. These questions are guided by her low scores on the HBS-IIR regarding intention, motivation, and self-efficacy. The interview yields idiographic and contextual information about the potential causal variables for nonadherence to daily flossing. She states that she never flosses. She brushes twice a day and doesn't see the added benefit of flossing. Some barriers to flossing stated were that she didn't have enough time in the morning and found flossing sometimes difficult, often getting stuck in between her teeth. The behavioral health specialist in collaboration with the hygienist also observes the patient flossing to see if self-report and direct observation converge.

Step 4

Now the behavioral health specialist selects the treatment he will be administering (see Tables 4.4 and 4.5). In collaboration with the dentist and his dental hygiene assistant, the specialist begins with bibliotherapy by giving the patient a brochure on flossing and tells her of the benefits of flossing daily such as decreasing risk of gum disease. He and the dental hygienist also model the correct way to floss to increase self-efficacy, and based on problem solving they suggest the use of waxed floss to overcome one stated barrier, the floss getting stuck between her teeth. To increase intention and motivation, the behavioral health specialist uses a motivational interviewing style to assist the patient in taking responsibility for dental health and to overcome ambivalence about flossing. The behavioral health specialist then gives the patient a reminder card that can be placed on the mirror in the bathroom to serve as a prompt. Finally, he chooses a treatment that has demonstrated effectiveness for enhancing adherence to dental hygiene, contingency management (see Tables 4.4 and 4.5). The behavioral health specialist discusses with the patient possible contingencies that would be relevant and motivating for her. He decided that it should be a daily contingency as the patient's motivation and intention was low and it wasn't currently a part of the patient's daily routine. During the interview, the patient had stated that she enjoyed using her computer at night to look at various websites for pleasure. The specialist suggested that she use this as a contingency. If she had flossed her teeth both in the morning and at night, then she would be allowed to use her computer to look at websites. If not, she would have to forgo this pleasure for the day. The patient agreed to this contingency. He also asked her to self-monitor her progress as another way to increase self-efficacy in the behavior. The self-monitoring form was a small, 5 × 3 inch, spiral bound notebook. Each page had 10 dates listed with AM and PM printed next to each date. The patient was to place a checkmark in the space next to AM after her morning flossing and then next to PM after her nightly flossing.

Table 4.4   Treatments Associated With Health Behavior Schedule-II Reduced (HBS-IIR) Items and Health Compliance Model-II (HCM-II) Variables and Components

HBS-IIR Item	HCM-II Variable	Model Component	Treatments
1.	Medical environment	FC/SD	Communication training Functional analysis Problem solving Self-management Stimulus control
2.	Active lifestyle	Sensory-motor	Behavioral chaining Behavioral contracting Generalization promotion Self-management Shaping
3.	Worry (AIDS)	Verbal-emotional	Cognitive restructuring Emotional regulation Motivational interviewing Multimodal behavior therapy Problem solving
4.	Global health value	Emotional-motivational	Harm reduction Mindfulness practice Motivational interviewing
5.	Worry (alcohol)	Verbal-emotional	Cognitive restructuring Emotion regulation Motivational interviewing Multimodal behavior therapy Problem solving
6.	Worry (lung)	Verbal-emotional	Cognitive restructuring Emotional regulation Multimodal behavior therapy Problem solving Motivational interviewing

(Continued)

Table 4.4 (Continued)

HBS-IIR Item	HCM-II Variable	Model Component	Treatments

7.	Self-care skills	Sensory-motor	Behavioral chaining
			Behavioral contracting
			Behavioral rehearsal
			Contingency
			  management
			Generalization
			  promotion
			Modeling
			Self-management
			Self-efficacy training
			Shaping

8.	Use of prompts	Sensory-motor	Behavioral chaining Behavioral contracting Generalization promotion Self-management Self-monitoring Shaping

9.	Health information
	  elicits negative
	  affect
		Emotional-
		  motivational
			Emotion regulation
			Cognitive restructuring
			Exposure
			Flooding
			Mindfulness practice
			Multimodal behavior
			  therapy
			Problem solving
			Relaxation training
			Stress inoculation
			  training
			Stress management
			Systematic
			  desensitization

10.	Embarrassment (with
	  gynecological exam)
		Emotional-
		  motivational
			Emotion regulation
			Cognitive restructuring
			Exposure
			Flooding
			Mindfulness practice
			Multimodal behavior
			  therapy
			Problem solving
			Relaxation training
			Systematic
			  desensitization

HBS-IIR Item	HCM-II Variable	Model Component	Treatments
11.	Self-goal	Language-cognitive	Acceptance
			Cognitive restructuring
			Harm reduction
			Mindfulness practice
			Motivational interviewing
			Multimodal behavior therapy
			Problem solving
			Self-efficacy training
12.	Understands purpose	Language-cognitive	Bibliotherapy
13.	Promised	Consequence	Assertiveness training
			Behavioral contracting
			Self-management
			Stimulus control
14.	Self-efficacy	Verbal-emotional	Behavioral chaining
			Behavioral contracting
			Behavioral rehearsal
			Cognitive restructuring
			Contingency management
			Generalization promotion
			Modeling
			Multimodal behavior therapy
			Problem solving
			Self-efficacy training
			Self-management
			Self-monitoring
			Shaping
15.	Risk	Verbal-emotional	Bibliotherapy
			Cognitive restructuring
			Harm reduction
			Multimodal behavior therapy
			Self-efficacy training
			Self-monitoring
			Relapse prevention
			Problem solving
16.	Self-reinforcement	Verbal-emotional	Self-management

(Continued)

Table 4.4 (Continued)

HBS-IIR Item	HCM-II Variable	Model Component	Treatments
17.	Intention	Language-cognitive	Bibliotherapy Cognitive restructuring Harm reduction Mindfulness practice Motivational interviewing Multimodal behavior therapy Problem solving Self-efficacy training
18.	Prescription	FC/SD	Assertiveness training Bibliotherapy Communication training
19.	Motivation	Emotional-motivational	Bibliotherapy Behavioral chaining Behavioral contracting Cognitive restructuring Contingency management Emotional regulation Harm reduction Mindfulness practice Modeling Motivational interviewing Multimodal behavior therapy Problem solving Self-efficacy training Self-management Shaping
20.	Pleasure during	Emotional-motivational	Mindfulness practice Self-management Self-monitoring
21.	Discomfort	Emotional-motivational	Behavioral rehearsal Mindfulness practice Modeling Problem solving

HBS-IIR Item	HCM-II Variable	Model Component	Treatments
			Relaxation training Self-management Self-monitoring Shaping Systematic desensitization
22.	Interference	Consequence	Assertiveness training Behavioral contracting Cognitive restructuring Multimodal behavior therapy Problem solving Self-management Stimulus control

Table 4.5   Treatments Found Effective for Increasing Health Behaviors and Selective Citations

Health Behavior	Effective Treatments	Selective Citations
1. Breast self-exam	Bibliotherapy	Worden et al. (1994)
	Contingency management	Hailey, Lalor, Byrne, and Starling (1992) and Solomon et al. (1998)
	Modeling	Worden et al. (1994)
	Multimodal behavior therapy	Worden et al. (1994)
	Self-management	Hailey et al. (1992) and Solomon et al. (1998)
2. Pap smear	Bibliotherapy	Yabroff, Kerner, and Mandelblatt (2000)
	Multimodal behavior therapy	Yabroff et al. (2000)
3. Medication	Harm reduction	Saounatsou et al. (2001)
	Multimodal behavior therapy	Saounatsou et al. (2001)
	Motivational interviewing	Safren et al. (2001) and DiLorio et al. (2003)
	Problem solving	Safren et al. (2001) and DiLorio et al. (2003)
	Self-management	Smith, Rublein, Marcus, Brock, and Chesney (2003)
	Self-monitoring	Safren et al. (2001) and DiLorio et al. (2003)
4. Not smoking	Modeling	Mermelstein, Hedeker, and Wong (2003)
	Motivational interviewing	Mermelstein et al. (2003)

(Continued)

Table 1.5 (Continued)

Health Behavior	Effective Treatments	Selective Citations
	Problem solving	Mermelstein et al. (2003)
	Self-efficacy training	Mermelstein et al. (2003)
5. Bike safety helmet	Bibliotherapy	Farley, Haddad, and Brown (1996)
	Modeling	Farley et al. (1996)
	Multimodal behavior therapy	Farley et al. (1996)
6. Sun protection	Bibliotherapy	Miller, Geller, Wood, Lew, and Koh (1999) and Weinstock, Rossi, Redding, and Maddock (2002)
	Generalization promotion	Lowe, Balanda, Stanton, and Gillespie (1999)
	Harm reduction	Lowe et al. (1999)
	Modeling	Miller et al. (1999) and Weinstock et al. (2002)
	Self-management	Lowe, Balanda, Stanton, and Gillespie (1999)
	Shaping	Lowe et al. (1999)
	Multimodal behavior therapy	Miller et al. (1999) and Weinstock et al. (2002)
7. Flossing teeth	Contingency management	Claerhout and Lutzker (1981) and Street, Sheaves, Konopasky, and Lenzer (1987)
8. Seatbelt	Bibliotherapy	Clark et al. (1999) and Williams, Wells, McCartt, and Preusser (2000)
	Modeling	Clark et al. (1999) and Williams et al. (2000)
	Multimodal behavior therapy	Clark et al. (1999) and Williams et al. (2000)
9. Moderate alcohol	Behavioral contracting	Ossip-Klein, Van Landingham, Prue, and Rychtarik (1984)
	Multimodal behavior therapy	Ossip-Klein et al. (1984)
	Problem solving	Koerkel (2002) and Dawe and Richmond (1997)
	Stimulus control	Koerkel (2002) and Dawe and Richmond (1997)
	Motivational interviewing	Dawe and Richmond (1997)
10. Safe sex practices	Bibliotherapy	Kim, Stanton, Li, Dickersin, and Galbraith (1997)
	Communication training	Kim et al. (1997)
	Problem solving	Holtgrave and Kelly (1996)
	Self-management	Holtgrave and Kelly (1996)

Health Behavior	Effective Treatments	Selective Citations
11. Exercise	Behavioral contingency	Hegel, Ayllon, VanderPlate, and Spiro-Hawkins (1986)
	Self-management	Baile and Engel (1978)
	Self-monitoring	Baile and Engel (1978)
12. Healthy diet	Bibliotherapy	Newell, Bowman, and Cockburn (2000) and Hegel, Ayllon, Theil, and Oulton (1992)
	Multimodal behavior therapy	Newell, Bowman, and Cockburn (2000) and Hegel, Ayllon, Theil, and Oulton (1992)
	Self-monitoring	Newell, Bowman, and Cockburn (2000) and Hegel et al. (1992)
	Shaping	Newell, Bowman, and Cockburn (2000) and Hegel et al. (1992)

At her 3-month follow-up appointment, the behavioral health specialist administered a posttest HBS-IIR. The scores revealed an increase in compliance enhancement skills as evidenced by an increase by 2 points in scores on Items 14 from a 2 to a 4, 17 from a 1 to a 3, and 19 from a 2 to a 4. The patient showed increased levels of flossing on HBS-IIR Item 23 and on her self-monitoring forms. Although she was very consistently flossing at night, she was having difficulty with her morning flossing. The behavioral health specialist inquired about this and the patient stated that she was often rushed in the morning and did not have time to floss every day. The specialist interviewed the patient about her morning routine to problem solve. He discovered that the patient had a break at 10 a.m. at work, and asked if it would be feasible for her to floss during her break at work. She stated that she would try this as an alternative. The behavioral health specialist also obtained results from the dental examination of her gumline, which indicated improvements and thus added support to the self-reported increase in flossing. The behavioral health specialist asked the patient to continue self-monitoring until her next 3-month appointment.

At the next 3-month appointment, the behavioral health specialist administered the HBS-IIR and found that the patient's scores had remained stable. Her self-monitoring also showed that her flossing had increased to almost 90%. The adjustment to flossing at her morning break had been successful and the patient stated she was able to floss almost every morning now and that flossing had become a part of her daily routine. Therefore, the treatment was deemed effective.

Suggested Readings

Myers, L. B., & Midence, K. (Eds.). (1998). *Adherence to treatment in medical conditions.* Amsterdam: Harwood Academic.

O'Donohue, W., Fisher, J., & Hayes, S. (Eds.). (2003). *Cognitive behavior therapy: Applying empirically supported techniques in your practice.* New York: Wiley.

References

Baile, W. F., & Engel, B. T. (1978). A behavioral strategy for promoting treatment compliance following myocardial infarction. *Psychosomatic Medicine, 40*(5), 413–419.

Bandura, A. (1991). Self-efficacy mechanism in psychological activation and health-promoting behavior. In J. Madden (Ed.), *Neurobiology of learning, emotion and affect* (pp. 229–269). New York: Raven Press.

Claerhout, S., & Lutzker, J. R. (1981). Increasing children's self-initiated compliance to dental regimens. *Behavior Therapy, 12*(2), 165–176.

Clark, M. J., Schmitz, S., Conrad, A., Estes, C., Healy, M. M., & Hiltibidal, J. (1999). The effects of an intervention campaign to enhance seat belt use on campus. *Journal of American College of Health, 47*(6), 277–280.

Conner, M., & Sparks, P. (1996). The theory of planned behavior and health behaviors. In M. Conner & P. Norman (Eds.), *Predicting health behavior: Research and practice with social cognition models* (pp. 121–161). Buckingham, UK: Open University Press.

da Costa, I. G., Rapoff, M. A., Lemanek, K., & Goldstein, G. L. (1997). Improving adherence to medication regimes for children with asthma and its effect on clinical outcome. *Journal of Applied Behavior Analysis, 30*(4), 687–691.

Dahlstrom, W. G., Welsh, G. S., & Dahlstrom, L. E. (1972). *An MMPI handbook: Clinical interpretation.* Minneapolis, MN: University of Minnesota Press.

Dawe, S., & Richmond, R. (1997). Controlled drinking as a treatment goal in Australian alcohol treatment agencies. *Journal of Substance Abuse Treatment, 14*(1), 81–86.

DiLorio, C., Resnicow, K., McDonnell, M., Soet, J., McCarty, F., & Yeager, K. (2003). Using motivational interviewing to promote adherence to antiretroviral medications: A pilot study. *Journal of the Association of Nurses in AIDS Care, 14*(2), 52–62.

DiMatteo, M. R. (1997). Health behaviors and care decisions: An overview of professional-patient communication. In D. S. Gochman (Ed.), *Handbook of health behavior research II: Provider determinants* (pp. 5–22). New York: Plenum Press.

Dubanoski, J., Kameoka, V., Heiby, E., & Wong, E. (1996). A cross-ethnic psychometric evaluation of the Elder Life Adjustment Interview Schedule. *Journal of Clinical Geropsychology, 2,* 247–262.

Dubbert, P. M., Rappoport, N. B., & Martin, J. E. (1987). Exercise and cardiovascular disease. *Behavior Modification, 11,* 329–347.

Eifert, G. H., & Evans, I. M. (Eds.). (1990). *Unifying behavior therapy.* New York: Springer.

Farley, C., Haddad, S., & Brown, B. (1996). The effects of a 4-year program promoting bicycle helmet use among children in Quebec. *American Journal of Public Health, 86*(1), 46–51.

Frank, M. R. (2000). Psychometric evaluation of the health behavior schedule-II for compliance with behavioral health regimens (Masters thesis, University of Hawaii). *Masters Abstracts International.*

Frank, M. R., Heiby, E. M., & Lee, J. H. (in press). Assessment of determinants of compliance to twelve health behaviors: Psychometric evaluation of the Health Behavior Schedule-II. *Psychological Reports.*

Gafarian, C. T., Heiby, E. M., Blair, P., Gallagan, R., & Singer, F. (1995, February). *Psychometric evaluation of the daily diabetes activity schedule.* Poster session presented at the convention of the Hawaii Psychological Association, Honolulu, HI.

Gafarian, C. T., Heiby, E. M., Blair, P., & Singer, F. (1999). The diabetes time management questionnaire. *The Diabetes Educator, 25,* 585–592.

Gochman, D. S. (Ed.). (1997). *Handbook of health behavior research II: Provider determinants.* New York: Plenum Press.

Hailey, B. J., Lalor, K. M., Byrne, H. A., & Starling, L. M. (1992). The effects of self-reinforcement and peer-reinforcement on the practice of breast self-examination. *Health Education Research, 7*(2), 165–174.

Haynes, S. N., & O'Brien, W. H. (Eds). (2000). *Principles and practice of behavioral assessment.* New York: Kluwer Academic.

Hegel, M. T., Ayllon, T., Theil, G., & Oulton, B. (1992). Improving adherence to fluid restrictions in male hemodialysis patients: A comparison of cognitive and behavioral approaches. *Health Psychology, 11*(5), 324–330.

Hegel, M. T., Ayllon, T., VanderPlate, C., & Spiro-Hawkins, H. (1986). A behavioral procedure for increasing compliance with self-exercise regimens in severely burn-injured patients. *Behaviour Research and Therapy, 24*(5), 521–528.

Heiby, E. M., & Carlson, J. G. (1986). The health compliance model. *The Journal of Compliance in Health Care, 1,* 135–152.

Heiby, E. M., & Frank, M. (2003). Compliance to health regimens. In O'Donohue, J. Fisher, & S. Hayes (Eds.), *Cognitive behavior therapy: Applying empirically supported techniques in your practice* (pp. 103–108). New York: Wiley.

Heiby, E. M., Gafarian, C. T., & McCann, S. C. (1989). Situational and behavioral correlates of compliance to a diabetic regimen. *The Journal of Compliance in Health Care, 4,* 101–116.

Holtgrave, D. R., & Kelly, J. A. (1996). Preventing HIV/AIDS among high-risk urban women: The cost-effectiveness of a behavioral group intervention. *American Journal of Public Health, 86*(10), 1442–1445.

Horne, R. (1998). Adherence to medication: A review of existing research. In L. B. Myers & K. Midence (Eds.), *Adherence to treatment in medical conditions* (pp. 285–309). Amsterdam: Harwood Academic.

Horne, R., & Weinman, J. (1998). Predicting treatment adherence: an overview of theoretical models. In L. B. Myers & K. Midence (Eds.), *Adherence to treatment in medical conditions.* UK: Harwood Academic.

Kim, N., Stanton, B., Li, X., Dickersin, K., & Galbraith, J. (1997). Effectiveness of the 40 adolescent aids-risk reduction interventions: A qualitative review. *Journal of Adolescent Health, 20,* 204–215.

Koerkel, J. (2002). Controlled drinking as a treatment goal in Germany. *Journal of Drug Issues, 32*(2), 667–688.

Lowe, J. B., Balanda, K. P., Stanton, W. R., & Gillespie, A. (1999). Evaluation of a three-year school-based intervention to increase adolescent sun protection. *Health Education and Behavior, 26*(3), 396–408.

McCaul, K. D., Schroeder, D. M., & Reid, P. A. (1996). Breast cancer worry and screening: Some prospective data. *Health Psychology, 15,* 430–433.

Meichenbaum, D., & Turk, D. C. (1987). *Facilitating treatment adherence: A practitioners' guidebook.* New York: Plenum Press.

Melamed, B. G., & Siegel, L. J. (1975). Reduction of anxiety in children facing hospitalization and surgery by use of filmed modeling. *Journal of Consulting and Clinical Psychology, 43*(4), 511–521.

Mermelstein, R., Hedeker, D., & Wong, S. C. (2003). Extended telephone counseling for smoking cessation: does content matter? *Journal of Consulting and Clinical Psychology, 71*(3), 565–574.

Miller, D. R., Geller, A. C., Wood, M. C., Lew, R. A., & Koh, H. K. (1999). The Falmouth safe skin project: Evaluation of a community program to promote sun protection in youth. *Health Education and Behavior, 26*(3), 369–384.

Murray, M., & McMillan, C. (1993). Health beliefs, locus of control, emotional control and women's cancer screening behavior. *British Journal of Clinical Psychology, 32,* 87–100.

Newell, S. A., Bowman, J. A., & Cockburn, J. D. (2000). Can compliance with nonpharmacologic treatments for cardiovascular disease be improved? *American Journal of Preventive Medicine, 18*(3), 253–261.

O'Brien, M. K., Petrie, K., & Raeburn, J. (1992). Adherence to medication regimens: Updating a complex medical issue. *Medical Care Review, 49,* 435–453.

O'Donohue, W., Fisher, J., & Hayes, S. (Eds.). (2003). *Cognitive behavior therapy: Applying empirically supported techniques in your practice* (pp. 103–108). New York: Wiley.

O'Donohue, W., & Kitchener, R. (1999). *Handbook of behaviorism.* San Diego, CA: Academic Press.

Ossip-Klein, D. J., Van Landingham, W. P., Prue, D. M., & Rychtarik, R. G. (1984). Increasing attendance at alcohol aftercare using calendar prompts and home based contracting. *Addictive Behaviors, 9*(1), 85–89.

Prochaska, J. O., Redding, C. A., Harlow, L. L., Rossi, J. S., & Velicer, W. F. (1994). The transtheoretical model of change and HIV prevention: A review. *Health Education Quarterly, 21,* 471–486.

Reidel, H. P. R., Heiby, E. M., Kopetskie, S. (2001). Psychological behaviorism theory of bipolar disorder. *The Psychological Record, 51,* 507–532.

Rimer, B. K., Demark-Wahnefried, W., & Egert, J. R. (1997). Acceptance of cancer screening. In D. S. Gochman (Ed.), *Handbook of health behavior research II: Provider determinants* (pp. 285–301). New York: Plenum Press.

Safren, S. A., Otto, M. W., Worth, J. L., Salomon, E., Johnson, W., Mayer, K., et al. (2001). Two strategies to increase adherence to HIV antiretroviral medication: Life-steps and medication monitoring. *Behaviour Research and Therapy, 39,* 1151–1162.

Saounatsou, M., Patsi, O., Fasoi, G., Stylianou, M., Kavga, A., Economou, O., et al. (2001). The influence of the hypertensive patient's education in compliance with their medication. *Public Health Nursing, 18*(6), 436–442.

Sheeran, P., & Abraham, C. (1996). The health belief model. In M. Conner & P. Norman (Eds.), *Predicting health behavior: Research and practice with social cognition models* (pp. 23–61). Buckingham, UK: Open University Press.

Smith, S. R., Rublein, J. C., Marcus, C., Brock, T. P., & Chesney, M. A. (2003). A medication self-management program to improve adherence to HIV therapy regimens. *Patient Education and Counseling, 50,* 187–199.

Solomon, L. J., Flynn, B. S., Worden, J. K., Mickey, R. M., Skelly, J. M., Geller, B. M., et al. (1998).

Assessment of self-reward strategies for maintenance of breast self-examination. *Journal of Behavioral Medicine, 21*, 83–102.

Staats, A. W. (1996). *Behavior and personality: Psychological behaviorism.* New York: Springer.

Staats, P. S., Hekmat, H., & Staats, A. W. (1996). The psychological behaviorism theory of pain: A basis for unity. *Pain Forum, 5*, 194–207.

Street, P. A., Sheaves, S., Konopasky, R. J., & Lenzer, I. (1987). Children's oral hygiene: Spot checks and contingency management are equivalent. *Psychological Reports, 61*(1), 300.

Van der Pligt, J. (1996). Risk perception and self-protected behavior. *European Psychologist, 1*, 34–43.

Wallston, K. A. (1992). Hocus-pocus, the focus isn't strictly on locus: Rotter's social learning theory modified for health. *Cognitive Therapy and Research, 16*, 183–199.

Weinstock, M. A., Rossi, J. S., Redding, C. A., & Maddock, J. E. (2002). Randomized controlled community trial of a multi-component stage matched intervention to increase sun protection among beachgoers. *Preventive Medicine, 35*, 584–592.

Weinstein, N. D. (1993). Testing four competing theories of health-protective behavior. *Health Psychology, 12*, 324–333.

Williams, A. F., Wells, J. K., McCartt, A. T., & Preusser, D. F. (2000). Buckle up now! An enforcement program to achieve high belt use. *Journal of Safety Research, 31*(4), 195–201.

Worden, J. K., Mickey, R. M., Flynn, B. S., Constanza, M. C., Vacek, P. M., Skelly, J. M., et al. (1994). Development of a community breast screening promotion program using baseline data. *Preventive Medicine, 23*(3), 267–275.

Yabroff, K. R., Kerner, J. F., & Mandelblatt, J. S. (2000). Effectiveness of interventions to improve follow-up after abnormal cervical cancer screening. *Preventive Medicine, 31*, 429–439.

PART III

Specific Strategies and Techniques for Promoting Treatment Adherence

5

Promoting Treatment Adherence Through Motivational Interviewing

Ana M. Bisonó

Jennifer Knapp Manuel

Alyssa A. Forcehimes

In medical settings, patient adherence is one of the greatest challenges to achieving treatment goals. According to Zweben and Zuckoff (2002), treatment adherence describes "the extent to which people follow through with agreed-on or prescribed actions, or do what providers expect them to do, where treatment is concerned" (p. 300). Motivational interviewing (MI) can be used to increase a variety of treatment compliant behavior, such as attending scheduled appointments and medication compliance (Zweben & Zuckoff, 2002). DiMatteo, Giordani, and Lepper (2002) conducted a meta-analysis to examine the relationship between patient adherence and medical treatment outcomes in 63 studies over a 30-year period. Results showed that on average 26% more patients had a better treatment outcome when adherence rates were high. The correlation was even stronger in studies that did not involve medications (e.g., behavior change interventions) and when the illness was chronic (e.g., hypertension, hypercholesterolemia, intestinal disease, and sleep apnea). Their review supports the simple yet important fact that treatment efficacy often depends on patient adherence. Given the strong correlation between treatment adherence and positive outcomes, what can practitioners do to increase patient adherence?

Importance of Motivational Interviewing in Increasing Adherence to Treatment

MI is a collaborative method that elicits from patients their own motivation or reasons for changing their behavior. Practitioners then reinforce patient reasons for change through the use of reflective listening. It can be thought of as a way of speaking so others hear and hearing when others speak. MI is a client-centered, directive style of counseling introduced by Miller (1983) for use in addressing substance abuse. Since then, this counseling style has been applied to areas beyond addictions, and over 70 clinical trials have established MI as an efficacious method for facilitating behavior change as well as increasing adherence to treatment. This method is intended for use particularly when patient motivation and adherence are important for treatment to be effective. Given that motivation is often a significant obstacle in behavior change, MI is particularly useful in dealing with many health problems related to lifestyle as well as in the prevention and treatment of many chronic illnesses (Miller, 2004).

Efforts to enhance motivation have received increasing attention in health care settings (Emmons & Rollnick, 2001). Findings have supported the efficacy of MI to increase retention in substance abuse treatment, smoking cessation treatment, HIV-risk prevention, diet, and exercise, as well as medication adherence. MI has been incorporated in health behavior interventions as a way of enhancing motivation for behavior change (Emmons & Rollnick, 2001). A number of clinical trials have found that adding even one session of MI at the early stages of treatment can improve the efficacy by increasing patient retention and adherence, thus improving outcomes (Miller, 2000).

Although there are many strategies that can be used in the application of this method, MI is not a technique so much as a style for practitioner-patient communication. The underlying spirit of MI is the key in carrying out this style of counseling in a meaningful way. This chapter offers a method to practitioners interested in increasing patient treatment adherence, which has shown promising positive results. The emphasis is to explain the spirit of MI and provide an overview of the techniques and skills used in its application.

Theoretical Basis of Motivational Interviewing

MI has been described as a client-centered counseling style used for eliciting behavior change by helping patients to explore and resolve ambivalence (Miller & Rollnick, 1991; Rollnick & Miller, 1995). Miller (2004) further described it as "a way of being with people, that is also directive in seeking to move the person toward change by selectively evoking and strengthening the patient's own reasons for change" (p. 4). To use this method, the practitioner and the patient work together to address the patient's health care needs, emphasizing a "side-by-side companionable approach" (Miller, 2004, p. 4).

According to Miller (2004), the approach fits with a few established models of psychotherapy. In particular, MI suits Carl Rogers' client-centered (1980) approach to psychotherapy and Daryl Bem's self-perception theory (1967). Rogers' approach (1980) highlights the spirit of MI, the way of being with another in an empathic and genuine manner. Bem's self-perception theory (1967) has parallels with the mechanisms of change in MI, emphasizing the process of change that occurs as individuals voice their opinions aloud.

In MI, the practitioner selectively elicits and reinforces (through reflective listening) positive self-statements, consequently directing the patient to move in a positive direction. However, the patient, not the practitioner, argues for change. Thus, MI is a patient-centered yet directive counseling style that seeks to explore and resolve the patient's ambivalence by eliciting and augmenting particular reasons for the patient's change in behavior.

The Spirit of Motivational Interviewing

The spirit of MI is based on three fundamental components: collaboration, evocation, and autonomy. MI is a collaborative approach, meaning that the practitioner does not assume an authoritarian or expert role in the relationship. Instead, the practitioner respects the patient's perspective and autonomy. In addition, the practitioner fosters a warm, comfortable environment in which the patient is able to communicate honestly and openly with the practitioner.

The second fundamental element of the spirit of MI is evocation. MI's evocative nature assumes that practitioners can draw out perspective and values from their patients. MI emphasizes that perspectives and values should be elicited from the patient rather than imparted. Instead of considering the patient's mind as an empty vessel ready to be filled with facts and feedback, the practitioner explores the patient's own intrinsic values to facilitate change. Two Latin verbs regarding education, *docere* and *ducere*, highlight the important difference between evoking and imparting information. *Docere* means to lead or impart knowledge or information, whereas *ducere* means to draw forth or evoke from within. The words express a subtle but important distinction of what MI is and is not. The spirit of MI focuses on *ducere*—the ability to draw forth rather than an emphasis on pulling the patient toward the goal (Miller, 2004; Miller & Rollnick, 2002).

The third fundamental element within the spirit of MI is autonomy. In MI, the practitioner understands that it is up to the patient to decide whether or not he or she wants to change, and how best to go about that change. The practitioner respects the patient's choices and decisions regarding self-direction, even if they are divergent from what the practitioner thinks best for the patient.

Principles of Motivational Interviewing

MI is based on four key principles that are consistent with the general spirit described above. This section provides a brief overview of these principles (see Table 5.1).

1. *Express empathy*: Expressing empathy involves actively listening to the patient and conveying an understanding of the patient's perspective, without judging, criticizing, or blaming. In MI, ambivalence about change is regarded as normal and a part of the change process; therefore empathic listening is used to understand and accurately reflect this ambivalence (Miller & Rollnick, 1991, 2002).

2. *Develop discrepancy*: A goal in MI is for patients to see a discrepancy between their personal goals and their present behavior. The objective is for the practitioner to direct the discussion in such a way that the patients perceive this discrepancy and the reasons to change their behavior without pressure from the practitioner. Eliciting reasons for change from the patient is more powerful than giving the patient prescribed reasons why change is necessary (Miller & Rollnick, 1991, 2002).

3. *Roll with resistance*: Avoiding pushing against resistance to change is a third MI principle. Rather than arguing with a patient who is resistant to change, practitioners roll with this resistance. Arguing in favor of a certain position with the patient—for instance, arguing to persuade patients to take medications—will likely result in defensiveness on his or her

part, a decreased desire to take the medication, and lower medication compliance. Practitioners can roll with resistance by reflecting or rephrasing the patient's arguments against change. They can also try to increase the patient's participation in problem solving so that the patient is generating solutions rather than refuting solutions offered by the practitioner. Patient resistance may also be a signal that the practitioner should modify his or her approach with the patient or accept more realistic outcome goals (Miller & Rollnick, 1991, 2002).

4. *Support self-efficacy*: Self-efficacy, a person's confidence in his or her ability to achieve a specific goal, is an important predictor of a successful treatment outcome. If a practitioner believes that the patient is able to change his or her behavior and expresses this support, the patient may feel empowered by the idea that change is possible. An objective in MI is to increase patients' confidence in their ability to change and support steps taken to change (Miller & Rollnick, 1991, 2002).

General Methods of Motivational Interviewing

A primary goal in MI is to shape the language that patients use to describe their dilemmas. "Change talk" occurs when clients give their own reasons and arguments for a behavioral change (Miller & Rollnick, 1991, 2002) and it generally falls into one of four categories: desire, ability, reasons, and need. Key words that are indicative of the desire change talk category are want, wish, and prefer. The ability change talk category refers to patient statements of self-confidence, such as able, can, and could. The reasons change talk category includes patient arguments for change, such as why the patient should change or benefits to changing. Utterances that fall into the need change talk category include words such as need

to, have to, and important. See Table 5.2 for examples of change talk. The four change talk categories predict patient commitment to change, which in turn predicts behavioral change by the patient (Amrhein, Miller, Yahne, Palmer, & Fulcher, 2003). When a patient offers a practitioner change talk, for example, "I sure would save a lot of money if I quit buying cigarettes," the practitioner then has the opportunity to reflect this change talk and thus reiterate the patient's own arguments for change. Reflections allow the patient to hear his or her change talk, which further reinforces what the patient has said (Miller, 2004).

Skills used in MI to elicit change talk from patients include the following: (1) asking open questions, (2) affirming, (3) listening reflectively, and (4) summarizing. These skills are often referred to by the acronym OARS (open questions, affirming, reflecting, and summarizing).

1. *Ask open questions*: Asking open questions, questions that cannot be answered with a simple "Yes" or "No," gives the patient the opportunity to elaborate and focus on what he or she feels is important. An open question allows a patient to give his or her own perspective without reacting to cues from the practitioner. Additionally, questions of this kind set the stage for a discussion in which the patient, rather than the practitioner, does most of the talking. Although it is also normal to ask closed questions (questions that elicit a "Yes"/"No" or short response), about half of all questions should be open ones. Examples of open questions include the following:

   "What brings you here today?"

   "If you decided you wanted to exercise more, how would you go about that?"

   "You mentioned that your weight has caused you a lot of problems. Tell me what that is like."

Table 5.1   Description of Motivational Interviewing (MI) Principles

MI Principle	Brief Description
Express empathy	Actively listen to the patient and understand his or her perspective
Develop discrepancy	Develop a discrepancy between the patient's goals and current behavior Reflect the patient's ambivalence about change Patient should give reasons or arguments for change
Roll with resistance	Reflect resistance from the patient Arguing with the patient for change is counterproductive
Support self-efficacy	Enhance the patient's confidence to change The patient should initiate change in behavior and the practitioner should support the patient's ability to initiate change

Table 5.2   Examples of Change Talk

Change Talk Category	Example of Change Talk
Desire	"I really want to quit smoking."
Ability	"I know that I can remember to take my medication every day."
Reasons	"Smoking is killing me. I can't breathe, I'm always out of breath, and it's expensive."
Need	"I have to exercise more."

2. *Affirm*: Affirmations are an important part of a practitioner-patient discussion. Affirmations can be direct compliments or appreciative statements. Practitioners can also affirm patients through reflective listening and statements that convey an understanding of the patient. Affirmations increase collaboration between the patient and practitioner and facilitate patient exploration (Miller & Rollnick, 2002). Often simple affirmations are used, such as letting the patients know you appreciate their openness or complimenting them when they make good choices:

"Thanks for coming in today."

"That's a great idea."

"This situation seems to be very difficult but you are handling it well."

3. *Listen reflectively*: Reflective listening is one of the most important, yet difficult, skills in MI. Reflective listening occurs when a practitioner makes a statement that is a guess at what the client has said. Ideally, reflections will move the session forward and shape the patient's speech in the direction of change. It is not imperative, or even desirable, that reflections relay the patient's exact idea. An incorrect reflection still conveys that the practitioner is listening to the patient and is trying to understand his or her perspective. Some reflective statements are similar to questions, except that there is a difference in inflection. Whereas in questions voice tone turns up at the end, in reflections the inflection is down at the end of a statement. The difference between inflections

can have substantial meaning in MI. For instance, if a practitioner reflects, "It is important to you to stay healthy," the practitioner is conveying that he or she understands what the patient is saying and is reflecting the patient's value of good health. However, if the practitioner said, "Is it important to you to stay healthy?" the practitioner is asking a question rather than communicating an understanding of the patient's perspective.

There are two main types of reflections: simple and complex reflections. Simple reflections simply repeat or rephrase what the patient has said, whereas complex reflections tend to continue the paragraph, meaning the practitioner anticipates the patient's train of thought. Although simple reflections repeat the patient's statements, the practitioner is still guiding the session by choosing what to reflect. Reiterating the patient's speech also reinforces what the client has said, especially if patient change talk is being repeated:

(a) Patient: "My wife wants me to stop smoking. She is always nagging me about it."

Practitioner: "Your wife is really concerned about you and wants to help you."

(b) Patient: "I want to lose weight; I just hate eating healthy foods. Why can't nutritious food taste good!"

Practitioner: "It's frustrating to you how healthy food tastes, yet losing weight is really important to you."

4. *Summarize*: The fourth OARS skill used in MI is summarizing. Summary statements are used to tie patients' statements together and communicate that the practitioner has been listening to the patient and understands his or her perspective. Summaries are also used to reinforce important material that has been discussed in consultation

between a practitioner and a patient. Summaries can be used to collect ideas, link together ideas, or as a transition, indicating a shift in the direction of the discussion or to wrap up a consultation.

Importance and Confidence Rulers

Although an understanding of the theory and principles of MI is necessary to effectively use a number of MI skills, others "may not require skillfulness in the overall method or even in understanding of the underlying theory to be used effectively in practice" (Miller, 2004, p. 5). For example, importance rulers are a widely used and relatively easy way to assess a patient's confidence, ambivalence, and readiness to change. This technique can be used to assess the importance of certain behaviors such as losing weight, quitting smoking, and reducing drinking. When using this ruler with a patient, the practitioner asks, "On a scale of zero to ten, where zero is not at all important and ten is very important, how important is it for you to quit smoking?" This question is then followed with a "backward" question that will elicit change talk from the patient. For example, if a patient responds with a five, then the practitioner would ask, "Why are you a five and not a zero?" This type of "backward" follow-up question sets up the patient to respond with change talk, rather than resistance. Asking why the patient is not at a higher number, would have the opposite and undesired effect of causing the patient to defend the status quo (Miller, 2004).

Confidence rulers are similar to importance rulers, except that they assess the patient's belief in his or her ability to change. For example, practitioners may ask, "On a scale from zero to ten, where zero is not at all confident and ten is extremely confident, how confident are you that you could quit smoking?" Practitioners can then ask why the patient did not choose a lower number. An additional follow-up question might be

"What would it take for you to go from a four to a six?" (Miller & Rollnick, 2002).

After the patient answers the practitioner's "backward question," the practitioner can follow up with an open question such as, "What else?" This type of question is intended to elicit further change talk from the patient. By listening reflectively and empathically to the patient, the practitioner will likely elicit reasons and argument to change from the patient. Following open questions, the practitioner may summarize the patient's statements, thus reinforcing his or her responses (Miller, 2004).

Brief Case Example

This example is a compilation of real interactions between practitioners and patients and exemplifies how quickly a practitioner can elicit change talk from a patient. This case example is illustrative of the empathic and supportive characteristics of MI. During this 2-min example, the practitioner guided the patient from being concerned about his smoking but unsure of how to quit, to listing all the reasons he should quit smoking, and discussing treatment options with his practitioner.

Practitioner:	"Hi Paul. How are you feeling today?"	Practitioner begins dialogue with an open question.
Paul:	"I'm feeling better."	
Practitioner:	"I would like to talk to you for a few minutes about your smoking. Would that be ok with you?"	Practitioner asks permission to discuss smoking with patient. This puts the patient in control and helps establish rapport with patient.
Paul:	"So you want to fuss at me about my smoking?"	Patient is resistant to subject matter.
Practitioner:	"You're concerned that I am going to lecture you. Well I have no intention of fussing at you, Paul. I was just hoping we could talk about how you feel about smoking for a few minutes."	Practitioner rolls with patient's resistance by reflecting the patient's concerns.
Paul:	"How I feel about smoking? Well I know it's terrible for my wife, my kids, and me. I've tried to quit before, it's just so hard."	Patient gives reasons for change: smoking is harmful to self and family.
Practitioner:	"So you would like to quit, but you've just had a hard time quitting in the past. How else do you feel about smoking?"	Simple reflection and open question.
Paul:	"It costs me a fortune, my wife hates it and is nagging at me all the time to quit but I'll never be able to do it."	Patient gives more reasons to change, but resistance regarding quitting.

(Continued)

(Continued)

Practitioner:	"So although you would really like to quit smoking, it's too hard so there's really no point in trying."	Practitioner gives an amplified reflection— an exaggeration of what the patient said.
Paul:	"Well I wouldn't say there's no point. I mean I think I could quit if I really tried."	Patient gives more change talk. Reflection.
Practitioner:	"So you're pretty sure you could quit smoking. How ready do you feel to quit?"	Practitioner assesses the patient's readiness to change.
Paul:	"Well I want to quit, I'm just not sure how."	Change talk.
Practitioner:	"Well I know of some treatments that have helped a lot of people quit smoking. Would you be interested in hearing about them?"	Practitioner asks permission to give the patient information regarding quitting smoking.
Paul:	"OK."	
Practitioner:	"You have a few different options and it's really up to you. You can choose whatever feels most comfortable to you or you can decide that none of these options are for you. You are the one who needs to decide what is best for you."	Emphasizes patient's control. Patient is the expert and knows what will work best for him.

Review of Empirical Evidence for the Effectiveness of Motivational Interviewing in Treatment Adherence Studies

As MI has expanded to populations other than substance abuse, numerous studies have been conducted to evaluate its effectiveness for a wide range of clinical problems. MI and adaptations of MI (AMIs) were first developed to promote change in alcohol and drug problems. One example of an AMI is to give the patient personalized feedback based on results from standardized measures, such as a serum chemistry panel. The feedback from the lab tests is given in an MI style, which includes processes such as reflective listening. The discussion between the practitioner and patient then incorporates the essential methods of MI, including open-ended questions, affirmations, reflective listening, and summaries (this process is described later in the chapter). The term *AMI* is used to refer to interventions that preserve

MI principles as a central part of treatment. Often, however, it is difficult to assess if these studies of AMIs are actually preserving the principles of MI, because fidelity of MI has seldom been documented (Burke, Arkowitz, & Dunn, 2002).

Recent studies have examined the role that MI plays in increasing treatment adherence, and the results have been generally positive. In a randomized pilot study, Smith, Heckemeyer, Kratt, and Mason (1997) studied whether treatment adherence and glucose control could be improved in a group of older obese women with noninsulin dependent diabetes mellitus (NIDDM) by adding MI strategies to a behavioral intervention for obese patients. Participants were randomly assigned to one of the two treatment modalities: to a standard 16-week behavioral group focusing on weight control or the same behavioral group plus three individual MI sessions. Participants in the MI group were significantly better than the standard group in the number of meetings attended (13.3 vs. 8.9), food diaries completed

(15.2 vs. 10.1), and blood glucose records kept (46.0 vs. 32.2 days). These results support the rationale for including an MI component to standard behavioral treatment programs.

Kemp, Kirov, Everitt, Hayward, and David (1998) conducted a randomized clinical trial comparing outcomes of treatment adherence in a group of patients diagnosed with psychiatric disorders. In this study, compliance therapy, a blend of MI and cognitive approaches to treating psychotic symptoms, was compared with treatment as usual. The results showed a significant effect for the compliance therapy treatment group post-treatment on measures of treatment compliance (19%), insight (18.8%), and drug attitudes (15.6%).

In a pilot study, Daley, Salloum, Zuckoff, Kirisci, and Thase (1998) studied the efficacy of an MI-based motivational therapy on treatment adherence and completion for patients dually diagnosed with depression and cocaine dependence. Participants were assigned to either motivational therapy or treatment as usual upon discharge from an inpatient psychiatric unit. Results from comparison between patients in the two conditions showed that the use of motivational therapy increased treatment adherence and completion rates in this population. Patients in the motivational therapy group were significantly more likely to complete outpatient treatment, attend more treatment sessions, and experience fewer rehospitalizations than the patients in the treatment as usual group. The researchers concluded that the findings from this pilot support motivational therapy to increase treatment adherence and completion in patients with depression and cocaine dependence.

Swanson, Pantalon, and Cohen (1999) conducted a randomized trial to study the effectiveness of MI on treatment adherence. Participants were psychiatric inpatients, the majority of whom were also diagnosed with substance abuse/dependence disorders. Treatment conditions included treatment-as-usual (which included prescription therapy, individual and group therapy, activities planning, milieu treatment, and planning for after discharge) and treatment-as-usual plus MI

(MI component consisted of brief feedback on the results of an MI-based assessment administered early in the hospitalization period and a one-hour motivational interview, using MI techniques, before discharge). Results illustrate that patients in the treatment-as-usual plus MI group were significantly more likely to attend the first outpatient appointment after discharge (47%) than the patients in the treatment-as-usual group. Based on these results, the authors concluded that brief MI-based interventions promote treatment adherence among psychiatric and dually diagnosed individuals.

In another study, Berg-Smith et al. (1999) used an MI-based intervention to increase treatment adherence and retention of adolescents in the "Dietary Intervention Study in Children." The participants were part of a multicenter clinical trial that implemented a family-based group approach aimed at lowering dietary fat to decrease levels of cholesterol in high-risk children. The MI-based intervention appeared to be an age-appropriate shift from a family-based intervention, and the adolescents in the study were satisfied with the approach.

In the area of exercise, Young, King, Sheehan, and Stefanick (2002) evaluated the association among baseline stage of motivation readiness for exercise and adherence to a 9-month exercise intervention. Results showed that although most of the men and about a third of women in the study reached the goals of the intervention, the stage of motivational readiness for exercise did not predict adherence to the intervention.

Dilorio, Resnicow, McDonnell, Soet, McCarty, and Yeager (2003) conducted a pilot study using an MI-based intervention to increase treatment adherence to antiretroviral medications. Patients were randomly assigned to either motivational enhancement therapy (MET) or a control group. Results indicated that although differences in missed medications were not significant between the two groups, patients in the MET condition reported that they were more likely to follow the prescription regimen as recommended by their health practitioner.

Who Might Benefit from Motivational Interviewing?

Numerous studies have examined the efficacy of MI using a wide range of populations. Studies support MI across several behavioral domains, including decreasing drinking, drug use, smoking and risky behaviors, and increasing exercise and fruit and vegetable intake (Belcher et al., 1998; Berg-Smith et al., 1999; Burke, Arkowitz, & Menchola, 2003; Butler et al., 1999; Carey et al., 1997, 2000; Colby et al., 1998; DiMatteo et al., 2002; Dunn, Deroo, & Rivara, 2001; Ershoff et al., 1999; Glasgow, Whitlock, Eakin, Lichtenstein, 2000; Harland et al., 1999; Kemp et al., 1998; Noonan & Moyers, 1997; Resnicow et al., 2001; Schubiner, Herrold, & Hurt, 1998; Smith et al., 1997; Valanis et al., 2001; Woollard et al. 1995; Young et al., 2002). These findings suggest that MI is applicable in a wide range of settings across diverse populations. In addition, MI may be particularly efficacious with individuals who are angry, resistant to treatment, and less ready for change (Heather, Rollnick, Bell, & Richmond, 1996; Project MATCH Research Group, 1997, 1998; Rollnick & Heather, 1992).

Contraindications of Motivational Interviewing

Despite MI's success in numerous studies across diverse populations, there are instances in which the use of MI is not suggested. For instance, MI may not be the ideal approach with patients who are already very ready to make a behavioral change (www.motivationalinterview.org; Project MATCH Research Group, 1997, 1998). Although empathic listening and a respect for the patient's autonomy are key components of MI, patients who are ready and willing to make a behavioral change may not want or need to talk about their ambivalence or confidence in changing. Although some techniques are unnecessary with eager and motivated patients, MI skills remain helpful as a way to interact with a patient and encourage continued

success. In addition, Miller and Rollnick (2002) state that there are certain situations in which using MI creates ethical dilemmas. It is not appropriate for MI to be used when a practitioner has a personal investment in the patient's decision or the relationship is coercive in nature (Miller & Rollnick, 2002).

Obstacles to Using Motivational Interviewing in Health Care Settings

Time

Health care practitioners may feel overwhelmed, knowing the average patient contact is 10 to 15 min and is often restricted to one visit with a particular patient (Emmons & Rollnick, 2001). Although time constraints may seem to be an obstacle for using MI in health care settings, MI has been shown to be an efficacious treatment to enhance patient retention, medical adherence, treatment adherence, and outcomes by incorporating even a single session of MI into active treatment (Miller, 2004). Brief AMIs that honor the spirit of MI are very useful and can be applied even in a short period of time (Miller, 2004).

Expert Role

The MI approach can be significantly different from traditional treatment provided in settings where individuals seek help for health behavior change (Emmons & Rollnick, 2001). Practitioners who follow the "expert-driven, practitioner-centered" model commonly used in medical settings can find it challenging to embrace the collaborative spirit of MI (Resnicow et al., 2002). Traditional counseling approaches place the practitioner in the "expert" role, leaving the patient in the position of complying with or ignoring the advice the "expert" offers. Instead, one of the central goals of MI is to put the patient in the role of the "expert," allowing the individual to interpret the information that is exchanged, and to decide whether or not this information is applicable to his or her current situation (Emmons & Rollnick, 2001). In this model, the patient does much of the mental work associated with his or her treatment (Resnicow et al., 2002). This is particularly useful in health care settings, in which patients may be ambivalent about changing their behaviors. The brevity of MI interventions facilitates patient and practitioner exploration of ambivalence regarding behavior change.

This is a difficult shift in roles, as the practitioner has expert knowledge of the results of particular behaviors. When met with ambivalence, practitioners are tempted to exclaim, "Can't you see that you must stop drinking—It's destroying your liver!" Although many doctors give advice to their patients and educate them on the reasons they should change their behaviors, patients often meet this advice and information with resistance and defensiveness. MI allows patients to explore their ambivalence about changing (Rollnick & Heather, 1992) and initiate movement toward change. According to Rollnick, Mason, and Butler (1999), some of the behavioral changes that practitioners and patients discuss include diet alterations, adjusting meal times, drinking less alcohol or abstaining from alcohol, exercising more, quitting smoking, taking or changing medications, monitoring glucose levels, abstaining from drugs, or increasing their liquid intake.

Some suggestions to avoid the expert role:

- Avoid arguing for change while the patient argues against it.
- Don't assume you have to come up with all the solutions for health behavior change.
- Avoid labeling the patient.
- Be careful not to assume that your patients ought to change, want to change, or that your patients' health is the prime motivating factor for them to change.
- Don't assume that if your patient decides not to change, the consultation has failed (Rollnick et al., 1999)

Mastery

Mastering the application of MI skills while honoring its spirit requires some practice. Some practitioners choose to attend MI training workshops and dedicate time to develop their skill level, but many do not have the time or desire to acquire a high level of MI expertise. For this reason, brief techniques that preserve the spirit of MI have been developed (Miller, 2004). An example of such technique is the "importance and confidence rulers" described earlier, which can be easily learned and applied. As previously mentioned, MI is a "way of being" with people, rather than a "step-by-step" approach, which allows the practitioner to use its techniques and to continue to improve his or her skill level.

Discussion

MI has emerged as a promising approach that facilitates internally motivated change, and increases treatment adherence in a variety of areas (i.e., diet, exercise, smoking cessation, and substance use reduction) and multiple settings (i.e., inpatient, outpatient and community clinics). However, as in all other approaches, MI is not a "fix all" that works in every area or for everyone.

Some caution in the interpretation of these results is warranted. In many of the trials conducted, the description of how MI and AMIs were implemented in the study protocol is missing, leaving the reader wondering what methods were actually used. Therefore, it is difficult to assess whether MI has worked in a given trial when it is not clear that MI was in fact used. Rollnick & Miller (1995) caution that care should be taken to only call "Motivational Interviewing" the approaches that honor and carry through the *spirit* of MI. Furthermore, treatment adherence is not measured consistently across studies. In many of these trials, adherence is assessed through patients' self-reports, treatment attendance, or outcomes (e.g., attributing weight loss to treatment adherence when factors other than "adherence" are the main contributing factors). Treatment adherence is not defined consistently across trials.

Nevertheless, MI is a well-established effective treatment method in the area of substance abuse, and research is illuminating its benefits in other domains. The use of MI in other areas is rather recent and therefore more research, correcting the above-mentioned problems, is needed. Why MI works as well as it does remains a puzzle that requires further investigation. Many trials of MI in multiple areas are underway and the results will continue to shed light on its effectiveness.

Suggested Readings

Emmons, K. M., & Rollnick, S. (2001). Motivational interviewing in health care settings. *American Journal of Preventive Medicine, 20*(1), 68–74.

Miller, W. R., & Rollnick, S. (1991). *Motivational interviewing: Preparing people to change addictive behaviors.* New York: Guilford Press.

Miller, W. R., & Rollnick, S. (2002). *Motivational interviewing: Preparing people for change* (2nd ed.). New York: Guilford Press.

Resnicow, K., Dilorio, C., Soet, J. E., Borrelli, B., Hecht, J., & Ernst, D. (2002). Motivational interviewing in health promotion: It sounds like something is changing. *Health Psychology, 21*(5), 444–451.

Rollnick, S., & Heather, N. (1992). Negotiating behavior change in medical settings: The development of brief motivational interviewing. *Journal of Mental Health, 1*(1), 25–38.

Rollnick, S., Mason, P., & Butler, C. (1999). *Health behavior change: A guide for practitioners.* New York: Churchill Livingstone.

References

Amrhein, P. C., Miller, W. R., Yahne, C. E., Palmer, M., Fulcher, L. (2003). Client commitment language during motivational interviewing predicts drug use outcomes. *Journal of Consulting and Clinical Psychology, 71*(5), 862–879.

Belcher, L., Kalichman, S., Topping, M., Smith, S., Emshoff, J., Norris, F., et al. (1998). A randomized trial of a brief HIV risk reduction counseling intervention for women. *Journal of Consulting and Clinical Psychology, 66*(5), 856–861.

Bem, D. (196). Self-perception: An alternative interpretation of cognitive dissonance phenomena. *Psychological Review, 74*(3), 183–200.

Berg-Smith, S. M., Stevens, V. J., Brown, K. M., Van Horn, L., Gernhofer, N., Peters, E., et al. (1999). A brief motivational intervention to improve dietary adherence in adolescents. *Health Education Research, 14*(3), 399–410.

Burke, B., Arkowitz, H., & Dunn, C. (2002). The efficacy of motivational interviewing and its adaptations: What we know so far. In W. R. Miller & S. Rollnick (Eds.), *Motivational interviewing: Preparing people for change* (2nd ed.). New York: Guilford Press.

Burke, B., Arkowitz, H., & Menchola, M. (2003). The efficacy of motivational interviewing: A meta-analysis of controlled clinical trials. *Journal of Consulting and Clinical Psychology, 71*(5), 843–861.

Butler, C. C., Rollnick, S., Cohen, D., Bachmann, M., Russell, I., & Stott, N. (1999). Motivational consulting versus brief advice for smokers in general practice: A randomized trial. *British Journal of General Practice, 49*, 611–616.

Carey, M. P., Braaten, L. S., Maisto, S. A., Gleason, J. R., Forsyth, A. D., Durant, L. E., et al. (2000). Using information, motivational enhancement, and skills training to reduce the risk of HIV infection for low-income urban women: A second randomized clinical trial. *Health Psychology, 19*(1), 3–11.

Carey, M. P., Maisto, S. A., Kalichman, S. C., Forsyth, A. D., Wright, E. M., & Johnson, B. T. (1997). Enhancing motivation to reduce the risk of HIV infection for economically disadvantaged urban women. *Journal of Consulting and Clinical Psychology, 65*(4), 531–541.

Colby, S. M., Monti, P. M., Barnett, N. P., Rohsenow, D. J., Weissman, K., Spirito, A., et al. (1998). Brief motivational interviewing in a hospital setting for adolescent smoking: A preliminary study. *Journal of Consulting and Clinical Psychology, 66*(3), 574–578.

Daley, D. C., Salloum, I. M., Zuckoff, A., Kirisci, L., & Thase, M. E. (1998). Increasing treatment adherence among outpatients with depression and cocaine dependence: Results of a pilot study. *American Journal of Psychiatry, 155*(11), 1611–1613.

Dilorio, C., Resnicow, K., McDonnell, M., Soet, J., McCarty, F., & Yeager, K. (2003). Using motivational interviewing to promote adherence to antiretroviral medications: A pilot study. *Journal of the Association of Nurses in AIDS Care, 14*(2), 52–62.

DiMatteo, M. R., Giordani, P. J., & Lepper, H. S. (2002). Patient adherence and medical treatment outcomes: A meta-analysis. *Medical Care, 40*(9), 794–811.

Dunn, C., Deroo, L., & Rivara, F. P. (2001). The use of brief interventions adapted from motivational interviewing across behavioral domains: A systematic review. *Addiction, 96,* 1725–1742.

Emmons, K. M., & Rollnick, A. (2001). Motivational interviewing in health care settings: Opportunities and limitations. *American Journal of Preventive Medicine, 20*(1), 68–74.

Ershoff, D. H., Quinn, V. P., Boyd, N. R., Stern, J., Gregory, M., & Wirtshafter, D. (1999). The Kaiser Permanente prenatal smoking-cessation trial: When more isn't better, what is enough? *American Journal of Preventive Medicine, 17*(3), 161–168.

Glasgow, R., Whitlock, E., Eakin, E., & Lichtenstein, E. (2000). A brief smoking cessation intervention for women in low-income planned parenthood clinics. *American Journal of Public Health, 90*(5), 786–789.

Harland, J., White, M., Drinkwater, C., Chinn, D., Farr, L., & Howel, D. (1999). The Newcastle exercise project: A randomized controlled trial of methods to promote physical activity in primary care. *Behavioral Medicine Journal, 319,* 828–832.

Heather, N., Rollnick, S., Bell, A., & Richmond, R. (1996). Effects of brief counselling among male heavy drinkers identified on general hospital wards. *Drug and Alcohol Review, 15,* 29–38.

Kemp, R., Kirov, G., Everitt, B., Hayward, P., & David, A. (1998). Randomised controlled trial of compliance therapy. *British Journal of Psychiatry, 172,* 413–419.

Miller, W. R. (1983). Motivational interviewing with problem drinkers. *Behavioural Psychotherapy, 11,* 147–172.

Miller, W. R. (2000). Rediscovering fire: Small interventions, large effects. *Psychology of Addictive Behaviors, 14*(1), 6–18.

Miller, W. R. (2004). Motivational interviewing in service to health promotion. The art of health promotion: Practical information to make programs more effective. *American Journal of Health Promotion, 18*(3), 1–10.

Miller, W. R., & Rollnick, S. (1991). *Motivational interviewing: Preparing people to change addictive behaviors.* New York: Guilford Press.

Miller, W. R., & Rollnick, S. (2002). *Motivational interviewing: Preparing people for change* (2nd ed.). New York: Guilford Press.

Noonan, W. C., & Moyers, T. B. (1997). Motivational interviewing. *Journal of Substance Misuse, 2,* 8–16.

Project MATCH Research Group. (1997). Project MATCH secondary a priori hypotheses. *Addiction, 92,* 1671–1698.

Project MATCH Research Group. (1998). Matching alcoholism treatments to client heterogeneity: Project MATCH three-year drinking outcomes. *Alcoholism: Clinical and Experimental Research, 22,* 1300–1311.

Resnicow, K., Dilorio, C., Soet, J. E., Borrelli, B., Hecht, J., & Ernst, D. (2002). Motivational interviewing in health promotion: It sounds like something is changing. *Health Psychology, 21*(5), 444–451.

Resnicow, K., Jackson, A., Wang, T., De, A. K., McCarty, F., Dudley, W. N., et al. (2001). A motivational interviewing intervention to increase fruit and vegetable intake through black churches: Results of the eat for life trial. *American Journal of Public Health, 91*(10), 1686–1693.

Rogers, C. (1980). *A way of being.* Boston: Houghton Mifflin.

Rollnick, S., & Heather, N. (1992). Negotiating behavior change in medical settings: The development of brief motivational interviewing. *Journal of Mental Health, 1*(1), 25–38.

Rollnick, S., Mason, P., & Butler, C. (1999). *Health behavior change: A guide for practitioners.* New York: Churchill Livingstone.

Rollnick, S., & Miller, W. R. (1995). What is motivational interviewing? *Behavioral and Cognitive Psychotherapy, 23,* 325–334.

Schubiner, H., Herrold, A., & Hurt, R. (1998). Tobacco cessation and youth: The feasibility of brief office interventions for adolescents. *Preventive Medicine, 17,* A47–A54.

Smith, D. E., Heckemeyer, C. M., Kratt, P. P., & Mason, D. A. (1997). Motivational interviewing to improve adherence to a behavioral weight-control program for older obese women with NIDDM: A pilot study. *Diabetes Care, 20*(1), 52–54.

Swanson, A. J., Pantalon, M. V., & Cohen, K. R. (1999). Motivational interviewing and treatment adherence among psychiatric and dually diagnosed patients. *Journal of Nervous and Mental Disease, 187*(10), 630–635.

Valanis, B., Lichtenstein, E., Mullooly, J., Labuhn P., Broody, K., Severson, H. H., et al. (2001). Maternal smoking cessation and relapse prevention during health care visits. *American Journal of Preventive Medicine, 20*(1), 1–8.

Woollard, J., Beilin, L., Lord, T., Puddey, I., MacAdam, D., & Rouse, I. (1995). A controlled trial of nurse counselling on lifestyle change for hypertensives treated in general practice: Preliminary results. *Clinical and Experimental Pharmacology and Physiology, 22,* 466–468.

Young, D. R., King, A. C., Sheehan, M., & Stefanick, M. L. (2002). Stage of motivational readiness: Predictive ability for exercise behavior. *American Journal of Health Behavior, 26*(5), 331–341.

Zweben, A., & Zuckoff, A. (2002). Motivational interviewing and treatment adherence. In W. R. Miller & S. Rollnick (Eds.), *Motivational interviewing: Preparing people for change* (2nd ed.). New York: Guilford Press.

6

Patient Education to Promote Adherence to Treatments

Megan L. Oser

Adequate adherence to effective treatment is necessary to improve patient outcomes. However, before patients can adhere to treatment they must be informed of the treatment plan and how to adhere to it. Surprisingly, a substantial number of patients lack basic knowledge about their medications and treatment plan. Patients obviously cannot be expected to comply with treatment that they do not understand. Therefore, knowledge of the treatment and how to adhere to the treatment is a prerequisite of treatment adherence. Treatment outcomes are ultimately dependent on the patient's willingness and ability to incorporate and maintain necessary adherence behaviors.

When a patient lacks the knowledge necessary to successfully adhere to a particular treatment, this not only places treatment effectiveness at risk but also considerably jeopardizes the patient's health. To further complicate the issue, poor adherence may lead to negative public health consequences. These larger public health consequences must not be minimized because patient nonadherence to treatment for transmittable diseases (e.g., HIV or streptococcal infection) involves the serious threat of building resistance to available medications and transmission of drug-resistant viruses and/or bacteria. A recent meta-analysis (DiMatteo, 2004) illustrates the magnitude of treatment nonadherence as a major health care problem. It was calculated that in the year 2000, there were over 759.3 million medical visits for the treatment of medical problems. Nonadherence prevalence rates are estimated to be at 24.8%. This means that as many as 188.3 million medical visits result in patients not following the medical instructions provided to them (DiMatteo, 2004). These data do not fault patients or the health professionals. Rather, these statistics indicate that there are serious flaws in the system of delivery of adherence information to patients.

A major reason for the growth in the field of treatment adherence is the increasing prevalence of chronic disease along with a general increase in the use of prescription medications (Gardner, 2002). Data indicate that poor adherence to medical recommendations often occurs when the treatment regimen is complex and requires patient decision making or self-administration. Improving patients' knowledge of specific adherence-related behaviors, such as the precise steps necessary to follow the treatment plan, and how to incorporate the self-management behaviors into one's lifestyle, may lead to improved adherence in patients following either a complicated or a simple treatment regimen (DiMatteo, 2004; Kravitz & Melinkow, 2004; Raynor, 1998). Providing adherence-related knowledge may benefit patients in several ways. Knowledge may serve to (a) fully inform patients about what to expect from treatment, (b) promote the development of adherence-related skills, (c) increase patient motivation, (d) improve adherence to medical and behavioral recommendations, and (e) increase satisfaction with the health care experience. More broadly, improving knowledge of treatment adherent behavior may result in better patient self-management, more efficient use of health care resources, and ultimately, substantial reductions in health care costs (Clark & Becker, 1998).

One of the most important objectives of this chapter is to explain that merely giving information about the treatment to a patient is not what is meant by providing information to patients. Simply delivering information about the treatment plan is necessary but not sufficient for improving adherence-related knowledge. Providing information is a comprehensive and multistep process that is tailored to each patient's needs. As discussed throughout this chapter, adherence to treatment includes adherence to (a) medication regimens, (b) medical and psychological treatment plans, and (c) the full range of self-management behaviors patients must undertake to effectively manage their health care. The purpose of this chapter is to discuss the empirical literature and theoretical underpinnings for increasing adherence-related knowledge.

This chapter also provides a set of practical guidelines and major strategies, informed by theory and empirical evidence, for health care providers to use for increasing adherence- and treatment-related knowledge with the aim of improving adherence to treatment.

Empirical Research on Adherence-Related Knowledge

Available data suggest that greater knowledge of disease and its treatment is often associated with improved adherence and, more specifically, that regimen-related knowledge is necessary for treatment compliance. However, increased knowledge of medication and treatment is not always associated with higher levels of adherence because several factors influence the outcome of providing information to patients, as discussed in detail below (Clark & Becker, 1998).

The evidence that patients want more information about their treatment is abundant. However, studies investigating patient knowledge show striking deficiencies in the basic understanding of one's medical condition (Raynor, 1998). These substantial gaps in knowledge may arise for various reasons. First, patients may be bombarded with a large number of sources of information, many varying widely in quality and accuracy. The inconsistency of this information impedes the patient's ability to know which information to use in making adherence-related decisions. In addition, adherence is not likely to improve as a result of large amounts of information being given, particularly when the information is superfluous, such as information about the etiology of the illness. Second, of all the aspects of medical care, patients express the most dissatisfaction with the information given to them by their health care providers. Providers are typically not well trained as to how best to educate patients, and consequently do not feel prepared for this role. The most common problem is that health care providers tend to underestimate the amount and type of information that patients want and need. Health care providers sometimes provide too much background and technical information, and insufficient information about how to adhere to treatment, with not enough time spent on ensuring that the information is being received and clarifying what the patient understands and wants to know. It is important to note that the amount and type of information provided to patients is related to not only patient adherence but also patient satisfaction with care, and overall recall and understanding of the information, thereby significantly affecting the patient's experience with receiving health care (Noble, 1998).

Furthermore, research has revealed that patients commonly do not feel their physicians explain treatment regimens in understandable terms. Many patients do not have the fundamental medical knowledge or know the basic technical terms that providers use to explain treatment plans (Hulka, Cassell, Kupper, & Burdette, 1976). The use of technical jargon by providers in their explanations to patients is a major barrier to the patient understanding medical instructions. Another large gap in patients' knowledge about their medication regimen is the lack of awareness and understanding of side effects. Knowledge of side effects is one component of knowing what to expect when incorporating a new treatment regimen into one's lifestyle (Raynor, 1998). Thus, increasing adherence-related knowledge requires that the information be presented in laymen's terms along with potential side effects and how they may interfere with adherence (Noble, 1998; Parker, 2000).

There is a common misconception that patients are less likely to adhere if they are fully informed about the treatment and its associated side effects because this information may lead to the realization that adherence is too difficult and/or not worth the risks of side effects. This common misconception that patients should not be given full information about their treatment has been disconfirmed by the following series of investigations. Ley (1982) summarized research in which patients were given all the information about treatment including the negative consequences. In areas such as terminal illness, investigative procedures, less serious illness, and medication, the provision of treatment information in its entirety has traditionally been considered "potentially harmful." Data suggest that there is no evidence of iatrogenic effects resulting from giving patients information in any of these areas. There is also no evidence that side effects will increase or that adherence will worsen by providing information about medication side effects. In fact, nonadherence is more likely to occur if a patient experiences side effects about which he or she has not been informed (Noble, 1998).

Knowledge about how to incorporate a medication regimen or treatment program into one's lifestyle is a more influential factor in accounting for treatment nonadherence than information about one's disease. For example, one study demonstrated that epileptic patients' adherence to medications was more influenced by events in their daily routine than by their doctors' advice, especially if the patient has a poor relationship with the provider (Garnett, 2000). Therefore, it is imperative to convey knowledge about how to integrate the demands of medication-taking behaviors into one's daily routine. This includes the specific behaviors the regimen requires, how and when to perform them, and how to manage potential problems. Simply put, patients need problem-solving knowledge about adherence (Meichenbaum &Turk, 1987). The most compelling reasons why there is a need to explicate effective strategies for improving adherence-related knowledge are as follows: (a) patients want treatment and adherence-related information, (b) often there is a discrepancy between the information the patient needs and the information actually given, (c) a better informed patient is typically a more satisfied patient, and (d) increasing adherence knowledge is more complex than merely giving information (Meichenbaum & Turk, 1987; Noble, 1998; Raynor, 1998).

Theoretical Underpinnings for Increasing Adherence-Related Knowledge

Implicit in all the health behavior models and a common component among many adherence interventions is a basic level of knowledge of the illness, the treatment, and how to adhere to the treatment. Most health behavior theories posit that knowledge functions as a predisposing factor influencing other health-related decisions such as adherence (Clark & Becker, 1998). The provision of information is especially important in three key health behavior models. First, according to the self-efficacy model (Bandura, 1977), enhanced self-efficacy leads to improved behaviors and the motivation to adhere properly. One tenet of building self-efficacy is to engage patients in feasible short-term behavior change plans. The successful completion of action plans increases self-efficacy. If a patient is provided with information about the skills necessary to adhere to treatment and successfully completes these tasks, then self-efficacy may be improved. Second, the health belief model (Becker, 1974) states that a person's willingness to adhere to a treatment plan is related to four factors: level of interest in one's health, perception of susceptibility to an illness, perception of severity of illness and its consequences, and consideration of advantages and disadvantages in engaging in adherence behaviors. There is evidence that identifying and addressing patients' health beliefs before beginning treatment is effective for improving adherence. This has direct implications for increasing patients' adherence knowledge. Providing accurate knowledge to patients helps change their inaccurate beliefs about adherence, allowing new accurate knowledge to be learned, which in turn may lead to better adherence. By discussing patient beliefs about health and adherence, the provision of information can be better tailored to address the patient's beliefs about health and adherence (Noble, 1998). Third, the transtheoretical model

(Prochaska & DiClemente, 1983) states that there are stages that patients progress through when changing their health-related behavior. These stages are discussed in detail in Whiteley, Williams, and Marcus, this volume. This model does not presume that patients receiving treatment have already decided that they need treatment. It suggests that the provider of information should tailor the information to the patient's current stage. For example, if a patient is still considering the consequences of not adhering to treatment, it would be ineffective to provide information about how exactly to integrate the treatment plan into his or her lifestyle (Noble, 1998). To change health-related decisions, health beliefs, self-efficacy, and self-management, knowledge of the illness, its treatment, and how to adhere to treatment is necessary.

Who Would Benefit From Increasing Adherence-Related Knowledge?

Improving adherence-related knowledge can enhance adherence among patients who want to adhere but need more and better information to do so, among patients who have fears and misconceptions about treatment, and among patients dissatisfied with their care due to lack of information (Raynor, 1998). Patients with complicated health problems and a complex treatment regimen are at the greatest risk of misunderstanding the instructions about how to adhere to treatment. It follows that the suggestions offered in this chapter would be of great benefit to populations of patients with extensive and complicated treatment plans or to those patients who cannot care for themselves, as in the case of elderly populations or those individuals with cognitive disorders. In addition, patients who overuse health care resources may benefit from improving adherence-related knowledge especially related to self-management behaviors. Providing information to high utilizers may enlighten them as to how to adhere to treatment better and avoid unnecessary visits to the provider resulting from a lack of positive treatment outcomes due to poor treatment adherence. Patients who hold the belief that adherence is not important or those who have low self-efficacy regarding their ability to adhere properly may benefit from knowledge about adherence and the necessary skills to integrate treatment into their lives.

Providers may assume that the majority of patient populations will benefit from gaining knowledge about treatment adherence if the knowledge is given in a way that best fits the needs of the patient. The patient populations mentioned above will particularly benefit from the approaches provided in this chapter because simply reading written information about the treatment plan, which is one standard method for providing knowledge in most health care environments, is unlikely to positively affect adherence in patients experiencing these types of difficulties.

Contraindications of Increasing Adherence-Related Knowledge

If the requirements to adhere to a treatment plan are complex and the negative consequences of not following a treatment plan are substantial, then some individuals may experience a decrease in self-efficacy about their ability to adhere to treatment, thereby limiting their ability to implement the changes in behavior necessary for treatment adherence. However, if the provider effectively assesses the patient's understanding of, and concerns about, adherence, then these difficulties with adherence are more likely to be resolved. In contrast, if the consequences of nonadherence are negligible and the requirements for treatment adherence are great, then relaying this knowledge might lead some patients to choose to not adhere to treatment.

An investigation by Gibbs, Waters, and George (1989) exemplifies this iatrogenic effect of information on adherence. The results indicated that written information on pharmacological treatment for arthritis caused a small number of patients to stop taking the medication. These patients were experiencing minor symptoms that did not warrant the risk of the side effects described, and so they decided to discontinue the medication. Giving too much information may also create a barrier to treatment adherence. As mentioned earlier, patients may not be able to process large amounts of information and may become overwhelmed as a result of too much of the wrong type of information for improving adherence.

Strategies to Increase Adherence-Related Knowledge

One of the most promising and commonly used strategies for enhancing treatment adherence is providing information to patients about how to adhere to treatment. There are numerous factors associated with poor treatment adherence, such as lack of skills to adhere to treatment, inaccurate health beliefs about the importance of adherence, and inadequate knowledge of how to adhere to treatment. Of all these factors, lack of knowledge appears to be more easily targeted and changed than most and therefore would be an important first step for improving patient adherence to treatment (Raynor, 1998). To this end, the goals of increasing adherence-related knowledge, such that treatment adherence is facilitated, are (a) ensuring that the knowledge provided actually helps change adherence behavior, (b) ensuring that the patient understands the consequences of nonadherence, (c) improving the relationship and communication between patient and provider, (d) providing information about which strategies to use when barriers to adherence are present, and (e) ensuring that the patient remembers the information provided (Kravitz & Melinkow, 2004; Raynor, 1998). To achieve these goals of improving knowledge about adherence, there are five key strategies:

1. Provide quality standards of information, such as what problems patients can anticipate and the basic skills for integrating adherence to treatment into one's lifestyle.

2. Use several methods for providing information to ensure an optimal transfer of adherence-related knowledge.

3. Facilitate a collaborative relationship with patients.

4. Accurately assess and tailor adherence information to each patient's needs, capabilities, and current lifestyle.

5. Improve information recall so that patients retain the information.

Guidelines and step-by-step procedures are presented below for each of these key strategies to improve adherence-related knowledge among patients.

Standards of Information

According to practiced medical standards, the minimum information to be provided to patients about their medication regimen includes: (a) name and dose; (b) purpose and benefits (treatment rationale); (c) how to take (adherence procedures); (d) special precautions and instructions, and (e) adverse effects (side effects) (Raynor, 1998). Along with the minimum standards of information, treatment information is more likely to affect patients if they are educated about the risks associated with discontinuation of treatment and importance of continuing medication for the entire duration prescribed. This includes information about the expected length of time until effects are notable. Patients

often discontinue treatment because of minimal alleviation of symptoms or a lack of positive effects in a given period of time. Likewise, it is just as important to explain to patients that it is necessary to continue treatment for the entire duration of time prescribed even if symptoms decrease or disappear early in treatment, as in the case of taking antibiotics. Providing information about problem-solving strategies for common adherence problems will further bolster the improvement of patients' adherence-related knowledge. One caveat to these recommendations is for patients adhering to a complex treatment regimen. Instructing these patients in all aspects of the treatment at one consultation may overwhelm the patient because large amounts of information are not easily remembered. Instead, break the information into its component parts and give the information over consecutive visits (Meichenbaum & Turk, 1987). These guidelines are practical enough to be extended to treatments beyond pharmacotherapy, such as behavioral recommendations (Raynor, 1998). See Table 6.1 for recommended standards of adherence-related information.

These guidelines for providing standards of information use a more comprehensive approach when discussing adherence to treatment with patients, and one criticism of this approach is that health care providers do not have the extra time to devote to providing this level of information to patients. However, the long-term benefits of patients' improved adherence outweigh the short-term time costs of fully communicating about adherence with patients. Long-term benefits may include faster recovery, fewer unproductive or unnecessary visits to the provider, and less chance of building resistance to medications due to poor adherence. Ultimately, more time may be saved when the provider uses a more comprehensive and proactive strategy of informing the patient about adherence at the beginning of treatment and reviewing treatment adherence throughout the duration of treatment.

Table 6.1   Recommended Standards of Adherence-Related Information

- Name and dose of medications
- Treatment rationale (e.g., purpose and benefits)
- Adherence procedures (e.g., how to take medications)
- Special precautions and instructions
- Side effects
- Risks associated with discontinuation of treatment before duration of treatment has ended
- Importance of treatment adherence for entire length of time prescribed
- Problem-solving strategies for common adherence problems

Methods for Conveying Information to Patients

Using verbal communication as well as providing written information will best orient the patient to pertinent information about adherence and also helps create a better understanding between the patient and the provider. Evidence supports the strategy that written information combined with verbal information is the most effective means of transmitting information to patients. From two seminal reviews of information and adherence (Morris and Halperin, 1979; Ley, 1988), written information reinforced with verbal information produced the highest level of knowledge and adherence. These data strongly suggest that to thoroughly educate a patient, written instructions must be accompanied by a verbal explanation. The combination of verbal and written information allows for a greater likelihood of increasing knowledge and improving adherence because the verbal repetition of information allows the patient to remember the information better and reinforces the relevance of the information. Furthermore, patients prefer the combination of the two methods (Raynor, 1998).

One method for delivering both verbal and written adherence information to patients is to give the verbal information first, then convey to the patient that the written information is important by highlighting the most important points with the patient. Another approach that

has been demonstrated to be both easy and effective is for health care providers to ask the patient to teach the provider how to adhere to the treatment. That is, in addition to asking the patients to read about how to adhere to treatment, providers can demonstrate to patients the desired skill for adhering to treatment (e.g., how to use an inhaler). The provider would then ask the patient to demonstrate the skill to determine his or her understanding. One way to ask the patient is, "Can you show me or tell me what I just went over with you? I need to see how well I explained this to you" (Parker, 2000).

Most patient education information, including adherence-related information, has used written materials at a reading level at or above the 10th grade. Such material is not useful to millions of Americans with a low level of health literacy. Health literacy, as defined by the National Library of Medicine, is the degree to which individuals have the capacity to obtain, process, and understand basic health information and services needed to make appropriate health decisions (Parker, 2000). When treating patients with low health literacy skills, some ways in which to convey important information and increase the chances that patients with poor health literacy understand the information include (a) providing nonwritten materials, such as straightforward picture books, videotapes, audiotapes or multimedia presentations; (b) providing written materials using language at or below the fifth-grade reading level; (c) using simple language and speaking slowly; and (d) including important family members or caregivers in discussions. Merely relying on patient education materials or the instructions written on the medication bottles will not be effective for patients with low health literacy (Parker, 2000).

Table 6.2 lists guidelines of how to deliver information both in written form and verbally.

Facilitating a Collaborative Relationship Between Patient and Provider

Providing adherence-related information to patients occurs in the context of the relationship between the provider and the patient. The nature of this relationship is a critical variable involved with the provision of information to patients. Patients are more likely to follow treatment recommendations when there is clear communication between the patient and the provider (Noble, 1998). This is especially true when communication centers on successful management of the treatment regimen. To make the transfer of knowledge as smooth and as effective as possible and maximize the benefits of adherence education, the communication between patient and provider should be a collaborative endeavor. This information exchange specifically involves the provider educating the patient about adherence procedures and also obtaining information from the patient to make certain that the patient is learning the information. According to a meta-analysis conducted by Hall, Roter, and Katz (1988), patients' understanding and ability to remember information provided by the health care provider was positively related to a collaborative relationship between the provider and the patient. In addition, patient levels of adherence were positively associated with doctors asking questions about adherence (Noble, 1998). Table 6.3 gives guidelines to improve communication with patients when educating them about following treatment (Clark & Becker, 1998).

Tailoring Information to Meet Patient Needs

Giving information about how to adhere to treatment without first considering the patient's capability to learn and apply the knowledge is premature and less likely to improve adherence. Providers must assess the patient's existing knowledge of treatment to know how to effectively provide knowledge to the patient. The individualized assessment involves identifying the environmental, social, individual, and treatment regimen factors to determine the approach for providing information best suited for the patient. Much of this patient data can be obtained from routine consultations with patients (Falvo, 1994). After a brief assessment of adherence-related knowledge, the type and method by which to provide information can be tailored to the individual patient's needs. For example, patients with low health literacy may be given medication reminder charts (explained below) in addition to verbal information. For some patients, the verbal information accompanied by written information may be sufficient, and for others a more thorough and intensive approach to provide information to solve adherence-related problems may be necessary.

Tailoring the language and pace of delivery of information to the level the patient will understand can be one of the most difficult tasks for providers. To effectively customize the information for the individual patient, the information should be detailed enough to enable a person to follow a detailed plan and, at the same time, variable enough to allow for individual circumstances (e.g., when and if to take a late dose, how to follow a recommended diet when on vacation) (Noble, 1998). Customizing information improves adherence because patients prefer personalized information that is adapted to their daily routine. Currently, the use of medicine reminder charts allows for the individualization of written information about medication regimens. Medicine reminder charts consist of a

Table 6.2 Guidelines for Delivering Information to Increase Adherence Knowledge

Verbal

- Use information that is clear, direct, and conversational
- Use simple words, no technical jargon, short sentences, and specific instructions
- Ensure that information is personally important; for example, the inclusion of a patient's name can be a powerful indicator of relevance
- Define the purpose of the material
- Focus on behaviors or actions instead of non-behavioral facts
- Limit the number of concepts
- Use examples to explain technical concepts
- Include a summary to review key ideas

Written

- Organize the information so that it is easy to read
- Use clear headings; headings in the form of a question are particularly effective
- Use plenty of white space; too much text on a page will be overwhelming to the reader
- Use bullet points; bulleted lists are better remembered and understood than paragraphs
- Use uppercase and lowercase letters
- Use bold type to emphasize important information
- Provide a question-and-answer format for interaction
- Use illustrations to reinforce or explain specific parts of the text in a different way
- Use cues such as color, underlines, and arrows to help the eye focus on relevant information
- Hand the written information to the patient in person

SOURCE: Adapted from Murphy, Chesson, Walker, Arnold, and Chesson (2000) and Myers and Midence (1998).

Table 6.3 Guidelines for Improving Communication with Patients

- Be attentive to the patient
- Elicit patient's immediate and underlying concerns about the illness and its treatment and express willingness to modify treatment based on patient concerns
- Provide reassurance to alleviate the patient's fears
- Engage the patient by using open-ended questions and simple language
- Obtain information from the patient about potential problems with dosing times or side effects of the medications to tailor the medication regimen to fit the patient's needs
- Use appropriate nonverbal and verbal reinforcement when the patient reports proper adherence strategies
- Review the long-term treatment plan so that the patient knows what to expect over time, the conditions under which the physician may modify treatment and can evaluate the success of treatment

SOURCE: Adapted from Shumaker, Schron, Ockene, and McBee (1998).

simple table showing a sample day's regimen (see Table 6.4). Empirical data show significant improvements in adherence through the use of medicine reminder charts. In one investigation, the percentage of patients who were given the medication reminder chart and demonstrated

Table 6.4   Medicine Reminder Chart

Medicine	Morning/Breakfast	Noon/Lunch	Evening/Dinner	Bedtime
Zoloft			Two tablets*	
Amoxcycillin	One capsule		One capsule	One capsule
Inhaler	Two puffs	Two puffs	Two puffs	Two puffs

SOURCE: Adapted from Myers and Midence (1998).

NOTE: This chart tells you when to take your medications. If there is a * by the dose, this means you should take the medicine with food.

Table 6.5   Questions for Providers Assessing Adherence-Related Knowledge

- Have the rationale for treatment, benefits of adherence, and costs of non-adherence been explained to and understood by the patient?
- Does the patient have misconceptions about the treatment that need to be addressed before providing new accurate information?
- Does the patient have the skills for remembering?
- Can the patient recite the name of the medication and when and how to take it?
- Have side effects been explained in a non-threatening way?
- Does the patient frequently miss appointments or is late on refills? This may be a red flag for poor adherence.
- How will the patient's lifestyle make it more or less likely to adhere to the treatment?

Questions to ask patients to determine knowledge level

- Tell me what your regimen is and how you will follow it.
- On a scale from 1 (least) to 10 (most), how informed of your treatment regimen are you?
- How confident do you feel that you can adhere to the treatment?
- What problems might you have in following the treatment plan?

complete knowledge of their regimen was almost twice that of patients who were not given the medication reminder chart (Raynor, 1998).

Assessment of adherence knowledge must continue throughout the patient's treatment for optimal treatment adherence because adherence will vary along with patients' changing situations and circumstances, and research shows that patients' adherence-related skills deteriorate over time. Even if the treatment regimen is simple, it is beneficial if patients are provided knowledge about how to follow the treatment plan (Clark & Becker, 1998). The list of questions given in Table 6.5 will help in the assessment of the patient's knowledge of treatment adherence, as well as any potential adherence-related difficulties, and will aid in the tailoring of the treatment plan to the individual patient.

Improving Information Recall

Oftentimes, patients cannot recall important information given by providers, even immediately following the consultation. Typically, information is not remembered because of poor recall (after 5 minutes patients forget approximately one half of the provider's instructions), poor recall due to the time when instructions were given (material presented in the first third of the discussion is best remembered), selective recall (patients remember diagnoses better than treatment recommendations), poor recall due to lack of categorizing information (reorganization of medical statements into categories enhances recall), and poor recall due to lack of repetition (Clark & Becker, 1998; Ley, Bradshaw, Eaves, & Walker, 1973). Enumerated below are several recommendations proposed by Ley (1977), based on the research cited above, to improve patients' processing and recall of important information:

1. Make the information as concrete as possible.

2. Provide patients with instructions at the beginning of the consultation.

3. Emphasize the importance of the instructions.

4. Give the patient the framework of the information to be provided and break down the information into its component parts. Signal the beginning of each new segment before providing the details.

5. Repeat important information.

Case Study

Here is a clinical example of a dialogue between a provider and a patient, in which the provider is prescribing a common beta-blocker for hypertension. This case example incorporates all the major strategies discussed in this chapter for improving adherence knowledge.

Provider: Before you begin this new treatment plan, it would help me to know what information you already have about your diagnosis and treatment. Could you tell about your understanding and beliefs of high blood pressure?

Patient: I know that high blood pressure increases one's risk of a heart attack and that it is a common condition. I've also heard that some high blood pressure medications have pretty severe side effects.

Provider: Yes, that is right, and I will address the issue of side effects in a moment. I'd like to start by going over some very important information with you so that you are fully informed about how to adhere to this treatment. Here is a pamphlet about the medication(s) you will be taking, why this particular treatment for hypertension is prescribed, and how to take these medications. Now I am going to highlight the most important parts of the written information, as well as some other information that I believe is very useful to help patients adhere to these medications. First, I am prescribing a common beta-blocker to treat your hypertension. You will take this medication once a day, preferably at the same time each day. Basically, the beta-blocker eases the workload of the heart. They are very effective in reducing blood pressure and are currently a standard of treatment for high blood pressure. As you commented earlier, there are side effects associated with beta-blockers. The most common side effects include fatigue, vivid dreams, depression, and memory loss. You may feel dizzy or lightheaded at times. Other side effects may include coldness in the extremities (i.e., legs and toes, arms and hands), asthma, gastrointestinal problems, and sexual dysfunction. If you begin to experience any of these side effects, please call me. There are many ways we can manage these side effects. It is very important that you do not stop taking these medications until I instruct you to do so. It is extremely important not to stop this medication abruptly. Angina, heart attack, and even sudden death have occurred in patients who discontinued treatment without gradual withdrawal. Also, if you forget to take a dose, take the missed dose as soon as possible. Do you have any questions about the information I have just given you?

Patient: No, it was all very clear.

Provider: Many patients have some difficulties adhering to treatments such as these. What do you see getting in the way of following this treatment plan?

Patient: I may forget to take the medication every day.

Provider: Yes, this is very common among patients. This medication reminder chart may be helpful to look at every day to remind you to take your medication at the prescribed time. Is this medication reminder chart something that you think can be useful in helping you to follow the treatment plan?

Patient: Sure. I'll try it. Thanks.

Provider: Great. Let's start with this approach and when you come in for a follow-up visit we can reassess how this plan is working for you. Do you have any other concerns or questions about this treatment?

Patient: No. Thanks for taking the time to provide me with all of this information.

Provider: Now, based on the information I just went over with you, can you tell me what your treatment plan is and why it is important to follow it as prescribed? Your answer will help me understand how well I have explained everything to you.

This example illustrates several important guidelines discussed in this chapter:

1. Assessment of patient's existing treatment knowledge
2. Providing a standard set of information to each patient (i.e., name and dose, treatment rationale, side effects)
3. Using a combination of written and verbal information (i.e., information pamphlet and provider verbally repeating information)
4. Facilitating a supportive and collaborative relationship between the patient and provider (i.e., providing reassurance and willingness to accommodate patient's needs)
5. Tailoring this information to meet the patient's needs (i.e., medication reminder chart)
6. Assessing patient's understanding and recall of important information (i.e., having patient restate the important information just provided)

Much more than simply repeating instructions or giving written information is involved with increasing adherence-related knowledge. Research and clinical experience indicate that increasing patients' knowledge about their illness and its treatment is necessary but often not sufficient to improve adherence. Several other factors discussed throughout this chapter must be considered when providing information about adherence to a patient to positively affect treatment adherence.

Suggested Readings

Falvo, D. R. (1994). *Effective patient education: A guide to increased compliance* (2nd ed.). Gaithersburg, MD: Aspen.

Myers, L., & Midence, K. (Eds.). (1998). *Adherence to treatment in medical conditions.* Amsterdam: Harwood Academic.

Meichenbaum, D., & Turk, D. (Eds.). (1987). *Facilitating treatment adherence.* New York: Plenum Press.

Shumaker, S. A., Schron, E. B., Ockene, J. K., & McBee, W. L. (Eds.). (1998). *Health behavior change.* New York: Springer.

References

Bandura, A. (1977). Self-efficacy: Toward a unifying theory of behavioral change. *Psychological Review, 84,* 191–215.

Becker, M. H. (1974). The health belief model and sick role behavior. *Health Education Monographs, 2,* 409–419.

Clark, N., & Becker, M. (1998). Theoretical models and strategies for improving adherence and disease management. In S. A. Shumaker, E. B. Schron, J. K. Ockene, & W. L. McBee (Eds.), *Health behavior change* (pp. 5–33). New York: Springer.

DiMatteo, M. R. (2004). Variations in patients' adherence to medical recommendations: A quantitative review of 50 years of research. *Medical Care, 42*(3), 200–209.

Falvo, D. R. (1994). *Effective patient education: A guide to increased compliance* (2nd ed.). Gaithersburg, MD: Aspen.

Gardner, J. (2002). Increased prescribing linked to more older patients, more multiple conditions, new drug choices, medical payment and delivery systems, and direct marketing to consumers. *Health Affairs, 21*(4), 210–222.

Garnett, W. R. (2000). Antiepileptic drug treatment: Outcomes and adherence. *Pharmacotherapy, 20,* 191–199.

Gibbs, S., Waters, W., & George, C. (1989). The benefits of prescription information leaflets. *British Journal of Clinical Pharmacology, 27,* 723–739.

Hall, J., Roter, D., & Katz, N. (1988). Correlates of provider behavior: A meta-analysis. *Medical Care, 26,* 657–675.

Hulka, B., Cassell, J., Kupper, L., & Burdette, J. (1976). Communication, compliance, concordance between physicians and patients with prescribed medications. *American Journal of Public Health, 66,* 847–853.

Kravitz, R., & Melnikow, J. (2004). Medical adherence research: Time for a change in direction? *Medical Care, 42*(3), 197–199.

Ley, P. (1977). Psychological studies of doctor-patient communication. In S. Rachman (Ed.), *Contributions to medical psychology* (Vol. 1). Oxford: Pergamon Press.

Ley, P. (1982). Satisfaction, compliance, and communication. *British Journal of Clinical Psychology, 21,* 241–254.

Ley, P. (1988). *Communicating with the patient.* London: Croom Helm.

Ley, P., Bradshaw, P., Eaves, D., & Walker, C. (1973). A method for increasing patients' recall of information presented by doctors. *Psychological Medicine, 3,* 217–220.

Meichenbaum, D., & Turk, D. (Eds.). (1987). *Facilitating treatment adherence.* New York: Plenum Press.

Morris, L., & Halperin, J. (1979). Effects of written drug information on patient knowledge and compliance, a literature review. *American Journal of Public Health, 69,* 47–52.

Murphy, P. W., Chesson, A. L., Walker, L., Arnold, C. L., & Chesson, L. M. (2000). Comparing the effectiveness of video and written material for improving knowledge among sleep disorders clinic patients with limited literacy skills. *Southern Medical Journal, 93*(3), 297–308.

Noble, L. (1998). Doctor-patient communication and adherence to treatment. In L. Myers & K. Midence (Eds.), *Adherence to treatment in medical conditions* (pp. 51–82). Amsterdam: Harwood Academic.

Parker, R. (2000). Health literacy: a challenge for American patients and their health care providers. *Health Promotion International, 15*(4), 277–283.

Prochaska, J. O., & DiClemente, C. C. (1983). Stages and processes of self-change of smoking: Toward an integrative model of change. *Psychotherapy: Theory, Research, and Practice, 19,* 276–288.

Raynor, D. K. (1998). The influence of written information on patient knowledge and adherence to treatment. In L. Myers & K. Midence (Eds.), *Adherence to treatment in medical conditions* (pp. 83–111). Amsterdam: Harwood Academic.

7

Skills Training to Promote Patient Adherence to Treatments

Kyle E. Ferguson

Heather Scarlett-Ferguson

Despite several decades of research, one of the greatest challenges in health care today remains poor adherence or nonadherence to prescribed treatments. Recent estimates suggest that medication adherence rates are approximately 50%, whereas adherence to lifestyle prescriptions are much lower, often less than 10% (Haynes, McDonald, & Garg, 2002). Although there is variance between groups, generally speaking, such low adherence rates are pervasive across health conditions, cultures, race, sex, intelligence, education, treatment regimens, and age groups (Dunbar-Jacob & Mortimer-Stephens, 2001; McDonald, Garg, & Haynes, 2002). Accordingly, nonadherence is a major public health concern, not only in the United States but also globally.

Definition of Adherence

Treatment adherence, as used in the literature, typically refers to the extent to which a patient's behavior is consistent with medical or health advice (Haynes, 1979). Behaving *consistently with medical or health advice* entails the following (Meichenbaum & Turk, 1987, pp. 20–21):

1. Entering into and continuing a treatment program

2. Keeping referral and follow-up appointments

3. Correct consumption of prescribed medication

4. Following appropriate lifestyle changes (e.g., in the areas of diet, exercise, stress management)

5. Correct performance of home-based therapeutic regimens

6. Avoidance of health risk behaviors (e.g., smoking, alcohol, drug abuse)

Intentional Versus Unintentional Nonadherence

A useful way of conceptualizing adherence or nonadherence in the above examples is to make the distinction between *intentional* and *unintentional nonadherence* (Wroe, 2002). Intentional nonadherence involves deliberately missing appointments, abstention from healthy lifestyle recommendations, or changing doses. Patients, for example, might alter the dose or dose schedule due to powerful medication side effects. Perhaps, as prescribed, the medication causes extreme nausea. By consuming less of the medication or taking it less frequently, patients are able to stave off such adverse effects, at least some of the time (e.g., during holidays).

Groups at particular risk of intentional nonadherence are alcohol and substance abusers and the elderly. Alcohol, for example, interacts with certain prescription medications, and the combination makes the person feel very ill. In elderly patients, polypharmacy is the rule, not the exception. Many drug "cocktails" prescribed for the elderly produce unpleasant side effects. Moreover, the elderly often have age-associated, increased susceptibility to adverse reactions (Merck, 2000). That is to say, the right dose for a comparable problem for an 80-year-old is often much lower than that for a 20-year-old. Many physicians without adequate gerontological training often make this mistake and overprescribe.

Unintentional nonadherence involves nondeliberate treatment alterations because of cognitive and/or socioeconomic factors. Patients with probable Alzheimer's disease, for example, usually forget to take their medication as prescribed due to the nature of their illness, particularly in the middle to later stages of the disease (Murray et al., 2004). Patients may lose the medication, become confused and take too much, or, due to delusional thinking (a common symptom of progressive dementia), throw it away, fearing that someone is trying to poison them. On the other end of the age continuum, children might be too young to care for themselves independently (i.e., unintentional nonadherence due to cognitive immaturity), as in the case of adhering to the highly complex regimen of cystic fibrosis treatment (Bernard & Cohen, 2004). Here, parental supervision is almost always required, overseeing the child's diet, airway clearance, and other therapeutic steps too numerous to mention. Other groups at risk for unintentional nonadherence are persons with mental retardation, moderate to severe brain injuries, severe mental illness, and cognitive impairment due to a general medical condition (e.g., congestive heart failure).

Unintentional nonadherence can also be due to economic and social factors (Jerant, von Friederichs-Fitzwater, & Moore, 2005). Some patients, for example, simply cannot afford to pay for medications due to cost or lack of insurance coverage. Relatedly, certain medications have to be taken with meals, at specific times. However, the homeless cannot be expected to coordinate these, as meals are intermittent at best.

Regarding social factors, some family members believe that helping the "sick" person might actually hinder his or her ability to cope and recover (Jerant et al., 2005). Hence, in spite of recommendations, individuals who would otherwise play a crucial role in implementing the treatment plan refuse to participate. Other unintentional nonadherence concerns spousal support. In traditional households, men typically do not cook and participate in grocery shopping. Accordingly, some men do not adhere to recommended diets because healthier choices are not readily available and they simply lack the instrumental skills to cook a meal for themselves or do their own shopping.

A Stepped-Care Approach to Adherence

The metaview of this chapter is based on the stepped-care delivery model of health care (O'Donohue, Cummings, Cucciare, Cummings, & Runyan, 2006). That is, all patients prescribed new medications or lifestyle changes are given the least intensive, most cost-efficient intervention(s) as the first line of defense. Should patients have problems adhering to the recommendations, a more intensive, costlier intervention is implemented. And should that fail, an even more intensive intervention, at greater cost, is employed.

Organization of This Chapter

Adherence is a complex phenomenon that involves patient variables, provider variables, environmental and community factors, and interactions between these (Meichenbaum & Turk, 1987; Milhalko et al., 2004). This chapter focuses on patient variables, in particular those self-management skills needed to effectively adhere to treatment prescriptions. Although this chapter touches on adherence skill sets at all levels of the stepped-care model, it is most pertinent in later stages, as patients receive greater attention for nonadherence. These skill sets will later be discussed within a behavior analytic theoretical framework. Of course, due to page limitations, every conceivable skill set is not taken up in this chapter. Rather, for the benefit of a wider audience, the authors have selected only a few that tend to traverse treatment regimens, conditions, and so forth.

The chapter is organized as follows. Theoretical underpinnings and purported mechanisms underlying these techniques, who might benefit from this form of training, and contraindications of its use are discussed first. The remainder of the chapter provides step-by-step guidelines in teaching self-management to clients, followed by a case study.

Theoretical Underpinnings and Underlying Mechanisms of Techniques

Barring a stay in the hospital under 24-hour supervision, managing any acute or chronic health condition involves varying degrees of self-management. Self-management, from a behavior analytic perspective, is the "personal and systematic application of behavior change strategies that result in the desired modification of one's own behavior" (Heward, 1987, p. 517). Technically speaking, the *behavior change strategies* are the *controlling responses*, and taking the medication as prescribed and engaging in recommended lifestyle changes are the *controlled responses*, that is, the *desired modification* (Holland & Skinner, 1961, p. 307).

The science of self-management is based on the empirical regularities discovered in the learning laboratory, involving human and nonhuman subjects. The two major mechanisms affecting treatment adherence are classical (respondent, Pavlovian) conditioning and operant conditioning.

Classical Conditioning

Classical conditioning is largely based on a two-term relationship between a stimulus and a response (S-R), where control is transferred from a reflex-eliciting, unconditioned stimulus (UCS) to an otherwise neutral stimulus, conditioned stimulus (CS) (Pierce & Epling, 1999). The nomenclature changes from unconditioned response (UCR) to conditioned response (CR) after the transfer of control (even though the response looks similar).

Classical conditioning is best illustrated in the development of anticipatory nausea and vomiting (ANV) in patients receiving chemotherapy (Stockhorst, Klosterhalfen, & Steingruber, 1998). ANV occurs in about one of every four cancer patients (Morrow, Roscoe, Kirshner, Hynes, & Rosenbluth, 1998). From a classical conditioning perspective, neutral stimuli (e.g., the look, sounds, and smells of the chemotherapy environment) come to elicit the CR (i.e., ANV) after a sufficient number of pairings with chemotherapy infusions (UCS). The infusions are considered the UCS because they can elicit nausea and vomiting (UCR) without prior conditioning.

From a behavioral point of view, the implications in treating ANV are relatively straightforward, namely, to block the association between potential CS and the UCS. One way of achieving this aim is to employ the counterconditioning technique called systematic desensitization, advanced by Wolpe (1958, 1990). Insofar as clients remain in a deep state of relaxation, it is believed to reciprocally inhibit and thus block the transfer of control from unconditioned stimuli to neutral stimuli (Wolpe, 1976).

As it turns out, systematic desensitization, among other relaxation-based techniques, is part and parcel of psychosocial interventions in cancer care (Fawzy, Fawzy, Arndt, & Pasnau, 1995). In one study, for example, Morrow and Morrell (1982) examined the effects of systematic desensitization as a strategy to reduce ANV. Sixty cancer patients were randomly assigned to one of three conditions: no-treatment control, counseling-only, and systematic desensitization as the counterconditioning technique. Only the patients in the systematic desensitization group showed significant reductions in frequency, severity, and duration of ANV.

Operant Conditioning

Patients also adhere and nonadhere to prescribed treatments due to prevailing contingencies of reinforcement (Meichenbaum & Turk, 1987). Contingencies are the "*relations* between responses and the events that follow them—their *consequences*—and the events that precede or accompany them—their *antecedents*" (Sulzer-Azaroff & Mayer, 1991, p. 98, italics in original). This linear relationship is depicted in the three-term contingency: antecedent → behavior →

consequence (Pierce & Epling, 1999). For the time being, let us reverse the order and work backward, starting with the consequences of behavior.

The consequences of behavior either increase or decrease the likelihood that the behavior will occur again under similar circumstances. If the behavior increased, either of two events has occurred. When the behavior is instrumental in gaining something from the environment (e.g., attention from others) and increases in frequency, the behavior has been *positively reinforced*[1] (Skinner, 1953). For example, if a patient goes for a walk and feels more energetic and, as a result, maintains or increases this mode of exercise, this denotes *positive reinforcement.*

If the behavior removes something from the environment and increases in frequency, the behavior has been *negatively reinforced.* For example, if a patient takes opioids (prescribed as needed, i.e., PRN) to escape or avoid pain and, as a result, increases the daily recommended dose, this is an instance of *negative reinforcement.*

In the absence of reinforcement, a previously reinforced behavior eventually ceases. When behavior terminates as a result of withholding reinforcement, the behavior undergoes *extinction* (Catania, 1992). Readers should note that extinction only occurs after a response has been maintained by reinforcement. For example, when parents begin ignoring the adherence behavior of their child with asthma—where parental attention served as the sole reinforcer for adherence—behavior will extinguish.

The antithesis of reinforcement is punishment. When the behavior decreases as a result of something aversive being presented in the environment, the behavior has been *positively punished* (Foxx, 1982). For example, many medications cause dizziness, insomnia, constipation, headache, blurred vision, among other powerful side effects. When patients stop taking medications as prescribed due to adverse reactions, the underlying behavioral principle is *positive punishment.*[2] To put it simply, adherence is punished by its consequences.

Similarly, if the behavior decreases as a result of removing something reinforcing from the environment, the behavior has been *negatively punished*. For example, sexual side effects, such as impotence, can lead to medication nonadherence. Technically speaking, adherence behavior is negatively punished by the medication's adverse effects (i.e., take the medication as prescribed—"performance" suffers—sexual activity, a powerful reinforcer, goes down).

Antecedents or discriminative stimuli begin the chain in the three-term contingency by evoking behavior (Sulzer-Azaroff & Mayer, 1991). Antecedents come in many forms. The physical and social environment, the time of day and season, and the internal economy of the individual (i.e., inner physiological processes; Michael, 1982, pp. 150–151) are antecedents that in concert affect the probability that an individual will adhere or nonadhere to treatment. For example, teenager diabetics may not inject themselves with insulin after a meal when out with peers, for fear of social stigma. By contrast, they might adhere better in the company of their parents.

Who Might Benefit From This Technique?

The adherence skills discussed in this chapter are seldom used on their own. They are usually combined with other procedures as part of a treatment package. Regarding the initial step in self-management training, every patient will benefit from being given a rationale for therapy and being educated about what to expect from therapy, the benefits of treatment, potential side effects, and when to contact their health care providers should significant complications arise. As for other techniques mentioned in the chapter, clients most likely to benefit are those for whom adherence has become a problem. Below, we provide a few examples of the beneficial outcomes of the techniques outlined here:

• *Providing a rationale and patient education*: Brief counseling about the importance of taking all of the medication as prescribed significantly improved adherence with antibiotics for streptococcal pharyngitis in patients undergoing acute care (Colcher & Bass, 1972).

• *Self-monitoring*: Consistent self-monitoring has been shown to improve weight management among obese weight controllers in relation to patients who do so inconsistently or not at all (Boutelle, Baker, Kirschenbaum, & Mitchell, 1999). Self-monitoring bolsters self-awareness with respect to adherence discrepancies and, as such, plays an integral role in most behaviorally oriented programs targeting nonadherence.

• *Goal setting and behavioral contracting*: A behavioral contract (taken up later) was employed with 10 children, diagnosed with hemophilia, over a 1-year period to improve adherence to prescribed therapeutic exercise (Greenan-Fowler, Powell, & Varni, 1987). As stipulated in the contract, points were awarded for adherence, which were later exchanged for reinforcers. Whereas adherence to the program was 55% during a 1-week baseline, adherence rose to 94% after commencing with behavioral contracting.

• *Stimulus control*: Chronic sleep deprivation increases the risk of cardiovascular disease and symptomatic diabetes, among many other health complications (Alvarez & Ayas, 2004). Stimulus control is the behavioral principle underlying sleep hygiene (e.g., using the bed for only sleep and sex), a core component in treating insomnia. Strom, Pettersson, and Andersson (2004) found that an Internet-based sleep management program employing stimulus control resulted in significant improvements in total sleep time and sleep efficiency (i.e., the quality of sleep).

• *Relapse prevention*: Relapse, or reverting back to heavy alcohol use patterns after a period of abstinence or moderate use, occurs in many patients in alcohol treatment programs (Larimer, Palmer, & Marlatt, 1999, p. 151). In a recent meta-analysis, Irvin, Bowers, Dunn, and Wang (1999) examined 26 published and unpublished relapse prevention (RP) studies. Their analyses revealed that RP programs are generally effective (i.e., small to medium effect sizes), with a few qualifications. Of particular note, RP was most effective when applied to alcohol or polysubstance use disorders.

Contraindications of the Strategies or Treatments

Whereas self-management has produced beneficial outcomes for most patients, some patients cannot be relied on to manage certain or most aspects of their treatment. Recall the notion of unintentional nonadherence. Patients who have difficulties with adherence due to cognitive impairment or immaturity should not be responsible for those elements of treatment that could prove potentially dangerous. Accordingly, such individuals should not be allowed free access to medications. Such use should be carefully monitored by a responsible party.

Restrictions notwithstanding, patients should be encouraged to participate as much as possible in treatment planning and in its execution. Whenever possible, provide choices for patients and let them decide among them. This point is particularly relevant in goal setting and contingency contracting, which are taken up later in the chapter.

Step-by-Step Procedures

Step 1: Providing a Rationale and Patient Education

After a routine exam and/or laboratory testing, primary health care providers inform patients of their diagnosis, give a brief overview of the treatment options available, and provide specific recommendations as to the proper use of the medications (e.g., two tablets twice daily with meals) and what lifestyle changes are required for healthier living (e.g., low-sodium diet along with 30 minutes of exercise three times weekly). Patients are usually given pamphlets, URL addresses of pertinent Web sites, and a self-help publication list at this time (see appendix), after which, should medications be prescribed, patients see a pharmacist next, who provides further guidance on how to safely take the medication, as well as information on possible side effects and drug interactions.

Points to Consider[3]

1. Review what would be considered an acceptable level of adherence, initially. Namely, at the outset, is the patient expected to adhere to the program 100% of the time, or is a lower percentage acceptable? Five minutes of exercise twice weekly, for example, might be appropriate if it establishes a behavioral momentum, eventually leading to 30 minutes of exercise three times a week.

2. Use the more neutral term *adherence* over the value-laden term *compliance*. *Noncompliance* may communicate that the patient is being defiant and intentionally difficult, which may further exacerbate patient nonadherence (Jenkins, 1995).

3. Write out prescriptions, in addition to just communicating verbally, as this has been shown to improve recall and adherence to recommendations.

4. Prescriptions should be written in simple language (e.g., fourth-grade reading level) and as parsimoniously as possible.

5. Is the patient responding appropriately on hearing the news? If not, explore why not? Perhaps, he or she does not care, is in denial of the problem, or simply questions the validity of the diagnosis and remains silent about it.

6. Ask if the patient places good health high on the list of priorities. If not, discuss why not (see Whiteley, Williams, & Marcus, this volume, about motivational interviewing strategies).

7. Have patients describe in their own words the medical regimen. Provide corrective feedback when needed and have them try again, until their descriptions are better aligned with recommendations.

8. Ask them if they think that the treatment is appropriate for their situation and whether or not it will work. Some individuals with chronic health problems, for example, believe that "it is too late," doubting that any intervention can improve matters.

9. Talk about potential barriers to adherence and help them problem-solve around these. Relatedly, ask about past nonadherence and whether they were able to overcome those barriers and achieve adherence (try to incorporate previously effective coping strategies in the present treatment plan). If they were not successful, talk about ways of avoiding similar mistakes.

10. Talk about what to expect if they miss a dose and how to correct for that. For example, do they simply miss the dose or do they take a double dose at the next opportunity?

11. Ask them if there are any potential side effects that are of concern (real or imagined).

12. Discuss what social support is available and ask how they will access it.

13. Schedule a follow-up appointment, either in person or over the phone, to assess whether patients are adhering to their treatment plan.

14. If you suspect substance abuse, address this first, as it will likely interfere with all treatment efforts (Cummings & Cummings, 2000).

A Caveat

Some patients require greater attention at the outset of treatment due to the nature of their condition, in which case, a rationale and patient education is not enough. Type I diabetics, for example, require assembling an intensive, costly health care team immediately comprising a diabetes educator, dietitian, pharmacist, exercise physiologist, mental health counselor, ophthalmologist, podiatrist, and dermatologist (American Diabetes Association, 2002). For such patients, begin training in self-monitoring and begin targeting other adherence skills (see below) as soon as possible.

Step 2: Self-Monitoring

As mentioned earlier, in the best of times about half the patients will not adhere to their prescriptions, in which case a more intensive and costly intervention becomes necessary. At this next step in the stepped-care model, group interventions, such as wellness classes, are usually recommended. Smoking cessation groups, stress management classes, weight watchers, Alcoholics Anonymous, and bereavement groups are a few such examples. In addition to classes, self-monitoring can also be beneficial. In particular, self-monitoring can increase awareness of the problem and draw patients' attention to the environmental determinants of adherence and nonadherence.

Accordingly, self-monitoring can serve two functions (Korotitsch & Nelson-Gray, 1999). Self-monitoring has assessment and therapeutic utility, due to reactivity. Reactivity is "the occurrence of behavior change initiated by the procedure of self-monitoring" (Nelson, 1977, p. 218). Simply observing just how bad the problem is can motivate some patients into behavior change (i.e., the so-called "valence" of the target behavior evokes more adaptive behavior; Nelson, 1977, p. 221).

Self-monitoring is the systematic observation and recording of one's own behavior. It involves two separate behavioral processes (Bornstein, Hamilton, & Bornstein, 1986). First, an individual must discriminate between the presence and absence of the targeted response. Second, the patient must then record the behavior after it has occurred. Patients need to be taught when to self-monitor, what to self-monitor, and how to self-monitor (Mahoney, 1977, p. 243).

Defining the Target

Accurately defining the target response is the initial step in teaching patients how to monitor their behavior. A useful heuristic in identifying a behavioral target is to ask yourself the following (Haynes & O'Brien, 2000). (1) What behaviors do you and your patient think are causally linked to adherence and nonadherence? Only target those that are. (2) Ask yourself if you have the resources or expertise to change the targeted behavior given the strictures of daily practice. Consider referring out to specialty care (e.g., substance abuse treatment program) if this is not the case.

The behavioral definition should be objective, clear, and complete (Hawkins & Dobes, 1975). *Objective* means to include only observable characteristics of the targeted response (Barlow & Hersen, 1984). For example, did the patient consume a serving of red meat on a given day? Definitions ought to be clear and easily paraphrased. For example, a brisk walk for 30 minutes three times a week is much more straightforward than defining exercise as a minimum of 30 minutes, three times weekly, at an intensity of 80% to 90% of the patient's maximum heart rate, given gender, age, and overall fitness level. A definition is complete when it sets the parameters of behavior. For example, a complete definition of insulin injection involves

the timing of the injection, injection site, and dose, all of which are inextricably tied and inseparable (American Diabetes Association, 2002).

Once the therapist and patient agree on an acceptable behavioral target or targets, the next step is to select an appropriate self-monitoring device. We recommend employing a variant of that developed by Bijou and colleagues (Bijou, Peterson, & Ault, 1968). It consists of three columns: (1) antecedent, (2) behavior, and (3) consequence (see Table 7.1). Document the context or situational determinants of adherence and nonadherence under the Antecedent column (Heidt & Marx, 2003). When does the target behavior usually occur? Where does it occur? Who is usually present at the time? The targeted behavior (or behaviors) is recorded under the Behavior column. Self-statements are also recorded here, as these can be helpful in pointing to the prevailing contingencies (e.g., feelings of embarrassment point to stigma or peer influence). The physical, interpersonal, and emotional consequences are recorded under the Consequence column. This section is thus used to identify reinforcers and punishers, as well as unconditioned and conditioned stimuli.

Although the ABC self-monitoring device yields the most data, it is labor intensive and may not be appropriate for every patient, particularly those who are not all that motivated to change. Consider using a simpler approach that requires less effort to implement, a scatter-plot

Table 7.1   A Self-Monitoring Form Commonly Used in Treatment Adherence

Antecedent	Behavior	Consequence
• forgot healthy lunch on the way to work	• went to McDonald's across the street	• I loved the food and later felt like a fat slob
• very hungry at lunchtime	• had two Big Macs and ate large fries	• I can't stick to a healthy diet, it's too hard
• only had 20 minutes to eat before conference call		

SOURCE: Modeled after Bijou et al. (1968).

assessment (Touchette, MacDonald, & Langer, 1985). A scatter plot, arranged in a matrix, can help identify behavioral patterns in natural settings by showing temporal distributions of behavior over the course of successive days (see Figure 7.1). When temporal patterns emerge, query further as to what might be going on at those particular times.

The observer records the time interval (broken down into a meaningful unit that is amenable to the participant's schedule; e.g., hours, 30 minutes, 15 minutes) and instances of behavior on the ordinate axis (y-axis); days of the week are set down on the abscissa (x-axis). Use a symbol, such as a hatch mark, to denote the behavioral target, or have patients write in the number.

2							IIIIIII
1							IIII
12 a.m.							IIIIIII
11							IIIIIIIII
10	IIIII	III		IIIIIIIII	IIIIIIIII		
9	IIIIIIIIIII	IIIIIIIIII	IIIIIII	IIIIIIIIIII		IIIII	
8	IIIII	IIIIIII			IIIIIIIII		
7	IIIII		IIIIIIIIIII				
6 p.m.					IIIIIIIII	III	
	Sun	Mon	Tues	Wed	Thurs	Fri	Sat

Figure 7.1   A Scatter-Plot Form. "I" Denotes a Cigarette in This Hypothetical Example

SOURCE: Modeled after Touchette et al. (1985).

Interpreting the Data

On reviewing the ABC or scatter-plot assessment data, the first question to ask is whether nonadherence is caused by a skills deficit or is due to faulty contingencies (Mager & Pipe, 1984). If the patient could adhere to the regimen if you paid him or her a trillion dollars, it is probably a skills deficit, in which case ask yourself whether the patient was able to adhere at some point in time (either recently or in the past). If so, provide refresher training. Are prompts necessary? If so, provide checklists, posted signs, reminders, and other antecedent stimuli.

After ruling out skills deficits, ask yourself whether performance is punishing. If so, try decreasing the "unpleasantness" of the activity whenever possible. For example, consider another medication with fewer side effects (see the case study at the end of the chapter). Employ relaxation should patients become highly nervous or upset during times when they should be engaging in adherence-relevant behavior.

One cannot assume that all patients are "motivated" to change, even in the worst cases, in which case, ask yourself: Is nonperformance reinforcing? The "sick role" can be very effective at getting attention from others. Moreover, there might also be financial incentives to nonadhere, in spite of the personal costs.

Points to Consider[3]

1. Training in self-monitoring improves accuracy. Role-play with the patient. Have patients practice filling out mock

forms. Provide corrective feedback when necessary

2. Always review self-monitoring data and let patients know this in advance; otherwise, you are communicating to patients that this activity is not important.

3. Enhance adherence to self-monitoring by having patients state this as an explicit goal in writing or verbally (see Hayes, Barlow, & Nelson-Gray, 1999, p. 381).

4. Patients are more likely to record positive over negative targets. For example, rather than record failed attempts at resisting the urge to smoke, have patients keep track of successes.

5. Targeting fewer behaviors bolsters reactivity.

6. Continuous (i.e., following every response) versus daily or weekly recording produces more reactivity.

7. Consider the timing of recording. Recording "urges" (i.e., premonitoring) as opposed to behavior after the fact can have more of a reactive effect on certain consumptive behaviors like overeating (see Bornstein et al., 1986, pp. 189–190).

8. The ultimate goal of self-management training is to get patients to monitor their own behavior and use these data to make treatment decisions. Accordingly, provide your input only after patients have had an opportunity to problem-solve "out loud." In other words, employ the Socratic method (e.g., "What do you think is going on? What makes you think that? What else might be going on?").

Step 3: Contingency Management

After attending classes and self-monitoring, many patients continue to have problems with adherence. Thus, the next step in the model is to increase the level of intensity yet again. For diabetics, this might entail having to schedule individual time with a diabetes nurse. An obese patient might be assigned a personal trainer and dietician. Patients with asthma might be referred to an asthma specialist for booster sessions, because they would have already worked with such a professional when first diagnosed. Should patients have adherence problems due to a psychological disorder (e.g., depression) or medical condition (e.g., suspected stroke), they are referred to an appropriate health care specialist (e.g., clinical psychologist or neurologist, respectively). Last, patients who require substantial support are referred to a case manager, who provides assistance with accessing financial aid, among other social services.

Behavioral contracts can also be employed at this time. A behavioral contract is a "negotiated explicit agreement between the patient and healthcare provider that specifies expectations, plans, responsibilities and contingencies for behavior to be changed" (Meichenbaum & Turk, 1987, p. 165). Specific elements usually include most, if not all, of the following (see Figure 7.2; Martin & Pear, 1978, p. 377):

- A clear statement of the targeted behaviors
- The method of data collection
- Reinforcers to be used, their schedule of delivery, and who will deliver them
- Potential problems and their resolution
- Bonus and/or penalty clauses
- A schedule of review for progress
- Signatures of all parties involved and the dates of the agreement

Points to Consider[4]

1. Negotiated, self-determined treatment goals are more likely to be carried out.

2. All goals should be specified behaviorally and in quantifiable terms; otherwise, it will be difficult determining whether goals have been achieved.

Patient: _____ Therapist: _____ Support Person: _____

Effective Dates: _____ to _____

Goals

Long-term: _____

Short-term: _____

Responsibility (Who, What, When, How Well)

1. _____

2. _____

3. _____

Reward: _____

Who will monitor behavior? _____

What records will be kept? _____

Who delivers the reward? _____

Signed: _____ Date: _____   _____ Date: _____

Patient   Therapist

_____ Date: _____

Support Person

The contract will be reviewed on: _____

Figure 7.2   A Behavioral Contract

SOURCE: Modeled after Sulzer-Azaroff and Mayer (1991).

3. Choose a contingency manager (support person in Figure 7.2), such as a parent, older sibling, spouse, or close friend, and have him or her participate in treatment planning. This way he or she will feel more invested in the program and better informed. Later on, adolescent and adult patients can serve in this role, providing self-reinforcement.

4. Involve significant others in goal and treatment selection. Such individuals will not only provide social support in time of need but also help identify possible contingencies affecting adherence or nonadherence, which may elude the patient. Or, such information will provide convergent validity of patients' self-reports.

5. Use positive reinforcement for adherence versus punishment for nonadherence in the patient's contingency plan. Punishment engenders avoidance behavior on the part of the patient (e.g., patients

begin avoiding the contingency manager and anything associated with the program that becomes associated with punishment).

Stimulus Control

In addition to behavioral contracting, teaching patients antecedent control strategies is also helpful (Watson & Tharp, 1997). Recall that antecedents evoke behavior. For example, the television can evoke eating behavior, especially when a person usually eats in front of it. Food is, after all, a powerful reinforcer. This evocative effect of the television can occur at other times, as well, when the individual reports not feeling hungry.

When stimuli come to evoke behavior, we call it stimulus control (Pierce & Epling, 1999). The contexts in which stimuli evoke behavior fall along a continuum ranging from a few situations to many. Although this range can be established fortuitously, one can systematically formulate these relations, restricting or broadening the range of stimulus control. The systematic restriction and expansion of stimulus control is called discrimination and generalization, respectively (Sulzer-Azaroff & Mayer, 1991, p. 249).

In our above example, an instance of overgeneralization (i.e., too many inappropriate generalizations), the intervention would entail discrimination training. That is, the individual should eat only at designated places and at designated times, establishing "tighter" stimulus control. At the start of the intervention, the television will continue to evoke much of the behavioral chain, which used to eventuate in consumption of the edible reinforcer (i.e., food). Over time, in the absence of the reinforcer, cravings and other behavior (e.g., rifling through the cupboards) will eventually recede. Ultimately, the television will lose stimulus control over eating behavior. Conversely, only the table will be associated with eating behavior.

Generalization training involves presenting the reinforcer in many situations, as a means of widening or spreading stimulus control.

Reinforcing blood glucose monitoring outside the home is one such example. We want patients to be able to engage in this behavior at all places and times.

Whereas discrimination and generalization training are more indirect paths affecting antecedent control, there are more direct strategies that involve directly manipulating antecedents: (1) presenting the antecedent that evokes the desired target behavior; (2) removing antecedents that evoke competing, undesirable behavior; (3) decreasing the response effort for the desirable behavioral target; (4) and increasing the response effort for competing behavior (Miltenberger, 2001, p. 386).

Donning one's workout clothes immediately after returning home from work is an example of the following: (1) A person is more likely to go running (target behavior) while wearing workout clothes versus a suit and tie. Avoiding the junk food aisle during shopping excursions is an example of the following: (2) Avoiding contact with junk food packaging, which has a long history of being paired with reinforcement, decreases the likelihood that one will purchase such items—the first link in the chain of behaviors that ends in consumption. Decreasing the number of pills a person has to take, by consolidating several into one capsule, is an example of the following: (3) Taking, say, two pills takes less effort than taking five or six. Placing individual cigarettes throughout the house is an example of the following: (4) It is much easier reaching in one's pocket than having to hunt around the house each time a person wants to light up.

Points to Consider[5]

1. The maintenance of stimulus control requires frequent pairings of the antecedent stimulus with reinforcement (e.g., every third or fourth time).

2. Decrease the power of problematic stimulus control by changing establishing operations (EOs). EOs are environmental events that affect behavior in two ways

(Michael, 1993). (a) EOs momentarily alter the reinforcing effectiveness or punishing qualities of events. For example, food deprivation increases the reinforcing properties of a person's favorite foods. By contrast, food can serve as a punisher after someone has overindulged on a heavy meal. (b) EOs also serve an evocative function. Food deprivation, for example, evokes behavior that has been successful at obtaining food in the past (e.g., rummaging through the freezer). After overindulging, the uncomfortable physical effects may evoke the behavior of searching for an antacid.

3. Teach patients distraction techniques. Distraction is a self-regulation technique designed to shift one's attention away from problematic antecedents. Some smokers, for example, distract themselves from stimuli that elicit cravings and evoke smoking behavior with pictures of family members (especially children and grandchildren) taped to the package.

Relapse Prevention

Many patients relapse after achieving and maintaining acceptable levels of adherence. Broadly defined, relapse is reverting back to problematic behavioral patterns after a period of success (Larimer et al., 1999). For alcoholics, this entails "falling off the wagon," after a period of abstinence. For dieters, this involves reverting back to a high-caloric diet, following adherence to a restricted diet. For patients on complex medication regimens, this entails slipping back into old patterns of not taking the medication as prescribed.

People typically relapse in four high-risk situations (Watson & Tharp, 1997, p. 289). The first situation is when patients are emotionally disregulated. Being angry, frustrated, or anxious can lead to relapse, because these interfere with one's ability to effectively problem-solve. The

second situation has to do with the social setting. Bars, for example, are notorious for all kinds of relapse, from smoking to unprotected sex, from drinking to intravenous drug use. The third situation is intoxication. Alcohol, for example, makes people less self-aware, impairs judgment, and fosters impulsivity (Hull, 1987). People are simply more inclined to give in to urges when under the influence. The last situation involves "unexpected encounters with temptation" (Watson & Tharp, 1997, p. 290). For example, a recovering alcoholic may inadvertently pick up someone else's drink, mistaking it for a soda and take a swallow.

RP training involves the following (Ellis, McInerney, DiGiuseppe, & Yeager, 1988, p. 66; Larimer et al., 1999):

- Identifying high-risk situations
- Developing alternative coping strategies, such as relaxation and assertiveness training
- Cognitive restructuring of the abstinence violation effect (AVE)
- Developing a relapse plan

The first step is to identify high-risk situations related to nonadherence. Structure queries around the four high-risk situations mentioned above (e.g., How are you feeling emotionally when you slip? Who's around and where are you at the time?). The second step is teaching patients alternative coping strategies. Relaxation is highly beneficial in coping with emotional disregulation. For relaxation, we recommend using Bernstein and Borkovec's (1973) standardized protocol. As far as the basic procedure is concerned, the following is the training sequence by which clients are taught to tense and release the various muscle groups (p. 25):

1. Dominant hand and forearm

2. Dominant biceps

3. Nondominant hand and forearm

4. Nondominant biceps

5. Forehead

6. Upper cheeks and nose

7. Lower cheeks and jaw

8. Neck and throat

9. Chest, shoulders, and upper back

10. Abdominal or stomach region

11. Dominant thigh

12. Dominant calf

13. Dominant foot

14. Nondominant thigh

15. Nondominant calf

16. Nondominant foot

Patients might also benefit from assertiveness training as a coping strategy, especially when nonadherence is related to passive interpersonal styles (e.g., not being able to say "no" when someone passes the patient a joint). See Duckworth (2003) for a detailed discussion on assertiveness skills training.

The third step involves teaching patients how to avoid the AVE. The AVE occurs when a one-time abstinence violation is seen as a total relapse (Ellis et al., 1988, p. 35). One way to prevent the AVE is to encourage the idea that adherence is a process. Teach patients to reframe lapses

not as failures or lack of willpower but as mistakes or errors in learning that signal the need for increased planning to cope more effectively in similar situations in the future. . . . This reframing of lapse episodes can help decrease the client's tendency to view lapses as a result of personal failing or moral weakness and remove the self-fulfilling prophecy that a lapse will inevitably lead to a relapse. (Larimer et al., 1999, p. 157)

Last, develop a relapse plan with the patient, outlining the steps of what to do in the event of

a relapse. Writing these instructions down on a reminder card is especially helpful in high-arousal situations (Watson & Tharp, 1997). In some circumstances, patients are invited to call the therapist right after a relapse, to examine the situation for clues as to what triggered the relapse (Larimer et al., 1999, p. 156).

Points to Consider[6]

1. Plan a relapse. For example, a binge eater might eat several bites of high-caloric food (e.g., piece of chocolate cake) and then set the fork down, at which point the patient employs coping strategies, such as relaxation, "cold" instead of "hot" cognitions (see Mischel, 1974), or cognitive distraction. This will provide practice and, when a patient is successful, can be efficacy enhancing.

2. Dispel myths about abstinence. Many patients believe if they muster enough "willpower" they can quit "cold turkey" the first time. Remind patients that although some people can eventually quit their habit of choice, it usually involves many attempts and much support on the part of others (i.e., coping model vs. mastery model).

3. Substance use usually arises when people are not living fulfilling lives. Help patients establish well-balanced lifestyles and get them involved in meaningful activities (e.g., community groups).

Concluding Remarks

Despite several decades of research, poor adherence continues to pose a formidable challenge in health care today. In all likelihood, adherence remains largely an unsolved clinical problem due to its sheer complexity. Indeed, adherence entails patient variables, provider variables, environmental and community factors, and interactions between these (Meichenbaum & Turk, 1987; Milhalko et al., 2004). The number of possible permutations is thus exponentially vast.

This chapter touched on patient variables that factor into the adherence equation, in particular adherence skill sets. These skills were discussed within a behavior analytic theoretical framework and within the context of a stepped-care health care model. With an understanding of the underlying principles of behavior, we hope readers will be able to incorporate this approach into case conceptualization and treatment planning, because contingency management is necessary for success. Let us now close with a case example, illustrating some of the techniques outlined in the chapter. In addition to highlighting techniques, this case study also illustrates some of the barriers therapists and clinicians face in day-to-day practice.

Case Study

Background

Mr. F. is a 54-year-old male smoker with a body mass index (BMI) of 25. He reportedly smokes an average of 20 cigarettes per day. He is a social drinker and was diagnosed with hypertension 2 years ago. He does not engage in regular exercise. His current medication regime includes hydrochlorothiazide (25 mg) and lisinopril (20 mg) daily to treat his hypertension. When he was diagnosed with hypertension, his blood pressure (BP) was 146/94.

Behavioral Targets

1. *Lifestyle issues*: Mr. F. is a moderately heavy smoker, which poses increased cardiovascular risk. He is on the upper quadrant of the BMI index. He should try to maintain a healthy weight. Diet is important in hypertension, especially sodium and fat. He states he is a social drinker, but the quantity consumed should be identified. There is no information concerning exercise, but regular fitness is important.

2. *Medication*: Mr. F. must be encouraged to take his medication on a regular basis, even if he does not have any symptoms that he is aware of. His medication may be causing side effects that have not been identified. A thorough, detailed, medication review should be performed.

3. *BP monitoring*: Mr. F. should regularly monitor his BP. This will be an indication that the medication and any lifestyle modifications are successful (or unsuccessful).

Case Conceptualization

When Mr. F. was initially diagnosed with hypertension, he was very shocked. He had no symptoms, felt he was "pretty healthy," and did not really understand what the "big deal" was. The fact that he had no overt symptoms made it difficult for him to understand the potential severity of the disease as well as the importance of adherence.

Treatment Planning

First Visit. The first step was education. Mr. F. was educated about the disease, the potential complications, prevention of progression, and strategies for improving health. Initially, the client was advised that his condition would improve if he increased his exercise regimen, which was reportedly "an occasional walk with my wife when she goes on a diet." Further investigation revealed that he walked for about 30 minutes twice a month. An increase to walking 30 minutes three times a week was recommended. He was also advised that reducing or, ideally, quitting smoking would be beneficial to his condition, as well as improving other facets of his health, such as reducing his risk for heart attack and stroke. He was also told that he should watch his salt intake by cutting out high-salt foods and follow a "no-added salt" diet. He was instructed to make an appointment with the hospital dietitian to learn about a healthy diet in hypertension. These strategies were to be employed for a 2-month time period and then evaluated. He was also advised not to gain any further weight as his BMI was borderline obese.

When faced with these options, Mr. F. said quitting smoking would be very difficult as he ran a bingo hall. He thought he might be able to watch the salt and maybe take the dog for a few more walks. The client was also given information regarding smoking cessation to read at his leisure. He was also given a pamphlet about hypertension and how it is a silent killer. A follow-up contact was made after his initial visit.

Second Visit. After the 2-month time period, the client's BMI fell to 24, but his BP was still elevated at 141/91. When questioned about what things he was able to do to improve his condition, he replied, "Well, I am walking more often, and that makes the dog happy. The salt thing has been kind of tough. Food just doesn't have enough flavor without salt. Oh, and yes, I'm still smoking." He stated he had seen a dietitian, and she had told him that he could put salt in foods when cooking them but should not add salt after the food was cooked. He said he did not realize that canned food had so much salt and that sodium and salt meant the same thing. When questioned about a follow-up visit to the dietitian, he said that it was unnecessary, for he felt he had changed his salt consumption adequately. When questioned about the frequency of exercise, he stated he walked the dog for 20 minutes three times a week. When asked about the number of cigarettes smoked in a day, he said that he still smoked about 20 cigarettes per day. He said he could not even think about quitting.

Third Visit. Because his BP was still elevated, but improved, he was instructed to self-monitor his BP on a more frequent basis. He was advised to purchase a BP cuff or go to a pharmacy with a BP chair. It was recommended that he keep a weekly record of his BP and bring it to his next visit, which was scheduled in 2 months. He was counseled that smoking cessation would improve his condition.

Fourth Visit. At his next visit, Mr. F.'s BP was 142/92. He forgot to bring in his record of BP measurements that were done over the last 2 months but said he only gone to the pharmacy "a couple of times." He said he was still consuming reduced sodium, but the weather was too cold to be walking the dog that often. He had also gained 4 pounds and his BMI was up to 25—the low end of obese. His smoking had remained unchanged.

Fifth Visit. Mr. F. was questioned again about BP monitoring and strongly advised to purchase a BP cuff he could use at home. This would avoid the bother of having to "go" somewhere to monitor his BP. He was asked if his pharmacists could be contacted to ensure he got proper counseling on how to use the device and how to accurately record the results.

Mr. F. was also asked to revisit the dietitian to come up with a weight reduction strategy. An appointment was arranged for him. The importance of exercise was reemphasized, and he was asked if he would like to attend a smoking cessation group. He refused. Because his BP was elevated, he was asked to return in 1 month for a follow-up visit. A telephone call was made to Mr. F. 1 week prior to his appointment to remind him of it and to ensure he brought his BP monitoring record.

Sixth Visit. Mr. F. returned 1 month later with a BP of 140/92. He had lost 3 pounds and credited it to his dietitian. He was monitoring his BP every other day and had seen the pharmacist twice to make sure he was doing it correctly. His exercise had increased slightly but was not as good as when he was first diagnosed. He still smoked 20 cigarettes per day.

Mr. F. was praised for his successes—weight loss and BP monitoring—and was encouraged to continue with these steps. Because his BP continued to be elevated, he was prescribed hydrochlorothiazide (25 mg) each morning. He was instructed to seek counseling from the pharmacist about the medication and smoking cessation. He was asked to return in 1 month.

Seventh Visit. Mr. F. returned in 1 month with a BP of 138/90 and a weight reduction of 5 pounds. He did complain, however, about the medication. He said all he did all day was "go to the bathroom," and he stated that he had trouble sleeping through the night because he was "always getting up to urinate." He didn't think he wanted to take medications because they made him feel worse than before. He was still routinely monitoring his BP at home, and the results were well documented.

Mr. F. was praised for his BP reduction and weight loss. It was reinforced that the medication probably was helping get his BP down, in addition to lifestyle changes. When carefully questioned, it was determined that Mr. F. often forgot to take his medication in the morning and remembered when he got home for dinner. As a result, its action peaked during the night, keeping him awake. He was instructed to "anchor" his medication regime with his daily morning routine (i.e., brushing teeth, picking up his car keys, eating breakfast) so that it would also become a routine for him. If this was not possible, he was asked to purchase a medication alarm system that would beep each morning to remind him. Follow-up was scheduled in 2 months' time.

Eighth Visit. After 2 months, Mr. F.'s BP was 139/90, with a further 2-pound weight loss but no change in smoking habits. He stated he was complying with the medication, and this was confirmed with refill medication checks with the pharmacist.

An additional medication was added to his regime, captopril (25 mg twice daily). Follow-up was scheduled in 1 month. He was praised for his successes and was once again encouraged to discuss smoking cessation with the pharmacist.

Ninth Visit. Mr. F. returned in 1 month with a BP of 137/89, maintaining his current weight and stating he was "smoking less because he coughs so much." Further questioning about the cough was done, and it was concluded that he was experiencing side effects from the captopril.

He was switched to lisinopril (10 mg daily) and instructed to discuss the new medication with the pharmacist. A follow-up call was made by the pharmacist to determine how well the new medication was suiting him. He was instructed to return in 1 month.

Tenth Visit. Mr. F. returned in 1 month with a BP of 139/90, stating that this pill was "way better than the last one; I don't cough all the time." His weight had dropped 2 more pounds, and his new BMI was 23. He stated he was smoking 15 cigarettes per day, and it really wasn't that bad.

His lisinopril dose was increased (to 20 mg daily) to bring his BP down. He was given information about smoking cessation counseling offered in his neighborhood. He was instructed to continue BP home monitoring and to return for a visit in 1 month.

Eleventh Visit. Mr. F. returned in 1 month with a BP of 135/85. He had maintained his weight, was monitoring his BP, had few medication side effects, but had not quit smoking. He had not gone to the smoking cessation group.

Mr. F.'s BP is acceptable given the circumstances. The only remaining recommended lifestyle change is smoking cessation. An appointment with a counselor was arranged so he could have intensive therapy. He was instructed to return every 3 months for a checkup.

Notes

1. Recall, the concept of UCS. Consequences that naturally increase the behavior they follow can also be unconditioned stimuli. Chocolate, for example, elicits salivation (UCR) and can increase the behavior that precedes it (e.g., a person will "work" for chocolate—chocolate thus serves as a reinforcer). The same can be said of conditioned stimuli.

2. Adverse mediation effects (UCS) also serve as a punisher. The same can be said of the CS (i.e., otherwise neutral stimuli associated with these effects).

3. Adapted from Cox, Tisdelle, and Culbert (1988), Jenkins (1995), and Meichenbaum and Turk (1987).

4. Adapted from Meichenbaum and Turk, 1987, Nelson (1977), Bornstein et al. (1986), Bloom, Fischer, & Orme (1995), and Hayes, Barlow, and Nelson-Gray (1999).

5. Adapted from Meichenbaum and Turk (1987), Martin and Pear (1978), Houmanfar, Maglieri, and Roman (2003), and Sulzer-Azaroff and Mayer (1991).

6. Adapted from Meichenbaum and Turk (1987), Ellis et al. (1988), Watson and Tharp (1997), and Larimer, Palmer, and Marlatt (1999).

References

Alvarez, G. G., & Ayas, N. T. (2004). The impact of daily sleep duration on health: A review of the literature. *Progress in Cardiovascular Nursing, 19*, 56–59.

American Diabetes Association. (2002). *American Diabetes Association complete guide to diabetes* (3rd ed.). Alexandria, VA: Author.

Barlow, D. H., & Hersen, M. (1984). *Single case experimental designs: Strategies for studying behavior change* (2nd ed.). New York: Pergamon Press.

Bernard, R. S., & Cohen, L. L. (2004). Increasing adherence to cystic fibrosis treatment: A systematic review of behavioral techniques. *Pediatric Pulmonology, 37*, 8–16.

Bernstein, D. A., & Borkovec, T. D. (1973). *Progressive relaxation training: A manual for the helping professions.* Champaign, IL: Research Press.

Bijou, S. W., Peterson, R. F., & Ault, M. H. (1968). A method to integrate descriptive and experimental field studies at the level of data and empirical concepts. *Journal of Applied Behavior Analysis, 1*, 175–191.

Bloom, M., Fischer, J., & Orme, J. G. (1995). *Evaluating practice: Guidelines for the accountable professional* (2nd ed.). Boston: Allyn and Bacon.

Bornstein, P. H., Hamilton, S. B., & Bornstein, M. T. (1986). Self-monitoring procedures. In A. R. Ciminero, K. S. Calhoun, & H. E. Adams (Eds.), *Handbook of April assessment* (2nd ed., pp. 176–222). New York: Wiley.

Boutelle, K. N., Baker, R. C., Kirschenbaum, D. S., & Mitchell, M. E. (1999). How can obese weight controllers minimize weight gain during the high-risk holiday season? By self-monitoring very consistently. *Health Psychology, 18*, 364–368.

Catania, A. C. (1992). *Learning* (3rd ed.). Englewood Cliffs, NJ: Prentice Hall.

Colcher, I. S., & Bass, J. W. (1972). Penicillin treatment of streptococcal pharyngitis. *Journal of the American Medical Association, 222*, 657–659.

Cox, D. J., Tisdelle, D. A., & Culbert, J. P. (1988). Increasing adherence to behavioral homework assignments. *Journal of Behavioral Medicine, 11*, 519–522.

Cummings, N. A., & Cummings, J. L. (2000). *The first session with substance abusers: A step-by-step guide.* San Francisco: Jossey-Bass.

Duckworth, M. P. (2003). Assertiveness skills and the management of related factors. In W. O'Donohue, J. E. Fisher, & S. C. Hayes (Eds.), *Cognitive behavior therapy* (pp. 16–22). Hoboken, NJ: Wiley.

Dunbar-Jacob, J., & Mortimer-Stephens, M. K. (2001). Treatment adherence in chronic disease. *Journal of Clinical Epistemology, 54,* S57–S60.

Ellis, A., McInerney, J. F., DiGiuseppe, R., & Yeager, R. J. (1988). *Rational-emotive therapy with alcoholics and substance abusers.* Boston: Allyn and Bacon.

Fawzy, I. F., Fawzy, N. W., Arndt, L. A., & Pasnau, R. O. (1995). Critical review of psychosocial interventions in cancer care. *Archives of General Psychiatry, 52,* 100–113.

Foxx, R. M. (1982). *Increasing behaviors of persons with severe retardation and autism.* Champaign, IL: Research Press.

Greenan-Fowler, E., Powell, C., & Varni, J. W. (1987). Behavioral treatment of adherence to therapeutic exercise by children with hemophilia. *Archives of Physical Medicine and Rehabilitation, 68,* 846–849.

Hayes, S. C., Barlow, D. H., & Nelson-Gray, R. O. (1999). *The scientist practitioner: Research and accountability in the age of managed care* (2nd ed.). Needham Heights, MA: Allyn and Bacon.

Haynes, B. R. (1979). Introduction. In B. R. Haynes, D. W. Taylor, & D. L Sackett (Eds.), *Compliance in health care* (pp. 1–10). Baltimore: Johns Hopkins University Press.

Haynes, R. B., McDonald, H. P., & Garg, A. (2002). Helping patients follow prescribed treatment: Clinical applications. *Journal of the American Medical Association, 288,* 2880–2883.

Haynes, S. N., & O'Brien, W. H. (2000). *Principles and practice of behavioral assessment.* New York: Kluwer Academic/Plenum Press.

Hawkins, R. P., & Dobes, R. W. (1975). Behavioral definitions in applied behavior analysis: Explicit or implicit. In B. C. Etzel, J. M. LeBlanc, and D. M. Baer (Eds.), *New developments in behavioral research: Theory, methods, and applications. In honor of Sidney W. Bijou.* Hillsdale, NJ: Erlbaum.

Heidt, J. M., & Marx, B. P. (2003). Self-monitoring as a treatment vehicle. In W. O'Donohue, J. E. Fisher, & S. C. Hayes (Eds.), *Cognitive behavior therapy* (pp. 361–367). Hoboken, NJ: Wiley.

Heward, W. L. (1987). Self-management. In J. O. Cooper, T. E. Heron, & W. L. Heward (Eds.), *Applied behavior analysis* (pp. 515–549). Columbus, OH: Merrill.

Holland, J. G., & Skinner, B. F. (1961). *The analysis of behavior.* New York: McGraw-Hill.

Houmanfar, R., Maglieri, K. A., Boyce, T. E., & Roman, H. R. (2003). Behavioral contracting. In

W. O'Donohue, J. E. Fisher, & S. C. Hayes (Eds.), *Cognitive behavior therapy* (pp. 40–45). Hoboken, NJ: Wiley.

Hull, J. (1987). Self-awareness model. In H. Blaine & K. Leonard (Eds.), *Psychological theories of drinking and alcoholism* (pp. 272–304). New York: Guilford Press.

Irvin, J. E., Bowers, C. A., Dunn, M. E., & Wang, M. C. (1999). Efficacy of relapse prevention: A meta-analytic review. *Journal of Consulting and Clinical Psychology, 67,* 563–570.

Jenkins, C. D. (1995). An integrated behavioral medicine approach to improving care of patients with diabetes mellitus. *Behavioral Medicine, 21,* 53–66.

Jerant, A. F., Friederichs-Fitzwater, M. M., & Moore, M. (2005). Patients' perceived barriers to active self-management of chronic conditions. *Patient Education and Counseling, 57*(3), 300–307.

Korotitsch, W. J., & Nelson-Gray, R. O. (1999). An overview of self-monitoring research in assessment and treatment. *Psychological Assessment, 11,* 415–425.

Larimer, M. E., Palmer, R. S., & Marlatt, G. A. (1999). Relapse prevention: An overview of Marlatt's cognitive-behavioral model. *Alcohol Research and Health, 23,* 151–160.

Mager, R. F., & Pipe, P. (1984). *Analyzing performance problems or you really oughta wanna* (2nd ed.). Belmont, CA: Pitman.

Mahoney, M. J. (1977). Some applied issues in self-monitoring. In J. D. Cone & R. P. Hawkins (Eds.), *Behavioral assessment: New directions in clinical psychology* (pp. 241–254). New York: Brunner/Mazel.

Martin, G., & Pear, J. (1978). *Behavior modification: What it is and how to do it.* Englewood Cliffs, NJ: Prentice-Hall.

McDonald, H. P., Garg, A., & Haynes, R. B. (2002). Interventions to enhance patient adherence to medication prescriptions: Scientific review. *Journal of the American Medical Association, 288,* 2868–2879.

Meichenbaum, D., & Turk, D. C. (1987). *Facilitating treatment adherence: A practitioner's guidebook.* New York: Plenum Press.

Merck. (2000). *The Merck manual of geriatrics* (3rd ed.). White House Station, NJ: Merck Research Laboratories.

Michael, J. L. (1982). Distinguishing between discriminative and motivational functions of stimuli. *Journal of the Experimental Analysis of Behavior, 37,* 149–155.

Michael, J. L. (1993). *Concepts and principles of behavior analysis.* Kalamazoo, MI: Association for Behavior Analysis.

Milhalko, S. L., Brenes, G. A., Farmer, D. F., Katula, J. A., Balkrishnan, R., & Bowen, D. J. (2004). Challenges and innovations in enhancing adherence. *Controlled Clinical Trials, 25,* 447–457.

Miltenberger, R. G. (2001). *Behavior modification: Principles and procedures* (2nd ed.). Belmont, CA: Wadsworth.

Mischel, W. (1974). Processes in delay of gratification. In L. Berkowitz (Ed.), *Advances in experimental social psychology* (Vol. 7, pp. 249–292). New York: Academic Press.

Morrow, G. R., & Morrell, C. (1982). Behavioral treatments for the anticipatory nausea and vomiting induced by cancer chemotherapy. *New England Journal of Medicine, 9,* 1476–1480.

Morrow, G. R., Roscoe, J. A., Kirshner, J. J., Hynes, H.E., & Rosenbluth, R.J. (1998). Anticipatory nausea and vomiting in the area of 5-HT3 antiemetics. *Supportive Care in Cancer, 6,* 244–247.

Murray, M. D., Morrow, D. G., Weiner, M., Clark, D. O., Wanzhu, T., Deer, M. M., et al. (2004). A conceptual framework to study medication adherence in older adults. *American Journal of Geriatric Pharmacotherapy, 2,* 36–43.

Nelson, R. O. (1977). Methodological issues in assessment via self-monitoring. In J. D. Cone & R. P. Hawkins (Eds.), *Behavioral assessment* (pp. 217–240). New York: Brunner/Mazel.

O'Donohue, W., Cummings, N. A., Cucciare, M. A., Cummings, J., & Runyan, T. (2006). *Integrated behavioral healthcare: A primer and resource guide.* Amherst, NY: Humanity Books.

Pierce, W. D., & W. F. Epling. (1999). *Behavior analysis and learning* (2nd ed.). Upper Saddle River, NJ: Prentice Hall.

Skinner, B. F. (1953). *Science and human behavior.* New York: Macmillan.

Stockhorst, U., Klosterhalfen, S., & Steingruber, H. J. (1998). Conditioned nausea and further side-effects in cancer chemotherapy: A review. *Journal of Psychophysiology, 12,* 14–33.

Strom, L., Pettersson, R., & Andersson, G. (2004). Internet-based treatment for insomnia: A controlled evaluation. *Journal of Consulting and Clinical Psychology, 72,* 113–120.

Sulzer-Azaroff, B., & Mayer, G. R. (1991). *Behavior analysis for lasting change.* New York: Harcourt Brace College Publishers.

Touchette, P. E., MacDonald, R. F., Langer, S. N. (1985). A scatter plot for identifying stimulus control of problem behavior. *Journal of Applied Behavior Analysis, 18,* 343–351.

Watson, D., & Tharp, R. G. (1997). *Self-directed behavior: Self-modification for personal adjustment* (7th ed.). Pacific Grove, CA: Brooks/Cole.

Wolpe, J. (1958). *Psychotherapy by reciprocal inhibition.* Stanford, CA: Stanford University Press.

Wolpe, J. (1976). *Theme and variations: A behavior therapy casebook.* New York: Pergamon Press.

Wolpe, J. (1990). *The practice of behavior therapy* (4th ed.). New York: Pergamon Press.

Wroe, A. L. (2002). Intentional and unintentional nonadherence: A study of decision making. *Journal of Behavioral Medicine, 25,* 355–372.

8

Increasing Resources and Supports to Improve Adherence to Treatments

Robin Shapiro

Marcia Herivel

At the beginning of the 21st century, medical providers have access to evidence-based knowledge, sophisticated equipment, elaborate technology, and customized protocols for defeating many illnesses. Medical treatment, however, occurs in the context of each patient's complex and particular life circumstances. Patients who lack tangible and intangible resources and supports are less likely to be able to follow a provider's treatment recommendations.

Without the concrete resources to sustain physical existence (food, housing, shelter) and the financial means to pay for them, as well as the supports to sustain personal well-being (emotional, social, community, and spiritual supports), patients may not be able to adhere to even the best- laid treatment plans. Two important factors in promoting treatment adherence are (1) increased, individualized resources and supports to enhance patients' ability to manage their medical needs and (2) providers who work with patients' individual circumstances.

To illustrate how increasing resources and supports can promote treatment adherence, let us consider the many ways in which the lack thereof creates barriers to adherence. Resource and support barriers to treatment adherence can be described in four areas: (1) concrete resources, (2) social/emotional supports, (3) individual circumstances, and (4) system deficits.

Concrete resources sustain basic existence. They include adequate and healthful food, safe and reliable shelter, transportation, and sufficient financial means to provide these resources for oneself and one's family. Having such basic amenities as a telephone or voice mail service can be critical to maintaining continuity of treatment, especially for chronically ill patients. Housing, in particular, is the key to treatment adherence. Economic trends coupled with current social policies (reduced public funds for poverty programs, severe shortages in public housing and its funding, and the third decade of deinstitutionalization of the mentally ill) have created unprecedented numbers of homeless people in this country. People without stable housing have greater difficulty keeping medical appointments, getting prescriptions filled, taking prescriptions regularly, or even keeping a pill bottle in their possession. Chronic and acute illnesses are widespread among the homeless, and they need a staggering level of additional resources to maintain basic health. If resources are not provided to link homeless people with outpatient care, it costs an enormous amount to treat them in emergency rooms (ERs) and inpatient hospital beds.

The same is true for the less tangible *emotional and social supports* that help individuals to maintain a sense of both personal well-being and connection to the larger society. These include the emotional support provided by family and friends and the social support gained through neighborhood and community involvement, church affiliation, and paid, political, and volunteer work.

Affiliation is an essential human need, without which people can become isolated, apathetic, and depressed. Lack of connection to other people hinders the ability to maintain all kinds of self-care, including following health care recommendations. Health care providers can assist patients to assess the social deficits in their lives, and to help correct them through appropriate referrals and follow-up. Affiliation can bring identification, information about and connection to a wider array of resources, warmth, and support.

The barriers to adherence created by *individuals' circumstances* may involve individual deficits, including cognitive impairments, illiteracy, limited English, or any limited ability to comprehend treatment rationales and recommendations. Providers in such cases need to tailor treatment plans and communication to match individuals' limitations, which can include the need for additional resources and support.

Mental illness as an individual circumstance can be an especially challenging barrier to treatment adherence. Major depression, for example, can erode the motivation to care for oneself and to manage one's life, including tending to medical needs. Severely bipolar patients are notorious for abandoning treatment protocols and medication regimes due to extreme mood variations and to the appeal of manic and hypomanic states for some bipolar patients. Obsessive-compulsive individuals may "ruminate" themselves out of taking prescribed medication. People with extreme social anxiety may not be able to reach out to anyone for help.

Maintaining treatment adherence in patients with personality disorders can be complex. Because many of these disorders (particularly borderline personality disorder) are formed in the context of early relationships with caregivers, their pathology tends to play out in the patient-provider relationship, with patients' emotional states and demands often eclipsing and hindering medical needs. When providers are armed with both the knowledge and appropriate resource information to help patients with serious mental illness, treatment adherence is much more likely, and providers' energies can be wisely used.

Substance abusers are especially hard to treat. Alcohol, opiates, or amphetamines may cause medical problems and become the primary blocks to treatment adherence. Smokers may continue to smoke through lung cancer treatment or emphysema. Other less physically destructive drugs or compulsive behaviors may cause too much internal disorganization for patients to follow treatment guidelines. Many addicted people avoid seeing medical providers because, "They'll just tell me I have to quit" or "They'll put me in the hospital, and I won't be able to smoke/drink there." Others are frequent users of expensive emergency medical care, while continuing to cause, by their substance use, the problems they come in for.

Patients' individual beliefs and perceptions about medicine and health care providers often exert a powerful influence as barriers to adherence. For example, a patient may believe that complying with a particular medical recommendation is an impediment to engaging in more enjoyable activities (e.g., quitting smoking or drinking makes it more difficult to socialize with friends in bars). He or she may perceive medical providers as authority figures to be challenged rather than as collaborative helpers because of past negative experiences. Without sufficient information, the patient may not see the need for a particular behavior change.

Patients may be loath to use community resources because of their beliefs about "handouts" and the importance of being independent. In the United States, there is a strong ethos that the poor are "not us," are not intelligent, and are "losers." As a country of immigrants, we have a strong sense that people should "pull themselves up by their bootstraps" and not need or accept help. There is a stigma about psychotherapy. I've heard, "But if I go to AA, then it means that I'm an alcoholic!" "If I go to therapy, it means that I'm crazy!"

Patients may perceive treatment (often rightfully) as unpleasant or harmful or dangerous. Most people possess anecdotal knowledge from other "nonmedical" sources that may contradict information from mainstream medical providers: the experiences of friends or family with illness and recovery, information from the media, intergenerational patterns of health behavior, naturopathic and homeopathic remedies, and healing practices linked to non-Western cultural and spiritual traditions. Frequently, such knowledge seems more valid than information obtained from health care professionals in a setting patients may perceive as intimidating, overwhelming, or irrelevant to their primary concerns.

Often, the barriers to adherence resulting from an individual's beliefs and perceptions about health care are powerful indicators of a mismatch between that individual's worldview and the good intentions of health care providers. This situation raises the need to explore the patient's willingness and ability to engage in treatment, an exploration that may require additional time, staff, or other resources.

A final barrier to adherence in the realm of individual circumstances is the simple lack of experience with positive behavioral change. Poverty itself can contribute to unpredictable and sometimes chaotic life circumstances, such as frequent changes of residence, inconsistent child care arrangements, and uneven finances. Such circumstances contribute over time to a perception of diminished control over one's life and, therefore, a limited ability to effect positive behavioral changes. Patients in health care settings where behavioral and lifestyle changes are an integral part of treatment will need increased resources and support to counter their inexperience with this approach to care.

A complete discussion of *system deficits* as a barrier to treatment adherence is beyond the scope of this chapter. The health care choices of individuals occur within the context of social and health policy. These policies affect both patients and providers. The most obvious system barriers to adherence for patients are the rising cost of health care and its decreasing availability to the poor, working poor, and self-employed. Patients and providers alike are caught in this gradual erosion of the public sector and privatization of health care. The results are incremental and widespread: decreased staffing of health and mental health facilities results in decreased time for patient-provider interaction, time to teach, explain, assess, and adapt treatments to individual patient needs. The work of linking patients with optimal resources and supports often falls to "adjunct" health care professionals, such as nurse educators, social workers, health promotion specialists, and case managers. In this era of diminishing funds, these adjunct positions are the first to be cut in a budget crisis.

While resources shrink, patient needs remain. When patients appear to be "noncompliant," they may in fact be caught in constraints imposed by systems and policies beyond their control. Likewise, when providers appear to be rushed or inaccessible, they may be struggling to balance their practice standards with incompatible system constraints. Under these circumstances, to talk at all about increasing resources and supports is to imply that both providers and patients must work together collaboratively and creatively to create relevant, realistic, and flexible treatment plans.

Empirical Evidence

In literature about treatment adherence, there is rare and tangential mention of the topic of resources available to patients. Donald Meichenbaum and Dennis Turk (1987) address the topic of social support, noting the importance of the patient's social environment. They point to the complexity of social support networks and caution that it is not the number of social supports but rather their quality that can enhance a person's ability to adhere to treatment regimens. The authors also state that although providing social support will be helpful for some patients, others may find it intrusive and a threat to their sense of self-sufficiency.

Whereas most of the adherence literature addresses strategies to assist patients to achieve various types and levels of behavioral change, some sources do make mention of the need for a variety of adjunct services and resources. Lin and Katon (1998) found that when primary care physicians collaborated with on-site mental health consultants to manage patients with depression and provided a multifaceted intervention (including patient guidelines, evidence-based provider education, quick diagnostic tools, patient education, and a consultant for complex patients), patients improved significantly.

Ribisl and Humphreys (1998) speak of their success in collaborating with the community organizations in which individuals participate in their private lives (churches, voluntary associations, and neighborhoods) to promote adherence in the treatment of diabetes. They posit this approach as a "third way" between the extremes of rugged individualism (total patient autonomy) and paternalism (greater social control).

Other sources speak of the power of the beliefs of both patients and providers in influencing adherence. Horne (1999) states that "patients' adherence behavior is likely to be the result of dynamic interaction between beliefs about the illness and treatment and perceptions of outcome, rather than the product of a single decision" (p. 493). A prior study by Horne suggested that "medication adherence is related to personal perceptions of the *necessity* of medication and *concerns* about potential adverse effects and the way in which each individual balanced the perceived benefits (*necessity* beliefs) against perceived risks (*concern*)" (p. 492).

Goldstein, DePue, Kazura, and Niaura (1998) note that physician recommendations are stronger predictors of women obtaining a screening mammography than women's beliefs and perceptions. These authors stress customizing interventions to patients' needs and using counseling skills to improve adherence.

Ciechanowski (1999) discusses attachment style in diabetic patients as it relates to treatment adherence. He found that of those patients with a "dismissing" attachment style (compulsively self-sufficient individuals with difficulty obtaining support from others), adherence was poorest in those who perceived that their provider had poor communication skills. He concludes that patient-provider communication modifies the relationship between adherence and attachment style.

Theoretical Underpinnings for Individualized Interventions

The key to effectively linking patients with needed resources is the relationship between provider and patient. It is possible to support that assumption from several theoretical perspectives. Those noted here are based in the mental health field but can apply to helping relationships in any field. Numerous theories have been developed to support the importance of the patient-provider relationship in strengthening adherence. Those presented here are merely a sampling, selected to remind providers that success of any intervention or suggestion to a patient will be colored by the many levels and aspects of the interaction.

Adults presenting for medical treatment are sometimes individuals with impaired early attachment to parental figures, generally as a result of limited or poor parenting skills in the primary caregiver. As a result, mistrust, ambivalence, and insecurities may temper their relationships with others, including in the patient-provider relationship. These dynamics may manifest as indirect communication, failure to follow up on treatment plans or even sabotage of treatment. It is important for providers to recognize that patients with serious attachment issues will likely require an enhanced level of communication on the part of the provider, and additional, extended efforts and services on the part of the health care team to ensure adherence.

From the psychodynamic perspective, the relationship between the psychotherapy client and the therapist is the core mediating variable in ensuring client involvement and engagement. From this perspective, the relationship between client and therapist is the medium in which change occurs. Without this trusting and open relationship, which is constantly explored as both metaphor and example of healthy communication, no amount of sophisticated techniques can facilitate change in the client. The parallel to the patient-provider relationship in the medical setting is clear. When there is an obvious mismatch between patient and provider, communication is difficult, whereas when the relationship works, continuity and cooperation occur easily.

The cognitive-behavioral therapy (CBT) perspective is particularly applicable to the challenges of improving adherence in medical settings. For CBT to be effective with psychotherapy clients, the ideal first step is a thorough assessment of clients' therapy goals for themselves. This assessment should include a review of options for achieving those goals and a discussion of the client's willingness and ability to engage in those options. The treatment plan is then formulated as a collaborative effort between client and therapist, targeting problematic behaviors and cognitions for treatment. Issues such as clients' "resistance" to perceived provider authority are thus minimized, and the clients' involvement in their own care plan is maximized. The therapist monitors the clients' engagement in the process throughout therapy and checks the ongoing relevance of goals and objectives. By maintaining this kind of collaborative dialogue, the clients take responsibility for the process and become invested in treatment outcome. The CBT approach is an ideal model to adapt for enhancing adherence in medical settings.

Eye movement desensitization and reprocessing (EMDR) works with a "future template" (Shapiro, 2001) in which the patient imaginally practices the new behavior, answering the questions, "How would you like to do that differently next time?" and "What stands in the way of going to that support group, keeping your appointment with DSHS, etc.?" Shapiro (2005) uses the two-hand interweave to help with ambivalence: "Hold wanting to make that appointment in one hand. Hold wanting to avoid it in the other hand. What do you notice now?"

Motivational interviewing (MI), a subset of CBT, incorporates theory from the transtheoretical model of Prochaska and Diclemente (1986) and was developed for the treatment of alcohol addiction. It helps "stuck" patients to enhance self-sufficiency, increase cognitive dissonance, and direct that dissonance toward behavior change (Goldstein et al., 1998). MI espouses five approaches: (1) express empathy, (2) develop discrepancy (between the desire to use and to abstain), (3) avoid argumentation, (4) roll with resistance, and (5) support self-efficacy. Through the use of open-ended questions, the provider aims to legitimize the patient's feelings and validate the patient's freedom to change or not, without judgment. This approach, like some cognitive-behavioral approaches, accepts and works with the patient's level of readiness for change and is, therefore, collaborative and empowering (Miller & Rollnick, 1991).

Contraindications of This Strategy

Using individualized interventions for increasing resources and support is not contraindicated so much as compromised by the limitations in the current health care environment. This is an approach requiring careful assessment, research of resources in the community and the patient's environment, and a trial and error process to link patients with workable resources. It can be time-consuming and labor-intensive. When adjunct staff (e.g., social workers, nurse educators, or case managers) are available to locate resources and connect patients with them, primary providers are able to perform their roles more easily. The challenge is to convince funders of the long-range cost savings possible by tailoring services in this way to individuals' needs.

Assessment Targets

Let's look at the possible needs that patients might have and the resources that may be available to meet those needs. Do they have enough money, food, housing, or clothing? Is there a way to pay for medications? Do they have transportation? Are they aware of the resources to contact to get these things? Other important questions address transportation, "Are you having trouble getting to your appointments?"; clothing, "You're going to need to stay warm/out of the sun. Do you have a thicker coat/long-sleeved shirt and hat?"; and medication, "Can I ask you how you are going to pay for the medication?" Some questions are specific to the patient's malady: "Who will be around to help

you out of bed for the first few days?" "You're going to be woozy for a while. Is there someone who can make sure you get your medication at the right time?"

Do they have the skills that would allow them access to support? Can they speak English, read, write, drive, parent, find work, or ask assertively for what they need? Are they new to the community, the country or their status (disabled, unemployed, homeless, or gravely ill)? Have they already bought the book or done a Web search on their condition or do they have no information? Do they need assistance to identify and contact services? Do they have social supports? Are there family members, friends, fellow employees, church members, neighbors, or institutional staff available for emotional or physical support? Is there already a support group that can rally around the client? (Alcoholics Anonymous [AA], cancer support group, big local family, church community, or book club.) Do they need one?

Are they sober enough, sane enough, or compliant enough to adhere to the treatment? Do they trust you, your relationship with them, or treatment modality enough to hear what you have to say?

Who, if anyone, has power of attorney if the person is incapacitated? Who will advocate for them in an inpatient setting or difficult social service maze? Are there people who could take responsibility for meals, medications, and transportation, if needed? Are the patients able to communicate these needs or do the support people need to accompany them to the treatment appointment?

Are there disease-related needs? Do the patients have multiple sclerosis, cancer, AIDS, or other issues that might occasion use of multiple new resources (home health, support groups, online information-sharing collectives?)

What internal resources do the patients have? Do they understand your suggestions? (Intelligence, language ability.) Will they be able to remember them? (Cognitive or emotional ability.) Are they too stunned by trauma or illness to take in what is being suggested? Are they able to get online to find and use the wealth of support and information resources there? Are they too psychotic to separate your suggestions from their hallucinations? Are you asking them to try one more "impossible" thing in a life of failure? Or are they too proud or contrary to do anything you, the authority figure, ask of them?

What are the cultural issues for your patients? Do they come from a culture where illness or mental illness is shameful; never to be discussed with anyone but close family members? Are they from a higher-class family, feeling entitled to good care and support? Do they come from a working or subsistence-class background and have less sense of entitlement and hope of help? Is the treatment or resource you want to suggest antithetical to a religious or cultural belief (i.e., birth control)? Is prayer or religious/spiritual practice an important component of their healing? Will they be using alternative health care services? Which ones? Do they support or clash with the treatment that you do?

How do you ask about these things? As a health care professional, you expect to ask about symptoms. To add a whole new level of assessment, when you are barely given time to deal with the physical assessment, can be overwhelming, if not impossible. If you run a one-person office, it's your job to do the assessment and make the referral. This may necessitate a whole appointment spent on the psychosocial assessment.

The Assessment

Your inquiries should be as matter-of-fact as any question about bodily functions or pain level. Be direct with your questions. Acknowledge that you are asking nosy, snoopy questions that might be embarrassing. Say that you need to know the whole person so that you can make a referral that fits. Normalize the questions: "Everybody needs support when they're dealing with this disease. Who is in your life that you can talk to about it?" Face your patient as you ask these questions. Make eye contact, unless the patient is from a non-eye-contact culture (some

Asian and some Native American cultures) or is too ashamed or distraught to look at you.

Work collaboratively. Find out what their solutions are. Assume solutions, but don't assume that the patient knows about available resources or is able to access them. Conversely, don't assume that the client is incompetent. Mild mental retardation or even psychosis does not necessarily mean incompetence. Some resourceful homeless people have a cooking set up at their tent and a regular round of dumpster diving and free hot meals. Others have no clear plan for a place to stay, no regular food, nor the ability to carry through with a plan. Some patients have a greater knowledge of the newest treatments, the best support groups, and the competency of disease-specific caseworkers than you do. Some are clueless about available resources and need comprehensive assistance. Pay attention!

Many agencies have a psychosocial and needs assessment form for practitioners to follow. The assessments can include current life circumstances, the family constellation, cultural identification, additional support systems, work and income source, mental health history and diagnosis, presence of developmental disability or substance abuse, and questions about the patients' awareness of and ability to use resources and supports. You may want to create your own form or checklist, to make sure you cover all appropriate bases.

Respond to the concerns of the patients. Ask them if there's anything missing in their support system: "What are you worried about in this process?" "What help do you need that you don't have?" "What haven't I asked you about, that I should have?"

A few months ago, while assisting my mother (with her heart attack symptoms) in a large university hospital ER, I heard a voice from a gurney in the hallway repeating, "Is anybody there?" I talked to the Bengali immigrant who had been rear-ended while driving a cabulance. He was much more distressed about lack of income, if he was laid up, and how he was going to get home to a distant suburb than the issue of his possibly broken neck. When I explained workman's comp and disability to him, he relaxed. When I told him later that we'd drive him home (with no broken neck), he was nearly ecstatic. No one in the busy, crowded ER had addressed his most urgent concerns.

Know the available services. If you're not familiar with the services, talk to a crisis center, senior services, or other multipurpose social service agency. Go online to see what's available in your area. You might be able to send the patients to a place that can connect them to everything they need. (Getting you off the hook!) If you obtain a release of information, you can often speed up the process by bringing the other agency's caseworker up to speed on your patients' circumstances and capabilities. Chart the referrals and if you see the patients again, ask what happened with them.

If your workplace is larger, there may be a nurse or secretary who is the external resource expert. Make sure that there is clear transfer of responsibility from one caregiver to the next. Don't leave the patient in a room and simply send in the resource expert. Tell the patient, "We need to find you a place to stay and some food. Let me introduce you to Julie Smith, who can help you with what you need."

In even larger institutions, there are resource experts, including social workers, discharge planners, and financial advisors. In hospitals, nurses often do psychosocial assessments as part of the discharge process. In other settings, your patients may need to go to another part of the institution to interact with these folks. It helps if you know the names of the people doing the work. You can then tell the patients that John Doe or Julie Smith will take care of them; they know the system better than you do. Patients will feel cared for and are more likely to transfer some of their positive feelings about you to the other provider.

When you are doing the assessment and you think that there is an available resource, ask the patients if they would be interested in the referral, "Did you know that there's an agency that deals with your disease? They have support groups, counseling, and transportation. Do you want to know more about them?" If the patients

endorse the need for and interest in the resource, you are on your way to a successful referral.

Connecting With Patients to Promote Use of Resources and Supports

Patients are more likely to do what you suggest to them if they like you, feel understood by you, and think that you care about them. Listen to their answers to your questions, address their concerns, and bring your whole attention to the interaction. Find a way to orient yourself in their direction. If you can make a human-to-human connection, even for a few minutes, you are likely to have that person's trust. If you see the patient more than once, read your notes before you meet again. People remember you. They want to be remembered by you. Asking a few questions, while looking at the patient, not the chart, will build connection and treatment adherence.

Make sure you listen to what they need. Don't assume a homeless person is helpless. Don't assume a middle-class person can navigate a particular social service maze without help. Don't assume that the patients share your assessment of their needs. Wrong assumptions on the part of the caregiver break intersubjectivity, the feeling that the patient and the health care worker are on the same page.

If you are the resource person to whom the patient has been referred, mention the referring doctor or therapist: "Dr. Jones told me that you need some support. He said that you need some money/food/etc. in your life. Let's see how we can get that for you. This is what he said you needed? Do I have that right? What else do you need to talk about? What else do you need?"

Making a Referral

The more your client likes and trusts you, the more likely that he will use your referral. If he understands and endorses the need for outside help, he's even more likely to use it. If he has successfully used resources in the past, feels entitled to them and has the ability to contact the resource, there's a high likelihood that he will accept the referral. Do your homework beforehand. Know the real needs and capabilities of your client.

In the easy cases, refer to the previous discussion and the patient's endorsement of the need. If you personally know the agency or the person to whom you are referring, say something good about them. "You said that you want some emotional support through this ordeal. I'm giving you the names of three good therapists who deal with your issues. They're great!" Then ask for them to make a specific time in which they'll use the referral: (When people commit to a particular timeline they are more likely to do a new behavior). "When will you be able to call them? . . ." This afternoon? Great!" If your patients are a bit hesitant, shy, or feeling hopeless, you might ask them to contact you to tell you when they have contacted the resource: "After you've called the therapist, leave me a message about how it went." It's harder for people to skip contacting the resource if they know that you're waiting for their call.

When your patients don't accept the referral, find out what's going on. Is it beyond their financial, energetic, cognitive, or emotional capabilities? Is it the wrong referral? Is it shaming or embarrassing? Are they in denial of the need? Are they in a power struggle with you, as authority figure? Do they feel too helpless or hopeless to try anything new or extra? A good question is "What stands in the way of trying this approach?" Sometimes the answer is very specific: "I don't have child care for my kids, so I can't go to a Thursday night group." "I'm a private person, I can't talk in front of a group of people." "I tried that before and it didn't work." "The Smiths do not take charity." "Don't tell me what to do!"

What do you do now? Sometimes, simple problem solving suffices. "This is a wonderful group, I think you'd fit in really well. Do you know anyone who could baby-sit for you on Thursdays? Could they make a weekly commitment to do that? Great! We'll sign you up." "It sounds like transportation is a problem. Do you know that AA has volunteers who will pick you up and take you to meetings?" "You're going to need all your friends and family to get through this. Who is the most organized friend that you have, who could set up the care committee for you?" "You're anxious calling people you don't know on the phone? Let me/my receptionist/my nurse place the call for you. I'll get it going and then put you on the line." "You're too anxious to go to a group? Would an online support group work for you?"

Sometimes it's necessary to listen to a litany of why people can't use a resource. Often, people have been traumatized by their interaction with a social service agency and are averse to another attempt to work with it. Listen to their story. Think about what you might do to intervene. Your offer to call or have a staff member intervene can make a world of difference to an overwhelmed or traumatized patient.

When people are in denial of the need, use MI (Chapter 12) to assist them to explore where they are to develop discrepancy. Unless you are in charge of an incarcerated patient, you can't force him or her to comply. A few helpful questions include, "It sounds like part of you thinks you need this help and part of you isn't ready. What percent thinks you ought to use this resource? What are the reasons? What percent wants to avoid it? What's going on with the avoidant part?" Don't give them a bunch of reasons and information unless they say they want it. Ask: "Would you like some information that might help in this decision?" You can use your authority as an "expert" to point out the real consequences of adherence or nonadherence. "People with your type of liver problems expect to live for years if they stop drinking, and months if they don't. Most people can't stop drinking on their own. Your life is at stake. That's why I'd like to send you to the treatment program." "I'm really afraid for you. I've known several women in abusive relationships similar to yours who have been killed. I know you love him and are very attached to him. Do you have a bottom line? What would be the final straw that would get you to a safe place?"

I'm quite fond of what I call creative enabling. It goes like this. "It sounds like you're not ready for this referral. Let's see how you get along without the treatment program/support group/chore service. You do the research and report to me next time about it." Three things can happen with creative enabling. The patient may realize that he or she needs the help and comply before or after the next visit with you. The patient may decide that he or she really doesn't need the service or dive deeper into denial. The patient may find his or her own solution to the problem and will proudly (and sometimes defiantly) report that "I've been sober for three weeks," "I got my three best friends together and we're meeting weekly until this deal is over," or "I've hired my neighbor girl to clean the house and run errands for me."

Some people obviously (to you) need the service and refuse to try it. In these cases you most often must learn to acknowledge your limitations, soothe your own frustration, and go back to the MI steps. Sometimes you do have leverage. Many mental health agencies and private therapists refuse services to people who refuse alcohol or drug treatment. Other agencies require participation in other outside programs. This "take it or leave it" approach is most helpful in the context of a caring rather than punitive stance: "I really want to continue our treatment, but in my experience it just won't work if you don't have these other supports. Is there any way I can talk you into going to those meetings so that we can keep working together?"

Note the issue and agreed-upon solution or currently deadlocked process in the chart and follow up at the next appointment, as you would with any other symptom. "How is your research project going?" Whether people are complying or not, they will usually answer with a smile.

Resources

Family comes first, as it is patients' most used resource. Next come friends and social networks, support and self-help groups, then professional, agency, and governmental supports. Urban areas will have many official services based in multiple locations and organizations. Suburban areas will have fewer, more spread out services. Rural areas and small towns will have the fewest agencies and governmental supports, possibly one multiservice center in the county seat. However, people in small towns and rural areas may have tight-knit circles of social support. People who are well integrated into the social life of a small town expect to help and be helped in times of need.

Family Support

Most patients rely on their families and closest relationships for concrete and emotional support. Parents, spouses, and grown or almost grown children naturally provide transportation, personal care, and other services. When family members are nonexistent, estranged, or far away, practitioners must find ways to help the client replace the family functions with other services. When families are available, you need to assess their capabilities to provide care. You may need to engage one or more family members in assessment and planning stages of treatment.

Here are some questions to consider: Is the family member up to the task? Sometimes a frail, elderly person becomes the caregiver for the formerly "competent" spouse. Can she lift him onto the bed? Deal with his dementia? Have the energy to provide round-the-clock care?

Is the caregiver emotionally stable enough to cope with the stresses of care giving? Is there an underlying mental illness? Is the person old enough to be of true help? Is the caregiver dismissive of other people's needs, projecting her own denial of the situation on a suffering family member? Is he "on board" with the treatment plan? Is she already working the "triple shift" of a job, children, and an elderly parent? Will this added responsibility be one burden too many?

Are the patients able to ask for what they need? Will they alert the family when necessary or not want to "bother" them? Are they too cognitively impaired or too stoic to accurately report the pain level or level of impairment?

What kind of support is available for the primary caregiver? Are there other family members or friends who can take a shift, run an errand, cook a meal, bring take-out, or offer an opportunity to debrief? If the caregiver needs extra help, what would fit the bill? Home health care? A care committee? An adult child or a parent moving in for the duration of the illness?

In many areas there are support groups for caretakers of sick kids, people with Alzheimer's disease, AIDS, and other illnesses. There may be adult day centers where ambulatory elderly people can spend 4 to 8 hours doing activities, having a meal, and being medically monitored, while the caregiver works, tends to other obligations, or simply rests. In some places there are similar services for people with AIDS or other chronic conditions.

When you assess these needs, be aware of the nuances of the patient's system. Some families pull together beautifully for the good of the patient. Some family members, caught in old dynamics, are too busy "winning the fight" to cooperate with any others. Some "families" contain no blood relatives. This can be true for some gay people, who may be estranged from their families. The caregivers may be a tight- or loose-knit web of friends, coworkers, neighbors, and/or church members. Psychotherapists and addiction specialists often refer to patient's natural support groups. They ask, "Which friends are best to call when you feel lonely or when you feel like celebrating if you get the promotion or need to be consoled if you don't?" "Who would be the best person to stay with until the suicidal urges pass?"

Care Committees

When sick, disabled, or elderly people have established social communities, formal and informal "care committees" may be created to help care for them. Care committees promote treatment adherence by taking the burden of care off one or two people and spreading the responsibility through the patient's community. A well-organized care committee can take responsibility for many aspects of the patient's well-being, including food, transportation, errand running, medication monitoring, house cleaning, and socializing. They may be convened by a family member, friend, physician, social worker, church committee, or the patient himself or herself. They may involve family members, friends, home health care professionals, and/or church members. They may "just happen" as people respond to the patient's perceived needs. For an organized group, the convener calls or e-mails a list of possible volunteers and asks them to a meeting. The group lists the concrete and less tangible needs of the patient. Does the person need meals, pharmacy runs, nonmedical personal care, house cleaning, dog walking, outings, shopping trips, transportation to the doctor, the church, or the support group, 24-hour care, reminders to take medication, or company? Who can take on which tasks? Is this a long-term or a short-term commitment? In case of chronic or wasting disease, what will happen when the patient needs a higher level of care? How will the committee members communicate? How will they communicate with health care professionals? Who, if the patient is unable, is in charge? How does the group deal with schedule changes? (E-mail has made this part much easier!) Often, a logbook, read by both committee members and home health care workers is kept at the patient's house. It can contain medication changes; notes about the patient's moods, food preferences, and physical state, or anecdotes about any events on the volunteers' shifts.

During the early years of the AIDS epidemic, I convened many care committees for friends and then for clients. The committee members were exceptionally dedicated and responsible. Experience gave us some important lessons. It was important that members set reasonable goals for themselves. It was useful if people had regular shifts and regular jobs such as "five to eight p.m. on Tuesday evenings including making dinner and washing the dishes." The closest friends were not always the best people for a particular job. Near strangers were sometimes more functional. "Little jobs" like pharmacy pickups at odd times, could be essential. When each member of the committee had the complete list of volunteers and their availability at hand, she could call others to swap shifts, make emergency runs, or update the crew with new information. "Hanging out with the patient" is a legitimate function of a care committee. Sometimes the social needs of the patient are overlooked when concrete needs are overemphasized.

Support Groups

Support or self-help groups serve many functions and cover almost every condition. They may serve to "plug in" new members to specific services and information and provide a place for identification and emotional support. They may be very structured, goal-oriented, and time-limited, and closed to new members. They may be open-ended or perpetual. Some are educational; some are emotional. Many serve both functions. Support groups may be unaffiliated or supported by an agency, church, or hospital. They may serve new moms, crime victims, family and friends of suicide victims, sexual minorities, or people who like to make scrapbooks. They offer affiliation, identification, and a place to belong.

AA is the most famous and prevalent of self-help groups. There is an AA group (or many) in nearly every city in the world and in nearly every American town. The groups are highly structured, peer led, and free to all addicts. Other 12-step groups include Al-Anon (for family and friends of alcoholics), Sex and Love Anonymous (sex addicts), Adult Children of Alcoholics, Alateen, Narcotics Anonymous, Nar-Anon (their family and friends), and more. When referring someone to a 12-step group, explain that not all groups are alike. In AA, they might want to shop for a home group that fits, whether they are female, gay, a businessperson, or a biker. Big cities might have 20 meetings each day of the week.

Computer-savvy shut-ins and people in rural or underserved areas have the new option of online support groups that offer support and information in chat rooms and forums. Patients with social anxiety may be more comfortable with online contact, and thus more likely to receive support.

Mental Health and Addiction Services

Mental health and addiction services help patients organize their brains and, thus, their lives. New medications help bipolar, depressed, anxious, and psychotic patients bring their moods and thoughts into manageable reality. Since the advent of EMDR, a trauma therapy, patients no longer need to suffer the debilitating flashbacks, nightmares, and cognitive distortions of posttraumatic stress disorder (PTSD). New research on attachment has increased the efficacy and efficiency of psychotherapy for personality disorders. Psychotherapists may be the first to notice changes in peoples' physical well-being and the ones who strongly suggest that a denying or avoidant patient contact a physician. They may work with patients on many self-care issues, including following medication regimes, eating, exercise, and sleeping habits, and cessation of self-destructive behaviors. Low-cost psychotherapy is most often available at community mental health centers, church-based clinics, and private, nonprofit agencies.

If people have the money, or the insurance, there are inpatient and outpatient treatment programs for nearly every addiction: alcoholism, narcotics, sex, pornography, and compulsive eating. There are low-cost treatment centers for alcohol and drug addiction, often with long waiting lists.

Advocacy Groups

Advocacy organizations organize themselves to serve a particular population. They may be governmental, private nonprofit, or all volunteer.

They may be well funded or struggling. For instance, every state is mandated to have a senior information and assistance office. Highly populated areas may have one office per county. Some offices may serve several sparsely populated counties. (Search for "eldercare locator" on the Web to find one in your area.) There's an organization for nearly every serious disease and social problem. Before you make a referral, know what services are available from an organization.

Concrete Resources

Concrete resources include food, housing, transportation, money, clothing and medication. Food and housing are tied together. If a patient doesn't have a kitchen, a food bank may be of little assistance and food stamps or other governmental relief may not be available. Health care providers need to ask patients about their solutions to food and housing dilemmas: "I want to prescribe you some antibiotics that you have to take with food. I know that you don't have a place to live. What are you doing about food? Are you getting three meals a day? [If not] Is there any way you can get three meals each day? These pills don't work/will give you a stomach ache if you're not eating." If the client doesn't know how or is unable to get regular food, either you or someone in your system should assist him or her. The client will feel seen and responded to, an important component of developing adherence. And the concrete need will be taken care of, to the best of your facility's ability. Food resources include food banks where people may go to pick up bags of food, church- or community-sponsored meals programs, food stamps, and food banks.

In urban areas, a savvy, mobile person could find several hot, reasonably nutritious meals once or twice a day at churches, missions, and volunteer kitchens. A person who had a place to cook could make the rounds of the food banks and find enough food to get by. Most of the meals would be high on carbohydrates and fats, low on fruit, vegetables, and protein. The fare at

food banks and meal programs depends on donations, which may vary seasonally. Urban areas often have a few variations on the "Meals on Wheels" programs that deliver a week's worth of prepared food for different client populations. In Seattle, the Senior Services agency and the Lifelong AIDS Alliance are the primary purveyors of meals to shut-ins.

In less populated areas, food stamps may be the most used food resource. If a church or a volunteer agency serves hot meals, it may be on a weekly rather than a daily basis. In rural areas, where they may be known, patients may avoid food resources out of embarrassment. In the city, it's easy to be anonymous.

Some people don't know how to eat inexpensively or healthily. They may not know that their food stamps will stretch to the end of the month if they cook beans and rice and oatmeal instead of prepared foods and boxes of cereal. They may not be organized or skilled enough in cooking and meal planning to use the resources available to them. These people need education along with their food assistance.

As stated before, it's hard to comply with any treatment regimen when you have no fixed place to stay. In urban areas, there are short- and long-term shelters and housing vouchers that are most often used in cheap hotels. The shelters vary from first-come, first-served mats on the floor, sometimes crowded and dangerous, to longer-term "transitional housing," which may include a modest private, lockable room, cooking facilities, or communal meals and on-site counseling. Some shelters cater to specific populations: women or men, families, teenagers, people with AIDS, people with mental illness, or alcoholic people. Depending on the available housing resources, some homeless people find it safer and more peaceful to sleep in their cars or camp in secluded places than to stay in a crowded dormitory-style shelter. The flophouses of yesteryear are scarce but still available in some areas. Some YMCAs and YWCAs function as low cost, homeless shelters. As the working poor get priced out of urban housing, more of them—sane, sober, competent people—find themselves living in homeless encampments, their cars, or a friend's backyard.

Homeless people need more than a bed. In urban areas, there is often a service center that provides showers, laundry facilities, and inexpensive mailboxes, or voice mail services (a necessity for job seekers). These services may be scattered around town or under one roof. In small towns or rural areas, these services may be scarce or less formal. Churches, fraternal organizations, or community volunteers may provide temporary housing, a handout, and/or food to those in need. Ungar, Manuel, Mealey, Thomas, and Campbell (2004) discuss community guides, nonprofessionals who mentor "excluded individuals back into the associational life of the community." These individuals can become regular referral sources for many services. They are often connected to extensive informal networks of potential donors, drivers, and other volunteers. Churches, whether the "big box" nondenominational churches with dozens of services and employees, or small rural community churches with one minister, may take on many of the concrete and nontangible services needed by an individual, whether the person is a member of the congregation, a believer, or completely unaffiliated.

Money is the root of all concrete resources. It's also the hardest one to get. Homeless shelters, transitional housing, food or clothing distributors, or bus vouchers are often immediately available. It can be difficult to connect to a financial source that meets or supplements those needs. The state/county department of social and health services (DSHS) is a good place to start. Despite shrinking budgets, they are mandated to provide minimal assistance to indigent people. They may provide food stamps, medical coupons, housing vouchers, bus passes, and financial assistance. Depending on the federal, state, and county funding levels, a referral to DSHS may be only the beginning of meeting a patient's concrete needs. If your patient is eligible for Social Security, Disability, state General Assistance to the Unemployable, or other welfare payments, find out why they're not hooked up with these financial resources. Sometimes one long, frustrating phone call from you can start the financial ball rolling for a disorganized, unassertive, or naive client.

Many DSHS forms are difficult to fill out, even for literate, highly functional people. Many DSHS offices are understaffed and appear to have a mandate to turn away as many applicants as possible. If this is true in your area, warn your patients that the process is difficult, that it's not about them, and that it is always necessary to keep trying. The more they know what to expect from the DSHS or other systems, the less they will take the built-in shaming process personally, or feel defeated by how difficult it is. Legitimate Disability claims are often rejected. Many people need to hire a lawyer to get their payments. Support them to get what they already paid for.

Work

Able-bodied patients may be able to find day work through private or nonprofit day labor offices. People may find under-the-table work, often construction or gardening work, at certain street corners in urban areas. For less able-bodied patients, who want to earn their way, there are 22 newspapers for the poor and homeless in U.S. cities. Vendors must agree to be sober and reasonably kempt. They make 50 to 75 cents profit on each newspaper they sell. Most of the newspapers provide an array of referral and support services for their vendors, as well as a social outlet. To see if there is a homeless newspaper in your city, check out www.nasna.org/.

Education

Many advocacy organizations offer orientation classes, pamphlets, and online information about their disease or issue.

Transportation

Transportation opportunities vary widely. In Manhattan or San Francisco, bus and subway tokens can get reasonably able-bodied patients to their appointments and back home again. Some cities or suburbs are nearly impossible to navigate without a car, an agency transportation service, or a scarce and expensive taxi ride. In rural areas, there may be no formal transportation services into town or between towns. Transportation assistance includes free or discounted bus passes or taxi vouchers (often available to anyone on welfare or disability); van transportation through the municipal Senior Services, or a disease-specific agency; and volunteer drivers, often connected to Senior Services organizations or church-based programs.

Physical Care

Home Health Care Services may cover nursing, physical and occupational therapies, and personal care assistance. Availability also varies widely between urban and rural settings. Urban areas have chore services for qualified disabled and elderly patients. Some organizations, such as Seattle's Lifelong AIDS Alliance or Senior Services, deliver meals, supervise volunteer or paid house cleaners, and provide errands or commodities-on-wheels services. In some cities there are home-sharing services that match up younger or more able-bodied boarders with elderly or disabled home owners, who may exchange services for room and board.

Examples

In the late 1980s, a 35-year-old man was diagnosed with AIDS. As a patient at a large HMO, he received generally good medical care. While he was still able to work and leave the house, he attended professionally facilitated AIDS support group meetings. Through those meetings he learned about the Seattle Treatment Exchange Program (STEP), a clearinghouse of AIDS treatment information, and began receiving their newsletter and attending briefing meetings. As he became quite ill and unable to work, the Northwest AIDS Foundation assisted him in signing up for Disability payments, a volunteer chore service, and a meals program. His lover asked a friend to organize a care committee. The patient made a list of 15 friends and coworkers, who were invited to a meeting. At the meeting, which the patient attended, his needs were discussed and the participants volunteered for "shifts" and tasks, including meal preparation, errand running, transportation to appointments, cat box cleaning, hanging out, and phone support of other volunteers. When the HMO refused to provide an expensive sight-saving medication (strongly recommended by the STEP newsletter) on the grounds that it was experimental, a representative of the care committee called the HMO doctor to offer support for releasing the medication. "We'll have media, the 15 people from the care committee and 25 people from ACT-UP (an advocacy group) in your lobby by noon tomorrow." The doctor thanked the committee for its "help." Within 2 hours, the medication was ordered. Within 2 days, it was administered. The patient kept his sight. As the illness progressed, the lover became the liaison with the HMO and Hospice. During his last weeks, his mother came from the other coast. The patient died at home attended by his mother, his lover, and a friend. The care committee was instrumental in supporting and planning the funeral.

While a 22-year-old man was in psychotherapy for PTSD, he lost his job and quickly became homeless. Quite proud, he refused free psychotherapy or handouts from his friends and family. A deal was made: for every 4 hours of volunteer service, he would receive an hour of therapy. He volunteered at a community food bank. He continued therapy and bartered food for sleeping privileges on the floors of friends. He was able to feel like a contributor and was quite proud of his resourcefulness. He eventually got a job with benefits, a girlfriend with a nice apartment, a car, and freedom from the symptoms of PTSD. He acknowledged that he would have distanced himself from all his friends if he hadn't been able to find a way to contribute to their households. The food bank work allowed him to eat, stay socially connected, continue in therapy, and participate in the community.

A 40-year-old married woman was hospitalized for depression, PTSD, and a serious suicide attempt. She was referred to psychotherapy and psychiatric care. Every week, she met with three members of her church for support and a check-in. As her symptoms improved, they met every other week, then monthly, then as needed. Group members were available for phone calls. When the patient had suicidal thoughts or thoughts of self-harm, she learned to call her group members and her therapist. She lived to move through her depression, her PTSD, and her suicidal impulses.

Conclusion

Medical intervention occurs in the context of the patient's broader circumstances. Patients need good internal and external resources to adhere to treatment regimens. Finding a good match between a patient's needs and external resources can be an important part of treatment. Practitioners who make a thorough assessment in the context of a connected relationship, who know the patient's and the community's resources and with whom the patient feels a connection are best able to make successful referrals that promote treatment adherence.

References

Ciechanowski, P. (1999). *The patient-provider relationship and adherence to treatment in patients with diabetes.* Unpublished master's thesis, University of Washington.

Goldstein, M. G., DePue, J., Kazura, A., & Niaura, R. (1998). Models for provider-patient interaction: Applications to health behavior change. In S. A. Shumaker, E. G. Schron, J. K. Ockene, & W. L. McBee (Eds.), *The handbook of health behavior change* (2nd ed., pp. 85–113). New York: Springer.

Horne, R. (1999). Patients' beliefs about treatment: The hidden determinant of treatment outcome. *Journal of Psychosomatic Research, 47*(6), 491–495.

Lin, H. B., & Katon, W. (1998). Beyond the diagnosis of depression. *General Hospital Psychiatry, 20,* 207–208.

Meichenbaum, D., & Turk, D. (1987). *Facilitating treatment adherence: A practitioner's guidebook.* New York: Plenum Press.

Miller, W. R., & Rolnick, S. (1991). *Motivational interviewing: Preparing people to change addictive behavior.* New York: Guilford Press.

Prochaska, J. O., & DiClemente, C. C. (1986). Toward a comprehensive model of change. In W. R. Miller & N. Heather (Eds.), *Treating addictive behavior: Processes of change* (pp. 3–27). New York: Plenum Press.

Ribisl, K. M., & Humphreys, K. (1998). Collaboration between professionals and mediating structures in the community: Toward a "third way" in health promotion. In S. A. Shumaker, E. G. Schron, J. K. Ockene, & W. L. McBee (Eds.), *The handbook of health behavior change* (2nd ed., pp. 535–554). New York: Springer.

Shapiro, F. (2001). *Eye movement desensitization and reprocessing: Basic principles, protocols and procedures* (Rev. ed.). New York: Guilford.

Shapiro, R. (2005). *EMDR solutions, pathways to healing.* New York: W.W. Norton.

Ungar, M., Manuel, S., Mealey, S, Thomas, G., & Campbell, C. (2004). A study of community guides, lessons for professionals practicing with and in communities. *Social Work, 49,* 550–561.

9

Problem Solving to Promote Treatment Adherence

Arthur M. Nezu

Christine Maguth Nezu

Michael G. Perri

Problem solving is the overt, self-directed process by which a person attempts to identify adaptive solutions for stressful or difficult problems in real life (Nezu, 2004). Problem-solving therapy (PST), a cognitive-behavioral intervention, helps individuals cope more effectively with such problems by teaching them to apply various skills. Effective coping can involve altering the nature of the problem (e.g., overcoming obstacles to a goal), changing one's reactions to it (e.g., acceptance that a goal cannot be reached), or both. Overarching goals of PST include (a) decreasing the negative impact (e.g., emotional distress) related to the experience of both major (e.g., undergoing a divorce) and minor (e.g., losing one's wallet at the train station) life events and problems; (b) increasing one's ability to cope more effectively with such

problems; and (c) minimizing the likelihood of similar problems occurring in the future (Nezu, Nezu, & Lombardo, 2003).

Problems can be single events (e.g., obtaining a loan from a bank), a series of related problems (e.g., continuous arguments with a spouse), or chronic situations (e.g., major chronic illness, such as cancer). They can originate from the environment (e.g., interpersonal difficulties) or from within the person (e.g., conflicting goals). Situations become problems when an effective response is required for the person to cope adaptively, but where such a response is not immediately available or identifiable due to the presence of various obstacles. Such obstacles can include ambiguity, unpredictability, conflicting demands, deficient skills, or lack of resources.

Rationale for Using Problem Solving to Increase Treatment Adherence

In reviewing the different types of problems that can exist, the potential relevance of PST as a means to enhance adherence to either a medical or a psychosocial treatment regimen is readily apparent. Conceptually, from a PST framework, problems in adhering to a treatment protocol can be classified into two types of difficulties: (a) difficulties in motivation (i.e., confusion or conflicting goals regarding whether or not one should enter into treatment or continue with treatment) and (b) difficulties in overcoming various barriers to successful adherence (i.e., obstacles that exist regarding limited resources, such as time, money, abilities, cognitive understanding, and so forth, that make successful adherence to treatment difficult). Obviously, one type of problem can easily engender or worsen problems of the other kind. For example, low motivation to continue to participate in a protocol that involves using steroidal medication as part of one's medical treatment for asthma can lead to the lack of searching for resources (e.g., advice for the health care team; searching the web for information) that can make dealing with negative iatrogenic effects easier. On the other hand, not having the time to engage in a treatment that requires more than a momentary gesture (e.g., taking a pill) can easily lower one's motivation to try to identify time during a busy schedule to adhere to a time-consuming activity.

PST, because it targets both motivational and pragmatic problematic issues, is ideally suited to help a patient overcome either or both sets of adherence problems. More specifically, PST, as a cognitive-behavior strategy, aims to help people adopt a more optimistic orientation toward the achievement of goals (which includes the identified goal for which an initial treatment is prescribed, such as smoking reduction, weight loss, pain management, anxiety reduction), as well as provide a systematic means by which they can devise effective solution plans geared to overcome existing barriers to achieve such goals. More recently, problem solving has been identified as a key ingredient in effective patient self-management of chronic diseases, such as asthma, diabetes, and arthritis (Bodenheimer, Lorig, Holman, & Grumbach, 2002).

Evidence for the General Efficacy of PST

With regard to the conceptual underpinnings of PST, a large number of studies have found problem-solving effectiveness and psychological distress and dysfunction to be significantly related (Nezu, 2004). Such converging findings have emerged from investigations using varying research designs and differing measures of problem solving. For example, some studies have looked at simple correlations between measures of distress and problem solving, whereas others have looked at differences in problem solving between reliably diagnosed patient groups (e.g., major depressive disorder; posttraumatic stress disorder, or PTSD). Furthermore, several studies have found problem solving to serve as a significant moderator of the relationship between stress and distress, such as depression and anxiety (i.e., at similar levels of high stress, effective problem solvers are less depressed and anxious than ineffective problem solvers) (Nezu, Wilkins, & Nezu, 2004).

As a function of this significant association between problem-solving effectiveness and emotional distress, a large number of controlled outcome studies have been conducted to evaluate the efficacy of PST. In general, this approach has been found to be an effective cognitive-behavioral intervention for a variety of psychological disorders (D'Zurilla & Nezu, in press; Nezu, D'Zurilla, Zwick, & Nezu, 2004). For example, a series of studies by Nezu and his colleagues have found PST to be especially effective in treating major depressive disorder (e.g., Nezu, Nezu, & Perri, 1989) and in improving the quality of life of adult cancer patients (Nezu, Nezu, Felgoise, McClure, & Houts, 2003).

Efficacy of PST to Promote Adherence

Research has also been conducted to specifically evaluate the efficacy of PST as a means to enhance treatment adherence. Although several investigators have included PST as part of a larger intervention package to foster adherence to treatment (e.g., Safren et al., 2001), more recently, researchers have conducted studies where PST was implemented in isolation. As such, these types of investigations provide for a more direct assessment of the efficacy of PST as a means of increasing adherence.

Perri et al. (2001), for example, based on a problem-solving model of obesity management (Perri, Nezu, & Viegener, 1992), conducted a study that compared two extended therapy programs for the long-term management of obesity with standard behavioral treatment (BT). More specifically, participants included 80 obese women who initially completed 20 weekly group sessions of BT. They were then randomly assigned to one of the three experimental conditions: (a) no further contact (BT-only); (b) a year-long, biweekly program of training in relapse prevention (RP); and (c) a year-long, biweekly program of PST. PST was conceptualized as helping the obese person negotiate the myriad of problems that often impede successful weight management (e.g., eating in reaction to stress, having difficulty finding time to exercise due to family obligations). Results indicated that participants in the PST condition had significantly greater long-term weight reductions than BT participants. In addition, a significantly larger percentage of PST individuals achieved clinically significant losses

of 10% or more in body weight than did BT participants. Moreover, further analyses indicated that the PST group demonstrated significantly better adherence to behavioral weight management strategies than did the BT group and that the effect of treatment condition on weight loss was significantly mediated by adherence to the initially taught behavioral strategies.

Another study using PST to enhance adherence focused on adolescent suicide. Specifically, Spirito, Boergers, Donaldson, Bishop, and Lewander (2002) conducted an investigation to determine whether PST would increase adherence to outpatient treatment for adolescents after a suicide attempt. Sixty-three participants were randomly assigned to a standard disposition planning protocol or a problem-solving-based compliance enhancement program. At a 3-month follow-up evaluation, after controlling for barriers to receiving treatment in the community (e.g., insurance coverage difficulties), adolescents in the PST condition were found to attend significantly more treatment sessions than the standard disposition-planning group (mean of 8.4 vs. 5.8 sessions, respectively). These results further support the efficacy of PST to foster treatment adherence.

Finally, Kazdin and Whitley (2003) conducted an investigation that focused on means to enhance therapeutic change regarding children referred to an outpatient clinic for aggressive and antisocial behavior. They conceptualized parental stress as a factor that can moderate treatment outcome both directly and indirectly, particularly with regard to the extent to which parents experience barriers in coming to treatment and actual treatment attendance. A sample of 127 children, aged 6 to 14 years, and their families received problem-solving skills training and the parents received parent training. Families were randomly assigned to receive or not receive a further problem solving based intervention (PPS) that focused specifically on parental stress over the course of treatment. Although the PPS intervention appeared to have no significant impact on treatment attendance, the PPS protocol was found to enhance therapeutic change for children and parents and did reduce the barriers that parents experienced during treatment, supporting the notion that PST helps enhance adherence.

Overall, the above body of research would seem to suggest that PST is an effective means to enhance adherence to other treatment protocols.

Theoretical Underpinnings of PST

Problem-solving outcomes are largely determined by two general, but partially independent, dimensions: (a) problem orientation and (b) problem-solving style (D'Zurilla & Nezu, in press; D'Zurilla, Nezu, & Maydeu-Olivares, 2004). *Problem orientation* is the set of relatively stable cognitive-affective schemas that represent a person's generalized beliefs, attitudes, and emotional reactions about problems in living and one's ability to successfully cope with such problems. This latter component involves self-perceptions of control over one's environment and invokes two aspects that are based on Bandura's (1997) concepts of self-efficacy and outcome expectancies. In social problem-solving theory, these two components are termed (a) *generalized problem-solving self-efficacy* or the general belief that one is capable of solving problems and implementing solutions effectively and (b) *generalized positive problem-solving outcome expectancy* or the general belief that problems in living are "solvable." In numerous studies, positive self-efficacy and outcome expectancies have been found to facilitate adaptive coping in stressful situations and to reduce anxiety and emotional distress, whereas negative self-efficacy and outcome expectancies, on the other hand, tend to increase anxiety, avoidance behavior, and other maladaptive responses in stressful problematic situations (Bandura, 1997).

As such, one's problem orientation can be either positive or negative. A *positive orientation* is one that involves a tendency to (a) appraise problems as challenges, (b) be optimistic in believing that problems are solvable, (c) believe in one's own ability to solve problems, and (d) believe that successful problem solving involves time and effort. Conversely, a *negative problem orientation* is one that involves the tendency to (a) view problems as threats, (b) expect problems to be unsolvable, (c) doubt one's own ability to solve problems successfully, and (d) become frustrated and upset when faced with problems. A positive orientation can lead to positive affect and approach motivation, which in turn can facilitate later problem-solving efforts. Conversely, a negative orientation can engender negative affect and avoidance motivation, which can later serve to inhibit or disrupt subsequent problem-solving attempts (D'Zurilla & Nezu, 2001).

Problem-solving style refers to those core cognitive-behavioral activities that people engage in when attempting to solve problems in living. There are three differing styles that our model describes—one of which is adaptive, whereas the remaining two reflect maladaptive ways of coping. *Rational problem solving* is the constructive problem-solving style that involves the systematic and planned application of certain skills, each of which makes a distinct contribution toward the discovery of an adaptive solution or coping response in a problem-solving situation. This model includes four specific rational problem-solving skills: (a) problem definition and formulation, (b) generation of alternatives, (c) decision making, and (d) solution implementation and verification.

The goal of *problem definition and formulation* is to delineate the reasons why a given situation is a problem (e.g., the presence of obstacles), as well as to specify a set of realistic goals and objectives to help guide further problem-solving efforts. The purpose of the *generation-of-alternatives* task is to create, using various brainstorming principles, a pool of possible solutions to increase the likelihood that the most effective ideas will be ultimately identified. The goal of *decision making* is to conduct a cost-benefit analysis of each alternative by identifying and then weighing their potential positive and negative consequences if carried out, and then, based on this evaluation, to develop an overall solution plan. Finally, the purpose of *solution implementation and verification* is to carry out the solution plan, monitor and evaluate its effectiveness, and troubleshoot if the outcome is unsatisfactory. In other words, if the solution is not effective, the individual needs to re-cycle through the various problem-solving tasks in order to determine where renewed efforts should be directed in order to solve the problem successfully. For example, insufficient alternatives may have been generated or the problem solver did not carry out the solution optimally. Similar to self-control theory, this model suggests that if the problem *is* solved, then the individual should engage in self-reinforcement.

Our model further specifies two additional problem-solving styles, both of which are dysfunctional or maladaptive in nature (D'Zurilla & Nezu, in press). An *impulsive/careless style* involves the generalized response pattern characterized by impulsive, hurried, and careless attempts at problem resolution. Although the individual characterized by this style actively attempts to apply various strategies to address problems, such attempts are narrow, hurried, and incomplete. For example, a person with this style is likely to consider only a few solution alternatives, often impulsively implementing the first idea that comes to mind. In addition, the narrow range of options and their consequences are scanned quickly, carelessly, and unsystematically.

Avoidance style is a second maladaptive problem-solving pattern, which is characterized by procrastination, passivity, and overdependence on others to provide solutions. This type of problem solver generally avoids problems rather than confronting them "head-on," puts off addressing problems for as long as possible, waits for problems to resolve themselves, and attempts to shift the responsibility for solving one's problems to other people. In general, both styles can lead to ineffective or unsuccessful problem resolution. In fact, they are likely to worsen existing problems or even create new ones.

Given the above model, then, the specific therapy objectives of PST are to (a) enhance one's positive orientation, (b) decrease one's negative orientation, (c) improve one's rational problem-solving skills, (d) decrease one's impulsive/careless style, and (e) decrease one's avoidance style. According to our model of PST, this is accomplished through a series of didactic explanations, skills training activities, role-play exercises, and homework assignments. In addition to fostering actual skill acquisition, PST attempts to foster generalized application of such skills across a multitude of intrapersonal and interpersonal problems (see D'Zurilla & Nezu, in press; Nezu et al., 1989, 1998, for examples of detailed PST manuals for professionals and Nezu, Nezu, & D'Zurilla, in press, for a patient-oriented self-help guidebook).

Who Can Benefit From PST?

In the literature, PST has been effectively applied as the sole intervention to a wide range of psychological problems including depression, suicidal ideation and behaviors, schizophrenia, emotional problems of primary care patients, social phobia, behavioral problems of adults with mental retardation, substance abuse, and behavioral disorders of children (Nezu et al., 2004). It has been used to improve the quality of life of patients with various medical problems, such as cancer, hypertension, head injuries, and arthritis. PST has also been combined with other cognitive-behavioral strategies for the treatment of borderline personality disorder, marital and family problems, HIV/AIDS risk behaviors (e.g., unsafe sex), and parent-adolescent conflict. PST has also been applied as a maintenance strategy to enhance the effects of other treatment approaches for weight loss. Researchers have also used PST to enhance the ability of individuals to serve as effective caregivers of persons with cancer, Alzheimer's disease, patients with dementia, adults with spinal cord injuries, and children with behavior problems (C. M. Nezu, Palmatier, & Nezu, 2004). PST has also been applied to enhance "normal" individual's coping and stress management skills, to decrease "vocational indecision," and to enhance social skills among shy young adolescents.

As a means to enhance treatment adherence, PST can be effective for a wide range of medical and psychiatric patient populations. Individuals experiencing medical or psychological problems often are confronted by a myriad of additional problems, some of which may impede successful adherence to their medical or psychosocial treatment, especially when such treatment involves self-care activities, such as taking medication, engaging in life-style behavioral changes, self-monitoring of treatment progress, or practicing various stress management strategies. As mentioned previously, such problems can be conceptualized as motivational (e.g., "I don't know if this medication is really helping me and it has such bad side effects!") or represents a specific barrier (e.g., "I don't know when I have the time to practice relaxation exercises when I have my job, my spouse, my children, and my friends that I have to deal with"). PST, by virtue of its specific focus (i.e., helping people to solve problems), is particularly relevant to helping people overcome both types of issues.

Contraindications

Because PST has been found to help individuals representing both a wide array of cognitive abilities (e.g., ranging from intellectually "normal" adults to persons with mild to moderate mental retardation) and psychological difficulties (e.g., ranging from "normal college students" to adults with schizophrenia), it would appear that few contraindications for this intervention exist at present (Nezu, 2004). Based on the authors' clinical experience, PST would not be recommended as the sole intervention for clinically significant anxiety disorders, such as simple phobias or obsessive-compulsive disorder.

Step-by-Step Guidelines

Assessment Issues

There are currently two major self-report inventories that measure global problem-solving abilities, each of which is a useful means to assess a patient's overall problem-solving strengths and weaknesses at a point when adherence problems are beginning to emerge.

The Social Problem-Solving Inventory— Revised (SPSI-R; D'Zurilla, Nezu, & Maydeu-Olivares, 2002) is a 52-item revision of the original D'Zurilla & Nezu (1990) 70-item, self-report SPSI that was directly linked to the model introduced by D'Zurilla and Goldfried (1971) and later expanded and refined by D'Zurilla and Nezu (1982, 1999). Based on a factor analysis of the SPSI, the SPSI-R currently contains five scales, including (a) *positive problem orientation* (PPO); (b) *negative problem orientation* (NPO); (c) *rational problem solving* (RPS); (d) *impulsivity/carelessness style* (ICS); and (e) *avoidance style* (AS). In addition, the RPS scale contains four subscales, each representing the four specific rational problem-solving tasks previously delineated (e.g., problem definition).

The Problem Solving Inventory (Heppner, 1988) is a self-report measure that assesses the construct of "problem-solving self-appraisal." In addition to a total score, this inventory provides for three scale scores: (a) *problem-solving confidence* (i.e., self-assurance while engaging in problem solving), (b) *approach-avoidance style* (i.e., the general tendency to approach or avoid problem-solving activities), and (c) *personal control* (i.e., the extent to which a person is in control of his emotions and behavior while solving problems).

Treatment Guidelines

Prior to training the specific PST components, the therapist should present an overall rationale describing the purpose, goals, and specific components of PST, emphasizing how it can be helpful for the unique circumstances of a given patient, especially in terms of helping the patient to adhere more successfully to an overall treatment protocol. Part of this rationale includes the notion that the experience of stressful events and difficult problems often leads to lowered motivation, emotional distress, and various behavioral problems. Moreover, PST is geared to teach people some new skills, as well as to help them to apply previously acquired problem-solving skills to new problems and stressful situations. Structurally, PST training can be broken into three major foci: (a) training in problem orientation, (b) training in the four specific rational problem-solving skills (i.e., problem definition and formulation, generation of alternatives, decision making, solution implementation, and verification), and (c) practice of these skills across a variety of problems.

In describing the treatment guidelines below, we offer suggested exercises that can facilitate skill acquisition regarding each of the various problem-solving abilities. We wish, however, to emphasize that it is the underlying principle associated with each skill area that is crucial to consider when conducting PST rather than viewing any of the techniques described as "equal to the therapy approach itself."

Training in Problem Orientation

Training in problem orientation is geared to foster (a) positive self-efficacy beliefs; (b) acceptance of the notion that it is "normal" to experience a wide range of problems, including those associated with difficulties regarding successful adherence; (c) the ability to identify problems accurately when they occur; and (d) the ability to minimize the likelihood that negative emotional reactions lead to impulsive or avoidant reactions. To achieve such objectives, training in this process can include several different techniques, as described below.

Reverse-Advocacy Role-Play

According to this strategy, the problem-solving therapist pretends to adopt a particular belief about problems (i.e., ones that tend to reflect a negative orientation) and asks the patient to provide reasons why that belief is irrational, illogical, incorrect, or maladaptive. Such beliefs might include the following types of statements: Problems are not common to everyone; if I have a problem, that means I'm crazy." "I shouldn't have to work so hard at this treatment." "All my problems are caused by me." "There must be a perfect solution to this problem." At times when the patient has difficulty generating arguments against the therapist's position, the counselor then adopts a more extreme form of the belief, such as "no matter how long it takes, even if it takes *forever*, I will continue to try and find the perfect solution to my problem." This procedure is intended to help individuals identify alternative ways of thinking and then to dispute or contradict previously held negative beliefs with more adaptive perspectives. Moreover, this task permits the individual to provide arguments in his or her own words against previously expressed maladaptive thoughts. Homework assignments geared to reinforce such learning is also encouraged, such as providing counterarguments to other negative problem-orientation beliefs (e.g., "People can't change" ; "Most people don't have problems") not specifically addressed in session.

ABC Method of Constructive Thinking

With this technique, patients are taught to view emotional reactions from the "ABC" perspective, where A = activating event (such as a problem), B = beliefs about the event (including what people say to themselves), and C = emotional and behavioral consequences. In other words, how individuals *feel and act* often are products of how they *think*. Using a currently experienced adherence problem, the PST therapist can use this procedure to diagnose negative self-talk and thoughts that are likely to lead to distressing emotions, lowered motivation, or other difficulties in adhering to a treatment protocol. Such cognitions often include highly evaluative words, such as "should" and "must," "catastrophic" words used to describe non-life-threatening events, and phrases that tend to be overgeneralizations (e.g., "I'm never going to quit smoking, ever! It's just too hard!"). By examining one's self-talk, the patient can learn to separate realistic statements (e.g., "I wish . . .") from maladaptive ones (e.g., "I must have . . .") as they pertain to problems with adherence. The patient can also be given a list of positive self-statements that could be used to substitute for or help dispute the negative self-talk (as in the reverse-advocacy role-play strategy). These can be placed on an index card that can be carried throughout the day or posted in a visible place to remind the individual to use this strategy outside the therapist's office. A useful homework assignment associated with this strategy would involve having the patient identify which negative thoughts were involved at times when he or she became emotionally distressed.

Visualization

As a means of enhancing patients' optimism, this technique is used to help them create the experience of successful problem resolution or ultimate goal attainment in their "mind's eye" and vicariously experience the reinforcement to be gained. Visualization in this context requests individuals to close their eyes and imagine that they have successfully achieved their ultimate goal (e.g., reduce smoking, change certain lifestyle habits, minimize pain, lose weight, decrease anxiety). The focus is on the end point—not on "how one got to the goal" but rather "focusing on the feelings of having *reached* the goal." To foster this, additional questions include: "How would your life be different if you achieved your goals?" "How would you feel about yourself having achieved these goals?" The central point of this strategy is to have patients create and "experience" their own positive consequences related to goal attainment as a motivational step toward enhanced self-efficacy. In essence, it helps create a visual image of "the light at the end of the tunnel."

Identifying Problems When They Occur

The purpose of this technique is to help "normalize" the experience of problems by discussing the various types of difficulties that can occur in general and specifically with regard to successful adherence to a particular treatment protocol. The therapist can create handouts that contain various types of problems that can occur with regard to successful treatment (e.g., peer pressure to continue smoking, nicotine withdrawal, lack of effective stress management tools, influence of alcohol on inhibition) as a springboard to discuss this issue, as well as to begin to assess for the specific problems that a given patient is currently experiencing regarding adherence.

To foster an individual's ability to recognize a problem, patients are taught to *use feelings as cues* (i.e., negative physical and emotional reactions) that a problem exists. In other words, rather than labeling one's negative emotions as "the problem" (e.g., "I get too angry and upset with myself when I overeat"), they are instructed to conceptualize such emotions as a "signal" that a problem exists and then to observe what is occurring in their environment in order to recognize the "real problem" that is causing such emotions (e.g., "When I get upset, I have to realize that something else is going on to make me feel this way, and I shouldn't just start eating to reduce my tension"). Patients are instructed to use the mnemonic "STOP and THINK" as a means of inhibiting avoidance or impulsive problem-solving behavior when they experience a particular emotion, whether affectively or physically. The "think" aspect of this phrase refers to the use of the four specific rational problem-solving skills described next.

Training in Problem Definition and Formulation

The importance of this first rational problem-solving skill can be expressed in the age-old proverb—*A problem well-defined is a problem half solved.* In other words, with a clear understanding of what is "wrong," one can then make attempts to make circumstances "right." Problem definition and formulation includes (a) gathering information about the problem, (b) objectively and concisely defining the problem, (c) separating facts from assumptions, (d) identifying the features that make the situation problematic, and (e) setting realistic goals.

In an effort to gain a comprehensive understanding of the problem, patients are instructed to use questions such as "*who, what, where, when, why, and how*" in order to gather important facts about a problem. Suggesting that the patient take on the role of "detective," "investigator reporter," or "scientist" can foster such efforts. When describing problems, patients are trained to separate *assumptions* (e.g., "I messed up my entire diet") from *facts* (e.g., "I overate at this one party"), as well as to use clear and unambiguous language (e.g., "I feel sad when I think about my father's death, which then makes me feel like giving up," versus "I feel all screwed up!").

In defining problems, patients are further taught to delineate specific goals and objectives that they would like to reach. These goals are specified in concrete and unambiguous terms, again, to minimize confusion. Clients are especially encouraged to state goals or objectives that are realistic and attainable.

The last step in problem definition and formulation training involves identifying those obstacles that exist in a given situation that prevent one from reaching the specified goals. The factors that make a situation a problem may involve *novelty*, as when one begins a new treatment regimen, *uncertainty*, often experienced with knowledge that the treatment prescribed is of an experimental nature, *conflicting outcomes*, which occur when negative side effects of a treatment begin to appear to outweigh the benefits of a drug, *lack of resources*, especially limited finances, or some other personal or environmental constraint or deficiency.

In identifying these obstacles, the therapist should be careful to help the patient accurately analyze the problem situation. Within this context, patients are taught to consider alternative problem formulations. In some cases, the problem focused on initially may not be the "real" problem (i.e., the basic, primary, or most important problem). The basic problem in some cases may be an earlier problem in a current cause-effect problem chain, where problem A is causing problem B, which in turn is causing problem C. Another possibility is that the more important problem may be a broader or more complex problem (e.g., significant fear that a treatment is not going to work) of which the specific problem focused on initially is only a part (e.g., feelings of frustration with slow progress). Once this broader, more complex problem is identified, it can then be dealt with as a whole, or it may be solved more effectively by breaking it down into more manageable subproblems and working on each of them one at a time.

Training in Generation of Alternatives

Once a problem is well-defined, patients are then instructed to use various "brainstorming principles" to foster creativity and flexibility and to minimize the tendency to react to stressful problems in previously maladaptive habitual ways. The overall objective of this problem-solving operation is to make available as many alternative solutions to the problem as possible to increase the likelihood that the most effective ones will eventually be identified. The specific principles include (a) the *quantity principle* (i.e., the more solution ideas that are identified, the more likely it is to develop an effective solution), (b) the *deferment-of-judgment principle* (i.e., refrain from evaluating solutions until a comprehensive list is generated), and (c) the *strategies-tactics principle* (i.e., ideas can be conceptualized as both general strategies and a variety of tactics or steps to carry out each of the strategies).

If patients have difficulty developing such a list, they are instructed to (a) combine ideas, (b) modify existing ideas, (c) identify how a role model (e.g., personal hero, family member) may approach a similar problem, or (d) use visualization. If severe emotional distress (e.g., anxiety) interferes with one's ability to be creative, the therapist may wish to engage in relaxation training. Homework assignments associated with this problem-solving task would include having the patient generate a comprehensive list of possible solution ideas with regard to the "well-defined problem(s)" previously identified.

Training in Decision Making

After developing a list of possible alternative solutions, the problem solver's next objective is to choose among these options in order to develop an overall solution plan. To accomplish this process, patients are first encouraged to identify potential consequences of these alternatives. This involves identifying various outcomes of both short- and long-term solutions, as well as both personal and social consequences.

Personal consequences that can be used as criteria regarding the value of an idea involve the effects of a given alternative on one's emotional well-being, the amount of time and effort involved, and the effects on one's physical well-being and personal growth. Social outcomes would entail the consequences associated with the well-being of other individuals and

their interpersonal relationships with the patient.

In addition, clients are taught to estimate both the likelihood that a given alternative would be effective in reaching their goals and whether they will actually be able to implement the solution optimally, evaluating their unique ability and desire to carry out a solution regardless of its effect on the problem.

Using these ratings, individuals are taught to develop an overall solution plan by first comparing the ratings of the various alternative solutions. If only a small number of ideas appear to be rated as potentially satisfactory, then the problem solver must ask several evaluative questions: "Do I have enough information?" "Did I define the problem correctly?" "Are my goals too high?" "Did I generate enough options?" At this point, the patient may need to go back and engage again in the previous problem-solving tasks.

If several effective or satisfactory alternatives are identified, then the client is encouraged to include a combination of potentially effective coping options for each subgoal to "attack" the problem from a variety of perspectives. Furthermore, a contingency plan complete with alternative coping options is often useful in the event the first group of options fails.

Training in Solution Implementation and Verification

This final rational problem-solving skill involves actually implementing the solution plan and then evaluating the effectiveness of its outcome. Specific operations include (a) carrying out the solution plan, (b) monitoring its outcome, (c) evaluating its effectiveness, and (d) troubleshooting if the solution is unsuccessful versus engaging in self-reinforcement if the problem is resolved.

The first part of this problem-solving task involves the actual performance of the chosen solution plan. In essence, the patient may be able to hypothetically develop an effective solution plan, but if it is never actually carried out, then the problem will never get resolved, nor will the individual receive important "natural" feedback (i.e., problem-solving success or failure).

At times, some patients, due to fear of failure or continued poor self-efficacy beliefs, inhibit their willingness to implement a solution plan. In such cases, we suggest that patients complete a "comparison worksheet," which requires them to list the consequences that will occur if the problem is *not* solved, versus the consequences if the problem is resolved successfully. Visualization can also be used to increase a patient's self-efficacy related to executing the solution, identifying and overcoming obstacles, and increasing the effectiveness of solution implementation. In addition, if relevant, the patient can practice, via role-playing, carrying out the chosen solution plan.

The second aspect entails the careful monitoring and evaluation of the actual solution outcomes. After the solution plan is carried out, individuals are encouraged to monitor the real-life consequences that occur as a function of the implemented solution. Clients are taught to develop self-monitoring methods that are relevant to a given problem that would include (a) ratings of the solution outcome itself (e.g., Did the plan achieve the specified goals? What were the positive consequences? What were the negative consequences?) and (b) evaluative ratings of one's emotional reactions to these outcomes (e.g., How do I feel about these outcomes? Do they make me happy? Am I less anxious?), and the degree to which outcomes match the consequences previously anticipated during the decision-making process (e.g., Did what I predict was going to happen actually happen?).

If the match is satisfactory, then the problem solver is encouraged to administer some form of self-reinforcement, such as self-statements of congratulation or a tangible gift or reward. On the other hand, if the match is unsatisfactory, then he or she is encouraged to either implement the previously identified contingency plan or to recycle through the entire problem-solving process. Particular care should be exercised to differentiate between difficulties with the *performance* or implementation of a coping option and the problem-solving *process* itself.

Structured Practice

After the majority of training has occurred, the remainder of PST can be devoted to practicing the newly acquired skills and applying them to a variety of adherence problems. As the 13th-century Persian poet, Saa'di, stated, "However much thou art read in theory, if thou hast no practice, thou art ignorant." This quote is to suggest that the more a patient applies these skills to various problem situations, the better he or she becomes at overall problem resolution. Beyond actually solving stressful problems, continuous in-session practice serves three additional purposes: (a) the patient can receive "professional" feedback from the therapist, (b) increased facility with the overall PST model can decrease the amount of time and effort necessary to apply the entire model with each new problem, and (c) practice fosters maintenance and generalization of the skills.

In addition to focusing on resolving and coping with current problems, these practice sessions should also allow for "future forecasting," whereby the patient is encouraged to look to the future and anticipate where potential adherence problems might arise (e.g., new negative side effects of a medication, change in health care team, slow overall progress, changes in one's work responsibilities) in order to apply such skills in a preventive manner. Continuous application of these skills is encouraged, for as the poet Emily Dickinson stated, "Low at my problem bending, another problem comes."

Case Study

The following is an example of applying PST as a means of fostering treatment adherence to a standard behavioral weight loss program.

Nicole S., a 39-year-old woman, lost 21 pounds over the course of 16 weeks of behavioral treatment for obesity. She and her therapist, Dr. K, had agreed to continue therapy, but Nicole changed her mind and called her therapist to say that she had decided to drop out of treatment. Dr. K viewed this seemingly unexpected turn of events in two ways. First, she viewed it as a clinical challenge that was a normal part of helping patients deal with obesity, a condition that often requires an ongoing problem-solving intervention for effective long-term management. Second, the therapist looked upon the situation as an opportunity to help Nicole acquire the problem-solving skills needed to manage the myriad of challenges that commonly arise in the course of weight-management interventions.

When Dr. K asked Nicole for more information about her decision to end therapy, she explained that she had "lost the motivation to continue." Rather than confronting the patient about the reasons for her change of heart, the therapist "normalized" the challenge facing Nicole as a common experience for many people dealing with weight management. Dr. K encouraged Nicole to view "the loss of motivation" as a problem that could be addressed and resolved through the use of "problem-solving therapy" (PST). Indeed, the first step of PST began with an "orientation" toward problems, specifically the adoption of a perspective that views problems as normal events for which there are a range of potential solutions, including some that may resolve the problem in an effective manner. Dr. K viewed Nicole's desire to end therapy as an avoidant approach to dealing with distressing problems. Thus, the therapist's first challenge was to engage the patient and get her to agree to work directly on the problem rather than running away from it. In this case, Dr. K invited Nicole to try an "experiment" that involved making a commitment to four additional sessions of therapy that would directly address her "loss of motivation" for continuing her weight management effort. Nicole agreed.

Dr. K worked with Nicole to reframe her perspective on the nature of problems and solutions. She then asked Nicole to focus on defining the particular problem that she experienced as a "loss of motivation." Nicole recalled the circumstances associated with her change in motivation. With the assistance of Dr. K's use of "fact-finding" questions (e.g., Who? What? When? Where? Why? How?), the patient related that her change in motivation came after she inadvertently overheard a coworker say, "Nicole has lost over 20 pounds. It's a shame that nobody has noticed." Nicole described herself as "devastated" by the remark. She had worked very hard at weight loss, and over the course of 4 months, she had reduced her weight from 216 pounds down to 195 pounds. Nicole's "loss of motivation" was directly tied to her expectation that others would notice her change in weight and would praise her for her accomplishments. Nicole was defining her weight-loss progress based on the reactions of others. Thus, Dr. K helped Nicole to redefine the problem and to set a goal of developing "a healthy set of expectations about weight loss" (i.e., appropriate expectations that would be independent of other people's reactions).

Next, Nicole and Dr. K engaged in a "brainstorming" exercise designed to generate a wide range of "healthy expectations." Nicole was encouraged to think creatively in generating a long list of potential options without regard to how silly or outrageous the option might seem at first glance. Indeed, her list of alternative solutions included some seemingly extreme alternatives, such as making a sign for her office door that read, "Nicole has lost 21 pounds—tell her how great she looks!" or taking a vow "I'm never going to diet or weigh myself again!" Her list also included the following options: "Tell myself it doesn't matter whether other people have noticed my loss." "I've noticed the weight loss, and that's what counts." "I'm not going to judge myself based on my appearance." "I'm a healthier person because I've lost weight." "There's no law that says other people have to notice when you've lost weight." "It's hard for people who see you everyday to notice changes in your weight." "Write positive sayings on index cards and read them whenever feeling a loss of motivation." "Look myself in the mirror everyday and say 'You are a beautiful, strong woman.'"

After carefully considering the potential advantages and disadvantages associated with the various options generated in the brainstorming exercise, Dr. K helped Nicole to decide on a solution. They initially decided to forgo the notion of posting a sign announcing her weight loss, and further agreed it made little sense to give up the weight control effort after having made considerable progress. Instead, the strategy that Nicole decided to employ involved a combination of tactics focused on positive self-talk. She chose to begin each morning with a "mirror exercise." As a prompt, she posted an index card on her mirror that read "You're a beautiful, strong woman!" In addition, she wrote out positive sayings with healthy expectations about weight loss on separate index cards. She placed them in her purse and agreed to read them over at least twice per day, and more often when experiencing "valleys" in her motivation for weight management.

Nicole agreed to implement the plan on a daily basis for 2 weeks. She also agreed that each time she made use of her positive affirmations, she would place a check mark near the date in her pocket calendar. Nicole and Dr. K decided that at the end of the 2-week period, they would evaluate how often Nicole implemented the plan and whether it was helping with her motivation to continue her weight-management efforts. If the outcome was not successful, Dr. K would work with Nicole to determine what factors seemed to be responsible for the lack of success (e.g., whether not implementing the specific tactics played a role) and together they would cycle through the relevant steps of the PST model to develop a new solution plan. If, on the other hand, the outcome were positive, Dr. K would have the opportunity to congratulate Nicole for successfully applying the problem-solving approach to an important challenge in weight management and have her engage in self-reinforcement as well.

References

Bandura, A. (1997). *Self-efficacy: The exercise of control.* New York: W.H. Freeman.

Bodenheimer, T., Lorig, K., Holman, H., & Grumbach, K. (2002). Patient self-management of chronic disease in primary care. *Journal of American Medical Association, 288,* 2469–2775.

D'Zurilla, T. J., & Goldfried, M. R. (1971). Problem solving and behavior modification. *Journal of Abnormal Psychology, 78,* 107–126.

D'Zurilla, T. J., & Nezu, A. (1982). Social problem solving in adults. In P. C. Kendall (Ed.), *Advances in cognitive-behavioral research and therapy* (Vol. 1, pp. 202–274). New York: Academic Press.

D'Zurilla, T. J., & Nezu, A. M. (1990). Development and preliminary evaluation of the Social Problem-Solving Inventory (SPSI). *Psychological Assessment: A Journal of Consulting and Clinical Psychology, 2,* 156–163.

D'Zurilla, T. J., & Nezu, A. M. (in press). *Problem-solving therapy: A positive approach to clinical intervention* (3rd ed.). New York: Springer.

D'Zurilla, T. J., & Nezu, A. M. (2001). Problem-solving therapies. In K. S. Dobson (Ed.), *The handbook of cognitive-behavioral therapies* (2nd ed., pp. 211–245). New York: Guilford.

D'Zurilla, T. J., Nezu, A. M., & Maydeu-Olivares, A. (2002). *Social Problem-Solving Inventory-Revised (SPSI-R): Technical manual.* North Tonawanda, NY: Multi-Health Systems.

D'Zurilla, T. J., Nezu, A. M., & Maydeu-Olivares, A. (2004). Social problem solving: Theory and assessment. In E. C. Chang, T. J. D'Zurilla, & L. J. Sanna (Eds.), *Social problem solving: Theory, research, and training* (pp. 11–27). Washington, DC: American Psychological Association.

Heppner, P. P. (1988). *The problem-solving inventory.* Palo Alto, CA: Consulting Psychologist Press.

Kazdin, A. E., & Whitley, M. K. (2003). Treatment of parental stress to enhance therapeutic change among children referred for aggressive and antisocial behavior. *Journal of Consulting and Clinical Psychology, 71,* 504–515.

Nezu, A. M. (2004). Problem solving and behavior therapy revisited. *Behavior Therapy, 35,* 1–33.

Nezu, A. M., D'Zurilla, T. J., Zwick, M. L., & Nezu, C. M. (2004). Problem-solving therapy for adults. In E. C. Chang, T. J. D'Zurilla, & L. J. Sanna (Eds.), *Social problem solving: Theory, research, and training* (pp. 171–191). Washington, DC: American Psychological Association.

Nezu, A. M., Nezu, C. M., & D'Zurilla, T. J. (in press). *Solving life's problems: A 5-step guide to enhanced well-being.* New York: Springer.

Nezu, A. M., Nezu, C. M., Felgoise, S. H., McClure, K. S., & Houts, P. S. (2003). Project Genesis: Assessing the efficacy of problem-solving therapy for distressed adult cancer patients. *Journal of Consulting and Clinical Psychology, 71,* 1036–1048.

Nezu, A. M., Nezu, C. M., Friedman, S. H., Faddis, S., & Houts, P. S. (1998). *Helping cancer patients cope: A problem-solving approach.* Washington, DC: American Psychological Association.

Nezu, A. M., Nezu, C. M., & Lombardo, E. R. (2003). Problem-solving therapy. In W. O'Donohue, J. E. Fisher, & S. C. Hayes (Eds.), *Cognitive behavior therapy: Applying empirically supported techniques in your practice* (pp. 301–307). New York: Wiley.

Nezu, A. M., Nezu, C. M., & Perri, M. G. (1989). *Problem-solving therapy for depression: Theory, research, and clinical guidelines.* New York: Wiley.

Nezu, A. M., Wilkins, V. M., & Nezu, C. M. (2004). Social problem solving, stress, and negative affective conditions. In E. C. Chang, T. J. D'Zurilla, & L. J. Sanna (Eds.), *Social problem solving: Theory, research, and training* (pp. 19–65). Washington, DC: American Psychological Association.

Nezu, C. M., Palmatier, A., & Nezu, A. M. (2004). Social problem-solving training for caregivers. In E. C. Chang, T. J. D'Zurilla, & L. J. Sanna (Eds.), *Social problem solving: Theory, research, and training* (pp. 223–238). Washington, DC: American Psychological Association.

Perri, M. G., Nezu, A. M., McKelvey, W. F., Schein, R. L., Renjilian, D. A., & Viegener, B. J. (2001). Relapse prevention training and problem-solving therapy in the long-term management of obesity. *Journal of Consulting and Clinical Psychology, 69,* 722–726.

Perri, M. G., Nezu, A. M., & Viegener, B. J. (1992). *Improving the long-term management of obesity: Theory, research, and clinical guidelines.* New York: Wiley.

Safren, S. A., Otto, M. W., Worth, J. L., Salomon, E., Johnson, W., Mayer, K., et al. (2001). Two strategies to increase adherence to HIV antiretroviral medication: Life-steps and medication monitoring. *Behaviour Research and Therapy, 39,* 1151–1162.

Spirito, A., Boergers, J., Donaldson, D., Bishop, D., & Lewander, W. (2002). An intervention trial to improve adherence to community treatment by adolescents after a suicide attempt. *Journal of the Academy of Child and Adolescent Psychiatry, 41,* 435–442.

10

Relapse Prevention to Promote Treatment Adherence

Arthur W. Blume

G. Alan Marlatt

Relapse prevention has been found to be an efficacious intervention to promote treatment adherence. Although the therapy was first developed for use to prevent relapse among patients abusing substances, such as alcohol and tobacco, relapse prevention has been used successfully to prevent relapses of other mental disorders after treatment and in the treatment of other health conditions. Empirical evidence for the efficacy of relapse prevention to promote adherence after treatment is reviewed subsequently.

Empirical Evidence for the Efficacy of the Relapse Model and Relapse Prevention

A substantial body of research has found support for the relationship of overt determinants, such as strong emotions and mood, environmental stressors, and interpersonal relationship stress, with subsequent relapse behavior (Larimer, Palmer, & Marlatt, 1999; Mackay & Marlatt, 1990; Maisto, O'Farrell, McKay, Connors, & Pelcovits, 1988; Marlatt, 1985d, 1996; Marlatt & Gordon, 1980; Schonfeld, Rohrer, Dupree, & Thomas, 1989; Smith & Frawley, 1993; Strowig, 2000; Vuchinich & Tucker, 1996). In addition, researchers identified covert determinants of relapse, including low self-efficacy (Allsop, Saunders, & Phillips, 2000; Greenfield et al., 2000; Marlatt, 1985a, 1985c, 1996; Marlatt & Barrett, 1994; Miller, McCrady, Abrams, & Labouvie, 1994), poor coping after treatment (e.g., Chaney, O'Leary, & Marlatt, 1978; Connors, Maisto, & Zywiak, 1996; Monti, Gulliver, & Myers, 1994; Walton, Blow, & Booth, 2000), and increased positive expectancies (Brown, 1985; Marlatt, 1985a, 1985c).

Reviews of the research literature support the efficacy of relapse prevention to maintain treatment effects and promote adherence. A review of the literature found that relapse prevention was effective for treating substance abuse and was especially effective in reducing the severity of relapses when they did occur and in enhancing the maintenance of treatment effects over time (Carroll, 1996). A meta-analysis of relapse prevention studies for substance use disorders found it to be a widely effective intervention, especially for alcohol use disorders (Irvin, Bowers, Dunn, & Wang, 1999). Relapse prevention has been used effectively among people with co-occurring substance use and psychotic disorders (Ho et al., 1999) and has shown effectiveness in controlled trials for other types of mental health problems and health behaviors, including depression (Katon et al., 2001) and managing obesity (Perri et al., 2001). In addition, relapse prevention has been used to promote adherence to recommended health behavior changes, such as increasing physical exercise (Belisle, Roskies, & Levesque, 1987) and managing Type II diabetes (Simmons & Owens, 1992).

Theoretical Underpinnings for the Technique

As a cognitive-behavioral therapy, relapse prevention includes many change strategies common to that family of therapies. Relapse prevention includes behavioral assessment and self-monitoring to identify potential risk areas, skills training, behavioral rehearsal, enhancement of self-efficacy to negotiate high-risk situations, and cognitive modification techniques to challenge unhelpful beliefs associated with relapse behavior. In addition, relapse prevention includes effective intervention strategies designed to manage and moderate the duration and severity of nonadherence when it does occur.

The following section reviews the empirically supported model for relapse as first proposed by Marlatt (1985c), which involves a generally linear progression of events toward a relapse. It is worth noting, however, that a recent article has suggested that relapse may result from highly complex and dynamic interactions between relapse risk factors and the determinants of relapse, which would be best explained using chaos or catastrophe theory (Witkiewitz & Marlatt, 2004).

Stage 1: Specific Vulnerabilities for Relapse

Research has found that certain vulnerabilities can place a client in a high-risk situation, which makes adherence to treatment recommendations difficult (Marlatt, 1985c, 1985d). The first of these vulnerabilities is called lifestyle imbalance, which occurs when patients do certain activities in excess at the expense of others, which in turn often causes fatigue and dissatisfaction. Balance across different life domains, such as participation in spiritual practices, intellectual pursuits, healthy diet and exercise, balanced emotional responses, and healthy relationships, seems critical for good health and quality of life. Related to lifestyle imbalances, a second area of vulnerability for relapse is a desire for indulgence. Lifestyle imbalances often prompt a desire to engage in pleasurable activities to offset the discomfort of the imbalances. Patients may be tempted to engage in unhealthy indulgences during periods of discomfort or to cope with stress or a negative mood. This may be particularly true for patients who find that adherence with medical advice contributes to the discomfort being experienced.

Another area of vulnerability can arise when patients experience cravings or temptations to return to old behavior. An example might be when a physician has suggested a diet for a patient to lose weight or control diabetes. Patients may experience temptations or cravings that will place them at risk of discontinuing the diet. Patients also make apparently irrelevant decisions that can place them in high-risk situations. These decisions often are made without awareness or concern for the potential for risk that may result from choices made. Apparently irrelevant decisions often are associated with setting up a relapse by putting oneself in a highly tempting situation that can later serve as an excuse for the patient's giving in to that temptation. Using the example of a diet, a patient may have no intention of lapsing when she buys cookies for her children, but she has increased her risk nonetheless by having the cookies so easily accessible.

Stage 2: High-Risk Situations

Three types of situations have been found to place patients at risk of relapse. The first occurs when a client experiences strong or negative moods and emotions. Negative moods and strong emotions make rational responses difficult, especially when learning and practicing new coping responses. A second high-risk situation can arise from stressful environmental conditions. Financial constraints, for example, can be a significant factor in nonadherence to treatment recommendations. A third type of high-risk situation involves interpersonal conflict, usually with family. Pressures brought to bear on patients by family members may have a significant impact on treatment progress. In some cases, family members may unwittingly interfere with the patient's adherence to treatment recommendations. An example might be a partner who ridicules the patient for use of prescribed prophylactic medications for asthma.

If the patient has sufficient skills and uses them appropriately with confidence and in a timely fashion in the high-risk situation, then treatment adherence may be maintained. Patients, however, frequently either do not have the skills necessary to succeed or do not know how and when to use the skills with confidence. Poor coping responses may cause a patient to advance toward relapse.

Stage 3: Changes in Self-efficacy and Expectancies

As the patient's confidence to cope successfully while maintaining adherence to treatment recommendations diminishes, positive expectancies related to nonadherent behavior arise. At this point, the patient may believe that nonadherence is the preferred path given the discomfort of ineffectual coping with the high-risk situation. For example, a bipolar patient who has not coped well with the side effects of a mood stabilizer may become increasingly discouraged from continued use of that medicine. The patient may be tempted to discontinue use of the medicine and return to using marijuana to "self-medicate" instead. As confidence in the prescribed mood stabilizer decreases, the patient experiences increased beliefs that a return to substance abuse is an attractive option.

Stage 4: Lapses and Goal Violation Effects

Lapse or slips into nonadherence can occur as a result of the lower self-efficacy in maintaining treatment gains and the increased positive expectancies about the desirability of nonadherence. Lapses may be transitory events or a precursor to a relapse from adherence. How patients and treatment professionals respond to and prepare for such a slip into nonadherence may determine whether the lapse progresses to a relapse. Lapses generally cause the experience of a goal violation effect, which can be detrimental to progress of patients. A goal violation effect occurs when the patient reacts emotionally to the slip with feelings such as guilt or remorse or with hopelessness about her or his ability to return to adherence. A dichotomous experience of a goal violation effect is when abstinence is violated during a lapse. Abstinence violation effects contribute to an all or nothing outcome, which ultimately may interfere with adherence to treatment recommendations. Goal violation effects leave patients vulnerable to relapse.

Stage 5: Relapse

Relapse represents a return to pretreatment behavior. Even during relapse, though, there are interventions that can help patients return to adherence. Relapse is not treatment failure but merely a sign that the relapse plan needs some fine tuning and that the patient may need to learn additional skills. In addition, professionals may need to use motivational enhancement techniques to encourage a return to adherence (e.g., Miller & Rollnick, 2002). Later in this chapter, relapse prevention strategies for maintaining treatment adherence will be described, including techniques to circumvent relapse processes prior to nonadherent behavior.

Who Might Benefit From Relapse Prevention?

Those at risk of nonadherence, such as patients with multiple problems and stressors who will likely encounter numerous high-risk situations for treatment relapse, would likely benefit from having relapse prevention integrated into the core of their treatment. In addition, most patients should benefit from using relapse prevention strategies after treatment to maintain behavior changes and to successfully promote adherence to treatment advice.

Contraindications for Relapse Prevention

The strategies of relapse prevention are broad in scope and pragmatic in application, so they will likely benefit most patients. The efficacy of relapse prevention among certain special populations, however, has yet to be tested. Relapse prevention methods may not be culturally relevant for some ethnic minority groups, and traditional relapse prevention methods may need to be culturally enhanced.

Relapse prevention also presumes that the patient will be able to at least provide partial self-care and have the cognitive abilities to reason and problem solve effectively under in vivo conditions. If patients are unable to effectively problem solve or to care for themselves, then relapse prevention methods may not be effective. Relapse prevention may be effective with these kinds of patients, however, if they are closely monitored by treatment professionals under structured conditions.

Step-by-Step Guide to Relapse Prevention

Step 1: Assessment

The first step for conducting relapse prevention is to thoroughly assess the patient's behavior to determine vulnerabilities for relapse and to determine high-risk relapse situations. A behavioral analysis is conducted to determine past relapse behavior related to the health behavior targeted for intervention. The function and context of past relapses are determined from this assessment, which will provide a clear picture for treatment professionals on where to intervene. Professionals want to identify emotional, environmental, and interpersonal vulnerabilities that may interfere with the maintenance of treatment gains. In addition, professionals assess for high-risk situations that patients may encounter and, in addition, how the patient may have responded in those situations before. At the same time, professionals will want to uncover situations in which patients have low self-efficacy in coping in an adherent fashion and to assess for positive expectancies related to nonadherent behavior. Self-monitoring, relapse fantasies, and relapse roadmaps, three techniques used to assess for relapse patterns, are described below.

Self-monitoring (or keeping track) of behavior, thoughts, and emotions is assigned between sessions in an effort to gather more data about vulnerabilities and high-risk situations. Self-monitoring is reviewed at the beginning of each session as part of the assigned homework review. Professionals assign patients to track high-risk cues or triggers on a daily basis and review them in session. Monitoring may be done in a diary form and often includes numeric ratings of the experience of discomfort, the level of stress, or the intensity of emotions or mood. In addition, professionals may ask patients to link these data with a numeric rating of thoughts about relapse.

Another useful way to understand high-risk relapse situations is to determine a patient's relapse roadmap. Relapse roadmaps analyze past relapse behavior chains using a behavioral analysis to examine the patient's relapse history for the targeted behavior. Different links along the behavior chain are mapped in an effort to uncover risky behavior, relapse warning signs, and appropriate points for intervention. Patients are taught that each chain, or intersection on the roadmap, allows a place for them to take a detour away from risk.

Relapse roadmaps also can be used to identify risks for apparently irrelevant decisions. The roadmap provides a concrete and systematic way to examine how a seemingly benign decision ultimately leads to harmful consequences. Patients may not be aware of how one decision ultimately leads to a risky situation, but a visually concrete strategy such as a relapse roadmap allows for examination of where the path may lead.

Professionals also should make it a point to ask patients about thoughts or fantasies about returning to nonadherent behavior. By understanding these relapse fantasies, professionals are able to build strategies into the relapse plan that will help patients avoid acting upon such fantasies in the future. Relapse fantasies also provide clues for possible apparently irrelevant decisions that patients may make that will place them at risk, and these fantasies expose positive expectancies patients have about nonadherent behavior.

In addition to assessing for relapse vulnerabilities and high-risk situations, professionals also will want to assess the patient's repertoire of skills to discover if the patient has ability to cope with the vulnerabilities and high-risk situations in question. Evidence for skills deficits may be uncovered by examining the relapse history of the patient. Role-playing in session to observe how she or he would respond to various high-risk situations may uncover skill deficits that would place the patient at risk.

Step 2: Orientation to Relapse Prevention

During the development of the relapse prevention plan, orient the patient to the relapse prevention model. As part of this orientation, the patient is told that relapse, although not inevitable, is normal, and does not represent a failure of treatment. Instead, lapse and relapse behaviors are part of learning how to change. Professionals can use an analogy, such as learning how to walk, to represent the process of learning new adherent behavior. Most toddlers will fall when learning how to walk before they get it right, but this does not mean that they will not be able to walk correctly in the future. Setbacks are part of progress.

Similarly, patients are taught that lapses and relapses are situational rather than systemic. Lapses occur because of poor coping in a specific situation. Attributing lapses and relapse to the patient only contributes to the toxicity of the goal violation effect. This is not a helpful strategy to encourage a return to adherence. Attributing lapses and relapses to situations can help define the problem that needs to be solved. Assigning blame to the person may cause the lapse to seem unsolvable to the patient and should be avoided. Orientating the patient early in treatment to this approach will help to reduce the goal violation effects if lapses do occur later in treatment.

In addition, professionals review the suggested relapse prevention plan and orient patients to the relapse process. Professionals will want to use the patient's own behavior to explain the different stages in the relapse process. An overview is provided for how the relapse chain can be intervened upon at each stage in that process. The professional provides an outline of how the interventions will occur. Patients are oriented to the importance of homework to practice adherence under real-world conditions.

Professionals will want to orient patients to the various signs warning of a risk of relapse, such as making apparently irrelevant decisions, coping ineffectively, and experiencing lowered self-efficacy or increased positive expectancies for nonadherent behavior. The warning signs that are taught should be individualized to the patient using the information gathered through assessment. The information about warning signs often is given to patients in written form. Suggest that patients place the list of warning signs in prominent places that they frequent (such as at home or in cars) as reminders.

Developing the Relapse Prevention Plan

Using the assessment for patient vulnerabilities and past high-risk situations as a guide, professionals then develop an individualized relapse prevention plan. The relapse prevention plan will include cognitive-behavioral strategies for exposure and prevention of response to high-risk cues that trigger urges for nonadherence, skills training for more effective coping and imaginal and in vivo rehearsal of skills usage to increase self-efficacy and skills generalization, and development of safety plans in the event of emergencies and also in the event that a lapse or relapse should occur.

Relapse rehearsal is one strategy used with patients to encourage use of a relapse prevention plan. The goal of a relapse rehearsal is to practice with a patient what he or she should do if a lapse or relapse should occur. The goal of this strategy is to manage the severity and duration of non-adherent behavior should it occur and to provide for continuity of care and regular contact with the patient during the slip. Relapse rehearsal also helps patients to stop a lapse or relapse before it happens by using the plan to break the chain of events earlier in the relapse process. Because the relapse plan is being rehearsed, it is more likely that the patient will respond skillfully and appropriately when a crisis does occur or perhaps respond in such a way as to avoid the crisis.

Professionals help patients develop a very specific step-by-step plan of action, generally presented to patients in written form and easily available for future reference, on what to do in the face of vulnerabilities, high-risk situations, decreased self-efficacy, or increased positive expectancies, or even during a slip or relapse. An important part of the plan is to provide for communication between the professional and the patient during the crisis. The plan should be comprehensive but simple enough for patients to follow and carry out effectively on their own. Rehearsals will allow professionals to observe the plan in action and determine if it is comprehensive and user friendly. Patients are reminded that relapse is a normative behavior but that it is not inevitable. Planning ahead for a crisis is prudent, even if the relapse plan is never used.

Reminder Cards in Case of Emergency

Relapse prevention also uses reminder cards on how to respond in case of a lapse or relapse. Reminder cards are meant to be portable and easily accessible, so they are small enough to fit in a wallet, pocket, or purse. The cards include brief step-by-step instructions on what to do, including calling a professional for help and support, getting away from the situation that has contributed to the lapse, and other brief individualized reminders to aid the patient under stressful conditions to respond appropriately. Several reminder cards are commonly created to be used, and these cards are placed strategically in areas frequented by the patient, such as cars, bedrooms, kitchens, and offices. Like other prompts, using the cards is practiced with patients frequently during treatment.

Relapse Contracts

Finally, using the relapse plan, a relapse contract is developed. The contract is written out, which can be signed by both the patient and the professional to gain commitment for carrying it out, and a copy is given to the patient. Most relapse contracts provide for mutually agreed upon action steps, including getting out of the context that prompted the lapse and contacting a professional by phone for help and support. The relapse contract is reviewed frequently during treatment so that the patient is very familiar with the plan prior to experiencing any difficulties.

Step 3: Using Cognitive-Behavioral Interventions

As a cognitive-behavioral therapy, relapse prevention relies heavily on empirically validated intervention techniques to effect change in a patient. In the following sections, cognitive and behavioral modification strategies commonly used in relapse prevention will be reviewed.

Cognitive Interventions: Challenging Expectancies

Use cognitive modification strategies to challenge expectancies related to adherence and nonadherence. One way to challenge expectancies is to present facts or use research to refute patient beliefs that may interfere with adherence. Use of this strategy, however, requires a diplomatic approach, such as using a motivational interviewing style (Miller & Rollnick, 2002) to avoid resistance and to encourage commitment to treatment recommendations. Professionals often assign as homework scientifically supported literature to aid in refuting unhelpful and errant expectancies that will interfere with treatment adherence.

In addition, other empirically supported cognitive modification strategies can be used to challenge expectancies. Hypothesis testing, for example, can be used by patients to test their assumptions about adherence versus nonadherence. Patients are taught to view their expectancies as beliefs to be examined and tested rather than facts to be acted on. Hypothesis testing relies on collecting data in support and in refutation of the assumption (expectancy) being tested. Patients are asked to test the veracity of their expectancies under real-world conditions, and then the results of their "experiment" can be discussed in session. Finally, the expectancy may sometimes be fulfilled by nonadherent behavior but not always. Under these conditions, professionals may suggest that patients track how often the expectancy does occur to provide a balanced perspective. Patients often operate under an assumption that the expectancy is 100% true, but when tested they find it is only true 30% of the time.

Another method to challenge expectancies involves allowing patients to examine evidence both in favor of and in opposition to maintaining adherence to treatment recommendations. In relapse prevention, this is generally carried out by means of a decision matrix. The decision matrix uses a 2 × 2 column approach to look at the pros and cons of adherence over the short term and then again over the long term. The matrix prompts patients to consider first what positive things may happen as a result of nonadherence over the short term, then what negative things may happen. In a similar fashion, the questions are restated, but this time asking how nonadherence will affect the patient over the long term (both pros and cons). Use of the decision matrix can be a particularly potent way to challenge positive expectancies about nonadherence and negative expectancies about adherence, especially over the long term, by providing for a balanced perspective on all the consequences of the patient's actions. Decision matrices also can be used after a lapse or relapse to encourage a return to adherent behavior.

Cognitive Restructuring

Cognitive restructuring is used in relapse prevention to modify noxious beliefs secondary to goal violation effects. The goal is to reframe the lapse so that patients view it as normative and an opportunity rather than a failure. Goal violation effects often bring about feelings of shame, failure, and hopelessness in patients. Cognitive restructuring allows patients to view the lapse in a more constructive way.

Professionals will want to normalize lapse and relapse as a common part of the change process, as mentioned in the orientation section. If this has been done, then the patient will be more likely to interpret a lapse or relapse constructively if it occurs, which will make it easier to avoid the toxic experiences of a goal-violation effect. Patients will see an opportunity to learn more about the change process, will remember their commitment to seek professional help in order to minimize the lapse or relapse behavior without massive levels of shame, and may have the self-efficacy to return to adherent behavior.

Finally, as mentioned in the orientation section, relapse prevention teaches patients to change the attribution for a lapse or relapse from a personal failure or shortcoming within themselves to a problem with coping with a particular situation. Relapse debriefing is the cognitive restructuring strategy used to dissect a lapse or relapse after it has occurred, and it helps in the process of modifying cognitions about the slip into nonadherent behavior. If the lapse is related to poor coping in a particular situation, then skills can be learned to overcome the problem in the future. Attributing lapses to situations rather than to self also aids in the development of self-efficacy in maintaining treatment gains over time even if setbacks should occur.

Labeling and Detachment

Professionals also teach patients to label and detach when they feel the urge to engage in non-adherent behavior. Labeling and detaching help patients to say out loud when they want to "quit" on adherence. Labeling this desire to give up on adherence sometimes allows patients to detach themselves from acting on the desire. Labeling the desire for nonadherence helps patients become detached observers of the desire, and they can view the desire as just a thought and not necessarily an outcome. Labeling and detaching publicly in front of supportive collaterals (or professionals) can be a very potent way to prevent acting on the desire, because then the patient is not alone in trying to stop the desire for nonadherence.

Behavioral Interventions: Skills Training

Relapse prevention skills for effectively coping with the different stages of the relapse process are taught. These skills vary according to individual need and the nature of the targeted behavior but likely will include average daily living skills, interpersonal effectiveness skills such as assertiveness training and refusal skills, emotion regulation skills such as anger management, and distress tolerance skills such as discomfort surfing.

The first type of skill set that may need to be trained include average daily living skills (ADLs). These are skills such as taking medicines as prescribed, balancing a checkbook register, being functionally literate, and preparing food. The ability to use these skills effectively cannot be taken for granted because deficits in ADLs can adversely affect the ability of a patient to comply with treatment recommendations.

Another set of skills that are important for relapse prevention are those needed to endure discomfort, which are often referred to as distress tolerance skills. Distress tolerance skills either provide a means to feel better during seemingly intolerable situations or allow patients to distract themselves while in those situations. Relaxation training or breathing retraining are examples of the former, whereas counting or thought stopping are examples of the latter. Distraction skills are useful for clients; however, they should not be used during cue exposure because that will diminish its effectiveness (see below).

One distress tolerance (and mindfulness—see later) skill specifically developed for relapse prevention was originally called "urge surfing" because it was used to ride out cravings for substances. Urge surfing also can be thought of as "discomfort surfing" (Blume, Anderson, Fader, & Marlatt, 2001) when used to ameliorate unpleasant experiences for a variety of health behaviors that are not necessarily related to cravings for substances. With this technique, professionals instruct patients to imagine that the discomfort they are experiencing will ebb and flow like a wave. Patients sometimes cannot imagine that discomfort will eventually subside, but personal discomfort tends to fluctuate or even eventually dissipate over time. The point is to postpone impulsive responses that may lead to nonadherence to treatment recommendations while in the height of the discomfort because the discomfort will likely fade naturally if the patient rides it out. Discomfort surfing can be used for a variety uncomfortable situations that patients may need to tolerate, such as pain, symptoms from other mental disorders, and even medication side effects.

Because interpersonal relationship stress is a strong predictor of relapse behavior, professionals find it important to conduct social skills training as a part of relapse prevention. Nonadherence may result from ineffectual interpersonal interactions that create frustration or that prevent patients from requesting the needed services. For example, assertiveness training may be important to promote treatment adherence. Problems with assertiveness can create significant interpersonal problems and even social isolation. Similarly, teach patients how to refuse to engage in nonadherent behavior, especially under circumstances where there are peer pressures to do so. Saying no can be difficult for some patients and practicing such a skill may be warranted. Additionally, many patients have difficulties with managing or identifying emotions, which can create havoc in social interactions.

Anger management training, for example, may be required to help some patients succeed after treatment. Many patients identified as "difficult" are so because of skill deficits, which lead to problems interacting with others.

Finally, mindfulness skills teach patients how to focus on the present moment and to concentrate on the task at hand. Presumably, this ability to concentrate would help patients remain adherent to treatment recommendations. Mindfulness skills include specific tasks designed to practice focusing on the present moment, such as observing breathing or concentrating intensely on a single object. Urge and discomfort surfing as well as meditation include strong mindfulness components that aid patients to focus on the present moment (Witkiewitz, Marlatt, & Walker, 2005).

In addition, teaching other types of skills can help prevent relapse and restore lifestyle balance (see below), such as teaching stress management. The key to successful relapse prevention is to match the skills training component to the needs of the patient in order to promote adherence. Adding new skills to a patient's repertoire and rehearsing those skills may allow the patient to respond calmly and effectively in the face of stressful situations in the real-world.

Stimulus Control and Cue Exposure

Professionals also will want to use stimulus control and cue exposure with patients in order to minimize temptations to relapse into old behavior triggered by environmental or intrapersonal cues. Stimulus control involves controlling the duration and conditions for which a patient is exposed to a cue that is linked to a response of nonadherence to treatment recommendations. At first the duration and circumstances of exposure to such a cue are artificially controlled in session or by the professional. The eventual goal is, however, to teach patients how to regulate exposure to threatening cues on their own in real-world conditions. In addition, professionals will want to help patients understand how some cues can be avoided altogether by changes in lifestyle and how to minimize exposure to other threatening cues when they occur.

Cue exposure, on the other hand, is an exposure technique designed to have patients confront the cue without responding with nonadherent behavior patterns, in order to weaken the conditioned response in the presence of the conditioned stimulus. Effective cue exposure can be done in vivo or imaginally. The goal is to expose a client to the relapse cue or trigger to the point of discomfort and to make the client stay with the discomfort for a period of time until it diminishes eventually to zero discomfort. The discomfort may be seen as an urge to escape or avoid, as anxiety, as an urge to return to nonadherent behavior, or simply as an increase in positive expectancies or fantasies about the nonadherent behavior. Another goal of cue exposure is response prevention, which simply means that professionals prevent the patient from responding with nonadherent behavior during exposure to the conditioned cue. By exposing the patient to the cue and preventing nonadherent behavior from occurring in the presence of that cue, the professional ensures that the cue begins to lose its power over time to elicit a nonadherent response in the patient.

At the same time, patients are encouraged to use new skills to cope with encountering relapse cues whenever possible. Skills are rehearsed under controlled clinical conditions at first, and then through homework assignments, these skills become generalized to nonclinical situations. A good rule of thumb for professionals is to use cue exposure techniques instead of stimulus control whenever cue exposure is safe for the patient and whenever there is a reasonable likelihood that the patient will be exposed to that cue after treatment. If the likelihood of exposure to the cue is remote, the cue can be completely avoided, and if the cue can be life threatening, then professionals may wish to use stimulus control techniques instead of exposure.

Using the Relapse Contract

If the patient slips, make sure to provide for continued contact and to encourage a face-to-face meeting as soon as possible to revise the relapse prevention plan in order to shorten the duration of the lapse/relapse and to mitigate its severity. At this face-to-face meeting, use the relapse contract to encourage a return to adherence. First, negotiate with the patient to end the lapse/relapse; if the patient is not prepared at that instant to return to adherence, then gain an agreement on when she or he is willing to end the lapse/relapse. Be concrete: Have the patient set a date and even an hour for the lapse/relapse to end. In the same way, negotiate with the patient on limiting the amount and type of nonadherent behavior that is being engaged upon during the lapse/relapse period. Again, gain specific commitments for limits on the behavior from the patient. Using these strategies allows for managing the duration and severity of the lapse/relapse, which in turn makes a return to adherence easier for the patient. After the lapse or relapse ends, conduct an analysis of the event to determine how to strengthen the relapse prevention plan. Remind the patient that the event allows an opportunity to grow and to improve the change plan. Revise the plan to include what has been learned. Finally, teach new skills to improve the patient's ability to cope with that situation if encountered again in the future.

Programmed Relapse

Under some circumstances, if a patient intends to relapse and there is no way to stop that behavior, then you may want to clinically manage how the relapse occurs. If the patient absolutely intends to relapse, then the experience could be educational if it were conducted in such a way as to challenge the positive expectancies about nonadherence that the patient may have. Relapse prevention provides for a strategy to do so, called a "programmed relapse."

A programmed relapse is meant to be conducted under clinical conditions, so it can be observed and reflected upon therapeutically. Programmed relapses have been used effectively with some types of addictive behaviors to control the severity and duration of the event.

To conduct a programmed relapse, first gain a commitment from the patient not to engage in nonadherence until he or she is in your presence (e.g., at the next session). At that session, before the lapse, ask the patient to describe all his or her expectancies for a return to the old nonadherent behavior, and document those for later use. Then, allow the patient to engage in the nonadherent behavior. Ask the patient to describe his or her beliefs and thoughts about the lapse throughout the process. Finally, compare the expectancies the patient had just prior to the experience with the actual experience of the nonadherent behavior as it occurred. In addition, discuss any goal violation effects that the patient may be experiencing after the lapse.

The goal is to use a programmed relapse to challenge the positive expectancies of the lapse by comparing them with the reality of the experience immediately after it has occurred. Many patients will reveal during such an experience that the reality of the lapse is not nearly as rewarding as they had anticipated before the lapse. When confronted with discrepancies between expectancies and reality, many patients choose to return to adherence after such a programmed relapse session. Remember that programmed relapse is meant to be an intervention of last choice, to be used when it is clear that the patient fully intends to relapse and that other interventions are not working to stop the relapse.

Step 4: Increasing Self-efficacy to Respond Effectively

Imagery can be used to prepare a client for facing a high-risk situation during or after treatment. Guided imagery can be used to model effective coping on how to respond appropriately in high-risk relapse situations and also by instilling confidence in the patient's ability to succeed under those conditions. Professionals use imagery to describe a situation in which the patient has used a skillful plan of action that leads to successful outcomes to enhance the patient's self-efficacy under those simulated conditions. Patients also learn how to use imagery to help themselves in real-world conditions.

Rehearsal of skills also enhances self-efficacy in maintaining treatment successes over time. Rehearsal of skills begins in session. Eventually, homework is assigned to practice the skills across different situations in order to generalize the use of those skills. As the patient develops competence and confidence in the use of the skills, self-efficacy will be enhanced. Professionals also can aid in promoting self-efficacy by reinforcing patient successes and progress during treatment.

Step 5: Restoring Lifestyle Balance

Part of circumventing relapse vulnerabilities and high-risk situations involves lifestyle changes, including restoring balance in the life of the patient (Marlatt, 1985b). Assess whether patients are balancing their time in healthy ways to reduce undue stress. Make sure the patient has balance between physical, spiritual, emotional, and intellectual pursuits during and after treatment and provide for a plan that balances work with play. Evaluate over time how well the client's activities remain balanced and whether the relapse prevention plans are effective at maintaining such a balance.

Related to restoring balance, teach patients skills for seeking substitute indulgences that avoid the risks of nonadherent behavior. Substitute indulgences are pleasurable activities meant to alleviate temptations for nonadherence when patients have desires to indulge in something pleasurable. Substitute indulgences are healthy alternatives to nonadherent behavior. When adherence is perceived as difficult or without pleasure by patients, it is important to build into the treatment substitute indulgences as alternative ways to feel good.

Alternative activities also are an important way to restore lifestyle balance and to structure a patient's time. Encourage patients to structure their free time with activities that will preclude nonadherent behavior. Alternative activities may have educational, vocational, recreational, social, or spiritual goals (to name but a few options); the type of activity is less important than the function, which is to fill patients' time with interesting and challenging activities that at the same time make nonadherent behavior difficult.

Summary

Relapse prevention improves patient outcomes after treatment. It improves adherence as a stand-alone intervention or as an adjunct with other types of interventions. Key elements of relapse prevention include assessment to determine individualized vulnerabilities and high-risk situations for relapse among patients, skills assessment and training in skills that may be absent but necessary to maintain behavior change over the long term, challenging those beliefs that interfere with adherence (such as expectancies), and using behavioral rehearsal and homework designed to generalize new skills in vivo and enhance self-efficacy in successfully coping with high-risk situations. The therapy not only can prevent relapse from occurring but also can minimize the severity and duration of a relapse when it does occur. To illustrate one way to use relapse prevention to promote treatment adherence, a brief case study is given.

Case Study

Jaine is a 35-year-old, moderately obese woman who was told by her physician that she needed to lose 50 pounds of weight and exercise regularly. She has tried crash dieting before, with short-term gains, but these diets historically ended in a relapse. Jaine had been physically active earlier in her life but has not exercised systematically for several years and has never attempted to reduce weight by the use of a combination of diet and exercise previously. She is motivated and committed to make the changes suggested by her physician but is somewhat discouraged by her history of previous relapses after diets.

She has joined a fitness center, which includes a personal trainer to supervise her exercise program and a nutritionist who is helping Jaine develop a healthy and nutritious diet to reduce caloric intake. It is important to incorporate relapse prevention strategies related to exercise and diet into Jaine's program to improve her chances of success in reaching her weight reduction and exercise goals. The first step in developing a relapse prevention plan is to assess what situations make Jaine vulnerable to slipping from both her dieting and her exercise routines. Roadblocks that may prevent her from using the fitness center resources or from following the recommendations of her personal fitness expert and nutritionist are determined by means of self-monitoring of daily activities, thoughts, and emotions and by identifying how these may relate to food cravings or disinterest in adherence; assessing relapse histories, fantasies, and roadmaps; and assessing for a history of apparently irrelevant decisions made prior to past diet relapses. In addition, Jaine's past exercise history is assessed to understand why exercise was important to her earlier in her life and what led to its cessation later in life, in order to identify potential roadblocks to maintaining a new exercise program. Finally, after a thorough assessment of past relapse behavior, an assessment of Jaine's skills in maintaining her diet and exercise program is conducted.

When the assessment is completed, Jaine is oriented to the relapse model, to cognitive-behavioral therapy, and to particular strategies and techniques designed to help her maintain her treatment gains. Key terms of the model are defined, and the philosophy of the model is shared, including the belief that lapses and relapses, although not necessarily inevitable, are a common and normative part of the change process. Following orientation, her relapse prevention plan will be developed collaboratively, with attention to details about potential vulnerabilities and high-risk situations that Jaine has shared during the assessment. Among other things, she has linked past diet relapses to such things as upset feelings, family discord, eating at restaurants when tired, and having junk food in the house. She gave up exercising because of time constraints but feels she will be able to maintain such a program by structuring time into her morning schedule to go to the fitness center. The relapse prevention plan will include skills training for assertiveness with her family; alternative activities to structure her time at home; distress tolerance skills to aid with upset feelings; time management techniques to help her build a daily schedule that includes morning exercise; behavior modification to avoid purchasing junk food or keeping it around the house; and a plan developed just in case of emergencies, which includes reminder cards around her home, in her car, and at work that tell her step-by-step what to do, including calling professionals, when she has a desire to lapse on her diet and exercise program.

The plan will be rehearsed frequently, as will be the skills that have been taught to her (such as assertiveness, time management, etc.). Homework will be assigned to practice these skills outside of session. In addition, cue exposure and response prevention techniques will be used to target cues that trigger food cravings or the urge toward nonadherent behavior. Exposure will be conducted until those cues no longer elicit a response that places Jaine at risk. As relapse prevention therapy progresses for Jaine, the plan will be periodically reevaluated to determine if it is sufficiently meeting her needs to maintain her weight loss and fitness gains, with the goal to improve the plan if needed. The combination of interventions to improve her diet and exercise regimens to improve her fitness along with relapse prevention strategies to maintain progress over time should allow a motivated and committed Jaine to meet the weight reduction and fitness goals suggested by her physician.

Suggested Readings

Marlatt, G. A., & J. R. Gordon (Eds.). (1985). *Relapse prevention: Maintenance strategies in the treatment of addictive behaviors.* New York: Guilford Press.

Marlatt, G. A., & D. M. Donovan (Eds.). (2005). *Relapse prevention: Maintenance strategies in the treatment of addictive behaviors* (2nd ed.). New York: Guilford Press.

References

Allsop, S., Saunders, B., & Phillips, M. (2000). The process of relapse in severely dependent male problem drinkers. *Addictions, 95*(1), 95–106.

Belisle, M., Roskies, E., & Levesque, J-M. (1987). Improving adherence to physical activity. *Health Psychology, 6*(2), 159–172.

Blume, A. W., Anderson, B. K., Fader, J. S., & Marlatt, G. A. (2001). Harm reduction programs: Progress rather than perfection. In R. H. Coombs (Ed.), *Addiction recovery tools: A practical handbook* (pp. 367–382). Thousand Oaks, CA: Sage.

Brown, S. A. (1985). Reinforcement expectancies and alcoholism treatment outcome after a one-year follow-up. *Journal of Studies on Alcohol, 46*(4), 304–308.

Carroll, K. M. (1996). Relapse prevention as a psychosocial treatment: A review of controlled trials. *Experimental and Clinical Psychopharmacology, 4*(1), 46–54.

Chaney, E. F., O'Leary, M. R., & Marlatt, G. A. (1978). Skills training with alcoholics. *Journal of Clinical and Consulting Psychology, 46*(5), 1092–1104.

Connors, G. J., Maisto, S. A., & Zywiak, W. H. (1996). Understanding relapse in the broader context of post-treatment functioning. *Addictions, 91*(Suppl.), S173–S189.

Greenfield, S. F., Hufford, M. R., Vagge, L. M., Muenz, L. R., Costello, M. E., & Weiss, R. D. (2000). The relationship of self-efficacy expectancies to relapse among alcohol dependent men and women: A prospective study. *Journal of Studies on Alcohol, 61*(2), 345–351.

Ho, A. P., Tsuang, J. W., Liberman, R. P., Wang, R., Wilkins, J. N., Eckman, T. A., et al. (1999). Achieving effective treatment of patients with chronic psychotic illness and comorbid substance dependence. *American Journal of Psychiatry, 156*(11), 1765–1770.

Irvin, J. E., Bowers, C. A., Dunn, M. E., & Wang, M. C. (1999). Efficacy of relapse prevention: A meta-analytic review. *Journal of Consulting and Clinical Psychology, 67*(4), 563–570.

Katon, W., Rutter, C., Ludman, E. J., Von Korff, M., Lin, E., Simon, G., et al. (2001). A randomized control trial of relapse prevention of depression in primary care. *Archives of General Psychiatry, 58*(3), 241–247.

Larimer, M. E., Palmer, R. S., & Marlatt, G. A. (1999). Relapse prevention: An overview of Marlatt's cognitive-behavioral model. *Alcohol Health and Research World, 23*(2), 151–160.

Mackay, P. W., & Marlatt, G. A. (1990). Maintaining sobriety: Stopping is starting. *International Journal of the Addictions, 25*(9A–10A), 1257–1276.

Maisto, S. A., O'Farrell, T. J., McKay, J. R., Connors, G. J., & Pelcovits, M. (1988). Alcoholic and spouse concordance on attributions about relapse to drinking. *Journal of Substance Abuse Treatment, 5*(3), 179–181.

Marlatt, G. A. (1985a). Cognitive factors in the relapse process. In G. A. Marlatt & J. R. Gordon (Eds.), *Relapse prevention: Maintenance strategies in the treatment of addictive behaviors* (pp. 128–200). New York: Guilford Press.

Marlatt, G. A. (1985b). Lifestyle modification. In G. A. Marlatt & J. R. Gordon (Eds.), *Relapse prevention: Maintenance strategies in the treatment of addictive behaviors* (pp. 280–348). New York: Guilford Press.

Marlatt, G. A. (1985c). Relapse prevention: Theoretical rationale and overview of the model. In G. A. Marlatt & J. R. Gordon (Eds.), *Relapse prevention: Maintenance strategies in the treatment of addictive behaviors* (pp. 3–70). New York: Guilford Press.

Marlatt, G. A. (1985d). Situational determinants of relapse and skills-training interventions. In G. A. Marlatt & J. R. Gordon (Eds.), *Relapse prevention: Maintenance strategies in the treatment of addictive behaviors* (pp. 71–127). New York: Guilford Press.

Marlatt, G. A. (1996). Taxonomy of high-risk situations for alcohol relapse: Evolution and development of a cognitive-behavioral model. *Addictions, 91*(Suppl.), S37–S49.

Marlatt, G. A., & Barrett, K. (1994). Relapse prevention. In M. Galanter & H. D. Kleber (Eds.), *The textbook of substance abuse treatment* (pp. 285–299). Washington, DC: American Psychiatric Press.

Marlatt, G. A., & Gordon, J. R. (1980). Determinants of relapse: Implications for the maintenance of behavior change. In P. O. Davidson & S. M. Davidson (Eds.), *Behavioral medicine: Changing health lifestyles* (pp. 410–445). New York: Brunner/Mazel.

Miller, K. J., McCrady, B. S., Abrams, D. B., & Labouvie, E. W. (1994). Taking an individualized approach to the assessment of self-efficacy and the prediction of alcoholic relapse. *Journal of Psychopathology and Behavioral Assessment, 16*(2), 111–120.

Miller, W. R., & Rollnick, S. (2002). *Motivational interviewing* (2nd ed.). New York: Guilford Press.

Monti, P. M., Gulliver, S. B., & Myers, M. G. (1994). Social skills training for alcoholics: Assessment and treatment. *Alcohol and Alcoholism, 29*(6), 627–637.

Perri, M. G., Nezu, A. M., McKelvey, W. F., Shermer, R. L., Renjilian, D. A., & Viegener, B. J. (2001). Relapse prevention training and problem-solving therapy in the long-term management of obesity. *Journal of Consulting and Clinical Psychology, 69*(4), 722–726.

Schonfeld, L., Rohrer, G. E., Dupree, L. W., & Thomas, M. (1989). Antecedents of relapse and recent substance use. *Community Mental Health Journal, 25*(3), 245–249.

Simmons, M. W., & Owen, N. (1992). Perspectives on the management of Type II diabetes. *Australian Psychologist, 27*(2), 99–102.

Smith, J. W., & Frawley, P. J. (1993). Treatment outcome of 600 chemically dependent patients treated in a multimodal inpatient program including aversion therapy and pentothal interviews. *Journal of Substance Abuse Treatment, 10,* 359–369.

Strowig, A. B. (2000). Relapse determinants reported by men treated for alcohol addiction: The prominence of depressed mood. *Journal of Substance Abuse Treatment, 19,* 469–474.

Vuchinich, R. E., & Tucker, J. A. (1996). Alcoholic relapse, life events, and behavioral theories of choice: A prospective analysis. *Experimental and Clinical Psychopharmacology, 4,* 19–28.

Walton, M. A., Blow, F. C., & Booth, B. M. (2000). A comparison of substance abuse patients' and counselors' perceptions of relapse risk: Relationship to actual relapse. *Journal of Substance Abuse Treatment, 19,* 161–169.

Witkiewitz, K., & Marlatt, G. A. (2004). Relapse prevention for alcohol and drug problems: That was Zen, this is Tao. *American Psychologist, 59*(4), 224–235.

Witkiewitz, K., Marlatt, G. A., & Walker, D. D. (2005). Mindfulness-based relapse prevention for alcohol and drug problems: The meditative tortoise wins the race. *Journal of Cognitive Psychotherapy, 19*(3), 211–228.

11

Promoting Adherence Through Collaborative Teams (PACT)

A Practice Model

Brian Giddens

Lana Sue I. Kaʻopua

Case Study: A Set-up for Failure

Marie is a 47-year-old African American widow with two teenage sons and one adult daughter. She works as a teller in a metropolitan bank. On detecting a breast lump, she goes immediately to a primary care physician. As she has not sought care for 6 years, the physician does a complete workup, which includes a clinical breast examination. A suspicious lump is confirmed and non-insulin-dependent diabetes mellitus is diagnosed. Following a diagnostic mammogram, referrals are made to an oncologist and an endocrinologist, each of whom practices at different medical facilities. Motivated by a family history of breast cancer and diabetes, Marie follows through with both referrals. The oncologist diagnoses Marie with breast cancer Stage I and recommends a lumpectomy plus radiation; tamoxifen is prescribed. The endocrinologist prescribes metformin and refers Marie to a lifestyle modification course. All treatment recommendations are initiated but not sustained. Notably, Marie misses several radiation appointments and almost all sessions of the lifestyle course. When asked about her nonadherence, she explains, "It's too much—there aren't enough hours in the day." Loss of energy, appetite, sleep, and pleasure are disclosed to the oncologist, who subsequently refers Marie to a mental health care center for evaluation and treatment of depression. Unfortunately, the sliding fee scale for counseling is based on income and does not consider patient expenses. Because she does not qualify for reduced rates and is worried about the cost of insurance co-payments already incurred, Marie declines further services even though she found the initial session helpful.

What's Wrong With This Picture?

Marie is initially motivated to adhere to treatment recommendations and has more health care resources than many patients. However, systems barriers hinder optimal use of available resources and contribute to nonadherent behavior. Overall service delivery is fragmented even though individual professionals are providing adequate care within their respective domain of expertise. Attention to the patient's overall plan of care is lacking the "three C's" crucial to enhancing adherence:

- Coordination of care
- Collaboration between health care providers and across service systems
- Communication to address the patient's evolving needs in a timely way

Systems approaches that incorporate these elements are warranted to improve treatment outcomes, especially among patients like Marie who have several life-threatening diagnoses, complex regimens, multiple providers associated with different health care systems, and a general lack of support for adhering to treatments (Gill, 2004; Institute of Medicine [IOM], 2001; Ko & Chaundhry, 2002; Koopman & May, 2004; Pogach et al., 2004; Wolfe, 1997). Systems approaches are aimed at modifying the ways in which services are delivered and systems of care interface and potentially prevent the development of medical conditions that require more costly acute care (Gill, 2004; IOM, 2001).

Premised on the value of care continuity, systems approaches that rely on collaboration, coordination, and communication between providers and across systems (Becker & Maiman, 1980; Ko & Chaundhry, 2002; Koopman & May, 2004) might be likened to the metaphorical helping network characterized in the adage "it takes a village."

This chapter describes a practice model for enhancing adherence, promoting adherence through collaborative teams (PACT), which translates the three Cs into relevant considerations.

The PACT practice model expands the conventional construct of the health care team to include providers within and across systems of care, as well as patients and their significant others. The theoretical and empirical literature on adherence, continuity of care, and care coordination that informed the development of the PACT practice model is briefly reviewed.

Review of Theoretical and Empirical Literature

Adherence

Patient adherence refers to the process of steady devotion to treatment recommendations, including those related to medication, diet, exercise, and medical visits (Ka`opua & Giddens, 2004; Ka`opua & Mueller, 2004). Although crucial to attaining therapeutic outcomes, adherence is often difficult to manage, even when patients intend to adhere (Becker & Maiman, 1975; DiMatteo & DiNicola, 1982; Ka`opua &

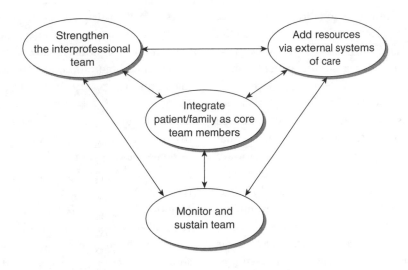

Figure 11.1   Promoting Adherence Through Collaborative Teams (PACT)

Mueller, 2004; Shumaker, 1990; Turk, Salovey, & Litt, 1986). Thus, patient adherence remains a focus for providers across professions and disciplines (Haynes, McKibbon, & Kanani, 1996; Linsk & Bonk, 2000; Wolfe, 1997), across specialty practice areas (Ko & Chaundhry, 2002; Koopman & May, 2004; Lester, Tritter, & Sorohan, 2004), and more recently, across systems of care (Gill, 2004; Nasmith et al., 2004).

Historically, research has focused on prediction of adherence, and the empirical literature falls into three broad categories of variables: disease characteristics, regimen-related factors, and patient characteristics (Ka`opua & Mueller, 2004; Linsk & Bonk, 2000). Most research indicates that adherence is more difficult to sustain when disease conditions are of a chronic nature, when distressing symptoms and/or treatment side effects are experienced, and when there are complex and/or multiple directives. Sustained follow-through is especially problematic when patients have a chronic condition because regimens tend to be open-ended and require adherence for an indefinite period of time. Emerging research indicates that patient characteristics such as sense of self-efficacy, knowledge of the disease and its treatments, treatment readiness, and social support are better predictors of adherence than are demographic characteristics like socioeconomic status, race or ethnicity, and gender, the last of which may be better understood as proxies for availability and access to care, cultural beliefs and practices, and health literacy. In supporting adherence, health care providers face the challenge of any combination of these disease-, regimen-, or patient-related factors. Thus, the challenge of assisting patients to adhere is a daunting one and potentially overwhelming for individual providers to manage on their own.

Systems and team approaches for enhancing adherence are indicated to augment the focus on individual behavioral change. Research suggests the efficacy of systems strategies, including assignment of specific roles and responsibilities for activities directed at treatment adherence, arranging for continuity of provider and other staff, a team approach to continuous monitoring of patient adherence, training to increase the development of an "active influence orientation" in each member of the health care team, and tailoring interventions to address adherence barriers (Becker, 1990; Becker & Maiman, 1980).

DiMatteo and DiNicola's (1982) social psychological model for achieving patient adherence suggests "why" systems approaches are relevant. Factors associated with adherence intent are distinguished from those associated with behavior. Intervention strategies that increase knowledge and positive attitudes toward treatment may influence intent but in some cases may be insufficient to effect behavioral change. Structural barriers in the social environment, including those related to access, availability, and acceptability of health services, may disable adherence intent. By extension, interventions that address these barriers through the provision of tangible, emotional, and informational support are facilitative of adherence behavior.

Interventions addressing structural barriers in service delivery systems and in the patient's social environment are also recognized as important in the ADHERE practice heuristic (Ka`opua & Giddens, 2004). Developed through a process of literature review and expert consensus on exemplary practices and programs (National Association of Social Workers, 2003), the heuristic considers patients with multiple chronic diagnoses (e.g., HIV, substance abuse, depression) and promotes a holistic understanding of the full range of patient needs (e.g., treatment, psychosocial, financial, housing) to sustain treatment adherence. Coordination and collaboration in developing and implementing a plan of care are recommended with involvement that optimally includes providers in health care systems and community-based treatment programs, as well as patients and their significant others.

Continuity of Care

According to the IOM (2001), health care systems in the United States are currently organized in a decentralized and fragmented way that inhibits patients' access to continuity of care or continuous healing relationships. Care continuity is especially inadequate in responding to the health needs of the growing number of those with chronic conditions, many of whom are also living with comorbid conditions. Collaborative management of disease by all relevant providers, including those involved in disease management, health education, and monitoring of health status, is identified as a systems strategy for generally bridging the chasm of quality care (IOM, 2001) and for more specifically influencing adherence (Gill, 2004; Gill & Mainous, 1998; Koopman, Mainous, Baker, Gill, & Gilbert, 2003; Mainous et al., 2004; Nasmith et al., 2004).

Although emerging research suggests that adherence is associated with continuity of care, current research has yet to explain the mechanism by which continuity of care influences adherence and other health outcomes (Gill, 2004). However, there is some indication that greater continuity may influence trust in the therapeutic relationship, which may be particularly critical to making important decisions such as those related to treatment initiation (Mainous et al., 2004). Continuity of care is associated with higher rates of adherence to prescriptions (Charney et al., 1967), routine cancer screening and improved disease control (Ko & Chaundhry, 2002; Mainous et al., 2004), management of chronic conditions like diabetes mellitus (Koopman et al., 2003; Mensing et al., 2001; Nasmith et al., 2004; Pogach et al., 2004), and management of mental health conditions, such as depression (Lester et al., 2004; Liu et al., 2003; Reich, Jaramillo, Kaplan, Arciniega, & Kolbasovsky, 2003).

Care Coordination

Coordination is regarded as essential to achieving continuity of care in the current landscape of decentralized and fragmented health care services (IOM, 2001). Coordination by care management teams may be a promising means to ensure optimal care for patients with multiple needs such as those diagnosed with chronic conditions (Nasmith et al., 2004; Wagner, 1996).

In the Cote-des-Neiges Diabetes Pilot Program, Nasmith et al. (2004) tested a service delivery model using an interprofessional team approach to coordination. Nurse liaisons were designated to coordinate care and facilitate communication between patients and physicians. Routine communication on adherence was accomplished through a variety of media (e.g., e-mail, fax, telephone contact, office visits to physicians). The stages of change model (Prochaska & DiClemente, 1982) undergirded patient education aimed at therapeutic behavioral change and assessment of patient adherence to treatment recommendations. As appropriate, patients were referred to other professionals and community resources (e.g., physical activity groups, patient support groups) that promoted adherence to treatment recommendations. Results suggest that coordinated care and integrated service delivery improve patient adherence to self-care behaviors (i.e., foot care and follow-through with nutritional consultation). Physicians and patients expressed satisfaction with the coordinated interprofessional team approach and improved access to community resources.

Even when such programs of care management are not in place, other research suggests that modest systems interventions such as planned case conferences and shared patient loads may improve coordination and quality of care. Such structural changes provide opportunities for interprofessional communication and collaboration (Parkerton, Smith, & Straley, 2004) and, by extension, allow for discussion of ways to improve monitoring, tailor treatments, and integrate supportive services that ultimately offer the prospect of sustaining patient's devotion to treatment recommendations.

Moving Toward a Collaborative Approach to Care

In applying the PACT practice model in a medical context, the first system to consider is that of the medical team. Many terms have been used to describe teams of health care professionals, including multidisciplinary, interdisciplinary, and most recently, interprofessional. The term interprofessional recognizes there is a relationship between team members and broadens the team to include a variety of professions within and external to a given health care system.

Which professions might care teams include? When referencing teams in a health care setting, a broader definition than what traditionally might be seen as a care team is presented. Certainly the physician, nurse, social worker, pharmacist, nutritionist, and rehabilitation professionals (occupational, physical, and speech therapists) constitute the traditional team. But in terms of enhancing an individual's ability to adhere to a plan it is imperative that the individual's larger circle of providers become engaged with the conventional care team. This would include, to varying degrees, the involvement of other systems of care. In the case of Marie, this might include the health educator, the mental health counselor, and a professional affiliated with the local American Diabetes Association. These professionals may have, or should be developing, a relationship with the patient that can serve to reinforce and monitor factors that affect adherence. If these providers do not know the plan, how can they help their patient adhere?

Finally, the team is not complete unless the patient and his or her significant "family" system are included. Family can include the traditional family structure of a spouse, parents, siblings, and children, or it can be an individual's chosen family, encompassing partners and/or friends. As will be illustrated, adherence starts and ends with the patient, and no plan is complete without the active participation of the individual being treated. The PACT practice model provides pertinent questions to ask of the team and the setting and demonstrates some tangible approaches to improving the interprofessional nature of health care delivery to allow for better patient outcomes.

Stage 1: Using an Interprofessional Team Perspective to Assess Adherence Barriers

The first step in reviewing the interprofessional capacity of the setting and the team is to ask some very basic questions:

- Who is on the team?
- Who is available to help?

In a solo practice, the immediate "team" may be limited to a physician and a nurse. What about the larger team? Are there community programs to draw from? For example, in the case of Marie, have relationships been developed with the American Cancer Society, an organization that might have services and programs to assist with transportation and emotional support? Is there a contact with the local community mental health center to find out if the patient has a case manager? Even in the smallest practice, teams can be developed to include external providers when mutual gains are determined.

- Are team members aware of each other's roles?

On any team, it is essential to know what team members can expect from one another. For example, does the physician really know what the social worker can do? Do team members understand the differences in practice between an occupational therapist and a physical therapist? There are many assumptions made in health care as to the roles and tasks of different disciplines. These assumptions, together with gaps in communication, can cause errors and inefficient follow-up. For example, a physician may assume that the social worker in the hospital setting screens all patients for financial needs. The physician may assess a patient, hear from the patient that he or she is underinsured, and assume that the patient's financial needs will be met by the social worker. The social worker may work in a busy medical service where screening of all patients is not possible and without a referral, may not even get involved. If the social worker did become involved, completing a financial aid application may not be within the scope of work. The result? The patient remains underinsured, the hospital adds another bill to "bad debt," the patient does not have funds to complete treatment, and as with the case of Marie, the significant initial efforts of the patient and the providers are wasted.

Several strategies have been implemented in health care institutions to improve interprofessional understanding of roles and tasks. In some settings, new resident orientations are beginning to include an interprofessional panel of providers to inform residents as to how best to use the skills of other professionals. Health science curricula are starting to provide training on how to work in a team and how to maximize one's service by incorporating the use of other professionals. In inpatient settings, interdisciplinary rounds are occurring with increasing frequency, fueled in part by the Joint Commission on Accreditation of Health Care Organizations' drive to increase interdisciplinary communication and the IOM's report detailing the importance of communication in preventing errors (IOM, 2000). Formalized efforts certainly help increase awareness and build team skills; even informal events, such as a clinic inviting chemical dependency counselors to a lunch for an information exchange, can be beneficial.

Patient needs optimally drive "who" is included on the health care team. For example, a practice that has a high incidence of publicly insured patients would benefit from having contacts within the state community services office so that when financial questions arise, clinic staff can obtain needed information. An oncology practice should be aware of what is offered by community nonprofit organizations serving persons with cancer; such organizations provide support for people with cancer and may offer respite for caregivers. An interprofessional approach requires having a working relationship with representatives from key systems of care and extends beyond making referrals.

Once the core team and potential external team members have been identified, and everyone is aware of who is available for what purpose, the team can concentrate on ensuring that the right questions are being asked. Here is a sample list of questions for a new patient that would be helpful in assessing for adherence barriers:

- Does the patient have funds for medications and other care needs?
- What is the patient's literacy level? Because nearly 50% of all adults may have problems understanding basic health information, does the patient fully understand the prescriptions, directives, treatment consents, and patient education materials? (Center for Health Care Strategies, 2003)
- Does the patient have a need for an interpreter?
- What is the patient's cultural perspective relating to health care?
- What has been the patient's prior experience with the health care system? Was it positive or negative?
- Who would the patient call if he or she were in need of assistance? The way this question is phrased will provide the interviewer with more tangible information about potential caregivers (i.e., team members) than asking the traditional question of "who" the family members are. With the latter question, there may be file information on who is legally related to the patient, but the significance of the contact to the patient would be unknown. Differentiating legal contacts from supportive and caregiving contacts is important.
- Does the patient work with any community programs or other medical providers? If the answer is affirmative, potential team members and systems of care are identified.

Although these questions are important examples of ways to understand up front any adherence barriers, the focus of this chapter is how to use a collaborative team approach in helping patients adhere to treatment. Thus, a review of this list can further clarify tasks and roles by determining who on the team is responsible for obtaining the information. A secondary gain from working collaboratively is that not only can a team introduce a variety of skills and talents into the mix, but the work of assessing and monitoring a patient can also be shared. For example, a medical center may have their admitting department ask about coverage for inpatient care, but they may not ask if the patient has medication insurance. A crisis erupts when the patient is educated the morning of discharge about medications. The team finds out that while the patient is covered for the hospital stay, the patient has no coverage for outpatient meds. The pharmacist is called because it relates to a medication issue, the social worker is contacted because the person is uninsured, the nurse is frustrated because the delay was not planned, and the physician is being paged (most likely by all parties) to confirm that all the medications are truly needed. Again, staff time is wasted, the patient feels the repercussions of the crisis, and adherence may be affected.

If the team identifies questions that are pertinent for identifying an adherence barrier, the team needs to ensure that it is one team member's responsibility to get the question answered and to communicate the information for the rest of the team to use as needed. Which member of the team would be likely to ask each of the preceding questions?

Stage 2: Integrating External Systems Into the Planning

There are many benefits in expanding an individual's care team, including the following:

- There is a coordinated approach to patient care.
- Everyone "speaks" the same language and understands the terminology of health care systems.
- Redundancy is decreased.

- Messages to the patient are consistent.
- Everyone is clear about the goals
- More input allows for more ideas on how best to reach the patient.

At the same time, there are inherent difficulties in adding more providers or other systems of care to the team:

- It takes time to identify who needs to be at the table.
- Someone has to assume responsibility for coordinating the providers.
- Disagreement might occur as to what the priority goals are for the patient (i.e., the substance abuse counselor may claim that the patient needs to admit he or she has an alcohol problem before any behavioral intervention might be appropriate; the nutritionist might want to wait on a gastric bypass surgery until the patient has been able to prove he or she understands how to eat healthier).
- There may be differences in values and philosophy between professional cultures.
- Disagreement can occur as to who should be the lead contact, provider, or organization.

Let us look at some of these barriers and review some practical ways to decrease their impact.

- Who has the time to get more providers involved?

Time is a valuable commodity for health care providers. But increased up-front time can decrease time spent farther down the treatment continuum and can lead to better patient outcomes and more efficient care (which are not opposing concepts). Planning for collaboration is key. As mentioned in Stage 1, just knowing who the team members are and what to expect of the team is a major step. Adding a coordinating responsibility to determine who the external providers might be, how involved they are in the

client's life, and what information they may have that might be beneficial for treatment planning could be done through assigning this task to an existing team member. Protocols could be developed to automatically obtain consent for releasing or obtaining information when certain provider types are identified, such as when a mentally ill patient is working with a mental health case manager. For some settings, decision tree diagrams can be created that cue a provider to make referrals based on the responses to the assessment questions. Some versions of electronic medical record systems can be configured to automatically notify a provider of a referral.

Deciding as to who else to bring to the table should be a team decision, based on the individual assessments of each team member. Gathering the team together for a "huddle" can take a minimum of time, if the time is organized and focused. Each professional should identify in advance what needs to be communicated. Team members who are new to the group should be prepped on the purpose of the team meeting so that they can come prepared. Scripted questions (e.g., Did the patient attend scheduled appointments this week? What barriers were identified in the patient's assessment? Who is responsible for following up on the identified barriers? What has been communicated to the patient?) may be used to avoid going off on tangents, and a time-keeper can be identified to prevent a 15-minute huddle from expanding to a 45-minute teaching round. Most settings will use the core team to identify key issues, and the extent to which external providers are brought in will be determined by the relationship of the provider to the patient, the degree to which the external provider could have an effect on the patient's adherence, and the mutual gain that can be achieved by combining treatment goals.

- When the "team" is involved, who coordinates the team?

The coordinator of a team is determined by the setting and the patient needs. A coordinator's responsibilities could include monitoring the patient's progress, communicating treatment plan changes or patient situational changes to the rest of the team, and in general ensuring a smooth flow of information while trying to avoid redundancy. Some larger hospitals have a coordinator position in place, but in settings without such a designated coordinator, the priority needs of the patient should determine the coordinator. If the medical care is fairly routine, but the patient's life is dysfunctional, perhaps the social worker should be the coordinator, with key responsibility for calling the team together when necessary and providing updates when the plan changes. If the patient requires ongoing blood pressure and glucose monitoring, perhaps the nurse can coordinate the team. If the coordinator is chosen based on patient needs, instead of the role existing within one team member's responsibilities, team members need to be aware of how the coordinator is selected, and they must all have the skills to coordinate (i.e., the ability to collaborate; the capacity for clear, strong communication; understanding of the value of all disciplines).

If multiple systems of care are involved, a decision will need to be made as to which institution should take the lead. Again, this should be determined by the patient's situation. Where will the patient spend most of his or her time? Which facility is most convenient and comfortable for the patient? What medical or psychosocial needs are most significant, and which organization, or system, can best manage most of those needs? Which system is best equipped with the resources needed to serve as the lead organization?

- What happens when there is disagreement as to the priority goals for the patient?

Just as with any workgroup, conflicts will occur in an interprofessional team and between systems of care. In the health care professions, there are also hierarchies, especially in traditional settings (i.e., the physician leads, everyone else follows). To truly adopt the interprofessional approach, team members need to listen and respect the contributions of all members. Physicians no longer have the time to be expected to know all the answers, and in the current health care climate, ideas for enhancing adherence from all members of the team should be encouraged. Providers must recognize that unless the care team "buys" into the treatment plan, the members will not be supporting the plan with the patient; disagreements need to be discussed. Given the time constraints on health care workers, an "agree to disagree" or a "let's try it and see what happens" decision may be adopted by the team, signaling that while there are questions still to be answered, the group is moving forward as a team.

- What about managing the differences between the professional cultures?

There has been much written about cultural competency in terms of ethnicity, gender, sexual orientation, age, and other factors, but very little attention has been paid to understanding and managing the differences between professional cultures. Consider the stereotypes. The hard-charging doctor who thinks he or she is God. The social worker in Birkenstocks who needs to "process." These are just a few of the stereotypes that persist in health care. Although these are extreme examples, the fact is that each profession has their own way of identifying and working through a problem, and sometimes cultures clash. A nurse who becomes emotionally connected to a bone marrow transplant patient might not understand why the social worker keeps a more objective stance. A physician may be used to speaking up and being listened to, whereas a nurse or a physical therapist may be hesitant to "take the lead" with a suggestion, assuming incorrectly that the physician is in charge and must have already considered the idea.

Resolving cultural clashes with other disciplines can be managed in the same manner as one would approach working with someone from a different country. The team member should be listened to with an open mind, avoiding previous stereotypes. Common ground should be established, understanding that both providers are working toward helping the patient. Needs and wants should be stated clearly. Assumptions should be confirmed to ensure accurate understanding. The ability of one party to meet the stated needs of the other party needs to be clarified. The best communication occurs when members of a team are able to "be present" with those of another. Avoiding assumptions about professional cultures will lead to more collaboration and prevent misunderstandings.

- What else needs to be considered in working with an expanded group of providers?

Obtaining consent to release and receive information is key to working with providers external to a closed system. For some clinics or hospitals, there may be clearly identified programs where information may be shared frequently, such as between the state health department and a community hospital. The Health Insurance Portability and Accountability Act allows for sharing of information relating to continuity of care or financing of care without requiring an additional specific consent for each agency or institution that a provider may collaborate with in coordinating care (except in cases where matters of "heightened confidentiality" may apply—as with substance use, mental health, or sexually transmitted diseases—check state laws pertaining to specific consent requirements for these areas).

Even in cases where a specific consent may not be required (beyond the general consent for care used in clinics, nursing homes, and hospitals), it is crucial to discuss with the patient and the support team who the medical team will be working with and why the information will be shared. By role modeling collaboration for the patient, the provider conveys to the patient that care is truly being coordinated by a team rather than by a disparate collection of providers.

Stage 3: Engaging the Patient and the "Family"

Throughout the assessment and care process, the PACT practice model focuses on the patient and the support system. Historically, health care systems have tended to foster dependence and passivity on the part of the patient; however, with the "baby boomer" generation, patients are beginning to ask for more inclusion in the treatment decision-making process. Unfortunately, it is not the stereotypical baby boomer who peruses the Internet for medical information and has the confidence to ask questions of his or her provider who tends to be a concern, in terms of adherence. It is often the persons who are overwhelmed by systems of care, who do not understand the complexities of medical care and treatment, or who have conflicting demands within their own personal situation that prevent them from making their own health care a priority.

Engaging the patient and the patient's support system is not difficult, but it requires planning, making use of available patient contact, and follow-up. Here are some practical, common sense suggestions for enhancing patient involvement in care:

- Prepare the patient prior to the visit. When a visit is scheduled, the scheduler should inquire as to any special needs, such as interpretation or payment questions. Patient information should be sent explaining what will happen during the visit, the questions the patient should be prepared to answer, and a sample list of questions many patients often ask. Materials should be language appropriate and written at a basic reading level.
- Encourage the patient to bring in a friend or a family member. This conveys the importance of involving the support system even before the first visit.
- Review the assessment questions, as indicated earlier in this chapter, to ensure that barriers to adherence are discussed. Be

prepared to seek assistance from other team members when barriers are discovered.

- When a barrier exists, engage the patient and the "family" in problem solving: "You have mentioned that because of what happened to your family members with diabetes, you are very afraid of complications from this disease. Yet you have not chosen to see the nutritionist or followed through on incorporating exercise into your daily activities. What might be standing in your way in following through with these suggestions?"

In the PACT practice model, the patient is seen as the "expert" and encouraged to problem solve. This is a shift from the traditional health care model where the patient is captive to the problem solving of the medical team and is expected to passively follow directions.

- Be specific about any expectations of the patient and her or his family member. At the end of the visit, or at discharge, the treatment team should have a list of what they are to do, and the patient and the family also should have a list of their responsibilities, making it clear that the plan is a joint effort.

Stage 4: Monitoring and Sustaining the Team

A systems approach to adherence involves monitoring not only the patient's outcomes relating to improved adherence but also the team's success. As mentioned earlier in the chapter, a successful team is one that integrates the three Cs of collaboration, coordination, and communication. A cut in staffing to a medical service, a change in team members, or an increased number of demands placed on a team can upset the functioning of the team. Keeping the team productive requires monitoring the team process. Once every quarter, the team could add a half-hour onto their daily huddles to check

in with each other about what is working and what is not working on their team. Quality improvement surveys might include a question to staff about their satisfaction with team functioning and decision making. External systems can be queried annually to evaluate their satisfaction with collaborative relationships.

Much of ongoing monitoring involves active problem solving when an issue occurs that impedes care or team functioning. If a team member continually is unprepared to follow through on his or her assigned tasks, someone on the team needs to take action to correct the problem, either by directly confronting the individual or by working with the team member's supervisor. If a problem team member, or system, is not dealt with, this conveys to the team that the behavior is tolerated, and at that point, there is no motivation for the rest of the team to meet expectations.

Monitoring the team includes obtaining feedback from the primary team member—the patient. Although patient outcomes are a necessary measure of a team's success, the patients should also be asked if they felt that they were listened to, if the team provided a consistent message throughout the care process, and if the concerns or questions of the patient received follow-up.

In settings where the same team members continue to work together over time, effort must be made to sustain ongoing productivity within the team. Collaboration although useful can also be exhausting, and as with familial relationships, "breaks" are needed to keep a team's energy high. Some ideas for sustaining a team include asking team members to share success stories of patients who benefited from a team approach or situations in which extra time put in by the team ended up improving patient outcomes. Food is a classic motivator. A plate of homemade cookies is a cheap and easy way to enliven a tired, overworked team or to defuse tensions between members of different systems.

The use of humor is essential, especially given the demands of health care, though it must be balanced with other team needs. Although this chapter has not focused on the subject of group dynamics, a key issue for a team is to ensure a mix of personalities and skills. A strong team will encompass a variety of personalities. A team that has too many comedians would never get the work done, but a team that is composed of primarily serious, analytical types would most likely not be a team that anyone would want to join.

Some teams may need to establish norms as to what is expected of team members, allowing the team to revisit the norms on a regular basis to ensure that they are being followed. Revisiting the norms allows the team to remember what they believe in, what they value. The norms also are useful for orienting a new team member to what the expectations of team members are.

Marie Revisited: Implementing the PACT Practice Model

If the PACT primary model is implemented, Marie's situation would be managed differently. Let us reconsider this situation and see how working with PACT, and incorporating the three Cs of communication, collaboration, and coordination can lead to a better outcome for patients and providers.

Marie notices a lump in her breast. She goes immediately to her primary care physician, who she has not seen in 6 years. Her physician confirms the lump, and does further testing, diagnosing Marie with non-insulin-dependent diabetes. The physician also asks Marie about her mental state and after realizing that Marie is a single mom, with some clear signs of depression and the likelihood of two significant diagnoses, asks the social worker to help evaluate Marie's ability to adhere to care. The social worker asks some basic questions related to practical matters, such as how Marie might get to and from appointments while working full-time. Questions are also asked about Marie's past perceptions of health care, and Marie is given the opportunity

to talk about the largely negative and hopeless impressions she has of her mother's and husband's deaths from cancer and of her uncle's amputation due to diabetes. Financial issues are reviewed, and it is acknowledged that money for co-pays may be an issue for Marie. The social worker confers with the primary care provider, and it is determined that referrals to specialists will need to be made that allow for ease of access and that this will require some ongoing monitoring to help Marie along the way.

Although the primary physician usually refers to a colleague at a different medical center for oncology needs, the physician asks the nurse to check for the availability of an oncologist who has a practice in the same medical center as the primary physician. The primary physician knows that Marie is more likely to follow up with appointments if all her care is in one place, with one medical record. The primary physician knows it is also more likely that the endocrinologist and the oncologist, and their attendant staff, will be aware of each specialty treatment plan if they have access to the same medical record.

The primary clinic nurse makes sure that the physician's and social worker's documentation are sent to the oncology and diabetes clinics, highlighting the joint referrals and asking that staff in both clinics arrange appointments so that Marie's visits to the hospital are kept to a minimum. The nurse also notes the social worker's suggestion that ongoing monitoring may be needed, recommending social work intervention in the clinic and consultation with a pharmacist regarding patient assistance programs for medications. Last, the nurse e-mails the patient care coordinator and asks that the patient be sent information regarding government assistance for medical costs and hospital "charity care" programs.

The oncologist and the endocrinologist make their recommendations but bring in the social worker and the pharmacist to consult as part of their team. The endocrinologist, knowing that

Marie may have trouble returning for the health education appointment, makes sure that the nurse provides Marie with written materials and a video on diet and exercise. Although Marie is encouraged to make an appointment for a health education consultation, the endocrinologist also makes a note for the health educator to follow up with Marie, providing the nurse with Marie's work phone number. Because both the diabetes and the oncology social workers work out of the same department, they agree that one of them should be the primary social worker for Marie such that duplication and confusion are minimized.

The social worker reviews the primary clinic notes and realizing that transportation may be an issue, talks with Marie about a free shuttle service from a clinic close to her office to the Medical Center. The social worker frankly discusses with Marie about her ability to go to daily radiation treatments and back to work again by bus or shuttle. They agree that Marie will be provided with one charity taxi voucher each week that she can use on "really bad days."

Because Marie is seen as high-risk given her two fairly recent diagnoses, the primary care clinic nurse checks back in with her to see how she is doing. When the nurse hears that nothing has been done yet about Marie's depression, the nurse calls the social worker at the medical center. The social worker acknowledges that counseling is needed but expresses concern that Marie has so many appointments already and has no additional funds to pay for counseling. After some consultation with both their colleagues, a cancer support group is found that meets on weekends in Marie's neighborhood. In addition, an appointment is made with the primary care physician to consider prescribing antidepressants. Marie is also asked what she wants to do, given the limited options. She is willing to talk with her primary doctor about beginning antidepressants. She also expresses that she will seek support from her adult daughter, who she admits "has been trying to help, but I've been trying to be so strong and haven't let her."

This scenario could continue given the ongoing nature of Marie's conditions and the universe of possibilities that could be sought to enhance Marie's chances of adherence. The difference between the two scenarios is clear. Efforts to promote adherence are grounded in the "three C's" of the PACT practice model illustrated in Table 11.1.

Table 11.1   Application of the PACT Practice Model

Coordination

- Services are arranged with patient access as a priority.
- Gaps in care are anticipated and solutions are immediately offered.
- Handoffs are clean, with each team member clear as to his or her role and responsibilities.

Communication

- The patient is queried about potential barriers to following the treatment plan.
- The patient's perception of disease and health is investigated.
- Follow-ups and reminders are regarded as necessary and routinely used.
- Chart notes are read by the interprofessional team and recommendations receive follow-through.

Collaboration

- Patients are part of the problem-solving team.
- Team members attend to details. The team knows that missed details can make a significant difference in patient adherence.
- Each team member contributes ideas that are used when appropriate.

Summary

Adherence is a critical issue for providers and for health care systems for several reasons. Health care costs are escalating. Nonadherence costs in terms of provider time (usually multiple providers), missed appointments, and poor outcomes, resulting in a higher-cost level of care being required. Providers get frustrated by patients who do not follow treatment plans, and these patients are thus often "typed" as nonadherent. Once a patient is stereotyped as nonadherent, other providers may not assess the patient objectively, thus perpetuating the problem.

"Silos" of care, between disease entities, health care systems, and among ancillary community programs, segment care and serve as barriers to care continuity and coordination. For example, the health care system does not integrate mental health and substance use providers into the general health care arena in any consistent manner. Adherence can be significantly affected by these issues, but as resources for mental health treatment and chemical dependency treatment decrease, more patients are coming into the general health care arena for care, and providers are not prepared to manage these co-occurring concerns.

Although coordination of care is important, continuity of care is equally necessary. It is a common practice to "reinvent the wheel" every time a patient has an exacerbation of a chronic illness, rather than looking historically at what has worked and what systems of care have been or are already in place. Monitoring adherence success encompasses the concept of continuity of care by ensuring that outcomes are evaluated as successful only when the patient is able to maintain her or his adherence over time.

The degree of education, monitoring, and patient support that can aid in patient adherence can be challenging, if not impossible, for a single provider to manage. A larger team reduces the burden on any single provider and, moreover, increases the likelihood that diverse perspectives and ideas are shared.

Adherence is known to be challenging for patients as well as the providers who serve them. Follow-through can be difficult to maintain across the illness trajectory. Factors influencing adherence are complex and include the patient's health beliefs, behavioral intention, resource access, chronicity of illness, relationship with the provider, treatment side effects, and social and familial supports.

Because of these many challenges, finding ways to collaborate with the patient to enhance adherence is crucial to increasing the likelihood of successful health outcomes. The PACT practice model recognizes the variety of relationships in a patient's life and promotes using these connections to help develop and sustain the plan of care. At the same time, the shared responsibility of supporting adherence through systems approaches that include collaborative team efforts is emphasized.

References

Becker, M. H. (1990). Theoretical models of adherence and strategies for improving adherence. In S. A. Shumaker, E. Br. Schron, & J. K. Ockene (Eds.), *The handbook of health behavior change* (pp. 5–43). New York: Springer.

Becker, M. H., & Maiman, L. A. (1975). Sociobehavioral determinants of compliance with health and medical care recommendations. *Medical Care, 13,* 10–24.

Becker, M. H., & Maiman, L. A. (1980). Strategies for enhancing patient compliance. *Journal of Community Health, 6,* 113–135.

Center for Health Care Strategies. (2003). *Fact sheet: Impact of low health literacy skills on annual health care expenditures.* Lawrenceville, NJ: Author.

Charney, E., Bynum, R., Eldredge, D., Frank, D., MacWhinney, J. B., McNabb, N., et al. (1967). How well do patients take oral penicillin? A collaborative study in private practice. *Pediatrics, 40,* 188–195.

DiMatteo, M. R., & DiNicola, D. D. (1982). Achieving patient compliance. *The psychology of the medical practitioner's role.* New York: Pergamon Press.

Gill, J. M. (2004). The structure of primary care: Framing a big picture. *Family Medicine, 36,* 65–68.

Gill, J. M., & Mainous, A. G. (1998). The role of provider continuity in preventing hospitalizations. *Archives of Family Medicine, 7,* 352–357.

Haynes, R. B., McKibbon, K. A., & Kanani, R. (1996). Systematic review of randomized trials of interventions to assist patients to follow prescriptions for medications. *Lancet, 348,* 383–386.

Institute of Medicine. (2001). *Crossing the quality chasm: A new health system for the 21st century.* Washington, DC: National Academy of Sciences.

Ka`opua, L. S., & Giddens, B. (2004). ADHERE: A practice model for enhancing client follow-through with recommended treatments. *NASW Mental Health Section Connection, Spring,* 3–7.

Ka`opua, L. S., & Mueller, C. W. (2004). Treatment adherence among native Hawaiians living with HIV. *Social Work, 49,* 55–64.

Ko, C., & Chaundry, S. (2002). The need for a multidisciplinary approach to cancer care. *Journal of Surgical Research, 105,* 53–57.

Koopman, R. J., Mainous, A. G., Baker, R., Gill, J. M., Gilbert, G. E. (2003). Continuity of care and recognition of diabetes, hypertension, and hypercholesterolemia. *Archives of Internal Medicine, 163,* 1357–1361.

Koopman, R. J., & May, K.M. (2004). Specialist management and coordination of "out-of-domain care." *Family Medicine, 36,* 46–50.

Lester, H., Tritter, J. Q., & Sorohan, H. (2004). Managing crisis: The role of primary care for people with serious mental illness. *Family Medicine, 36,* 28–34.

Linsk, N. L., & Bonk, N. (2000). Adherence to treatment as social work challenges. In V. J. Lynch (Ed.), *HIV/AIDS at year 2000* (pp. 211–227). Boston: Allyn and Bacon.

Liu, C. F., Hedrick, S. C., Chaney, E. F., Heagerty, P., Felker, B., Hasenberg, N., et al. (2003). Cost-effectiveness of collaborative care for depression in primary care veteran population. *Psychiatric Services, 54,* 698–704.

Mainous, A. G., Kern, D., Hainer, B., Kneuper-Hall, R., Stephens, J., & Geesey, M. E. (2004). The relationship between continuity of care, trust, and stage of cancer at diagnosis. *Family Medicine, 36,* 35–39.

Nasmith, L., Cote, B., Cox, J., Inkell, D., Rubenstein, H., Jimenez, V., et al. (2004). The challenge of promoting integration: Conceptualization, implementation, and assessment of a pilot care delivery model for patients with Type 2 diabetes. *Family Medicine, 36,* 40–45.

National Association of Social Workers HIV/AIDS Spectrum: Mental Health Training and Education of Social Workers Project. (2003). *The role of social work in medication treatment adherence.* Washington, DC: Author.

Parkerton, P. H., Smith, D. G., & Straley, H. L. (2004). Primary care practice coordination versus physician continuity. *Family Medicine, 36,* 15–21.

Pogach, L., Charns, M. P., Wrobel, J. S., Robbins, J. M., Bonacker, K. M., Hass, L., et al. (2004). Impact of policies and performance measurement on development of organizational coordinating strategies for chronic care delivery. *American Journal of Managed Care, 10,* 171–180.

Prochaska, J. O., & DiClemente, C. C. (1982). Transtheoretical therapy: Toward a more integrative model of change. *Psychotherapy: Theory, Research, and Practice, 19,* 276–288.

Reich, L.H., Jaramillo, B.M., Kaplan, L.J., Arciniega, J., Kolbasovsky, A. D. (2003). Improving continuity of care: Success of a behavioral health program. *Journal of Healthcare Quarterly, 25,* 4–9.

Shumaker, S. A. (1990). Lifestyle change and adherence: The broader context. In S. A. Shumaker, E. B. Schron, & J. K. Ockene (Eds.), *The handbook of health behavior change* (pp. 405–408). New York: Springer.

Turk, D. C., Salovey, P., & Litt, M. D. (1986). Adherence: A cognitive-behavioral perspective. In K. E. Gerber & A. M. Nehemkis (Eds.), *Compliance. The dilemma of the chronically ill* (pp. 44–72). New York: Springer.

Wagner, E. H., Austin, B. T., & Von Korff, M. (1996). Improving outcomes in chronic illness. *Managed Care Quarterly, 4,* 12–35.

Wolfe, G. S. (1997). The case manager's role in adherence. *Journal of the Association of Nurses in AIDS Care, 8,* 24–28.

PART IV

Promoting Adherence to Specific Treatments

12

Adherence to Medications

Paul F. Cook

As Sir William Osler (1849–1919) noted, "The desire to take medication is perhaps the greatest feature which distinguishes man [and woman] from animals" (Cushing, 1940, p. 342). But regardless of humans' tendency to medicate themselves, adherence to prescribed medications can be a particularly challenging aspect of adherence to medical treatment regimens. This has been recognized since the time of Hippocrates (ca. 200 BCE) who admonished physicians to "keep watch also on the fault of patients which often makes them lie about taking of things prescribed" (Henrichs, 1985, p. 71). Unlike adherence to other aspects of a treatment regimen, such as completing office visits, adhering to a specific diet, or maintaining an exercise routine, taking medication is most often a behavior done in private, and one that must be maintained over a long period of time—often daily—with little external reward or punishment for performing or not performing the behavior. Studies with diabetic patients, who often have a multifaceted treatment regimen involving diet, exercise, blood glucose testing,

and medication, have shown that medication adherence is not highly correlated with adherence to other aspects of the regimen (Glasgow, McCaul, & Schafer, 1987).

Problems of Nonadherence to Medications

Summary results from many years of research demonstrate that across medical conditions, 50% or more of all patients stop taking prescribed long-term medications within the first year (Meichenbaum & Turk, 1987; National Council on Patient Information and Education [NCPIE], 1995). This holds true not just in treatments for asymptomatic conditions like hypertension (Takala, Niemelä, Rosti, & Sievers, 1979), hyperlipidemia (Kruse, 1991), osteoporosis (Scott-Levin, 2001), and glaucoma (Gordon & Kass, 1991), but also for conditions where one might expect a higher adherence rate, such as treatments for migraine (Packard & O'Conell, 1986), epilepsy (Leppik, 1990), arthritis (Belcon,

Haynes, & Tugwell, 1984), and depression (Tierney, Melfi, Signa, & Crognah, 2000). In addition, a percentage of patients never start treatment at all, even after receiving a first prescription. This percentage has been estimated to be 20% or greater (Koop, 1985), and although it can be difficult to collect data about the number of patients who never start treatment, similarly high nonfulfillment rates have been confirmed in published studies on lipid-lowering (Kruse, 1991) and hormone-replacement drugs (Ravnikar, 1987).

Nonadherence to prescribed medication regimens includes both total nonadherence (not starting treatment or discontinuing against medical advice) and partial nonadherence (taking less than the recommended dose or taking the medication less frequently than prescribed). The term *nonadherence* is also sometimes used to include overuse of medication, sharing medications with others, and nonadherence to medication-related limitations regarding food, drink, physical activity, or other medications that interact with the target drug. One study reported that among older adults, 40% of patients discontinue medications inappropriately, up to 10% take medication prescribed for someone else, and more than 20% take medications that are not currently prescribed (old pills, etc.) (Salzman, 1995). Although the assessment of adherence has been a subject of debate (see, e.g., Cook, 2001; Roth, 1987; Riekert, this volume), high rates of medication nonadherence have been documented using so many different methods—including patient reports, physician reports, pill counts, pharmacy refill data, serum blood levels of target drugs, direct observation of patients' behavior, and electronic devices that surreptitiously record pill bottle openings, inhaler puffs, or eyedropper use—and for so many drug categories and medical conditions that the high incidence of nonadherence for all medications no longer seems an issue for debate.

Consequences of Nonadherence to Medications

High levels of medication nonadherence can be frustrating for treatment providers (Rollnick, Mason, & Butler, 1999), and may also contribute to decreased patient satisfaction and negative treatment outcomes. When patients do not take medication as it is prescribed, the results of treatment may not match those obtained in clinical trials. As noted by former U.S. Surgeon General C. Everett Koop (1985, p. 1), "drugs don't work if people don't take them." Independent of patients' adherence to other aspects of the treatment regimen, nonadherence to prescribed medications alone is responsible for 11% of all hospital admissions (Col, Fanale, & Kronholm, 1990) as well as 23% of all nursing home admissions (Smith, 1985), and it accounts for 125,000 cardiac deaths per year (Smith, 1989), as well as $47 billion annually (1993 dollars) in direct health care costs (Friend, 1995) plus an additional $53 billion in estimated indirect costs due to impaired functioning and disability (NCPIE, 1995). Among older adults, medication nonadherence is the cause of 40% of all hospital admissions, with an average cost per admission of around $2,150 in 1987 dollars (Col et al., 1990).

Causes of Medication Nonadherence

To design successful interventions for medication nonadherence, it is necessary to first understand why patients do not take medications as they are prescribed. Although the incidence and consequences of medication nonadherence are well documented, researchers have found the causes of nonadherence to be more elusive. Many people spontaneously attribute medication nonadherence to characteristics of the medication itself, most notably treatment efficacy and side effects. Increasing numbers of patients also complain about the high costs of prescription drugs. Alternately, some writers have suggested that "prescription noncompliance can be primarily attributed to lack of patient education" (Mazzeo-Caputo, 1998, p. 57). Finally, there are a number of psychological variables that predict treatment adherence or nonadherence. Each of these sources of difficulty will be examined as a basis for interventions to improve adherence.

Logistical Barriers to Medication Adherence: Drug and Regimen Factors

Medication-related causes for nonadherence have been the primary focus of the pharmaceutical industry. For instance, Abbott Laboratories executive Milton Henrichs predicted in the mid-1980s that new medications would improve treatment compliance through "longer-acting drugs, . . . tablets and capsules that are smaller, that are coated to be more readily swallowed, that have distinctive shapes and colors, . . . drug products refined to eliminate adverse events, . . . combination products to reduce the frequency of drug taking, and special packaging to eliminate confusion" (Henrichs, 1985, p. 71). One only needs to view pharmaceutical manufacturers' host of direct-to-consumer advertisements to know that all these predictions have come to pass: many medications are now available in weekly or monthly formulations, they have more targeted chemical mechanisms of action resulting in better efficacy and fewer side effects, they include combination drugs that consolidate complex medication regimens into a single pill, and they are available in convenient formulations such as capsules that dissolve under the tongue or patches that deliver pharmaceuticals through the skin. Other improvements have also been made, such as pills designed in distinctive shapes and colors so that patients can easily recognize them, and pharmacies or health care providers packaging all of patients' medications in one convenient dispenser labeled with the days and times when they must be taken.

Despite these advances, research has not shown a corresponding improvement in treatment adherence. As an example, antidepressant medications have seen major advances over the past 20 years, with a new class of selective serotonin reuptake inhibitors (SSRIs) replacing the older class of tricyclic antidepressants (TCAs) as the first-line treatment for depression based on a more specific mechanism of action and a reduced chance of serious side effects. However, rates of SSRI adherence (Thompson, Buesching, Gregor, & Oster, 1996; Tierney et al., 2000) are in general no better than adherence rates for TCAs (Frank et al., 1990; Johnson, 1973; Montgomery & Kasper, 1995). Similarly, pharmacological treatments for hypertension have improved, with newer acetylcholinesterase (ACE) inhibitors having more specific mechanisms of action and fewer systemic side effects than older beta-blocking and diuretic medications. However, rates of compliance for ACE inhibitors (Cheng, Kalis, & Feifer, 2001) are similar (and possibly slightly worse) than rates of compliance for the older classes of drugs (Levine et al., 1979; Logan, Achber, Milne, Campbell, & Haynes, 1979). A third example can be found in studies of medication for diabetes, where newer antidiabetic drugs have a more specific mechanism of action than insulin treatment, and also have the advantage of being taken orally rather than by injection. However, older studies of insulin and phosphate medication adherence (Hartman & Becker, 1978; Tagliacozzo, Luskin, Lashof, & Ima, 1974) show treatment attrition rates that are very similar to those observed with new oral antidiabetic medications ("The Medicine Isn't Going Down," 2000). In these drug classes and others, the past 20 years have seen substantial improvements in the quality of treatments but no corresponding improvement in medication adherence rates.

Financial Barriers to Medication Adherence: Prescription Drug Costs

Although most medication-related variables do not seem to be strongly associated with treatment adherence, it is important to recognize that medication cost can be an important factor in patients' decision to take or not take medications. This is particularly true in recent years with increasing numbers of people taking multiple medications, increased use of costly brand-name "blockbuster" drugs, and increases in pharmacy copayments based on changes in the benefit design of many commercial health insurance plans. These increased costs have led to reported increases in nonadherence (Dalzell, 1999). In two surveys reported by Levy (1991), only 8% of patients said that cost was the main reason they didn't take their medications as prescribed. But a decade later, a Harris Poll showed that 22% of patients did not fill prescriptions due to drug costs, 16% said they had taken doses less often to save money, and 14% said they had taken smaller doses because of cost. Even among patients earning $75,000 or more per year, 12% said they did not fill a prescription in the past year because of cost (Kaiser Family Foundation, 2001). In another study, patients who made under $30,000 per year were only 60% likely to remain in treatment, but patients who made over $30,000 were 80% likely to remain in treatment. This study is noteworthy not only because it shows that economic disparities can reduce medication adherence but also because it shows that some people will be compliant despite the economic hardships created by their treatment: Even in the low-income group, 60% of patients were adherent (Ballinger, 2002). The cost of treatment clearly has an impact on compliance, and this seems to have become a more significant problem in recent years. However, it appears that even when financial costs present a significant barrier to medication adherence, for some patients the perceived benefits of treatment still outweigh the costs.

Educational Barriers to Medication Adherence: Lack of Knowledge

It is a truism among health professionals that increased patient knowledge does not automatically translate to behavior change. However, this insight has not been routinely incorporated into strategies for improving medication adherence. Among patients who understand and agree with their treatment, adherence to medication regimens is only about 75% (Cramer, 1995). Even among physicians and nurses, who are presumably the best-educated consumers of prescription medications, documented rates of medication adherence are only 77% for short-term medications and 84% for long-term medications, with no significant differences between physicians and nurses in their level of adherence (Corda, Burke, & Horowitz, 2000).

Nevertheless, educational interventions to improve medication adherence were widespread in 1987, when Henrichs commented that "a wealth of brochures, pamphlets, books, audiotapes, videotapes, and media of every sort, prepared specifically for patient consumption, does not appear to have influenced a great many to comply with prescribed regimens" (Henrichs, 1985, p. 72). A meta-analysis of educational interventions conducted 20 years ago (Mullen, Green, & Persinger, 1985) concluded that educational materials, particularly print materials presented alone, had modest effects (Cohen's d effect size = +0.42), and that simply giving patients the drug package insert—which is filled with useful medical information—had approximately zero effect on compliance ($d = -0.03$). A study with older adults specifically showed no correlation between patients' knowledge of their medication regimens and their level of adherence after an educational intervention ($r = .14$: Wolfe & Schirm, 1992). Another study reached this tongue-in-cheek conclusion: "drug compliance not so bad, knowledge not so good." This study reported that 27 of 30 older adults interviewed after hospital discharge achieved excellent medication adherence "despite the fact that most did not understand the purpose of their drug therapy" (Smith & Andrews, 1983, p. 336).

Despite findings from the 1970s onward showing that patient education does not improve medication adherence, educational interventions are still a mainstay of interventions to improve treatment adherence, including booklets, pamphlets, brochures, Web sites, and recorded telephone messages sponsored by pharmaceutical manufacturers, medical associations, and managed care organizations. In fact, with the advent of educational disease management programs promoted by health insurers and pharmaceutical manufacturers, as well as the availability of enormous amounts of health information through the Internet, patients may be better educated about their diseases now than at any previous time in the history of medicine. For example, in a well-publicized disease management program sponsored by Pfizer in the state of Florida, 113,000 patients with asthma, hypertension, diabetes, and heart failure received quarterly newsletters about their disease and its treatment, as well as access to an automated telephonic health information line, in-person health fairs and educational seminars, and a 24-hour telephonic nurse triage service; some patients also received case management by phone (Pfizer, 2003). The Pfizer study documented a modest reduction in participants' self-report of barriers to medication adherence—a change of about one-half point on a 12-point self-report scale (Pfizer, 2003)—but the program was also criticized for implementation problems and weaker-than-expected outcomes ("Florida to Pull Plug," 2004). Perhaps because of disease management programs' focus on patient education rather than patient behavior change, a recent report from the Congressional Budget Office (CBO) concluded that despite these programs' popularity there was insufficient evidence to conclude that they reduce overall health care costs (CBO, 2004).

Psychological Barriers to Medication Adherence

From the literature reviewed above, there is ample reason to conclude that medications have become more convenient and less unpleasant to take than they were 20 years ago, and that people have more opportunities to become knowledgeable about their health and prescribed medications. However, the continued low rates of medication adherence reported in the literature lead to the inescapable conclusion that better medications and more knowledge about medications do not translate to any meaningful improvement in medication adherence; other factors are clearly involved. One such factor is clearly drug costs, which present a greater burden today than 20 years ago, but as the studies reviewed indicate, drug cost alone is probably not the determining factor in patients' decision to adhere or not adhere to medication regimens. Instead, the demonstrated lack of improvement in medication adherence in the past 20 years supports the conclusion that a great deal of nonadherence results from psychological factors—people's habits, attitudes, and beliefs about taking medication.

Cognitive Factors

Patient beliefs about treatment are one important psychological cause of nonadherence. For example, Levy (1991) reported the results of two patient surveys—one conducted by a pharmaceutical company and the other by the American Association of Retired Persons (AARP). Across the two surveys, 68% of respondents said that the main reasons they didn't take their medications as prescribed were because they didn't think they needed the medications, because they didn't understand the treatment, or because they didn't believe the medications would help. Various cognitive theories of health-related behavior (e.g., the theory of reasoned action, the health belief model, protection motivation theory: see Weinstein, 1993 for an analysis of several cognitive models' partially overlapping constructs) posit that patients' beliefs are the primary reason for nonadherence to treatment. These theories suggest that patients are more likely to make needed changes in their health-related behavior when (a) they perceive a threat against their health that seems salient to them, (b) they believe that they are able to take some type of action to reduce the threat, and (c) they have adequate self-efficacy to believe that they will be successful in performing the action. In numerous tests, cognitive constructs have been shown to predict people's intentions to perform a number of prevention-related behaviors, and in some studies to predict actual performance of health behaviors (see, e.g., Aiken, West, Woodward, Reno, & Reynolds, 1994; Conner, Norman, & Bell, 2002; Sheeran, Conner, & Norman, 2001). Cognitive therapy expert Judith Beck (2000) gives a number of examples of core beliefs that interfere with medication adherence, such as the belief that "taking medication means I'm defective/crazy/sick/weak/inferior/broken," the belief that "medication is toxic/addictive," or the belief that "I should always solve problems myself" and not rely on medications (p. 2). Beck suggests specific strategies to help providers challenge each of these beliefs.

Cognitive models can also help explain a discrepancy about the impact of drug side effects. Although the research discussed above shows that drugs with fewer side effects do not necessarily have better adherence rates, many patients still report that side effects are a major reason for medication nonadherence. Several studies show that patients' *fear* of side effects may be a more important determinant of medication adherence than the actual chemical properties of the medication. In the AARP survey reported by Levy (1991), 30% of patients said they were nonadherent to medication regimens because they were *worried* about potential side effects, not because they were actually experiencing side effects. Similarly, another study found that patients with schizophrenia attributed their medication nonadherence primarily to side effects that they feared they would experience, that they had previously experienced on other medications, or that they had heard about from other mental health consumers (Davidhizar, 1987). They were less concerned about side effects that they were actually experiencing, and many of the side effects that worried them most were not pharmacologically associated with their actual treatment regimens. Another study found that patients' level of distress about side effects was not directly proportional to the side effects' "objective" medical severity. For instance, sexual problems, weight gain, and dry mouth (regarded by medical professionals as inconvenient) were rated as more subjectively distressing than the more potentially medically serious side effects of muscle rigidity and akathisia (Marder, 2002). Based on these studies, patients' beliefs and concerns about side effects may be reasonably considered a causal factor in nonadherence, independent of the actual physiological effects of the medications taken.

Emotional Factors

In addition to patient beliefs, emotional factors are a second potential cause of medication nonadherence; according to these theories, "perceived threat" of illness is more than a cognitive belief about one's susceptibility to disease. Theories such as the self-regulatory model (Cameron, Leventhal, & Leventhal, 1993) and the cognitive social health information processing model (Miller, Shoda, & Hurley, 1996) suggest that people react emotionally to information about health threats and attempt to reduce distress through their thoughts and actions. If a given piece of information creates anxiety, the person will either (a) act to reduce the anxiety or (b) discount the information. What a given person does in a given situation depends on his or her tolerance for uncertainty, on his or her typical style for coping with health-related concerns, and on various environmental factors that make the health-related threat more or less salient. Miller et al. (1996) give examples of patients acting in ways that seem contrary to their best interests—for instance, patients who routinely "monitor" their health status generally fare better than patients who tend to "blunt" affective reactions to health threats, but in situations of high anxiety (e.g., being confronted with a diagnosis of breast cancer), the "monitors" may be overwhelmed with anxiety and, therefore, unable to cope effectively. In this situation, the "blunters" may actually cope more effectively by not focusing excessively on the health threat. Another study demonstrated that after participants with high levels of health concern were given a blood pressure reading, they had slower reaction times for health-related words on a Stroop task. This finding suggests that health-conscious individuals experienced cognitive interference in processing health-related information once they had been given information that caused concern about their own health (Lecci & Cohen, 2002). In another illustration of emotional interference with accurate cognitive processing, Croyle and Sande (1988) demonstrated that individuals who are told they tested positive for a (fictional) health risk called *TAA enzyme deficiency* are more likely to minimize the risks of the condition than other participants who are given the same information about the deficiency, but who are told they tested negative for it. Similar results have been found among participants tested for actual health risk factors, such as high blood pressure (Croyle, 1990). These counterintuitive findings can be explained based on the higher level of anxiety induced in the participants who are led to believe that they have the deficiency, which in turn leads these participants to protect themselves by focusing on nonthreat information—e.g., the participant's sense that "I feel fine," which has no relevance for an asymptomatic condition, or a belief that "if I haven't heard of the disorder, it can't be that serious," which confuses statistical frequency with severity.

Emotional factors help to explain the paradoxical finding that "the greater the effect of an illness on a patient's ability to perform everyday activities, the more likely that patient is to waver or default" on medication regimens (Henrichs, 1985, p. 72). For instance, in one study only 42% of glaucoma patients took their eye drops after being told that they would go blind without the treatment. Shockingly, among patients who already *had* gone blind in one eye due to their glaucoma, the adherence rate rose only to 58% (Vincent, 1971, cited in Meichenbaum & Turk, 1987). Similarly, poor adherence rates have been found in more recent studies of breast cancer (Lebovits, Strain, Schleifer, Tanaka, Bhardwaj, & Meese, 1990) and emphysema (Tashkin et al., 1991). Even patients with life-threatening medical conditions, who are clearly aware of the dire consequences associated with nonadherence, are prone to nonadherence. Davis (1968) hypothesized that this pattern resulted from the fact that

> some patients were unable to accept the information which the doctor had given them. Because of the fear or anxiety associated with illness, such patients might tend to disengage themselves from situations which might remind them of their role obligations [as patients]. (p. 121)

Although this pattern has been repeatedly observed over at least 35 years, some health care providers still believe that the best way to motivate patients is to "put the fear of God into them" by stressing disastrous consequences of nonadherence. Research has not shown this strategy to be effective (Rollnick et al., 1999). There is some evidence that fear-based patient education tactics may actually be counterproductive. Fear-based appeals may motivate behavior change when the patient is already engaged in healthy behavior but tend to be discounted by those patients who are currently engaged in unhealthy behavior and, therefore, are most in need of behavior change (Keller, 1999). This finding also fits with evidence that health threats lead to behavioral coping efforts only when the patient has a high level of belief in his or her ability to change; when the patient feels unable or unwilling to change, health threat information leads to emotion-focused coping by discounting the information (Rippetoe & Rogers, 1987).

Behavioral Factors

Habits and learned behaviors are a third potential determinant of medication nonadherence. Behaviorist theories suggest that health-related behaviors are a function of (a) a person's learned behavioral repertoire, (b) the environmental cues that prompt or remind a person to engage in a specific behavior, and (c) the reinforcers that draw out and then maintain a particular behavior over time (Cameron & Best, 1987). If patients do not experience suitable reinforcement (e.g., an immediate reduction in symptoms), they are less likely to persevere in treatment over time. Similarly, if patients experience negative consequences of their behavior (such as side effects or inconvenience), the behavior is likely to be extinguished. Finally, it is well-known that immediate reinforcers have a stronger impact on behavior than delayed reinforcers. Based on this finding, it is logical that long-term reinforcers (such as reduced chance of illness or death) would be neglected in favor of short-term reinforcers (such as the reduced hassle and financial cost associated with stopping medications), and that, therefore, patients will tend to drop out of long-term medical treatments (Meichenbaum & Turk, 1987). Accordingly, behavioral interventions have been designed to improve medication adherence by teaching patients how to take their medications correctly and to monitor their own medication use, by helping them design cues in their home environment that will remind them to take medication, by enlisting the patient's spouse or other family members to support the patient's efforts, by offering incentives for adherence, and by instructing the patient to reward himself or herself for successful adherence (Cameron & Best, 1987; Haynes, Wang, & Gomes, 1987).

Motivational Factors

Motivational factors are a final potential factor influencing medication compliance. Patients' motivation for treatment is implicated by several theories: For instance, the transtheoretical model (see Prochaska & DiClemente, 1984; Prochaska, Prochaska, & Johnson, this volume) suggests that people pass through a predictable series of motivational stages—precontemplation, contemplation, decision, action, and maintenance—in their efforts to change health-related behaviors, and that specific methods may be useful in helping people to progress from each stage to the next. Persons in the *precontemplation* stage with respect to a particular behavior need help identifying personally meaningful reasons for initiating a change, rather than education about the benefits of change or instruction in how to perform specific behaviors. These additional interventions may, however, be helpful to persons in other stages of change. The transtheoretical model's stages successfully predict changes in a variety of health behaviors, from exercise and diet to safe-sex practices to smoking cessation (Prochaska et al., 1994; Rosen, 2000).

Prospect theory (Kahneman & Tversky, 2000) implicates other motivational factors. In the face of minor threats to their health status, people tend to be risk averse and, therefore, may prefer to endure their symptoms (a minor loss) rather than to take medications that have potentially uncertain benefits and side effects (perceived as a greater risk). On the other hand, if people view a health situation as a potentially serious loss, they will become risk seeking, and may prefer to take chances. Ironically, in this situation, a risky treatment that promises a small chance of cure may look more attractive than a more predictable regimen for managing a chronic illness. These reversals have been documented even among medical professionals. Physicians prefer a treatment that guarantees 18 years of survival over a treatment with just an 80% chance of 30 years' survival (risk aversion for lower risk of losses), but they prefer to take a chance on a treatment that offers only a 20% chance of 30 years' survival versus a treatment where the survival rate is higher (25%) but the expected benefit of 18 years' survival is lower (risk seeking for higher risk of losses: Tversky & Kahneman, 2000). On the other hand, if a treatment offers the chance to improve one's health status (rather than to prevent a loss), people are also more likely to seek risks. This may explain patients' aversion to prescription medications at the same time they seek out herbal and alternative therapies— medical treatment is unfortunately experienced by most Americans as a way to prevent losses in health status whereas herbal treatments may be perceived as a method for increasing energy or health. Another interesting finding of prospect theory is that people prefer risk (known probabilities of loss) to uncertainty (unknown probabilities of loss: Fox & Tversky, 2000)—this may lead people to prefer their current symptoms, which are at least familiar, to medical treatment, which may carry uncertain outcomes. To date, prospect theory has been tested only in a limited way in health psychology, but the results have been promising so far. For example, Detweiler, Bedell, Salovey, Pronin, and Rothman (1999) reported on an intervention to prevent sunburn in which messages emphasizing health-related gains from using sunscreen were more effective than messages that stressed the negative consequences of nonuse. The threat of a major loss with an unknown probability (skin cancer) may lead people to take their chances about sunburn, whereas emphasizing a potential gain (healthy skin) may lead people to take the minor risk of trying something new (sunscreen). Interestingly, if a minor loss had been emphasized (e.g., flaking skin), people might have been more willing to use sunscreen than when a major illness was threatened. This also would be in line with prospect theory's predictions.

Strategies to Improve Medication Adherence

Various methods have been attempted to improve medication adherence ranging from automated e-mail reminders to several sessions of in-person medication counseling by a pharmacist or other professional, and several articles have reviewed the literature on interventions to improve medication adherence. An initial meta-analysis of interventions to improve adherence was conducted in 1985, reviewing 70 studies published between 1961 and 1984 (Mullen et al., 1985). These authors found that one-to-one counseling was the most efficacious intervention ($d = +1.13$), with more modest efficacy for group education ($d = +0.75$), counseling or group education plus printed materials ($d = +0.73$), behavior modification or self-monitoring interventions ($d = +0.51$), and written and/or audiovisual educational materials ($d = +0.42$).

This review highlights a key concern in analyzing the efficacy of interventions to improve adherence. Although many of the interventions described were clearly based on psychological (behaviorist) theories or involved one-to-one interventions with patients, the authors characterized all these methods as "patient education." When interventions involve one-on-one interaction between a patient and a health educator, "education" may not be an accurate description of the process—as the authors of one early study noted, "nurse teaching sessions, the relatively complex design notwithstanding, unfolded into complex processes of interaction" between the patient and the health educator (Tagliacozzo et al., 1974, p. 598). Many interventions designed by medical professionals use the term *education*, which is more familiar in the medical field, but have adopted research-based psychological strategies to promote behavior change. For example, an excellent textbook by Lorig (1996), written for a target audience of nurses and health educators, describes a complex algorithm for selecting an intervention based on the patient's knowledge, beliefs, and features of the medication regimen. Lorig's suggested "educational" interventions include problem-solving steps, modeling, reframing physical symptoms, seeking social support, self-talk, and contingency management. This expanded concept of patient education may be very helpful to practitioners, but contributes to some confusion in the literature. More problematic is a recent tendency to characterize purely educational interventions (newsletters, etc.) as "behavior change." Proponents of disease management have adopted some of the language of psychological interventions, such as the stages of change, but do not use psychological techniques (Cummings, 2004). Newsletters, videotapes, and telephonic patient education activities may have some impact; however, for the remainder of this review, interventions will be characterized as *educational* if they impart information and *psychological* only if they use specific psychological techniques to promote behavior change. Because of the loose definition of *educational* in Mullen et al.'s (1985) review, it is difficult in this meta-analysis to compare psychological techniques to educational ones.

A more recent unpublished meta-analysis of the literature on interventions to improve treatment adherence was conducted by the author (Cook, 2000). This meta-analysis included 43 studies published between 1975 and 2000. Studies were specifically excluded if they focused only on patient education (i.e., no techniques used other than imparting information to the patient) and included only if medication adherence was the target outcome. Most studies used a randomized control group design, although some pre- and posttest studies were also included. Only eight of the studies in this review (19%) were also included in the Mullen et al. (1985) review; therefore, this meta-analysis presents largely independent conclusions about a body of research that specifically examined psychological techniques to improve medication

adherence. The overall analysis showed a moderate effect for psychologically based interventions (average $d = 0.74$), with significant heterogeneity among the various studies examined ($\chi^2 = 61.8$, $p < .001$). Although all studies included in this review were based on psychological principles for behavior change, some ($n = 15$) used a stimulus-control method such as pill dispensers, calendars, or a beeping reminder device. These assistive technologies make use of well-supported behaviorist principles, but do represent a purely environmental manipulation rather than a personalized interaction with the patient. They produced significantly weaker effects (average $d = 0.68$) than interventions that included direct contact between the patient and a health educator, nurse, pharmacist, or other counselor (average $d = 0.82$, which was significantly greater than the effect for reminder technologies, $Z = 1.75$, $p = .04$).

The interpersonally based psychological interventions were still significantly heterogeneous ($\chi^2 = 3.27$, $p < .001$), which led to a follow-up analysis to identify specific techniques with greater efficacy. Table 12.1 gives average effect sizes and heterogeneity statistics for each category of treatment.

As shown in Table 12.1, the strongest effects were produced by interventions that trained participants to monitor their own behavior and by interventions that used cognitive-behavioral principles to address participants' beliefs about medication and to design customized adherence plans. Such approaches help patients to realistically evaluate the costs and benefits of taking medication and also likely increase a sense of agency and control over decisions affecting one's own health. Reminder strategies were found to be less efficacious than behavioral, family-oriented, and cognitive interventions. Alternative packaging was found to be only slightly less efficacious than cognitive-behavioral techniques; this unexpected finding may be because of the fact that in 4 of 11 studies, alternative packaging was actually combined with either self-monitoring

Table 12.1   Average Effect Sizes for Psychological Interventions

Intervention Strategy	No. of Studies	Average Effect	Heterogeneity
Self-monitoring (SM)	12	$d = 1.09$	$\chi^2 = 1.04$
Cognitive-behavioral treatment (CBT)	20	$d = 0.97$	$\chi^2 = 1.01$
Alternative packaging (AP)	11	$d = 0.93$	$\chi^2 = 1.12$
Family counseling (FC)	4	$d = 0.79$	$\chi^2 = 0.17$
Assertiveness training (AT)	2	$d = 0.78$	$\chi^2 = 0.003$
Reminders and support (RS)	14	$d = 0.59$	$\chi^2 = 1.04$
Motivational interviewing (MI)	1	$d = 0.57$	N/A
Self- (or external) reward (SR)	2	$d = 0.44$	$\chi^2 = 0.02$

SOURCE: Adapted from Cook (2000).

or cognitive-behavioral counseling. It is also important to note that the results on motivational interviewing, self-reward, and assertiveness training come only from one or two studies each and that, therefore, the stability of these findings is unknown. One other important finding from this review was that combinations of techniques were more efficacious than single techniques used alone. This finding argues for using a package of the more efficacious strategies in combination.

Finally, an even more recent review of the literature reviewed seven of the studies included in the Cook (2000) paper, plus 25 others, with most of the reviewed studies being published since 1990 (McDonald, Garg, & Haynes, 2002). Unfortunately, the authors of this up-to-date review concluded that "studies were too disparate to warrant meta-analysis" (p. 2868) and, therefore, presented only the finding that 49% of the interventions showed statistically significant improvement in medication compliance as a result of the intervention. From the narrative review, it appears that several of the interventions that showed no significant differences between treatment and control actually provided educational interventions only (e.g., group patient education meetings). The authors also note that several studies had low statistical power. The authors did conclude that "almost all of the interventions that were effective for long-term care were complex, including combinations of more convenient care, information, counseling, reminders, self-monitoring, reinforcement, family therapy, and other forms of additional supervision or attention" (p. 2877). This review used more methodologically strict inclusion criteria than the Cook (2000) review and reached more guarded substantive conclusions, but the two reviews' basic findings are compatible: interventions that use a combination of psychological (rather than educational) techniques have the best results.

Case Examples

Based on the findings described above, the author and his colleagues designed a multicomponent psychological intervention—"*Script*Assist"—to improve patients' adherence to prescribed medications. The author's initial meta-analysis pointed to the efficacy of psychological techniques for improving medication adherence, and recent studies on lipid-lowering drugs (Blumi, McKenney, & Cziraky, 2000), arthritis medication (Maisiak, Austin, & Heck, 1996), and antidepressants (Katzelnick et al., 2000) demonstrated that one-to-one telephonic patient counseling is efficacious. Therefore, to control costs and to include patients in widespread geographic areas, *Script*Assist was designed as a psychological, telephonic patient counseling program.

Components of the Intervention

The *Script*Assist program was designed around three key components—*predicting* medication nonadherence before it occurs, *detecting* nonadherence once it has occurred, and *promoting* successful medication adherence over time through psychological interventions. To predict noncompliance, the author and his colleagues developed a screening tool that uses psychological and demographic variables to prospectively determine which patients are at high risk for medication nonadherence. An initial set of 45 variables was selected based on their published association with medication nonadherence, including patient history variables, health-related locus of control, current treatment complexity, and social support. A CART statistical procedure was used to produce a classification algorithm so that each patient can be asked a unique series of no more than four questions (with each subsequent question selected based on the participant's response to the prior question) to obtain a prediction of nonadherence that is approximately 80% accurate. To date, the predictive algorithm has shown evidence of stability across psychiatric and nonpsychiatric populations. Prediction of nonadherence was considered an essential program component in order to deliver more support to those patients who were most likely to drop out of treatment, while keeping overall program costs low.

To detect nonadherence, the *Script*Assist program provides a series of follow-up telephone calls in which the patient interacts with the same telephonic counselor over time. The nature of the telephonic interaction tends to promote honest responding, even about sensitive issues. Studies have shown that people find relatively anonymous forums such as the Internet to be helpful in discussing sensitive health-related topics (Davison, Pennebaker, & Dickerson, 2000; Rosson, 1999). To further promote honest discussion of medication adherence, nurses were trained to provide the intervention. Although there is no reason why a nursing degree is required to speak with patients about their medication adherence, it was our belief that patients would feel more comfortable speaking with a nursing professional about medication issues. There is also research evidence that nurses are relatively good at detecting medication nonadherence. In one study, physicians were correct in their judgments about treatment adherence only 59% of the time, whereas nurses in the same medical practices were accurate 70% of the time (Valenti, 2001). This may reflect a tendency to perceive nurses as supportive and knowledgeable peers, whereas physicians may be perceived as authority figures. Providing a series of interactions with the same nurse over time was believed to promote honest discussion based on the development of a helping relationship. Finally, nurses were trained to use nonjudgmental interviewing techniques to elicit accurate information about patients' medication adherence. Nurses were instructed to use warm tones of voice, to convey interest in the patient's report, and to make introductory statements like the following: "Many patients have told me that they find it difficult to take all their medicines exactly as the doctor prescribed. Do you find it hard, too?" (Fletcher, Pappius, & Harper, 1979).

Finally, to promote patients' medication adherence, including both initial behavior change to adopt a new medication regime and ongoing maintenance of medication adherence, nurses were trained in various psychological techniques from the literature reviewed above. Although the author and his colleagues initially provided a multimodal training stressing cognitive, behavioral, and emotion-focused counseling techniques drawn from the psychotherapy literature, they eventually adopted a training model based primarily on Miller and Rollnick's

(2002) motivational interviewing procedure. There were several reasons for this approach. First, although motivational interviewing showed relatively poor results in the one study included in the author's meta-analysis on medication adherence (Cook, 2000), it has been demonstrated to have beneficial results in studies on related variables such as dietary adherence, exercise program adherence, and treatment attendance (Zweben & Zuckoff, 2002). Second, motivational interviewing draws on the framework of Prochaska's transtheoretical model, which provides rules for matching interventions ("processes of change") to clients' stage of change (see Prochaska, Prochaska, & Johnson, this volume), and therefore readily incorporates cognitive, behavioral, and other interventions when these are appropriate (e.g., for persons in the contemplation, action, or maintenance stages of change). However, motivational interviewing is the only available intervention specifically designed for use with persons in the very common precontemplation stage of change. Third and perhaps most important, motivational interviewing teaches a way of interacting with patients that is radically different from the traditional medical model in which most nurses have been trained (Rollnick et al., 1999). Nurses can readily teach patients cognitive, behavioral, or emotion-focused coping techniques and help them to practice these techniques, as this is very similar to the nurse's traditional role as a patient educator, but patients who are not yet convinced of the need for change require a very different approach. Motivational interviewing teaches counselors to regard every patient as being ambivalent about change, whether the patient is currently highly adherent or has not yet filled the first prescription. Skillful attention to both sides of the patient's ambivalence helps to build patients' own motivation for change, and can be accomplished in a very brief period of time. Motivational interviewing also trains counselors to avoid common "traps" that result from a medical model, such as trying to act as an expert who can "fix" the patient's behavior, labeling or blaming the patient for being noncompliant, or "taking sides" by acting exclusively as a cheerleader for change but not acknowledging the patient's ambivalence. From the perspective of motivational interviewing, even educating patients can be a trap—when patients are passive recipients of information about the benefits of treatment and their concerns or opinions are not actively solicited, this can drive them deeper into the resistant side of their ambivalence. On the other hand, if patients themselves ask questions to learn more about their treatment, it can increase their investment in treatment and their motivation for behavior change.

Results With Psychiatric Conditions

When developing the *Script*Assist program, the author and his colleagues first conducted a pilot study with antidepressant medication (Cook, Berdie, Dubin, & Wirecki, 2000). This study recruited patients with depression from two outpatient psychiatric practices in Denver and randomly assigned them to receive either treatment as usual or the *Script*Assist telephone intervention in addition to their regular psychiatric treatment. Apart from their depression, patients were relatively high-functioning: all had commercial health insurance and were able to attend outpatient treatment, and patients with substance abuse or personality disorders were specifically excluded. All patients were recruited at the start of treatment and gave informed consent to participate; they were told that the study was about patients' experiences with medication but not that medication adherence was the specific outcome of interest. A customized intervention was designed for antidepressant adherence, including specific strategies to address expected barriers to treatment such as the immediate side effects of antidepressant treatment, the relatively slow remission of depressive symptoms after the onset of treatment, and the need for maintenance treatment for several months beyond the point of symptom remission. Four months after the start of treatment, only 57% of control group participants were still in treatment, whereas 88% of the participants in the intervention group were still in treatment. This pilot study provided important initial support for the telephone intervention but had several important limitations. First, it was limited to a mental health condition (depression) where a counseling intervention might have been more acceptable or helpful to participants than it would be to patients with a medical condition unrelated to mental health. Second, it was a very small-scale study ($N = 18$) in a limited population, with inadequate statistical power and carefully selected participants who were probably not representative of the general population. Finally, the difference between intervention and control groups was based on patient self-report. Clearly, the findings of this pilot study required replication and extension.

In another small-scale study with a psychiatric population, again conducted in Denver, a *Script*Assist program was implemented for patients with schizophrenia and bipolar disorder who were prescribed an antipsychotic medication. The core *Script*Assist program was again customized for this population, in this case with additional intervention protocols focused on managing symptoms of psychosis, coping with antipsychotic medication side effects, and relapse prevention. Patients were recruited through community mental health centers, were either Medicaid recipients or uninsured, and were generally at lower socioeconomic and functional levels than participants in the previous study with antidepressants. This was again a small-scale study ($N = 16$). In this case, participants' results were compared with a baseline rate of adherence to antipsychotic medications, estimated from published studies to be approximately 55%. This low baseline rate for atypical antipsychotics was later confirmed by examining pharmacy data available through *Script*Assist's parent company, Centene Corporation—of 752 Medicaid patients prescribed the target antipsychotic medication over a 9-month period, 57% were adherent. Among participants receiving the customized *Script*Assist intervention, however, 74% were

adherent up to 9 months. This study extended the previous results by demonstrating that the telephonic patient counseling program could be of benefit even in a relatively lower-functioning population with severe psychiatric difficulties, and compared patient-reported adherence with a baseline compliance level established by pharmacy refill data. However, the study again had the limitations of a small and potentially nonrepresentative sample (in this study patients were not referred at the very beginning of treatment, so there was reason to suspect that the sample was biased in favor of patients who were already stabilized and adherent to their antipsychotic regimens), a psychiatric population rather than a general medical population, and the use of patient self-report to assess adherence in the intervention group.

Results With a Medical Condition: Chronic Pelvic Pain

A large-scale pilot study ($N = 1,118$ patients nationwide) was conducted to improve adherence to medication for chronic pelvic pain. Women with chronic pelvic pain are a special population with acute symptoms that would seem likely to promote compliance with medical advice, but the problem of treatment nonadherence is the same in this population as in many others. Pharmacy fill data showed that patients taking medication for endometriosis and uterine fibroids—two common causes of pelvic pain—discontinue treatment at a rate of about 60% within the first 5 months of treatment. Women with endometriosis or uterine fibroids drop out of treatment despite the fact that they generally experience acute exacerbations of pain, the fact that their treatment is comparatively short term (6–12 months), the fact that treatment is infrequent (monthly or even just once per 3 months), and the fact that they have often received multiple other treatments that were unsuccessful or only partially successful in alleviating their pain. Psychological factors again interfere with treatment adherence. First, patients may have concerns about the common menopause-like side effects of the medication (which are regularly experienced but generally tolerated by patients), or they may have fears about possible side effects that are much less common. Second, we also hypothesized that emotional distress could contribute to nonadherence, as many women with a diagnosis of endometriosis or uterine fibroids have undergone numerous unsuccessful treatments, including exploratory laparoscopic surgery, and may have received a number of misdiagnoses (potentially including the assertion that "it's all in the patient's head") before receiving the present course of treatment. Under these circumstances, patients might be more likely to feel pessimistic about the likelihood that treatment will help and, therefore, might avoid the treatment or might focus more on negative treatment experiences than on expected benefits. Third, although behavioral factors are less likely to have an impact on adherence to a once-monthly than to a once-daily treatment, we hypothesized that some women might report nonadherence to treatment because of the "hassle factor" associated with monthly trips to the physician's office; alternately, we hypothesized that some patients might have difficulty keeping track of when their next dose of medication was scheduled, precisely because the treatment occurs so infrequently. Finally, we hypothesized that patients who were less motivated for treatment (e.g., because they saw fewer benefits and more drawbacks associated with taking the medication) would become nonadherent.

A customized intervention was again designed to improve adherence to the medication for endometriosis and uterine fibroids, focusing on the psychological factors described above and making use of the same core motivational interviewing and cognitive-behavioral techniques. A total of 683 physicians' offices throughout the United States were contacted by the staff of a pharmaceutical manufacturer, and they began to enroll patients into the program. For the initial pilot program, physicians were asked to describe the program to all patients taking the specific medication that was the focus of the study and to send in a patient consent form. This was done to minimize any possible volunteer bias where patients who self-enrolled in the program would be more likely to be compliant. However, physicians requested other methods where patients could self-enroll, and after the conclusion of the pilot program, additional methods—such as a patient self-enrollment form, 800 number, and Web site enrollment—were implemented. For the physician-referred patients who participated in the initial pilot program, the 6-month medication adherence rate was 71.3%. This was a significant improvement compared with a baseline 6-month adherence rate (from pharmacy data) of 46.0%. These results, obtained with a large, geographically and ethnically diverse sample of patients in treatment for a medical condition, provided a demonstration of the *Script*Assist program's effects that had much greater external validity. However, because the intervention group's adherence rate was based on interview data whereas the baseline adherence rate was established using pharmacy data, internal validity was still lacking.

Results With a Chronic, Asymptomatic Medical Condition: Osteoporosis

A second study examining adherence to medication for a medical condition, osteoporosis, was conducted in 2003–2004. In this study a separate nationwide group of 55 physicians was contacted with the assistance of pharmaceutical sales representatives, and these physicians enrolled patients prescribed a medication for osteoporosis (current $N = 137$ patients with complete data). Patients were then provided with telephonic nursing support to promote osteoporosis medication adherence. Osteoporosis is a particularly interesting test case for medication adherence in that most patients with the condition have no symptoms or vague symptoms (e.g., back pain, posture changes), the medication produces no immediate symptom relief, and the goal of treatment is primarily to prevent or delay future deterioration in the patient's health. Although the treatment has no immediate benefit that can be perceived by the patient, it can cause gastrointestinal distress or other side effects, and it has dosing instructions that can be inconvenient to the patient (e.g., do not eat or lie down for at least 30 minutes after taking the medication). The medication is available in a once-a-week dosing form, which can reduce inconvenience for the patient but can make it more difficult to remember because it is not part of a daily routine. A customized *Script*Assist intervention manual was designed to address these unique factors using the program's core psychological techniques. In this study, pharmacy data on patients' prescription refills was obtained by the participating physicians' offices, with patients' consent. Patients who participated in the *Script*Assist intervention had an adherence rate of 69% after 6 months, compared with a baseline adherence rate obtained from national pharmacy data of 49% at 6 months. This study showed that even when using the same nonpatient-reported standard (pharmacy data) for both the baseline and intervention measures, the *Script*Assist intervention produced a significant improvement in medication adherence.

Conclusion

The reviewed research suggests that nonadherence to prescribed medications is frequent for all drug classes and all chronic disease states, that the reasons for nonadherence are primarily psychological (rather than based on drug properties or patients' knowledge about treatment), and that counseling interventions adapted from the psychotherapy literature can produce significant improvements in compliance. Building on this body of knowledge, the author and his colleagues developed a psychologically based telephone counseling model to promote medication adherence, which has now been tested with treatments for depression, bipolar disorder, schizophrenia, endometriosis, uterine fibroids, and osteoporosis. To date, these *Script*Assist programs have produced an average effect size of $d = 1.05$ (or $r = .46$), which is similar to the best effect sizes seen for psychological interventions in previous meta-analyses. Although none of the studies conducted to date have been free of methodological problems, the current results provide preliminary support for a multimodal telephonic counseling intervention, adapted to address the particular psychological issues involved in adherence to each class of medications, as a way to improve medication adherence across a range of medical and psychiatric conditions. Future studies with this model will continue to evaluate large-scale programs with a high degree of generalizability, while incorporating additional design features such as pharmacy-based measurement of adherence and appropriate control groups to increase internal validity.

References

Aiken, L. S., West, S. G., Woodward, C. K., Reno, R. R., & Reynolds, K. D. (1994). Increasing screening mammography in asymptomatic women: Evaluation of a second-generation, theory-based program. *Health Psychology, 13,* 526–538.

Ballinger, M. (2002, January). Compliance dwindles as drug costs escalate. *Managed Healthcare Executive,* 9–10.

Beck, J. (2000, August). Improving medication compliance with cognitive techniques. *Open Minds Advisor,* 1–3.

Belcon, M. C., Haynes, R. B., & Tugwell, P. (1984). A critical review of compliance studies in rheumatoid arthritis. *Arthritis and Rheumatism, 27,* 1227–1233.

Blumi, B. M., McKenney, J. M., & Cziraky, M. J. (2000). Pharmaceutical care services and results in Project IMPACT: Hyperlipidemia. *Journal of the American Pharmaceutical Association, 40,* 157–165.

Cameron, R., & Best, J. A. (1987). Promoting adherence to health behavior change interventions: Recent findings from behavioral research. *Patient Education and Counseling, 10,* 139–154.

Cameron, L., Leventhal, E. A., & Leventhal, H. (1993). Symptom representations and affect as determinants of care seeking in a community-dwelling, adult sample population. *Health Psychology, 12,* 171–179.

Cheng, J. W. M., Kalis, M. M., & Feifer, S. (2001). Patient-reported adherence to guidelines of the sixth joint national committee on prevention, detection, evaluation, and treatment of high blood pressure. *Pharmacotherapy, 21,* 828–841.

Col, N., Fanale, J. E., & Kronholm, P. (1990). The role of medication noncompliance and adverse drug reactions in hospitalizations of the elderly. *Archives of Internal Medicine, 150,* 841–845.

Congressional Budget Office. (2004). *An analysis of the literature on disease management programs.* Retrieved March 27, 2006, from www.cbo.gov/ftpdocs/59xx/doc5909/10-13-DiseaseMngmnt.pdf

Conner, M., Norman, P., & Bell, R. (2002). The theory of planned behavior and healthy eating. *Health Psychology, 21,* 194–201.

Cook, P. F. (2000). *Psychosocial interventions to improve medication compliance: A meta-analysis.* Retrieved April 3, 2006, from www.scriptassistllc.com/files/research/ComplianceMeta-Analysis.pdf

Cook, P. F. (2001). *Methods for assessing medication compliance.* Retrieved April 3, 2006, from www.scriptassistllc.com/files/research/WhitePaper.pdf

Cook, P. F., Berdie, M. J., Dubin, M. D., & Wirecki, T. S. (2000). *Effect of telephone outreach counseling on patients' adherence to antidepressant medication.* Retrieved April 3, 2006, from www.scriptassistllc.comfiles/research/PilotStudyWrite-Up1.pdf

Corda, R. S., Burke, H. B., & Horowitz, H. W. (2000). Adherence to prescription medications among medical professionals. *Southern Medical Journal, 93,* 585–589.

Cramer, J. A. (1995). Optimizing long-term patient compliance. *Neurology, 45*(Suppl. 1), S25–S28.

Croyle, R. T. (1990). Biased appraisal of high blood pressure. *Preventive Medicine, 19,* 40–44.

Croyle, R. T., & Sande, G. N. (1988). Denial and confirmatory search: Paradoxical consequences of medical diagnosis. *Journal of Applied Social Psychology, 18,* 473–490.

Cummings, N. A. (2004, May). In W. O'Donohue (Chair), panel discussion. Conducted at Conference on Psychological Approaches to Disease Management, University of Nevada, Reno.

Cushing, H. (1940). *Life of Sir William Osler* (Vol. 1). Cambridge, UK: Oxford University Press.

Dalzell, M. D. (1999). Pharmacy copayments: A double-edged sword. *Managed Care Magazine.* Retrieved November 2, 1999, from www.managedcaremag.com/archiveMC/9908/9908.pharcopay.html

Davidhizar, R. E. (1987). Beliefs, feelings and insight of patients with schizophrenia about taking medication. *Journal of Advanced Nursing, 12,* 177–182.

Davis, M. S. (1968). Physiologic, psychological and demographic factors in patient compliance with doctors' orders. *Medical Care, 6,* 115–122.

Davison, K. P., Pennebaker, J. W., & Dickerson, S. S. (2000). Who talks? The social psychology of illness support groups. *American Psychologist, 55,* 205–217.

Detweiler, J. B., Bedell, B. T., Salovey, P., Pronin, E., & Rothman, A. J. (1999). Message framing and sunscreen use: Gain-framed messages motivate beach-goers. *Health Psychology, 18,* 189–196.

Fletcher, S. W., Pappius, E. M., & Harper, S. J. (1979). Measurement of medication compliance in a clinical setting: Comparison of three methods in patients prescribed digoxin. *Archives of Internal Medicine, 139,* 635–638.

Florida to pull plug on Medicaid DM initiative. (2004). *Disease Management News, 9*(19), 1, 4.

Fox, C. R., & Tversky, A. (2000). A belief-based account of decision under uncertainty. In D. Kahneman & A. Tversky (Eds.), *Choices, values, and frames* (pp. 118–142). Cambridge, UK: Cambridge University Press.

Frank, E., Kupfer, D. J., Perel, J. M., Cornes, C., Jarrett, D. B., Mallinger, A. G., et al. (1990). Three-year outcomes for maintenance therapies in recurrent depression. *Archives of General Psychiatry, 47,* 1093–1099.

Friend, T. (1995, October 3). Health and education. *USA Today,* p. D4.

Glasgow, R. E., McCaul, K. D., & Schafer, L. C. (1987). Self-care behaviors and glycemic control in Type I diabetes. *Journal of Chronic Disease, 40,* 399–412.

Gordon, M. E., & Kass, M. A. (1991). Validity of standard compliance measures in glaucoma compared with an electronic eyedrop monitor. In J. A. Cramer & B. Spilker (Eds.), *Patient compliance in medical practice and clinical trials* (pp. 163–173). New York: Raven Press.

Hartman, P. E., & Becker, M. (1978). Non-compliance with prescribed regimen among chronic hemodialysis patients: A method of prediction and educational diagnosis. *Dialysis & Transplantation, 7,* 978–989.

Haynes, R. B., Wang, E., & Gomes, M. D. M. (1987). A critical review of interventions to improve compliance with prescribed medications. *Patient Education and Counseling, 10,* 155–166.

Henrichs, M. J. (1985). Compliance programs and strategies of the pharmaceutical industry. In *Improving medication compliance: Proceedings of a symposium* (pp. 71–75). Reston, VA: National Pharmaceutical Council.

Johnson, D. A. W. (1973). Treatment of depression in general practice. *British Medical Journal, 2,* 18–20.

Kahneman, D., & Tversky, A. (2000). *Choices, values, and frames.* Cambridge, UK: Cambridge University Press.

Kaiser Family Foundation. (2001). Harris interactive survey shows many adults do not fill prescriptions, cut back on doses because of costs. Retrieved November 30, 2001, from www.kaiser-network.org

Katzelnick, D. J., Simon, G. E., Pearson, S. D., Manning, W. G., Helstad, C. P., Henk, H. J., et al. (2000). Randomized trial of a depression management program in high utilizers of medical care. *Archives of Family Medicine, 9,* 345–351.

Keller, P. A. (1999). Converting the unconverted: The effect of inclination and opportunity to discount health-related fear appeals. *Journal of Applied Psychology, 84,* 403–415.

Koop, C. E. (1985). Keynote address. In *Improving medication compliance: Proceedings of a symposium* (pp. 1–4). Reston, VA: National Pharmaceutical Council.

Kruse, W. H.-H. (1991). Compliance with treatment of hyperlipoproteinemia in medical practice and clinical trials. In J. A. Cramer & B. Spilker (Eds.), *Patient compliance in medical practice and clinical trials* (pp. 175–186). New York: Raven Press.

Lebovits, A. H., Strain, J. J., Schleifer, S. J., Tanaka, J. S., Bhardwaj, S., & Meese, M. R. (1990). Patient compliance with self-administered chemotherapy. *Cancer, 65,* 17–22.

Lecci, L., & Cohen, D. J. (2002). Perceptual consequences of an illness-concern induction and its relation to hypochondriacal tendencies. *Health Psychology, 21,* 147–156.

Leppik, I. E. (1990). How to get patients to take their medication. *Postgraduate Medicine, 88,* 253–256.

Levine, D. M., Green, L. W., Deeds, S. G., Chwalow, J., Russell, R. P., & Finlay, J. (1979). Health education for hypertensive patients. *Journal of the American Medical Association, 241,* 1700–1703.

Levy, R. A. (1991). Failure to refill prescriptions: Incidence, reasons and remedies. In J. A. Cramer & B. Spilker (Eds.), *Patient compliance in medical practice and clinical trials* (pp. 11–18). New York: Raven Press.

Logan, A. G., Achber, C., Milne, B. J., Campbell, W. P., & Haynes, R. B. (1979). Work-site treatment of hypertension by specially trained nurses. *Lancet, ii,* 1175–1178.

Lorig, K. (1996). *Patient education: A practical approach.* Thousand Oaks, CA: Sage.

Maisiak, R., Austin, J., & Heck, L. (1996). Health outcomes of two telephone interventions for patients with rheumatoid arthritis or osteoarthritis. *Arthritis and Rheumatism, 39,* 1391–1399.

Marder, S. (2002, May). Approaching the adherence challenge. In *The adherence challenge: Chronic issues and emerging solutions with antipsychotic therapy.* Symposium presented at the meeting of the American Psychiatric Association, Philadelphia.

Mazzeo-Caputo, S. E. (1998). In the know: Goals & guidelines for improving patient education. *Pharmaceutical Executive, 18*(7), 57–62.

McDonald, H. P., Garg, A. X., & Haynes, R. B. (2002). Interventions to enhance patient adherence to medication prescriptions. *Journal of the American Medical Association, 288,* 2868–2879.

Meichenbaum, D. C., & Turk, D. (1987). *Facilitating treatment adherence: A practitioner's guidebook.* New York: Plenum Press.

Miller, S. M., Shoda, Y., & Hurley, K. (1996). Applying cognitive-social theory to health-protective behavior: Breast self-examination in cancer screening. *Psychological Bulletin, 119,* 70–94.

Miller, W. R., & Rollnick, S. (2002). *Motivational interviewing: Preparing people for change* (2nd ed.). New York: Guilford Press.

Montgomery, S. A., & Kasper, S. (1995). Comparison of compliance between serotonin reuptake inhibitors and tricyclic antidepressants: A meta-analysis. *International Clinical Psychopharmacology, 9*(Suppl. 4), 33–40.

Mullen, P. D., Green, L. W., & Persinger, G. S. (1985). Clinical trials of patient education for chronic conditions: A comparative meta-analysis of intervention types. *Preventive Medicine, 14,* 753–781.

National Council on Patient Information and Education. (1995). *Prescription medication compliance: A review of the baseline of knowledge.* Washington, DC: Author.

Packard, R. C., & O'Conell, P. (1986). Medication compliance among headache patients. *Headache, 26,* 416–419.

Pfizer. (2003). *Florida: A healthy state of the program, summer 2003* [Brochure]. New York: Author.

Prochaska, J. O., & DiClemente, C. C. (1984). *The transtheoretical approach: Crossing traditional boundaries of therapy.* Homewood, IL: Dow Jones-Irwin.

Prochaska, J. O., Velicer, W. F., Rossi, J. S., Goldstein, M. G., Marcus, B. H., Rakowski, W., et al. (1994). Stages of change and decisional balance for 12 problem behaviors. *Health Psychology, 13,* 39–46.

Ravnikar, V. A. (1987). Compliance with hormone therapy. *American Journal of Obstetrics and Gynecology, 156,* 1332–1334.

Rippetoe, P. A., & Rogers, R. W. (1987). Effects of components of protection-motivation theory on adaptive and maladaptive coping with a health threat. *Journal of Personality and Social Psychology, 52,* 596–604.

Rollnick, S., Mason, P., & Butler, C. (1999). *Health behavior change: A guide for practitioners.* New York: Churchill Livingstone.

Rosen, C. S. (2000). Is the sequencing of change processes by stage consistent across health problems? A meta-analysis. *Health Psychology, 19,* 593–604.

Rosson, M. B. (1999). I get by with a little help from my cyber-friends. *Journal of Computer-Mediated Communication, 4*(4). Retrieved September 3, 2004 from http://jcmc.indiana.edu/vol4/issue4/rosson .html

Roth, H. P. (1987). Measurement of compliance. *Patient Education and Counseling, 10,* 107–116.

Salzman, C. (1995). Medication compliance in the elderly. *Journal of Clinical Psychiatry, 56*(Suppl. 1), 18–22.

Scott-Levin. (2001). [Data on patient persistency with Evista and Fosamax (osteoporosis drugs)]. Unpublished raw data.

Sheeran, P., Conner, M., & Norman, P. (2001). Can the theory of planned behavior explain patterns of health behavior change? *Health Psychology, 20,* 12–19.

Smith, D. (1989). Compliance packaging: A patient education tool. *American Pharmacy, NS29*(2), 127.

Smith, M. (1985). The cost of noncompliance and the capacity of improved compliance to reduce health care expenditures. In *Improving medication compliance: Proceedings of a symposium* (pp. 35–42). Reston, VA: National Pharmaceutical Council.

Smith, P., & Andrews, J. (1983). Drug compliance not so bad, knowledge not so good—the elderly after hospital discharge. *Age and Ageing, 12,* 336–342.

Tagliacozzo, D. M., Luskin, D. B., Lashof, J. C., & Ima, K. (1974). Nurse intervention and patient behavior: An experimental study. *American Journal of Public Health, 64,* 596–603.

Takala, J., Niemelä, N., Rosti, J., & Sievers, K. (1979). Improving compliance with therapeutic regimens in hypertensive patients in a community health center. *Circulation, 59,* 540–544.

Tashkin, D. P., Rand, C., Nides, M., Simmons, M., Wise, R., Coulson, A. H., et al. (1991). A nebulizer chronolog to monitor compliance with inhaler use. *American Journal of Medicine, 91*(Suppl. 4A), 33S–36S.

The medicine isn't going down. (2000). *American Science News, 158,* 11.

Thompson, D., Buesching, D., Gregor, K. J., & Oster, G. (1996). Patterns of antidepressant use and their relation to costs of care. *American Journal of Managed Care, 2,* 1239–1246.

Tierney, R., Melfi, C. A., Signa, W., & Crognah, T. (2000). Antidepressant use and use patterns in naturalistic settings. *Drug Benefit Trends, 12,* 7–12.

Tversky, A., & Kahneman, D. (2000). Rational choice and the framing of decisions. In D. Kahneman & A. Tversky (Eds.). *Choices, values, and frames* (pp. 209–223). Cambridge, UK: Cambridge University Press.

Valenti, W. M. (2001). Treatment adherence improves outcomes and manages costs. *AIDS Reader, 11,* 77–80.

Weinstein, N. D. (1993). Testing four competing theories of health-protective behavior. *Health Psychology, 12,* 324–333.

Wolfe, S. C., & Schirm, V. (1992). Medication counseling for the elderly: Effects on knowledge and compliance after hospital discharge. *Geriatric Nursing, 13*(3), 134–138.

Zweben, A., & Zuckoff, A. (2002). Motivational interviewing and treatment adherence. In W. R. Miller & S. Rollnick (Eds.), *Motivational interviewing: Preparing people for change* (2nd ed., pp. 299–319). New York: Guilford Press.

13

An Ecological Approach to Adherence in Diabetes Management

Perspectives From the Robert Wood Johnson Foundation Diabetes Initiative

Edwin B. Fisher

Carol A. Brownson

Mary L. O'Toole

Victoria Anwuri

Gowri Shetty

Richard R. Rubin

C omplexity of management regimen has long been recognized as a challenge to adherence and self-management (Dailey, Kim, & Lian, 2001; Donnan, MacDonald, & Morris, 2002; Melikian, White, Vanderplas, Dezeii, & Chang, 2002). However, a dimension of the complexity of diabetes management that has received somewhat less attention is its extension throughout the settings of daily life—family, neighborhoods, workplaces, and communities.

This chapter reviews previous research on adherence in diabetes, frames that within an ecological approach to self-management developed through the Diabetes Initiative of the Robert Wood Johnson Foundation, and describes several promising approaches to extend support for adherence from projects of the Diabetes Initiative.

Rubin (2005) recently identified several characteristics of diabetes management that have strong impacts on adherence. First is the individual's comprehension of the effects diabetes may have on her or his welfare, the pertinence of those effects to the proposed treatment, and the benefits of the treatment. Second is the complexity of regimens. For example, in a paper cited by Rubin, electronic monitoring of medication taking showed that adherence rates were 79% in regimens involving once-daily doses of medication, decreasing to 66% for twice-daily doses, and 38% in regimens involving 3 doses per day (Paes, Bakker, & Soe-Agnie, 1997).

Medication costs constitute a third factor that discourages adherence. Eleven percent of respondents to a survey of adults with Type 2 diabetes reported limiting their glucose-lowering medications in the previous year because of costs (Piette, Heisler, & Wagner, 2004). Disproportionate prevalence among low-income and disadvantaged populations makes this an especially critical barrier for diabetes management.

As also noted by Rubin (2005), diabetes and its treatment often entail a variety of adverse events that can deter adherence. For example, "tight" glucose control often increases the frequency of mild hypoglycemia, disturbing and compromising quality of life even if not clinically serious. Other adverse events include drug interactions and problems with medication tolerance. Also, medications for conditions that frequently co-occur with diabetes (e.g., hypertension, high cholesterol) may bring additional adverse events (gastrointestinal problems, sexual problems, drowsiness). Research suggests that people who are not totally adherent to all their medications tend to have just one medication they skip frequently, and it is the one that they perceive to be producing the greatest side effects (Grant, Devita, Singer, & Meigs, 2003).

Emotional well-being is an important dimension of diabetes management that has strong relationships with adherence but often receives insufficient attention in diabetes care. In one study, almost 70% of adults with diabetes reported that psychological problems limited their treatment adherence (Peyrot, Rubin, & Siminerio, 2002). Almost 50% of this same sample reported specific psychological problems (e.g., depression) or poor psychological well-being, but only 10% reported systematic treatment for these.

Rubin (2005) described a number of approaches to meeting the challenges of improving adherence. These include verifying comprehension and recall of regimens and their rationales, clarifying treatment benefits, simplifying regimens, using electronic monitoring to enable follow-up to focus on specific areas of adherence problems, minimizing costs, discussing and mitigating adverse events, and combining both treatment of emotional distress and supporting "healthy coping" (American Association of Diabetes Educators, n.d.).

Complementary to approaches for clinicians to take in improving adherence in diabetes, ecological perspectives point to broader influences on behavior. From an ecological approach, the behavior of the individual is surrounded by layers of influence from family, social network, neighborhood, community and organizations such as workplaces, cultural factors, policy, and government (Glasgow, 1995; McLeroy, Bibeau, & Steckler, 1988; Sallis & Owen, 2002; Stokols, 1996). This perspective suggests additional ways to promote adherence, such as ongoing support from peers and health workers or community or policy approaches to addressing costs and some of the other barriers identified by Rubin. Integration of this broad, ecological perspective with interventions of individual professionals in clinical settings has been a focus of the Diabetes Initiative of the Robert Wood Johnson Foundation.

The Robert Wood Johnson Foundation Diabetes Initiative

The Diabetes Initiative extends self management and support for diabetes care to 14 real world settings serving diverse audiences in the United States. Based on extensive research showing the importance of self management both in diabetes care and prevention (e.g., Glasgow et al., 1999), the Initiative was developed by the Foundation to demonstrate successful models of self management programs as a way of stimulating further dissemination of state-of-the-art programs, especially reaching disadvantaged groups that experience a disproportionate burden of diabetes. In particular, projects were chosen to "demonstrate that comprehensive models for diabetes self-management can be delivered in primary care settings and can significantly improve patient outcomes."[1] Recognizing that diabetes management takes place throughout the daily settings of individuals' lives, projects were also chosen to "extend support for diabetes management beyond the clinical setting into the communities where people with diabetes live."[2] In light of the status of diabetes as an ideal model for chronic disease care (Fisher, Delamater, Bertelson, & Kirkley, 1982; Glasgow et al., 1999), the Initiative's projects also were anticipated to serve as demonstrations of self-management support and community support, two components of Wagner's chronic care model (Wagner, 1998) that have received somewhat less attention than its more clinical components. In addition to evaluations of the individual sites and of lessons to be learned from their projects, a cross-site evaluation is being conducted by RTI International.

To guide the integration of services provided to individuals in clinical settings with services and supports provided through families, workplaces, and other community settings, the Diabetes Initiative developed an ecological model of self-management organized from the perspective of the individual's need for "resources and supports for self-management" (RSSM) (Fisher et al., 2005, p. 1523). RSSM include individualized assessment, collaborative goal setting, enhancing skills for self-management (including a wide range of skills such as those required for physical activity, healthy eating, problem solving, and healthy coping), ongoing follow-up and support, access to resources (such as those required for healthy eating and physical activity), and continuity of quality clinical care. The remainder of this chapter focuses on approaches developed by projects of the Diabetes Initiative to provide RSSM in clinical and community settings. These include enhancing the focus on self-management and adherence of the clinician during the outpatient visit, group medical visits, attention to emotional distress in diabetes care and management, use of community health workers (CHWs) in diabetes management, and providing ongoing follow-up and support for sustained diabetes management.

Making the Primary Care Doctor Count: Enhancing Focus on Self-Management in the Outpatient Visit

The limited time available in outpatient medical encounters poses substantial challenges to efforts to encourage adherence and self-management. The Diabetes Initiative project of St. Peter Family Medicine Residency Program in Olympia, Washington, has developed ways of enhancing the focus on self-management in the patient-physician interaction. The process begins with the provider and medical assistant reviewing patient goals and developing a plan for medical intervention. The medical assistant then contacts patients and invites them to a "planned visit." During this planned visit, the medical assistant follows a standing order protocol that includes taking a history, recording immunizations, performing foot checks and vital signs, and obtaining needed laboratory testing and specialist referrals and ends with an introduction to self-management goal setting. If appropriate, the patient considers committing himself or herself to a specific goal. The medical assistant follows standard cues for self-management goal setting based on the transtheoretical model. A typical planned visit currently takes approximately 15 minutes.

The medical assistant enters data directly into a standing order form and inputs lab results into an electronic medical record after the visit. When the patient is scheduled to see the physician 1 week later, the medical assistant provides the physician the completed standing order form and lab results along with a graphic display of these and previous results. With this information already brought together, the physician is then free to focus on updating treatment plans and self-management plans with the patient. This includes collaborative setting of self-management goals with the patient. Both the goals and a rating of their quality (based on pertinence and specificity) are included in clinical records from the encounter.

Following the medical visit, the medical assistant confers with the physician about follow-up strategies and then calls the patient 2 weeks later to review self-management goals, provide support and encouragement, and attend to any need of the patient for greater knowledge or skills to pursue his or her goals. The process is repeated with each medical visit, approximately every 3 or 4 months.

All medical assistants at St. Peter Family Medicine are trained to conduct planned visits. Based on experience with this approach, the planned visits appear to organize care and improve efficiency so that the provider is afforded more time for disease management and self-management support.

Group Medical Visits

In group medical visits (Beck et al., 1997), all patients in a particular category, say, those with diabetes, are scheduled for a group visit in a 2- or 3-hour block of time. Physicians and other staff carry out basic assessments and individual medical visits within this group visit that also includes educational and supportive discussions or other activities. Evaluation of group medical visits relative to usual care have indicated impressive impacts on glucose control as well as other measures (Trento et al., 2001, 2004).

Diabetes Initiative projects have developed several approaches to implement group medical visits and have expanded group visits to cover a greater range of RSSM. At Open Door Heath Center in Homestead, Florida, patients with Type 2 diabetes are divided into four groups, which are each assigned a Tuesday of the month for their group visit. Patients attend the "group support visit" every other month, alternating with bimonthly individual provider visits. These are open sessions, and family members are encouraged to participate. The group support visit includes blood sugar checks before and after a group walk and a discussion around one of a rotating series of topics of the day. The group is lead by a professional "lifestyle coach" (dietitian/ health educator) who is assisted by a peer CHW. Patients can also pick up medications and/or see the physician who holds the Tuesday times available for such contact as needed.

Each of the three clinical teams at St. Peter Family Medicine Residency Program offers its patients a group medical visit staffed by a faculty physician, two medical assistants, and three resident physicians who receive oversight from the faculty member. Eight to fourteen patients attend each session. One of the medical assistants has adapted the content of the chronic disease self-management program (Lorig & Holman, 2003) to develop patient education "modules" for the group visit sessions. These are the base for solution-focused activities with patients in the group visits.

In the project of New River Health Association and the Department of Family and Community Health at Marshall University School of Medicine in Huntington, West Virginia, group visits are offered twice a month and last 2 to 2.5 hours. They are staffed with teams consisting of a physician, a nurse, and a facilitator. The group visits include the same services that are delivered during routine individual office visits but are organized to provide a supportive group setting. Patients' most recent lab values are posted, vital signs are taken, and foot inspections are performed. Twelve to fifteen patients generally participate in each visit. Patients have the option of seeing their physician privately or electing one or the other type of visit as their preferred mode of receiving medical care. For physicians and other health care professionals, group visits are billable services that increase the time available for direct patient education.

The group visit at New River Health Association typically allows 20 minutes for health education discussions that address patient's questions, as well as risk assessment, medical decision making, and collaborative goal setting that helps patients make action plans. As part of every group visit, there is education about lab values, nutrition, and physical activity, with other topics addressed as they emerge. Patients talk to one another and hear the answers to questions that may not have occurred to them or that they may be reluctant to ask. Experience at New River indicates that group visits provide several advantages including an improved system for follow-up of diabetes care, time for patient education and discussion, more time with the medical care team, improved access, greater patient and provider satisfaction, and fewer urgent care visits. Additionally, patients who attend group visits appear to be more likely to pursue self-management activities.

New River Health Association has seen the use of group visits expand from one group visit on chronic illness care to group visits addressing mental health, black lung disease, and chronic pain and from one clinical team to seven. New River has provided consultation and education about group visits to other clinics in their system.

In spite of the apparent benefits of group visits, some patients find the group visit intimidating and overwhelming with so many patients and so many activities going on simultaneously. Some find the 2- to 2.5-hour duration too time-consuming, and others prefer to see their primary care provider each time they come to the clinic. In response, St. Peter Family Medicine Residency Program designed two variations of the group visit: the "mini" group visit and the "open-access, open-office" session.

The mini group session brings together three or four patients with a physician and a medical assistant for a more intimate 1-hour group medical session. With patients' consent, their medical information is shared with the group. Barriers to and successes with lifestyle change are explored, and previous self-management goals are reviewed. New goals are set, and if patients are willing, contact information is exchanged. Patients may choose to call each other between visits to "check in," offer support, and share successes and frustrations. Medical management is part of the mini visit, as it is during a routine provider visit, but it occurs openly with the input of other patients. Counter to concerns that those with emotional problems might be reluctant to express them in such a setting, experience shows that problems with depression and social stressors surface more easily so that patient-selected goals often focus on stress reduction and counseling. Teams have witnessed some very intense and touching connections between patients (tears, hugs, laughter, etc.) and anticipate that these new relationships will lead to improved disease (diabetes, depression, etc.) management and better outcomes. The following is an example of interactions within and progress through the mini group visit:

> Maggy (aged 27), her uncle Henry (aged 61), and Cynthia (aged 48) were the first to attend a mini visit. Maggy had made a recent breakthrough with regard to her depression, and

her diabetes was under better control. She believed her uncle's recent diagnosis and her relative "expertise" with diabetes, along with counseling, had given her a new perspective on her disease. She shared her story with Cynthia, who was suffering from severe depression with profound feelings of hopelessness. Cynthia ended the session feeling inspired and made a new commitment to follow through with counseling at Behavior Health Resources. Henry, who was under excellent glycemic control, was quite taken by the experience and offered to call Cynthia to check in with her in a week or two. Self-management goals, phone numbers, and hugs were exchanged. All three pledged to return in 3 to 4 months for another mini visit.

The open-access, open-office group session is quite different in that patients are asked to bring their own questions to a group session where the provider has no prepared medical agenda or plan. All 300 of St. Peter Family Medicine patients with diabetes are invited to come over a 2-hour period for as long as they need, where they will have the attention of two providers. Patient's charts are available if needed. Many topics have been discussed, including diet fads, alternative medicine/herbal treatments, exercise/safety, medications (types and mechanism of actions, interactions), labs, depression and social stressors, barriers to successful lifestyle changes, and success stories. Patient feedback has been very positive, prompting St. Peter Family Medicine to hold further sessions. Individualized chart notes are dictated after each session and reflect the information or discussion specific to each patient. St. Peter Family Medicine has been successful in billing for services based on these notes.

An important feature of the several types of group visits is their creating a menu of choices for patients to customize their medical care to best meet their needs. By combining a planned visit with a provider visit, followed by a medical assistant's phone call of support and then having an open-office session a few months later,

patients are able to gain control of their medical issues and be supported and encouraged in the process. Some patients may choose a combination of planned and provider visits with a "traditional" group session, whereas other patients may prefer a combination of planned visits with mini group visits with their provider. Providing patients choices among care patterns constitutes more personalized, customer-driven service that will likely lead to improved patient satisfaction, engagement in care, and treatment adherence.

Use of Community Health Workers

A popular and effective approach to extending the range of providers to enhance follow-up and support is through nonprofessionals such as CHWs, also called lay health workers, *promotoras*, health coaches, or lay health educators. In a number of settings, CHWs have been found to be effective in individualized assessment, goal setting, and teaching skills as well as for providing follow-up and support (Corkery et al., 1997; Swider, 2002; Zuvekas, Nolan, Tumaylle, & Griffin, 1999). Observations from sites of the Robert Wood Johnson Foundation Diabetes Initiative indicate their widespread use and utility in patient education and problem solving as well as in ongoing support and encouragement. CHWs are used to provide individual services, including monitoring, patient education, assistance in problem solving, and encouragement for ongoing self-management. They are also used in a number of settings to run group self-management classes. At Maine General Health, a program focused on promoting physical activity as a part of diabetes management centers on lay health educators who work with individuals seeking to increase their activity levels. At Campesinos sin Fronteras, a community-based diabetes program in Arizona, *animadoras* are program participants who assist with group programs and have the opportunity to be trained to become *promotoras*.

Key characteristics of CHWs may be the time they spend with patients and, connected to this, their availability to discuss a wide range of issues, not just details of disease management. Research on adherence implicates the importance of time (Ludmerer, 1999). Growing recognition of the importance of stress and negative emotion, both as barriers to disease management and as direct influences on clinical status (Williams, Barefoot, & Schneiderman, 2003) also point to the utility of CHWs addressing wide-ranging problems in people's lives. Linked to time available and flexibility to discuss diverse problems, research indicates several additional characteristics of CHWs that may be especially beneficial including easy access to them (Fisher, 1996) and support that is nondirective (cooperating without taking control, accepting the recipient's perspectives rather than prescribing correct courses of action) (Fisher, La Greca, Greco, Arfken, & Schneiderman, 1997; Fisher, Todora, & Heins, 2003) or that enhances autonomy (Williams, Rodin, Ryan, Grolnick, & Deci, 1998).

Attention to Emotional Distress in Diabetes Care

During the initial phases of their projects, Diabetes Initiative grantees focused attention on how depression complicated self-management both through adding problems needing to be addressed and through interfering with efforts to motivate ongoing self-management. This has led to plans for screening for depression in primary care, providing interventions for those with depression, and exploration of the roles of community health workers and others outside the primary care setting in identifying and assisting those with depression. Across all these, an important observation has been the integration of attention to depression with the rest of diabetes self-management. In contrast to viewing depression as automatically requiring separate treatment or even as precluding self-management pending satisfactory treatment of

depression, there has been increased recognition of the overlap between self-management tasks and improvement in depression. For example, physical activity has mood-elevating effects as well as improving glucose metabolism.

In addition to the effects on mood of some aspects of diabetes management, the very process of setting individualized goals and realizing success in achieving them that is intrinsic to virtually all approaches to self-management is also central to several leading approaches to treating depression. For example, problem-solving therapy for depression (D'Zurilla & Nezu, 1999) emphasizes a standard approach to setting goals, identifying alternative ways of pursuing goals, choosing a strategy, implementing plans, reevaluating, and reassessing, which is standard in virtually all approaches to self-management dating from the 1970s (Etzwiler, 1986; Fisher., 1986; Lorig et al., 1999). This recognition of the overlap of addressing depression and promoting self-management has led to broader views of approaches to treating depression, ranging from screening and medication provided through primary care to assistance provided by CHWs, in some cases without the word *depression* ever being used.

Faced with significant numbers of patients with a new diagnosis of depression, 9 of the 14 sites of the Diabetes Initiative have shared experiences in developing their approaches to dealing with depression. All nine sites use the PHQ9 (Kroenke, Spitzer, & Williams, 2001) for screening. This has indicated prevalence of moderate to severe depression well above the range of 18% to 31% reported in the literature (Anderson, Freedland, Clouse, & Lustman, 2001), as high as 70% in one site.

Across the treatment approaches of the nine sites, several key themes emerged. First is the importance of the primary care setting in identifying and treating depression. For many patients, the primary care setting is the only and/or most convenient and/or preferred point of access to services, including mental health services. Recognizing this, several of the grantees have focused on enhancing and expanding their primary care services and resources for treating depression. All nine sites provide antidepressant medication as needed. Beyond this, the sites have provided varying additional services, including referral to psychologists or other counselors or psychiatrists; group treatment; and at Community Health Center, Inc. in Connecticut, integration of psychological counseling into primary care through close consultation between the psychologist and other care providers, offering psychological counseling within the primary care setting, and integrated medical records. All the nine sites provide some variety of psychotherapy, group therapy, or counseling to their patients in addition to medication for depression.

An important extension of CHW interventions is their role with individuals coping with depression and negative emotions. Services include referrals from CHWs to primary care providers, with a query as to the need for mental health services, or directly to mental health providers. They also include referral to CHWs from mental health and other providers for ongoing support and/or enrollment in self-management classes likely to help them.

At Gateway Community Health Center in Laredo, Texas, *promotoras* have been incorporated into the clinic staff, to teach a 10-week diabetes self-management course in the clinic and administer the PHQ9 twice during the 10-week course. Patients who screen positive for depression are referred to their primary care provider for further evaluation. After treatment has been initiated, *promotoras* follow a depression protocol to follow up with patients. This protocol involves weekly phone contact emphasizing mood improvement, troubleshooting of antidepressant medications, and suicide prevention. At Campesinos sin Fronteras, a community-based organization in Arizona, *promotoras* also visit patients in their homes to provide depression assessment, advice, and support.

Beyond depression, per se, Diabetes Initiative projects have been influenced by recognition of the more general role of negative emotions and

emotional distress in diabetes as in other chronic diseases, including cardiovascular disease (Williams et al., 2003) for which diabetes is a major risk factor and antecedent. Anxiety, stress, hostility all contribute to heightened morbidity and mortality along with depression. Especially in the low-income populations served by the Diabetes Initiative projects, social, economic, and family stressors also add to the burden of negative emotion complicating disease management and adding to the risk of more severe disease (Wright & Fisher, 2003). Parallel to this wide range of negative emotions, a wide range of skills including problem-solving skills, stress management skills, and skills in cognitive management of negative emotion (Beck, Rush, Shaw, & Emery, 1979; Lustman, Griffith, Freedland, Kissel, & Clouse, 1998; Nezu, Nezu, Felgoise, McClure, Houts, 2003; Penedo et al., 2004) are pertinent to those with diabetes.

In reflection, understanding of the role of depression and negative emotion in the Diabetes Initiative has progressed through several stages:

1. Recognition that depression is a barrier to self-management

2. Recognition of the centrality of goal setting and problem solving in both depression and diabetes self-management so that interventions can focus on both

3. Recognition that depression and its treatment are a part of a broader range of negative emotions and skills for coping with them that are widely pertinent to those with diabetes

This recognition of the wide range of negative emotions and coping skills pertinent to diabetes management leads finally to a normalization of negative emotion in diabetes and recognition of the central role of such skills in diabetes management. In contrast then to the view of depression as a comorbidity requiring separate treatment and perhaps precluding "normal" efforts at self-management, negative emotion is seen as a routine part of the experience of many of those with diabetes. Approaches to preventing or alleviating negative emotion become, in turn, routine parts of skills to be taught for diabetes management. This is expressed positively in the American Association of Diabetes Educators (n.d.) having included healthy coping among its AADE7 Self-Care Behaviors™.

Ongoing Follow-Up and Support

The ecological perspective and several of the interventions described here reflect the fact that diabetes management is "24/7," involved in every aspect of individuals' lives. The most important aspect of diabetes, however, may be that it is "for the rest of your life." A vigorous combination of medical treatment, adherence, and self-management does not "solve" the problem. Rather, those with diabetes face a lifelong challenge of maintaining their management patterns and coping with unpredictable changes in their disease status, which is an intrinsic characteristic of the disease even with the best self-management. Reflecting this, major meta-analyses of self-management programs in diabetes (Norris, Engelgau, & Narayan, 2001; Norris, Lau, Smith, Schmid, & Engelgau, 2002) found that the only program feature that was uniquely predictive of success was duration of contact. "Interventions with regular reinforcement are more effective than one-time or short-term education" (Norris et al., 2001, p. 583). This mirrors meta-analyses of smoking cessation. As Kottke and his colleagues put it aptly in a major review of smoking cessation interventions (Kottke, Battista, & DeFriese, 1988), "Success was not associated with novel or unusual interventions. It was the product of personalized smoking cessation advice and assistance, repeated in different forms by several sources over the *longest feasible period* [italics added]" (pp. 2888–2889).

Self-management and adherence in chronic disease require "chronic" ongoing follow-up and support. It makes no more sense to assume self-management patterns will be sustained in the absence of ongoing follow-up and support than it makes to assume that improvements in blood sugar levels brought on through medications will be sustained in the absence of the medication. As Baer, Wolf, and Risley (1968) put it in some of the earliest writings in behavior modification, "Generalization [or maintenance of behavior change] should be programmed, rather than expected or lamented" (p. 97).

Several of the programmatic approaches described in this chapter appear to have particular utility in providing ongoing follow-up and support. Group medical visits and offering patients a variety of types of visits (planned individual; group; mini group; open access, open office as at St. Peter Family Medicine Residency Program) provide an opportunity for conveniently accessing care and consultation and alternatives that may fit changes in need or preference over time. Similarly, CHWs provide individualized, flexible social support, "troubleshooting," problem solving, and review of management plans. Programs are often organized so that CHWs have ample time to listen to and discuss individuals' problems, including those that may not be directly related to diabetes but, as we increasingly understand the diffuse roles of stress and negative emotion (Williams et al., 2003; Wright & Fisher, 2003), may be very important influences on self-management and adherence. Several Diabetes Initiative sites provide CHW services as long as the client needs or wishes. This is an important feature in providing follow-up and support for diabetes that is "for the rest of your life."

Paradoxically, "high-tech" approaches may provide new opportunities for the ongoing support that we may tend to see as the "warm, fuzzy" of diabetes care. Phone calls (Wasson et al., 1992; Weinberger et al., 1995) and the Internet (McKay, Feil, Glasgow, & Brown, 1998) have been shown to be valuable in providing ongoing support. In one study, follow-up from nurses included calls twice a week for 1 month, and then weekly. Relative to controls, the intervention achieved significant improvements in glucose control and improved diet (Kim & Oh, 2003). In another study, phone calls from nurses were scheduled at least monthly and reviewed patient education, adherence, and general health status as well as problem solving and access to care. Relative to controls they also improved glucose control (Weinberger et al., 1995). The combination of automated phone monitoring with nurse follow-up was successful in reaching low-income and minority patients and achieving benefits not only in blood glucose levels but also in increased self-efficacy and reduced levels of depression (Piette, McPhee, Weinberger, Mah, & Kraemer, 1999; Piette et al., 2000).

A critical aspect of "for the rest of your life" is the fact that changes in life circumstances (e.g., children moving away from home, divorce, widowhood, retirement) and development of problems with diabetes (e.g., vision problems, problems with sexual function) will provoke emotional distress as individuals move through life. Flexible, accessible approaches to recognizing emotional distress and making assistance available, such as those described in the programs of several Diabetes Initiative grantees, should provide helpful *ongoing* resources. The American Association of Diabetes Educators (n.d.) takes this further through a prospective approach to negative emotion and stress, teaching and promoting skills for healthy coping as a normal part of diabetes care throughout the life span.

As important as ongoing follow-up and support are for management of a chronic disease, little research in diabetes management has addressed them (Fisher et al., 2005). The ecological perspective of RSSM suggests exciting approaches to enhancing ongoing follow-up and support through family, community, organizational, and policy channels. These should combine with excellent, ongoing clinical care and be recognized as critical parts of the comprehensive resources and support people with diabetes need to manage their disease throughout their lives—"24/7" and "for the rest of your life."

Concluding Thoughts

This paper has posed several extensions of our ways of looking at adherence. One extension entails broadening our views from thinking about adherence to medication to thinking about engagement in a way of life (self-management) that includes effective use of medicines as well as all the other things individuals can do to manage diseases like diabetes, prevent disease, and enhance their lives. A second extension entails the ecological perspective and RSSM that identify the importance of a wide range of influences, including clinical care, in giving people what they need to lead healthy and satisfying lives. From adherence to engagement in life, ecological perspectives expand our view of how behavioral science can enable people to do—and continue doing—the things that will improve their health and well-being.

Notes

1. Call for Proposals, Advancing Diabetes Self Management, the Robert Wood Johnson Foundation, July 2002, p. 3.
2. Call for Proposals, Building Community Supports for Diabetes Care, the Robert Wood Johnson Foundation, July 2002, p. 4.

References

American Association of Diabetes Educators. (n.d.). AADE7™ self-care behaviors. Retrieved April 14, 2006, from www.aadenet.org/AADE7/#AADE7

Anderson, R. J., Freedland, K. E., Clouse, R. E., & Lustman, P. J. (2001). The prevalence of comorbid depression in adults with diabetes: A meta-analysis. *Diabetes Care, 24*(6), 1069–1078.

Baer, D. M., Wolf, M. M., & Risley, T. R. (1968). Some current dimensions of applied behavior analysis. *Journal of Applied Behavior Analysis, 1,* 91–97.

Beck, A. T., Rush, A. J., Shaw, B. F., & Emery, G. (1979). *Cognitive therapy of depression.* New York: Guilford Press.

Beck, A., Scott, J., Willliams, P., Robertson, B., Jackson, D., Gade, G., et al. (1997). A randomized trial of group outpatient visits for chronically ill older HMO members: The Cooperative Health Care Clinic. *Journal of the American Geriatric Society, 45*(5), 543–549.

Corkery, E., Palmer, C., Foley, M. E., Schechter, C. B., Frisher, L., & Roman, S. H. (1997). Effect of a bicultural community health worker on completion of diabetes education in a Hispanic population. *Diabetes Care, 20,* 254–257.

Dailey, G., Kim, M. S., & Lian, J. F. (2001). Patient compliance and persistence with antihyperglycemic drug regimens: Evaluation of a Medicaid population with Type 2 diabetes mellitus. *Clinical Therapy, 23,* 1311–1320.

Donnan, P. T., MacDonald, T. M., & Morris, A. D. (2002). Adherence to prescribed oral hypoglycaemic medication in a population of patients with Type 2 diabetes: A retrospective cohort study. *Diabetic Medicine, 19,* 279–284.

D'Zurilla, T. J., & Nezu, A. M. (1999). *Problem-solving therapy* (2nd ed.). New York: Springer.

Etzwiler, D. D. (1986). Diabetes management: The importance of patient education and participation. *Postgraduate Medicine, 80,* 67–72.

Fisher, E. B., Jr. (1986). A skeptical perspective: The importance of behavior and environment. In K. A. Holroyd & T. L. Creer (Eds.), *Self-management of chronic disease: Recent developments in health psychology and behavioral medicine.* New York: Academic Press.

Fisher, E. B. (1996). A behavioral-economic perspective on the influence of social support on cigarette smoking. In L. Green & J. H. Kagel (Eds.), *Advances in Behavioral Economics* (Vol. 3, pp. 207–236). Norwood, NJ: Ablex.

Fisher, E. B., Brownson, C. A., O'Toole, M. L., Shetty, G., Anwuri, V. V., & Glasgow, R. E. (2005). Ecological approaches to self management: The case of diabetes. *American Journal of Public Health, 95*(9), 1523–1535.

Fisher, E. B., Jr., Delamater, A. M., Bertelson, A. D., & Kirkley, B. G. (1982). Psychological factors in diabetes and its treatment. *Journal of Consulting and Clinical Psychology, 50,* 993–1003.

Fisher, E. B., Jr., La Greca, A. M., Greco, P., Arfken, C., & Schneiderman, N. (1997). Directive and nondirective support in diabetes management. *International Journal of Behavioral Medicine, 4,* 131–144.

Fisher, E. B., Todora, H., & Heins, J. (2003). Social support in nutrition counseling. On the cutting edge. *Diabetes care and education, 24*(4), 18–20.

Glasgow, R. E. (1995). A practical model of diabetes management and education. *Diabetes Care, 18*(1), 117–126.

Glasgow, R. E., Fisher, E. B., Anderson, B. J., La Greca, A., Marrero, D., Johnson, S. B., et al. (1999). Behavioral science in diabetes: Contributions and opportunities. *Diabetes Care, 22,* 832–843.

Grant, R. W., Devita, N. G., Singer, D. E., & Meigs, J. B. (2003). Polypharmacy and medication adherence in patients with Type 2 diabetes. *Diabetes Care, 26,* 1408–1412.

Kim, H. S., & Oh, J. A. (2003). Adherence to diabetes control recommendations: Impact of nurse telephone calls. *Journal of Advanced Nursing, 44,* 256–261.

Kottke, T. E., Battista, R. N., & DeFriese, G. H. (1988). Attributes of successful smoking cessation interventions in medical practice: A meta-analysis of 39 controlled trials. *Journal of American Medical Association, 259,* 2882–2889.

Kroenke, K., Spitzer, R. L., & Williams, J. B. (2001). The PHQ-9: Validity of a brief depression severity measure. *Journal of General Internal Medicine, 16,* 606–613.

Lorig, K. R., & Holman, H. (2003). Self-management education: History, definition, outcomes, and mechanisms. *Annals of Behavioral Medicine, 26,* 1–7.

Lorig, K. R., Sobel, D. S., Stewart, A. L., Brown, B. W. B., Jr., Bandura, A., Ritter, P., et al. (1999). Evidence suggesting that a chronic disease self-management program can improve health status while reducing hospitalization: A randomized trial. *Medical Care, 37,* 5–14.

Ludmerer, K. M. (1999). *Time to heal: American medical education from the turn of the century to the era of managed care.* New York: Oxford University Press.

Lustman, P. J., Griffith, L. S., Freedland, K. E., Kissel, S. S., & Clouse, R. E. (1998). Cognitive behavior therapy for depression in Type 2 diabetes mellitus: A randomized, controlled trial. *Annals of Internal Medicine, 129*(8), 613–621.

McKay, H. G., Feil, E. G., Glasgow, R. E., & Brown, J. E. (1998). Feasibility and use of an Internet support service for diabetes self-management. *Diabetes Educator, 24,* 174–179.

McLeroy, K., Bibeau, D., & Steckler, A. (1988) An ecological perspective on health promotion programs. *Health Education Quarterly, 15,* 351–377.

Melikian, C., White, T. J., Vanderplas, A., Dezeii, C. M., & Chang, E. (2002). Adherence to oral antidiabetic therapy in a managed care organization: A comparison of monotherapy, combination therapy, and fixed-dose combination therapy. *Clinical Therapy, 24,* 460–467.

Nezu, A. M., Nezu, C. M., Felgoise, S. H., McClure, K. S., & Houts, P. S. (2003). Project Genesis: Assessing the efficacy of problem-solving therapy for distressed adult cancer patients. *Journal of Consulting and Clinical Psychology, 71,* 1036–1048.

Norris, S. L., Engelgau, M. M., & Narayan, K. M. (2001). Effectiveness of self-management training in Type 2 diabetes: A systematic review of randomized controlled trials. *Diabetes Care, 24,* 561–587.

Norris, S. L., Lau, J., Smith, S. J., Schmid, C. H., & Engelgau, M. M. (2002). Self-management education for adults with Type 2 diabetes: A meta-analysis of the effect on glycemic control. *Diabetes Care, 25,* 1159–1171.

Paes, A. H., Bakker, A., & Soe-Agnie, C. J. (1997). Impact of dosage frequency on patient compliance. *Diabetes Care, 20,* 1512–1517.

Penedo, F. J., Dahn, J. R., Molton, I., Gonzalez, J. S., Kinsinger, D., Roos, B. A., et al. (2004). Cognitive-behavioral stress management improves stress-management skills and quality of life in men recovering from treatment of prostate carcinoma. *Cancer, 100,* 192–200.

Peyrot, M., Rubin, R., & Siminerio, L. (2002). Physician and nurse use of psychosocial strategies and referrals in diabetes [Abstract]. *Diabetes, 51*(Suppl. 2), A446.

Piette, J. D., Heisler, M., & Wagner, T. H. (2004). Problems paying out-of-pocket medication costs among older adults with diabetes. *Diabetes Care, 27,* 384–391.

Piette, J. D., McPhee, S. J., Weinberger, M., Mah, C. A., & Kraemer, F. B. (1999). Use of automated telephone disease management calls in an ethnically diverse sample of low-income patients with diabetes. *Diabetes Care, 22,* 1302–1309.

Piette, J. D., Weinberger, M., & McPhee, S. J. (2000). The effect of automated calls with telephone nurse follow-up on patient-centered outcomes of diabetes care: A randomized, controlled trial. *Medical Care, 38,* 218–230.

Piette, J. D., Weinberger, M., McPhee, S. J., Mah, C. A., Kraemer, F. B., & Crapo, L. M. (2000). Do automated calls with nurse follow-up improve self-care and glycemic control among vulnerable patients with diabetes? *American Journal of Medicine, 108,* 20–27.

Rubin, R. R. (2005). Adherence to pharmacologic therapy in patients with Type 2 diabetes mellitus. *The American Journal of Medicine, 118*(Suppl. 5), 27–34.

Sallis, J. F., & Owen, N. (2002). Ecological models of health behavior. In F. M. L. K. Glanz & B. K. Rimer (Eds.), *Health behavior and health education: Theory, research, and practice* (3rd ed., pp. 462–484). San Francisco: Jossey-Bass.

Stokols, D. (1996). Translating social ecological theory into guidelines for community health promotion. *American Journal of Health Promotion, 10*(4), 282–298.

Swider, S. M. (2002). Outcome effectiveness of community health workers: An integrative literature review. *Public Health Nursing, 19,* 11–20.

Trento, M., Passera, P., Borgo, E., Tomalino, M., Bajardi, M., Cavallo, F., et al. (2004). A 5-year randomized controlled study of learning, problem solving ability, and quality of life modifications in people with Type 2 diabetes managed by group care. *Diabetes Care, 27,* 670–675.

Trento, M., Passera, P., Tomalino, M., Bajardi, M., Pomero, F., Allione, A., et al. (2001). Group visits improve metabolic control in Type 2 diabetes: A 2-year follow-up. *Diabetes Care, 24,* 995–1000.

Wagner, E. H. (1998). Chronic disease management: What will it take to improve care for chronic illness? *Effective Clinical Practice, 1*(1), 1–4.

Wasson, J., Gaudette, C., Whaley, F., Sauvigne, A., Baribeau, P., & Welch, H. G. (1992). Telephone care as a substitute for routine clinic follow-up. *Journal of American Medical Association, 267*(13), 1788–1793.

Weinberger, M., Kirkman, M. S., Samsa, G. P., Shortliffe, E. A., Landsman, P. B., Cowper, P. A., et al. (1995). A nurse-coordinated intervention for primary care patients with non-insulin-dependent diabetes mellitus: impact on glycemic control and health-related quality of life. *Journal of General Internal Medicine, 10,* 59–66.

Williams, R. B., Barefoot, J. C., & Schneiderman, N. (2003). Psychosocial risk factors for cardiovascular disease: More than one culprit at work. *Journal of the American Medical Association, 290,* 2190–2192.

Williams, G. C., Rodin, G. C., Ryan, R. M., Grolnick, W. S., & Deci, E. L. (1998). Autonomous regulation and long-term medication adherence in adult outpatients. *Health Psychology, 17,* 269–276.

Wright, R. J., & Fisher, E. B. (2003). Putting asthma into context: Community influences on risk, behavior, and intervention. In I. Kawachi & L. F. Berkman (Eds.), *Neighborhoods and health* (pp. 222–262). New York: Oxford.

Zuvekas, A., Nolan, L., Tumaylle, C., & Griffin, L. (1999). Impact of community health workers on access, use of services, and patient knowledge and behavior. *Journal of Ambulatory Care Management, 22,* 33–44.

14

Adherence Challenges in Asthma Treatment

Susan D. Schaffer

Asthma is a clinical disorder characterized by chronic airway inflammation, episodic wheezing, hyperresponsiveness of airways to a variety of stimuli, and largely reversible obstruction of airways (Agency for Healthcare Research and Quality [AHRQ], 2001). In 1997, 26.7 million Americans reported having received a physician diagnosis of asthma at some point, representing an increase in prevalence of 73% since 1980; 11 million reported experiencing an attack within the past year (Centers for Disease Control and Prevention [CDC], 2002). Continuing asthma morbidity for adults is also evident in the increasing number of outpatient and emergency visits for asthma, in the work-absence days related to asthma that more than doubled between 1980 and 1996, and in the increasing percentage of adults who report asthma-related activity limitations (CDC, 2002). Children, however, particularly inner-city children, bear a disproportionate burden of asthma morbidity and mortality (CDC, 2002). Uncontrolled asthma in children causes hospitalization, unscheduled visits to health providers, disturbed sleep, days lost from school, and decreased participation in physical activity and sports (Bauman et al., 2002; Robertson et al., 1998).

Because asthma is a chronic condition, symptom management and improved function are the focus of health provider interventions. Although avoidance of allergen/irritant exposure and appropriate recognition and treatment of asthma exacerbations are important, successful symptom management of asthma is largely determined by patient adherence to prescribed anti-inflammatory medications that can prevent attacks (Kohler, Davies, & Bailey, 1996). Inhaled corticosteroids (ICS), which have been recommended as first-line treatment for adults and children with persistent asthma, stabilize underlying inflammation and improve lung functioning (National Institutes of Health National Asthma Education and Prevention Program [NIH NAEPP], 2002). Results from large clinical trials have demonstrated that the use of ICS reduces morbidity and mortality associated with asthma (O' Byrne et al., 2001, Pauwels et al., 2003; The Childhood Asthma Management Program Research Group, 2000).

Continuing asthma morbidity has been linked to the failure of providers to prescribe ICS for patients with persistent asthma (Yuksel, Ginther, Man, & Tsuyuki, 2000) and the failure of these patients to use these medications on a regular basis (Anis et al., 2001; Bauman et al., 2002; Bender, 2002). The costs of nonadherence go beyond negative clinical outcomes for patients. In 1998, the total annual cost in economic terms of asthma hospitalizations was estimated to be almost $2.7 billion (Weiss & Sullivan, 2001). Although there is no generally recognized minimum level of adherence that provides clinical benefit, 80% to 85% has been used as a benchmark for asthma adherence (Creer & Levstek, 1997). However, researchers who have examined patient adherence to preventive asthma therapies report that rates of nonadherence are often over 50% (Creer, 1993; Jerome, Wigal & Creer, 1987; Rand & Wise, 1996).

Barriers to Asthma Treatment Adherence

Asthma medication nonadherence is associated with multiple socioeconomic, disease-, treatment-, provider-, and patient-related barriers (Bender, 2002; World Health Organization [WHO], 2003). Socioeconomic barriers include cultural and lay beliefs about illness and treatment, inability to afford medications or regular provider visits, and lack of transportation (Wallace, Scott, Kinnert, & Anderson, 2004; WHO, 2003). The most significant disease-related barrier is the variable nature of symptoms, which causes patient confusion about the accuracy of the diagnosis and the need for ongoing treatment. Treatment-related barriers include complex regimens, adverse medication effects, perceived medication effects, and delayed onset of action of ICS.

Provider-related barriers include lack of easy access to providers, treatment by multiple providers, provider communication difficulties, and short patient visits that limit asthma teaching. Patient-related barriers include poor understanding of the need for treatment, lack of confidence in the provider or medication, persistent misunderstandings about side effects, comorbid (especially psychological) problems, and lack of motivation to change behavior.

Although all these factors must be addressed to maximize adherence, patient motivation may be the most critical (Bender, 2002). A number of researchers have thus recommended that interventions focus on motivation to adhere (Blessing-Moore, 1996; Donaldson, Rutledge, & Pravikoff, 2000). Motivational interventions shape or reinforce behavior and include adherence contracts, reinforcement of psychomotor performances such as the skill of using a metered-dose inhaler (MDI), and reinforcement of perceptions of medication usefulness and of the patient's ability to manage a regimen or, for example, an asthma episode (Schaffer & Yoon, 2001). Patient-provider communication is at the heart of motivational interventions to enhance adherence.

Disease-Related Barriers

Intermittent symptoms are characteristic of asthma, yet patients may regard asymptomatic periods as remission or cure of asthma (Leickly et al., 1998). Mild or stable asthma symptoms can become normalized to such an extent that the effects of the disease are not noticed or are perceived as not burdensome (Steven, Morrison, & Drummone, 2002). Patients with severe asthma, particularly those with recurrent exacerbations, have blunted perception of dyspnea and find it difficult to determine when they should take treatment-related action (Veen et al., 1998).

Treatment-Related Barriers

Preventive medications like ICS do not relieve symptoms acutely, so patients may not view them as effective (Leickly et al., 1998). The requirement that medications be taken on an ongoing basis is a challenge to adherence; studies demonstrate that adherence to chronic medication decreases over time (Haynes et al., 2000; Jonasson, Carson, & Mohinckel, 2000). In addition, some treatment regimens require multiple doses of multiple medications, making it difficult for the patient to remember regimens (Eisen, Miller, Woodward, Spitznagel, & Przybeck, 1990; Pullar, Birtwell, Wiles, Hay, & Feely, 1988). Finally, current NAEPP (2002) recommendations that asthma medication regimens be "stepped down" to the least medication necessary to maintain control may contribute to patient perceptions that their asthma is cured or not problematic.

Inhaled ICS at low to moderate doses have been shown to have minimal systemic side effects. Studies encompassing 6 years of observation demonstrate no adverse effects on bone mineral density, no increased incidence of subcapsular cataracts or glaucoma, and no sustained effects on growth velocity in children (NIH NAEPP, 2002). Although the effects of ICS on hypothalamic-pituitary-adrenal axis function are measurable, these effects are clinically insignificant (NIH NAEPP, 2002). However, fear of cortisone-related side effects continues to deter adherence, particularly among parents of children with asthma.

Provider-Related Barriers

Failure of providers to prescribe ICS according to standardized treatment guidelines continues to be a national and international problem. One study of 1,022 patients showed that ICS had been prescribed for only half the patients who presented to an emergency room for acute asthma (Yuksel et al., 2000). Another study of nearly 11,000 Medicaid patients showed that fewer than half the patients with asthma were prescribed more than one puff of ICS per day (Shireman, Heaton, Gay, Cluxton, & Moomaw, 2002). Although a meta-analysis of randomized, controlled trials showed that written asthma

action plans are associated with improved asthma outcomes (Jones, Pill, & Adams, 2000), fewer than half the adults and children surveyed in multiple studies reported having a written action plan (Douglass et al., 2002; Haby, Powell, Oberklaid, Waters, & Robertson, 2002; Ruffin, Wilson, Southcott, Smith, & Adams, 1999).

The health care environments within which providers work may make it difficult for providers to provide the patient-centered counseling likely to optimize adherence (Belcher, 1990). The structure of that environment dictates whether patients see a consistent provider, whether appointments are of sufficient length for provision of asthma-related teaching, and whether written educational materials are available. Patient dissatisfaction with the patient-provider relationship can also decrease adherence to medication. Rand (2004) reports that providers do more than 60% of the talking during visits, rarely address psychosocial issues related to treatment, and fail to name the medication or give dosing instructions 50% of the time. Patients who do not understand provider instructions or who feel uncomfortable expressing concerns about medications are less likely to adhere (Apter, Reisine, Affleck, Barrows, & Zuwallack, 1998).

Patient-Related Barriers

For individuals with asthma, perceptions of the illness, of the illness' effects on everyday activities, and of their ability to control asthma symptoms are important determinants of adherence behavior (Rand & Butz, 2000; Steven et al., 2002). Steven et al. (2002) found that people with asthma may reject preventive medication because they do not accept that they have asthma, dislike relying on medication, or feel that asthma symptoms are not burdensome or asthma has little effect on their lives.

Patient misunderstanding of inhaled anti-inflammatory medications is associated with reduced adherence to its daily use (Farber et al., 2003). Wallace et al. (2004) found that patients were concerned that ICS are addictive. Horne and Weinman (1999) found that individuals with asthma who had been prescribed ICS had more concerns about taking their medications than renal, cardiac, or oncology patients had about theirs and were more likely to perceive that the costs of their medication outweighed the benefits. Another study found that participants were concerned with a number of side effects, including tremors, mouth or throat soreness, hoarseness, osteoporosis, or other effects less clearly related to the actual pharmacological effects of ICS (Goeman et al., 2002). This study also found that the cost of medication was an issue for nearly two thirds of the participants.

Although drug manufacturing companies are developing dry powder formulations for inhaled medications that are relatively easy to use, standard MDIs require a multistep process and hand-eye coordination to deliver effective doses. Patients who are not carefully educated about using MDIs often have inadequate technique, resulting in suboptimal doses of medication reaching the lungs and suboptimal asthma control even though they use the MDI as frequently as recommended (Giraud & Roche, 2002; Minai, Martin, & Cohn, 2004).

Patients with complicated lives have been shown to have particular problems with asthma medication adherence. For example, caring for an ill spouse is associated with considerable reduction in adherence (Barr, Somers, Speizer, & Camargo, 2002). Comorbidities requiring multiple medications for multiple medical conditions also decrease adherence to ICS (Balkrishnan & Christensen, 2000). Depression is particularly associated with nonadherence to asthma medication (Bosley, Fosbury, & Cochrane, 1995).

Measuring Treatment Adherence in Asthma

Although nonadherence to ICS deprives patients of the anticipated therapeutic benefits, providers often fail to question patients about adherence, and patients rarely volunteer this information (Steele, Jackson, & Gutmann, 1990). In any case, simply asking about medication usage does not ensure an accurate response. Self-report is prone to biases such as social desirability, interviewer technique, and psychological factors such as health beliefs or memory (Vitolins, Rand, Rapp, Ribisl, & Sevick, 2000). Self-report is, however, generally more valid for nonadherence than adherence (Rand & Butz, 2000). In requesting adherence information from a patient, it is helpful if the provider normalizes the possibility of missed doses to minimize the effect of social desirability (Quittner et al., 2000). Walewski et al. (2004) found significant correlations between pharmacy-verified medication refill patterns and responses to the following three questions: (1) How long does a canister of ICS usually last? (2) What percentage of doses do you estimate that you forget? (3) When was the last time you used short-acting bronchodilator medication (>12 hours ago correlates with low adherence). To promote accurate recall of adherence behavior in an interview setting, it may be ideal to limit questions to behavior occurring in the previous week (Rudd, 1993). Daily medication diaries eliminate recall bias, but it is difficult for patients to remember to maintain them, they can be falsified, and they are tedious for patients to use over the long term.

Assessing pharmacy refill patterns is increasingly recognized as a valid measure of adherence. Although refill patterns may overestimate use because medication purchased is not necessarily medication used and patients may use multiple pharmacies, records that reveal infrequent refilling of medication strongly suggest poor adherence (Sherman, Hutson, Baumstein, & Hendeles, 2000). Pharmacy refill is calculated as days of medication obtained (i.e., number of doses obtained divided by daily dosage) divided by the number of days between refill and date of office visit.

Electronic monitors that attach to MDIs can provide an accurate representation of patient usage and may directly increase adherence in those users informed of the capabilities of the device (Nides et al., 1993). These devices record the time, date, and number days of medication obtained of puffs taken, which enables providers to identify patients who "dump" medication from their MDI before a scheduled visit. Although they are expensive and unnecessary for most patients, the expense may be worthwhile in persons with severe asthma and multiple hospitalizations.

MDILog and Doser CT are the currently available monitoring devices, with mean accuracy ranging from 90.1 for the MDILog to 94.3 for the Doser CT (Julius, Sherman, & Hendeles, 2002). MDILog II (Medtrac Technologies, Lakewood, Colorado) is compatible with only two of the many preventive medication MDIs currently on the market (Medtrac Technologies, 2003). Doser CT (NewMed Corporation, Newton, Massachusetts) is an equally reliable but simpler device that can be attached to most standard MDIs by the participant when refills are obtained. It is automatically activated to record each inhalation taken each day and stores daily usage information for 45 days. Many asthma medications are being reformulated as non-aerosol, dry-powder inhalers. As these often incorporate dose counters, electronic devices may become less important.

Implementing Asthma Adherence Interventions

Patients whose asthma is well controlled should have minimal chronic symptoms, normal or near-normal lung function as measured by spirometry or peak flow reading, infrequent exacerbations, minimal need for "quick-relief" beta-agonist medications, no limitations on activities (including exercise) with no school or work missed due to asthma, and minimal adverse effects from medication (British Thoracic Society, 2003; NIH NAEPP, 2002). The most promising interventions to achieve these goals, according to current research, are multifaceted, incorporating patient education, contracts, self-monitoring, social support, telephone follow-up, tailoring of treatment to meet patient needs, and good provider-patient communication (see Miller, Hill, Kottke, & Ockene, 1997, for expert panel on compliance).

Provider Adherence Interventions: Education

Although knowledge alone does not ensure patient adherence, knowledge of the disease and of the treatment regimen is a necessary component of successful disease management (WHO, 2003). In 1997, the NAEP standardized the content areas about which clinicians should routinely educate their patients with asthma to enhance their self-management skills. These areas include basic facts about asthma, roles of medications, self-monitoring and inhaler skills, and environmental control strategies.

Teaching points related to asthma pathophysiology, asthma medication, using a standard inhaler, and environmental control measures are summarized in Table 14.1. Generally, providers should ensure that their patients with asthma understand that asthma is a chronic condition that cannot be cured but can be controlled and that symptoms may include coughing, wheezing, chest tightness, and shortness of breath. Patients must understand the differences and appropriate use of both controller (ICS) and quick-relief (i.e., short-acting bronchodilator) medications. Those who have normal lung function and who have symptoms ≤2 days/week or ≤2 nights/month and those who have exercise-induced symptoms only do not require daily medications. For all others, providers should emphasize that daily use of controller medications (usually ICS) is necessary to control asthma (NIH NAEPP, 2002). Providers should also ensure that patients are able to use their

Table 14.1   Asthma Knowledge Teaching Points

Key points on asthma pathophysiology

- The airways in the lungs are inflamed or swollen all the time even when the patient feels normal.
- Due to the inflammation in the airways patients are hyperresponsive to irritants like smoke, dust, and pollen.
- During an asthma attack the airways constrict, or become smaller, which causes coughing, wheezing, chest tightness, and shortness of breath.

Key points on asthma medications

Short-acting or quick-relief medications	*Long-acting or preventive medications*
• Quick-relief medications are taken *only* when symptoms of asthma are present and are intended to provide relief of symptoms. • The patient should take this medication when symptoms begin and are mild, to avoid a bad asthma attack. • Quick-relief medications last only about 4 hours and *do not* prevent symptoms from reoccurring. • The patient should notify the provider if quick-relief medications are needed more often than usual. This is a sign that long-term medications need to be added or changed. • Use of a peak flow meter will facilitate recognition of asthma exacerbations and help to determine when short-acting relief medications or additional actions are necessary.	• Preventive medications prevent symptoms and control asthma. • They must be taken every day, even if the patient feels well, to keep the asthma under control. • The patient should establish a daily routine for taking long-term control medicine. • It usually takes several weeks before the full effects of the medication are felt. • Steroid inhalers are not effective in relieving the symptoms of an acute exacerbation. • The patient should rinse the mouth and spit each time after using an inhaled steroid to help prevent side effects such as throat irritation and local fungal infection (thrush).

MDIs or dry powder inhalers or nebulizers appropriately and can identify and avoid things that make their asthma worse (environmental controls). See Table 14.2 (using metered dose inhalers) and Table 14.3 (key environmental control measures).

In addition to this basic knowledge about the disease and its treatment, patients must know how to monitor their symptoms and recognize and treat asthma exacerbations. An asthma action plan guides patient decision making related to asthma exacerbations and may be used for both patients who monitor symptoms and those who monitor peak flow readings. Figure 14.1 contains asthma action plan templates for adults and children.

Provider Adherence Interventions: Communication

Patient-provider communication can enhance patient knowledge and satisfaction with treatment and influence beliefs about treatment; however, poor patient-provider communication is common. Miller et al. (1997) recommend that providers relate to patients in an approachable, friendly, or supportive manner; inquire about patient concerns and treatment goals; actively listen to patient views; and use joint problem-solving strategies to enhance adherence. Providers should develop asthma action plans in concert with patients, acknowledging their patients' personal experiences with the disease (Douglass

Table 14.2   Key Points on Standard Inhalers

Steps for Using a Standard Inhaler	Cleaning the Inhaler	Replacing the Inhaler
For proper use of the inhaler, the patient should • Shake the inhaler before using it • Exhale all the way • Hold the inhaler 1–2 in. in front of his or her open mouth[a] • Begin to breathe in *slowly* as he or she presses down on the inhaler *once* (one puff)[b] • Keep breathing in *slowly*, as deeply as possible, until the lungs are full • Hold his or her breath and count to 10 slowly, if possible • Wait about 1 min between puffs for quick-relief medication (this is not necessary for the long-acting medications)	• To determine if the inhaler needs to be cleaned, the patient should look at the hole where the medicine sprays out; if he or she sees powder, it does need to be cleaned • The patient should remove the mouthpiece from the canister and rinse *only* the mouthpiece and cap in warm water • He or she should let the mouthpiece and cap dry overnight and then attach the canister to the mouthpiece and put the cap on	• The patient should note the available doses in the canister and calculate the number of days the canister will last (e.g., a canister containing 60 doses that is used twice daily will last 30 days) • The patient should dispose of the canister after the calculated date, even if it does not seem empty • Neither shaking the canister nor placing it in water is a reliable method of determining if the canister is empty

a. The inhaler may also be placed in the mouth if the patient finds the recommended technique difficult.

b. If a holding chamber/spacer is used, first press down on the inhaler, then begin to breathe in slowly within 5 seconds.

Table 14.3   Key Points on Environmental Control Measures

• If the patient smokes, the provider should encourage and assist him or her to stop.

• Smoking should not be allowed in the patient's home or in the patient's immediate vicinity.

• Mattresses and pillows should be incased in a special dustproof cover to reduce dust-mite exposure.

• If the patient is unable to purchase special covers for the pillows and mattress, then bed linen should be washed each week in hot water (130°F) to kill the mites.

• The bedroom should be kept as free of environmental asthma precipitants as possible.

• The patient should keep all food and furred or feathered pets out of the bedroom and keep the bedroom door closed.

• If pets reside in the house, the patient should replace the carpet with hard-surface floors or keep the pets out of rooms that have a carpet or cloth-covered furniture.

• The patient should replace carpets that have a moldy smell, as these may precipitate asthma exacerbation.

• Someone other than the patient should vacuum the home because vacuuming may precipitate an asthma attack.

(Continued)

Table 14.3 (Continued)

- The patient should keep windows closed during the night and stay inside with windows closed at midday and in the afternoon hours when pollen and some mold spore counts are the highest.
- Air-conditioned air circulated through regularly cleaned filters helps to decrease exposure to potential allergens.
- Patients should be informed about all medicines—such as aspirin, cold medicine, and eye drops—that may precipitate an asthma attack.
- Patients should clean moldy surfaces with bleach-containing cleaners.

SOURCE: Adapted from NAEPP (1997a) by Dinah Welch. Used with permission.

et al., 2002). In addition, providers should provide culturally appropriate written instructions about the treatment regimen that are tailored to the patient's level of literacy (WHO, 2003). It is also important that providers and health care facilities allow sufficient time for patient education and discussion related to disease and treatment during patient visits and ensure that mechanisms are established for easy phone access for patient questions (Apter et al., 1998; Korsch & Nagrete, 1972). Use of other health care providers such as nurses and pharmacists to supplement the efforts of providers can provide the kind of social support that improves adherence (DiMatteo, 2004).

Provider Interventions: Behavioral

Patients with asthma should be clinically assessed at least every 6 months because patients' memories and self-management practices fade with time (NIH NAEPP, 1997b). Treatment adherence should be assessed at every visit. More frequent visits are needed for patients who are newly diagnosed or poorly controlled (NIH NAEPP, 1997b, *Practical Guide*) and for patients whose medication regimens have changed (Barber, Parsons, Darracott, & Horne, 2004). Reinforcement, review, and reminders are needed for as long as chronic drug therapy is needed (Haynes et al., 2000; NIH NAEPP, 1997b, *Practical Guide*).

Providers should ask patients whether they are able to afford prescribed medications

(Stevens, Sharma, & Kesten, 2003; Tseng, Brook, Keeler, Steers, & Mangione, 2004). Patients who have cost concerns should receive sample medications if available. In the United States, many drug manufacturers provide chronic medications at minimal or no cost to patients who document financial need. Information may be obtained from drug company representatives or by accessing drug company Web sites.

Patient medication regimens should be as simple as possible, requiring patients to use medications no more than twice daily (Pullar et al., 1988; Sherman et al., 2000). Inhalers that contain multiple medications, which are becoming increasingly available, should be considered. These combined medications may be less expensive than the medications would be separately and may enhance adherence through their simplicity (Stoloff, Stempel, Meyer, Stanford, & Rosenzweig, 2004). Providers should advise patients to keep medications in locations (such as on the bedside table or next to the toothbrush or coffee pot) that allow medication taking to be associated with other routine activities (Roter et al., 1998; Schaffer & Yoon, 2001).

Patients who miss appointments should be contacted and offered new appointments because patients who lack prescriptions are unlikely to be taking their medication as prescribed (Haynes et al., 2000). Patients who have multiple health conditions, who have depression or other mental health issues, or who have had repeated acute visits for asthma exacerbations

ASTHMA ACTION PLAN FOR _____ Doctor's Name _____ Date _____

Doctor's Phone Number _____ Hospital/Emergency Room Phone Number _____

GREEN ZONE: Doing Well

- No cough, wheeze, chest tightness, or shortness of breath during the day or night
- Can do usual activities

And, if a peak flow meter is used,
Peak flow: more than _____
(80% or more of my best peak flow)
My best peak flow is: _____

Take These Long-Term-Control Medicines Each Day (include an anti-inflammatory)

Medicine	How much to take	When to take it

| Before exercise | ☐ 2 or ☐ 4 puffs | 5 to 60 minutes before exercise |

⇧

YELLOW ZONE: Asthma Is Getting Worse

- Cough, wheeze, chest tightness, or shortness of breath, or
- Waking at night due to asthma, or
- Can do some, but not all, usual activities

-Or-

Peak flow: _____ to _____
(50% - 80% of my best peak flow)

Add: Quick-Relief Medicine - and keep taking your GREEN ZONE medicine

☐ _____ ☐ 2 or ☐ 4 puffs, every 20 minutes for up to 1 hour
(short-acting beta$_2$-agonist) ☐ Nebulizer, once

If your symptoms (and peak flow, if used) *return to GREEN ZONE* **after 1 hour of above treatment:**
☐ Take the quick-relief medicine every 4 hours for 1 to 2 days.
☐ Double the dose of your inhaled steroid for _____ (7-10) days.

-Or-

If your symptoms (and peak flow, if used) do not return to GREEN ZONE after 1 hour of above treatment:
☐ Take: _____ ☐ 2 or ☐ 4 puffs or ☐ Nebulizer.
(short-acting beta$_2$-agonist)
☐ Add: _____ mg. Per day For _____ (3-10) days
(oral steroid)
☐ Call the doctor ☐ before/ ☐ within _____ hours after taking the oral steroid.

⇧

RED ZONE: Medical Alert!

- Very short of breath, or
- Quick-relief medicines have not helped, or
- Cannot do usual activities, or
- Symptoms are same or get worse after 24 hours in Yellow Zone

-Or-

Peak flow: less than _____
(50% of my best peak flow)

Take this medicine:

☐ _____ ☐ 4 or ☐ 6 puffs or ☐ Nebulizer.
(short-acting beta2-agonist)
☐ _____ mg.
(oral steroid)

Then call your doctor *NOW.* Go to the hospital or call for an ambulance if:
■ You are still in the red zone after 15 minutes AND
■ You have not reached your doctor.

DANGER SIGNS

- Trouble walking and talking due to shortness of breath
- Lips or fingernails are blue

⇧ ■ Take ☐ 4 or ☐ 6 puffs of your quick-relief medicine *AND*
■ Go to the hospital or call for an ambulance (_____) *Now!*

National Asthma Education and Prevention Program: National Heart, Lung, and Blood Institute; NIH Publication No. 97-4053

Figure 14.1 Asthma Action Plan

are particularly at risk for nonadherence and benefit from more frequent provider contact (Bosley et al., 1995; Cochrane, 1996). Providers should provide peak flow meters to patients who have difficulty recognizing asthma exacerbations to facilitate self-monitoring. Patients should be instructed to measure peak flow each morning and record readings in a log, which they should bring to each visit with the provider to assess treatment efficacy.

Provider Interventions: Children

Families with involved, supportive parents are optimal for effective treatment of asthmatic children. Clinicians must make a deliberate effort to ensure that both parents are educated about and have access to medication if they are separated or divorced (George, 1998). Many parents have specific fears about giving their child steroid medication that should be addressed individually (Goeman et al., 2002). Clinicians should emphasize that routine use of ICS can protect their child from coughing through the night and may prevent emergency room visits and hospitalizations (Divertie, 2002). In addition, parents may have misconceptions about asthma, believing that their child should not go outside or participate in sports (Buston & Wood, 2000). A crucial aspect of achieving optimal control of the disease for children with asthma is thus assessing parent knowledge about asthma and providing relevant factual information.

Model Provider Questions for Enhancing Patient Adherence

As mentioned above, patient-provider communication is one of the keys to optimal management of asthma. By asking targeted questions during patient visits, the provider can determine the patient's level of knowledge about the disease and treatment, assess patient goals, assess asthma control, and address issues that have been shown to affect adherence to the treatment regime. A table of model questions is provided in Table 14.4. Protection motivation theory (PMT) (Prentice-Dunn & Rogers, 1986) was used to develop and organize adherence-focused questions and can be helpful as a construct within which providers can develop their own strategies for working with patients to manage their asthma. PMT, which has been used in disease prevention and health promotion research for over two decades, combines features of the health belief model (Rosenstock, 1974) with self-efficacy theory and other constructs. It proposes that an individual must perceive some level of threat to health to be motivated to adhere to treatment. Protection motivation (motivation to behave in a healthy or adherent fashion) depends on perceptions of the severity of the health problem, vulnerability to the health problem, efficacy of the recommended treatment (response efficacy), ability to make recommended behavioral changes (self-efficacy), and costs of making the behavioral changes (response costs). PMT also acknowledges that there may be rewards associated with maintaining the unhealthy behavior that must be overcome. In a recent meta-analysis of 65 studies (N = approximately 30,000) that applied PMT, either fully or in part, the authors found that, in general, increases in threat severity, threat vulnerability, response efficacy, and self-efficacy facilitated adherent intentions or behaviors (Floyd, Prentice-Dunn, & Rogers, 2000).

Conclusions

ICS stabilize underlying inflammation and improve lung functioning in persons with persistent asthma and have been recommended as a first-line treatment since 1991. Nevertheless, inadequate patient adherence to prescribed medication is a major cause of poor clinical outcomes in the treatment of asthma. There are multiple disease-, treatment-, provider-, socio-

Table 14.4   Enhancing Adherence During Patient Care Visits

Visit 1

Knowledge	*Construct*
What do you know about asthma?	Identify patient perceptions/ misconceptions
What medications are you (your child) currently using for asthma? Tell me what you know about these medications. What else are you doing to help your asthma (or your child's asthma)? (identifies complementary or alternative treatments and environmental-control efforts)	
Treatment goals What do you expect your (your child's) asthma treatment to achieve?	Identify patient goals
Asthma control Ask about frequency of day/night/exercise symptoms, frequency of quick-relief medication use, missed school or work, emergency asthma visits.	Assess severity and control of asthma
Adherence-enhancing strategies How severe do you think your (your child's) asthma is? What worries you the most about your (your child's) asthma? (Reinforce or correct perceptions regarding use of spirometric, peak flow, or symptom data.)	Severity/vulnerability
Is there anything your asthma prevents you from doing?	Possible rewards of nonadherence
How would your life be different if your asthma were better controlled?	
What is keeping you from reaching your goals? (Assess concerns regarding medications such as side effects, costs.)	Response costs
Reinforce efficacy of prescribed medications. (e.g., the medication you are taking is the best for your asthma)	Response efficacy
Review and reinforce MDI or dry-powder inhaler technique.	Self-efficacy
Assess self-reported adherence during past week and time of dose(s) most often missed; work with patient to problem-solve and create a plan to enhance medication adherence. Seek endorsement that patient feels able to make and plans to make changes *in the next week* to improve adherence. Use statements such as "People like you have tried this and succeeded."	Self-efficacy

Visit 2

Content	*Construct*
Asthma control Ask about frequency of day/night/exercise symptoms, frequency of quick-relief medication use, missed school or work, emergency asthma visits. Adjust medications as necessary.	Asthma control
Adherence-enhancing strategies Inquire about medications and doses currently used; assess perceived purposes of medications; correct misconceptions as needed.	Self-efficacy

(Continued)

Table 14.4   (Continued)

Content	Construct
Inquire about use of asthma action plan; inquire about usefulness of plan; reinforce plan.	
Assess concerns regarding medications such as side effects, costs.	Response costs
Assess self-reported adherence (number of doses missed in the past week, time of dose that is most often missed). Assess success of adherence strategies agreed upon during previous visit. Ask how the patient will remember medication taking in atypical situations such as vacations or rotating work schedules. Develop strategies with the patient to improve adherence. Seek endorsement that the participant feels able to make and plans to make changes *in the next week* to improve adherence. Use statements such as "People like you have tried this and succeeded."	Self-efficacy
Reinforce efficacy of prescribed medications.	Response efficacy
Review and reinforce MDI technique.	Self-efficacy
Assess environmental triggers (e.g., Have you noticed anything in your home, work, or school that makes asthma worse?). Discuss relevant environmental-control strategies and provide handout.	Self-efficacy

Subsequent visits

Content	Theoretical Construct

Asthma control
    Ask about frequency of day/night/exercise symptoms, frequency of quick-relief medication use, missed school or work, emergency asthma visits.
    Adjust medications as necessary.
	Asthma control

Adherence-enhancing strategies
    Inquire about medications and doses currently used; assess perceived purposes of medications; correct misconceptions as needed.
    Inquire about use of asthma action plan; reinforce plan.
	Self-efficacy

Assess concerns regarding medications such as side effects, costs.	Response costs
Assess self-reported adherence (number of doses missed in the past week, time of dose that is most often missed).	Self-efficacy
Assess success of adherence strategies agreed upon during previous visit. Problem-solve strategies to improve adherence. Seek endorsement that the participant feels able to make and plans to make changes *in the next week* to improve adherence. Use statements such as "People like you have tried this and succeeded."	
Reinforce efficacy of prescribed medications.	Response efficacy
Review and reinforce MDI technique.	Self-efficacy
Assess environmental triggers (e.g., How are you controlling your exposure to things that make your asthma worse?)	Self-efficacy

Case Example

Bernie M. is a 38-year-old African American man, who originally presented to the family practice complaining of heartburn symptoms and hyperpigmented lines on his fingernails. A routine systems review revealed that he had had asthma as a child, with recurrent bouts of bronchitis but had not taken medications since adolescence. He acknowledged occasional wheezing and exercise-related dyspnea that interfered with his ability to play recreational basketball. Although his lungs were clear during physical examination, preliminary screening with a peak flow meter demonstrated a peak flow of 320 (normal value for his age, height, and sex is 620). Asked about his perceptions of asthma, he stated that he believed he had outgrown asthma and that his exercise-related symptoms were due to being "out of shape." However, when shown his peak flow results and advised that he could breathe much better than he was currently, he agreed to try a rescue inhaler. He was prescribed an albuterol inhaler, taught about symptoms that indicate the need to use rescue medication, and taught about MDI technique, which he demonstrated satisfactorily with a placebo inhaler. He was scheduled for spirometry, which demonstrated a forced expiratory volume in 1 second (FEV_1), which was 80% of predicted, with a 12% improvement in FEV_1 after use of albuterol. He was advised that this test confirmed that he still had asthma, and I suggested that he would benefit from treatment. He was asked to continue using his albuterol inhaler as needed and scheduled for a revisit in 1 month.

At the 1-month follow-up visit, Bernie reported that he found the albuterol very helpful and was using it at least three times weekly. He had not used albuterol the day of the visit, however, and his peak flow was 380 (still quite abnormal). I advised that his baseline lung function would improve if he used small doses of ICS daily. He was reluctant to use daily medication because he thought his asthma was "not that bad" but agreed when the provider suggested that he "just try it" for 1 month. He was given a 1-month supply of ICS after he satisfactorily demonstrated his MDI technique. Differences between controller medication (ICS) and rescue medication (albuterol) were carefully explained. He was given an asthma action plan with his medications written in and asked to return in 1 month.

After 1 month, he reported having missed only 2 to 3 ICS doses in the past week. He reported that he was breathing better than he had in years and had reduced his albuterol use to once weekly. His improved peak flow of 480 was used to demonstrate medication efficacy. He agreed to use the medication regularly and said that leaving his inhaler next to his toothbrush would help him remember to use it twice daily. He reported concern about medication affordability. Because he met drug company eligibility requirements, he was helped to complete an application for his ICS to be provided at no cost and was given another ICS sample. I reviewed his action plan with him and verified his MDI skill. He was given a booklet about environmental controls and agreed to consider keeping his dog out of his bedroom.

At his next visit 3 months later, he acknowledged that he had stopped using the ICS. He denied having troubling side effects or concern about medication and said that he had received a 90-day supply by mail. However, he said, he did not want to be dependent on medication. He was advised that his ICS medication was not addictive, and his improved quality of life on medication was stressed. Noting that he was again experiencing some shortness of breath and seeing that his peak flow had returned to pretreatment baseline, he agreed to reinstate his ICS, using memory strategies to maintain adherence that had worked for him previously.

economic-, and patient-related barriers to preventive medication adherence; all these barriers must be systematically addressed to maximize adherence.

Suggested Readings/ Resources

Logan, D., Zelikovsky, N., Labay, L., & Spergel, J. (2003). The Illness Management Survey: Identifying adolescents' perceptions of barriers to adherence. *Journal of Pediatric Psychology, 28,* 383–392.

Twenty-seven-item self-report measure of perceived barriers to asthma treatment that is recommended for use by providers or researchers to quantify issues that adolescents perceive as the greatest barriers to regimen adherence.

References

Agency for Healthcare Research and Quality (AHRQ). (2001). *Management of chronic asthma: Evidence report/technology assessment number 44* (Publication No. 01-E044). Rockville, MD: U.S. Government Printing Office.

Anis, A. H., Lynd, L. D., Wang, X. H., King, G., Spinelli, J. J., Fitzgerald, M., et al. (2001). Double trouble: impact of inappropriate use of asthma medication on the use of health care resources. *Canadian Medical Association Journal, 64,* 625– 631.

Apter, A. J., Reisine, S. T., Affleck, G., Barrows, E., & Zuwallack, R. L. (1998). Adherence with twice-daily dosing of inhaled steroids: Socioeconomic and health-belief differences. *American Journal of Respiratory and Critical Care Medicine, 157,* 1810–1817.

Balkrishnan, R., & Christensen, D. B. (2000). Inhaled corticosteroid use and associated outcomes in elderly patients with moderate to severe chronic pulmonary disease. *Clinical Therapeutics, 22,* 452–469.

Barber, N., Parsons, J., Darracott, R., & Horne, R. (2004). Patients' problems with new medication for chronic conditions. *Quality and Safety in Health Care, 13,* 172–175.

Barr, R. G., Somers, S. C., Speizer, F. E., & Camargo, C. A. (2002). Patient factors and medication guideline adherence among older women with asthma. *Archives of Internal Medicine, 162,* 1761–1768.

Bauman, L. J., Wright, E., Leickly, F. E., Crain, E., Kruszon-Moran, D., Wade, S., et al. (2002). Relationship of adherence to pediatric asthma morbidity among inner-city children. *Pediatrics, 110,* e6.

Belcher, D. W. (1990). Implementing preventive services. Success and failure in an outpatient trial. *Archives of Internal Medicine, 150,* 2533–2541.

Bender, B. G. (2002). Overcoming barriers to nonadherence in asthma treatment. *Journal of Allergy and Clinical Immunology, 109*(Suppl. 6), s554–s559.

Blessing-Moore, J. (1996). Does asthma education change behavior? To know is not to do. *Chest: The Cardiopulmonary Journal, 109*(1), 9–11.

Bosley, C. M., Fosbury, J. A., & Cochrane, G. M. (1995). The psychological factors associated with poor compliance with treatment in asthma. *European Respiratory Journal, 8,* 899–904.

British Thoracic Society, Scottish Intercollegiate Guidelines Network. (2003). British guideline on the management of asthma. *Thorax, 58*(Suppl. 1), 1–94.

Buston, K., & Wood, S. (2000). Non-compliance among adolescents with asthma: Listening to what they tell us about self-management. *Family Practice, 17,* 177.

The Childhood Asthma Management Program Research Group. (2000). Long-term effects of budesonide or nedocromil in children with asthma. *New England Journal of Medicine, 343,* 1054–1063.

Centers for Disease Control and Prevention. (2002). Surveillance for asthma—United States, 1980–1999. *Morbidity and Mortality Weekly Report, 51*(SS01), 1–13.

Cochrane, G. M. (1996). Compliance and outcomes in patients with asthma. *Drugs, 52*(Suppl. 6), 12–19.

Creer, T. L. (1993). Medication compliance and childhood asthma. In N. A. Krasnegor, L. Epstein, S. B. Johnson, & S. J. Yaffe (Eds.), *Developmental aspects of health compliance behavior* (pp. 303–333). Hillsdale, NJ: Erlbaum.

Creer, T. L., & Levstek, D. (1997). Adherence to asthma regimens. In D. S. Gochman (Ed.), *Handbook of health behavior research* (Vol. II, pp. 132). New York: Plenum Press.

DiMatteo, M. R. (2004). Social support and patient adherence to medical treatment, a meta-analysis. *Health Psychology, 42,* 207.

Divertie, V. (2002). Strategies to promote medication adherence in children with asthma. *American Journal of Maternal Child Nursing, 27,* 10–18.

Donaldson, N. E., Rutledge, D. N., & Pravikoff, D. S. (2000). Principles of effective adult-focused patient education in nursing. CINAHL Information Systems, Glendale, CA. Accessed March 19, 2006.

Douglass, J., Aroni, R., Goeman, D., Stewart, K., Sawyer, S., Thien, F., et al. (2002). A qualitative study of action plans for asthma. *British Medical Journal, 324,* 1003–1007.

Eisen, E. A., Miller, D. K., Woodward, R. S., Spitznagel, E., & Przybeck, T. R. (1990). The effect of prescribed daily dose frequency on patient medication compliance. *Archives of Internal Medicine, 150,* 1881–1884.

Farber, H. J., Capra, A. M., Finkelstein, J. A., Lozano, P., Quesenberry, C. P., Jensvold, N. G., et al. (2003). Misunderstanding of asthma controller medications: Association with nonadherence. *Journal of Asthma, 40,* 17–25.

Floyd, D. L., Prentice-Dunn, S., & Rogers, R. W. (2000). A meta-analysis of research on protection motivation theory. *Journal of Applied Social Psychology, 30*(2), 407–429.

George, M. (1998). Removing obstacles to care and promoting adherence. *Asthma Care and Education, 1,* 25.

Giraud, V., & Roche, N. (2002). Misuse of corticosteroid metered-dose inhaler is associated with decreased asthma stability. *European Respiratory Journal, 19,* 246–251.

Goeman, D. P., Aroni, R. A., Stewart, K., Sawyer, S. M., Thien, F. C. K., Abramson, M. J., et al. (2002). Patients' views of the burden of asthma: A qualitative study. *Medical Journal of Australia, 177,* 295–299.

Haby, M. M., Powell, C. V. E., Oberklaid, F., Waters, E. B., & Robertson, C. F. (2002). Asthma in children: Gaps between current management and best practice. *Journal of Paediatrics and Child Health, 38,* 284–289.

Horne, R., & Weinman, J. (1999). Patients' beliefs about prescribed medicines and their role in adherence to treatment in chronic physical illness. *Journal of Psychosomatic Research, 47,* 555–567.

Haynes, R. B., Montague, P., Oliver, T., McKibbon, K. A., Brouwers, M. C., & Kanani, R. (2000). Interventions for helping patients to follow prescriptions for medications (Cochrane Review). *Cochrane Database of Systematic Reviews, 3.*

Jerome, A., Wigal, J. K., & Creer, T. L. (1987). A review of medication compliance in children with asthma. *Pediatric Asthma, Allergy & Immunology, 1,* 193–211.

Jonasson, G., Carlsen, K. H., & Mowinckel, P. (2000). Asthma drug adherence in a long term clinical trial. *Archives of Disease in Childhood, 83,* 330–333.

Jones, A., Pill, R., & Adams, S. (2000). Qualitative study of views of health professionals and patients on guided self management plans for asthma. *British Medical Journal, 321,* 1507–1510.

Julius, S. M., Sherman, J. M., & Hendeles, L. (2002). Accuracy of three electronic monitors for metered dose inhalers. *Chest, 121*(3), 871–876.

Kohler, C. L., Davies, S. L., & Bailey, W. C. (1996). Self-management and other behavioral aspects of asthma. *Current Opinion in Pulmonary Medicine, 2*(1), 16–22.

Korsch, B. M., & Nagrete, V. F. (1972). Doctor-patient communication. *Scientific American, 227,* 66–74.

Leickly, F. E., Wade, S. L., Crain, E., Kruszon-Moran, D., Wright, E. C., & Evans, R. (1998). Self-reported adherence, management behavior, and barriers to care after an emergency department visit by inner city children with asthma. *Pediatrics, 101,* 1–8.

Medtrac Technologies. (2003). Electronic monitoring of metered dose inhaler use and technique. Retrieved December 30, 2003, from www.tri-nim .com/productlibrary/literature/westmed/mdilog .pdf

Miller, N. H., Hill, M., Kottke, T., & Ockene, I. S. (1997). The multilevel compliance challenge: Recommendations for a call to action: A statement for healthcare professionals. *Circulation, 95,* 1085–1090.

Minai, B. A., Martin, J. E., & Cohn, R. C. (2004). Results of a physician and respiratory therapist collaborative effort to improve long-term metered-dose inhaler technique in a pediatric asthma clinic. *Respiratory Care, 49,* 600–605.

National Institutes of Health National Asthma Education & Prevention Program. (1997a). *Expert panel report II: Guidelines for the diagnosis and management of asthma* (NIH Publication No. 97–4051). Bethesda, MD: Government Printing Office.

National Institutes of Health National Asthma Education & Prevention Program. (1997b). *Practical guide for the diagnosis and treatment of asthma* (NIH Publication No 97–4053). Bethesda, MD: Government Printing Office.

National Institutes of Health National Asthma Education and Prevention Program. (2002). *Guidelines for the diagnosis and management of asthma—update on selected topics* (NIH Publication No. 02–5075). Bethesda, MD: Government Printing Office.

Nides, M., Toshkin, D., Simmons, M., Wise, R. A., Li, V. C., & Rand, C. S. (1993). Improving inhaler adherence in a clinical trial through the use of nebulizer chronolog. *Chest, 104,* 501–507.

O'Byrne, P. M., Barnes, P. J., Rodriguez-Roisin, R., Runnerstrom, E., Sandstrom, T., Svensson, K., et al. (2001). Low dose inhaled budesonide and formoterol in mild persistent asthma: The OPTIMA randomized trial. *American Journal of Respiratory and Critical Care Medicine, 164*(8, Pt. 1), 1392–1397.

Pauwels, R. A., Pedersen, S., Busse, W. W., Tan, W. C., Chen, Y. Z., Ohlsson, S. V., et al. (2003). Early intervention with budesonide in mild persistent asthma: A randomized, double-blind trial. *Lancet, 361,* 1071–1076.

Prentice-Dunn, S., & Rogers, R. W. (1986). Protection motivation theory and preventive health: Beyond the health belief model. *Health Education Research, 1*(3), 151–163.

Pullar, T., Birtwell, A. J., Wiles, P.G., Hay, A., & Feely, M. P. (1988). Use of a pharmacologic indicator to compare compliance with tablets prescribed to be taken once, twice, or three times daily. *Clinical Pharmacology and Therapeutics, 44,* 540–545.

Quittner, A. L., Drotar, D., Levers-Landis, C., Slocum, N., Seidner, D., & Jacobsen, J. (2000). Adherence to medical treatments in adolescents with cystic fibrosis: The development and evaluation of family-based interventions. In D. Drotar (Ed.), *Handbook of research methods in pediatric and child clinical psychology.* New York: Plenum Publishing.

Rand, C. (2004, April). *The central role of the practitioner in improving patient adherence.* Paper presented at conference titled Innovations and Best Practices in Patient Adherence, Washington, DC.

Rand, C. S., & Butz, A. M. (2000). Psychosocial factors in chronic asthma. In K. B. Weiss, A. S. Buist, & S. D. Sullivan (Eds.), *Asthma's impact on society: The social and economic burden.* New York: Marcel Dekker.

Rand, C. S., & Wise, R. A. (1996). Adherence with asthma therapy in the management of asthma. In

S. J. Szefler (Ed.), *Severe asthma: Pathogenesis and clinical management: Lung biology in health and disease* (8th ed., pp. 435–464). New York: Marcel Dekker.

Robertson, C. F., Dalton, M. F., Peat, J. K., Haby, M. M., Bauman, A., Kennedy, J. D., et al. (1998). Asthma and other atopic diseases in Australian children (Australian arm of the International Study of Asthma and Allergy in Childhood [ISSAC]). *Medical Journal of Australia, 168,* 434–438.

Rosenstock, I. M. (1974). Historical origins of the health belief model. *Health Education Monographs, 2,* 328–335.

Roter, D. I., Hall, J. A., Merisca, R., Nordstrom, B., Cretin, D., & Svarstad, B. (1998). Effectiveness of interventions to improve patient compliance: A meta-analysis. *Medical Care, 36,* 11138–11161.

Rudd, P. (1993). The measurement of compliance: Medication taking. In M. A. Krasnegor, L. Epstein, S. B. Johnson, & S. J. Jaffe (Eds.), *Developmental aspects of health compliance behavior* (pp. 185–213). Hillsdale, NJ: Erlbaum.

Ruffin, R. E., Wilson, D., Southcott, A. M., Smith, B., & Adams, R.J. (1999). A South Australian population survey of the ownership of asthma action plans. *Medical Journal of Australia, 171,* 348–351.

Schaffer, S. D., & Yoon, S. L. (2001). Evidence-based methods to enhance medication adherence. *The Nurse Practitioner: The American Journal of Primary Health Care, 26*(12), 44–54.

Sherman, J., Hutson, A., Baumstein, S., & Hendeles, L. (2000). Telephoning the patient's pharmacy to assess adherence with asthma medications by measuring refill rate for prescriptions. *Journal of Pediatrics, 136,* 532–536.

Shireman, T. I., Heaton, P. C., Gay, W. E., Cluxton, R. J., & Moomaw, C. J. (2002). Relationship between asthma drug therapy patterns and healthcare utilization. *Annals of Pharmacotherapy, 36,* 557–564.

Steele, D. J., Jackson, T. C., & Gutmann, M. C. (1990). Have you been taking your pills? The adherence-monitoring sequence in the medical interview. *Journal of Family Practice, 30,* 294–299.

Steven, K., Morrison, J., & Drummone, N. (2002). Lay versus professional motivation for asthma treatment: A cross-sectional, qualitative study in a single Glasgow general practice. *Family Practice, 19,* 172–177.

Stevens, D., Sharma, K., & Kesten, S. (2003). Insurance status and patient behavior with asthma medications. *Journal of Asthma, 40,* 789–793.

Stoloff, S. W., Stempel, D. A., Meyer, J., Stanford, R. H., & Rosenzweig, J. R. C. (2004). Improved refill persistence with fluticasone propionate and salmeterol in a single inhaler compared with other controller therapies. *Journal of Allergy and Clinical Immunology, 113,* 245–251.

Tseng, C. W., Brook, R. H., Keeler, E., Steers, W. N., & Mangione, C. M. (2004). Cost-lowering strategies used by Medicare beneficiaries who exceed drug benefit caps and have a gap in drug coverage. *Journal of the American Medical Association, 292,* 952–960.

Veen, J. C., Smits, H. H., Ravensberg, A. J., Hiemstra, P. S., Sterk, P. J., & Bel, E. H. (1998). Impaired perception of dyspnea in patients with severe asthma. Relation to sputum eosinophils. *American Journal of Respiratory and Critical Care Medicine, 158,* 1134–1141.

Vitolins, M. Z., Rand, C. S., Rapp, S. R., Ribisl, P. M., & Sevick, M. A. (2000). Measuring adherence to behavioral and medical interventions. *Controlled Clinical Trials, 21,* 188S–194S.

Walewski, K. M., Cicutto, L., D'Urzo, A. D., Heslegrave, R. J., & Chapman, K. R. (2004). Evaluation of a questionnaire to assess compliance with anti-asthma medications. *Journal of Asthma, 41,* 77–83.

Wallace, A., Scott, J., Kinnert, M., & Anderson, M. E. (2004). Impoverished children with asthma: A pilot study of urban healthcare access. *Journal for Specialists in Pediatric Nursing, 9,* 50–58.

Weiss, K. B., & Sullivan, S. D. (2001). The health economics of asthma and rhinitis. I. Assessing the economic impact. *Journal of Allergy and Clinical Immunology, 107*(1), 3–8.

World Health Organization. (2003). *Adherence to long-term therapies: Evidence for action.* Geneva, Switzerland: Author.

Yuksel, N., Ginther, S., Man, P., & Tsuyuki, R. T. (2000). Underuse of inhaled corticosteroids in adults with asthma. *Pharmacotherapy, 20,* 387–393.

15

Adherence to Smoking Cessation Treatments

Whitney M. Waldroup

Elizabeth V. Gifford

Preety Kalra

C igarette smoking is a leading cause of morbidity and mortality. Worldwide, tobacco causes an estimated 4.9 million deaths annually with 440,000 deaths occurring in the United States alone (Centers for Disease Control [CDC], 2004). Adult male smokers will lose an average of 13.2 years of life due to smoking-related illnesses, whereas adult women will lose 15.4 years of life (CDC, 2002). "Every 6.5 seconds one person dies and many others fall ill or suffer diseases and disability due to tobacco use" (World Health Organization [WHO], 2004). As the most preventable cause of premature death

and disability worldwide (Killen et al., 2000), it is widely believed that a reduction in the prevalence of tobacco use would be the single most effective public health measure (Fornai et al., 2001).

The health risks associated with cigarette smoking are well documented. In the United States, 20% of all deaths are attributable to smoking-related illnesses (CDC, 2002), including one third of all deaths from cancer and heart disease. More than 8.6 million Americans have at least one serious illness caused by smoking (CDC, 2004). Cigarette use increases the risk of a multitude of diseases including cancers of the

Authors' Note: Requests for reprints should be sent to Elizabeth Gifford, Center for Health Care Evaluation, Palo Alto Veterans Administration and Stanford University School of Medicine, 795 Willow Road (152), Menlo Park, California 94025. Preparation of this manuscript was supported by the Department of Veterans Affairs.

lung, esophagus, bladder, kidney and stomach, coronary heart disease, stroke, chronic obstructive pulmonary disease, and peptic ulcer disease. An estimated 70% to 90% of lung cancer, 56% to 80% of chronic respiratory diseases, and 22% of cardiovascular diseases are attributable to tobacco smoking (WHO, 2002).

In addition to the health impacts of cigarette smoking, the economic impact to society is staggering. Each pack of cigarettes sold in the United States is estimated to cost $7.18 in medical care costs and lost productivity (CDC, 2002). From 1995 to 1999, cigarette smoking caused over $150 billion in annual health-related economic losses, including $75.5 billion in excess medical expenditures in 1998 (CDC, 2002). The estimated annual economic cost per smoker in the United States is $3,391 (CDC, 2002). Despite the well-recognized health risks of tobacco use, as well as the economic toll to the individual and society, the prevalence of smoking remains approximately 23% in the United States. In 2001, approximately 22.8% of the U.S. adult population, an estimated 46.2 million adults, were current smokers (CDC, 2003). Although this is a reduction from the 25.5% prevalence in 1994 (Goldstein, 1998), the overall decline in smoking is not occurring at a rate fast enough to meet the national goal of Healthy People 2010, which calls for a population prevalence of less than 12% (U.S. Department of Health and Human Services [USDHHS], 2000). In the United States, current smoking prevalence (cigarette use within the past month) is highest among American Indians/Alaska Natives (37.1%) and lowest among Asians (17.7%). Caucasians, Black or African Americans, and Hispanics have rates of current smoking closer to the national average, 26.9%, 25.3%, and 23%, respectively (Substance Abuse and Mental Health Services Administration, 2003) Current smoking is highest in persons living in poverty, in younger persons, and in persons with lower levels of education (CDC, 2003).

Effective Smoking Cessation Treatments

Many of the effects of smoking are reversible. For example, 15 years after quitting smoking the risk of death among ex-smokers is no greater than that among nonsmokers (USDHHS, 2000). Because of the numerous short- and long-term health benefits and economic benefits that accompany the cessation of tobacco use (Fagerstrom, 2002), much attention has been focused on the development of effective smoking cessation treatments. Research in smoking cessation over the past two decades has demonstrated that appropriate treatments can help smokers achieve abstinence from cigarettes (WHO, 2003). Smoking cessation treatments are among the most cost-effective health care interventions, considered to be a "gold standard" of chronic disease prevention interventions (Fiore, 2000).

The USDHHS established the *Treating Tobacco Use and Dependence Clinical Practice Guideline*, which identified effective treatment strategies designed to be implemented in health care settings. *The Guideline* identified five first-line and two second-line smoking cessation medications for tobacco users attempting to quit. First-line medications, those that have proven safe and effective and are approved by the Food and Drug Administration (FDA) for smoking cessation, include two forms of pharmacotherapy: bupropion hydrochloride sustained release (Bupropion SR), an antidepressant, and nicotine replacement therapy (NRT).

Antidepressants

Bupropion is a selective re-uptake inhibitor of dopamine and noradrenalin that is thought to prevent or reduce cravings and other features of nicotine withdrawal (Richmond & Zwar, 2003). Nicotine triggers the release of dopamine in the brain, and the pleasurable sensations that result are thought to be a driving force in establishing addiction (Caskey et al., 2002). Currently, it is hypothesized that bupropion, by inhibiting the uptake of dopamine, affects the pleasure and reward activity in the mesolimbic system and nucleus accumbens, which is responsible for its efficacy in smoking cessation (Pontieri, Orzi, & Di Chiara, 1996). Quitting smoking results in subnormal dopamine levels, producing withdrawal symptoms, and antidepressant therapy is thought to restore these levels, thereby reducing craving and associated symptoms (Patkar, Vergare, Batra, Weinstein, & Leone, 2003). Currently available as Zyban™, slow-release bupropion is the same medication previously marketed as the antidepressant Wellbutrin™. Two large multicenter studies showed that the use of Bupropion SR doubles long-term cessation rates compared with placebo when given in combination with counseling (Hurt et al., 1997; Jorenby et al., 1999). Bupropion is given in twice-daily 150-mg doses, after three initial days of 150 mg/day only. Bupropion is contraindicated in persons with any medications or medical diagnosis or history (e.g., head injury) that lowers their seizure threshold.

Nicotine Replacement

Nicotine replacement strategies are based on the principle that nicotine is the dependence-producing constituent of cigarette smoking and that smoking cessation and abstinence can be achieved by providing nicotine without the harmful impurities in cigarette smoke (Ziedonis, Wyatt, & George, 1998). Providing an alternative form of nicotine in the form of a relatively stable, fixed dose over a period of 16 or 24 hours may relieve withdrawal symptoms in a smoker abstaining from tobacco, and the smoking cessation process is eased (Cinciripini & McClure, 1998; Rigotti, 2002). Several forms of delivery of NRT are available, including the nicotine patch, gum, spray, and oral inhaler. Nicotine gum delivers nicotine through transbuccal absorption.

The recommended dose is 10 to 12 pieces of gum per day for 1 to 3 months, and each piece is chewed for 30 minutes and then discarded. The nicotine patch is available in three active forms (7, 14, and 21 mg) and delivers a steady state of nicotine for the entire 16- or 24-hour period that the patch is worn. Treatment with the nicotine patch lasts 8 to 12 weeks when 24-hour patches are used and 16 to 20 weeks with a 16-hour patch. Oral inhalers provide 10 mg of nicotine as an inhalant and treatment may last from 4 to 24 months. The efficacy of NRT is well established. A recent Cochrane Review of 103 clinical trials of nicotine replacement for smoking cessation found all forms of nicotine replacement to increase the odds of quitting for 6 months of follow-up approximately 1.5- to 2-fold regardless of setting. Use of the nicotine patch and gum was approximately 80% more effective than placebo, whereas nasal spray, inhaled nicotine, and nicotine sublingual tablet or lozenge more than doubled the rates of cessation (Silagy, Lancaster, Stead, Mant, & Fowler, 2004). Combining the use of two NRTs (i.e., patch with either nicotine gum or nasal spray) may increase long-term cessation rates compared with a single form of NRT (Cofta-Gunn, Wright, & Wetter, 2004). In addition to NRT and bupropion, two second-line pharmacotherapies, nortriptyline and clonidine, have some preliminary evidence for efficacy in treating tobacco dependence but have not been approved by the FDA for this purpose (Cofta-Gunn et al., 2004).

Psychosocial Treatments

Several forms of behavioral treatment have been developed to aid in smoking cessation. Even brief clinical interventions consisting of physician advice (less than 3 minutes) and low-intensity interventions (lasting 3–10 minutes) significantly increase long-term cessation. Analyses of contact time and number of treatment sessions show a strong dose-response relationship between treatment intensity and outcome, with sessions that last longer than 10 minutes and at least four sessions per treatment being the most effective (Cofta-Gunn et al., 2004). Other psychosocial interventions include telephone, group, and individual counseling, all of which substantially increase smoking cessation compared with no intervention. Three counseling modalities have substantial proven efficacy: cognitive behavioral problem solving (Antonuccio & Danton, 1999), interpersonal support (Tsoh et al., 1997), and aversive conditioning techniques such as rapid smoking (Gifford & Schoenberger, 2003). Cognitive behavioral treatments typically focus on identifying the antecedents and consequences of smoking and on developing coping skills for resisting cravings and other triggers. Treatments emphasizing social support are typically less structured. Aversive treatments are highly structured behavioral treatments that involve considerable commitment and expertise. Among the different types of behavioral therapies and counseling, practical counseling, intratreatment social support, and help with finding extratreatment social support are the most efficacious and should be offered to all smokers (Cofta-Gunn et al., 2004). Multiple counseling sessions (at least four) are encouraged by *The Clinical Practice Guideline for Treating Tobacco Dependence.*

Problems With Adherence in Smoking Cessation Treatment

The majority of Americans who still smoke report that they would like to quit. Annually, 40% of smokers in the United States make a quit attempt (CDC, 2002). Long-term cessation rates, generally defined as sustained abstinence after 1 year, however, are poor because the majority of these quit attempts are unsuccessful. Among the 90% of smokers who attempt to quit smoking without any treatment, only 3% to 5%

will be abstinent after 1 year (Lichtenstein & Glasgow, 1992). Only 10% to 30% of those who use a pharmacological or behavioral treatment are successful at abstaining in the long term (Fiore, Smith, Jorenby, & Baker, 1994). The successful quitter has attempted to quit smoking an average of six times (Fiore, 2000; Fiore et al., 1990).

Adherence to smoking cessation treatment, or lack thereof, may help explain these poor rates of successful cessation. With smoking cessation treatment, as with any other therapy for chronic conditions, poor adherence severely compromises the effectiveness of treatment (WHO, 2003). Conversely, good compliance with the rules of smoking cessation programs predicts treatment success (Pomerleau, Adkins, & Pertshuck, 1978). This chapter focuses on adherence to the two types of programs identified in *The Clinical Practice Guideline: Pharmacotherapy*, which includes treatment with Bupropion SR or NRT and behavioral treatment.

Multiple studies have shown effects for rates of adherence on abstinence from cigarettes. Patients with better rates of adherence to antidepressant medication used to aid in smoking cessation, as determined by higher blood levels of these medications, have a greater likelihood of completing behavioral treatment and are more likely to be abstinent (Hitsman, Spring, Borrelli, Niaura, & Papandonatos, 2001; Killen et al., 2000). Higher rates of abstinence from cigarettes have been found in participants who used the patch more frequently (Alterman, Gariti, Cook, & Cnaan, 1999). In fact, the best predictor of smoking cessation with the use of the nicotine patch is wearing the patch every day (Cummings, Biernbaum, Zevon, Deloughry, & Jaen, 1994). Yet several studies have shown considerable nonadherence in the use of the patch (Cummings et al., 1994; Orleans et al., 1994; Stapleton et al., 1995) and in the use of bupropion (Hurt et al., 1997). Even when the importance of adhering to patch treatment is stressed prior to commencing treatment, less than half the patients who enter treatment wear the patch as prescribed most of the time (Alterman et al., 1999). The contribution of adherence to abstinence, however, can be difficult to assess because many clinical trials do not adequately define adherence or provide consistent means for assessing adherence.

Adherence Criteria

Definitions of adherence or nonadherence differ depending on treatment. In general, adherence is described by WHO (2003) as "the extent to which a person's behavior corresponds with agreed recommendations from a health care provider" (p. 17, based on Haynes, 1979; Rand, 1993). Adherence to NRT is commonly defined as its continuous use for the entire prescribed period, generally 12 to 16 weeks. Adherence to Bupropion SR is defined as the extent to which patients take the prescribed daily dose of Bupropion, generally 300 mg in the form of twice-daily 150-mg pills, for the entire prescribed course of treatment. The recommended duration of treatment with Bupropion SR is between 7 and 12 weeks (Richmond & Zwar, 2003). In most research studies, subjects are considered to be treatment adherent based on a high percentage of days of correct NRT or medication use. Because Bupropion SR requires a lead-in period of 3 days, in which patients take a smaller 150-mg dose (to prevent seizures), patients who fail to comply with Bupropion must recycle through the ramp-up period. Behavioral treatments do not carry such risks. There is, however, insufficient research on patient adherence to behavioral treatment components (e.g., completing homework). Therefore, for the purpose of this chapter we define adherence to behavioral smoking treatment as participation as measured by attendance.

Adherence Trajectories

Adhering to treatment is important for achieving maximal smoking treatment efficacy. Attending more smoking cessation classes, for example, increases the likelihood of being abstinent from cigarettes at the end of a behavioral treatment and at 3-month follow-up (Bushnell, Forbes, Goffaux, Dietrich, & Wells, 1997; Kamarck & Lichtenstein, 1988). Conversely, decline in adherence over time is a common problem in smoking cessation treatment and a barrier to successful treatment outcome. The World Health Organization suggests that adherence to smoking cessation therapies is a logarithmic function of the number of weeks of treatment, showing a rapid decrease during the first 6 weeks of treatment, followed by a slower decline after 24 weeks (WHO, 2003). In studies of nicotine patch adherence, self-reports of compliance with patch use show that use decreases steadily over successive follow-up visits. One study of active patch users had rates of compliance of 92% in the first week of treatment, decreasing to 61% by Week 12 (Stapleton et al., 1995). Although smokers may report wearing the patch every day as instructed (for the entire 16- or 24-hour period), oftentimes they will do so for fewer weeks than recommended by their treatment provider (Cummings et al., 1994). In a study of 1,070 older adults, continuous use of the patch occurred for 5 out of 12 recommended weeks of treatment, with patients using the patch for a median of 30 days out of a possible 84 (Orleans et al., 1994). Typically, nonadherence to patch treatment leads to unsuccessful smoking outcome (Kenford et al., 1994; Stapleton et al., 1995).

Adherence to Bupropion SR shows similar declines through the treatment period. In a recent study comparing Bupropion SR plus counseling with Bupropion SR alone, overall rates of adherence to medication were 75% at Week 3, decreasing to 40% at Week 7 and 28% at Week 10 (Gifford, Antonuccio, Kohlenberg, Hayes, & Piasecki, 2002). This study was notably different from other medication trials in that participants were not paid weekly for participation (reflecting more real-world conditions, as of course patients are not generally paid weekly to report whether they are taking their medication). Of the participants who completed medication treatment, 53% were abstinent from cigarettes at the end of treatment (Week 10) compared with 28% abstinence for those who did not adhere to medication (Gifford et al., 2002).

Although the mechanisms relating adherence and outcome are not clear (Klesges, Ward, & DeBon, 1996), it does appear that adherence is related to outcome in both psychosocial and pharmacological treatments. In combined treatments, which are widely considered the gold standard in smoking cessation, adherence to different components of the treatment may have an additive effect. In a recent study, participants in a combined behavioral and pharmacological treatment for smoking cessation clinical trial who attended at least 6 of 10 individual counseling sessions were 6 times more likely to be abstinent at posttreatment than those who attended 2 or fewer sessions (Gifford et al., 2002). Hughes (1995) described possible reasons why multicomponent treatments may be more effective, including the idea that one treatment may increase adherence to the other. For example, reductions in withdrawal symptoms or placebo effects may increase smokers' self-efficacy, which may improve their adherence to behavioral skills training. Alternatively, a supportive relationship context with a treatment provider may increase patients' motivation to adhere to medications.

Risk Factors for Nonadherence

Several factors have been demonstrated to influence patients' level of adherence to smoking cessation treatment. These include level of nicotine dependence, intensity of cravings, sociodemographic variables such as education level and age, depression, and concerns about weight gain. By recognizing these factors and tailoring treatment to account for these potential barriers, providers may be able to increase cessation rates through improved treatment adherence.

Level of Nicotine Dependence

Smokers who are more highly addicted have a harder time abstaining from cigarettes, which

may affect adherence to smoking cessation treatment. A high degree of nicotine dependence, discomfort with withdrawal symptoms, inadequate dose, notably increased cravings and appetite, and side effects are thought to be associated with poor patch adherence (Cummings, 1994; Fiore et al., 1994; Orleans et al., 1994; Stapleton et al., 1995). Patients who smoke more cigarettes daily and have higher expired carbon monoxide (CO) levels and salivary and urinary cotinine levels and higher Fagerstrom Tolerance Questionnaire (FTQ) scores are more likely to drop out of treatment (Fagerstrom, 1978). Smoking a greater number of cigarettes prior to beginning treatment with the nicotine patch is predictive of poorer rates of adherence (Alterman et al., 1999). More physiologically dependent smokers are more likely to drop out before the end of behavioral treatment (Hitsman et al., 2001).

Sociodemographic Factors

Differences in treatment adherence may also be due to sociodemographic factors. In one study of adherence to a multicomponent smoking cessation treatment for women with a history of depression (Ginsberg et al., 1997), age was found to be the primary predictor of attendance. Other studies have found that smokers who are older and have higher levels of education have better rates of adherence to treatment (Bushnell et al., 1997), though some studies have failed to find this effect (Hitsman et al., 2001). Race and gender have been hypothesized to influence adherence to treatment as well as smoking cessation outcome; however, studies have shown mixed results for the level of significance of either of these two factors. Patch use does not appear to differ for African American versus Caucasian smokers or by gender (Alterman et al., 1999). In studies of substance abuse treatment, however, African American ethnicity is an independent predictor of early treatment drop-out, with African American clients being five times more likely to drop out of treatment early compared with Caucasians (King, Polednak, Bendel, Vilsaint, &

Nahata, 2004). Although a significant amount of evidence exists showing that women have more difficulty achieving and maintaining abstinence from smoking (Blake, 1989), large population studies have not shown consistent gender differences in cessation, and clinical trials yield mixed results. Gender disparities in quit rate and adherence may be confounded by concerns of postcessation weight gain (Borelli, Spring, Niaura, Hitsman, & Papandonatos, 2001).

Depression

Current depression is associated with smoking (Breslau, 1993), and there is evidence that smokers with elevated levels of depressive symptoms have an increased risk of smoking cessation treatment failure (Anda et al., 1990; Rausch, Nichinson, Lamke, & Matloff, 1990). Depression is associated with low rates of adherence to treatments for multiple medical conditions (discussed in other chapters), an effect that may also affect adherence to smoking cessation treatment. Patients suffering from depressive disorders may discontinue antidepressant treatment due to the unpleasant side effects of these medications (Nemeroff, 2003), which in bupropion use include insomnia, gastrointestinal distress, dry mouth, dizziness, and in rare cases, seizures. Smokers who are depressed may use cigarettes to self-medicate or prevent or reduce depressive episodes (Dilsaver, Pariser, Churchill, & Larson, 1990), and depressed mood may provoke relapse following cessation (Hall, Munoz, Reuss, & Seuss, 1993). It is important to consider not only the effects of current depression but also the history of depression in smokers. Among participants in smoking cessation programs, the prevalence of a history of depression ranges from 33.2% to 61% (Covey, Glassman, Stetner, & Becker, 1993; Dalack, Glassman, Rivelli, Covey, & Stetner, 1995; Glassman et al., 1988; Hall, Munoz, & Reus, 1994). Women with a history of depression report heavier smoking and a longer history of smoking (Ginsberg et al., 1997); thus, increased dependence on nicotine may lead to decreased treatment adherence as well as treatment failure.

Weight Gain

For many smokers, a major barrier to treatment or cessation is postcessation weight gain. Because nicotine increases energy turnover, weight control after quitting cigarettes may become more difficult (Fagerstrom, 2002), and about 80% of people gain weight post cessation (U.S. Public Health Service, 1990). Therefore, weight gain concerns may interfere with cessation efforts (Klesges et al., 1988). Smokers who are concerned about cessation-related weight gain are more likely to drop out early in treatment (Mizes, Sloan, & Segraves, 1998). The literature surrounding the role of postcessation weight gain, treatment adherence, and relapse is controversial, and some studies have found that greater postcessation weight gain is actually associated with continued abstinence rather than relapse. The effect of greater weight gain among those who complete treatment may be explained by the idea that it is weight gain concern, rather than actual postcessation weight gain, that predisposes relapse; and those who are the most highly concerned may self-select out of treatment. Gender differences in relapse have been shown with regard to weight gain. For men, every kilogram increase in weight increased the risk of relapse by 17%, whereas for women, every kilogram of weight gained decreased risk of relapse by 2% (Borelli et al., 2001). The seemingly protective effect of weight gain for women, however, is likely explained by the phenomenon of women with high levels of weight gain concern self-selecting out of treatment. In clinical trials, smokers who were treated with Bupropion SR gained significantly less weight than those who received a placebo. Weight gain is inversely related to daily dose of bupropion (100, 150, or 300 mg). Those who received NRT in combination with bupropion gained the least amount of weight (Hurt, 1999; Jorenby et al., 1999).

Promoting Adherence to Smoking Cessation Treatment

Adherence Assessment

Several strategies have been developed to assess levels of adherence to smoking cessation treatment. Although information on adherence can be obtained by self-report, patient estimates tend to substantially overestimate their actual adherence (Haynes, McDonald, & Garg, 2002). Thus, obtaining objective information beyond self-report is desirable. Implementing the use of a patch-monitoring log, where the number of patches prescribed for a certain time period is recorded, can monitor nicotine patch use and non-use. Patients who are prescribed patches by a health care provider may be asked to bring in used patches at subsequent appointments, and the number of actual used patches can be compared with the number of patches prescribed to be used in the same time period. The same strategy can be used for assessing adherence to nicotine gum. The number of prescribed doses of nicotine gum can be compared with the number of pieces of returned chewed gum (Ginsberg et al., 1997).

Similarly, having patients return their unused medication and comparing the number of unused pills with the total number of pills that were prescribed for that treatment period can monitor bupropion medication-taking behavior. Additional information about adherence can be obtained by asking patients to record the number of pills taken daily on a calendar. Although this can be done with the provider at the appointment at which the unused medication is returned, patients may be able to provide a more accurate report if they are given a calendar at the time of the prescription and asked to fill it in daily. The act of filling out a daily calendar may serve as a reminder to take medication that might have been otherwise forgotten. The calendar can also serve as a tool for recording any adverse events with the medication. By recording symptoms as they occur, the patient is providing a more accurate record of his or her history with the medication, which will allow the provider to best decide how to proceed with therapy.

Medication adherence is most easily and commonly determined by self-report, but this may also involve techniques such as monitoring blood levels for prescribed medications for smoking cessation treatment. To assess levels of adherence to medication such as bupropion, drug levels can be determined by serum assay. This technique is effective only for medications such as Bupropion SR, because therapeutic levels of NRT cannot be confirmed biologically.

Despite the ease of obtaining self-report data on adherence, problems exist in obtaining an accurate record of medication-taking behavior or NRT use. In general, self-reports of adherence tend to be exaggerated (Gao, Nau, Rosenbluth, Scott, & Woodward,, 2000; Waterhouse, 1993), possibly due to recall bias or a desire to avoid criticism and please the provider. Patients may err in their self-report of medication-taking behavior if the time period between retrospective self-report and the actual events is too long. Patients have been known to dispose of medication before adherence check to make it appear that they have adhered (Rand et al., 1992). Therefore, in some cases it may be helpful to have a method of verifying patient self-reported information. As discussed previously, biological confirmation of antidepressant drug levels can be obtained by serum assay. Although studies that include therapeutic drug monitoring are rare in the depression treatment literature, it may prove useful to monitor medication levels when treating nicotine dependence with antidepressant medication in order to improve treatment compliance (Killen et al., 2000). Although levels of adherence with NRT cannot be biologically confirmed, self-reports of abstinence from smoking can be confirmed by a variety of techniques. The simplest of these techniques is the measurement of expired CO. CO levels are measured using a Smokerlyser (Bedfont Scientific Ltd., Upchurch, U.K.) by having patients inhale maximally, hold breath for 15 seconds, and then exhale through the mouthpiece. CO readings of less than 10 parts per million are considered as not smoking. Levels of cotinine, the major proximate metabolite of nicotine, can be measured in body fluids, such as plasma, saliva, and urine, as a biomarker of inhaled or ingested nicotine (Benowitz, Jacob, & Perez-Stable, 1996; Jarvis, Tunstall-Pedoe, Feyerabend, Vesey, & Saloojee, 1987). Cotinine is readily detectable in smokers, with distribution of levels quite distinct from that of nonsmokers (Jaakkola et al., 2003).

Technology may also play an important role in assessing adherence. One novel strategy for assessing medication-taking behavior used an interactive voice response system. This system would automatically dial patients' phone numbers each night and ask, "Did you take your pill last night?" (Killen et al., 2000). This system provided a daily measure of patients' adherence to smoking cessation medication, eliminating the need for direct contact between the provider and the patient and decreasing the risk of patient error, which is more common when the self-reporting of behavior is delayed.

Adherence Promotion

Strategies for promoting adherence to smoking cessation therapies include assessing patient motivation, monitoring by provider (see previous section), establishing supportive relationships, multifaceted treatment programs, patient education, and recognition and discussion of potential barriers to adherence.

Assessing Motivation

Motivation influences patient's commitment to treatment. For example, patients' desire to attend classes or therapy sessions increases significantly when providers are skillful at facilitating client engagement (Miller & Rollnick, 1991).

Motivation to quit smoking also appears to be positively related to treatment adherence. Assessing smokers' readiness to change may provide useful information about the likelihood of adherence to treatment and may inform strategies for improving adherence.

A widely used measure of motivation is the University of Rhode Island Change Assessment (URICA), which measures motivation or readiness to change in each of four stages: precontemplation, contemplation, action, and maintenance (DiClemente & Hughes, 1990). Smokers who are more motivated at the beginning of treatment, as measured by the URICA commitment phase score, are more likely to adhere to treatment. For example, patients with a higher commitment phase score use more patches than patients who report lower levels of readiness to change (Alterman et al., 1999). Offering NRT or intensive behavioral counseling to patients in the precontemplation stage is less likely to be successful. Appropriate brief interventions in the precontemplation stage, however, can facilitate increases in patient motivation. Even busy physicians can offer the following effective interventions: educating the patients about the effects of smoking, recommending changes in behavior, listing options for achieving behavioral change, discussing the patients' reactions to the providers' feedback and recommendations, and following up to monitor and reinforce behavioral change. These interactions should always be conducted with an empathic, rather than a confrontational, interpersonal style (Malin, 2002).

Provider Support

Provider support is a key factor in improving adherence. Patients who receive more physician advice (Bushnell et al., 1997), and have more frequent contact with physicians and pharmacists (Orleans et al., 1994), are more likely to adhere to medication and NRT. This may be the result of patients feeling more support from their caregiver or feeling more informed about their treatment.

Providers are also able to adjust medications to patients' motivation level and treatment plan. Although compliance to NRT can be difficult to assess when self-administered (Curry, Ludman, & McClure, 2003), having providers prescribe NRT and follow patients for appropriate dosing may increase adherence and success.

A client's racial identity has been shown to be a major factor in predicting success in establishing a positive therapeutic relationship. Practitioner cultural competence involves recognition and acceptance of nonnormative behaviors in minority populations (Blank, Mahmood, Fox, & Guterbock, 2002). The cultural responsiveness hypothesis asserts that the efficacy of psychotherapy is in the therapist's ability to communicate an understanding of cultural background (Sue, Fujino, Hu, Takeuchi, & Zane, 1991), and lack of it may account for racial differences in the premature termination of treatment (Blank et al., 2002). As stated earlier in this chapter, African American clients are five times more likely to drop out of treatment early than Caucasians (King et al., 2004).

Treatment providers may be able to affect treatment adherence through their communication style with patients. In studies of the correlation of adherence to antidepressant medication for depression, physician initial communication style has been reported to positively influence client knowledge and initial beliefs about the medication. Clients with more positive beliefs about the treatment are more likely to see the physician in follow-up and are more satisfied with treatment after attempting medication use. Physician follow-up communication style and client satisfaction are both predictive of better medication adherence (Bultman & Svarstad, 2000).

Multifaceted Treatment Programs

In all smoking cessation treatment programs, the degree of provider contact is associated with adherence and self-reported treatment success (Glasgow, Schafer, & O'Neill, 1981). This is certainly the case in behavioral treatment programs,

where a dose-response relationship curve is observed, and in combined medication and psychosocial treatments. Although patients receiving more intense adjunctive psychological support or medical treatment are more adherent to patch treatment (Alterman et al., 1999), even minimal behavioral support results in similar or higher treatment adherence rates (WHO, 2003).

A vital factor in increasing patients' level of engagement in treatment is to provide treatment to motivated patients in a timely manner. Improving access to care can be accomplished by enrolling inpatients through specialty clinics, such as cardiovascular or pulmonary clinics with on-site counselors available to enroll interested patients into behavioral treatment programs when patients have scheduled medical visits. Providing behavioral treatment programs or NRT through innovative methods such as telephone smoking cessation programs can also increase the number of patients who are able to enroll and facilitate reaching those patients who are unable to attend treatment clinics. As stated earlier, patients who are more motivated at the beginning of treatment are more likely to adhere to patch treatment (Alterman et al., 1999) and be more involved in the therapeutic process (Joe, Simpson, Greener, & Rowan-Szal, 1999).

Although one of the goals of treatment programs is to capture patients while their motivation level is high, tailoring treatment programs to match patients' level of motivation may also increase adherence to cessation programs. For example, matching patients' motivation, level of dependence, and past quit attempts to different levels of care such as minimal, moderate, or maximal specialized care could optimize adherence rates by appropriately matching patients to treatment programs tailored to their specific motivation level through a stepped-care model (Abrams, Clark, & King, 1999).

Some smoking cessation programs have developed treatments in which patients become financially responsible for attending treatment sessions. This is accomplished by having patients, who can afford to, give a deposit at the beginning of treatment (i.e., $20–$50). By having patients commit their own resources, they are investing in their care. Patients then receive the full deposit at the end of treatment or in increments at every completed visit. Financial incentives may also increase motivation. A program that provides incentives such as small amounts of money, coupons, or gift certificates for attendance at therapy sessions or adherence to medication or NRT may be able to increase patient retention and adherence to treatment.

Patient Education

Adequate patient education is essential for adherence to medication or NRT. Inadequate instruction given to patients on proper patch use leads to patch nonadherence (Alterman et al., 1999). Patients who understand and are able to recognize potential side effects are better equipped to deal with these effects without abandoning treatment. Patient education can be accomplished in a variety of ways:

- Information pamphlet detailing how to take medication or NRT and potential side effects
- Consultation with a physician, with simple instructions on medication-taking behavior that the patient can recite back to the physician
- Consultation with pharmacists about correct medication-taking behavior
- Resources to contact in case bothersome side effects do occur
- Magnet for fridge with important numbers to contact for information about side effects or dosing schedules
- Twenty-four-hour contact number for physician
- Strategies for dealing with side effects outlined clearly by the practitioner

A potential barrier to adherence to any therapy or medication is cost. Although the cost of NRT is essentially equivalent to the cost of smoking (WHO, 2003), removing cost as a potential barrier and providing free access to NRT increases adherence (Bushnell et al., 1997). It is feasible to believe that the same relationship would be found with pharmacotherapy such as bupropion and behavioral treatment. Smokers may be motivated by the economic gain of quitting smoking; being forced to pay for NRT, behavioral treatment, or bupropion may counteract this motivation and lead to treatment nonadherence. Patient education should emphasize the fact that treatment is no more expensive than cigarettes and that the long-term gains (both health and economic) will more than offset the cost of treatment.

Recognition and Discussion of Patient Barriers

In line with patient education is the need to identify and develop strategies for any potential barriers to adherence to treatment. Improving adherence requires a continuous dynamic process and no single intervention strategy has been shown to be effective across all patients, conditions, or settings (WHO, 2003). Although the literature on specific methods for promoting adherence to smoking cessation is limited, several factors have been shown to be predictive of increased treatment adherence. Recognizing and incorporating these factors into the treatment plan may positively affect adherence and outcome.

Patients and treatment providers who work together to proactively determine potential barriers and develop solutions for dealing with these problems as they occur are better prepared to maintain the prescribed treatment. By prospectively addressing issues such as side effects, cost, cravings, weight gain, or time commitment to treatment, both the patient and the provider can identify areas in which the provider and the patient can modify or intensify treatment to plan for these potential hang-ups, which might have otherwise derailed treatment adherence. Proactive steps to counteract future issues allow patients and providers to target these problem areas and reassess them throughout the course of treatment.

For example, because cessation may induce depressive symptoms (Killen et al., 2000), it is of particular importance for providers to assess current or previous depression and take steps to prevent or alleviate depression. Although no relationship was seen between history of depression and adherence to a cognitive behavioral treatment program and nicotine gum for women who did not report any current depression (Ginsberg et al., 1997), current and previous depression may affect adherence and should be assessed prior to commencing treatment. Weight gain is a concern for smokers of both sexes and effective treatment should address these concerns. To counteract the negative influences of weight gain, smoking cessation may be combined with a low-energy diet or an exercise program for long-term weight management. Treatment with Bupropion SR may also attenuate the weight gain associated with cessation for patients with these concerns.

Another barrier to treatment adherence is distance to clinics and time commitment for behavioral treatment programs and renewal of NRT. Instituting programs that simultaneously provide smoking cessation treatment with other medical services could reduce the time for enrollment for motivated patients (Gifford, Palm, & Diloreto, in press). Telephone counseling is another useful strategy for overcoming barriers (Zhu et al., 1996).

Measures

The following measures may assist treatment providers in helping their patients achieve maximum adherence to smoking cessation treatment. Motivation and level of tobacco use are both associated with adherence; assessment of these variables can provide insight into appropriate treatment and potential challenges prior to commencement of treatment.

The URICA (Diclemente & Scott, 1997): This is a 24-item measure that identifies patient's stage of change, with four subscales corresponding to precontemplation, contemplation, action, and maintenance. Responses are given on a 5-point Likert scale.

The Fagerstrom Test for Nicotine Dependence: This is a six-item scale designed to determine level of nicotine dependence (Heatherton, Kozlowski, Frecker, & Fagerstrom, 1991). The Brief Fagerstrom Test for Nicotine Dependence is a two-item test for primary care providers interested in quickly ascertaining nicotine dependency (see Mallin, 2002).

Case Study

Mrs. C is a 43-year-old woman who began a combined program of Bupropion SR and behavioral treatment at her physician's recommendation. Mrs. C had been smoking two packs per day for over 20 years. She often smoked while watching television with her husband after dinner as a way of "relaxing after a hard day." Mrs. C expressed excitement about commencing treatment and was highly motivated to stop smoking because she had recently lost her good friend to lung cancer and was motivated by her desire to "stick around a lot longer" for her friends and family. She had previously quit smoking approximately 3 years ago, but she relapsed after a month when she found that she had "just switched from smoking to eating all the time." Because of the level of dependence and the history of relapse, her physician referred her to a combined treatment using bupropion and intensive counseling with the clinic behavioral counselor.

At the time of her first visit with the clinic smoking cessation therapist, Mrs. C had been taking Bupropion SR for 3 days and had thus far experienced only mild side effects, which included dry mouth and some difficulty sleeping. Despite these effects, she expressed commitment to treatment and stated her goal of taking her medication as scheduled and attending the group and individual treatment sessions. Her quit date was set for 5 days later, on Day 8 of her medication regimen.

Despite Mrs. C's apparent commitment to treatment, in her discussion with the clinic therapist she revealed a high level of concern about postcessation weight gain. Mrs. C had struggled with her weight throughout her life and stated that if she were to gain more than 10 pounds, she would be motivated to drop treatment and start smoking again, because she believed weight gain to be just as harmful to her body as cigarette smoking. Mrs. C and her therapist agreed that she would meet with a dietician at her primary care physician's office to begin a low-energy diet and that she would continue to walk daily for exercise. The therapist also informed Mrs. C that although weight gain is common, bupropion has been shown to decrease the amount of weight gained in smoking cessation. Mrs. C also informed her therapist that although she was not busy at the moment, she was about to start a new job and was concerned that with her new schedule, she might forget to take her medication. She felt that the therapist's suggestion to record her medication schedule in a daily log would provide structure and serve as a reminder to her to take her pills twice daily. She also appreciated her therapist's suggestion that she track her exercise in the same log and report back to her therapist on her successes and challenges in implementing this positive behavioral change.

At subsequent visits, Mrs. C reported on her activities as recorded in her log. This provided opportunities to discuss problems that arose, including managing on the holidays, finding time for herself, and her vulnerability to relapse when she felt "emotional." In spite of these barriers, the 10-week treatment was successful. When asked what helped her quit and stay quit at her 3-month follow-up, Mrs. C. reported appreciating the support from both her physician and her therapist and that her therapist "believed that she could really do it" and "helped her through the rough spots." Although she didn't like taking the medication, she also felt it was beneficial as it "made her cigarettes taste funny so she didn't even want to smoke them." She had retained the habit of using a daily log to record her exercise and eating at the suggestion of both the dietician and her behavioral counselor. She reported that she and her husband now regularly walked in the early evening, which helped her avoid smoking and eating while watching television during the critical window after dinner.

Conclusions and Further Research

Much remains to be learned about mechanisms of adherence in behavioral, pharmacological, and combined smoking cessation treatments. The current research literature, however, contains few studies that report adequate monitoring of adherence. Only a small number of reports provide detailed data on adherence such as the number of prescribed doses taken within a monitored period, days during which the correct number of doses are taken, or whether or not the prescribed intervals between doses are respected (WHO, 2003). Adherence is often not sufficiently measured in studies of smoking cessation programs, particularly those involving NRT, this in spite of the fact that such information is essential when comparing the relative effectiveness of smoking cessation treatments across programs (Fiore et al., 1994).

What is clear is that adherence to smoking treatments enhances treatment outcomes. In particular, interpersonal support is an essential component of adherence to all forms of treatment, including pharmacotherapies. Along with providing educational information, practitioners are advised to assess previous patient quit attempts, assess patient motivation to participate in smoking cessation treatment, and identify the presence of barriers to adherence that can inform the type of treatment prescribed and the course of therapy attempted. Engagement and empathy with the patients related to their current level of motivation and dependence will improve the likelihood of positive treatment outcomes.

Suggested Readings

Abrams, D. B., Clark, M. M., & King, T. K. (1999). Increasing the impact of nicotine dependence treatment: Conceptual and practical considerations in a stepped-care plus treatment-matching approach. In J. L. Tucker, D. M. Donovan, & G. A. Marlatt (Eds.), *Changing addictive behavior: Bridging clinical and public health strategies* (pp. 307–330). New York: Guilford Press.

Alterman, A. I., Gariti, P., Cook, T. G., & Canaan, A. (1999). Nicodermal patch adherence and its correlates. *Drug and Alcohol Dependence, 53*(2), 159–165.

Diclemente, C. C., & Scott, C. W. (1997). Stages of change: Interactions with treatment compliance and involvement. In L. S. Onken, J. D. Baline, & J. J. Boren (Eds.), *Beyond the therapeutic alliance: Keeping the drug-dependent individual in treatment* (pp. 131–156). Rockville, MD: National Institute on Drug Abuse.

Lichtenstein, E., & Glasgow, R. E. (1992). Smoking cessation: What have we learned over the past decade? *Journal of Consulting and Clinical Psychology, 60*(4), 518–527.

Mallin, R. (2002). Smoking cessation: Integration of behavioral and drug therapies. *American Family Physician, 65*(6), 1107–1114.

References

Abrams, D. B., Clark, M. M., & King, T. K. (1999). Increasing the impact of nicotine dependence treatment: Conceptual and practical considerations in a stepped-care plus treatment-matching approach. In J. L. Tucker, D. M. Donovan, &

G. A. Marlatt (Eds.), *Changing addictive behavior: Bridging clinical and public health strategies* (pp. 307–330). New York: Guilford Press.

Alterman, A. I., Gariti, P., Cook, T. G., & Canaan, A. (1999). Nicodermal patch adherence and its correlates. *Drug and Alcohol Dependence, 53*(2), 159–165.

Anda, R. F., Williamson, D. F., Escobedo, L. G., Mast, E. E., Giovino, G. A., & Remington, P. L. (1990). Depression and the dynamics of smoking. A national perspective. *Journal of the American Medical Association 26,* 1541–1545.

Antonuccio, D. O., & Danton, W. G. (1999). Adding behavioral therapy to medication for smoking cessation. *Journal of the American Medical Association, 281,* 1983–1984.

Benowitz, N. L., Jacob, P., III, & Perez-Stable, E. (1996). CYP2D6 phenotype and the metabolism of nicotine and cotinine. *Pharmacogenetic, 6,* 239–242.

Blake, S. M., Klepp, K. I., Pechacek, T. F., Folsom, A. R., Luepker, R. V., Jacobs, D. R., et al. (1989). Differences in smoking cessation strategies between men and women. *Addictive Behaviors, 14,* 409–418.

Blank, M. B., Mahmood, M., Fox, J. C., & Guterbock, T. (2002). Alternative mental health services: the role of the black church in the South. *American Journal of Public Health, 92,* 1668–1672.

Borrelli, B., Spring, B., Niaura, R., Hitsman, B., & Papandonatos, G. (2001). Influences of gender and weight gain on short-term relapse to smoking in a cessation trial. *Journal of Consulting and Clinical Psychology, 69*(3), 511–515.

Breslau, N., Fenn, N., & Peterson, E. L. (1993). Early smoking initiation and nicotine dependence in a cohort of young adults. *Drug and Alcohol Dependence, 33,* 129–137.

Bultman, D. C., & Svarstad, B. L. (2000). Effects of physician communication style on client medication beliefs and adherence with antidepressant treatment. *Patient Education and Counseling, 40,* 173–185.

Bushnell, F. K., Forbes, B., Goffaux, J., Dietrich, M., & Wells, N. (1997). Smoking cessation in military personnel. *Military Medicine, 162,* 715–719.

Caskey, N. H., Jarvik, M. E., Wirshing, W. C., Madsen, D. C., Iwamoto-Schaap, P. N., Eisenberger, N. I., et al. (2002). Modulating tobacco smoking rates by dopaminergic stimulation and blockade. *Nicotine & Tobacco Research, 4*(3), 259–266.

Centers for Disease Control. (2002). Annual smoking-attributable mortality, years of potential life lost, and economic costs—United States, 1995–1999. *Morbidity and Mortality World Report 51*(14), 300–303.

Centers for Disease Control. (2003). Cigarette smoking among adults—United States, 2001. *Morbidity and Mortality World Report, 52*(42), 1025.

Centers for Disease Control. (2004). *Targeting tobacco use: The nation's leading cause of death 2004.* Atlanta, GA: Author.

Cinciripini, P. M., & McClure, J. B. (1998). Smoking cessation: Recent developments in behavioral and pharmacologic interventions. *Oncology, 12*(2), 249–256, 259; discussion 260, 265, 272.

Cofta-Gunn, L., Wright, K. L., & Wetter, D. W. (2004). Evidence-based recommendations for the treatment of tobacco dependence. In J. A. Trafton & W. Gordon (Eds.), *Best practices in the behavioral management of chronic disease (Vol. 1): Neuropsychiatric disorders.* Los Altos, CA: Institute for Brain Potential.

Covey, L. S., Glassman, A. H., Stetner, F., & Becker, J. (1993). Effect of history of alcoholism or major depression on smoking cessation. *American Journal of Psychiatry, 150,* 1546–1547.

Cummings, K. M., Biernbaum, R. M., Zevon, M. A., Deloughry, T., & Jaen, C. R. (1994). Use and effectiveness of transdermal nicotine in primary care settings. *Archives of Family Medicine, 3*(8), 682–689.

Curry, S. J., Ludman, E. J., & McClure, J. (2003). Self-administered treatment for smoking cessation. *Journal of Clinical Psychology, 59,* 305–319.

Dalack, G. W., Glassman, A. H., Rivelli, S., Covey, L., & Stetner, F. (1995). Mood, major depression, and fluoxetine response in cigarette smokers. *American Journal of Psychiatry, 152,* 398–403.

DiClemente, C. C., & Hughes, S. O. (1990). Stages of change profiles in alcoholism treatment. *Journal of Substance Abuse, 2,* 217–235.

Diclemente, C. C., & Scott, C. W. (1997). Stages of change: Interactions with treatment compliance and involvement. In L. S. Onken, J. D. Baline, & J. J. Boren (Eds.), *Beyond the therapeutic alliance: Keeping the drug-dependent individual in treatment* (pp. 131–156). Rockville, MD: National Institute on Drug Abuse.

Dilsaver, S. C., Pariser, S. F., Churchill, C. M., & Larson, C. N. (1990). Is there a relationship between failing efforts to stop smoking and depression? *Journal of Clinical Psychopharmacology, 10,* 153–154.

Fagerstrom, K. (1978). Measuring degree of physical dependence to tobacco smoking with reference to individualization of treatment. *Addictive Behaviors, 3,* 235–241.

Fagerstrom, K. (2002). The epidemiology of smoking. *Drugs, 62*(Suppl. 2), 1–9.

Fiore, M. C. (2000). U.S. Public Health Service clinical practice guideline. Treating tobacco use and dependence. *Respiratory Care, 45*(10), 1200–1262.

Fiore, M. C., Smith, S. S., Jorenby, D. E., & Baker, T. B. (1994). The effectiveness of the nicotine patch for smoking cessation. A meta-analysis. *Journal of the American Medical Association, 271*(24), 1940–1947.

Fiore, M. C., Novotny, T. E., Pierce, J. P., Giovino, G. A., Hatziandreu, E. J., Newcomb, P. A., et al. (1990). Methods used to quit smoking in the United States. Do cessation programs help? *Journal of the American Medical Association, 263,* 2760–2765.

Fornai, E., Desideri, M., Pistelli, F., Carrozzi, L., Puntoni, R., Avino, S., et al. (2001). Smoking reduction in smokers compliant to a smoking cessation trial with nicotine patch. *Monaldi Archives of Chest Diseases, 56*(1), 5–10.

Gao, X., Nau, D. P., Rosenbluth, S. A., Scott, V., & Woodward, C. (2000). The relationship of disease severity, health beliefs and medication adherence among HIV patients. *AIDS Care, 12,* 387–398.

Gifford, E. V., Antonuccio, D. O., Kohlenberg, B. S., Hayes, S. C., & Piasecki, M. M. (2002, November). *Combining Bupropion SR with acceptance based behavioral therapy for smoking cessation: Preliminary results from a randomized controlled trial.* Paper presented at the Association for the Advancement of Behavior Therapy, Reno, NV.

Gifford, E. V., Palm, K., & Di Loreto, A. R. (in press). Smoking cessation in primary care. In W. T. O'Donohue, N. Cummings, D. Henderson, & M. Byrd (Eds.), *Behavioral integrative care: Treatments that work in the primary care setting.* New York: Taylor & Francis.

Gifford, E. V., & Schoenberger, D. (2003). Rapid smoking treatment for smoking cessation. In W. O'Donohue, J. Fisher, & S. C. Hayes (Eds.), *Cognitive behavior therapy: Applying empirically supported techniques in your practice.* New York: Wiley.

Ginsberg, J. P., Klesges, R. C., Johnson, K. C., Eck, L. H., Meyers, A. W., & Winders, S. A. (1997). The relationship between a history of depression and adherence to a multicomponent smoking-cessation program. *Addictive Behavior, 22,* 783–787.

Glasgow, R. E., Schafer, L., & O'Neill, H. K. (1981). Self-help books and amount of therapist contact in smoking cessation programs. *Journal of Consulting and Clinical Psychology. 49,* 659–667.

Glassman, A. H., Stetner, F., Walsh, B. T., Raizman, P. S., Fleiss, J. L., Cooper, T. B., et al. (1988). Heavy smokers, smoking cessation, and clonidine. Results of a double-blind, randomized trial. *Journal of the American Medical Association, 20,* 2863–2866.

Goldstein, M. G. (1998). Bupropion sustained release and smoking cessation. *Journal of Clinical Psychiatry, 59*(Suppl. 4), 66–72.

Hall, S. M., Munoz, R. F., & Reus, V. I. (1994). Cognitive-behavioral intervention increases abstinence rates for depressive-history smokers. *Journal of Consulting and Clinical Psychology, 62,* 41–46.

Haynes, R. B. (1979). *Determinants of compliance: The disease and the mechanics of treatment.* Baltimore, MD: Johns Hopkins University Press.

Haynes, R. B., McDonald, H. P., & Garg, A. X. (2002). Helping patients follow prescribed treatments: Clinical applications. *Journal of the American Medical Association, 288,* 2880–2883.

Heatherton, T. F., Kozlowski, L. T., Frecker, R. C., & Fagerstrom, K. O. (1991). The Fagerstrom Test for nicotine dependence: A revision of the Fagerstrom Tolerance Questionnaire. *British Journal of Addiction, 86*(9), 1119–1127.

Hitsman, B., Spring, B., Borrelli, B., Niaura, R., & Papandonatos, G. D. (2001). Influence of antidepressant pharmacotherapy on behavioral treatment adherence and smoking cessation outcome in a combined treatment involving fluoxetine. *Experimental Clinical Psychopharmacology, 9*(4), 355– 362.

Hughes, J. R. (1995). Combining behavioral therapy and pharmacotherapy for smoking cessation: An update. *NIDA Research Monographs, 150,* 92–110.

Hurt, R. D. (1999). New medications for nicotine dependence treatment. *Nicotine and Tobacco Research, 1*(Suppl. 2), S175–S179; discussion S207–S210.

Hurt, R. D., Sachs, D. P., Glover, E. D., Offord, K. P., Johnston, J. A., Dale, L. C., et al. (1997). A comparison of sustained-release bupropion and placebo for smoking cessation. *New England Journal of Medicine, 337,* 1195–1202.

Jaakkola, M. S., Ma, J., Yang, G., Chin, M. F., Benowitz, N. L., Ceraso, M., et al. (2003). Determinants of salivary cotinine concentrations in Chinese male smokers. *Preventative Medicine, 36,* 282–290.

Jarvis, M. J., Tunstall-Pedoe, H., Feyerabend, C., Vesey, C., & Saloojee, Y. (1987). Comparison of tests used to distinguish smokers from nonsmokers. *American Journal of Public Health, 11,* 1435– 1438.

Joe, G. W., Simpson, D. D., Greener, J. M., & Rowan-Szal, G. A. (1999). Integrative modeling of client engagement and outcomes during the first 6 months of methadone treatment. *Addictive Behavior, 24* (5), 649–659.

Jorenby, D. E., Leischow, S. J., Nides, M. A., Rennard, S. I., Johnston, J. A., Hughes, A. R., et al. (1999). A controlled trial of sustained-release bupropion, a nicotine patch, or both for smoking cessation. *New England Journal of Medicine, 340*(9), 685–691.

Kamarck, K. W., & Lichtenstein, E. (1988). Program adherence and coping strategies as predictors of success in a smoking treatment program. *Health Psychology, 7,* 557–574.

Kenford, S. L., Fiore, M. C., Jorenby, D. E., Smith, S. S., Wetter, D., & Baker, T. B. (1994). Predicting smoking cessation. Who will quit with and without the nicotine patch. *Journal of the American Medical Association, 271*(8), 589–594.

Killen, J. D., Fortmann, S. P., Schatzberg, A. F., Hayward, C., Sussman, L., Rothman, M., et al. (2000). Nicotine patch and paroxetine for smoking cessation. *Journal of Consulting and Clinical Psychology, 68*(5), 883–889.

King, G., Polednak, A., Bendel, R. B., Vilsaint, M. C., & Nahata, S. B. (2004). Disparities in smoking cessation between African Americans and Whites: 1990–2000. *American Journal of Public Health, 94,* 1965–1971.

Klesges, R. C., Brown, K., Pascale, R. W., Murphy, M., Williams, E., & Cigrang, J. A. (1988). Factors associated with participation, attrition, and outcome in a smoking cessation program at the workplace. *Health Psychology, 7,* 575–589.

Klesges, R. C., Ward, K. D., & DeBon, M. (1996). Smoking cessation: A successful behavioral/pharmacologic interface. *Clinical Psychology Review, 16,* 479–496.

Lichtenstein, E., & Glasgow, R. E. (1992). Smoking cessation: What have we learned over the past decade? *Journal of Consulting and Clinical Psychology, 60*(4), 518–527.

Mallin, R. (2002). Smoking cessation: Integration of behavioral and drug therapies. *American Family Physician, 65*(6), 1107–1114.

Miller, W. R., & Rollnick, S. (1991). *Motivational interviewing: Preparing people to change addictive behavior.* New York: Guilford Press.

Mizes S., Sloan D. M., & Segraves, K. (1998). The influence of weight-related. variables on smoking cessation. *Journal of Behavioral Therapy, 29,* 371–385.

Nemeroff, C. B. (2003). Improving antidepressant adherence. *Journal of Clinical Psychiatry, 64*(Suppl. 18), 25–30.

Orleans, C. T., Resch, N., Noll, E., Keintz, M. K., Rimer, B. K., Brown, T. V., et al. (1994). Use of transdermal nicotine in a state-level prescription plan for the elderly. A first look at 'real-world' patch users. *Journal of the American Medical Association, 271*(8), 601–607.

Patkar, A. A., Vergare, M. J., Batra, V., Weinstein, S. P., & Leone, F. T. (2003). Tobacco smoking: Current concepts in etiology and treatment. *Psychiatry, 66*(3), 183–199.

Pomerleau, O., Adkins, D., & Pertshuck, M. (1978). Predictors of outcome and recidivism in smoking cessation treatment. *Addictive Behavior, 3*(2), 65–70.

Pontieri, F., Orzi, F., & Di Chiara., G. (1996). Effects of nicotine on the nucleus accumbens and similarity to those of addictive drugs. *Nature, 382,* 255–257.

Rand, C. S. (1993). Measuring adherence with therapy for chronic diseases: Implications for the treatment of heterozygous familial hypercholesterolemia. *American Journal of Cardiology, 72*(10), 68D–74D.

Rand, C. S., Wise, R. A., Nides, M., Simmons, M. S., Bleecker, E. R., Kusek, J. W., et al. (1992). Metered-dose inhaler adherence in a clinical trial. *American Review of Respiratory Disease, 146,* 1559–1564.

Rausch, J. L., Nichinson, B., Lamke, C., & Matloff, J. (1990). Influence of negative affect on smoking cessation treatment outcome: A pilot study. *British Journal of Addiction, 85,* 929–933.

Richmond, R., & Zwar, N. (2003). Review of bupropion for smoking cessation. *Drug and Alcohol Review, 22*(2), 203–220.

Rigotti, N. A. (2002). Clinical practice. Treatment of tobacco use and dependence. *New England Journal of Medicine, 346*(7), 506–512.

Silagy, C., Lancaster, T., Stead, L., Mant, D., & Fowler, G. (2004). Nicotine replacement therapy for smoking cessation. *Cochrane Database Systematic Review,* Issue 3, Article No. CD000146.

Stapleton, J. A., Russell, M. A., Feyerabend, C., Wiseman, S. M., Gustavsson, G., Sawe, U., et al. (1995). Dose effects and predictors of outcome in a randomized trial of transdermal nicotine patches in general practice. *Addiction, 90*(1), 31–42.

Substance Abuse and Mental Health Services Administration. (2003). *Results from the 2002 National Survey on Drug Use and Health.* U.S. Department of Health and Human Services, Substance Abuse and Mental Health Services Administration. Retrieved March 23, 2006, from www.oas.samhsa.gov/nhsda/2k2nsduh/Results/2k2Results.htm

Sue, S., Fujino, D. C., Hu, L. T., Takeuchi, D. T., & Zane, N. W. (1991). Community mental health services for ethnic minority groups: A test of the cultural responsiveness hypothesis. *Journal of Consulting and Clinical Psychology, 59,* 533–540.

Tsoh, J. Y., McClure, J. B., Skaar, K. L., Wetter, D. W., Cinciripini, P. M., Prokhorov, A. V., Friedman, K., & Gritz, E. (1997). Smoking cessation 2: Components of effective treatment. *Behavioral Medicine, 23,* 15–27.

U.S. Department of Health and Human Services. (2000). *Healthy people 2010: With understanding and improving health and objectives for improving health* (2nd ed., 2 vols.). Washington, DC: Author.

U.S. Public Health Service. (1990). The Surgeon General's 1990 Report on the Health Benefits of Smoking Cessation Executive Summary: Introduction, overview, and conclusions. *CDC MMWR, 39*(RR-12), 2–10.

Waterhouse, D. M., Calzone, K. A., Mele, C., & Brenner, D. E. (1993). Adherence to oral tamoxifen: A comparison of patient self-report, pill counts, and microelectronic monitoring. *Journal of Clinical Oncology, 11,* 1189–1197.

World Health Organization. (2002). *The World Health Report 2002: Reducing risks, promoting healthy lifestyle.* Geneva, Switzerland: Author.

World Health Organization. (2003). *Adherence to long-term therapies: Evidence for action.* Geneva, Switzerland: Author.

World Health Organization. (2004). *The World Health Organization says that tobacco is bad economics all around 31 May—World No Tobacco Day 2004: The vicious circle of tobacco and poverty.* Retrieved March 21, 2006, from http://www.who.int/media centre/ news/releases/2004/pr36/en/print.html

Zhu, S. H., Stretch, V., Balabanis, M., Rosbrook, B., Sadler, G., & Pierce, J. P. (1996). Telephone counseling for smoking cessation: Effects of single-session and multiple-session interventions. *Journal of Consulting and Clinical Psychology, 64,* 202–211.

Ziedonis, D., Wyatt, S. A., & George, T. P. (1998). Current issues in nicotine dependence and treatment. In E. F. McCancelor-Katz (Ed.), *New treatments for chemical addictions* (pp. 1–34). Arlington, VA: American Psychiatric Publishing.

16

Adherence to Hypertension Treatments

Barry L. Carter

Blood pressure (BP) control in the United States has improved over the past 30 years; however, only 34% of patients with hypertension have BP controlled below 140/90 mmHg (Chobanian et al., 2003). Furthermore, BP control is even more difficult to achieve in patients with diabetes, renal insufficiency, or congestive heart failure (CHF) where there are more aggressive BP goals (<130/80 mmHg) (Chobanian et al., 2003). There is major concern that the prevalence of stroke, CHF, and end-stage renal disease is increasing due, in part, to poorly controlled BP.

Clinical trials (efficacy studies) have demonstrated that BP can be controlled in 70% to 80% of patients when there is close follow-up and forced drug titration (Black et al., 2001; Carter et al., 1994; Carter & Zillich, 2004; Grimm et al., 2001; Hansson et al., 1998). Traditionally, the two common explanations for poor BP control

have been limited access to care and poor patient adherence (Anonymous, 1997; Carter & Zillich, 2004; Miller, Hill, Kottke, & Ockene, 1997). However, one study recently found that most cases of uncontrolled BP occur in patients over 65 years of age who have access to health care and who have frequent contact with physicians (Hyman & Pavlik, 2001). Two other studies have confirmed that BP remained poorly controlled despite up to six visits to physicians per year (Berlowitz et al., 1998; Oliveria et al., 2002). These findings suggest that access to care or frequency of visits is not the primary reason for poor BP control. These two studies also question the explanation that poor adherence is a major cause of poor BP control in the population. Oliveria and coworkers found that patient factors (adherence, patient acceptance, regimen complexity) were uncommon (9%) barriers

Author's Note: The author would like to acknowledge Gail Ardery, RN, PhD, and Jessica Milchak, Pharm.D., who provided thoughtful comments on this chapter.

cited by physicians or patients (Oliveria et al., 2002). The primary barrier (91% of patient visits) was related to physician satisfaction with poorly controlled BPs. Another study found that those with poor BP control have similar adherence to those with good control (Nuesch, Schroeder, Dieterle, Martina, & Battegay, 2001). One study conducted in patients referred to a specialized hypertension center found that the most common reasons for resistant BP were drug-related, including suboptimal regimens (61%), patient nonadherence (13%), secondary hypertension (7%), or other (18%) (Garg, Folker, Izhar, Elliott, & Black, 2002). These findings suggest that problems with patient adherence contribute to a small percentage of cases of poorly controlled BP. These studies, however, might overestimate adherence because patients were engaged within a health system and they may have had greater motivation to adhere than patients who are lost to follow-up or who are not enrolled in an organized study.

Clearly, many patients do discontinue therapy, omit doses, forget their medications, or do not adhere to lifestyle modifications. Persistence over time is a particular concern. Data from Italy found that 42% to 65% of patients discontinued their medications after 1 to 3 years (Degli Esposti, Sturani, et al., 2002; Degli Esposti, Degli Esposti, et al., 2002). Another study found that 78% of patients with newly diagnosed hypertension and 97% with established hypertension persisted with therapy after one year, which is a higher persistence rate than is seen with many studies (Caro, Salas, Speckman, Raggio, & Jackson, 1999). This same study found that persistence rates declined to 46% and 82% in those with newly diagnosed or established hypertension, respectively, at 4.5 years. In these cases, BP deteriorates and control is difficult to achieve, which may lead to increased complications, hospitalizations, and medical costs (Flack, Novikov, & Ferrario, 1996).

Adherence to lifestyle modifications and medications is very important to achieving good BP control and reducing complications such as stroke, myocardial infarction, heart failure, kidney failure, and blindness (Flack et al., 1996). Patients who effectively adhere to lifestyle modifications also are much more likely to be able to withdraw antihypertensive medications (Espeland et al., 1999).

This chapter will focus on barriers to adherence to hypertension treatments and strategies to improve adherence for patients with hypertension. Several of the barriers and strategies to assess adherence are not unique to hypertension and are covered in other chapters of this book. This chapter will primarily focus on strategies as they have been studied and applied to patients with hypertension. Most of the literature on adherence in hypertension involves adherence to antihypertensive medications. However, because lifestyle modifications are a very important strategy for patients with hypertension or prehypertension, this literature will also be discussed (Chobanian et al., 2003).

Assessing Adherence in Patients With Hypertension

Patients seen for hypertension are frequently not adequately assessed for adherence to lifestyle modifications and medications. Often, the extent of assessment involves questions such as "Are you still watching your salt?" or "Are you taking your medications?" The systematic evaluation of adherence requires specific tools and expertise and is time-consuming, perhaps explaining why patients are often inadequately assessed.

The strategies used to assess adherence in hypertension are the same as for other chronic conditions: (1) patient self-report, (2) prescription database assessment, (3) pill counts, and (4) electronic monitoring (Billups, Malone, & Carter, 2000; Carter, Barnette, Chrischilles, Mazzotti, & Asali, 1997; Choo et al., 1999; Grymonpre, Didur, Montgomery, & Sitar, 1998; Kim, Hill, Bone, & Levine, 2000; Lee et al., 1996; Monane et al., 1997; Morisky, Green, & Levine,

1986; Ogedegbe, Mancuso, Allegrante, & Charlson, 2003; Park, Kelly, Carter, & Burgess, 1996; Port, Palm, & Viigimaa, 2003; Steiner & Prochazka, 1997; Svarstad, Chewning, Sleath, & Claesson, 1999; Vaur et al., 1999; Wang et al., 2004). These methods have primarily been used as research tools to evaluate adherence to various interventions and are not often used in the clinical setting. In addition, some of these strategies are time-consuming or expensive and would not lend themselves to routine clinical use. This section will review each strategy.

Perhaps the method used most commonly to assess adherence in clinical practice is patient self-report. A common question that can be used is "How many times in the last week (month) have you missed your medication?" This question should be asked for each medication and followed by specific questioning if problems are identified. Morisky validated a self-report in patients with hypertension that has been commonly used as a research tool (Morisky et al., 1986). The tool has four questions: "Do you ever forget to take your medicine?" "Are you careless at times about taking your medication?" "When you feel better do you sometimes stop taking your medicine?" "Sometimes if you feel worse when you take the medicine, do you stop taking it?" This tool demonstrated a strong predictive validity for BP control at both 2 and 5 years in a population of 290 patients seen in outpatient clinics (Morisky et al., 1986). This and one other study (Shea, Misra, Ehrlich, Field, & Francis, 1992) are important because they demonstrate a good relationship between self-reported adherence and actual BP control.

The Brief Medication Questionnaire (BMQ) was used to evaluate adherence to antihypertensive medications compared with the electronic Medication Events Monitoring System (MEMS) (Svarstad et al., 1999). The questionnaire had a high sensitivity as a method to assess adherence. The Medication Adherence Self-Efficacy Scale (MASES) was used to evaluate self-efficacy and enabling factors and their relationship with adherence to antihypertensive medications by African Americans (Ogedegbe et al., 2003). Although long (26 questions), this tool is particularly helpful in identifying barriers to adherence and strategies to enable patients to better adhere to their antihypertensive regimen. The Hill-Bone Compliance to High Blood Pressure Therapy Scale is unique in that it includes questions about not only medication-taking behavior but also the ability to reduce sodium intake and keep appointments (Kim et al., 2000). Using this tool, high compliance scale scores were shown to predict lower BP and better BP control. However, the reliability of patient self-report of adherence to antihypertensive medication has been poor when compared with prescription refills (Wang et al., 2004), but this may simply reflect the fact that prescription refills overestimate medication consumption (Grymonpre et al., 1998; Steiner & Prochazka, 1997).

Although self-report may overestimate adherence, it is the most convenient and cost-effective approach to use in the clinical environment (Choo et al., 1999; Dunbar-Jacob, Dwyer, & Dunning, 1991; Grymonpre et al., 1998). An admission of forgetfulness or intentional non-adherence has good predictive value and allows the clinician to identify barriers to adherence and strategies to overcome adherence problems (Choo et al., 1999).

A second method used to assess adherence is pharmacy refill records (Billups et al., 2000; Choo et al., 1999; Grymonpre et al., 1998; Monane et al., 1997; Steiner & Prochazka, 1997). Automated pharmacy refill records are convenient and can screen large populations but typically are used only for research purposes. Refill records cannot identify timing errors; they overestimate adherence if patients "stockpile" medications and underestimate adherence if there are other sources for the medications (e.g., samples). In addition, physicians may verbally change dose instructions in the midst of a prescription fill that is not reflected on the label directions, and this renders the refill information inaccurate.

Pill counts can be used clinically but have primarily been used in research studies (Choo et al., 1999; Grymonpre et al., 1998; Lee et al., 1996). Pill counts have only moderate correlations with other adherence measures due to inherent limitations. Pill counts may overestimate adherence if patients remove pills and place them in other containers (Choo et al., 1999; Grymonpre et al., 1998). In addition, unless each and every fill date is known precisely, pill counts will be inaccurate. Therefore, pill counts have been commonly used in large, multicenter clinical trials in hypertension where patients are dispensed their BP medications from study investigators. The African American Study of Kidney Disease and Hypertension (AASK) study found that acceptable adherence was achieved in 68% of patients with pill counts and 47% with MEMS (Lee et al., 1996). Interestingly, only 16% to 18% of patients who were found to be nonadherent using either or both methods achieved BP control, whereas 50% of those who were adherent to both methods achieved BP control.

Electronic monitoring is often considered the gold standard for assessing adherence, enabling measurement of overall adherence and the actual time when a dose is taken (Choo et al., 1999). Unfortunately, electronic monitoring is only accurate if patients consume the proper dose each time the cap is opened. Sources of error include patient opening the cap without consuming the medication, incomplete closure of the cap (some patients leave the cap off for convenience), or removing several doses of pills with one cap opening. Because the cost for an electronic monitor is high, this method has been primarily used for research purposes.

In summary, the use of a validated questionnaire is the most convenient and cost-effective strategy to evaluate adherence clinically. The modest to poor correlation between techniques for assessing adherence reflects their unique limitations rather than their relative worth. For this reason, research studies in hypertension should ideally use two different and complementary methods to assess adherence (Grymonpre et al., 1998).

Factors That Contribute to Poor Adherence in Hypertension

Barriers to adherence that have been identified in patients with hypertension are summarized in Table 16.1 (Flack et al., 1996). Many of these barriers are especially problematic in patients with newly diagnosed hypertension. Keeping the barriers in mind can help clinicians focus and streamline their interventions with patients who have poor BP control.

Patient Demographics

There are conflicting data on the influence of gender on adherence in hypertension. Some studies found higher levels of adherence in females than males (Caro et al., 1999; Flack et al., 1996), but others have not found such a relationship (Degli Esposti, Sturani, et al., 2002; Vaur et al., 1999). Women are generally more aware of hypertension, visit a physician more frequently, and adhere to treatment regimens at higher rates than men (Flack et al., 1996).

Most studies have found that older individuals with hypertension tend to adhere better to hypertension treatment than younger subjects (Billups et al., 2000; Caro et al., 1999; Degli Esposti, Degli Esposti, et al., 2002; Vaur et al., 1999), but other studies have found lower adherence in the elderly (Knight et al., 2001).

Individuals living in large urban centers have lower adherence levels than those in smaller cities or urban areas (Vaur et al., 1999). There appears to be a strong link between low income, depression, poor adherence, and poor BP control, at least in urban, hypertensive black men (Kim, Han, Hill, Rose, & Roary, 2003).

Patient Knowledge and Beliefs

Negative beliefs about hypertension (including inaccuracies about medications) and inadequate knowledge of hypertension are barriers to adherence (Ogedegbe et al., 2003; Ogedegbe,

Table 16.1   Adherence Barriers and Facilitators in Hypertension

Barriers to Adherence	Facilitators That Improve Adherence
Insufficient knowledge	Multiple chronic conditions (especially prior cardiovascular event)
Negative beliefs about hypertension or its treatment	Patients who are involved with treatment decisions
Lack of single provider	Strong provider-patient relationship
Lack of self-efficacy and control	Self-monitoring of BP
Complicated medication regimens	Female gender
Adverse drug reactions	Higher education
High medication costs	Higher socioeconomic status
Rapid lowering of BP (and/or excessive initial medication dose)	Married
Younger age	Patient knows goal BP
Male gender	Higher levels of BP
Minority race	Clinic and refill reminders, pillboxes
Large city dwellers	Monotherapy or combination therapy
Low socioeconomic status	
Depression	
Alcohol or substance abuse	
Cognitive impairment	
Smokers	

SOURCE: Flack et al. (1996) and Ogedegbe et al. (2003, 2004a, 2004b).

Harrison, Robbins, Mancuso, & Allegrante, 2004a, 2004b). Patients who lack knowledge about their target BP are more likely to have lower adherence levels (Alexander, Gordon, Davis, & Chen, 2003; Knight et al., 2001; Ogedegbe et al., 2003). Those who believe they have more control in their ability to reduce their BP may reduce their reliance on medications, leading to nonadherence (Patel & Taylor, 2002).

One study that used the health belief model found that African Americans were more oriented toward the present than whites (Brown & Segal, 1996). Individuals who were present oriented were less likely to believe they were susceptible to the complications of hypertension, they had greater faith in home remedies and they did not believe in the benefits of antihypertensive medications. Patient fears that

medications may cause a future ill-defined side effect, long-term damage to organs or their body, or addiction frequently lead to discontinuation of BP medications (Ogedegbe et al., 2003).

Medication Regimen

Complex antihypertensive regimens, multiple daily dosing, and the inconvenience of taking medications away from home are significant barriers to adherence (Knight et al., 2001; Nuesch et al., 2001; Ogedegbe et al., 2003, 2004a, 2004b). However, some patients taking more medications have higher adherence rates (Billups et al., 2000; Caro et al., 1999; Degli Esposti, Degli Esposti, et al., 2002). This latter observation might be explained by the health belief model that suggests that patients who feel they are ill or have worse disease are more likely to be concerned about their health (Billups et al., 2000).

Prescription drug costs have increased dramatically in recent years and prescription noncompliance has increased due to lack of affordability (Kennedy, Coyne, & Sclar, 2004; Ogedegbe et al., 2003). The influence of drug costs on adherence in hypertension will primarily influence those who lack prescription drug coverage (Raji, Kuo, Salazar, Satish, & Goodwin, 2004).

Drug Choice and Adverse Drug Reactions

The relationship between drug class and discontinuation (persistence) is unclear due to conflicting findings. One large study found no influence of drug class on persistence rates (Benson, Vance-Bryan, & Raddatz, 2000). Major changes in physician prescribing of various medication classes between 1986 and 1992 had little impact on persistence rates (60–69%) or BP control (Alderman, Madhavan, & Cohen, 1996). Studies have also found opposing rates of discontinuation for calcium channel blockers, alpha blockers, diuretics, and angiotensin blockers (Degli Esposti, Sturani, et al., 2002; Degli Esposti, Degli Esposti, et al., 2002; Monane et al., 1997; Ross, Akhras, Zhang, Rozinsky, & Nalysnyk, 2001). These conflicting findings might be explained by selection bias. For instance, if a diuretic is selected and the patient is told he or she may have a "mild case" of hypertension, the patient might preferentially discontinue that class more often based on the health belief model.

It is commonly believed that adverse drug events (ADEs) cause a high percentage of patients to stop therapy. However, one large study found that a diuretic (1.1%), a beta blocker (2.2%), or an angiotensin-converting enzyme (ACE) inhibitor (4.8%) was associated with lower ADEs than a placebo (6.5%), a calcium channel blocker (6.5%), prazosin (13.8%), or clonidine (10.1%) (Materson et al., 1993). Adverse reactions that lead to nonadherence are always a concern. Patients with treated hypertension have more distressful symptoms and lower scores on quality

of life measures than nonhypertensive controls (Erickson, Williams, & Gruppen, 2001). However, symptoms of distress were much lower and quality of life scores higher in hypertensive patients with controlled BP than in those with uncontrolled BP (Erickson et al., 2001). These findings suggest that hypertension is not an asymptomatic condition and patient symptoms may improve when BP is improved (Neaton et al., 1993). Unfortunately, such symptoms are often attributed to medications and may lead to discontinuation. Thus, placebo-controlled studies are very important to evaluate whether specific medication classes are associated with poorer adherence. Studies that were not placebo controlled have significant limitations.

Regardless, some patients clearly do have adverse reactions (e.g., dry cough with an ACE inhibitor or fatigue in an athlete on a beta blocker). Others firmly believe that one of their medications is causing a problem and the clinician must address this by patient education, dosage adjustment, or changing therapy. If a patient is going to discontinue a medication (presumably due to adverse events but perhaps for any other barrier), it is likely to occur early in therapy (Caro et al., 1999). Thus, frequent follow-up and communication early in the management and titration process are important.

Hypertension With Coexisting Conditions

Patients with hypertension and other chronic conditions, especially those with severe symptoms or sequelae from hypertension (angina, past myocardial infarction, or stroke) tend to have much higher rates of adherence than those without these concomitant conditions (Billups et al., 2000; Degli Esposti, Degli Esposti, et al., 2002; Knight et al., 2001). Notable exceptions are depression and/or substance abuse, which are associated with poor medication and dietary adherence and poor BP control (Kim et al., 2003; Wang et al., 2002). Patients who consume more alcohol and/or illicit drugs have low levels of dietary compliance (Kim et al., 2003).

Strategies to Improve Adherence in Patients With Hypertension

Many strategies can be used to improve adherence to lifestyle modification and medications in patients with hypertension. A Cochrane review has evaluated the literature on adherence in hypertension (Schroeder, Fahey, & Ebrahim, 2004) and an expert panel on compliance from the American Heart Association has provided specific recommendations to improve adherence (Table 16.2) (Miller et al., 1997).

Ethical Issues of Low Adherence

Not all cases of poor adherence are due to forgetfulness or barriers. Some patients with hypertension weigh the risks and benefits of treatment and choose not to take medications for valid reasons, at least as they perceive them (Bernardini, 2004). For these patients, additional education will not be effective unless their fundamental beliefs about their condition or the benefits of treatment change. For these patients, the clinician must include the patient in treatment and management decisions.

Table 16.2   Actions to Increase Adherence With Prevention and Treatment Recommendations for Hypertension

Actions by Patients	Specific Strategies
Patients must engage in essential prevention and treatment behaviors.	
• Decide to control risk factors • Negotiate BP goals with provider • Develop skills for adopting and maintaining recommended behaviors • Monitor progress toward BP goals • Resolve barriers to achieving BP goals	• Understand rationale, importance of commitment • Develop communication skills • Use reminder systems • Develop problem-solving skills, use social support networks • Define own needs on the basis of experience • Validate rationale for continuing to follow recommendations

Actions by Providers	Specific Strategies
Providers must foster effective communication with patients.	
• Provide clear, direct messages about importance of a behavior or therapy • Include patients in decisions about prevention and treatment goals for BP • Incorporate behavioral strategies into counseling	• Provide verbal and written instruction, including rationale for treatments • Develop skills in communication and counseling • Use tailoring and contracting strategies • Negotiate BP goals and a plan • Anticipate barriers or occasional low adherence and discuss solutions
Providers must document BP goals and respond to patient's progress toward goals.	
• Create an evidence-based practice • Assess patient's adherence at each visit • Develop reminder systems to ensure identification and follow-up of patient status	• Determine methods of evaluating hypertension outcomes • Use self-report on adherence, pill counts, or electronic data • Use telephone follow-up

(Continued)

Table 16.2 (Continued)

Actions by Health Care Organizations	Specific Strategies
Health care organizations must . . .	
• develop an environment that supports hypertension prevention and treatment interventions. • ensure continuity with one provider. • provide tracking and reporting systems. • provide education and training of providers. • provide adequate reimbursement for allocation of time for all health care professionals.	• develop training in behavioral science, office setup for all personnel. • use preappointment and refill reminders. • use telephone follow-up. • Schedule evening/weekend office hours. • provide group counseling for patients and families. • develop computer-based systems such as electronic medical records. • require continuing education courses in communication, behavioral counseling. • hire behavioral counselors to provide adherence counseling. • develop incentives tied to desired patient and provider outcomes.
Health care organizations must adopt systems to rapidly and efficiently incorporate innovations into medical practice.	
	• Incorporate nurse and/or pharmacist case management of hypertension • Implement pharmacy patient profile and recall review reminder systems • Effectively store and document BP data obtained from patient self-monitoring • Obtain patient data on lifestyle behaviors before visit • Provide continuous quality improvement training

SOURCE: Adapted from Carter (2001), Carter and Zillich (2004), and Miller et al. (1997).

Social Support and Self-Efficacy

Good social support from family, friends, and caregivers serves to facilitate good adherence in patients with hypertension (Ogedegbe et al., 2003). There is also a strong relationship between patient-reported self-efficacy and BP control (Ogedegbe et al., 2003). Behavioral strategies to improve self-efficacy should be strongly considered for patients with low adherence (Ogedegbe et al., 2003).

One study found that African Americans were more present-oriented than whites and indicated that focusing on the consequences of hypertension may not be very effective unless the patient or a close associate has experienced such a complication (Brown & Segal, 1996; Knight et al., 2001). This may explain why the Cochrane review found patient education alone to be an unsuccessful approach to improve adherence (Schroeder et al., 2004). For these patients, it may be much more effective to focus on overcoming the issues and problems of daily treatment of hypertension. Motivational strategies appear to be effective (Schroeder et al., 2004).

Patients should be taught to measure their own BP and keep a log of administration times and BP values. These strategies engage patients in their own care and improve adherence and BP control (Haynes et al., 1976). The use of telecommunication systems by which patients measure their BP at home, transmit these values via the telephone, and answer specific questions from the computer-controlled speech system has been shown to significantly improve BP control (Friedman et al., 1996).

Medication Regimen

The starting dose and dosage range listed in the product labeling for many antihypertensives is too high and often much higher than recommended by national guidelines (Chobanian et al., 2003; Cohen, 2001). The clinician must balance the need to start with low doses with the fact that this may require longer titration periods and, perhaps, more patient frustration. Additionally, slower dosage increases are less likely to cause side effects that limit adherence (Flack et al., 2000).

Regimens with less frequent daily administration (e.g., once daily dosing) clearly improve adherence, but many patients can effectively adhere to a twice-daily regimen (Carter, 2001; Carter et al., 1994; Carter & Zillich, 2004; Eisen, Miller, Woodward, Spitznagel, & Przybeck, 1990). Regimens using three or four times daily dosing should be avoided at all cost. Patients who take more antihypertensive medications have poorer BP control, which has been attributed to both lower adherence and resistant BP (Knight et al., 2001). When hypertension regimens become complex, it is advisable to consider combination pills or other strategies to simplify regimens (Chobanian et al., 2003; Schroeder et al., 2004). Combination products may actually lower medication costs. Providers should design regimens that are inexpensive, including agents like diuretics and beta blockers, because cost of medications is a significant predictor of adherence in patients with hypertension (Carter, Zillich, & Elliott, 2003; Chobanian

et al., 2003; Kennedy et al., 2004; Ogedegbe et al., 2003; Raji et al., 2004).

Reminder systems such as pillboxes, refill reminders, unit of use packaging, and administration routines help adherence (Murray, Birt, Manatunga, & Darnell, 1993; Ogedegbe et al., 2003; Schroeder et al., 2004). Electronic medication devices that remind patients when they took each BP medication are effective but used infrequently, primarily due to cost (McKenney, Munroe, & Wright, 1992).

Provider-Patient Relationships and Health Care Organization

Patients who see their physician more frequently have better rates of long-term adherence than those with less frequent visits (Caro et al., 1999; He et al., 2002). In addition, patients who have good relationships and communication with one physician have higher rates of adherence (He et al., 2002; Ogedegbe et al., 2003). When providers encourage family support, better provider-patient communication, and small group discussions, adherence is improved (Ward, Morisky, Lees, & Fong, 2000). The provider should work closely with the patient and family to establish a goal-oriented approach to their management including the desired goal BP, weight loss, and dietary changes (Singer, Izhar, & Black, 2002).

Health care systems should improve patient convenience, reduce waiting times, provide continuous care, provide clinic reminders, and telephone patients to reschedule them when they miss appointments (Ward et al., 2000). Individualized counseling about lifestyle modification and medications and home visits are also effective strategies to improve kept appointments and adherence for patients with hypertension (Jones, Jones, & Katz, 1987; Ward et al., 2000).

Multidisciplinary Approaches to Improve Adherence

Multidisciplinary teams can markedly improve both adherence and BP control. Nurse specialists or clinical pharmacy specialists located in physician offices are particularly effective at coordinating and assisting with hypertension management (Carter et al., 1997, 2001, 2003; Carter & Zillich, 2004; Miller et al., 1997).

The chronic care model has been used to improve adherence and disease control for patients with chronic conditions (Bodenheimer, Wagner, & Grumbach, 2002). The model sometimes uses a layperson as the primary contact person and liaison for patients to navigate the health system (Haynes et al., 1976). Nurses then see patients and measure BP and provide primary patient education and follow-up. Clinical pharmacists who are located in the office or clinic see patients who have resistant hypertension, complex medication regimens, drug interactions, or adverse reactions. These pharmacists assist with regimen design and monitoring to improve adherence and BP control. Several studies have found that when clinical pharmacists and physicians provide comanagement, there is a significant improvement in adherence and BP control (Borenstein et al., 2003; Carter et al., 1997, 2003; Erickson, Slaughter, & Halapy, 1997; McKenney, Slining, Henderson, Devins, & Barr, 1973; Park et al., 1996). In these models, pharmacists see patients between physician visits and provide regimen design, dosage adjustment, and monitoring in collaboration with the physician. Behavioral counselors, nutritionists, and social workers are consulted for complex adherence problems or social barriers to adherence. In this model, physicians focus on physical examinations, diagnoses, and patients with complications.

Summary

Patients with hypertension experience many barriers to adherence. Providers should develop good communication and continuity of care for patients with hypertension, establish mutually agreed upon goals, and establish close follow-up. Improving adherence can be very time-consuming, and multidisciplinary teams can improve adherence and BP control.

References

Alderman, M. H., Madhavan, S., & Cohen, H. (1996). Antihypertensive drug therapy. The effect of JNC criteria on prescribing patterns and patient status through the first year. *American Journal of Hypertension, 9*(5), 413–418.

Alexander, M., Gordon, N. P., Davis, C. C., & Chen, R. S. (2003). Patient knowledge and awareness of hypertension is suboptimal: Results from a large health maintenance organization. *Journal of Clinical Hypertension, 5*(4), 254–260.

Anonymous. (1997). The sixth report of the Joint National Committee on prevention, detection, evaluation, and treatment of high blood pressure. *Archives of Internal Medicine, 157*(21), 2413–2446.

Benson, S., Vance-Bryan, K., & Raddatz, J. (2000). Time to patient discontinuation of antihypertensive drugs in different classes. *American Journal of Health-System Pharmacy, 57*(1), 51–54.

Berlowitz, D. R., Ash, A. S., Hickey, E. C., Friedman, R. H., Glickman, M., Kader, B., et al. (1998). Inadequate management of blood pressure in a hypertensive population. *New England Journal of Medicine, 339*(27), 1957–1963.

Bernardini, J. (2004). Ethical issues of compliance/adherence in the treatment of hypertension. *Advances in Chronic Kidney Disease, 11*(2), 222–227.

Billups, S. J., Malone, D. C., & Carter, B. L. (2000). The relationship between drug therapy noncompliance and patient characteristics, health-related quality of life, and health care costs. *Pharmacotherapy, 20*(8), 941–949.

Black, H. R., Elliott, W. J., Neaton, J. D., Grandits, G., Grambsch, P., Grimm, R. H., Jr., et al. (2001). Baseline characteristics and early blood pressure control in the CONVINCE trial. *Hypertension, 37*(1), 12–18.

Bodenheimer, T., Wagner, E. H., & Grumbach, K. (2002). Improving primary care for patients with chronic illness: The chronic care model, Part 2. *Journal of the American Medical Association, 288*(15), 1909–1914.

Borenstein, J. E., Graber, G., Saltiel, E., Wallace, J., Ryu, S., Archi, J., et al. (2003). Physician-pharmacist comanagement of hypertension: A randomized, comparative trial. *Pharmacotherapy, 23*(2), 209–216.

Brown, C. M., & Segal, R. (1996). Ethnic differences in temporal orientation and its implications for hypertension management. *Journal of Health and Social Behavior, 37*(4), 350–361.

Caro, J. J., Salas, M., Speckman, J. L., Raggio, G., & Jackson, J. D. (1999). Persistence with treatment for hypertension in actual practice. *Canadian Medical Association Journal, 160*(1), 31–37.

Carter, B. L. (2001). Management of essential hypertension. In K. Bertch, T. Dunsworth, S. Fagan, et al. (Eds.), *The pharmacotherapy self-assessment program* (4th ed., pp. 1–39). Kansas City, MO: American College of Clinical Pharmacy.

Carter, B. L., Barnette, D. J., Chrischilles, E., Mazzotti, G. J., & Asali, Z. J. (1997). Evaluation of hypertensive patients after care provided by community pharmacists in a rural setting. *Pharmacotherapy, 17*(6), 1274–1285.

Carter, B. L., Billups, S. J., Malone, D., Valuck, R., Barnette, D. J., & Sintek, C. D. (2001). Recommended guidelines for pharmacists who provide care for patients in the IMPROVE study. *Federal Practitioner, 18*, 38–46.

Carter, B. L., Frohlich, E. D., Elliott, W. J., Moore, M. A., Mann, R. J., & Roberts, R. W. (1994). Selected factors that influence responses to antihypertensives. Choosing therapy for the uncomplicated patient. *Archives of Family Medicine, 3*(6), 528–536.

Carter, B. L., & Zillich A.J. (Eds.). (2004). Management of essential hypertension. In B. J. Zarowitz, et al. (Eds.), *The pharmacotherapy self-assessment program* (5th ed., pp. 129–159). Kansas City, MO: American College of Clinical Pharmacy.

Carter, B. L., Zillich, A. J., & Elliott, W. J. (2003). How pharmacists can assist physicians with controlling blood pressure. *Journal of Clinical Hypertension, 5*(1), 31–37.

Chobanian, A. V., Bakris, G. L., Black, H. R., Cushman, W. C., Green, L. A., Izzo, J. L., Jr., et al. (2003). The Seventh Report of the Joint National Committee on Prevention, Detection, Evaluation, and Treatment of High Blood Pressure: The JNC 7 report. *Journal of the American Medical Association, 289*(19), 2560–2572.

Choo, P. W., Rand, C. S., Inui, T. S., Lee, M. L., Cain, E., Cordeiro-Breault, M., et al. (1999). Validation of patient reports, automated pharmacy records, and pill counts with electronic monitoring of adherence to antihypertensive therapy. *Medical Care, 37*(9), 846–857.

Cohen, J. S. (2001). Adverse drug effects, compliance, and initial doses of antihypertensive drugs recommended by the Joint National Committee vs the Physicians' Desk Reference. *Archives of Internal Medicine, 161*(6), 880–885.

Degli Esposti, L., Degli Esposti, E., Valpiani, G., Di Martino, M., Saragoni, S., Buda, S., et al. (2002). A retrospective, population-based analysis of persistence with antihypertensive drug therapy in primary care practice in Italy. *Clinical Therapeutics, 24*(8), 1347–1357; discussion 1346.

Degli Esposti, E., Sturani, A., Di Martino, M., Falasca, P., Novi, M. V., Baio, G., et al. (2002). Long-term persistence with antihypertensive drugs in new patients. *Journal of Human Hypertension, 16*(6), 439–444.

Dunbar-Jacob, J., Dwyer, K., & Dunning, J. (1991). Compliance with antihypertensive regimen: A review of the research in the 1980s. *Annals of Behavioral Medicine, 13*, 31–39.

Eisen, S. A., Miller, D. K., Woodward, R. S., Spitznagel, E., & Przybeck, T. R. (1990). The effect of prescribed daily dose frequency on patient medication compliance. *Archives of Internal Medicine, 150*(9), 1881–1884.

Erickson, S. R., Slaughter, R., & Halapy, H. (1997). Pharmacists' ability to influence outcomes of hypertension therapy. *Pharmacotherapy, 17*(1), 140–147.

Erickson, S. R., Williams, B. C., & Gruppen, L. D. (2001). Perceived symptoms and health-related quality of life reported by uncomplicated hypertensive patients compared to normal controls. *Journal of Human Hypertension, 15*(8), 539–548.

Espeland, M. A., Whelton, P. K., Kostis, J. B., Bahnson, J. L., Ettinger, W. H., Cutler, J. A., et al. (1999). Predictors and mediators of successful long-term withdrawal from antihypertensive medications. TONE Cooperative Research Group. Trial of Nonpharmacologic Interventions in the Elderly. *Archives of Family Medicine, 8*(3), 228–236.

Flack, J. M., Novikov, S. V., & Ferrario, C. M. (1996). Benefits of adherence to anti-hypertensive drug therapy. *European Heart Journal, 17*(Suppl. A), 16–20.

Flack, J. M., Yunis, C., Preisser, J., Holmes, C. B., Mensah, G., McLean, B., et al. (2000). The rapidity of drug dose escalation influences blood pressure response and adverse effects burden in patients with hypertension: The Quinapril Titration Interval Management Evaluation (ATIME) Study. ATIME Research Group. *Archives of Internal Medicine, 160*(12), 1842–1847.

Friedman, R. H., Kazis, L. E., Jette, A., Smith, M. B., Stollerman, J., Torgerson, J., et al. (1996). A telecommunications system for monitoring and counseling patients with hypertension. Impact on medication adherence and blood pressure control. *American Journal of Hypertension, 9*(4, Pt. 1), 285–292.

Garg, J. P., Folker, A. C., Izhar, M., Elliott, W. J., & Black, H. R. (2002). Resistant hypertension revisited. *American Journal of Hypertension, 15*(4, Suppl. 1), A25.

Grimm, R. H., Jr., Margolis, K. L., Papademetriou, V. V., Cushman, W. C., Ford, C. E., Bettencourt, J., et al. (2001). Baseline characteristics of participants in the Antihypertensive and Lipid Lowering Treatment to Prevent Heart Attack Trial (ALLHAT). *Hypertension, 37*(1), 19–27.

Grymonpre, R. E., Didur, C. D., Montgomery, P. R., & Sitar, D. S. (1998). Pill count, self-report, and pharmacy claims data to measure medication adherence in the elderly. *Annals of Pharmacotherapy, 32*(7–8), 749–754.

Hansson, L., Zanchetti, A., Carruthers, S. G., Dahlof, B., Elmfeldt, D., Julius, S., et al. (1998). Effects of intensive blood-pressure lowering and low-dose aspirin in patients with hypertension: Principal results of the Hypertension Optimal Treatment (HOT) randomised trial. HOT Study Group. *Lancet, 351*(9118), 1755–1762.

Haynes, R. B., Sackett, D. L., Gibson, E. S., Taylor, D. W., Hackett, B. C., Roberts, R. S., et al. (1976). Improvement of medication compliance in uncontrolled hypertension. *Lancet, 1*(7972), 1265–1268.

He, J., Muntner, P., Chen, J., Roccella, E. J., Streiffer, R. H., & Whelton, P. K. (2002). Factors associated with hypertension control in the general population of the United States. *Archives of Internal Medicine, 162*(9), 1051–1058.

Hyman, D. J., & Pavlik, V. N. (2001). Characteristics of patients with uncontrolled hypertension in the United States. *New England Journal of Medicine, 345*(7), 479–486.

Jones, P. K., Jones, S. L., & Katz, J. (1987). Improving follow-up among hypertensive patients using a health belief model intervention. *Archives of Internal Medicine, 147*(9), 1557–1560.

Kennedy, J., Coyne, J., & Sclar, D. (2004). Drug affordability and prescription noncompliance in the United States: 1997–2002. *Clinical Therapeutics, 26*(4), 607–614.

Kim, M. T., Han, H. R., Hill, M. N., Rose, L., & Roary, M. (2003). Depression, substance use, adherence behaviors, and blood pressure in urban hypertensive black men. *Annals of Behavioral Medicine, 26*(1), 24–31.

Kim, M. T., Hill, M. N., Bone, L. R., & Levine, D. M. (2000). Development and testing of the Hill-Bone Compliance to High Blood Pressure Therapy Scale. *Progress in Cardiovascular Nursing, 15*(3), 90–96.

Knight, E. L., Bohn, R. L., Wang, P. S., Glynn, R. J., Mogun, H., & Avorn, J. (2001). Predictors of uncontrolled hypertension in ambulatory patients. *Hypertension, 38*(4), 809–814.

Lee, J. Y., Kusek, J. W., Greene, P. G., Bernhard, S., Norris, K., Smith, D., et al. (1996). Assessing medication adherence by pill count and electronic monitoring in the African American Study of Kidney Disease and Hypertension (AASK) Pilot Study. *American Journal of Hypertension, 9*(8), 719–725.

Materson, B. J., Reda, D. J., Cushman, W. C., Massie, B. M., Freis, E. D., Kochar, M. S., et al. (1993). Single-drug therapy for hypertension in men. A comparison of six antihypertensive agents with placebo. The Department of Veterans Affairs Cooperative Study Group on Antihypertensive Agents. *New England Journal of Medicine, 328*(13), 914–921.

McKenney, J. M., Munroe, W. P., & Wright, J. T., Jr. (1992). Impact of an electronic medication compliance aid on long-term blood pressure control. *Journal of Clinical Pharmacology, 32*(3), 277–283.

McKenney, J. M., Slining, J. M., Henderson, H. R., Devins, D., & Barr, M. (1973). The effect of clinical pharmacy services on patients with essential hypertension. *Circulation, 48*(5), 1104–1111.

Miller, N. H., Hill, M., Kottke, T., & Ockene, I. S. (1997). The multilevel compliance challenge: Recommendations for a call to action. A statement for healthcare professionals. *Circulation, 95*(4), 1085–1090.

Monane, M., Bohn, R. L., Gurwitz, J. H., Glynn, R. J., Levin, R., & Avorn, J. (1997). The effects of initial drug choice and comorbidity on antihypertensive therapy compliance: Results from a population-based study in the elderly. *American Journal of Hypertension, 10*(7, Pt. 1), 697–704.

Morisky, D. E., Green, L. W., & Levine, D. M. (1986). Concurrent and predictive validity of a self-reported measure of medication adherence. *Medical Care, 24*(1), 67–74.

Murray, M. D., Birt, J. A., Manatunga, A. K., & Darnell, J. C. (1993). Medication compliance in elderly outpatients using twice-daily dosing and unit-of-use packaging. *Annals of Pharmacotherapy, 27*(5), 616–621.

Neaton, J. D., Grimm, R. H., Jr., Prineas, R. J., Stamler, J., Grandits, G. A., Elmer, P. J., et al. (1993). Treatment of Mild Hypertension Study. Final results. Treatment of Mild Hypertension Study Research Group. *Journal of the American Medical Association, 270*(6), 713–724.

Nuesch, R., Schroeder, K., Dieterle, T., Martina, B., & Battegay, E. (2001). Relation between insufficient response to antihypertensive treatment and poor compliance with treatment: A prospective case-control study. *British Medical Journal, 323*(7305), 142–146.

Ogedegbe, G., Harrison, M., Robbins, L., Mancuso, C. A., & Allegrante, J. P. (2004a). Barriers and facilitators of medication adherence in hypertensive African Americans: A qualitative study. *Ethnicity & Disease, 14*(1), 3–12.

Ogedegbe, G., Harrison, M., Robbins, L., Mancuso, C. A., & Allegrante, J. P. (2004b). Reasons patients do or do not take their blood pressure medications. *Ethnicity & Disease, 14*(1), 158.

Ogedegbe, G., Mancuso, C. A., Allegrante, J. P., & Charlson, M. E. (2003). Development and evaluation of a medication adherence self-efficacy scale in hypertensive African-American patients. *Journal of Clinical Epidemiology, 56*(6), 520–529.

Oliveria, S. A., Lapuerta, P., McCarthy, B. D., L'Italien, G. J., Berlowitz, D. R., & Asch, S. M. (2002). Physician-related barriers to the effective management of uncontrolled hypertension. *Archives of Internal Medicine, 162*(4), 413–420.

Park, J. J., Kelly, P., Carter, B. L., & Burgess, P. P. (1996). Comprehensive pharmaceutical care in the chain setting. *Journal of the American Pharmaceutical Association (Wash), NS36*(7), 443–451.

Patel, R. P., & Taylor, S. D. (2002). Factors affecting medication adherence in hypertensive patients. *Annals of Pharmacotherapy, 36*(1), 40–45.

Port, K., Palm, K., & Viigimaa, M. (2003). Self-reported compliance of patients receiving antihypertensive treatment: Use of a telemonitoring home care system. *Journal of Telemedicine and Telecare, 9*(Suppl. 1), S65–66.

Raji, M. A., Kuo, Y. F., Salazar, J. A., Satish, S., & Goodwin, J. S. (2004). Ethnic differences in antihypertensive medication use in the elderly. *Annals of Pharmacotherapy, 38*(2), 209–214.

Ross, S. D., Akhras, K. S., Zhang, S., Rozinsky, M., & Nalysnyk, L. (2001). Discontinuation of antihypertensive drugs due to adverse events: A systematic review and meta-analysis. *Pharmacotherapy, 21*(8), 940–953.

Schroeder, K., Fahey, T., & Ebrahim, S. (2004). How can we improve adherence to blood pressure-lowering medication in ambulatory care? Systematic review of randomized controlled trials. *Archives of Internal Medicine, 164*(7), 722–732.

Shea, S., Misra, D., Ehrlich, M. H., Field, L., & Francis, C. K. (1992). Correlates of nonadherence to hypertension treatment in an inner-city minority population. *American Journal of Public Health, 82*(12), 1607–1612.

Singer, G. M., Izhar, M., & Black, H. R. (2002). Goal-oriented hypertension management: Translating clinical trials to practice. *Hypertension, 40*(4), 464–469.

Steiner, J. F., & Prochazka, A. V. (1997). The assessment of refill compliance using pharmacy records: Methods, validity, and applications. *Journal of Clinical Epidemiology, 50*(1), 105–116.

Svarstad, B. L., Chewning, B. A., Sleath, B. L., & Claesson, C. (1999). The Brief Medication Questionnaire: A tool for screening patient adherence and barriers to adherence. *Patient Education and Counseling, 37*(2), 113–124.

Vaur, L., Vaisse, B., Genes, N., Elkik, F., Legrand, C., & Poggi, L. (1999). Use of electronic pill boxes to assess risk of poor treatment compliance: Results of a large-scale trial. *American Journal of Hypertension, 12*(4, Pt. 1), 374–380.

Wang, P. S., Benner, J. S., Glynn, R. J., Winkelmayer, W. C., Mogun, H., & Avorn, J. (2004). How well do patients report noncompliance with antihypertensive medications? A comparison of self-report versus filled prescriptions. *Pharmacoepidemiology and Drug Safety, 13*(1), 11–19.

Wang, P. S., Bohn, R. L., Knight, E., Glynn, R. J., Mogun, H., & Avorn, J. (2002). Noncompliance with antihypertensive medications: The impact of depressive symptoms and psychosocial factors. *Journal of General Internal Medicine, 17*(7), 504–511.

Ward, H. J., Morisky, D. E., Lees, N. B., & Fong, R. (2000). A clinic and community based approach to hypertension control for an underserved minority population: Design and methods. *American Journal of Hypertension, 13*(2), 177–183.

17

Cancer-Related Adherence

Background, Clinical Issues, and Promotion Strategies

David Victorson

Amy H. Peterman

Cancer patients are living longer, with roughly 50% to 60% of those diagnosed surviving up to 5 years or more, depending on the stage, type of disease, and sociodemographic factors (American Cancer Society [ACS], 2004b). In addition to medical advances in anticancer therapies (e.g., multidrug chemotherapy, bone marrow transplantation), this has also been accomplished in part by increased cancer screening, surveillance, and prevention efforts, which have led to earlier-stage diagnoses and more treatable conditions (ACS, 2004a). Despite the life-threatening nature of cancer, in the year 2000 there were an estimated 4.5 million cancer-related clinic visits that resulted in patients not following all the treatment recommendations provided by their physicians (DiMatteo, 2004). In fact, roughly 21% of cancer patients do not adhere to some aspect of their treatment, such as failing to complete a full course of prescribed adjuvant therapy, returning for follow up appointments or engaging in necessary lifestyle changes or health promotion behaviors (Demark-Wahnefried, Peterson, McBride, Lipkus, & Clipp, 2000; DiMatteo, 2004). Suboptimal adherence rates to cancer treatment can vary widely but tend to resemble the general medical population with regard to certain health behaviors, such as taking oral medications and attending follow-up appointments (Peterman & Cella, 1998). Failure to adhere to cancer treatment recommendations can result in higher mortality rates, may increase the likelihood of recurrence, or may delay identification of possible latent disease effects or other complications (e.g., secondary tumors, chronic pain, thrombosis, osteoporosis) (Adsay et al., 2004; Ballantyne, 2003; de Csepel, Tartter, & Gajdos, 2000; Hershman & Narayanan, 2004; McCready et al., 2000; Payne, 2000; Van Gerpen & Mast, 2004).

Nonadherence also results in enormous monetary waste and can mislead important clinical research findings (Dunbar-Jacob & Mortimer-Stephens, 2001; Farmer, 1999).

In the past decade there has been growing interest in issues related to cancer-related adherence (CRA) (Peterman & Cella, 1998; Richardson & Sanchez, 1998). Defining and operationalizing CRA have been difficult and can depend on several factors (DiMatteo, 2004). The lexicon has evolved from the term *compliance* to *adherence* along with concomitant changes in the conceptualization and measurement of CRA. Historically, the term compliance has implied a passive and uninformed position of the patient, who had little, if any, input in treatment decisions. More recently, the term adherence has gained appeal and suggests a more patient-active commitment to a treatment regimen or recommended behavior, with a reasonable degree of input and negotiation. Although these differences are semantic to some degree, they expand the role of adherence responsibility to include not only the patient, but also caregivers, providers, and the health care delivery system at large. In this chapter, CRA is broadly defined as a dynamic and collaborative commitment to a recommended treatment and signifies an active partnership between patient, provider, and health care delivery system (Abrams et al., 1998).

CRA is affected by a complex set of factors and spans the full cancer spectrum, from issues of disease treatment and control, symptom management, prevention and health promotion, quality of life, palliative care, and death and dying (de Haes & Koedoot, 2003; Greene & Adelman, 2003; Peterman & Cella, 1998). This chapter is based on the premise that the oncology treatment team has an important role in maintaining and improving CRA. It offers practical and user-friendly guidelines aimed at members of the medical team, including information on different types of CRA issues common to treatment, known barriers, and effective methods of CRA assessment. Special attention is given to CRA-promoting strategies, which are brought to life through a clinically relevant case example.

CRA Problems and Predictors

There is a considerable range of behaviors expected of the cancer patient, first and foremost being an agreement to accept the prescribed course of treatment. With more effective self-administered treatments being developed, many aspects of medical care continue to transition from inpatient to outpatient settings. This increases patient responsibility as well as potential for error (Dunbar-Jacob & Mortimer-Stephens, 2001). Although many chemotherapeutic agents are administered intravenously at treatment clinics, patients are also responsible for correctly taking oral chemotherapy medications (e.g., Gefitinib, Hydroxyurea, Lomustine, Temozolomide), steroids (e.g., Dexamethasone, Prednisone), hormone therapies (e.g., Bicalutamide, Flutamide, Megestrol, Tamoxifen), and other supportive medications (e.g., Diphenhydramine Hydrochloride, Erythropoietin, Filgrastim, Lorazepam, Hydrocodone, Fluoxetine). Additional patient responsibilities might include scheduling and attending multiple treatment and follow-up visits and making lifestyle changes known to improve treatment efficacy and reduce the likelihood of morbidity and recurrence (e.g., timely reporting of symptom changes, improved diet, physical activity, sun protection, smoking cessation, emotional management) (Peterman & Cella, 1998). Although the patient is ultimately accountable for adhering to recommendations, the provider and health care delivery system can also affect CRA outcomes and unintentionally contribute to nonadherence. This can be manifested through inadequate distribution of information; delayed diagnosis, treatment, and follow-up; divergence from evidence-based guidelines and best practices; and lack of resources and institutional support (Arndt et al., 2003; Dugan & Cohen, 1998). An overview of each contributor is provided in the following section organized by patient, provider, and system factors. Unfortunately, there is relatively little empirical work on CRA. Findings from research on adherence in other chronic or life-threatening diseases (see Carter, this volume; Levensky, this volume; Whiteley, Williams, & Marcus, this volume) are likely to be relevant to cancer, but this has also not been demonstrated empirically.

Patient Factors

Some research has been devoted to identifying patient-centered factors that may affect CRA. Examples include the role of personality (Courneya, Friedenreich, Sela, Quinney, & Rhodes, 2002; Wiebe & Christensen, 1996), psychological distress (DiMatteo, Lepper, & Croghan, 2000), social support (Taylor et al., 2004), sociocultural and demographic variables (Cress, O'Malley, Leiserowitz, & Campleman, 2003; Meyerowitz, Richardson, Hudson, & Leedham, 1998), disease and treatment-related factors (McDonald, Amit, & Haynes, 2002), cognitive-behavioral influences (Kirsh, Whitcomb, Donaghy, & Passik, 2002), and the patient-provider relationship (DiMatteo et al., 1993).

Studies on CRA and personality, psychological distress and social support are sparse in the cancer literature, whereas research on sociocultural and demographic characteristics comprises the majority of empirical work on CRA. However, these factors have generally been unreliable in predicting adherence, and results seem to depend largely on the type of adherence behavior examined (Dunbar-Jacob & Mortimer-Stephens, 2001; McDonald et al., 2002; Meyerowitz et al., 1998). For example, the relationship between race/ethnicity and adherence to preventive screenings, follow-up of abnormal findings, and active cancer treatment has by and large been insignificant, weak, and attributed to mediating factors like income/access to heath care (e.g., inadequate child care, transportation, insurance coverage), knowledge and beliefs (e.g., belief that breast cancer primarily results from

breast feeding or excessive fondling), and physician recommendation (e.g., whether or not patients were advised to get regular screenings) (Jennings-Dozier & Lawrence, 2000; Meyerowitz et al., 1998). Research suggests that older cancer patients are less likely to receive treatment although certain types of cancer (e.g., ovarian, colon) have demonstrated adequate tolerability of chemotherapy regardless of age (Cress et al., 2003; Sargent et al., 2001). This has largely been attributed to fear and overestimation of toxicity and side effects by patients and providers. Although it is often believed that comorbid medical conditions mediate the age-adjuvant therapy relationship, Ayanian et al. (2003) found that after stratifying for comorbid conditions, older colon cancer patients continued to receive less chemotherapy than younger patients. Other reasons for this have included medication beliefs, cognitive changes, and nihilism (Dunbar-Jacob & Mortimer-Stephens, 2001; Murdaugh, 1998). Additional sociocultural variables such as acceptance of death and suffering, fatalism, strong family orientation, and indigenous folk healing practices have been reported to affect aspects of quality of life but have not been significantly associated with changes in CRA rates (Meyerowitz et al., 1998).

In general, disease severity has been found to be unrelated to CRA (DiMatteo et al., 1993). However, poorer prognosis has been linked with higher rates of treatment discontinuation and refusal (Peterman & Cella, 1998). One of the primary reasons for modifying or stopping treatment altogether is the toxic side effects. Many prescribed antineoplastic medications produce unpleasant reactions, including nausea, vomiting, pain, anemia, diarrhea, alopecia, leukopehia, thrombocytopenia, anorexia, cachexia, loss of taste, and suppuration (Yasko, 1998). There is an important distinction between treatment discontinuation due to the provider's objective toxicity assessment (does not constitute nonadherence) versus treatment discontinuation or variance as a result of the patient's subjective toxicity assessment (constitutes nonadherence).

It is believed that side effect-related nonadherence is mediated by the degree to which symptoms are unmanageable or interfere with normal activities of daily life (Richardson & Sanchez, 1998). Because of this, great efforts are taken to help facilitate normalcy during cancer treatment, which in and of itself can augment CRA rates (e.g., allowing schedule disruptions so a patient can attend a family gathering or take a long-awaited vacation). Additional treatment-related variables known to negatively affect CRA are asymptomatic status, length and type of treatment, and regimen complexity (Dunbar-Jacob & Mortimer-Stephens, 2001; McDonald et al., 2002; Peterman & Cella, 1998).

Several studies have investigated the relationship between cognitive-behavioral variables (motivation, self-efficacy, attitudes and beliefs, history of adherence, memory impairment) and CRA. Self-efficacy has been associated with higher CRA rates in relation to smoking cessation (Ockene et al., 1991), exercise (Blanchard, Courneya, Rodgers, & Murnaghan, 2003; Ott et al., 2004), participation in screening (Hay et al., 2003), and regular attendance to hospital appointments (Lev, 1997). Medication beliefs regarding the potential for dependence have predicted nonadherence (Horne & Weinman, 1999), especially as they relate to adherence to analgesic regimens (Kirsh et al., 2002). Cognitive impairment has also been linked with unintentional, under- or overmedication use, particularly among the elderly and those with substance abuse problems (Bruera, Moyano, & Seifert, 1995; Conn, Taylor, & Miller, 1994; Lundberg & Passik, 1997). In previous studies, intention to adhere and prior history of adherence have been positively related to CRA behaviors (DiMatteo et al., 1993; Myers et al., 1990).

Little empirical research exists on the association between the patient-provider relationship and CRA (DiMatteo, 2003). However, the relationship is believed to affect CRA through variables such as communication (DiMatteo, 2003), relationship satisfaction and trust (Beckman &

Frankel, 2003; Roter, 1992) cultural attitudes toward medical authorities (from deference to distrust) (Meyerowitz et al., 1998), and preferential modes of interaction (e.g., degree of touch, friendliness, amount of questioning) (DiMatteo, 2003; Steiner & Earnest, 2000). Interestingly, in an adherence questionnaire validation study (DiMatteo et al., 1993), the interpersonal aspects of care did not explain a significant proportion of adherence behaviors among patients who already had cancer or those at risk but were disease free. However, it did correlate with increased adherence to follow up after abnormal pap smears among low-income women. Findings such as these suggest that the quality of the patient-provider relationship may have its greatest impact on CRA when there is an imminent threat to developing cancer, such as receiving abnormal results.

Provider Factors

Comprehensive health care and multidisciplinary team approaches are increasingly becoming the standard in medical treatment (see Blume & Marlatt, this volume, for a more detailed discussion of this topic). For this reason, the term *provider* is defined not only as the primary care physician or medical, surgical, or radiation oncologist, but also the oncology nurses, pharmacists, nutritionists, and psychosocial service professionals (psychiatrists, psychologists, social workers, mental health counselors, health educators, etc.).

Oncology providers are the cancer patients' first line of credible and accurate information regarding their disease status, treatment options, and recommended behaviors. The distribution of information and shared decision making can be negatively influenced by hectic practice settings, time pressure in the clinical encounter, underdeveloped counseling and communication skills, lack of knowledge and training in the implementation of recommended behaviors (e.g., smoking cessation), and the sheer amount of new information published regularly (Dugan & Cohen, 1998). Provider beliefs and biases can also intentionally and unintentionally affect information delivery, such as skepticism about using new computer technologies or complementary approaches (Ben-Arye, Frenkel, & Stashefsky Margalit, 2004; Street, 2003). Provider delay in diagnosis and treatment has also been shown to affect survival rates and tends to affect those who are younger in age and present with false-negative biopsies (Wingo, Ries, Parker, & Heath, 1998). Divergence from treatment guidelines and best practices is another way in which providers may contribute to nonadherence, which is only complicated by data suggesting that many providers tend to overestimate their adherence to guidelines (Dugan & Cohen, 1998).

Health Care Delivery System Factors

The health care delivery system comprises the organizational structures responsible for supporting or not supporting health care services and recommended behaviors. No research has been conducted on these factors, but they may have an enormous impact on CRA. On a microlevel, it can affect everything from protected time and resources for continued education and training; adequate treatment space, coverage, and patient-provider ratios; performance enhancement, data management, and tracking procedures; and attempts to lower the cost of medications and copayments. On a macrolevel, it can influence the allotment of safe and accessible community areas for exercise and physical activity, the availability of healthier food options at inexpensive fast-food chains where many economically marginalized individuals frequent regularly, legislation and social marketing campaigns targeting tobacco company advertisement practices, and so on. To truly improve CRA, it is essential to broaden the scope of intervention to institute change within the micro- and macrolevels of the health care delivery system.

Measurement of CRA

CRA measurement has proven to be difficult and involves more than recording attendance and using rates of a particular treatment (DiMatteo, 2004; Farmer, 1999; Peterman & Cella, 1998). Methods can be grouped into direct and indirect approaches. Examples of direct measurement include the detection of drug metabolite or biologic markers in the blood or urine or simply observing the patient partaking in CRA behavior. Indirect approaches involve patient self-report, report from collateral sources, pill count, electronic monitoring, and medical chart review. Direct methods have been shown to be effective in qualitatively determining the presence or absence of a particular substance at a given time; however, they lack precision to quantitatively assess the manner in which medications are taken (Farmer, 1999). For example, pharmacologic tracers would not be effective in determining whether someone missed a pill every now and then, reduced the dosage, or discontinued medications completely (Steiner & Earnest, 2000). Among indirect methods, those involving self-report (clinical interview, diary, questionnaire) have demonstrated variable degrees of accuracy and depend on factors such as the demand characteristics of the setting, cognitive deficits (e.g., forgetfulness), and social pressures like avoiding embarrassment or seeking approval from medical staff. Interviews are simple in design but are confounded by interviewer ability, social pressure, and question wording (e.g., statements that sound blaming versus those that support and normalize). Garber, Nau, Erickson, Aikens, and Lawrence (2004) reported that interview-based reports of medication adherence were significantly nonconcordant with electronic measures, whereas questionnaires and diaries demonstrated moderate to high concordance rates with external correlates. DiMatteo et al. (1993) developed a theoretically driven self-report questionnaire (Adherence Determinants Questionnaire) to measure variables that might be related to CRA (interpersonal care, susceptibility, disease severity, cost-utility analysis, social norms, adherence intentions, barrier/support assessment). In their study, cancer patient populations and healthy persons at some risk for developing cancer reported that the variables most associated with adherence intentions were perceived utility of recommendations, perceived susceptibility, and prior history of adherent behavior.

The use of collateral reports from family, friends, and other health care providers has been infrequent in the cancer literature but has generally resulted in inaccurate estimations in findings from other medical populations (Farmer, 1999; Peterman & Cella, 1998). Furthermore, a good deal of nonadherence behaviors go undetected, even among the most clinically experienced physicians (Steele, Jackson, & Gutmann, 1990). Other indirect methods such as reviewing charts, counting pills, checking refills, weighing canisters, and electronic monitoring procedures have also demonstrated varying adherence rates although the use of electronic pill bottles has been shown to be particularly effective with adherence to oral chemotherapy medications (Lee, Nicholson Souhami, & Deshmukh, 1992). One reported drawback of electronic monitoring is that some individuals may experience increased psychological distress secondary to knowing their behavior is being observed (Ockene et al., 1991). As previously mentioned, each of these approaches has its advantages and disadvantages, and largely depends on the specific CRA behavior in question. There has been a growing movement toward an integrative, multimodal CRA measurement approach, which combines various aspects of direct and indirect procedures throughout the treatment process (Farmer, 1999; Peterman & Cella, 1998).

CRA Promoting Strategies

Over the past two decades, adherence-enhancing strategies have been studied across several medical conditions (Roter, Hall, Merisca, Nrodstrom, Cretin, & Svarstad, 1998) with recommendations to measure and conceptualize adherence as a multifactorial construct (Miller, Hill, Kottke, & Ockene, 1997). Reflecting this movement, strategies to promote CRA should also be multifaceted. Although no one intervention has led to large adherence improvements, those that have been complex and incorporated cognitive, behavioral, affective, and educational components have been most effective (McDonald et al., 2002).

Cognitive-behavioral strategies have included reinforcement-contingency principles (e.g., establishing a treatment contract; providing incentives and reinforcers), self-monitoring, and management procedures; problem solving and decision making; self-efficacy enhancement; goal setting; relapse identification; and establishing a system of cues and reminders (Clark & Becker, 1998; Marlatt & Gordon, 1980). Educational approaches have entailed the following: one-on-one and group education; use of verbal, written, audiovisual, and computerized methods; and mailings and telephone counseling. In fact, in a meta-analysis of adherence interventions across several medical conditions, Roter et al. (1998) reported that written information was less effective than other modalities and that group and telephone counseling demonstrated particularly strong effects. Affective-based CRA interventions have focused on strengthening social support resources through enlisting family members and providing counseling to couples and family (Ballard-Reisch & Letner, 2003).

Before CRA can be effectively promoted, consensus is necessary at the patient, provider, and system levels regarding what CRA outcomes are most important. At the patient level this might include adherence to (1) medications, (2) follow-up appointments, (3) speedy reporting of symptom changes, and (4) lifestyle modifications, particularly in the areas of diet, exercise, distress management, reduction or cessation of harmful substances (tobacco, alcohol, illicit drugs), and sun protection. At the provider level, this could include adherence to (1) use of effective counseling skills or other relationship-building strategies to enhance information delivery, (2) ongoing exploration of health beliefs and bias that could negatively affect the patient-provider relationship, (3) earlier diagnoses and initiation of treatment, and (4) convergence to best practices and treatment guidelines. At the system level, this might involve adherence to (1) the allowance of time and resources for staff education and training, (2) sufficient treatment space, staff coverage, and patient-provider ratios, (3) ongoing performance enhancement activities, (4) efforts to reduce patient medication/treatment costs, and (5) community and legislative involvement aimed at health promotion and harm reduction activities.

Patient-Centered Approaches

CRA Barrier and Promoter Evaluation

At the onset of treatment, the first step toward affecting change at the patient level is to evaluate potential CRA barriers and promoters and assist the patient in understanding their possible deleterious effects. Such an evaluation should be iterative (either every visit or predetermined critical junctures), multimodal (e.g., interview, questionnaire, collateral report), and stem from a coordinated effort by each member of the multidisciplinary team during initial contact with the patient. Based on the literature, important information to collect will include (1) level of psychological distress; (2) perception and satisfaction of social support; (3) income/access to health care; (4) knowledge, insight, and beliefs about medical status; (5) age; (6) degree of anticipated goal interference/life disruption secondary to treatment or side effects; (8) treatment-related coping self-efficacy in terms of medication use, symptom management, and lifestyle changes; (9) motivation, readiness, and intent to adhere; and (10) prior history of adherence in other medical circumstance or areas of life. Subsequent assessment of patient-provider communication and satisfaction factors will also prove important as this

relationship develops. Given the cognitive, behavioral, and psychosocial nature of this information, it seems appropriate that psychosocial personnel assume primary responsibility for collecting, synthesizing, and disseminating findings to medical team members.

Distribution of Information

Each patient should receive information and education about the importance of CRA as well as practical advice, encouragement, and reinforcement regarding barrier reduction or promoter maintenance strategies. This information should be provided in a structured and well-planned manner (so as not to overwhelm) through verbal, written, and audiovisual channels. Each member of the medical team should assume responsibility for discipline-specific CRA aspects (nurses review medication-specific tasks, nutritionists review dietary guidelines, etc.) although primary oncologists should attempt to cover all possible areas given their especially influential and venerated status among patients. If done well, this information would increase patients' sense of control and treatment efficacy, both of which are known to positively affect CRA outcomes.

Effective information dissemination should incorporate factors such as the patient's educational background, cultural worldview (e.g., emic and etic perspectives) and should be available in languages that reflect the population being treated. To this end, translation services should also be readily accessible and used regularly. Patients with lower literacy skills should be accommodated through the use of audio, visual, and interactive health communication (IHC) aids. One example is an innovative computer program called the *Talking Touchscreen*, a multimedia computer application designed for outcomes assessment with cancer patients lacking adequate literacy skills (Hahn et al., 2004). Other forms of IHC include e-mail, videoconferencing, CD-ROM programs, and Internet-based education and support (Street, 2003).

Important technical aspects of information delivery are timing and clarity as well as the use of lay terminology, repetition, and ongoing assessment of the patient's information preference/processing style. Basic counseling and interviewing skills can also enhance the presentation and receptiveness of information through attention to nonverbal communication (eye contact, body language, use of gestures, vocal tone, warmth, etc.) and active listening skills, such as paraphrasing and summarizing (Beckman & Frankel, 2003).

Cognitive, Behavioral, and Affective Skill Enhancement

Prior to beginning treatment, a patient-provider agreement should be established and operationalized through the joint development of treatment goals that are linked to specific CRA outcomes. At a minimum, all patients should be encouraged to have goals to take their medications correctly, return for all follow-up appointments consistently, alter diet appropriately, begin or continue physical activity program, manage stress effectively, abstain or reduce intake of harmful substances, and use sun protection. One approach would be to educate patients on the use of self-monitoring charts, which could be used to organize, log, and track goal progress and identify relapses. They would also serve as tangible reminders and facilitate regular CRA assessment for team members. To reinforce the importance of CRA goals and self-monitoring, the patient and provider should review charts at each appointment (or at critical treatment junctures) in a collegial and nonjudgmental manner consistent with motivational interviewing practices (see Rollnick & Miller, 1995). From this perspective, relapses or setbacks should be met with empathy, followed by a discussion of discrepancies between target goals and current behaviors with an emphasis on problem solving and patient efficacy support. Depending on the nature of the patient's social support resources, affective strengthening strategies should also be considered. Examples include enlisting other caregivers to become more involved in CRA responsibilities; providing a group venue for ongoing discussion and support; and linking patients to available community resources and assistance. Follow-up telephone counseling (especially at the beginning of treatment) can also be effective in answering questions about medications, symptoms, or self-monitoring procedures. An innovate application of telephone technology can be seen in an ongoing research study (Chang et al., 2002) where advanced lung cancer patients are asked to call weekly to complete a brief, prerecorded symptom monitoring survey over the phone. A research nurse tracks responses daily and score elevations are used to rapidly identify and triage those with deteriorating symptoms.

Provider-Centered Approaches

To enact the aforementioned patient-centered strategies, providers must also be committed to assuming responsibility for CRA and participate in attitudinal and behavioral change and skill development. Just as patients are encouraged to take medications as prescribed, providers should attempt to simplify treatment regimens whenever possible, such as consolidating related medications or coordinating dispensation intervals into one primary time per day. CRA communication among team members should be supported through ongoing dialogue and periodic CRA-specific rounds where performance data can be presented on various outcomes. Oftentimes, cancer patients receive treatment by medical professionals outside of the oncology area (primary care physician, nephrology, etc.). Effort should be taken to maintain communication with these services to enlist their support, compare adherence behaviors, and stay attuned to their other treatment goals and medication schedules. Basic training may be needed in patient-centered communication (e.g., delivery of bad news, working with family members, supporting informed choices, assisting in the transition to palliative care), counseling and education, motivational interviewing, relapse prevention, and stages of change principles (Beckman & Frankel, 2003; Prochaska, & DiClemente, 1986). Providers would also benefit from continued education and training on multicultural and diversity issues (e.g., culture-specific health beliefs, communication style, use of indigenous and folk healing practices) especially as they relate to their own cultural worldview and biases and ways they may intentionally or unintentionally influence patient-provider interactions.

System-Centered Approaches

The health care delivery system can also significantly affect CRA (Goldstein, DePue, Kazura, & Niaura, 1998; Street, 2003). Affecting change at this level can be complicated, especially because bureaucratic and institutional obstacles are omnipresent in any large organization. To begin with, it is central that institutions allocate sufficient time and resources for ongoing staff education and training, including burnout prevention programs targeting treatment delivery staff. To address the need for multifocused intervention strategies, it is also important to reinforce multidisciplinary team approaches through hiring and compensating sufficient adjuvant professionals, such as psychologists, social workers, nutritionists, and health educators. Unfortunately, at times cancer center outpatient waiting lobbies can feel like a busy airline terminal with overbooked flights. Because coming to chemotherapy or radiation treatment can be distressing enough, treatment environments should be relaxing, comfortable, and foster a sense of well-being and community for patients and staff alike. Environmental conditions such as soft lighting, background music, uncluttered areas, and free or discounted parking can go a long way. The ratio of staff and treatment rooms to the number of patients being scheduled should be adequate so that no patient waits an unreasonable amount of time, receives treatment in nonsanctioned areas, or has inadequate time with medical team members. Institutions should make dedicated efforts to support intervention research focusing on CRA barrier reduction (e.g., emotional distress, health beliefs, patient-provider communication) and CRA measurement issues. Health care institutions should use ties with local media and organizations for CRA-based social marketing campaigns that address issues of screening and prevention, risk-reduction, and health promotion. In this vein, relationships should be established with local churches, synagogues, and mosques to reach the members of the community that might otherwise lack access to health care. Finally, the health care delivery system should take advantage of its legislative power to attend to increasing health care costs, disparities, and the effects of societal factors such as urban sprawl, the tobacco industry, and unhealthy food marketing practices.

The Case of Sandra Gonzalez

Sandra Gonzalez is a 33-year-old, married, Spanish-speaking female who was born and raised in Mexico and came to the United States at the age of 15 years. She is undocumented and works as a fulltime nanny for a family with three young children. In Mexico, she only completed 6 years of education and has difficulty reading and writing in her native language. During her time in the United States she has not had the opportunity to learn English well because of work obligations but is able to communicate at a basic level. She is married and has four children ranging in age from 4 to 12 years. Her husband works in construction and is also undocumented. Neither has health insurance. She has several other family members in the area, including her mother, sister, and many cousins. She was raised as a Catholic and attends mass weekly. She also periodically frequents a local botanica (spiritual folk healing store) in her neighborhood where she consults with a curandero (healer) and is occasionally prescribed herbs, teas, and prayers for her mental, physical, and spiritual well-being. She does not drink alcohol or smoke, and has never exercised regularly or paid much attention to her diet.

In the past 8 months she has experienced intermittent vaginal bleeding and pain, which eventually prompted her to go to a community public health clinic that serves lower-income individuals. Her pap smear came back abnormal, which led to a subsequent pelvic exam, biopsy, and CT scan. Results came back with evidence of Stage IIIb cervical cancer due to which Mrs. Gonzalez was understandably upset. The clinic helped arrange an appointment with a gynecological oncologist to discuss treatment options.

One week prior to her consult, administrative staff from the cancer treatment center mailed a reminder to her home with appointment and contact information. They also called to confirm the meeting, answer questions, and verify her insurance status. They called several times before finally reaching the patient's 12-year-old daughter. The fact that it took so many times to reach anyone raised a red flag regarding potential CRA problems. The staff member made a note of this in Mrs. Gonzalez's chart under a section devoted to CRA issues. Her daughter spoke English well and was able to write down the appointment date and time. She stated that evenings are the best time to contact her mother but did not know about her insurance coverage status. Following standard protocol, the administrative staff person asked if there was any need for transportation assistance or translation services at the initial consult. The daughter offered that her mother does not speak English well but has a car and could drive. Translation services were requested for this appointment and every appointment thereafter. An additional chart entry was added regarding her English language ability.

On the day of her scheduled appointment, Mrs. Gonzalez did not show up. A staff member placed several calls over the next few days and was finally able to reach the patient one evening. With the help of her daughter, she stated that she was unaware of her appointment and never received the message. She reported that she does not have insurance. The staff member informed her of the hospital's outpatient clinic for uninsured individuals and gave her contact information to set up an appointment so she could apply for a special card. Her consult was rescheduled for the following week. The staff member made another chart entry where she indicated her low-income and uninsured status and reported that messages left with her children may not be reliably transmitted.

She arrived on time for her consult and brought her four children, husband, mother, and sister. An interpreter greeted them and stated that a nurse would be out shortly when the doctor was ready. The waiting area was pleasant and comfortable with updated furniture and wall hangings. Natural and soft lighting created a peaceful atmosphere with classical music playing quietly in the background. A treatment nurse came to get them within a reasonable amount of time and escorted them back to a consultation room. Initially, Sandra stood up alone until the nurse asked if she wished any of her family members to accompany her. Relieved and thankful, she brought her husband and sister, leaving her children with her mother. At the onset of the meeting, the gynecological oncologist made an effort to make them feel comfortable by engaging them in a warm, professional manner. He made it a point to speak naturally and directly to them and not solely to the translator. A background history was taken, which included questions regarding her use of complementary herbs or nutritional supplements. Because of the physician's openness and nonjudgmental manner, Sandra felt comfortable telling him that she occasionally takes special herbs purchased from a botanica. This facilitated a relationship-building discussion regarding the various cross-cultural healing practices, of which she was very appreciative. She was explained her treatment options and with the help of her doctor and family members, agreed to begin a course of radiation followed by chemotherapy. She was educated on possible side effects of treatment and was also given ample time to ask additional questions. One question dealt with her ability to continue working throughout treatment, as her family desperately needs the money. Her physician educated her on the possibility of fatigue and its debilitating nature. He also informed her that treatment could be scheduled to best accommodate her work schedule and needs. She felt relieved about this. To conclude the meeting, the oncologist educated her on the importance of CRA-specific goals she should keep in mind throughout the treatment, such as taking medications correctly, returning to appointments consistently, and engaging in health promotion behaviors, including diet, physical activity, and emotional management. When asked about her thoughts on this, she acknowledged that these would all be goals for her during treatment. She was told to arrive 1 hour before her first treatment to have blood work done and to fill out routine intake paperwork. She informed the nurse that she had been unable to get in touch with anyone from the outpatient clinic to discuss payment options and was feeling overwhelmed because of her language difficulties. Consequently she was accompanied by a staff social worker to the clinic office to help her make an appointment and fill out necessary paperwork. After their meeting, the oncologist entered her CRA goals into her medical chart.

On the day of her first appointment, Mrs. Gonzalez arrived with her four children and mother. After having blood drawn, she was given a New Patient Folder with information in Spanish. She was informed that she could either complete a paper/pencil intake packet included in the folder or use a computer terminal with an interactive bilingual assessment program in which questions are heard through headphones and choices are selected by touching images on the screen. Given her difficulties with reading and writing, she opted to use the computer program. After a basic tutorial on its use, she completed demographic questions about her age and income, a brief psychological distress screener, questions about social support, her expected level of life disruption because of treatment, how confident she was in her abilities to take medication correctly, monitor symptoms, and make lifestyle changes, and how motivated she was to adhere to treatment. This produced a brief CRA report, which was electronically sent to the psychosocial services office and reviewed by a team psychologist. The psychologist noted that although Sandra reported some CRA promoters (strong social support network, high motivation to begin treatment, moderate self-efficacy in certain areas), she also reported several financial stressors as well as a high degree of psychological distress related to her medical status and treatment. The psychologist reviewed the CRA-specific entries from her chart, which noted,

> Patient has limited English speaking abilities and is most comfortable speaking in Spanish. All future mailed reminders should be in Spanish. Translation services have been requested for every visit. . . . It is difficult to reach patient at home during the daytime (no answering machine, her children may be unreliable for leaving messages). The best time to reach her is after 8:00 p.m. . . . Patient is uninsured (in process of getting clinic card); has difficulty reading and writing in native language.

All these factors prompted a face-to-face meeting.

While receiving treatment Sandra was educated once again on the different medications she would be given by her nurse. She also met and spoke with the staff pharmacist and nutritionist about discipline-specific CRA goals. Later, she was introduced to the team psychologist, who took a brief psychosocial history and reviewed her responses and previously established CRA goals. When she had difficulty remembering some, the psychologist refreshed her memory by having her goals on hand from the initial conversation with her oncologist. Her psychological distress was assessed further and she was referred to the team psychiatrist for evaluation for antianxiety medication. She was also taught cognitive behavioral stress management strategies and would be followed regularly by psychosocial services. She was educated on the use and importance of self-monitoring charts and together they began making a one-page chart for each goal, which were later inserted into a three-ring binder that she would bring to each appointment. At the top of each chart was a graphic depiction of each goal (at the top of the nutrition chart was a symbol for food, etc.). It was decided that she would keep these charts on her bedside table so she would remember to enter information into them daily. She was also encouraged to educate her family members on how these charts should be completed in case she needed assistance at some point. The following evening, Sandra received telephone calls from the staff pharmacist and nutritionist to review medications and dietary guidelines and field any questions. That same day a postcard was mailed to her home with a reminder of her next appointment date and time. When she returned for treatment the next week, she brought her binder, which was jointly reviewed with team members and later entered into a central CRA tracking database to monitor individual progress over the long term. According to her report, she was able to take supportive oral medications correctly and implement dietary changes but had trouble attaining her physical activity goals. She also had questions regarding whether she had completed her charts accurately and was provided assistance and encouragement. She was reinforced for having remembered and completed these in addition to meeting the majority of her CRA goals. Her physical activity goals were reviewed and additional barriers were identified. This regular review and modification continued throughout the course of her treatment. Having used her charts as regular CRA measurement tools, it was possible to quickly identify and remediate barriers, relapses, and setbacks, which in turn, increased her efficacy and feelings of control. Prior to ending treatment, staff members provided exit counseling to Sandra and her family about her treatment experience, future follow-up appointments, and strategies to maintain lifestyle changes.

References

Abrams, D. B., Borrelli, B., Shadel, W. G., King, T., Bock, B., & Niaura, R. (1998). Adherence to treatment for nicotine dependence. In S. A. Shumaker, E. B. Schron, J. K. Okene, & W. L. McBee (Eds.), *The handbook of health behavior change* (2nd ed., pp. 137–165). New York: Springer.

Adsay, N. V., Andea, A., Basturk, O., Kilinc, N., Nassar, H., & Cheng, J. D. (2004). Secondary tumors of the pancreas: An analysis of a surgical and autopsy database and review of the literature. *Virchows Archiv: An International Journal of Pathology, 444,* 527–535.

American Cancer Society. (2004a). *Cancer detection & early prevention facts and figures.* Atlanta, GA: Author.

American Cancer Society (ACS). (2004b). *Cancer facts and figures.* Atlanta, GA: Author.

Arndt, V., Sturmer, T., Stegmaier, C., Ziegler, H., Becker, A., & Brenner, H. (2003). Provider delay among patients with breast cancer in Germany: A population-based study. *Journal of Clinical Oncology, 21*(8), 1440–1446.

Ayanian, J. Z., Zaslavsky, A. M., Fuchs, C. S., Guadagnoli, E., Creech, C. M., Cress, R. D., et al. (2003). Use of adjuvant chemotherapy and radiation therapy for colorectal cancer in a population-based cohort. *Journal of Clinical Oncology, 21*(7), 1293–1300.

Ballantyne J. C. (2003). Chronic pain following treatment for cancer: The role of opioids. *Oncologist, 8*(6), 567–575.

Ballard-Reisch, D. S., & Letner, J. A. (2003). Centering families in cancer communication research: Acknowledging the impact of support, culture and process on client/provider communication in cancer management. *Patient Education and Counseling, 50,* 61–66.

Beckman, H. B., & Frankel, R. M. (2003). Training practitioners to communicate effectively in cancer care: It is the relationship that counts. *Patient Education and Counseling, 50,* 85–89.

Ben-Arye, E., Frenkel, M., & Stashefsky Margalit, R. (2004). Approaching complementary and alternative medicine use in patients with cancer: Questions and challenges. *Journal of Ambulatory Care Management, 27*(1), 53–62.

Blanchard, C. M., Courneya, K. S., Rodgers, W. M., & Murnaghan, D. M. (2003). Determinants of exercise intention and behavior in survivors of breast and prostate cancer: An application of the theory of planned behavior. *Cancer Nursing, 25*(2), 88–95.

Bruera, E., Moyano, J., & Seifert, L. (1995). The frequency of alcoholism among patients with pain due to terminal cancer. *Journal of Pain Symptoms Management, 10,* 599–603.

Chang, C. H., Cella, D., Masters, G., Laliberte, B. A., O'Brien, P., Peterman, A., et al. (2002). Application of quality of life assessment in advanced lung cancer. *Clinical Lung Cancer, 4*(2), 104–109.

Clark, N. M., & Becker, M. H. (1998). Theoretical models and strategies for improving adherence and disease management. In S. A. Shumaker, E. B. Schron, J. K. Okene, & W. L. McBee (Eds.), *The handbook of health behavior change* (2nd ed., pp. 5–32). New York: Springer.

Conn, V., Taylor, S., & Miller, R. (1994). Cognitive impairment and medication adherence. *Journal of Gerontology Nursing, 20*(7), 41–47.

Courneya, K. S., Friedenreich, C. M., Sela, R., Quinney, H. A., & Rhodes, R. E. (2002). Correlates of adherence and contamination in a randomized controlled trial of exercise in cancer survivors: An application of the theory of planned behavior and the five factor model of personality. *Annals of Behavioral Medicine, 24,* 257–268.

Cress, R. D., O'Malley, C. D., Leiserowitz, G. S., & Campleman, S. L. (2003). Patterns of chemotherapy use for women with ovarian cancer: A population-based study. *Journal of Clinical Oncology, 21*(8), 1530–1535.

de Csepel, J., Tartter, P. I., & Gajdos, C. (2000). When not to give radiation therapy after breast conservation surgery for breast cancer. *Journal of Surgical Oncology, 74*(4), 273–277.

de Haes, H., & Koedoot, N. (2003). Patient centered decision-making in palliative cancer treatment: A world of paradoxes. *Patient Education and Counseling, 50,* 43–49.

Demark-Wahnefried, W., Peterson, B., McBride, C., Lipkus, I., & Clipp, E. (2000). Current health behaviors and readiness to pursue life-style changes among men and women diagnosed with early stage prostate and breast carcinomas. *Cancer, 88*(3), 674–684.

DiMatteo, M. R. (2003). Future directions in research on consumer-provider communication and adherence to cancer prevention and treatment. *Patient Education and Counseling, 50*(1), 23–26.

DiMatteo, M. R. (2004). Variations in patients' adherence to medical recommendations: A quantitative review of 50 years of research. *Medical Care, 42*(3), 200–209.

DiMatteo, M. R., Hays, R. D., Gritz, E. R., Bastani, R., Crane, L., Elashoff, R., et al. (1993). Patient adherence to cancer control regimens: Scale development and initial validation. *Psychological Assessment, 5*(1), 102–112.

DiMatteo, M. R., Lepper, H. S., & Croghan, T. W. (2000). Depression is a risk factor for noncompliance with medical treatment: Meta-analysis of the effects of anxiety and depression on patient adherence. *Archives of Internal Medicine, 160*(14), 2101–2107.

Dugan, E., & Cohen, S. J. (1998). Changing physician behavior to increase guideline implementation. In S. A. Shumaker, E. B. Schron, J. K. Okene, & W. L. McBee (Eds.), *The handbook of health behavior change* (2nd ed., pp. 283–304). New York: Springer.

Dunbar-Jacob, J., & Mortimer-Stephens, M. K. (2001). Treatment adherence in chronic disease. *Journal of Clinical Epidemiology, 54,* S57–S60.

Farmer, K. C. (1999). Methods for measuring and monitoring medication regimen adherence in clinical trials and clinical practice. *Clinical Therapeutics, 21*(6), 1074–1090.

Garber, M. C., Nau, D. P., Erickson, S. R., Aikens, J. E., & Lawrence, J. B. (2004). The concordance of self-report with other measures of medication adherence: A summary of the literature. *Medical Care, 42*(7), 649–652.

Goldstein, M. G., DePue, J., Kazura, A., & Niaura, R. (1998). Models for provider-patient interaction: Applications to health behavior change. In S. A. Shumaker, E. B. Schron, J. K. Okene, & W. L. McBee (Eds.), *The handbook of health behavior change* (2nd ed., pp. 85–113). New York: Springer.

Greene, M. G., & Adelman, R. D. (2003). Physician-older patient communication about cancer. *Patient Education and Counseling, 50,* 55–60.

Hahn, E. A., Cella, D., Dobrez, D., Shiomoto, G., Marcus, E., Taylor, S. G., et al. (2004). The talking touchscreen: A new approach to outcomes assessment in low literacy. *Psychooncology, 13*(2), 86–95.

Hay, J. L., Ford, J. S., Klein, D., Primavera, L. H., Buckley, T. R., Stein, T. R., et al. (2003). Adherence to colorectal cancer screening in mammography-adherent older women. *Journal of Behavioral Medicine, 26*(6), 553–576.

Hershman, D., Narayanan, R. (2004). Prevention and management of osteoporosis in women with breast cancer and men with prostate cancer. *Current Oncology Reports, 6*(4), 277–284.

Horne, R., & Weinman, J. (1999). Patients' beliefs about prescribed medicines and their role in adherence to treatment in chronic physical illness. *Journal of Psychosomatic Research, 47*(6), 555–567.

Jennings-Dozier, K., & Lawrence, D. (2000). Socio-demographic predictors of adherence to annual cervical cancer screening in minority women. *Cancer Nursing, 23*(5), 350–356.

Kirsh, K. L., Whitcomb, L. A., Donaghy, K., & Passik, S. D. (2002). Abuse and addiction issues in medically ill patients with pain: Attempts at clarification of terms and empirical study. *Clinical Journal of Pain, 18*(4), S52–S60.

Lee C. R., Nicholson P. W., Souhami R. L. Deshmukh, A. (1992). Patient compliance with oral chemotherapy as assessed by a novel oral technique. *Journal of Clinical Oncology, 10,* 1007–1013.

Lev, E. L. (1997). Bandura's theory of self-efficacy: Applications to oncology. *Scholarly Inquiry Nursing Practice, 11*(1), 21–37.

Lundberg, J. C., & Passik, S. D. (1997). Alcohol and cancer: A review for psycho-oncologists. *Psycho-oncology, 6,* 253–266.

Marlatt, G. A., & Gordon, J. R. (1980). Determinants of relapse: Implications for the maintenance of behavior change. In P. O. Davidson & S. M. Davidson (Eds.), *Behavioral medicine: Changing health lifestyles* (pp. 410–452). New York: Brunner/Mazel.

McCready, D. R., Chapman, J. A., Hanna, W. M., Kahn, H. J., Yap, K., Fish, E. B., et al. (2000). Factors associated with local breast cancer recurrence after lumpectomy alone: Postmenopausal patients. *Annals of Surgical Oncology, 7*(8), 562–567.

McDonald, H. P., Amit, G. X., & Haynes, R. B. (2002). Interventions to enhance patient adherence to medication prescriptions. *Journal of the American Medical Association, 288*(22), 2868–2879.

Meyerowitz, B. E., Richardson, J., Hudson, S., & Leedham, B. (1998). Ethnicity and cancer outcomes: Behavioral and psychosocial considerations. *Psychological Bulletin, 123*(1), 47–70.

Miller, N. H., Hill, M., Kottke, T., & Ockene, I. S. (1997). The multilevel compliance challenge: Recommendations for a call to action. A statement for healthcare professionals. *Circulation, 95*(4), 1085–1090.

Murdaugh, C. L. (1998). Problems with adherence in the elderly. In S. A. Shumaker, E. B. Schron, J. K. Okene, & W. L. McBee (Eds.), *The handbook of health behavior change* (2nd ed., pp. 357–376). New York: Springer.

Myers, R. E., Trock, B. J., Lerman, C., Wolf, T., Ross, E., Engstrom, P. F. (1990). Adherence to colorectal cancer screening in an HMO population. *Preventive Medicine, 19*(5), 502–514.

Ockene, J. K., Kristeller, J., Goldberg, R., Amick, T. L., Pekow, P. S., Hosmer, D., et al. (1991). Increasing the efficacy of physician-delivered smoking interventions: A randomized clinical trial. *Journal of General Internal Medicine, 6*(1), 1–8.

Ott, C. D., Lindsey, A. M., Waltman, N. L., Gross, G. J., Twiss, J. J., Berg, K., et al. (2004). Facilitative strategies, psychological factors, and strength/weight training behaviors in breast cancer survivors who are at risk for osteoporosis. *Orthopedic Nursing, 23*(1), 45–52.

Payne, R. (2000). Chronic pain: Challenges in the assessment and management of cancer pain. *Journal of Pain Symptom Management, 19,* S12–S15.

Peterman, A. H., & Cella, D. (1998). Adherence issues among cancer patients. In S. A. Shumaker, E. B. Schron, J. K. Okene, & W. L. McBee (Eds.), *The handbook of health behavior change* (2nd ed., pp. 462–482). New York: Springer.

Prochaska, J. O., & DiClemente, C. C. (1986). Towards a comprehensive model of change. In W. R. Miller & N. Heather (Eds.), *Treating addictive disorders: Processes of change* (pp. 3–27). New York: Plenum Press.

Richardson, J. L., & Sanchez, K. (1998). Compliance with cancer treatment. In J. Holland (Ed), *Psycho-oncology* (pp. 67–77). New York: Oxford University Press.

Rollnick S., & Miller, W. R. (1995). What is motivational interviewing? *Behavioural and Cognitive Psychotherapy, 23,* 325–334.

Roter, D.L. (1992). Commentary: Improving communication with cancer patients about diagnosis, prognosis, and treatment. *Oncology,* 6, 88-89.

Roter, D. L., Hall, J. A., Merisca, R., Nrodstrom, B., Cretin, D., & Svarstad, B. (1998). Effectiveness of interventions to improve patient compliance: A meta-analysis. *Medical Care, 36*(8), 1138–1161.

Sargent, D. J., Goldberg, R. M., Jacobson, S. D., Macdonald, J. S., Labianca, R., Haller, D. G., et al. (2001). A pooled analysis of adjuvant chemotherapy for resected colon cancer in elderly patients. *New England Journal of Medicine, 345,* 1091–1097.

Steele, D. J., Jackson, T. C., & Gutmann, M. C. (1990). Have you been taking your pills? The adherence-monitoring sequence in the medical interview. *Journal of Family Practice, 30,* 294–299.

Steiner, J. F., & Earnest, M. A. (2000). The language of medication-taking. *Annals of Internal Medicine, 132*(11), 926–930.

Street, R. L. (2003). Mediated consumer–provider communication in cancer care: The empowering potential of new technologies. *Patient Education and Counseling, 50,* 99–104.

Taylor, V. M., Yasui, Y., Burke, N., Nguyen, T., Acorda, E., Thai, H., et al. (2004). Pap testing adherence among Vietnamese American women. *Cancer Epidemiology, Biomarkers & Prevention, 13*(4), 613–619.

Van Gerpen, R., & Mast, M. E. (2004). Thromboembolic disorders in cancer. *Clinical Journal of Oncology Nursing, 8*(3), 289–299.

Wiebe, J. S., & Christensen, A. J. (1996). Patient adherence in chronic illness: Personality and coping in context. *Journal of Personality, 64,* 815–835.

Wingo, P. A., Ries, L. A., Parker, S. L., & Heath, C. W. (1998). Long-term cancer patient survival in the United States. *Cancer Epidemiology, Biomarkers & Prevention, 7*(4), 271–282.

Yasko, J. M. (1998). *Nursing management of symptoms associated with chemotherapy.* Bala Cynwyd, PA: Meniscus Health Care Communications.

18

Adherence to HIV/AIDS Treatments

Eric R. Levensky

Highly active antiretroviral therapy (HAART) has produced substantial improvements in treatment outcomes for HIV/AIDS patients in a number of clinical trials and has become the standard of care for the treatment of HIV/AIDS infection (Carpenter et al., 1997). These medications have been shown to (1) reduce the rate of viral replication (often bringing the HIV virus to undetectable levels), (2) decrease the incidence of opportunistic infections, (3) delay the progression to AIDS, (4) lead to general improvements in overall health, and (5) reduce health care costs (Carpenter et al., 1997; Deeks, Loftus, Cohen, Chin, & Grant, 1997; Deeks, Smith, Holodniy, & Kahn, 1997; Valenti, 2001).

Despite these promising effects of HAART, however, the treatment is typically quite complex and difficult to adhere to. HAART regimes can involve taking 10 to 20 pills a day on complex dosing schedules and often involve following food and fluid restrictions and requirements.

There are also a number of side effects caused by taking HAART, including headaches, nausea, vomiting, diarrhea, fatigue, metallic taste, and oral numbness, which can make adherence difficult. The consequence of the demanding nature of HAART is that the actual effectiveness of this treatment has been limited for many HIV/AIDS patients in real-life clinical settings by poor adherence to the regimen. A number of studies have found that to experience the beneficial effects of HAART, patients need to take at least 90% of the prescribed doses (see Andrews & Friedland, 2000; Barlett, 2002). However, 30% to 60% of HIV/AIDS patients in clinical settings do not maintain this level of adherence, and many patients do not consistently take the medication at the prescribed times or follow food and fluid requirements, both of which are known to affect the effectiveness of the treatment (Andrews & Friedland, 2000; Bartlett, 2002; Kastrissios et al., 1998; Malow et al., 1998).

Poor adherence to HAART not only substantially limits the treatment's effectiveness in producing the positive health outcomes described above, but can also make the patients become resistant to the medication by producing mutations in the virus (Condra et al., 1995; Jacobsen et al., 1996). Additionally, if an individual becomes resistant to one type of HAART medication, he or she can potentially become resistant to other, and possibly all, available HAART medications (Deeks, Loftus, et al., 1997; Deeks, Smith, et al., 1997; Hirsch, 1997). The end result of a patient's poor adherence to HAART can, therefore, be that this particular treatment is no longer effective for that individual and few other treatment options may exist. Furthermore, the treatment-resistant virus can then be transmitted to other people.

Given that high levels of patient adherence to HAART have proven to be both critically important and highly challenging to achieve, it is essential that clinical work with HIV/AIDS patients includes effective facilitation of adherence to this treatment. To this end, clinicians working with HIV/AIDS patients need to understand the common barriers to patient adherence as well as be knowledgeable and competent in specific methods of facilitating adherence. This chapter will briefly review the literature on adherence barriers and interventions in the treatment of chronic illness generally and will then discuss in more detail adherence issues of particular relevance and importance in the treatment of HIV/AIDS.

Overview of Common Treatment Adherence Barriers and Interventions

As discussed in Levensky and O'Donohue (this volume), a number of factors have been repeatedly identified as related to poor adherence in patients across many chronic illness populations and treatments, including HIV/AIDS, and a variety of interventions have been developed

and evaluated to address these barriers (see also Christiansen, 2004; Laurence, 2004; Meichenbaum & Turk, 1987; Roter et al., 1998; Shumaker, Schron, Ockene, & McBee, 1998; World Health Organization, 2003 for excellent reviews of this literature).

Factors that have been identified as being related to poor adherence can be organized as those related to the following domains (Ickovics & Meisler, 1997):

- **The patient** (e.g., inadequate adherence-related skills, resources, and support; problematic beliefs about health and treatment; stressful life events; depression; substance abuse; fear of stigma; medication is reminder of illness)
- **The treatment regimen** (e.g., complex and demanding regimen requiring significant behavioral change; poor fit between regimen requirements and patient's lifestyle/routines; frequent and severe side effects)
- **The disease** (e.g., not serious or health/life threatening; long in duration; lack of symptoms)
- **Patient-provider relationship** (e.g., poor communication and rapport; lack of adequate patient education and assessment of adherence by provider; patient has difficulty discussing problems, lacks trust in provider, and is uncertain the provider can help)
- **The clinical setting** (e.g., limited accessibility to services, such as limited availability of appointments and hours of operations, and long waits for service; poor continuity of care; unfriendly or unhelpful staff)

Interventions that have been developed and have some empirical support for their efficacy (as parts of multicomponent interventions or as stand-alone interventions) in improving treatment adherence in chronic illness populations, including HIV/AIDS, include the following (again, in addition to the chapters included in this volume, see also Christiansen, 2004; Laurence,

2004; Meichenbaum & Turk, 1987; Shumaker et al., 1998; World Health Organization, 2003):

- **Assessing readiness to begin treatment** (e.g., assessing patterns and barriers to past adherence, anticipating and addressing current adherence barriers, conducting "practice trials" to identify and address barriers before initiating treatment)
- **Educating the patient** (e.g., regarding the nature of the health problem and action of the treatment, specific requirements of the treatment, importance of adherence, and management of likely side effects)
- **Increasing adherence-related skills** (e.g., using pillboxes, treatment diaries, alarms, stickers, notes, and other treatment cues; integrating treatment into daily activities; communicating effectively with providers; problem solving; anticipating, avoiding, and managing slips in adherence)
- **Increasing resources and support** (e.g., referrals for assistance with accessing financial, dietary, housing, transportation, and child care resources; regular provider or clinic contact with patient; enlisting patient's family or friends to assist with and encourage adherence; referrals to "peer support," support groups, or individual counseling)
- **Increasing patient motivation** (e.g., gaining trust and developing rapport with patient; simplifying and tailoring regimen to fit patient's lifestyle and needs; treating side effects and reducing other barriers and aversive consequences of adherence; orienting patient to personal benefits of adherence and costs of poor adherence; enhancing self-efficacy; encouraging patient to take an active role in treatment; helping patient to reframe problematic beliefs about treatment and adherence; treating substance abuse and depression)
- **Maintenance** (e.g., regular follow-up contacts with patient and assessing

adherence and barriers to adherence; working with patient on ongoing basis to manage barriers to adherence)

A working knowledge of the common adherence barriers and interventions described above can be extremely useful in that it orients clinicians to the domains of barriers to consider and assess for when working with patients on HAART regimens (or soon to be), as well as to techniques and strategies that may facilitate these patients' adherence. However, as discussed in detail in the introductory chapters of this volume (e.g., Levensky & O'Donohue; Heiby & Lukens; and Ferguson & Scarlett-Ferguson), it is important use the adherence barriers and interventions listed above as *guidelines* for developing *individualized* interventions tailored to the specific circumstances and needs of each patient as opposed to using a one-size-fits-all approach to adherence counseling. Research and clinical practice have demonstrated that adherence tends to involve a complex and multidetermined set of factors and patient behaviors, and that HIV/AIDS and other chronic illness patients tend to be heterogeneous populations with regard to *whether* and *the manner in which* these common factors actually interfere with adherence, as well as the sorts of interventions that will be most helpful in improving adherence (Andrews & Freiland, 2000; Fogarty et al., 2002; Ickovics & Meisler, 1997; Meichenbaum & Turk, 1987). Therefore, a thorough assessment of the nature and function of each patient's individual adherence barriers, using known common barriers as a guideline, can be a critical component of any effective adherence intervention. This assessment should include determining whether or not potential barriers exist (e.g., substance abuse or depression) as well as whether and the way in which those potential barriers actually function to interfere with the patient's adherence (e.g., forgetting doses, apathy, sleeping through doses). Adherence interventions should then be tailored to the individual patient's identified adherence barriers, needs, and style. There is strong theoretical and clinical, and some empirical, support for this as a useful approach (e.g., Beutler & Harwood, 2000; Hayes, Nelson, & Jerrett, 1987).

There are a number of other, more stylistic strategies that may also be helpful in conducting effective adherence counseling. Because a thorough description of these strategies is beyond the scope of this chapter, the strategies are only listed here (see Heiby & Lukens; Bisono, Manuel, & Forchehimes; Oser; and Nezu, Nezu, & Perri of this volume, for more detailed discussion of these strategies)

- Using an appropriate language level
- Using reflective listening
- Maintaining a nonjudgmental stance and communicating empathy
- Validating and affirming the patient
- Responding to resistance with reflection and support rather than confrontation
- Working collaboratively with the patient and supporting self-efficacy
- Problem solving *with* the patient
- Helping patients adhere with barriers in place as well as with reducing adherence barriers
- Developing *concrete and behaviorally specific* treatment and adherence plans
- Obtaining strong commitments from the patient for agreed-upon plans

Issues of Particular Relevance in Facilitating Adherence to HAART

Parts I to III of this volume provide detailed discussions on the adherence barriers and interventions described above as well as methods for conducting individualized adherence counseling. As mentioned earlier, these adherence barriers and interventions have generally been found to apply to many chronic illness populations and treatments including HIV/AIDS. There are, however, a number of adherence issues that are particularly relevant and important in the treatment of HIV/AIDS patients that are highlighted and expanded on here (see Fogarty et al., 2002; Laurence, 2004; World Health Organization, 2003 for reviews of the literature on which this discussion is based).

Critical Importance of Facilitating Adherence

Although patient adherence is important in the treatment of nearly every chronic illness, it is of utmost importance in the treatment of HIV/AIDS. As discussed in the introduction of this chapter, nearly perfect adherence to HAART must be maintained for the treatment to be effective, and a lack of this level of adherence can result in treatment failure and resistance, disease progression, and potentially death. Furthermore, HAART regimens are typically some of the most complex and demanding treatments for patients to adhere to. Not only do typical regimens require patients to take multiple pills each day but the dosing frequency and schedule can be different for each medication. Additionally, many HAART regimens require that patients follow dietary restrictions, such as taking pills on an empty stomach or with food, or eating or not eating specific types of foods. Adhering to these regimens is often particularly challenging for those patients who are in the earlier stages of the disease and are asymptomatic, because HAART often produces a number of distressing side effects. The result of this is that rather than the medication helping to ameliorate unpleasant symptoms for these patients, it produces them, which can result in discontinuation of the medication. For all the above reasons, it is critical that the effective promotion of adherence be a primary focus in the treatment of HIV/AIDS patients.

Definitions of Adherence

Adherence to HAART is most often defined as the extent to which the prescribed number of pills is taken in the prescribed number of daily doses. Within this definition, nonadherence typically includes not filling or initiating the medication, missing doses, taking too many or too few pills in a dose, and terminating treatment prematurely. However, to be most effective, HAART regimens often require that patients are adherent to other recommendations, such as following strict dosing schedules (i.e., with rather narrow time windows during which doses must be taken) and following food and fluid intake requirements and restrictions. Therefore, taking doses too early or too late and not following food requirements should be regularly assessed and addressed as well.

Assessment of Adherence

Given the critical importance of high levels of adherence to HAART regimens, patients often feel uncomfortable reporting adherence problems to their providers. Additionally, because many HAART regimens require taking multiple medications in two or more doses per day, it can be extremely difficult for patients to remember if and when doses were missed. As a result of these factors, patients' estimates of their rates of adherence tend to be artificially high. Furthermore, health outcomes such as viral load and CD4 cell count are not reliable measures of adherence, because factors other than adherence can significantly affect these outcomes (e.g., drug resistance, problems with absorption or metabolism, drug interactions). Given the significant difficulty of adhering to HAART and the high rates of nonadherence, it is crucial that adherence to this treatment is assessed frequently and effectively (see Riekert, this volume, for a detailed discussion of methods for assessing patient adherence to medications).

Minimizing the Complexity and Demands of the Regimen

Research has clearly shown that the less complex and less demanding a treatment regimen is, the more likely it is to be adhered to, and this is certainly the case with HAART regimens (World Health Organization, 2003). Getting HIV/AIDS patients on regimens that involve the fewest pills at each dose, fewest doses per day (1–2), easiest administration (e.g., easiest to swallow), least food restrictions, and fewest (or least severe) side effects possible can go a long way in facilitating patient adherence. It can also be useful to select a medication regimen that fits best within a patient's lifestyle (e.g., dietary habits), daily routines (e.g., sleep, work, and play schedule), and resources (e.g., stability of housing, access to regular meals, refrigeration). The clinician should work *with* the patient in selecting a regimen because the patient often knows best what type of regimen will most likely be followed. In some cases, it may be possible to modify the dosing schedule of the prescribed regimen such that it fits better within a patient's routines. For patients with a significant history of adherence problems or substantial current adherence barriers, it may be worth considering starting them on a less complex and demanding regimen, even if it is not the first-choice treatment option. That is, a second-choice treatment option that is adhered to well can be more effective than a first-choice treatment option that is adhered to poorly.

Educating Patients About the Disease and the Treatment

Patients can fail to adhere to HAART medications because they do not understand the need for the treatment, the importance of adhering to the treatment, the specific requirements of the regimen, or how to integrate the regimen into their lives and manage adherence barriers, such as side effects. Unfortunately, this information is often not adequately conveyed to patients. Oser (this volume) provides an overview of methods for effectively educating patients on their treatments and treatment requirements; however, there are several issues relevant to patient education in the treatment of HIV/AIDS that are worth addressing here.

First, it is important that the patient has a basic understanding of HIV/AIDS, how HAART works to treat this illness, the importance of adherence, and the consequences of poor adherence. This information should be presented to the patient verbally and in writing. Useful points to make with regard to these issues are as follows:

- HIV is a virus that causes AIDS.
- Once HIV is in the body it makes copies of itself quickly.
- HIV attacks and destroys white blood cells called CD4 cells (also called T cells), which are an important part of the body's immune system.
- As the amount of HIV in the blood increases, more and more CD4 cells are destroyed and the body's immune system is weakened. The immune system is what keeps the body from getting sick when exposed to germs.
- As the body's immune system weakens, opportunistic infections begin to invade the body and the body is not able to fight them off.
- When a person gets certain types of infections, or the amount of CD4 cells in the blood get low enough, he or she is diagnosed with AIDS.
- The good news is that HIV medications stop HIV from copying itself, which allows more CD4 cells to be created, strengthens the immune system, and helps keep the body healthy.
- However, for the medications to be effective, the dosing instructions must be followed very carefully and consistently.

- Missing doses can cause an increase in the amount of HIV in the body and can cause the virus to become resistant to the medication.
- If the virus becomes resistant to the medication, then the medication is no longer effective, and other HIV medications may also be no longer effective.

Second, the patient should be clearly instructed on the specific requirements of the regimen, including (1) the name, color, and shape of each medication; (2) the number of pills of each medication to be taken at each dose; (3) the number of doses to be taken each day; (4) the times of day doses are to be taken; and (5) any special dosing instructions (e.g., food and fluid restrictions). This information should be provided verbally and in clear written form, and the patient's comprehension of this information should be assessed. It can be extremely useful to provide this information using the actual medication or pictures of the medication as visual aids. Many pharmaceutical companies provide medication charts with color pictures of the medications and dosing instructions.

Third, patients should be provided with verbal and written information on strategies for integrating the regimen into their lives and managing barriers (see the *Increasing Adherence—Related Skills, Resources, and Support* section of this chapter). This should include educating patients on side effects they are likely to experience and how to best manage these (see the *Managing Side Effects* section of this chapter). When discussing with patients the integration of the regimen into their lives, it can be useful to have them describe their typical daily routines, such as morning and nighttime rituals, meal patterns, work, social, and other activity schedules, and make a detailed plan for when and how dosing and other regimen requirements will occur within these routines. It is also important to discuss how and when the regimen will be followed during nontypical days, such as weekends, travel, and outings.

Assessing Readiness to Begin Treatment

Given that poor adherence to HAART can lead to treatment resistance, in addition to treatment failure and disease progression, it is often advisable to delay the initiation of treatment until the patient fully understands the requirements of the regimen, has a concrete and tenable plan for integrating the treatment in his or her life and successfully managing possible barriers (including side effects), and is clearly committed to adhering to the treatment. Therefore, the clinician should spend time with the patient discussing these issues prior to beginning the treatment. For those patients who have histories of poor adherence or significant current or anticipated barriers, it can be useful to conduct a "trial run" for 1 to 2 weeks using jelly beans or some other candy as a substitute for the medication. In this way, adherence plans can be practiced, and adherence problems and unanticipated barriers can be identified and addressed prior to initiating the actual treatment. If a trial run is conducted, a different or different color candy should be used to represent each medication and the regimen should be set up and followed exactly as the actual treatment would be (e.g., same dosing schedule, number of pills in each dose, food restrictions and requirements). See Prochaska and Johnson (this volume) for an additional guideline on assessing readiness to begin treatment.

Addressing Problematic Beliefs About HIV/AIDS and HAART

Patients can have certain beliefs about HIV/AIDS or HAART that result in their not adhering to the treatment (Janz & Becker, 1984). These beliefs can include the following: their HIV will not worsen if gone untreated; HIV is not a serious threat to their health; they do not have the ability to adhere to the regimen; the medication is not effective in treating HIV; the relative costs of taking the medication outweigh the benefits; or it is not necessary to take the medication as prescribed to be effective. It is important that patients' beliefs about HIV/AIDS and HAART are assessed both prior to initiating and during treatment, as well as the reasons for these beliefs. If these beliefs appear to be unfounded and interfering with patients' adherence, patients should be provided with accurate information. It is often important that this is done in a nonconfrontational manner (see Heiby & Lukens, this volume, for guidelines). In cases where problematic beliefs are the result of a lack of self-efficacy or depressive symptoms (e.g., hopelessness or apathy), strategies such as increasing self-efficacy and clarification of values or goals may be useful.

Increasing Motivation to Adhere

A fundamental challenge in facilitating adherence to HAART is that rather than ameliorating aversive symptoms, as is the case with many medical treatments, it often produces a number of distressing symptoms in previously asymptomatic patients. This, in addition to the ongoing challenges of following the otherwise demanding regimen, as well as in some cases depression and substance abuse, results in patients having trouble staying motivated to adhere. Because of this, it is important for clinicians working with these patients to regularly assess and enhance motivation to follow the treatment. Bisono, Manuel, and Forchehimes (this volume) provide a detailed discussion of methods for improving patient motivation to adhere to treatment and make behavioral changes generally. Strategies for improving motivation to adhere that are particularly relevant to the treatment of HIV/AIDS patients include regularly providing them with feedback on their viral loads and CD4 cell counts so that adherence can be reinforced and consequences of poor adherence can be made "real." It also may be useful to help patients identify and orient to their longer-term goals and values as motivators to maintain adherence despite current barriers and lack of reinforcement. These can include travel, educational, and work-related goals, as well as values such as taking care of a loved person or pet, being with family and friends, good health, and the ability to continue engaging in other specific activities.

Increasing Adherence—Related Skills, Resources, and Support

As has been discussed throughout this chapter, HAART regimens are typically complex and can require a significant amount of behavioral change and self-management on the part of patients. Many patients may not have had significant experience following a similar regimen, and may not possess the requisite skills for successfully adhering to HAART. Additionally, patients may be lacking in basic needs, such as food, housing, finances, and transportation, which can make following a complex regimen even more difficult. Clinicians can often facilitate patients' adherence considerably by providing them with basic adherence skills and tools, as well as referrals and assistance in accessing social services. Ferguson and Scarlett-Ferguson (this volume) and Shapiro and Herivel (this volume) discuss in detail methods for increasing patients' adherence skills, resources, and support.

Skills that can be particularly helpful for patients to learn are those that assist them in developing an organizational system for remembering and being able to take doses on time. Indeed, some ofthe most commonly sited reasons HIV/AIDS patients give for missing doses include (1) simply forgetting, (2) sleeping through doses, (3) being away from home and not having the medication with them, (4) having a change in the dailyroutine, and (5) being busy with other things (Levensky et al., 2002). Useful organizational and memory-aid skills include using alarms, notes, and stickers as cues for dosing; linking doses to daily activities such as morning and bedtime routines, meals, and television shows; keeping a diary to monitor

dosing; and using a pillbox as a reminder to take medication and as a reminder that the medication has been taken. Other adherence skills that can be useful to discuss with patients are integrating the regimen in their lifestyle (e.g., eating and sleeping patterns, work schedule, activities); taking the medication without others noticing and answering unwanted questions about the purpose of the medication (if this is an issue for the patient); anticipating, avoiding, and managing slips in adherence; using problem solving skills; and communicating effectively with providers (e.g., asking questions, reporting problems) (see Oser; Ferguson & Scarlett-Ferguson; and Blume & Marlatt of this volume for more detailed discussions of teaching these and other adherence skills to patients).

Prior to teaching these skills to patients, it is important to determine what skills are needed. This can be determined by having the patient describe a typical day of adherence and a typical day of nonadherence, and discuss the specific types of circumstances in which doses have been missed. Additionally, the effectiveness of the patient's current medication organizational/memory-aid system can be evaluated by assessing the extent to which doses are missed due to forgetting to take the dose, forgetting whether doses have been taken, being away from home and not having the medication available, running out of medication, sleeping through doses, being too busy, and having changes in daily routines. The extent to which these factors affect whether patients take their medications at the correct times and follow the food and liquid requirements can also be assessed in this way.

For those patients who are lacking in adequate resources and supports (e.g., money, food, housing, transportation, medication storage, emotional and practical social support, assistance and encouragement for following regimen), clinicians should attempt to increase these. There are a number of ways this may be accomplished, including referring patients to social services or a social worker for assistance with accessing resources (e.g., financial, housing, transportation, child care); enlisting patients' family and friends to assist them in following their regimens, reinforce adherence, and provide emotional support; increase clinic staff contact with patient through additional appointments, telephone "check-ins," and home visits; and referring patients to peer or other support groups, or to individual counseling (see Shapiro & Herivel, this volume).

Managing Side Effects

As discussed earlier, the experiencing of frequent or severe side effects is one of the most common reasons HIV/AIDS patients miss doses or discontinue their medication altogether, especially for those who are in the earlier and asymptomatic stages of the disease. Therefore, it is important that clinicians select medication regimens that produce the fewest and least severe side effects possible, and closely monitor and treat patients' side effects. Table 18.1 includes a list of side effects and other symptoms patients commonly experience while taking HAART, as well as a scale for measuring the severity of each. This can be a useful tool for regularly assessing patients' experiencing of side effects. It is also important to educate patients on the types of side effects they may experience and how to manage these. Although some symptoms experienced by patients may be related to the disease or other factors (e.g., related illnesses, other medications, drug interactions) rather than HAART, patients may attribute these symptoms to this treatment and as a result miss doses or discontinue the medication. Therefore, educating patients about the causes of their symptoms can be useful.

Side effects that are most frequent and tend to cause the most distress include upset stomach, nausea, diarrhea, and fatigue. Fortunately, these symptoms typically subside after the first few weeks of the treatment, and can be treated for the

Table 18.1   Assessment Measure for HAART Medication Side Effects

Symptom	Severity			Symptom	Severity		
	Mild	Moderate	Severe		Mild	Moderate	Severe
Headaches	☐	☐	☐	Skin rashes	☐	☐	☐
Nausea	☐	☐	☐	Changes in fat distribution	☐	☐	☐
Vomiting	☐	☐	☐	Weakness	☐	☐	☐
Diarrhea	☐	☐	☐	Tingling in hands or feet	☐	☐	☐
Abdominal pain	☐	☐	☐	Changes in taste	☐	☐	☐
Heartburn	☐	☐	☐	Dry or numb mouth	☐	☐	☐
Loss of energy	☐	☐	☐	Decreased appetite	☐	☐	☐
Muscle or joint pain	☐	☐	☐	Kidney stones	☐	☐	☐
Dizziness	☐	☐	☐	Anxiety	☐	☐	☐
Trouble sleeping	☐	☐	☐	Difficulty concentrating	☐	☐	☐
Fevers or chills	☐	☐	☐	Other: _____	☐	☐	☐
Night sweats	☐	☐	☐	Other: _____	☐	☐	☐
Vivid dreams	☐	☐	☐	Other: _____	☐	☐	☐

NOTE: Patient is instructed to indicate only symptoms experienced at least "mildly."

most part. In some cases, encouraging patients to think about side effects as "signs the medication is working" can be useful in helping the patients tolerate the effects, as can encouraging patients to discuss and think about how continuing to take the medications is linked to their long-term goals and values (e.g., health, family, friends).

Another side effect that can seriously impede adherence is lipodystrophy, which affects about half of patients on HAART. Lipodystrophy involves accumulations of fat in the upper back, neck, stomach, and chest areas and loss of fat in the face, arms, legs, and buttocks areas. Selecting regimens that minimize or do not produce lipodystrophy can go a long way in improving adherence, especially for those patients who fear these effects. As is the case with regimen complexity, a first-choice regimen with frequent and severe side effects may be less effective because of poor adherence than a second-choice regimen with fewer and less-severe side effects and better adherence. Patients differ in terms of how distressing they find different types of side effects and the extent to which different side effects will affect their adherence. It is important to discuss these issues with each patient before initiating or changing a regimen.

Addressing Substance Use and Depression

Although it is beyond the scope of this chapter to discuss the assessment and management of substance abuse and depression as it pertains to facilitating adherence, these behavioral health conditions are highly associated with poor adherence, and therefore are certainly worth mentioning here. If these conditions are identified, the clinician should not only offer treatment options to the patient (in a supportive, nonjudgmental, and nonconfrontational manner) and assist the patient in accessing them, but also work with the patient on adhering to the treatment in the context of these conditions, if possible. This will likely involve assessing the ways in which these conditions affect adherence (e.g., forgetting, apathy,

sleeping through doses, concerns about adverse interactions) and developing targeted interventions to address these barriers.

Follow-Up and Maintenance

Patients' adherence to HAART can increase or decrease over time as changes occur in factors such as their disease progression and symptoms, family and other relationships, work schedule, lifestyle and resources, mental health, and goals and values, to name a few. Therefore, it is important that clinicians have regular contact with patients and assess their adherence to the regimen, current and anticipated barriers to adherence, and the effectiveness of adherence plans that have been developed. Clinicians should then work with patients on modifying and developing new adherence plans to address identified barriers and problems as needed.

Conclusions

Knowledge of the common adherence barriers and interventions described in this chapter can be useful in that it orients clinicians to the domains of barriers to consider and assess for when working with patients on HAART regimens, as well as to techniques and strategies that may facilitate these patients' adherence. However, it is important that these common barriers and interventions are used as *guidelines* for developing *individualized* interventions tailored to the specific circumstances and needs of each patient as opposed to using the one-size-fits-all approach to adherence counseling. Adherence tends to involve a complex and multidetermined set of factors and patient behaviors, and patients tend to be heterogeneous with regard to whether and the manner in which common barriers actually interfere with adherence as well as the sorts of interventions that will be most helpful in improving adherence. Therefore, the nature and function of each patient's individual barriers should be thoroughly assessed, and then interventions should be tailored to address the nature and function of that patient's identified adherence barriers, as well as to his or her needs and style.

References

Andrews, L., & Friedland, G. (2000). Progress in HIV therapeutics and the challenges of adherence to antiretroviral therapy. *Infectious Disease Clinics of North America, 14*(4), 901–928.

Bartlett, J. (2002). Addressing the challenges of adherence. *Journal of Acquired Immune Deficiency Syndromes, 29*, 2–10.

Beutler, L., & Harwood, T. (2000). *Prescriptive psychotherapy: A practical guide to systematic treatment selection*. Oxford: Oxford University Press.

Carpenter, C. C., Fischl, M., Hammer, S. M., Hirsch, M., Jacobsen, D., Katzenstein, D., et al. (1997). Antiretroviral therapy for HIV infection in 1997: Updated recommendations of the International AIDS Society: USA panel. *Journal of the American Medical Association, 227*, 1962–1969.

Christensen, A. J. (2004). *Patient adherence to medical treatment regimens: Bridging the gap between behavioral science and biomedicine*. New Haven, CT: Yale University Press.

Condra, J. H., Schleif, W., Blahy, O., Gabryelski, L. J., Graham, D. J., Quintero, D. J., et al. (1995). In vivo emergence of HIV-1 variants resistant to multiple protease inhibitors. *Nature, 374*, 569–571.

Deeks, S., Loftus, R., Cohen, T., Chin, S., & Grant, R. (1997). *Incidence and predictors of virologic failure to indinavir or ritonavir in an urban health clinic.* Paper presented at the 37th annual meeting of the Interscience Conference on Antimicrobial Agents and Chemotherapy, Toronto, ON, Canada.

Deeks, S., Smith, M., Holodniy, M., & Kahn, J. (1997). HIV-1 protease inhibitors: A review for clinicians. *Journal of the American Medical Association, 276*, 146–154.

Fogarty, L., Roter, D., Larson, S., Burke, J., Gillespie, J., & Levy, R. (2002). Patient adherence to HIV medication regimens: A review of published and abstract reports. *Patient Education and Counseling, 46*, 93–108.

Hayes, S. C., Nelson, R. O., & Jarrett, R. B. (1987). The treatment utility of assessment: A functional approach to evaluating assessment quality. *American Psychologist, 42*(11), 963–974.

Hirsch, M. S. (1997). Selecting combination therapy using data from in vitro studies. *AIDS Reader, 7*, 116–120.

Ickovics, J. R., & Meisler, A. (1997). Adherence in AIDS clinical trials: A framework clinical research and clinical care. *Journal of Clinical Epidemiology, 50*, 385–391.

Jacobsen, H., Hanggi, M., Ott, M., Duncan, I. B., Owen, S., Andreoni, M., et al. (1996). In vivo resistance to an HIV-1 proteinase inhibitor: Mutations, kinetics and frequencies. *Journal of Infectious Disease, 173*, 1379–1387.

Janz, K. N., & Becker, M. H. (1984). The Health Belief Model: A decade later. *Health Education Quarterly, 11*(1), 1–47.

Kastrissios, H., Suarez, J. R., Katzenstein, D., Girard, P., Sheiner, L. B., & Blaschke, T. F. (1998). Characterizing patterns of drug-taking behavior with a multiple drug regimen in an AIDS clinical trial. *AIDS, 12*(17), 2295–2303.

Laurence, J. (Ed.). (2004). *Medication adherence in HIV/AIDS*. New York: Mary Ann Liebert.

Levensky, E. R., O'Donohue, W., Scott, J., Weisberg, M., Bolan, R., & Knox, L. (2002, December). *Increasing adherence to HAART with a brief assessment-based intervention: A preliminary evaluation.* Poster presented at Elements of Success, an international conference on adherence to antiretroviral therapy, Dallas, TX.

Malow, R. M., Baker, S. M., Klimas, N., Antoni, M. H., Schneiderman, N., Penedo, F. J., et al. (1998). Adherence to complex combination antiretroviral therapies by HIV-positive drug abusers. *Psychiatric Services, 49*(8), 1021–1022, 1024.

Meichenbaum, D., & Turk, D. (1987). *Facilitating treatment adherence: A practitioner's guidebook.* New York: Plenum Press.

Roter, D. L., Hall, J. A., Merisca, R., Nordstrom, M., Cretin, D., & Svarstad, B. (1998). Effectiveness of interventions to improve patient compliance: A meta-analysis. *Medical Care, 36*(8), 1138–1161.

Shumaker, S., Schron, E., Ockene, J., & McBee, W. (Eds.). (1998). *The handbook of health behavior change.* New York: Springer.

Valenti, W. (2001). Treatment adherence improves outcomes and manages costs. *AIDS Reader, 11*, 77–80.

World Health Organization (2003). *Adherence to long-term therapies: Evidence for action.* Geneva, Switzerland: Author. Retrieved June 7, 2005, from www.who.int/chronic_conditions/adherencereport/en

19

Adherence to Treatment of Substance Use Disorders

Steven J. Lash

Jennifer L. Burden

The Importance of Adherence in Substance Use Disorder Treatment

Treatment for substance use disorders (SUD) clearly has been shown to be effective (e.g., Holder, Longabaugh, Miller, & Rebonis, 1991) and to produce cost savings for society and treatment providers (e.g., Holder & Blose, 1992). Furthermore, a number of highly effective treatment approaches for SUD have been developed (for reviews, see Allen & Litten, 1999;

Fuller & Hiller-Sturmhofel, 1999). The effectiveness of these approaches, however, is substantially hampered by poor adherence to treatment. In clinical settings, adherence to SUD treatment is typically very poor, and this may explain why naturalistic studies often find only about 40% of clients are abstinent from substance use 1 year after beginning treatment (e.g., Moos, Finney, Ouimette, & Suchinsky, 1999).

Onken, Blaine, and Boren (1997) have compared the importance of adherence in SUD treatment with that of adherence to medications. Just

Authors' Note: We thank the staff of the Salem Veterans Affairs Medical Centers (VAMCs) Substance Abuse Residential Rehabilitation Treatment (SARRTP) for their help in the development of the CPR (contracting + prompting + reinforcing) intervention and Stephanie Fearer, PhD, for her comments on an earlier draft of this chapter. Preparation of this chapter was supported in part by a grant from the Department of Veterans Affairs, Veterans Health Administration, Health Services Research and Development Service (99–282–2). The views expressed in this article are those of the authors and do not necessarily represent the views of the Department of Veterans Affairs.

as the effectiveness of medications depends on individuals taking them over a specified time period, there is increasing evidence for a minimum effective dose of SUD treatment. Although additional research is still needed to identify the minimum effective duration and frequency of SUD treatment, a number of large-scale SUD treatment studies have found that 3 months of treatment is the minimum amount typically associated with improved outcome (e.g., Ershoff, Radcliffe, & Gregory, 1996; Simpson et al., 1997; Simpson, Joe, Fletcher, Hubbard, & Anglin, 1999). Because individuals with SUD are most vulnerable to relapse within the first 3 months of initiating abstinence (see Marlatt, 1985), continuing treatment and support during this period is critical. Research studies also suggest that adherence to treatment beyond 3 months offers increasing benefits. For instance, in a large-scale naturalistic study of SUD treatment programs in the U.S. Department of Veterans Affairs Medical Centers (VAMCs), the largest treatment effects were seen in those clients who participated in treatment for 12 months or more (Moos et al., 1999; Ritsher, Moos, & Finney, 2002). In another large-scale community-based study, longer durations of care were associated with better outcomes, even 8 years later (Moos & Moos, 2003).

Adherence to treatment, however, is a significant problem in SUD treatment. Only a small number of clients who enter treatment remain in treatment for at least 3 months (for reviews, see Carroll, 1997, 1998; Donovan, 1998; Stark, 1992). In two large-scale studies completed in the past decade, less than 30% of patients completed 3 months of treatment (Ershoff et al., 1996; Moos et al., 1999). In general, many individuals fail to complete initial intensive inpatient or outpatient treatment programs, and among those who do complete initial treatment, few participate in continuing care (i.e., outpatient aftercare services or support groups such as Alcoholics Anonymous [AA] or Narcotics Anonymous [NA]). The duration of SUD aftercare (i.e., individual and/or group therapy following initial treatment) and support group

attendance in VAMC treatment programs have been shown to be independently associated with better outcomes. Among clients who attended both aftercare and self-help groups following 3 or 4 weeks of intensive treatment, 63% were abstinent for at least 3 months at a 1-year follow-up assessment, compared with only 24% of those who did not attend any continuing care (Moos et al., 1999).

A relationship between treatment adherence and treatment outcome has been established, and interventions designed to increase continuing care participation often produce dramatic improvements in treatment outcomes. For instance, Ahles, Ossip, and their colleagues compared patients who signed a behavioral contract to attend aftercare and had a significant other prompt and reinforce attendance with those in standard care (Ahles, Schlundt, Prue, & Rychtarik, 1983; Ossip, Van-Landingham, Prue, & Rychtarik, 1984). The intervention group showed an 88% increase in attendance and a 3.5 times higher 1-year abstinence rate compared with the standard care group. Impressive results also have been found when family members are included in aftercare (O'Farrell, Choquette, Cutter, Brown, & McCourt, 1993) and when reinforcement vouchers are used contingent on abstinence (for a review, see Higgins, Alessi, & Dantona, 2002).

Given the relationship between treatment adherence and outcome, and the difficulty inherent in keeping clients engaged in treatment, a crucial task for treatment providers is to retain clients in treatment and to structure treatment programs in ways that enhance the likelihood that clients will participate in at least 3 months (and preferably 1 year) of treatment. Accomplishing this goal, however, is difficult. Although most treatment programs recommend that their clients participate in continuing care, they tend to place much more emphasis on initial intensive treatment. In addition to the need for a shift in priorities among treatment providers, barriers to long-term treatment adherence are significant and diverse among clients with SUDs.

Types of Adherence Problems and Barriers to Adherence

The reasons for and types of adherence problems in SUD treatment are diverse (Carroll, 1997). Often clients fail to present for treatment following the recommendation of an outside service provider. Once they apply for initial inpatient or outpatient treatment, they often fail to begin or complete it. Even among those who complete initial treatment, most fail to follow through with continuing care recommendations (Carroll, 1997; Ershoff et al., 1996; Fortney, Booth, Blow, & Bunn, 1995; Moos et al., 1999). Although many client characteristics have been identified as predictors of poor treatment adherence, research findings have been inconsistent. Client characteristics associated with poor adherence often are markers of environmental barriers to treatment adherence (e.g., homelessness) or identify a mismatch between the client and a particular treatment setting or program (Carroll, 1997; Klein, diMenza, Arfken, & Schuster, 2002). A part of the challenge of motivating clients to attend treatment for significant periods of time is that clients often struggle with treatment recommendations that require significant behavioral changes such as maintaining total abstinence, changing their lifestyles to avoid triggers for substance use, and obtaining social support for abstinence. In this context one explanation for poor treatment adherence is fairly straightforward: *Many clients do not necessarily want to stop abusing substances or make significant changes in their lifestyles.* Substance use is reinforcing on many levels, and the decision to change involves a complex process of examining the costs and benefits of changing problem behaviors. Influencing this decision are a multitude of personal and environmental factors that often impede motivation for and adherence to treatment.

Clients with SUD often present with complex treatment needs that can significantly affect the treatment process. Many are homeless and have limited financial and vocational resources, making it difficult to engage them in continuing care. These factors also affect the clinician's ability to implement some of the strategies that we have suggested in this chapter because these clients are difficult to contact given their transient lifestyles. Other factors such as limited child care and transportation resources also can significantly limit or affect clients' adherence to treatment (Kabela & Kadden, 1997). Furthermore, SUD clients often present with other mental health and medical problems that can significantly interfere with adherence to treatment. Estimates suggest that approximately 40% of SUD clients have other comorbid mental health disorders and that comorbid psychiatric problems significantly affect compliance with SUD treatment recommendations and treatment outcome (for a review, see Modesto-Lowe & Kranzler, 1999; Rosenthal & Westreich, 1999). In addition, clients with multiple medical problems often struggle with recommendations of total abstinence in the face of persistent problems such as chronic pain. Finally, clients often present for treatment at different stages in the change process and may not be ready to make all the changes necessary for successful treatment outcome. The impact of motivation has been discussed in detail in earlier chapters; however, attitude toward treatment and motivation to change can significantly affect SUD treatment adherence and outcome (see Connors, Donovan, & DiClemente, 2001; Prochaska, DiClemente, & Norcross, 1992).

In addition to a multitude of client factors, a number of treatment program factors significantly affect SUD treatment adherence. First, when a client seeks treatment, the length of time until the first session is scheduled determines whether a client follows through with SUD treatment (Kabela & Kadden, 1997). The sooner a client can be seen, the more likely he or she is to follow through with treatment. Furthermore, it is important to schedule individual and group therapy at times and in locations that are accessible and convenient for clients. Clients often need the option of attending treatment either in the evenings or during weekends and in community settings that are easily accessible or on a bus route. The therapeutic alliance between the client and treatment staff also has been identified as a significant mediator of treatment adherence on treatment outcome (Connors, Carroll, DiClemente, Longabaugh, & Donovan, 1997). Finally, the treatment program philosophy can significantly affect adherence to treatment. As discussed earlier, clients vary in their motivation to change, and they often present at different stages in the change process and with different expectancies about treatment (Connors et al., 2001). It is important for treatment providers to assess these factors and to address them early in the treatment process.

Assessment Issues

An initial assessment is essential in determining potential barriers to ongoing treatment that the client may face. Because detailed discussion of assessment strategies has been presented elsewhere in this book, we will emphasize a limited number of critical assessment issues. First, readiness to change, or motivation, should be a primary component of any initial assessment. Several measures are available for assessing readiness for change, including the University for Rhode Island Change Assessment (URICA; McConnaughy, Prochaska, & Velicer, 1983). The URICA is the most commonly used measure for assessing readiness for change and has been shown to significantly predict treatment outcome (Connors et al., 2001). In addition, assessment of expectancies about treatment can provide an important understanding of the client's acceptance and understanding of the treatment process. Furthermore, clinicians should assess environmental barriers to treatment participation, including housing status, employment, finances, transportation, child care, and environmental triggers for substance use. The Addiction Severity Index (McLellan et al., 1992)

is a structured clinical interview that can provide most of this information during initial contact with the client. Finally, potential comorbid psychiatric and medical conditions should be assessed given their significant impact on treatment adherence and outcome. Brief screening measures such as the Brief Symptom Inventory (Derogatis, 1993; Derogatis & Melisatatos, 1983) provide relatively brief screens for current psychiatric symptoms.

Contracting, Prompting, and Reinforcing Treatment Adherence

Once critical assessment issues are addressed, the next step is to implement clinical strategies that will increase adherence to SUD treatment. The CPR (contracting + prompting + reinforcing) intervention was developed to motivate clients to remain in treatment. CPR was designed with clinical settings in mind: it takes little additional therapist and staff time to implement, it is inexpensive, and it can be used with inpatient- and outpatient-based treatment programs. Although it is based on principles of behavior therapy and social learning theory (Bandura, 1986), the CPR intervention is compatible with most approaches to SUD treatment. CPR was designed specifically to facilitate any SUD treatment program or clinician's work by keeping clients in treatment long enough for treatment to be effective. There are several components of the CPR intervention. First, a treatment contract educates clients about the recommended duration and amount of treatment and the expected benefits of treatment. Next, adherence to therapy is routinely prompted with reminder phone calls and with appointment cards and letters. Finally, inexpensive social reinforcers and recognition are used regularly to motivate clients toward completing treatment adherence goals. A number of clinical trials have supported the effectiveness of CPR in increasing adherence to SUD treatment, and these increases in adherence have been associated with improvements in treatment outcome (Lash, 1998; Lash & Blosser, 1999; Lash, Burden, Monteleone, & Lehmann, 2004; Lash, Petersen, O'Connor, & Lehmann, 2001). The following describes application of the CPR intervention to increase adherence to outpatient aftercare therapy and 12-step support group participation following initial residential SUD treatment.

Contracting for Treatment Participation

The purpose of treatment contracting in CPR is to motivate clients to attend treatment by providing them with treatment outcome results, or abstinence rates, associated with adhering to treatment and by asking them to set a goal of attending initial treatment and continuing care at a specified frequency and for a specified duration. When completing the contract, the therapist guides the client in planning for treatment and continuing care and in committing to follow through with his or her plan. Because it often is hard for clients to initially commit to long-term treatment, at our treatment center they are encouraged to commit to participate in treatment for 90 days, or 3 months. Once they have achieved this goal, they are encouraged to commit to completing the remainder of 1 year of treatment in a second contract. We complete these contracts during individual therapy sessions, and each contract takes less than 20 minutes to complete. The therapist reads and explains the contract to the client and answers his or her questions. As part of an overall aftercare orientation and treatment planning process, we typically explain how aftercare is conducted at our site, help the client select an aftercare and an AA or NA support group, schedule his or her individual therapy sessions, schedule follow-up needs such as medical and mental health appointments, and problem solve how to overcome obstacles to continuing care participation. Introducing our prompts and reinforcers is an important part of the contracting session. The therapist shows or describes to the client what types of prompts or appointment reminders he or she will receive and explains the duration and frequency of aftercare attendance required to earn each reinforcer. Similarly, the therapist shows the client examples of each of the available reinforcers. We also have conducted a similar procedure for committing to initial SUD treatment (Lash, Gilmore, Burden, Weaver, Blosser, & Finney, 2005), and others have used similar contracts with family/significant other involvement (Ahles et al., 1983; Ossip et al., 1984) and with adolescents (Donohue et al., 1998) with success.

Our 90-day contract, shown in Figure 19.1 provides an example of the treatment contracting process. We present 1-year abstinence rates for clients who participate in no continuing care, aftercare only, AA or NA only, or aftercare plus AA or NA, based on a large-scale naturalistic study of clients in VAMC treatment programs (Ouimette, Moos, & Finney, 1998). The therapist explains that the abstinence rates are based on past research and may not reflect any one person's chances of success. In other settings with other populations, the appropriate abstinence rates should be presented when available, or these abstinence rates should be presented more cautiously. The therapist then asks the client to commit to participate in weekly AA or NA support group meetings, weekly aftercare group therapy sessions, and monthly individual therapy sessions for at least 9 weeks. This 2-month period following our 1-month long residential program is aimed at keeping the client in treatment for at least 3 months, the minimum duration of treatment associated with improved treatment outcome (e.g., Simpson et al., 1997, 1999). In addition, the therapist informs the client that continuing in treatment beyond 3 months plays a large role in the abstinence rates presented and that he or she will be encouraged to contract for additional continuing care at the end of 3 months of treatment.

At the conclusion of the contracting session, the therapist asks the client to sign and date the

3 Month Aftercare Contract

Facts: I, _____, understand that among veterans attending VA residential substance abuse treatment programs, the following percent of veterans are abstinent from alcohol and drugs 1 year later*:

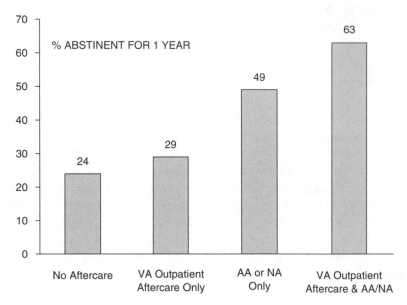

The program recommends that I set a goal to go to outpatient aftercare group therapy and AA or NA at least once a week for 9 weeks. This will help me through the first 3 months of recovery when most relapses occur. If I attend at least 7 outpatient groups & 2 individual sessions within 2 months, I will receive an aftercare certificate. If I attend 9 aftercare groups and 3 individual sessions within 3 months, I will receive an aftercare medallion.

Please circle your CHOICE above.

Going to aftercare is important to my sobriety. I will go to the below outpatient aftercare group and AA or NA meeting at least once a week for 9 weeks. I will only miss these if an emergency occurs. I will make this missed group up the same week, if possible. I will attend individual counseling once every month.

My outpatient aftercare group will be: _____ (Day of week, location & time).

My 12-step group will be: _____ (Day of week, location & time).

My first individual appointment will be:_____ (Therapist, date & time).

By signing this contract, I promise I will do my best to complete this plan.

Signed: _____ Date: _____ Witnessed: _____

*For at least the last 3 months. Source: Ouimette, Moos & Finney (1998).

Contract by S. J. Lash & J. L. Burden, funded by VA's HSR&D grant (IIR 99-282-2), Steven. Lash@med.va.gov

Figure 19.1 Ninety-Day Treatment Contract

SOURCE: Ouimette, Moos, and Finney (1998).

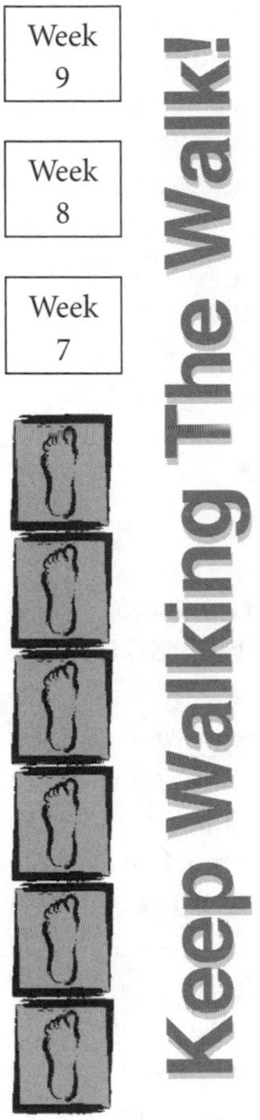

Week
9

Week
8

Week
7

Keep Walking The Walk!

John,

You have attended 6 weeks of aftercare. You need to attend 1 more week of group by 6/18/04, to reach your goal of attending at least 7 out of 9 weeks of group. Then you will receive your 90-Day Treatment certificate and have your name placed on the 90-Day Honor Roll.

Your next group is scheduled for Thursday 6/3/04 at 2:00 pm (Bldg. 9-1, room 127A).

Your next Individual meeting is scheduled for 6/3/04 at 1:00 pm with Bill (Bldg. 9-1, room 131).

Please call Bill at (533) 999-2222, extension 2589 if you need to reschedule your appointment.

Figure 19.2   Attendance Prompt With Feedback

contract, and the therapist signs it as a witness. The contract is given to the client, and he or she is asked to post it in a prominent location in his or her home (e.g., the refrigerator) as a reminder of his or her commitment to and the importance of following through with continuing care. Finally, the therapist shows and explains to the client our appointment reminders as well as our certificates and medallions that are used as reinforcers. Our 1-year contract is similar to our 90-day contract, except that it consists of separate aftercare and AA/NA sections. These sections present the respective 1-year abstinence rates of VAMC SUD clients who participate in ongoing aftercare and AA or NA (based on Moos et al., 1999).

Prompting of Treatment Adherence

Prompting in the CPR intervention consists of continuing care attendance reminders with clear feedback on the individual's progress toward achieving his or her treatment goals (see Figure 19.2). Cards, letters, and phone calls are used to remind and to motivate clients to attend scheduled aftercare and support group sessions and to encourage them to return to treatment following any missed sessions. Therapists send a brief handwritten letter to our clients a few days prior to their first aftercare appointment. This letter is personalized and congratulates them for completing the 28-day residential program and for committing to participate in continuing care and welcomes them to aftercare. These letters are well received by clients and are aimed at strengthening the therapeutic alliance. Appointment cards are sent prior to all scheduled individual and group aftercare sessions and before all AA or NA meetings. The cards list the location, day of the week, date and time of each appointment, as well as a phone number to call to cancel or reschedule a session. They also include feedback on how many aftercare sessions the client has attended and how many sessions still remain to earn the next available reinforcer. We mail appointment cards in envelopes to protect patient confidentiality and aim to have them arrive about 2 days prior to each session. We also use an automated phone messaging system that telephones each client 3 days before individual and group aftercare therapy appointments to remind him or her of each appointment in our program. Because someone other than the client may answer these phone calls, the type of appointment and the exact location of the appointment are not stated.

When a client misses an aftercare group or individual therapy session, we have found it critical that his or her therapist phone him or her that day, or the next day, to check with the client about why the session was missed and to encourage him or her to reschedule the appointment or to attend the next scheduled session. Phone contact allows the therapist to assess why the appointment was missed and to intervene in an appropriate way. An obstacle to participation may have arisen, such as a conflict with the client's work schedule. The therapist can then assist the client in problem solving how to resume continuing care. Alternatively, the client may have skipped the aftercare session and may feel guilty about having done so, or he or she may have relapsed and may believe that he or she has failed in treatment. The therapist can then encourage the client's return to aftercare and help him or her change his or her treatment-defeating negative beliefs (the reader is referred to the chapter by Blume and Marlatt, this volume,

on relapse prevention). If the therapist is unable to reach the client, he or she sends a personalized letter, expressing concern and encouraging the client to reschedule or return for his or her next appointment, and asks the client to call the therapist. Frequently, clients are impressed with the concern demonstrated by the therapist in personally contacting them, thus strengthening the therapeutic relationship.

Reinforcement of Aftercare Attendance

AA and NA support groups have long provided recognition for members who achieve various lengths of abstinence with medallions and key chains. Similarly, we provide treatment certificates and medallions for clients who complete various amounts of treatment and regularly verbally recognize clients for attending treatment in our CPR intervention. Reinforcement of aftercare participation by significant others (e.g., Ahles et al., 1983; Ossip et al., 1984) and reinforcement of negative substance use tests during initial treatment and aftercare (Higgins et al., 2002) have been shown to improve aftercare attendance and treatment outcome. When clients complete 90 days of treatment in our program, their group therapist presents them with an inexpensive framed certificate during group therapy. After the client receives the certificate, he or she is given an opportunity to share the ways treatment has been helpful to him or her, and other group participants are asked to provide the client feedback. Typically, group members praise the client for his or her treatment gains and encourage him or her to remain in treatment. Additionally, the client posts his or her name on the group's 3 months of treatment honor roll. This honor roll is posted prominently in the group therapy room. In addition to reinforcement for completing 3 months of treatment, clients are reinforced at several other points. When a client first joins an aftercare therapy group, the group therapist introduces him or her to the group members, praises him or her for following through with his or her initial aftercare commitment, and encourages other group members to do the same. Similarly, clients are acknowledged when they are halfway to completing 90 days of treatment. After the first 90 days of treatment, we recognize each client for completing 6, 9, and 12 months of treatment with certificates or medallions. We were initially surprised by the power of social reinforcement during group therapy sessions, but we have consistently seen that our clients take great pride in being recognized. Social reinforcement provides them with motivation during the early stages of recovery from SUD,

when they are dealing with many negative physical and social aftereffects of their substance use. Frequent reinforcement at this critical point helps transition them toward more natural reinforcers that occur as a result of maintaining abstinence and working in therapy, such as new and improved relationships, improved mental health, improved finances, and better physical health. We currently are integrating social reinforcement of abstinence into our CPR approach based on the contingency management work of Higgins and Budney (for a review, see Higgins et al., 2002).

Case Study: Our Program's Transition From Poor to Good Adherence and the Impact on Outcome

Our SUD treatment program in the early 1990s emphasized a 28-day residential program and also offered intensive outpatient treatment and outpatient aftercare therapy. Like many other programs, we provided excellent initial treatment from a biopsychosocial approach. Treatment included individual and group therapy; education about recovery from SUD; leisure and life skills training; as well as medical, psychiatric, and general mental health treatment. Despite admitting 350 clients each year, however, only about 6 to 10 clients attended our single aftercare group each week, and individual aftercare counseling was scarcely attended. Despite our recommendations that clients go to aftercare and AA or NA, few did. We were particularly concerned because we knew that continuing care was critical to treatment success, and we set out to change this by conducting a series of studies that examined practical interventions focused on motivating clients to start and remain in continuing care. We randomly assigned clients to treatment as usual or to treatment as usual plus an adherence intervention, and we measured how frequently they attended group therapy for the first 2 months following our 1-month initial program. Once we found an effective adherence intervention, this became our new treatment as usual, or standard treatment, and each new innovation was compared with it. If an intervention did not improve treatment adherence over treatment as usual, we did not continue to use it. Because clinical time was limited, only those interventions that were effective were continued.

Our first attempts to improve aftercare adherence failed (Lash & Dillard, 1996). Only about 27% of our clients ever attended aftercare, and the average number of sessions they attended was 1.2. We then introduced an early version of our treatment contract, which improved initiation of aftercare to 70% of our clients and the average number of sessions over the first 2 months of aftercare to 3.0 (Lash, 1998). Although these were significant improvements, few of our clients were remaining in treatment for at least 3 months. Contracting for aftercare attendance served primarily to get clients to begin aftercare, but it had less impact on keeping them in treatment (see Donovan, 1998). We sought to improve on contracting by adding attendance prompts with feedback to see if this would motivate clients to remain in aftercare longer (Lash & Blosser, 1999). We found that essentially

100% of our clients now began aftercare, and they attended an average of 4.4 weekly group sessions during the first 2 months of aftercare. For the first time, we also assessed the impact on a measure of treatment outcome. The average number of rehospitalizations for any reason over the next year was 0.75 when contracting alone was provided but only 0.25 when clients received contracting plus prompts. Next, we added social reinforcers to contracting and prompting (Lash et al., 2001, 2004). This further increased the average number of weekly groups attended to 5.5. We also comprehensively measured treatment outcome. Although the intervention produced no additional improvement in rehospitalization rates, 68% of participants in the CPR condition were abstinent at a 6-month follow-up compared with only 32% of participants who received the contract and prompts alone. Although attendance dropped after we stopped the intervention, it remained higher than in the comparison group. Unpublished results and clinical experience with the CPR intervention suggest that it improves the therapeutic bond between our clients and staff and that it helps clients maintain their motivation and commitment to change. Currently, we are completing a large-scale clinical trial of CPR versus standard treatment without our treatment contract, prompts, or reinforcers (Lash, Stephens, Burden, Grambow, & Horner, 2006).

Our use of a treatment contract, prompts, and social reinforcement to promote continuing care attendance is one example of how the CPR intervention can be applied. Other applications of this intervention may be equally or more effective. Implementing CPR and monitoring treatment attendance to recognize and prompt clients serves the dual purpose of providing therapists and treatment programs with feedback on how effective their efforts are in improving treatment adherence. We currently are developing a version of our contract to be used with patients whose initial treatment is provided in an outpatient setting. Copies of our contracts, prompts, and reinforcers and detailed instructions for their use are available from the authors at Steven.Lash@med.va.gov or Jennifer.Burden@med.va.gov. It is our belief that CPR can facilitate SUD treatment. Only if clients are kept in treatment and are abstinent for a minimum period of time can they fully benefit from treatment and begin receiving the naturally occurring benefits of decreased substance use. Keeping clients in treatment longer helps them acquire the skills needed to overcome problems (see Higgins & Petry, 1999) and make the lifestyle changes targeted by SUD treatment.

Suggested Readings

Carroll, K. M. (Ed.). (1997). *Improving compliance with alcoholism treatment.* Bethesda, MD: National Institute of Alcohol Abuse and Alcoholism.

Donovan, D. M. (1998). Continuing care: Promoting the maintenance of change. In W. R. Miller & N. Heather (Eds.), *Treating addictive behaviors* (2nd ed., pp. 317–336). New York: Plenum Press.

Onken, L. S., Blaine, J. D., & Boren, J. J. (Eds.). (1997). *Beyond the therapeutic alliance: Keeping the drug-dependent individual in treatment* (NIDA Monograph No. 165). Rockville, MD: National Institute on Drug Abuse-Division of Clinical and Services Research.

References

Ahles, T. A., Schlundt, D. G., Prue, P. M., & Rychtarik, R. G. (1983). Impact of aftercare arrangements on the maintenance of treatment success in abusive drinkers. *Addictive Behaviors, 8,* 53–58.

Allen, J. P., & Litten, R. Z. (1999). Treatment of drug and alcohol abuse: An overview of major strategies and effectiveness. In B. S. McCrady & E. E. Epstein (Eds.), *Addictions: A comprehensive guidebook* (pp. 385–395). New York: Oxford University Press.

Bandura, A. (1986). *Social foundations of thought and action: A social cognitive theory.* New Jersey: Prentice Hall.

Carroll, K. M. (1997). Compliance and alcohol treatment: An overview. In K. M. Carroll (Ed.),

Improving compliance with alcoholism treatment (pp. 5–12). Bethesda, MD: National Institute of Alcohol Abuse and Alcoholism.

Carroll, K. M. (1998). Enhancing retention in clinical trials of psychosocial treatments: Practical strategies. In L. S. Onken, J. D. Blaine, & J. J. Boren (Eds.), *Beyond the therapeutic alliance: Keeping the drug-dependent individual in treatment* (pp. 4–24). Rockville, MD: U.S. Department of Health & Human Services.

Connors, G. J., Carroll, K. M., DiClemente, C. C., Longabaugh, R., & Donovan, D. M. (1997). The therapeutic alliance and its relationship to alcoholism treatment participation and outcome. *Journal of Consulting and Clinical Psychology, 65,* 588–598.

Connors, G. J., Donovan, D. M., & DiClemente, C. C. (2001). *Substance abuse treatment and the stages of change.* New York: Guilford Press.

Derogatis, L. R. (1993). *BSI: Brief Symptom Inventory: Administration, scoring, and procedures manual.* Minneapolis, MN: National Computer Systems.

Derogatis, L. R., & Melisatatos, N. (1983). The brief symptom inventory: An introductory report. *Psychological Medicine, 13,* 595–605.

Donohue, B., Azrin, N. H., Lawson, H., Friedlander, J., Teichner, G., & Rindsberg, J. (1998). Improving initial session attendance of substance abusing and conduct disordered adolescents: A controlled study. *Journal of Child and Adolescent Substance Abuse, 8,* 1–13.

Donovan, D. M. (1998). Continuing care: Promoting the maintenance of change. In W. R. Miller & N. Heather (Eds.), *Treating addictive behaviors* (2nd ed., pp. 317–336). New York: Plenum Press.

Ershoff, D., Radcliffe, A., & Gregory, M. (1996). The Southern California Kaiser-Permanente chemical dependence recovery program evaluation: Results of a treatment outcome study in an HMO setting. *Journal of Addictive Disease, 15,* 1–25.

Fortney, J. C., Booth, B. M., Blow, F. C., & Bunn, J. Y. (1995). The effect of travel barriers and age on the utilization of alcoholism treatment aftercare. *American Journal of Drug and Alcohol Abuse, 21,* 391–406.

Fuller, R. K., & Hiller-Sturmhofel, S. (1999). Alcoholism treatment in the United States: An overview. *Alcohol Research & Health, 23,* 69–77.

Higgins, S. T., Alessi, S. M., & Dantona, R. L. (2002). Voucher-based incentives: A substance abuse treatment innovation. *Addictive Behaviors, 27,* 887–910.

Higgins, S. T., & Petry, N. M. (1999). Contingency management: Incentives for sobriety. *Alcohol Health and Research World, 23,* 122–127.

Holder, H. D., & Blose, J. O. (1992). A reduction of health care costs associated with alcoholism treatment: A 14-year longitudinal study. *Journal of Studies on Alcohol, 53,* 293–302.

Holder, H., Longabaugh, R., Miller, W. R., & Rebonis, A. V. (1991). The cost effectiveness of treatment for alcoholism: A first approximation. *Journal of Studies on Alcohol, 52,* 517–540.

Kabela, E., & Kadden, R. (1997). Practical strategies for improving client compliance with treatment. In K. M. Carroll (Ed.), *Improving compliance with alcoholism treatment* (pp. 15–50). Bethesda, MD: National Institute of Alcohol Abuse and Alcoholism.

Klein, C., diMenza, S., Arfken, C., & Schuster, C. R. (2002). Interaction effects of treatment setting and client characteristics on retention and completion. *Journal of Psychoactive Drugs, 34,* 39–50.

Lash, S. J. (1998). Increasing participation in substance abuse aftercare treatment. *American Journal of Drug and Alcohol Abuse, 24,* 31–36.

Lash, S. J., & Blosser, S. L. (1999). Increasing adherence to substance abuse aftercare group therapy. *Journal of Substance Abuse Treatment, 16,* 55–60.

Lash, S. J., Burden, J. L., Monteleone, B. R., & Lehmann, L. P. (2004). Social reinforcement of substance abuse treatment participation: Impact on outcome. *Addictive Behaviors, 29,* 337–342.

Lash, S. J., & Dillard, W. (1996). Encouraging participation in aftercare group therapy among substance-dependent men. *Psychological Reports, 79,* 585–586.

Lash, S. J., Gilmore, J. D., Burden, J. L., Weaver, K. R., Blosser, S., & Finney, M. L. (2005). The impact of contracting and prompting substance abuse treatment entry: A pilot trial. *Addictive Behaviors, 30*(3), 415–422.

Lash, S. J., Petersen, G. E., O'Connor, E. A., & Lehmann, L. P. (2001). Social reinforcement of substance abuse aftercare group therapy attendance. *Journal of Substance Abuse Treatment, 20,* 3–8.

Lash, S. J., Stephens, R. S., Burden, J. L., Grambow, S. C., & Horner, R. D. (2006). *Improving substance abuse treatment aftercare adherence and outcome* (Project IIR 99–282–2). Unpublished data.

Marlatt, G. A. (1985). Relapse prevention: Theoretical rational and overview of the model. In G. A. Marlatt & J. R. Gordon (Eds.), *Relapse prevention* (pp. 3–70). New York: Guilford Press.

McConnaughy, E. A., Prochaska, J. O., & Velicer, W. F. (1983). Stages of change in psychotherapy: Measurement and sample profiles. *Psychotherapy: Theory, Research and Practice, 20,* 368–375.

McLellan, A. T., Kushner, H., Metzger, D., Peters, R., Smith, I., Grisson, G., et al. (1992). The fifth edition of the Addiction Severity Index. *Journal of Substance Abuse Treatment, 9,* 199–213.

Modesto-Lowe, V., & Kranzler, H. R. (1999). Diagnosis and treatment of alcohol dependent patients with comorbid psychiatric disorders. *Alcohol Research & Health, 23,* 144–149.

Moos, R. H., Finney, J. W., Ouimette, P. C., & Suchinsky, R. J. (1999). A comparative evaluation of substance abuse treatment: I. Treatment orientation, amount of care, and 1-year outcomes. *Alcoholism: Clinical and Experimental Research, 23,* 529–536.

Moos, R. H., & Moos, B. S. (2003). Long-term influence of duration and intensity of treatment on previously untreated individuals with alcohol use disorders. *Addiction, 98,* 325–337.

O'Farrell, T. J., Choquette, K. A., Cutter, H. S. G., Brown, E. D., & McCourt, W. F. (1993). Behavioral marital therapy with and without additional couples relapse prevention sessions for alcoholics and their wives. *Journal of Studies on Alcohol, 54,* 652–666.

Onken, L. S., Blaine, J. D., & Boren, J. J. (1997). Treatment for drug addiction: It won't work if they don't receive it. In L. S. Onken, J. D. Blaine, & J. J. Boren (Eds.), *Beyond the therapeutic alliance: Keeping the drug-dependent individual in treatment* (NIDA Monograph No.165, pp. 1–2). Rockville, MD: National Institute on Drug Abuse, Division of Clinical and Services Research.

Ossip, D. J., Van-Landingham, W. P., Prue, D. M., & Rychtarik, R. G. (1984). Increasing attendance at alcohol aftercare using calendar prompts and home based contracting. *Addictive Behaviors, 9,* 85–89.

Ouimette, P. C., Moos, R. H., & Finney, J. W. (1998). Influence of outpatient treatment and 12-step group involvement on 1-year substance abuse treatment outcomes. *Journal of Studies on Alcohol, 59,* 513–522.

Prochaska, J. O., DiClemente, C. C., & Norcross, J. C. (1992). In search of how people change: Applications to addictive behaviors. *American Psychologist, 47,* 1102–1114.

Ritsher, J. B., Moos, R. H., & Finney, J. W. (2002). Relationship of treatment orientation and continuing care to remission among substance abuse patients. *Psychiatric Services, 53,* 595–601.

Rosenthal, R. N., & Westreich, L. (1999). Treatment of persons with dual diagnoses of substance use disorder and other psychological problems. In B. S. McCrady & E. E. Epstein (Eds.), *Addictions: A comprehensive guidebook* (pp. 439–476). New York: Oxford University Press.

Simpson, D. D., Joe, G. W., Broome, K. M., Hiller, M. L., Knight, K., & Rowan-Szal, G. A. (1997). Program diversity and treatment retention rates in the Drug Abuse Treatment Outcome Study (DATOS). *Psychology of Addictive Behaviors, 11,* 279–293.

Simpson, D. D., Joe, G. W., Fletcher, B. W., Hubbard, R. L., & Anglin, M. D. (1999). A national evaluation of treatment outcomes for cocaine dependence. *Archives of General Psychiatry, 56,* 507–514.

Stark, M. J. (1992). Dropping out of substance abuse treatment: A clinically oriented review. *Clinical Psychology Review, 12,* 93–116.

20

Adherence to Exercise Regimens

Jessica A. Whiteley

David M. Williams

Bess H. Marcus

The American College of Sports Medicine (ACSM, 2000) defines exercise as "planned, structured and repetitive bodily movement done to improve or maintain one or more components of physical fitness" (p. 4). Exercise is viewed as a subclass of physical activity, which is defined as "bodily movement that is produced by the contraction of skeletal muscle and that substantially increases energy expenditure" (ACSM, 2000, p. 4). According to these definitions, walking briskly for 20 minutes is an example of exercise. This behavior would also be considered physical activity; however, other nonexercise behaviors, such as walking from the car to the grocery store, painting a house, and gardening are also considered to be physical activities. A further distinction is made regarding intensity.

Any activity that is of the same intensity as a brisk walk (3–4 mph) and/or results in slight to moderate increases in heart rate or sweating is considered moderate intensity physical activity. Some moderate intensity physical activities include raking leaves, gardening, ice-skating, and doubles tennis. Moderate intensity physical activity can also be thought of as any activity resulting in 55% to 69% maximum heart rate, whereas vigorous activity is defined as 70% to 89% maximum heart rate, which for most people feels the same as jogging or running. Vigorous intensity physical activities include splitting wood, competitive basketball, high-impact aerobics, or singles tennis. As you can see, both moderate and vigorous intensity physical activities can include planned exercise; however, moderate intensity activities are more likely to include activities that can be incorporated into everyday life. Because exercise is encompassed by physical activity, the broader term, physical activity, will be used throughout this chapter, except when referring exclusively to exercise.

It was once thought that health benefits were best obtained through prescribing structured exercise programs. However, the recommendations have broadened to better meet the needs of those individuals who are unable to participate in structured exercise programs. Research has shown that moderate intensity physical activity that is incorporated into one's daily lifestyle can produce significant health benefits. The ACSM (Pate et al., 1995) currently recommends an accumulation of at least 30 minutes of moderate physical activity on most, preferably all days of the week. For vigorous activity, the ACSM (1990) guidelines recommend at least 20 minutes of vigorous activity 3 or more days per week. In addition, the 30 minutes of moderate intensity activity can be continuous or accumulated in three, 10-minute bouts. Those who follow these guidelines will experience the many benefits of regular physical activity, including decreased risk of cardiovascular disease, osteoporosis, obesity, depression, and breast and colon cancer.

Despite the numerous benefits of physical activity, prevalence rates in the United States have been dismal. A report by the Surgeon General in 1996 indicated that 60% of adults in the United States are not regularly physically active and that 25% of adults are completely sedentary. The important health benefits of physical activity, coupled with low prevalence rates have prompted health care professionals to recognize increasing rates of adherence to regular physical activity as one of the leading health objectives in *Healthy People 2010* (U.S. Department of Health and Human Services [USDHHS], 2000).

Although this goal sounds straightforward, defining adherence to physical activity can be complicated, because people are not usually prescribed a specific physical activity or exercise regimen. Moreover, regular physical activity is an ongoing and lifelong behavior. Thus, it becomes difficult to define adherence in dichotomous terms, that is, whether someone did or did not adhere to an exercise regimen. Instead, physical activity adherence may be thought of as the rate of physical activity over a period of time. For health care practitioners, adherence to physical activity may involve helping a client to initiate physical activity, to increase regularity of physical activity, to return to regular activity after a period of inactivity, or to maintain an already active lifestyle in the face of current or impending barriers. Although these scenarios are somewhat different, they all involve promotion of physical activity adherence.

Barriers

Whether someone is trying to begin an exercise program or struggling to maintain regular activity, the most commonly endorsed barrier to adherence is lack of time. Clients often report that adherence to physical activity takes time away from other activities, such as working, child care, watching television, or spending time with friends and family. People often have difficulty making physical activity a priority, especially when they find the activity aversive, because it is perceived as painful, uncomfortable, or boring. Another major barrier to physical activity adherence is lack of social support. People whose friends and family are not active and do not believe in the benefits of physical activity are less likely to be active themselves. Lack of equipment or a suitable place in which to work out are additional barriers to physical activity. Although walking is the most common form of physical activity and is presumably readily available, many people feel they do not have a place to walk that is safe, free from traffic, has flat and smooth terrain, or is attractive and conducive to walking. Still others are afraid they will experience muscle soreness or do not like the feeling of perspiration. Thus, there are a number of barriers experienced by individuals that make exercise adherence problematic. We will discuss the means of addressing these barriers later in the chapter.

Assessment Issues

In addition to the multiple barriers to exercise promotion and maintenance, assessment of physical activity continues to be controversial, because a "gold standard" measure does not exist. There are a number of brief, written self-report questionnaires that assess physical activity levels and can be completed within 5 to 10 minutes (see Marks & Caspersen, 1997). These questionnaires can be useful in large research studies, in which participants are asked to complete numerous questionnaires at one time. Although self-report questionnaires help give a general account of the overall amount of physical activity behavior, they often do not provide a detailed account of specific physical activity behaviors. Another self-report technique, the physical activity recall (PAR) interview, is a structured interview that more thoroughly assesses light, moderate, hard, and very hard physical activity over the course of the previous 1-week period (see Marks & Caspersen, 1997). The PAR has specific instructions for prompting clients about their physical activity and calls for extensive and standardized training of administrators. Although the PAR has shown good reliability and has been accepted as the most valid self-report measure, the extensive training that is necessary and the time-consuming nature of the interview (on average 15–20 minutes) are major drawbacks to this assessment tool.

Physical activity diaries, in which clients are asked to keep a daily record of all their physical activity over the course of 1 week, also provide a thorough assessment of a client's daily physical activity. Teaching clients to use physical activity diaries may take some time initially; however, teaching clients to self-monitor their activity can have benefits beyond simply gathering information (see next section). In addition to written and oral self-report, a number of objective measures of physical activity have recently been developed. Rigorous research protocols often use the doubly labeled water method to calculate the total energy expenditure over a period of time, or call for measurement of maximum oxygen consumption to assess changes in levels of physical fitness. Although these measures are highly accurate and reliable, they are also highly expensive and require extensive technical training and equipment. A more commonly used objective physical activity assessment tool is the step-counter or pedometer. Although pedometers lack the accuracy of some of the more expensive methods, they are inexpensive, easy to use, and provide a good tool for assessing walking behavior. In addition, pedometers can provide an excellent means of measuring and providing feedback on walking during an exercise program. In general, exercise assessment, although not perfect, is an important tool for promoting and tracking physical activity. Later we will discuss how exercise assessment can be integrated into adherence-promotion strategies.

In summary, rates of physical activity in this country continue to be low, despite the ever-increasing research base indicating that regular activity yields numerous health benefits. Researchers are continuously working to uncover the strategies that will work best to help people overcome the numerous barriers to physical activity adherence. In the sections that follow, we present the most recent, evidence-based strategies for promoting physical activity adherence. We will also provide a case example that illustrates how some of these strategies can be effectively implemented.

Adherence Promoting Strategies

The promotion strategies that have been shown to have the most support for exercise include principles from the stages of change model, social cognitive theory, and the relapse prevention model (Bandura, 1997; Marcus & Forsyth, 2003; Marcus & Lewis, 2003; Trost, Owen, Bauman, Sallis, & Brown, 2002). We will discuss how to assess your clients' motivational readiness to begin physical activity, their physical activity level, and then how to help them increase and maintain physical activity levels. In working with a client, we encourage you to determine goals that are appropriate for that particular person given his or her own barriers and circumstances. We do not recommend simply prescribing 5 days of moderate intensity activity, 30 minutes each session and not working with the client to determine an action plan for accomplishing this goal. Instead, we encourage you to assess your clients' readiness for change and activity level and then work with them to problem solve the barriers, increase their confidence in their abilities, and set meaningful short- and long-term goals. These strategies are what we know to be most effective in working toward adherence to a regular physical activity routine.

Assessment

Preliminary Assessment

As we discussed earlier, there are a number of ways to assess physical activity. When seeing a client for the first time, you can begin by performing a quick assessment of frequency and duration of physical activity. For example, you could ask, "How many times per week are you physically active? By physically active, I mean activity such as a brisk walk, biking, swimming, or any other activity where your heart rate and breathing increase." After the client responds you could then ask, "For about how many minutes are you active each time?" Finally, you can ask, "What are your typical activities?" In this way, you have a rough idea of his or her activity level and whether or not he or she is currently meeting the Centers for Disease Control (CDC)/ACSM guidelines.

Another way of quickly assessing a person's activity level and motivational readiness for change

(see Cook, this volume, for more details) is to ask a series of questions that will determine a person's stage of change (Marcus & Forsyth, 2003). The questions are as follows:

1. Are you currently physically active?

2. Do you intend on becoming more physically active in the next 6 months?

3. Do you currently engage in regular physical activity? For exercise to be regular, it must add up to a total of 30 minutes or more per day and be done at least 5 days per week. For example, you could take one 30-minute walk or take three 10-minute walks for a daily total of 30 minutes.

4. Have you been regularly physically active for the past 6 months?

The scoring for these questions is presented in Table 20.1. If a client answers "no" to Questions 1 and 2, he or she is in *precontemplation*; if he or she answers "no" to 1 and "yes" to 2, he or she is in *contemplation*; if he or she answers "yes" to 1 and "no" to 3, he or she is in *preparation*; if he or she answers "yes" to 1 and "yes" to 3, he or she is in *action*; and if he or she answers "yes" to 1, "yes" to 3, and "yes" to 4, he or she is in *maintenance*. After determining a client's stage of change, it is possible to provide motivational behavior change strategies that are tailored to the person's own readiness and motivation, as we will discuss in more detail later.

Tracking Activity

One of the primary tools for practical physical activity assessment that also provides means of physical activity promotion and maintenance is self-monitoring. Self-monitoring serves several important functions. First, it is a good way to determine a client's baseline physical activity. Monitoring also helps to identify opportunities for reducing sedentary behavior. Second, once the client is tracking his or her activity, it can become

Table 20.1.   Scoring for Stages of Change

Question			Response		
1	No	No	Yes	Yes	Yes
2	No	Yes	—	—	—
3	—	—	No	Yes	Yes
4	—	—	—	No	Yes
Stage =	Precontemplation	Contemplation	Preparation	Action	Maintenance

an excellent tool for maintaining adherence to the exercise program. Logging activity can help the client track progress, determine if goals are being reached, and set new goals. This can help maintain motivation as well as provide an element of accountability. Third, for the practitioner, the self-monitoring logs can be a tool for providing corrective feedback and praise. Thus, self-monitoring is one of the most powerful tools for promoting and maintaining exercise regimens. Self-monitoring can become cumbersome to the client, so that working with the client to create a quick and easy way to monitor his or her activity will be important. In addition, continued monitoring should be strongly encouraged. Initially, there are different types of self-monitoring that can be implemented to determine the client's baseline activity level.

If a client is particularly sedentary, some programs (Blair, Dunn, Marcus, Carpenter, & Jaret, 2001) will have clients begin by monitoring all their daily activities both at work and leisure. If you choose to do this you may want to suggest that they monitor 2 weekdays and 1 weekend day to reduce the burden. In this way, it is possible to work with your client to determine opportunities for increasing physical activity and decreasing sedentary behavior. For sedentary clients, you may have the clients fill out logs in which they track their activities in 1- or 2-hour blocks of time for the three chosen days. They may note types of activities (e.g., getting ready for work, driving, sitting at a desk, carrying heavy objects, walking, watching television), whether or not these activities were of moderate intensity or more, and the

duration of each activity. When clients monitor their activities they become more aware of their own habits and may be able to identify opportunities for increasing physical activity. For instance, if a client notices that he or she is consistently logging 2 hours of television watching per night, he or she may identify this time as an opportunity to eliminate some of this sedentary behavior and replace it with physical activity. Depending on a client's motivational readiness and fitness level, this activity can range from a 2-minute walk during commercial breaks to eliminating one 30-minute show and replacing it with a 30-minute walk outside or 30-minute ride on a stationary bicycle during a 30-minute program.

For clients who report that they are doing some activity, but not regularly, you could also have them conduct the activity logging discussed above. However, if they seem to have progressed to the point where they are already active and need encouragement to increase their frequency or duration to meet CDC/ACSM guidelines, this type of monitoring may be less useful. Instead, at the first meeting with an irregularly active client, you can have him or her track his or her weekly activity that reaches a moderate intensity or more. Have clients log the day of the week, time of day, type of activity, and duration of the activity on their self-monitoring logs. You may want to provide your clients with blank logs to facilitate the process.

Beyond the initial consultation and behavior initiation, self-monitoring is beneficial for additional reasons as well. Self-monitoring provides a way to monitor progress, set goals, and adhere to a regimen once the behavior is initiated. Finally, self-monitoring also provides the means for knowing what corrective feedback and problem solving may be needed to maintain adherence. We will talk more about these skills in the sections to follow.

Pedometers

If your clients are primarily walking for their activity, pedometers provide a nice way of tracking the steps they take on a daily basis. A pedometer, or step-counter, is a small device that sits on the waistband of your left hipbone. Clients should attach the device to the outside of their waistband or belt. There are many pedometers available that include a variety of tools to measure such things as distance and calories burned in addition to step counts. We recommend the basic Digi-Walker brand pedometer that measures only step counts (see www.digiwalker.com for more information). This particular brand has been tested and shown to be accurate and consistent. Pedometers should be combined with self-monitoring such that a client would log the number of steps he or she has taken each day. You may want a client to note the number of steps taken in purposeful exercise within the daily step total.

The overall goal for health benefits is 10,000 steps per day (Tudor Locke, 2002). A 30-minute walk will average 3,100 to 4,000 steps depending on length of stride (Tudor-Locke, 2002). Many sedentary individuals or individuals with chronic diseases may take 3,500 to 5,000 steps per day (Tudor-Locke, 2002). Therefore, we caution promoting 10,000 steps per day initially for the sedentary individual. This is a difficult goal and could be discouraging rather than motivating for someone doing few steps per day. Thus, for those individuals under 5,000 steps, you may want to determine an interim goal of 5,000 steps per day. Clients could work up to this goal by adding 500 steps per day. For those individuals who are above 5,000 steps but not to the ultimate goal of 10,000 steps, an interim goal could

be to encourage your client to increase his or her steps by 2,000 to 4,000 steps.

Exercise Plan

To best work with your client, we recommend that you use the strategies that will be described in the sections to follow. The goal of an exercise program would be to reach the CDC/ACSM guidelines described earlier of at least 5 days per week, 30 minutes each time of moderate or greater intensity. One acronym that has been developed to touch on these different elements is "FIT": *Frequency* (times per week), *Intensity* (heart rate, sweating, perceived exertion or speed), and *Time* (duration of the exercise session). For most individuals, it will be best to start at a low intensity for less frequent and shorter bouts of activity rather than beginning with the guidelines. It may also be very helpful to explain that equal health benefits can be gained from three, 10-minute bouts of moderate exercise. For many clients, a 10-minute walk may seem more manageable to fit into their schedule than 30 continuous minutes and is therefore an excellent way to begin an exercise program. Many individuals progress to longer sessions but some remain with three, 10-minute bouts. The strategies described below will give a better indication of how to implement these exercise recommendations.

Stage-Matched Strategies

Earlier, we presented the staging algorithm to determine your client's motivational stage of readiness for change. This information can be used to better determine what types of strategies can be used to promote your client's physical activity. It has been shown that individuals who are in the earlier stages of change, precontemplation and contemplation, are more likely to use what are called the cognitive processes of change, which include increasing knowledge and comprehending the benefits. As your clients progress or if they are starting in preparation or action, they are more likely to be engaging in what are called the behavioral processes of change, which include enlisting social support and substituting alternatives (Marcus & Forsyth, 2003). If you are able to target the strategies you use to an individual's stage of change, you are able to meet the individual at his or her own level of readiness, which can promote motivation and adherence to the goals you set together. See Table 20.2 for examples of stage-matched strategies you can use with your clients.

Decisional Balance

The stages of change model suggests that the decision to engage in a behavior is one in which an individual must determine if the benefits, or pros, outweigh the barriers, or cons (Marcus & Forsyth, 2003). If the pros outweigh the cons, the individual is more likely to engage in the behavior. Typically the more pros and the fewer cons that are endorsed for a behavior, the more advanced an individual is likely to be in his or her stage of change.

Benefits

One motivating technique for promoting activity is to have a client list the benefits or outcomes he or she expects to achieve from being physically active. To do this, you might have clients simply list their perceived benefits on an index card that they can easily refer to at a later time. Some benefits might be as follows: "I will feel better about myself." "I will have more energy." "My health will improve." "I will be less stressed." "I will be a role model for others." These benefits will be important to identify to promote activity but will also be important to come back to if a person starts to lose motivation for becoming physically active. Encouraging clients to revisit their original list of benefits can assist them in remembering why physical activity was important to them, thereby reinforcing their commitment to adherence.

Barriers

In addition to identifying the benefits to physical activity, it is also important to identify an individual's barriers to physical activity. Earlier, we discussed some of the more common barriers to physical activity. If a client's barriers are not addressed, then becoming physically active is unlikely. It will be important to help your clients learn the problem-solving strategies described below to learn how to deal with these barriers to initiating physical activity and to deal with new or continued barriers to maintain their activity level. One simple means of assessing barriers is to have a client write them down on an index card. This list can then become the starting place for a conversation about overcoming the barriers.

Problem Solving

One technique for solving problems is to follow four steps as symbolized by the acronym IDEA (Marcus & Forsyth, 2003). The first step is to *Identify* the problem. It is important to have the client try to assess and describe the problem as fully as possible. The next step is to *Develop* solutions for the problem in a brainstorming session. In this step, the client is not evaluating the practicalities of the solutions but rather simply trying to generate as many solutions as possible no matter how seemingly unrealistic. The next step is to *Evaluate* the solutions. This is the point at which the client determines which of the solutions are more realistic than the others and implements the solution or solutions that seem most appropriate. In the final step, the client has to *Analyze* the solution to determine if it was effective. Not all solutions will work as intended. It will be important to reevaluate the problem if necessary and refine the solutions. This process not only helps clients to learn to overcome obstacles that they have identified when initiating physical activity but also provides the skills to overcome obstacles that may threaten exercise adherence in the future.

Table 20.2.   Stage-Matched Strategies

Stage	Stage-Specific Goal	Sample Stage-Specific Strategies
Precontemplation	Help client to begin *thinking* about becoming physically active	✓ Assess and discuss the pros and cons of exercise ✓ Educate on the PA benefits including reduced risk of CVD, hypertension, cholesterol, osteoporosis ✓ Assess barriers to PA such as lack of time, lack of enjoyment, expense of equipment, fear of injury ✓ Set specific, realistic goals (e.g., read article about PA)
Contemplation	Increase the likelihood that the individual will take steps to become physically active	✓ Consider the pros and cons of PA ✓ Educate about starting a PA program ✓ Advise how to make PA part of daily life ✓ Decide on activities that are a good match to lifestyle ✓ Set specific, realistic goals (e.g., buy pair of walking shoes, talk to family members about exercise plan, or walk for 5 minutes) ✓ Set up reward plan for exercise (e.g., if I exercise for 10 minutes 3 times next week, I will rent a movie) ✓ Elicit social support for being physically active
Preparation	Increase exercise to the recommended levels (30 minutes or more of PA on most, preferably all days of the week)	✓ Many of the strategies from the contemplation stage can be applied ✓ Should carefully consider the goal differences between the stages ✓ Key is to overcome barriers that prevent the patient from progressing from some to regular activity (e.g., problem solve overcoming barrier of bad weather or unexpected events at work or home) ✓ Set specific, realistic goals that are daily, weekly, and/or monthly exercise goals ✓ Self-monitor activity
Action	To maintain their PA	✓ Identify risk factors for future relapse (e.g., vacations, stressful life events, illness, boredom of the PA routine) ✓ Set specific goals, both short- and long-term goals ✓ Can set secondary gain goals (e.g., decrease blood pressure) ✓ Self-monitor activity
Maintenance	To maintain their PA	✓ Identify any additional risk factors for relapse ✓ If relapsed in the past, identify what caused the client to stop exercising and what helped getting started again ✓ Continue to set goals and monitor exercise (e.g., set goals to do new activities to decrease risk of boredom)

NOTE: CVD, cardiovascular disease; PA, physical activity.

Confidence

Another critical area to address in exercise adherence is a client's confidence in his or her abilities to be active (Bandura, 1997). Confidence, or self-efficacy, can be increased in several ways (Bandura, 1997). First, verbal encouragement can be helpful. Thus, taking the time to address physical activity with your clients and encouraging them to become active or maintain their activity are important. Second, confidence can be built by watching role models. So you may want to encourage your clients to identify individuals in their life who are active and to learn from them how they first became active, what they like about exercising, and how they find the time to be active. Learning how others have been successful helps a client build his or her own confidence. Third, correctly interpreting physical and emotional symptoms can build confidence, particularly when moving from an early, sedentary stage such as precontemplation or contemplation to preparation or action. Sedentary individuals may incorrectly interpret muscle soreness for an injury or get discouraged if they do not perform as well as they did when they were younger. If you can work with a client initially to provide information, such as starting slowly, building endurance, or warming up to avoid muscle soreness, it will help to build his or her confidence. Finally, one of the most important factors for increasing confidence is practicing the behavior and learning to overcome obstacles. Thus by problem solving and setting goals as we will describe below, clients learn that they are able to adhere to an exercise routine and this knowledge will, in turn, increase their confidence and therefore serve to maintain their activity.

Goal Setting

Setting goals is another critical step in the process of adopting and maintaining physical activity. There are several characteristics of a goal that should be followed to maximize impact. A goal should be specific, short term, challenging, and realistic (Bandura, 1997). We recommend that you have clients write down a goal, or action plan, for the following week. An example of a goal that meets these criteria for someone who has been completely sedentary is "I will walk 10 minutes per day, three weekdays next week on my lunch break." If you contrast this goal with the common goals clients might make of "I will start walking," you can see that this first goal is more specific, short term, and seems realistic. For someone who has not been active, it is important to set manageable goals. If previously sedentary clients set the goal of 30 minutes of walking 5 days per week, you might ask them "Is this realistic for you? Describe to me when you think you will do your activity." If they do not appear to have solid answers to these questions, we recommend that you let them know that working up to that goal might be a better idea and to think of how to start off with a goal that is more likely to be accomplished. As a client progresses, it will be important to provide feedback and reinforcement for meeting goals as well as to work together to establish new goals that challenge that individual. If barriers appear to prevent accomplishing the goals, the problem-solving strategies discussed above can be implemented to address these barriers and to set realistic goals. Goal setting can maintain motivation and physical activity behavior and therefore exercise adherence.

Enjoyment

Another aspect of exercise adherence is making sure that your clients do activities that they enjoy (King, Taylor, Haskell, & DeBusk, 1988; Marcus & Forsyth, 2003). If the activity is not pleasurable, the dropout rate is likely to be fairly high. You can have clients identify an activity that they really enjoy or identify ways to try and make an activity more enjoyable. For example, a client might enjoy walking but get bored staying in his or her neighborhood. To solve this, he or she might try to think of a place he or she can walk that is pleasurable such as a park or trail, he or she might try to walk with friends or family, he or she might walk listening to music or a recorded book. For clients who have trouble identifying any activities they enjoy, we suggest having them think back to activities they may have enjoyed in the past. Finally, it will be important to assess this over time. If an activity becomes monotonous, other activities should be added or substituted to keep physical activity pleasurable so that it remains something that can be looked forward to, thereby making it reinforcing in and of itself.

Social Support

Another strategy that is important for exercise adherence is finding social support (Sallis, Grossman, Pinski, Patterson, & Nader, 1987). This can take several forms, and we suggest that you work with your clients to think of multiple ways in which they can enlist social support. For example, a client might walk with a friend, discuss the possibility of taking a half-hour to walk at lunch with a boss in exchange for working an extra half-hour, find someone to provide child care while walking, or ask someone to praise him or her if they notice him or her being active. Identifying many strategies for encouraging social support will be an important means of promoting and maintaining physical activity (Blair et al., 2001).

Relapse Prevention

As described by Nezu, Nezu, and Perri (this volume), relapse prevention requires that the issue of promoting adherence be addressed (Marlatt & Gordon, 1985). As we have discussed earlier, physical activity is a multifaceted behavior. One important step in working with clients is to help them try to identify, in advance, situations during which activity will be difficult. For instance, an upcoming vacation might be a situation that would disrupt an established exercise routine. Identifying this situation in advance and problem-solving solutions may help to prevent a cease in activity. Thus, you could work with the client to problem solve the barriers and set goals specific to their vacation. However, there will be times when clients are not able to exercise for a period of time. It will be important to let them know that although stopping activity is not recommended, situations may arise that make activity impossible for a period of time. What will be critical is to initiate their exercise regimen again as soon as possible and to not relapse into a sedentary lifestyle. Tracking their activity again, setting goals, and problem-solving barriers are all strategies to prevent a permanent relapse.

Case Example

The following is a sample of a few sessions between a health practitioner (P) and her client (C).

Session 1

P: I would like to talk to you for a while today about your current participation in physical activity and some of the benefits of physical activity. Physical activity reduces the risk of heart disease, stroke, diabetes, some cancers, obesity, depression, and anxiety. Therefore, it is something I would like to work with you to increase. Are you currently physically active?

C: No, I don't really do any activity except for stuff around the house.

P: What kinds of activities do you do around the house?

C: Housecleaning and gardening.

P: Does any of the cleaning or gardening reach a moderate intensity where your heart rate or breathing increases?

C: No, not really.

P: Do you intend to become more physically active?

C: I guess so, if I could find a way to fit it into my schedule.

P: Have there been times in the past when you have exercised regularly?

C: Yes. When I was younger I used to walk with friends and play softball sometimes. Now that I have two kids and work full-time I just don't have the time anymore.

P: Well, we can look to see if there are any windows of time where you can fit something in. I would like you to start this week by choosing three days to keep track of your activity. Please write your activity down in 2-hour blocks on two weekdays and one weekend. Write everything down, including time spent with your children, cleaning, driving, watching television, and so forth. Then, next week when you come in, we can take a look at it together and come up with a plan of how you can add some physical activity into your schedule for the week. I am also wondering what you think are the pros and cons of exercise for you. I am going to hand you an index card. On one side please list your pros and on the other list your cons.

C: OK.

P: All right, why don't you tell me what you have listed for some of your benefits, or pros, to being physically active.

C: I would like to improve my health, feel less stressed, improve my energy, and lose weight.

P: Great. Now what are some of your cons?

C: I don't think I have enough time, I don't have child care for the kids, and I am worried I may not be able to have the stamina I used to have.

P: That is a good start. Over the next week I would like you to start by keeping track of your activity and if you think of additional pros and cons, add them to the lists. Don't worry about doing any exercise this first week.

Session 2

P: How did it go writing down your activity?

C: well, it took a while to just write stuff down, but I think it was good.

P: Really, how so?

C: I realized that I spend a lot of time running errands each day and I sit down more than I realized too!

P: It isn't unusual to make such discoveries. That is why we had you write everything down. Now, based on what you learned, if I asked you to look for a place to decrease a time when you aren't active and substitute a 5-minute walk, do you think you could find one?

C: Well, I was thinking that if I go to the grocery store near the park, I could take my kids for a walk before shopping.

P: That's a great idea and just the kind of thing I was hoping you might be able to do. Are there other similar ideas?

C: I guess I could take the kids in the double stroller with me for a walk like that two other times before I do errands.

P: Well, you have done a great job of identifying three times to do a 5-minute walk. Do you think this will be realistic for you?

C: I think so. It won't be easy but since I have to get them in the stroller anyhow and the park is a nice place to walk, it might even be fun.

P: Great. What kinds of things might get in your way?

C: Well, if it rains that wouldn't be fun with the kids.

P: If that happens, what could you do instead?

C: Hmm. I used to have an exercise tape that I enjoyed. Maybe I could use that on the days when it is raining.

P: How many minutes would you do that for?

C: There are different length sessions. If I remember correctly there is a quick one for 10 minutes. I should be able to fit that in.

P: That sounds good as a backup plan. It is important to try and think about the obstacles in advance and make plans so those obstacles don't take you by surprise. I would also like you to think about talking to someone you know about becoming active, maybe you have a friend who is active and you can get tips from her, or find some articles about walking to read from the internet or a magazine. Is that possible?

C: Sure, I do have a friend who I can talk to—that will be even easier than fitting in exercise, and, I already have figured out how to do that!

P: Good. So, to summarize, for this week you will try walking for 5 minutes with your kids before your errands or using your exercise tape in the event of rain. You are also going to talk to your friend and get some exercise tips. Also, I would like you to keep track of the activity you do this week. Write down the day of the week, the activity you do, and how long you do it for.

C: OK.

Session 3

C: Here is my log. It wasn't as good as I had hoped.

P: Well, I am really glad you worked on it and brought it in today, let's take a look. It looks like you took two walks for 10 minutes each. How did that go?

C: It was fine, the kids liked it and it didn't take up too much extra time. I just didn't get a third day in because it rained. When I put my exercise tape in I realized that the quick version was too advanced, I couldn't keep up so I got frustrated and turned it off.

P: That is good information for us. When you start exercising again after a while it is important to start slowly and work up to your previous fitness and stamina levels. Let's think then if you can come up with some other ideas for bad weather. List anything at first as a brainstorm and we can evaluate the ideas later.

C: I could walk in the rain, buy a new video, dance with the kids, join a gym, walk in the mall, or walk a different day.

P: OK, great. Now, of those, which are more realistic for you? Which do you think you can afford, fit into your schedule, and will enjoy?

C: I really don't like walking in the rain; I would rather walk another day. I guess that would be my first choice but if it was an entire week of rain I could buy another, easier video to have as a backup plan.

P: That sounds good. Let's have you try that this next week and we'll revisit that again. Now, did you talk to your friend?

C: Yes, she gave me some tips but her kids are older so I'm not sure they will be helpful.

P: Was there anything that applied to you?

C: I guess just hearing that she struggled at first and now she really has made exercise a priority and part of her life. She said it gives her energy, I'm not sure if I believe it but that would be nice.

P: Often people who become regularly active find exercise does help their energy. So, even if you are feeling tired you might remind yourself that if energy is an important benefit to you, exercising will help you with this goal. Let's talk now about your goals for next week. Can you still exercise three times per week but increase the minutes?

C: I was thinking of doing something like that. Maybe I could move up to 15 minutes.

P: Will that be realistic for you?

C: Actually, I think it will. Once I get the kids strapped in, it is almost easier to go a little longer than to stop after only 5 minutes.

P: Great. Also, do you have anyone you can talk to about exercising or a friend or family member who can join you?

C: I thought about asking my neighbor to come to the park with me but I have been timing it around my errands. It might get really complicated.

P: Maybe it is something to keep in mind, particularly as we add on a couple of more days in the future. Having someone to walk with makes it more of a commitment and also makes it more fun. So, for this week you will exercise three times for 15 minutes, buy a new video, and think if there are other people with whom you can talk for exercise tips, maybe some mothers with small children like you.

C: Sounds good.

This case example shows the use of self-monitoring, decision-making, stage-specific strategies for someone in contemplation, goal setting, improving confidence, problem solving, and attention to social support and enjoyment of the activities. The sessions would progress from here by attending to continued goal setting, confidence building, and relapse prevention.

Summary

In summary, physical activity has a host of health benefits but only 25% of the population is active enough to realize these benefits. We discussed some of the common barriers and assessment issues as well as provided some adherence-promoting strategies that have been proven to be effective. These strategies include self-monitoring, using stage-matched techniques, decisional balance, problem solving, goal setting, confidence building, social support, enjoyment, and relapse prevention. All of these strategies can be used to help clients gradually achieve the CDC/ACSM guidelines of at least 5 days per week of moderate intensity activity for at least 30 minutes each time.

References

American College of Sports Medicine. (1990). American College of Sports Medicine position stand: The recommended quantity and quality of exercise for developing and maintaining cardiorespiratory and muscular fitness in healthy adults. *Medicine and Science in Sport and Exercise, 22*(2), 265–274.

American College of Sports Medicine. (2000). *ACSM's guidelines for exercise testing and prescription* (6th ed.). Baltimore: Williams & Wilkins.

Bandura, A. (1997). *Self-efficacy: The exercise of control.* New York: W. H. Freeman.

Blair, S. N., Dunn, A. L., Marcus, B. H., Carpenter, R. A., & Jaret, P. (2001). *Active living every day. 20 Weeks to lifelong vitality.* Human Kinetics: Champaign, IL.

King, A. C., Taylor, C. B., Haskell, W. L., & DeBusk, R. F. (1988). Strategies for increasing early adherence to and long-term maintenance of home-based exercise training in healthy middle-aged men and women. *American Journal of Cardiology, 61,* 628–632.

Marcus, B. H., & Forsyth, L. H. (2003). *Motivating people to be physically active.* Human Kinetics: Champaign, IL.

Marcus, B. H., & Lewis, B. A. (2003). Stages of motivational readiness to change physical activity behavior. *President's Council on Physical Fitness and Sports Research Digest, 4*(1), 1–8.

Marks, James S., & Caspersen, Carl J. (Eds.). (1997). A collection of physical activity questionnaires for health-related research [Special issue]. *Medicine and Science in Sports and Exercise, 29*(6), S89–S100.

Marlatt, G. A., & Gordon, J. R. (1985). *Relapse prevention: Maintenance strategies in the treatment of addictive behaviors.* New York: Guilford Press.

Pate, R. R., Pratt, M., Blair, S. N., Haskell, W. L., Macera, C. A., Bouchard, C., et al. (1995). Physical activity and public health: A recommendation from the Centers for Disease Control and Prevention and the American College of Sports Medicine. *Journal of the American Medical Association, 273,* 402–407.

Sallis, J. F., Grossman, R. M., Pinski, R. B., Patterson, T. L., & Nader, P. R. (1987). The development of scales to measure social support for diet and exercise behaviors. *Preventive Medicine, 16,* 825–836.

Trost, S. G., Owen, N., Bauman, A., Sallis, J. F., & Brown, W. (2002). Correlates of adults' participation in physical activity: Review and update. *Medicine and Science in Sports and Exercise, 34*(12), 1996–2001.

Tudor-Locke, C. (2002). Taking steps towards increased physical activity: Using pedometers to measure and motivate. *President's Council on Physical Fitness and Sports Research Digest, 3,* 17.

U.S. Department of Health and Human Services. (1996). *Physical activity and health: A report from the surgeon general.* Atlanta, GA: Author.

U.S. Department of Health and Human Services. (2000). *Healthy people 2010.* Washington, DC: Author.

21

Adherence to Dietary Recommendations

Barbara S. McCann

Dietary recommendations are frequently provided within the context of giving medical advice. Such recommendations are important in the management of a number of medical conditions. The most common of these include diabetes, hyperlipidemia, hypertension, and obesity. Even surgical treatments for obesity require substantial changes in daily dietary practices for surgery to be successful. This chapter provides a step-by-step description of procedures useful for adherence to dietary recommendations. Because of the widespread problem of obesity and obesity-related diseases in the United States (including the aforementioned diabetes, hyperlipidemia, and hypertension), recent interest in surgical approaches to weight loss, and the irony of requiring strict dietary adherence following surgery in individuals who heretofore have been extremely unsuccessful in controlling their food intake, many of the comments, suggestions, and examples contained herein will be made with the assumption that the primary goal of adherence to dietary recommendations is weight loss.

Experiences from clinical and research settings have demonstrated time and again that it is difficult for patients to follow dietary recommendations. This is due to many factors reflecting a range of biopsychosocial issues. These include intra- and interpersonal factors, economic constraints, cultural preferences regarding food, social influences, environmental constraints, and a host of psychological factors that are, as yet, poorly understood. Current systems of health delivery also affect patients' ability to follow dietary recommendations. For example, many insurance plans cover few or no interventions aimed at achieving weight loss or, in some cases, provide coverage only for more drastic interventions (such as weight loss surgery).

Common Adherence Problems

Virtually any type of dietary change for the purpose of improving health or managing a chronic condition requires one or both of the following: changing (usually decreasing) the quantity of food consumed and making appropriate food choices based on nutritional advice. Decreasing the amount of food consumed is required for weight loss because this is an effective means of reducing total daily caloric intake. Patients are sometimes encouraged to limit their intake of specific macronutrients, such as sodium (in the case of hypertension), protein (in renal disease), or saturated fat (in hyperlipidemia). Dietary recommendations for the purpose of losing weight usually require both types of changes, with patients frequently counseled to limit their intake of dietary fat as well as decrease the amount of food consumed. Because dietary fat is calorie dense, limiting dietary fat usually produces an overall reduction in total caloric intake.

It stands to reason then that the most common adherence problems seen when recommending dietary changes are consumption of too much food or selection of the "wrong" types of food. Rarely, patients may take recommendations to the extreme, by severely limiting food intake or the intake of specific macronutrients. Given advice to cut back on food intake to limit weight loss, many patients initially start out with the best of intentions. They may successfully decrease snacking between meals, cut back on second helpings, and limit portion sizes. Advice to limit sodium intake may prompt some to diligently avoid salty foods such as potato chips, olives, and prepackaged meals. Most patients, however, quickly encounter several barriers to following dietary recommendations and within a period of several days to several weeks may find themselves returning to their more familiar eating habits. Similar problems are encountered when attempting to limit the intake of specific macronutrients. Patients readily return to entrenched dietary practices.

Barriers to Adherence

Barriers to dietary adherence are often environmental. Patients sometimes find that appropriate foods are not readily available. For example, patients from our hospital, the majority of whom are living below the poverty level, must rely on food banks to supplement their monthly food purchases. Food banks typically have a very limited selection available. Grocery stores in impoverished areas often have a more limited selection of products than stores in affluent areas.

Internal cues also thwart efforts to adhere to dietary recommendations. The most salient of these are hunger cues. Many emotional states trigger consumption of "taboo" foods in individuals who are attempting to follow dietary recommendations. Generally speaking, patients report ignoring dietary recommendations when they experience emotional extremes. For example, patients will often overeat, or eat calorie-dense foods, when they feel sad, depressed, or angry. Conversely, patients report tossing dietary recommendations aside when attending parties, special occasions, or other celebrations where one would expect to find positive affect. Ironically, patients also report ignoring dietary recommendations when feeling bored, tired, lethargic, or indifferent. It would seem that there is no limit to the range of emotional states that can interfere with following solid dietary recommendations.

Social factors have a major impact on patients' ability to follow dietary recommendations. People often report dietary lapses in the context of watching others eating or being offered food by others or while attending social events in which food is present. Many patients describe family get-togethers as occasions for setting aside dietary advice.

Assessing and Enhancing Dietary Adherence

A review of numerous research studies and treatment materials reveals a number of common components designed to promote adherence to dietary recommendations and maximize maintenance of these changes. A practical framework for thinking about the organization of these various components is useful. In the following sections, we provide an overview of the phases commonly used to promote adherence to dietary recommendations. Not every patient will require all the phases, and some patients may need to repeat many of these phases over the course of their lives. Following a description of the phases, the specific treatment components will be detailed.

Treatment Phases

In the *introductory phase*, the patient discovers and accepts that dietary changes are needed and enters into a period of knowledge acquisition. An important first step is *motivational enhancement* so that the need for change is accepted by the patient. All dietary recommendations require some degree of *nutrition education*, and the specific requirements of a given set of dietary changes can be quite complex. Some rudimentary *self-monitoring* and *goal setting* are often introduced at this point. In many cases, patients who feel motivated to pursue dietary recommendations, have a good understanding of the changes needed, and have relatively solid support from family members are able to make a sufficient number of improvements in their dietary habits to effect significant improvements in their health.

If substantial changes aren't observed following the introductory phase, a brief *assessment phase* is generally needed to identify unique problem areas that patients may be encountering. This generally requires evaluation by a dietitian and may require the additional services of someone trained in more advanced behavioral issues. The assessment phase may require additional *dietary assessment* and self-monitoring. A *behavioral interview* may be needed to help identify underlying psychosocial problems or psychiatric difficulties and highlight areas that need to be addressed during the *intensive implementation phase*.

The intensive implementation phase will generally require frequent meetings between the patient and a health care provider. Components commonly used during the intensive implementation phase include goal setting and self-monitoring and additional use of motivational enhancement strategies and nutrition education. During this phase, *stimulus control*, *problem solving*, *cognitive strategies*, and *relapse prevention* are generally introduced and covered at length. Special topics such as *social support* and *underlying emotional issues* may need to be addressed during this phase.

Once patients have achieved a comfortable level of success at following dietary recommendations, either at the end of the introductory phase or during the intensive implementation phase, they are ready to enter into a *maintenance phase*. Research to date on a variety of dietary recommendations has demonstrated that longer treatment programs are associated with better maintenance of new behaviors. A variety of approaches to achieve extended contact can be used: telephone contact, mail and e-mail contact, contact in person, and even having patients form their own support networks for ongoing monitoring of dietary changes (peer support). In many cases, the most practical format for continued support is in-person contact with a member of the health care team. During this phase, patients are seen during intervals generally ranging in frequency from every 1 to 6 months. Any of the specific treatment components may be used during this phase, depending on the patient's progress. In some situations, problems surface during the maintenance phase that require re-entry into the assessment phase or *intensive intervention phase*. Often, setbacks due to illness or other major life changes, or "falling off the wagon" while vacationing, will lead to sustained problems with maintaining dietary recommendations.

Specific Treatment Components

Motivational Enhancement

Initial dietary recommendations to improve health are usually delivered in the physician's office. Patients often hope, and even expect, their physicians to come up with medications that will alleviate their ills. Patients with severe obesity are increasingly looking to surgical interventions to address their health problems. Suggestions for renewed efforts at diet and exercise fall short of these expectations. This calls for considerable skill in delivering the health message in a way that will interest the patient in behavior change. Motivational enhancement or motivational interviewing skills are useful during the introductory phase of treatment. Such skills also are useful throughout treatment, at any point when the patient's interest or commitment begins to wane.

Nutrition Education

The cornerstone of all dietary interventions with individuals is nutrition education. At a minimum, patients are provided with verbal instructions to cut back on food intake or on specific macronutrients. Often, such vague and general instructions fail to produce any noticeable improvement. Providing patients with written materials detailing the required changes is an improvement over this approach. Ideally, patients will be provided with an opportunity to have one or more sessions with a dietitian.

Patients often have a wide range of misconceptions about dietary recommendations. The market is flooded with products touting health claims that are often misleading. Dietitians can assist patients in identifying overly optimistic health claims, in reading and interpreting often complex nutritional labeling, and in selecting the types of foods most appropriate in managing their health condition. Dietitians can also provide a wealth of information regarding shopping strategies and methods of food preparation, making it easier for patients to follow dietary recommendations. Simply put, without knowing what, when, or how much to eat, patients will be unable to profit from dietary recommendations. Dietitians can help fill this knowledge gap. Ongoing visits with dietitians enable patients to address new questions and

assumptions that may arise in the course of making dietary changes.

Self-Monitoring

Self-monitoring of dietary intake is an essential component of programs promoting dietary change. Self-monitoring generally takes one of two forms: recording of certain macronutrients, such as grams of fat, calories, sodium, or protein, or an exchange system, in which participants are given a recommended daily number of servings of various food groups, along with examples of serving sizes.

Each approach has its advantages and disadvantages. The advantage of recording specific macronutrient quantities lies in its apparent precision. If weight reduction is the overarching goal, carefully recording caloric intake will go a long way toward helping patients attain weight loss. One reason for this is self-monitoring of any behavior will affect the frequency of the behavior being monitored. The downside of recording macronutrient quantities is that it is very labor-intensive. Keeping track of calories, for example, requires careful reading of labels and frequently necessitates carrying around a small reference booklet for estimating the caloric content of items that don't carry nutritional labels. Handheld devices for tracking calories and grams of fat hold some promise of added convenience. These are, however, limited by the extent to which the databases on which they are based are complete and whether they are user-friendly overall. The exchange system is often regarded as less challenging for people to use than counting macronutrients. In exchange systems, people typically eat a maximum number of servings of given food groups per day. By recording these throughout the day, people can avoid exceeding their maximum number of servings. The limitation of exchange systems is that they are frequently inaccurate because of the wide variety of foods available to the public. Often, exchange systems are based on standard serving sizes that are much smaller than what people are served in restaurants or dish out to their own families. Thus, patients may feel that they are dutifully following dietary recommendations when in fact they are greatly exceeding recommended daily intakes.

Several things are important to keep in mind in order to make self-monitoring successful and useful to the patient. First, patients need to understand that self-monitoring instruments are tools, not "report cards." That is, patients should use them throughout the day to aid in directing their food selections. Self-monitoring records that are completed the night before meeting with the health care provider serve no useful purpose whatsoever. The importance of accurate self-monitoring needs to be stressed throughout all phases of treatment in which it is used. Frequently, lulls in patient progress can be overcome by paying close attention to the accuracy of self-monitoring. Finally, it is extremely important that clinicians pay close attention to self-monitoring records at each visit. This reinforces the importance of such records in the patient's mind and provides early opportunities for corrective nutrition education. Despite its limitations and challenges, regular self-monitoring has been identified as a key factor in dietary adherence in a number of health conditions. Self-monitoring of diet is often combined with self-monitoring of the activities or settings in which eating takes place. Such information is valuable in implementing a number of other intervention components, including goal setting and stimulus control.

Goal Setting

Once the patient's initial dietary intake is known, specific goals can be established. Goals may be based on current recommendations for specific conditions, such as the National Cholesterol Education Program guidelines, or general guidelines such as the *Dietary Guidelines for Americans*. When weight loss is a goal of the intervention, specific calorie and fat intakes may be recommended based on ideal body weight, desired percentage of weight loss, or the participant's desired target. Other goals may target maximum intakes of calories, fats, sodium, or protein.

Dietary goals do not have to be based on stringent monitoring of grams of fat, calories, or number of servings of numerous food groups. The National Cancer Institute's "5 a Day" program is one such example. In this program, participants are simply encouraged to consume five (or more) servings of fruits and vegetables per day. Through careful review of patients' self-monitoring records, clinicians can often suggest very specific week-by-week goals that can be easily met by patients and bring about rapid progress. For example, a patient who tends to skip meals during the day can be instructed to strive toward eating three meals and two snacks per day. This particular goal is useful in addressing the onset of sudden intense hunger that may precipitate poor food choices or binge eating.

As with self-monitoring, it is important that clinicians review patients' progress toward goals at each visit. In many instances, patients will think of goals in terms of specific goals for weight loss. Although there is nothing wrong with establishing weight loss goals, such overarching desired effects of treatment should not be confused with the discrete, attainable goals that need to be established throughout the treatment in order to shape patients' behavior and provide them with several small successes along the way. Also, it is important to keep in mind that patients often have weight loss goals for themselves that are unrealistic. Patients can often achieve substantial health benefits from losing relatively small amounts of weight (e.g., 10% of starting weight) but would often need to lose much more (e.g., 50% or more of starting weight) in order to reach the elusive "ideal body weight."

Dietary Assessment

The initial assessment of dietary intake, before initiating a dietary intervention, enables the clinician to determine the individual participant's "starting point." Traditional methods of dietary assessment include multiday food diaries, 24-hour recalls, and food frequency questionnaires. On the basis of this assessment, individually tailored goals can be established. Each dietary assessment method has its advantages and disadvantages. Food frequency questionnaires can provide an estimate of dietary intake without being overly detailed and labor-intensive. They, however, provide only a global picture of dietary intake. Multiday food diaries are fairly precise (when completed correctly) but are subject to patients' desires to "look good." Patients will generally improve their food intake while completing food diaries. Their disadvantage is that they are quite time-consuming to complete and time-consuming to analyze. Twenty-four-hour food recalls, in which patients are asked to recall all foods eaten in the past 24 hours, have the advantage of little or no prospective recording bias. They are, however, subject to inaccurate recall, usually consisting of failure to remember items (and therefore underestimating food intake). Also, they may not be particularly representative of a person's overall intake.

In conducting a dietary assessment, it is important to keep in mind that underreporting of food intake is common. Women are more likely to underreport dietary intake than men, and underreporting is also associated with greater body weight. This phenomenon is not restricted to the reporting of the quantity of food consumed. Comparisons between self-reported sodium intake and urinary excretion of sodium indicate that people with high blood pressure frequently underreport their intake of salt.

Behavioral Interview

I use the term *behavioral interview* to refer to a variety of data-gathering methods that may be needed to identify specific problem areas and assist with treatment planning. It is important to differentiate a behavioral interview from *nutrition assessment*. The nutrition assessment will generally be used to evaluate the total calories consumed and the macronutrient content of the diet. The nutrition assessment gets at the end product of a set of behaviors. These behaviors include such things as grocery shopping, preferences regarding time and location of eating, food selection, and food preparation. Although a good nutritional assessment will address many of these behaviors, the task of linking these behaviors to the environment and to underlying emotional and cognitive constructs will usually be left to the behavioral interview. During the behavioral interview, the interviewer will attempt to identify factors that influence poor food choices and overconsumption of food.

More advanced interviewing techniques may be employed during the behavioral interview. If an underlying psychiatric disorder is suspected, for example, a formal evaluation by a psychiatrist or psychologist may be needed. This will be useful in identifying ancillary issues, such as the need for medication management of depression, to increase the likelihood of success in following dietary recommendations. Specific eating disorder interviews may be needed if binge eating or other eating disorders are suspected.

Stimulus Control

Stimulus control refers to limiting exposure to settings or situations that are associated with eating inappropriate foods or inappropriate quantities of food. Generally, stimulus control strategies are introduced early in treatment. Stimulus control generally refers to altering or structuring the environment in such a way as to decrease the likelihood of falling back into older, maladaptive behaviors. For example, a patient who finds it difficult to refrain from snacking on cookies at the end of the workday may benefit from storing such food items in a pantry or cupboard or refrain from buying them altogether. A patient who cannot refrain from dipping into the secretary's candy dish on the way to the mailroom may wish to consider a different route in order to avoid temptation. Other stimulus control strategies that are useful for adherence to dietary recommendations include positioning oneself at a considerable distance from buffet tables, avoiding grocery shopping while hungry, and shopping with preprepared grocery lists.

Problem Solving

Problem solving training generally entails clinician- or patient-generated descriptions of scenarios in which adherence may be problematic, followed by discussion of ways in which adherence can be maintained in such situations. An important element of problem solving training is to encourage participants to use these skills whenever they encounter situations that threaten adherence. Problem solving requires several key elements. The first of these is careful identification of the problem. Although at first glance this may seem relatively straightforward, it can be easy to rush past this step. Suppose a patient states that his problem is he is too tired when he gets home from work to cook and therefore relies too heavily on picking up meals at fast food restaurants on the drive home. The novice clinician may jump in at this point and suggest strategies such as preparing meals ahead of time or having several "quick-fix" recipes on hand for such occasions. Further assessment, however, may reveal that in this case the patient's failure to eat lunch on a consistent basis is leaving him both hungry and exhausted by the end of the day. This may suggest a set of other strategies altogether, such as packing lunch and a healthy midafternoon snack each morning before heading off to work.

Once a problem has been accurately identified, the patient and clinician should come up with several potential solutions. It is important for the clinician to encourage creative brainstorming here. Otherwise, patients may come up with a very limited set of potential solutions based on previous failed attempts at solving the problem. It is sometimes helpful to encourage patients to come up with outrageous solutions (such as hiring a personal chef), because these may lead to novel but practical solutions (such as sharing cooking duties during the week with a close friend or neighbor).

Problem-solving solutions must be tested and evaluated before the process is complete. This requires careful attention to assigning practical homework between sessions. Patients should be encouraged to choose one or more solutions to try out, describe when and where they will attempt the solution during the coming week, and then asked about their experience with the problem-solving attempt at the following session. If the solution does not work, this should be addressed in a similar problem-solving fashion.

Cognitive Strategies

Techniques adapted from cognitive therapy are frequently useful in helping individuals follow dietary recommendations. As noted earlier, one purpose of the behavioral interview is to identify cognitive and emotional antecedents to poor food choices. Several cognitive strategies can be used to modify these antecedents. One strategy is to help patients identify self-statements that give them "permission" to make poor food choices. For example, a patient who is feeling irritable because he has lost three quarters in a washing machine may find himself purchasing a candy bar from a vending machine with the accompanying thought, "My day is going so lousy. I deserve a treat to perk myself up." It is helpful to encourage patients to come up with more adaptive statements such as, "Losing three quarters is a hassle. But I'm not going to let something that trivial blow my diet." Patients should be encouraged to identify maladaptive self-statements and practice modifying them. A host of similar cognitive strategies can be used to assist patients in identifying common themes that trigger undesirable behaviors.

Relapse Prevention

According to Alan Marlatt's relapse prevention model (Marlatt & George, 1984), individuals maintain perceived control over behavior until they encounter a high-risk situation that threatens control and increases the risk of relapse. Lapses are inevitable in the face of long-term dietary change. Individuals who have made dietary changes face a number of high-risk situations that can lead to lapses. Therefore, relapse prevention training is important to include prior to ending the intensive intervention phase. Relapse prevention training consists of assisting patients in predicting personally salient high-risk situations they may encounter in the future and developing several strategies for dealing with such situations. Encouraging participants to regard lapses in dietary adherence as "educational opportunities" to aid in avoiding future lapses is a key component of the training.

One goal of relapse prevention training, and indeed all treatment components, is to enhance self-efficacy for making dietary changes. Self-efficacy refers to the belief that one can execute a certain behavior required to produce particular outcomes (Bandura, 1991), and it has been shown to predict the ability to initiate and maintain changes in a variety of health-related behaviors. All the intervention elements discussed thus far enhance self-efficacy. The most critical components to enhance self-efficacy for long-term maintenance include relapse prevention and problem solving. In addition, during all phases of treatment, patients should be encouraged to test new skills (e.g., ordering low-fat food in a restaurant) to enhance their confidence in their ability to maintain dietary changes.

Social Support

Social support, particularly support from spouses, is an important factor in dietary adherence. Active inclusion of the patient's spouse, or the individual in the household who is most responsible for cooking, shopping, and meal planning, is important. An incidental benefit of any dietary change is that changing the diet of one family member may have beneficial effects on other family members as well. As the entire family shifts toward healthier eating habits, the task of the identified patient becomes much easier.

Underlying Emotional Issues

Underlying emotional or psychiatric issues that may interfere with the patient's ability to adhere to dietary recommendations are often identified early on in treatment. In the case of psychiatric disorders, patients may benefit from a referral to an appropriate treatment provider to manage such conditions. Binge eating is fairly common among patients who need to lose weight in order to improve their health. Many of the strategies discussed thus far in this chapter can be used to address the rapid consumption of large amounts of food when feeling distressed. To do so, it is important to accurately identify binge-eating episodes and determine their antecedents (behavioral interview), alter environmental contingencies to reduce the likelihood that binges will occur (stimulus control), and modify self-statements that may precede binges (cognitive strategies).

Case Example

John, aged 45 years, had always been heavy. His mother had gestational diabetes during her pregnancy with him, and he weighed 14 pounds when he was born. He weighed between 260 and 320 pounds in high school. In spite of his weight, he was physically active and successful in high school sports. After high school, he became more sedentary and slowly but steadily started to gain weight. When he was first seen in the Weight Disorders Clinic, at age 40, he weighed 663 pounds. At 6 feet tall, his body mass index was 90 kg/m². He described significant episodes of binge eating and was consuming upward of 6,000 calories per day. He was bed bound at home and needed a wheel-chair to travel more than a few feet. John had Type 2 diabetes and hyperlipidemia, both managed with medications. He also had marked edema in his lower extremities and abdomen. He was beginning to have significant breakdown and weeping of his skin in these areas, and particularly in the scrotal area, which was quite painful. He was admitted to the inpatient unit for 1 week for further evaluation of his health and for diuresis to reduce the edema.

Once John was out of the hospital, he was evaluated by a dietitian and an endocrinologist. This represented the introductory phase of treatment. John was highly motivated to lose additional weight. Through careful assessment, his endocrinologist learned that John frequently engaged in binge eating. He referred John to our program for evaluation and treatment of his binge eating. This represented the beginning of the intensive intervention phase for John. He met weekly for 3 months with a postdoctoral fellow in clinical psychology, who addressed his binge eating with cognitive behavioral therapy. He also received monthly counseling from a dietitian. During this time, he kept daily logs of his food intake, recording fat grams and calories. He also kept track of his physical activity, which initially consisted of walking short distances. He quickly gained control of his eating habits and stopped binge eating. Less than a month after leaving the hospital, his weight was 650 pounds; much of this was probably due to diuresis during his hospital stay. By 3 months posthospitalization, John's weight was down to 632 pounds.

During his 3 months of working with the postdoctoral fellow on his binge eating, John was encouraged to continue with his detailed self-monitoring of his food intake. His therapist also worked with him on identifying high-risk situations that triggered binge eating. They worked together on identifying salient body image issues that may affect his continued progress. John and his therapist also discussed potential relapse issues that may crop up once their weekly meetings ended. Five months after John's hospitalization, his weight had decreased to 600 pounds. He was now entering into the maintenance phase.

John continued to work on increasing his physical activity level. He also kept up with his daily self-monitoring of food intake. Eight months following his initial contact with our facility, he achieved an important personal goal when his weight finally dropped below 600 pounds, to 585. He met monthly with a dietitian during this time. This level of support continued to work well for him. Nearly 1 year after he had been admitted to the hospital, his weight was down to 567 pounds. But by 15 months posthospitalization, his overall rate of weight loss had slowed down, and he was down to 552 pounds. At this point, John and his dietitian felt that his caloric consumption had probably started to creep up slightly. His trajectory of weight loss continued to plateau, with his weight reaching 542 pounds at 15 months posthospitalization. One bright spot during this plateau in his weight loss was John's ability to walk increasingly greater distances. He started taking up golf, and given his past history of competitive sports, this was an excellent match for him. A year and a half after his initial presentation, John's weight was 540 pounds, and he described himself as "addicted to golf."

Despite his overall success, John contacted me again approximately 20 months after his hospitalization. This was in keeping with John's relapse prevention plan, which encouraged him to contact us if he felt discouraged about his progress. John was particularly concerned because he had stopped self-monitoring, and he was well aware of its importance for maintaining his progress. When we started meeting again, John and I mutually decided to meet every 2 weeks. He agreed to step up his self-monitoring efforts. To increase his accuracy at self-monitoring, I encouraged John to purchase a digital food scale from a restaurant supply store. John's weight was down to 532 pounds a month later. John's renewed efforts at detailed and accurate self-monitoring revealed that his actual caloric intake had crept up to between 3,500 and 4,500 per day. Our ensuing visits were spent reviewing his self-monitoring records, identifying areas where he could improve, and problem solving for anticipated high-risk situations, such as holidays and celebrations. We also spent time addressing some increased stressors in his life, which included financial concerns and his father's deteriorating health. John's weight crept back up to 539 pounds 2 years after his initial hospitalization with us. At month 27, however, he finally broke an important barrier when his weight dropped to 529 pounds, below 530 pounds for the first time in many years. He was maintaining his weight at this level at his 30-month visit. His weight crept back up to 535 pounds in the ensuing 3 months, due to a variety of stressors including his father's continued deterioration. John remained out of touch with us for the following 7 months. During this time, his father died. His weight increased to 552 pounds. Although this weight regain was disappointing, the big picture was one of success. Compared with 3 years earlier, John had lost 111 pounds (nearly 17% of his initial body weight), was physically quite active, and was enjoying his passion for golf.

Comment

John's story illustrates several important points regarding adherence to dietary recommendations. Perhaps the two most important points are the need for ongoing program contact and the value of due diligence when it comes to self-monitoring, on the part of both the patient and his or her treatment team. It is unlikely that John could have achieved his weight loss goals without being sufficiently committed to the day-to-day tedium of recording his food intake. Another likely factor in John's success was the collaborative approach to his treatment. John was willing to agree to weight loss goals that both were realistic and conferred significant health benefits.

Suggested Readings

Bandura, A. (1991). Self-efficacy mechanisms in physiological activation and health-promoting behavior. In J. Madden (Ed.), *Neurobiology of learning, emotion, and affect* (pp. 229–270). New York: Raven Press.

Cooper, Z., Fairburn, C. G., & Hawker, D. M. (2003). *Cognitive-behavioral treatment of obesity: A clinician's guide.* New York: Guilford.

Fairburn, C. G., & Wilson, G. T. (Eds.). (1993). *Binge eating: Nature, assessment, and treatment.* New York: Guilford.

Marlatt, G. A., & George, W. H. (1984). Relapse prevention: Introduction and overview of the model. *British Journal of Addictions, 79,* 261–273.

Leahy, R. L. (2003). *Cognitive therapy techniques: A practitioner's guide.* New York: Guilford.

Miller, W. R., & Rollnick, S. (2002). *Motivational interviewing: Preparing people for change* (2nd ed.). New York: Guilford.

References

Bandura, A. (1991). Self-efficacy mechanisms in physiological activation and health-promoting behavior. In J. Madden (Ed.), *Neurobiology of learning, emotion, and affect* (pp. 229–270). New York: Raven Press.

Marlatt, G. A., & George, W. H. (1984). Relapse prevention: Introduction and overview of the model. *British Journal of Addictions, 79,* 261–273.

22

Adherence to Dialysis Treatment of End-Stage Renal Disease

Jamie A. Cvengros

Alan J. Christensen

More than 300,000 Americans are currently receiving dialysis for the treatment of end-stage renal disease (ESRD). For the majority of these patients, ESRD is the result of complications from another chronic disease, most commonly diabetes or hypertension. These patients must undergo life-sustaining renal replacement therapy to compensate for their own kidneys' inability to adequately filter the blood of excess fluid and toxins. The available renal replacement options include hemodialysis (the most common treatment), peritoneal dialysis, and transplantation. Both hemodialysis and peritoneal dialysis require active participation on the part of the patient through adherence to the behavioral demands of the treatment and in some cases through direct involvement in the treatment. Largely because of the shortage of donor organs, the large majority of ESRD patients (around 80%) receive some form of dialysis for the treatment of their condition. Moreover, the behavioral demands of dialysis are greater and more complex than those following a successful renal transplant.

Common Adherence Problems Among Patients Receiving Dialysis

For many patients, adherence to the complex behavioral and medical regimen associated with dialysis is extremely difficult. Studies have suggested that 30% to 60% of patients receiving dialysis fail to adhere to the behavioral and medical guidelines of their health care providers (Moran, Christensen, & Lawton, 1997; Friend, Hatchett, Schneider, & Wadha, 1997). The majority of these studies have examined nonadherence to three aspects of the hemodialysis regimen: (a) medications, (b) dietary restrictions, and (c) restriction of fluid intake.

Medications

For individuals with functioning kidneys, excess phosphorus (P) in the blood is excreted through urine. However, while undergoing dialysis treatment, the body is unable to excrete P in this way; therefore, patients are required to take regular doses of phosphate-binding medication. Failure to adhere to this medication regimen can lead to dangerous levels of P in the blood, which have been associated with complications such as bone demineralization and osteodystrophy (Johnson & Freehally, 2000). Clinically, serum P levels greater than 6.0 mg/dl are considered to represent significant nonadherence.

Dietary Restriction

In addition to phosphate-binding medications, patients are encouraged to control levels of P in their blood via dietary restrictions. Specifically, patients are instructed to reduce intake of high-P foods, such as a peanuts, colas, and dairy products. Additionally, patients with ESRD are unable to filter excess potassium (K) from their blood. To prevent hyperkalemia (i.e., serum K levels greater than 5.5 mEq/L), patients are encouraged to restrict their intake of K-rich foods, such as tomatoes, potatoes, and bananas. High levels of serum K are associated with cardiac arrhythmias, which can be fatal (Johnson & Freehally, 2000).

Fluid Intake Restriction

Fluid restriction is likely the most difficult aspect of the regimen for patients on hemodialysis. Specifically, because their kidneys can no longer function to remove excess fluid from the blood, patients undergoing hemodialysis are required to limit their intake of fluids from both drink and food to 1.0 to 1.5 L/day. Adherence to fluid restriction is assessed by computing the *interdialytic weight gain* (IWG), or weight gain between hemodialysis sessions. This measure is believed to be an accurate indicator of the amount of fluid a patient has consumed between dialysis sessions and may be a more valid indicator of adherence than biochemical markers such as serum P and serum K (Manley & Sweeney, 1986). IWG values greater than 2.5 kg are generally considered to be indicative of problematic nonadherence. Significant nonadherence to fluid restriction is associated with complications such as hypertension, congestive heart failure (CHF), pulmonary edema, and shortened survival (Wolcott, Maida, Diamond, & Nissenson, 1986).

Common Barriers to Dialysis Treatment Adherence

Patients with ESRD may face many barriers to successful treatment adherence. For example, some patients have limited access to adequate health care and medications. For those patients who live in rural areas, the nearest hemodialysis center may be several hours away. Additionally, many patients with ESRD must rely on friends or family for transportation to and from dialysis sessions. Second, although the costs of hemodialysis for patients with ESRD are covered under Medicare, patients may have limited financial resources to pay for medications and other treatment needs. Studies of patients undergoing hemodialysis have found that these barriers (e.g., long distance from home to clinic and medication cost) are associated with poorer adherence (Cummings, Becker, Kirscht, & Leven, 1982). Another common pragmatic barrier to treatment is needle phobia. In a study of patients currently undergoing center hemodialysis, 47%

of patients indicated that needle phobia was a significant reason for not changing treatment modalities from center dialysis to home (self-care) hemodialysis (McLaughlin, Manns, Mortis, Hans, & Taub, 2003).

In addition to these pragmatic barriers to adherence, potential psychosocial barriers to adherence also exist. For example, social stigma or embarrassment related to the disease and its treatment may play a role. Patients may be embarrassed to take medications or impose dietary restrictions when around others. One preliminary study examined the effect of these social influences on treatment adherence among patients with ESRD. This research has suggested that certain social influences do have detrimental effects on dietary and medication adherence among patients undergoing dialysis treatment (Johnson & Christensen, 2003). Another study found that perception of a family environment that is supportive (higher cohesion and expressiveness, less conflict) is associated with better fluid intake adherence among patients with ESRD (Christensen et al., 1992).

Special Assessment Issues Related to Dialysis Adherence

There are several adherence-related assessment issues relevant to dialysis treatment. Many of these issues parallel the unique barriers to adherence to the dialysis regimen as mentioned above. For example, it is important to assess the impact of practical and social barriers on a patient's treatment adherence. This can be accomplished using clinical observation and unstructured interview techniques.

In addition, it is important to assess the cognitive functioning of a patient undergoing dialysis. Because the population of ESRD patients is aging (U.S. Renal Data System [USRDS], 2004), and there is evidence that degree of renal failure is associated with impaired cognitive function

(Hart, Pederson, Czerwinski, & Adams, 1983), it is important to assess the cognitive capacity of the patients. Patients with impaired cognitive functioning may have difficulty in understanding and remembering the demands of the dialysis behavioral regimen. For example, patients with impaired cognitive function may not remember when to take medications or may not understand how to limit fluid intake. A quick estimate of cognitive function can be obtained using the Mini Mental Status Questionnaire (Folstein, Folstein, & McHugh, 1975), a 30-item measure that assesses short-term memory, working memory, and general orientation. For patients who demonstrate some cognitive decline on this measure, additional neuropsychological testing may be warranted.

Finally, from a behavioral standpoint, to ascertain the potentially modifiable factors underlying a patient's nonadherence, it may be useful to conduct a "functional analysis" of the behavior (Fordyce, 1982). First, it is important to assess the *temporal pattern* of the nonadherence. For example, is the patient most nonadherent over the weekend or during the holidays when social activity is greater? In addition, it is important to assess the *environmental responses* to the behavior. For example, might something in the patient's social environment be inadvertently reinforcing nonadherence? Assessment of these and other contextual issues may make management of nonadherence more successful and provide useful information for intervention strategies.

Implementing Adherence-Promoting Strategies

Research has suggested that behaviorally oriented interventions have modest success at increasing adherence among patients with ESRD undergoing dialysis (Christensen & Ehlers, 2002). Specifically, nonadherence has been conceptualized as a behavioral skill deficit, and some researchers have proposed that some patients may lack the self-control or self-regulation skills to adequately follow a behavioral regimen (Christensen, Moran, Wiebe, Ehlers, & Lawton, 2002; Kaplan De-Nour & Czaczkes, 1972). One study used an 8-week group "self-regulation" behavioral intervention to increase fluid intake adherence (Christensen et al., 2002). The results of this study suggested that those patients exposed to the behavioral intervention exhibited significantly better adherence to the fluid intake regimen at 8-week follow-up than the matched controls. The behavioral protocol was largely derived from the theory of self-regulation (or self-management) of behavior (Kanfer & Gaelick, 1991), which proposes that the successful completion of a behavior is a function of three self-regulatory processes: (a) self-monitoring, (b) goal setting, and (c) self-reinforcement.

First, patients must engage in self-monitoring; they must be able to effectively and accurately monitor their own behavior in relation to their treatment regimen. For example, patients must be able to accurately monitor their daily fluid intake from liquids and food. Second, patients must effectively engage in goal setting. Specifically, they must be able to choose appropriate and reasonable behavioral goals regarding their treatment regimen. For example, patients with ESRD must be able to make practical and attainable dietary goals (i.e., reducing P intake by eliminating soda from their diet). Finally, patients must engage in self-reinforcement for the achievement of their goals. Specifically, patients must be able to choose appropriate and meaningful rewards for their adherent behavior and must be able to administer these reinforcements effectively. Patients with a behavioral skill deficit in any of these three areas (self-monitoring, goal setting, and self-reinforcement) may have difficulty adhering to the behavioral demands of the dialysis regimen. The remainder of this section is dedicated to a step-by-step description of how to implement this behavioral approach with nonadherent patients. Although this approach is described in a group format, it can readily be modified for individual treatment.

This example uses the fluid intake restriction component of the regimen to illustrate this adherence promotion protocol.

Session 1: Introduction to the Self-Regulation Approach and Dialysis Regimen

In this session, provide patients with a summary of the self-regulation rationale. Specifically, provide a summary of the self-regulation theory that includes a description of each of the stages: self-monitoring, goal setting, and self-reinforcement. Patients should also be given a summary of the topics to be covered in the remaining sessions with an explanation as to how each of these topics is relevant to the self-regulation theory. In addition, review the behavioral components of the dialysis treatment regimen and the rationale for these behaviors. For example, explain why excess fluid and certain foods must be restricted. Specifically, instruct patients in the specific aspects of the behavioral regimen. For example, remind patients that they should generally consume only 1.0 to 1.5 L of fluid per day, including fluid found in foods such as popsicles, vegetables, fruits, and soup. In addition, it is important to review the medical consequences of inadequate fluid restriction, such as hypertension, cramping during dialysis, pulmonary edema, fatigue, and CHF.

Session 2: Introduction to Self-Management and Self-Monitoring

Begin the session with a review of the self-management rationale. Specifically, review the three components of the self-regulation model and emphasize the effect self-monitoring has on enhancing awareness and perceived control over behavior. In addition, highlight the association between self-reinforcement and the likelihood of repeating a behavior in the future. As part of this introduction to self-monitoring, encourage patients to share their previous experiences with self-monitoring. Provide patients with materials to aid in the self-monitoring of fluid intake, such as handouts or daily diaries, and assign the first "self-monitoring exercise." Ask the patients to record their fluid intake between this session and the next. An example of the worksheet provided to patients is provided in Figure 22.1. Finally, as an introduction to goal setting, provide patients with a copy of their recent IWG and laboratory reports to review. Patients should review these reports with the group leader and be asked to consider possible areas for behavioral improvement; however, explicit behavioral goals should not be set in this session.

Session 3: Continued Self-Monitoring and Review of Progress

Instruct patients to continue the use of the daily diaries to record daily fluid intake. In addition, encourage patients to record what they are doing and how they are feeling at the time of the fluid intake as well as the setting and antecedents relevant to the fluid intake. During this session, allow the group members to discuss their self-monitoring experience. Ask patients to discuss their degree of compliance with the monitoring exercise and to identify any barriers to consistent monitoring. In addition, assist patients in identifying any patterns of behavior (e.g., excessive drinking in the evening) and any antecedent stimuli (e.g., excessive drinking after arguments with their spouse) elucidated by their self-monitoring diaries.

Using these baseline monitoring data and IWG reports, emphasize the close association between fluid intake and IWG. In particular, have patients review their two or three most recent IWG values compared with their IWG values prior to self-monitoring. Most likely, patients will see a decrease in their most recent IWG values, indicative of a decrease in fluid intake. Discuss the reasons for this decrease, such as the phenomenon that behavior decreases simply after a period of self-monitoring. Patients should be encouraged to continue monitoring

Date: _____

Time	Fluid	Amount	Situation/Activity	Circle Mood Rating (1 = very low to 5 = very high)
				1 2 3 4 5
				1 2 3 4 5
				1 2 3 4 5
				1 2 3 4 5
				1 2 3 4 5
				1 2 3 4 5
				1 2 3 4 5
				1 2 3 4 5
				1 2 3 4 5

Total Fluid: _____

Figure 22.1   Daily Self-Monitoring Log

their fluid intake and continue contrasting these records with their IWG values. The last part of the session may be dedicated to role-playing potential "self-management problems." Have patients each identify one potential barrier to self-management and rehearse these behavioral coping techniques as a group.

Session 4: Introduction to Goal Setting

In this session, review with patients the importance of goal setting and the characteristics of an appropriate goal. For example, teach patients that a "good" goal has several components: (a) it is personally relevant, (b) it is positive, (c) it is realistic given their current behavior, (d) it is behaviorally specific, and (e) it is under the control of the patient. For example, if a patient is currently ingesting 2.5 L of fluid a day, "reduce my fluid intake" is an inadequate goal. Rather, "I will decrease my fluid intake by 0.5 L a day by having only one drink with each meal so that I have less cramping during dialysis" is a more realistic, specific, and personally relevant goal. For homework, invite patients to choose one treatment-related goal and one personal (non-treatment-related) goal and complete a goal-setting worksheet for each. In addition, encourage patients to discuss these goals with their health care provider before the next group session. An example of a goal-setting worksheet is provided in Figure 22.2.

Session 5: Introduction to Self-Reinforcement

Reintroduce patients to the concept of self-reinforcement and provide instruction for choosing rewards or reinforcers. Inform patients that reinforcers may be tangible (e.g., treating oneself to a movie after a week of adherence IWG values) or mental (e.g., giving oneself a

---

Focus Goal Worksheet

I want to _____

_____

_____

This will benefit me because _____

_____

_____

Break Down Into Subgoals (realistic, positive, specific, within your control)

Subgoal	By When?
1. _____	_____
2. _____	_____
3. _____	_____
4. _____	_____
5. _____	_____

Figure 22.2 Focus Goal Worksheet

compliment or mental "pat on the back"). Also, educate the patients on what makes a "good" reinforcement. Specifically, a good reward is something that is (a) enjoyable to the patient, (b) appropriately matched to the goal to which it is paired, (c) under the control of the patient, and (d) guilt free. In addition, good reinforcements should be as close to the completion of the goal as possible. For example, for meeting the goal of three consecutive IWG values at 2.5 kg or less, an appropriate reward may be a trip to the movie theater. A 32-oz triple-thick chocolate shake would be a less appropriate reward! Once patients understand the concept of an appropriate reinforcement, encourage them to construct a "reward menu" or a list of appropriate rewards for each goal. Finally, ask patients to choose a goal and matching reinforcement to work on as homework for the next session.

Session 6: Training in Behavioral Coping Skills

In this session, teach patients two specific behavioral coping strategies. First, teach patients to use stimulus control strategies to control their fluid intake. For this skill, patients learn to control or eliminate from their environment stimuli that elicit nonadherent behavior. For example, suggest that patients restrain their drinking to one modest-sized container. Also, encourage patients to remove drinking-related cues (e.g., glasses, milk jugs, wine bottles) from the dining table. These cues may be general cues pertinent to all patients on dialysis or may be personally relevant cues discovered through the self-monitoring exercises. It may also be important to encourage patients to avoid situations that promote fluid intake. For example, encourage patients to avoid "coffee breaks" around the water cooler at work. Second, teach patients to use the behavioral skill of self-instruction. Discuss ways in which patients can use cues or reminders in their household to promote fluid adherence. For example, patients may place a card with the words "edema" and "hypertension" on the refrigerator to be seen each time they reach for a soda.

Session 7: Relapse Prevention Strategies

In this session, invite patients to discuss their experiences using the self-management skills over the prior 7 weeks. Ask them to identify what was most and least helpful from the intervention. Finally, engage the group in a discussion of how to respond to "slipups." It is assumed that patients will have nonadherent periods where they do not meet their fluid intake goals. Provide skills to respond to these slipups and tips for preventing a relapse into previous nonadherent behavior. For example, urge patients to avoid the belief that "once I've messed up, it is all over and I might as well forget it." In addition, encourage patients to identify potential barriers to long-term maintenance of the behavior. Have each patient rehearse these relapse prevention strategies with the group.

Case Study: George

George is a 75-year-old man who has been undergoing renal dialysis for 5 years. His ESRD is a long-term complication of his Type 2 diabetes, which was diagnosed at age 50. He is married and lives with his wife, Louise, who is in good health. George retired only 5 years ago from his job as a high school mathematics teacher. Although he had no desire to quit teaching, due to the intense time commitment, he had no choice but to retire when he began dialysis. George receives dialysis treatments on Mondays, Wednesdays, and Fridays at a center located 75 miles from his home. In the past,

Louise has driven him to and from these appointments, but she has recently joined a women's organization that meets on Wednesdays. On these days, George relies on his neighbors and friends to take him to dialysis. Although he was initially very adherent to his dialysis regimen (e.g., IWG values consistently around 2.0 kg), George has recently become very nonadherent, particularly to the fluid intake restrictions. For example, his average IWG values over the last 3 months have been near 5.0 kg.

In response to George's recent behavioral change, his physician suggested that George meet with the staff psychologist, Dr. Skinner. Dr. Skinner met with George to assess his current behavior and provide suggestions for improving George's adherence to the dialysis regimen. During his assessment, Dr. Skinner inquired about several areas of George's life that may be related to his recent behavior. For example, when asked how he felt about dialysis, George replied,

> I know it is important, but dialysis really interferes with my week. I drive an hour and a half to get to the clinic, sit here doing nothing for four hours, and then drive home. When I get home, I am so tired that I can't do anything for the rest of the day. Then, two days later I get up and do the whole thing again.

In addition, George made several comments about how he feels like a child during his dialysis sessions. For example, he commented that "the nurses act like I can't do anything for myself. They even take my shoes off for me."

In an attempt to better understand George's pattern of fluid intake nonadherence, Dr. Skinner requested that George keep a daily diary of fluid intake for 2 weeks. Specifically, for each drink, Dr. Skinner asked George to record his mood and behavior prior to the drink and the setting in which he had the drink. Dr. Skinner provided George with a notebook to help with his self-monitoring exercise. When Dr. Skinner reviewed this diary with George at their follow-up appointment, they discovered some interesting patterns. Specifically, George did most of his drinking during the afternoons after dialysis and during the weekend. He reported that on dialysis days, he spent most of the afternoon watching TV or doing a puzzle while Louise worked in the garden or visited with friends. George stated that he was interested in doing these activities with her but was too tired. Therefore, he stayed at home and reported feeling "useless, bored, and incompetent." On the weekends, George spent much of his time working in the garden. While he was working, he would drink two or three large glasses of water or lemonade out of habit. In the afternoon, he would watch football on television. During the game, he would snack on peanuts or pretzels, which made him thirsty, and so he would drink a fair amount of soda. He reported eating and drinking on these days "just because that is what you do during the game."

In reviewing this diary, Dr. Skinner identified two key elements in George's nonadherence. First, Dr. Skinner suspected that nonadherence may help George to regain some sense of personal control or freedom, particularly given George's expressed feelings of incompetence and feeling "like a child." Second, Dr. Skinner suggested that simple behavioral interventions may help reduce George's fluid intake. Thus, Dr. Skinner made two recommendations to the referring physician.

First, Dr. Skinner suggested that to the extent possible, George should be actively involved in his treatment. For example, George could be taught how to set up the dialyzer, how to monitor his symptoms, or how to insert the needle. If the resources were possible, George might be a good candidate for home hemodialysis given the fact that he desires an active role in his care and is burdened by the 3-hour round trip to the dialysis center. Second, Dr. Skinner recommended that George be taught self-regulation skills. Specifically, George should continue to use self-monitoring of his fluid intake. In addition, George should work with his health care providers to set behavioral goals and engage in self-reinforcement. In addition, George may benefit from particular behavioral skills such as stimulus control and self-instruction. For example, when he works in the garden over the weekend, he should only drink his water or lemonade from a small container that must be refilled and reused. This would help him to adequately monitor how much he consumes. In addition, rather than snacking on salty foods during the football games, which only increase his thirst, George should snack on low-sodium foods like fruit, vegetables, or unsalted nuts.

Dr. Skinner's recommendations were incorporated into George's care. For example, George was taught how to set up the dialyzer and monitor his symptoms during his dialysis sessions. George reported to his physician that these changes made him feel more involved in his health care. After a few weeks of this new protocol, he said to his nurse, "I finally feel like a competent adult again." In addition, George continued to monitor his fluid intake. He also worked with his health care providers to set reasonable fluid intake goals. He began to drink water only from a small 4-oz glass while gardening and watching TV and carefully monitored the amount of fluid he ingested throughout the day. In addition, he began to eat low-sodium snacks or chewed on hard candy or crushed ice while watching TV, which lessened his thirst. After implementing the behavioral intervention, George's physicians found that his IWG values were significantly lowered. In fact, George's average IWG following the intervention was 2.0 kg, which was well within the "adherent" range.

Suggested Readings

Christensen, A. J. (2004). *Patient adherence to medical treatment regimens.* New Haven, CT: Yale University Press.

Christensen, A. J., & Johnson, J. A. (2002). Patient adherence with medical treatment regimens: An interactive approach. *Current Directions in Psychological Science, 11,* 94–97.

Kirschenbaum, D. S. (1991). Integration of clinical psychology into hemodialysis programs. In J. Sweet, R. Rozensky, & S. M. Tovian (Eds.), *Handbook of clinical psychology in medical settings* (pp. 567– 586). New York: Plenum Press.

Michenbaum, D. H., & Turk, D. C. (1987). *Facilitating treatment adherence: A practitioner's guidebook.* New York: Plenum Press.

References

Christensen, A. J., & Ehlers, S. L. (2002). Psychological factors in end-stage renal disease: An emerging context for behavioral medicine research. *Journal of Consulting & Clinical Psychology, 70,* 712–724.

Christensen, A. J., Moran, P. J., Wiebe, J. S., Ehlers, S., & Lawton, W. J. (2002). Effect of a behavioral self-regulation intervention on patient adherence in hemodialysis. *Health Psychology, 21,* 393–397.

Christensen, A. J., Smith, T. W., Turner, C. W., Holman, J. M., Gregory, M. C., & Rich, M. A. (1992). Family support, physical impairment, and adherence in hemodialysis: An investigation of main and buffering effects. *Journal of Behavioral Medicine, 15,* 313–325.

Cummings, M. K., Becker, M. H., Kirscht, J. P., & Leven, N. W. (1982). Psychosocial factors affecting adherence to medical regimens in a group of hemodialysis patients. *Medical Care, 20,* 567–580.

Folstein, M. F., Folstein, S. E., & McHugh, P. R. (1975). Mini-Mental State: A practical method for grading the state of patients for the clinician. *Journal of Psychiatric Research, 12,* 189–198.

Fordyce, W. E. (1982). A behavioural perspective on chronic pain. *British Journal of Clinical Psychology, 21,* 313–320.

Friend, R., Hatchett, L., Schneider, M. S., & Wadha, N. K. (1997). A comparison of attributions, health beliefs, and negative emotions as predictors of fluid adherence in renal dialysis patients: A prospective analysis. *Annals of Behavioral Medicine, 19,* 344–347.

Hart, R. A, Pederson, J. P., Czerwinski, A. W., & Adams, R. L. (1983). Chronic renal failure, dialysis, and neuropsychological function. *Journal of Clinical Neuropsychology, 5,* 301–312.

Johnson, J. A., & Christensen, A. J. (2003, March). *Development and validation of the Perceived Social*

Barriers to Adherence Scale. Student Meritorious Paper presented at the Society of Behavioral Medicine Conference, Salt Lake City, UT.

Johnson, R. J., & Freehally, J. (2000). *Comprehensive clinical nephrology*. New York: Harcourt.

Kanfer, F. H., & Gaelick, L. (1991). Self-management methods. In F. Kanfer & A. Goldstein (Eds.), *Helping people change* (4th ed., pp. 305–360). New York: Pergamon Press.

Kaplan De-Nour, A., & Czaczkes, J. W. (1972). Personality factors in chronic hemodialysis patients causing noncompliance with medical regimen. *Psychosomatic Medicine, 34*, 333–344.

Manley, M., & Sweeney, J. (1986). Assessment of compliance in hemodialysis adaptation. *Journal of Psychosomatic Research, 30*, 153–161.

McLaughlin, K., Manns, B., Mortis, G., Hans, R., & Taub, K. (2003). Why patients with ESRD do not select self-care dialysis as a treatment option. *American Journal of Kidney Disease, 41*, 380–385.

Moran, P. J., Christensen, A. J., & Lawton, W. J. (1997). Conscientiousness, social support, and adaptation to chronic illness. *Annals of Behavioral Medicine, 19*, 333–338.

U.S. Renal Data System. (2003). *USRDS annual report*. Bethesda, MD: National Institutes of Health, National Institute of Diabetes and Digestive and Kidney Diseases.

Wolcott, D. W., Maida, C. A., Diamond, R., & Nissenson, A. R. (1986). Treatment compliance in end-stage renal disease patients on dialysis. *American Journal of Nephrology, 6*, 329–338.

PART V

Promoting Adherence With Specific Populations

23

Treatment Adherence in Children and Adolescents

Tonya S. Watson

Nancy Foster

Patrick C. Friman

T reatment effectiveness is a moot issue if treatment recommendations are not followed. Research indicates that approximately half the families receiving psychological services do not to adhere to treatment recommendations (Kazdin, 1996). Although treatment adherence is problematic across clinical populations, it is particularly challenging with children and adolescents because there are at least two sources of nonadherence, the children and their parents. Thus, establishing acceptable levels of adherence requires examining parent and child variables that either facilitate or impede adherence to treatment recommendations.

In the extant literature, three of the most salient terms are adherence, compliance, and integrity. *Compliance* and *adherence* are fundamentally synonymous, and we will use *adherence* here. *Adherence* and *integrity* are not synonymous because treatment integrity refers to the fidelity with which a clinician delivers treatment. Adherence refers to the extent to which clients accurately and consistently follow the prescribed steps of treatment. For example, routine treatment for oppositional behavior in preschool children includes multiple steps (e.g., alpha commands, time in, time-out) and a prescription for the regular application of treatment. Assessing treatment adherence involves determining the number of prescribed steps actually followed (accuracy) and the regularity of applications (consistency).

Treatment Integrity

Historically, client noncompliance has been the focus of treatment adherence research; however, clinicians and researchers alike now realize the clinician should also be a target. As indicated above, clinician issues are subsumed under the general category of treatment integrity. Clinicians are an integral component of client adherence and can increase the probability of adherence by prescribing protocols accurately and consistently.

Some seemingly self-evident variables that contribute to treatment integrity include clinician training and experience, but we will not explore those here. Other not so self-evident, and possibly more manipulable, variables include the specificity of treatment recommendations, the standardization of treatment protocols, and the provision of supportive instructional aids such as handouts, audio recordings, videotapes, and e-mail or Web-based communications. For example, a common problem presenting in pediatric psychology clinics involves incontinence, and there are empirically supported treatment protocols for both urinary (enuresis) and fecal (encopresis) incontinence. Briefly, these treatments include information on relevant physiology, diet, toileting schedules, behavioral contingencies, activity levels, and parental involvement. To maximize integrity, a clinician would verbally supply information covering all these details and supplement the verbal recommendations with supportive instructional aids. There are a variety of other examples (e.g., empirically supported treatments for anxiety, depression, and oppositional behavior).

Types of Adherence Problems and Associated Barriers

When providing psychological services to children and their families, two general types of adherence problems confront the clinician: parental adherence and child adherence. For parents and children, there are both common and unique barriers that affect adherence. This section describes both types of adherence problems (i.e., parental and child) and the barriers associated with each.

Parental Adherence

A number of variables directly and indirectly affect parental adherence. Foremost among these are availability of economic and social resources. Although the influence of socioeconomic status on parental adherence is one of the most widely studied variables, it is unfortunately the least manipulable. Generally, parents with greater resources exhibit better adherence than do parents with fewer resources. Parental expectations are also important. For example, outcomes of behavioral treatment for nocturnal enuresis typically occur gradually. Parents who are uninformed about the likelihood of gradual outcomes and who expect full and early continence may become frustrated as they implement treatment and possibly drift from adherence. Parental cognitive ability may influence understanding of the treatment, and lower ability may result in diminished adherence. Finally, over the last 20 years adherence researchers have increasingly addressed the social acceptability of psychological treatments and learned that parents (clients in general) are reluctant to adhere to treatments deemed unacceptable.

Child Adherence

Several of the variables that affect parental adherence also affect child adherence. These include socioeconomic status, cognitive functioning, motivation, and perhaps expectations. In addition to these variables, however, there are some that are unique to children, such as general instructional compliance and developmental. Although children are often the targets of intervention, they either may not be aware that they have a problem (e.g., many oppositional children) or they may be fully aware of the problem but not motivated to work on it (e.g., older thumb-sucking children). For example, a relatively common clinical complaint is delayed toilet training. Toilet training is a complex process with multiple steps that have to be followed by the child, including disrupting current activity, sitting on a ceramic surface, partial undressing, and cleaning up. Children are not naturally motivated to do these things. Therefore, inaugurating a toilet-training program requires the child to be under good instructional control or the child will often not comply with the program. As another example, exposure and response prevention protocols used for some child anxiety disorders also require children to approach situations that they are more naturally inclined to avoid (e.g., remain in the presence of a feared event). If the child is not under sufficient instructional control, the protocol can be subverted through oppositional behavior.

Developmental level also influences treatment adherence, especially when treatments require the child to actively participate. For example, treatment programs for hair pulling in younger children often produce better outcomes than hair-pulling programs for older children. A key reason may be that parents are primarily responsible for implementing treatments for young children, which reduces the importance of active child participation. Older hair-pulling children, however, are responsible for major aspects of their own treatment, and thus they can readily undermine or avoid it or pull hair covertly, resulting in less-accessible targets for assessment and treatment.

Adherence-Related Assessment

Rating Scales and Observations

Although there are a variety of ways to assess adherence, most of these methods can be grouped into three major categories: self-report, parent or teacher report, and behavioral observations.

Self-report measures include rating scales and checklists and assess the presenting symptoms as well as demographic, familial, and personal information relevant to the reason for referral. Commonly used self-report measures include the Child Behavior Checklist (CBCL)—Youth Self-Report Form (Achenbach, 1991) and the Behavioral Assessment System for Children (BASC)—Self-Report of Personality (Reynolds & Kamphaus, 1998). By reporting his or her own behaviors, the child may be able to identify variables that could affect adherence.

Some of the most common standardized parent report measures include the CBCL—Parent Report Form (Achenbach, 1991), BASC—Parent Report (Reynolds & Kamphaus, 1998), Eyberg Child Behavior Inventory (ECBI) (Eyberg & Ross, 1978), and Conners Rating Scales—Revised (CRS-R) (Conners, 1997). An unstandardized measure includes the "typical day interview," which provides qualitative details about home routines that may provide information regarding parental strengths and weaknesses and other factors in the environment that may be relevant for treatment adherence (e.g., the extent to which the parents follow a well-established daily routine). Rating scales and behavior checklists can also be completed by teachers, providing the clinician with information on problematic symptoms occurring at school and possible variables that may affect adherence.

Behavioral observations obtained by the clinician may be one of the most valuable resources to assess treatment adherence. For example, the clinician may provide instructions or tasks and assess the child's responses and/or establish situations for the parent to demonstrate skills. Observing these samples of behavior can reveal parent instructional style, child responses, and parent follow-up or lack thereof.

Functional Assessment

A critical concern in the treatment for older children and especially adolescents is determining who will be the primary change agent. With young children, it is typically the parents. With older children and adolescents, it may be the child or adolescent, the parents, or both. Regardless of the targeted change agent, the clinician may assess treatment adherence by examining the contextual factors that are unique to each client and that may lead to treatment nonadherence. Conducting a functional assessment of the behaviors associated with nonadherence (resistant behaviors) may enhance the efficacy of therapeutic interventions. Regardless of the type or complexity of the assessment, clinicians may find it helpful to target the following: (a) nonadherent behaviors, (b) antecedents that trigger nonadherence, (c) individual differences that contribute to the occurrence of nonadherence (i.e., a skill or a motivation deficit, lack of support, the treatment being time intensive), and (d) any secondary gains from treatment refusal. Identifying the relationship between unique characteristics of the individual and the variables that elicit, maintain, and strengthen resistant behavior in children and adolescents can lead to the development of treatment plans that are ultimately implemented with greater adherence.

Approaches and Techniques to Facilitate Treatment Adherence

Setting the stage for enhancing treatment adherence with children and adolescents generally involves attending to three broad areas: (a) relationship building and support, (b) education, and (c) skills training and motivation. A meta-analysis involving 153 studies measuring treatment adherence suggested that when interventions use more than one strategy for improving adherence, they are more effective (Roter et al., 1998).

Relationship Building and Support

Effective treatment depends on building a relationship with the individual who will be implementing treatment. As previously mentioned, when treating problems in young children, the parents are typically responsible for treatment implementation. Thus, building rapport with young children may not be an integral part of promoting adherence. However, in situations where the child is responsible for a particular component of treatment (e.g., using a competing response when treating a habit), the clinician should focus on building rapport with the child to enhance the integrity of that component. Because adolescents are more actively involved in psychological treatments, establishing rapport with adolescents is almost always helpful in increasing treatment adherence.

Establishing rapport can be achieved in a variety of ways, one of which is identifying at least one of the adolescent's desirable qualities, attributes, or skills and allowing the adolescent access to direct and indirect acknowledgment of that quality by the clinician. Additionally, "normalizing" the problem by communicating that many teens have similar issues can improve rapport. Clinicians can also increase rapport between adolescent clients and their parents by altering parents' perceptions of previously ignored or forgotten positive traits of their child.

Therapists should be cautioned, however, that therapeutically experienced adolescents will often detect disingenuous rapport-building attempts (e.g., using street language, claiming to listen to certain types of music) by a clinician and may subsequently disregard related advice and treatment recommendations. If the clinician suspects a lack of participation or resistance, either verbally or nonverbally, this should not be ignored. The clinician should communicate that it is often difficult to discuss personal information with a new person and that many adults often struggle with this. Initial meetings should be less demanding with a gradual increase in information requested and participation required.

Frequent contact with the person responsible for implementing treatment, whether it is parent or adolescent, has also been shown to increase treatment adherence. At a minimum, the contact should entail answering questions about the treatment, asking questions to assess adherence, and expressing approval for correct implementation of components/treatment. Most typically, this is done via phone calls and follow-up visits. Additionally, e-mail offers an inexpensive, unobtrusive, and confidential means of contacting the person responsible for treatment.

Treatment Education

Although providing the necessary treatment information and recommendations does not guarantee treatment adherence, it can have a positive effect. Clinicians can enhance the extent to which information is understood by using nontechnical language whenever possible, providing written supplements to accompany instructions issued in session, having the parent or adolescent review the instructions during the session, and ensuring that all recommendations are specific.

Adolescents in therapy may be skeptical of any recommendations or directions from adults, thus supplying persuasive rationales can reduce skepticism. Rationales should be presented in a way that does not suggest the clinician is attempting to impose the intervention. In many situations, an effective approach is for the clinician to refer to a third party when explaining a treatment. For example, the clinician may say, "Some adolescents in your situation have found it useful to . . ." "The reason they found it useful was . . ." "When they decided to change their behavior, this is how they did it. . . ." Presenting rationales in this manner may allow the adolescent to objectively evaluate the information without immediately dismissing it as just another attempt by adults to control behavior. When the recommendations have been delivered, adolescents should then be given an opportunity to ask questions about treatment components and to discuss possible difficulties they may have with implementation.

As indicated above, parents may expect immediate changes, and thus, when appropriate, clinicians should modify such expectations and communicate the possibility of gradual change,

resistance to treatment, and possible positive and negative side effects associated with treatment. Even parents who are prepared for slow and steady improvements may become frustrated if they are not prepared for temporary increases in the frequency, intensity, or duration of problem behaviors. As just one example, initial use of time-out, a very common treatment for oppositional behavior, can result in temporary increases in tantrumlike behavior. Preparing parents to expect and respond appropriately to such reactions can reduce the possibility that these negative reactions will diminish adherence.

Skills Training and Motivation

Adherence is significantly affected by two psychological variables, skill and motivation. That is, some clients lack the skills to implement a treatment protocol, whereas others have sufficient skill but lack motivation. A skills deficit exists when a client does not know how to implement the treatment or a specific component(s) of the treatment. A motivation deficit exists when the client possesses sufficient skill but for some reason fails to implement treatment. The following methods may be used to teach skills or to enhance motivation.

Increasing Skills

A variety of direct instructional techniques can improve skill deficits that impede adherence. The most frequently used of these are verbal instructions, modeling, performance feedback, and scripting. Effective verbal instructions involve (a) a description of each step required in treatment with enough detail to allow completion of the step, (b) brevity, (c) only one or two steps at a time, and (d) statements about the positive impact of each step on success. Scripting is a more specific and comprehensive type of written instruction, and it involves supplying parent and/or child with a literal, written transcript of what to do and say for each component of treatment. Modeling involves initially requiring that the child and/or parent observe the trainer display treatment steps, imitating the steps themselves and receiving feedback from the therapist. Performance feedback involves evaluative commentary supplied by the clinician based on observation of the performance of treatment-related behavior or the results (or lack thereof) of treatments implemented.

Motivation

Reduced motivation may be broadly attributed to a number of interrelated factors that affect the parent's and child's participation with a treatment protocol. Some of the most common factors include the amount of time and effort required to implement treatment, the degree to which the treatment interferes with ongoing or preferred activities, and the results (e.g., experiential benefits, secondary gain) generated by the targeted behaviors.

General strategies for dealing with factors that reduce motivation include establishing a rewarding contingency favoring adherence, modifying an existing contingency (e.g., using new rewards), and simplifying the treatment protocol. When using rewards, motivational strategies such as token economies and behavioral contracting leading to rewards can improve adherence. Token economies involve a reward system in which children are provided with tokens or points for engaging in desirable behaviors. The tokens (or points) can then be exchanged for preferred items and activities that parents are willing to supply or arrange. Token economies are particularly useful when children are older than 7 years and the behaviors targeted

in treatment are either difficult or burdensome to the child (as indicated above).

Regarding simplifying treatment, the goal is typically to modify treatments so that they are less complex, require less effort, and involve less disruption to typical child and family schedules. For example, the most empirically supported treatment for habits in children is a multistep procedure called habit reversal. Components of habit reversal include self-monitoring, awareness training, relaxation training, competing response, and social support. A substantial body of literature demonstrates that an abbreviated habit reversal procedure consisting of just five components is as effective as the original 13-step protocol (Miltenberger, Fuqua, & Woods, 1998). Modified habit reversal procedures can improve adherence because they are simpler and fit more easily into daily routines than the full version. As another example, empirically supported treatment for bed-wetting involves a multiple-step procedure that includes use of a urine alarm and several other treatment components (e.g., Kegel exercises, urine retention training, a waking schedule, a monitoring system). Abundant research shows that the full treatment is highly effective, but there is corresponding research showing that a combination of just the urine alarm and a wake-up schedule can be as effective as the full version (Bollard & Nettlebeck, 1982). There are many other examples.

The following case example involves a child who was referred for chronic hair pulling. The most likely barriers to adherence during each stage of the treatment process will be highlighted as well as appropriate strategies for addressing them.

Case Example: Referral

Susie, age 13, was referred for treatment of trichotillomania or chronic hair pulling. Her mother reported that Susie had been pulling her hair for approximately 2 years and that a large bald spot had developed at the base of Susie's head.

Problem Identification

The assessment included standard intake information, a clinical interview with Susie and her mother, review of a typical day in Susie's life, direct observations of Susie, the CBCL completed by the mother, a review of the mechanics and logistics of Susie's hair pulling, examination of Susie's scalp, and photographs of the area of scalp with hair loss. The intake revealed unremarkable medical and developmental histories. Susie was an only child and lived at home with her natural parents. She was in sixth grade at a local public elementary school, and hair pulling was not a problem at school. Results of the CBCL and clinical interview were not clinically significant. Susie and her mother reported that Susie was most likely to pull her hair while watching TV; while reading; or when she was nervous, sad, bored, or angry. After pulling her hair, Susie typically briefly rubbed it between her fingers and then dropped it where it typically landed on her clothing, her bed, or the floor. To obtain a pretreatment baseline, we requested that the mother collect all pulled hair for a week prior to treatment and record all observations of hair pulling during that period. The results included an average of more than 300 hairs a day and at least five hair-pulling episodes a day. Additionally, during the initial session a clinician discreetly observed Susie while she watched television and her mother completed the behavior problem checklist. Consistent with the referral information, Susie pulled hair twice during the observation period. Measurement of Susie's bald spot yielded a circumference of 6 centimeters.

Possible Barriers to Adherence

The assessment information revealed at least four possible barriers to adherence. First, Susie's hair pulling appeared to provide pleasurable sensations or relief from unpleasant experiences. Additionally, it was often conducted during activities from which Susie would be unlikely to readily disengage (e.g., watching television) in order to practice treatment-related activities. Second, and perhaps related to the first, Susie was only moderately motivated to stop pulling. Third, because of her experience with Susie during stressful or emotionally reactive periods, the mother was reluctant to pursue treatment procedures at those critical times. Fourth, prior to the pursuit of treatment, Susie's hair pulling was readily observable at home, but hair-pulling adolescents typically become much more covert about pulling once treatment is begun.

Problem Analysis

Review of the assessment information indicated that Susie was moderately motivated to quit pulling hair and her mother was very motivated to help. Additionally, the clinical assessment information ruled out underlying psychopathology or other clinically significant associations, and therefore hair pulling could be addressed as an isolated clinical problem. The most empirically supported treatment for hair pulling as an isolated problem is the habit reversal procedure described above. Because of Susie's limited motivation and the high level of independent practice required for some of the components of habit reversal, we prescribed only three components, awareness training, practice of competing responses in response to the urge to pull, and social support.

Treatment Implementation

The first step in treatment involved supplying Susie and her mother with health education about the developmental course and causes of habits such as hair pulling, the normal course of hair development including normal daily hair loss (i.e., 100–150 hairs), and the likely success from full compliance with treatment. Susie and her mother were also informed that Susie's hair pulling did not appear to be related to underlying psychological problems. Supplying this type of information can increase motivation to participate because it can "normalize" the target problem, thus avoiding the pathologized perspective on hair pulling (and most other child behavior problems) found in the media and creating a sense that the problem can be solved by direct treatment. The entire habit reversal treatment procedure was presented to Susie and her mother, and jointly we agreed on the three components mentioned above. Additionally, we also agreed on three treatment goals, normal daily hair loss, absence of hair pulling, and elimination of the bald spot in 2 months.

As each of the three treatment components were delivered, written instructions were supplied to Susie and her mother. Treatment began with awareness enhancement. Habits such as hair pulling are often conducted with limited client awareness, and increasing it can make the habit more accessible for other components of treatment. Additionally, there is substantive literature showing that increasing awareness of clinical problems can have a reductive effect on those problems. Subsequently, the competing response procedures were begun. Two procedures were selected: the first for situations involving boredom, and it required that Susie occupy her hands in a way other than for pulling hair, such as sitting on them or holding a book. The other competing response procedure was for situations involving stress, sadness, or anger, and it required conscious breathing and deep muscle relaxation (both taught to Susie in the clinic). To address the possibility of covert practice, we requested that Susie's mother conduct random checks and recommend the appropriate competing response if hair pulling was either incipient or actually occurring. Susie and her mother both agreed to this step.

The final component, social support, was added to address all the barriers to adherence, especially reduced motivation. For Susie, the component actually had two components, one primarily social and the other material. The social component involved a general increase in parental deliveries of affection, positive regard, and appreciation to Susie. Additionally, admiration for her efforts and acknowledgment of her progress were to be delivered regularly. The material component involved a reward system that provided Susie benefits for any progress on the targets of treatment (i.e., reduced hairs pulled, reduced instances of pulling, and reduced size of bald spot). Benefits ranged from delayed bedtime and curfew to movies and special outings. Compliance with treatment steps was also rewarded, especially if it occurred at difficult times (e.g., practicing breathing and relaxation when highly upset). A social support system was also established for the mother. Specifically, one therapist maintained telephone contact with her at least every 2 days during the first weeks of treatment and at least once a week for 3 months thereafter. During the calls, questions were answered, feedback delivered, and admiration for effort was shared. If issues that could thwart adherence were not resolved during a call, a clinic visit was quickly established.

Outcome

Progress was measured in the same ways in which initial assessment information was obtained (i.e., daily counts of hairs lost, observations of pulling, and measures of the size of the bald spot). Hairs per day fell to around 100–150 within the first week of treatment, observations of hair pulling initially reduced to one or zero within the same period (reducing to zero within 4 weeks), and the bald spot was completely grown over within 3 months.

Summary

Treatment outcomes are dependent on treatment adherence. Dually influenced by clinician and client characteristics, adherence is maximized when clinicians combine careful assessment and a system of checks and balances to ensure that (a) protocols are administered consistent with client ability and level of functioning; (b) detailed instructions are provided, including "take-home" descriptions; (c) child instructional control is assessed and established; and (d) clinicians and clients agree on treatment outcomes. By assessing and reducing initial barriers to treatment, clinicians successfully increase adherence through proactively addressing potential problems.

We have attempted to show that adherence is multiply determined and that a broad range of variables can be manipulated to increase its occurrence. Strategically addressing these variables does not guarantee full adherence, but it does improve the chances that clients will engage in sufficient adherence to increase the probability of a positive outcome.

References

Achenbach, T. M. (1991). *Manual for the Child Behavior Checklist/4-18 and 1991 profile.* Burlington: University of Vermont, Department of Psychiatry.

Bollard, J., & Nettlebeck, T. (1982). A component analysis of dry-bed training for treatment of bed wetting. *Behavior Research and Therapy, 20,* 383–390.

Conners, C. K. (1997). *Conners' rating scales—revised: Technical manual.* North Tonawanda, NY: Multi-Health Systems.

Eyberg, S. M., & Ross, E. A. (1978). Assessment of child behavior problems: The validation of a new inventory. *Journal of Clinical Child Psychology, 11,* 130–137.

Kazdin, A. E. (1996). Dropping out of child therapy: Issues for research and implications for clinical practice. *Clinical Child Psychology and Psychiatry, 1,* 133–156.

Miltenberger, R. G., Fuqua, R. W., & Woods, D. W. (1998). Apply behavior analysis to clinical problems: Review and analysis of habit reversal. *Journal of Applied Behavior Analysis, 31,* 447–470.

Reynolds, C. R., & Kamphaus, R. W. (1998). *BASC: Behavior Assessment System for Children: Manual including preschool norms for ages 2–6 through 3–11.* Circle Pines, MN: American Guidance Service.

Roter, D. L., Hall, J. A., Merisca, R., Nordstrom, B., Cretin, D., & Svarstad, B. (1998). Effectiveness of interventions to improve patient compliance. *Medical Care, 36,* 1138–1161.

24

Strategies for Enhancing Medication Adherence in the Elderly

Hillary LeRoux

Jane E. Fisher

Medication adherence in older adults is a complex and poorly understood problem. The high prevalence of nonadherence in this population is not surprising given the demands of managing multiple medications. Most people, regardless of age, would be challenged to adhere to the complicated medication regimens encountered by many older adults. Elderly persons receive a greater number and variety of medications than any other population (Lo, 2001). Persons aged 65 years and older comprise approximately 13% of the population but consume 30% of all prescribed medications (Williams, 2002). The majority of elderly persons (61%) take at least one prescription medication (Williams, 2002). In addition, elderly persons have consumed 40% of over-the-counter medications, herbal therapies, and/or some form of dietary supplement within the past year (Lo, 2001; Williams, 2002). The high numbers of prescription medications, nonprescription medications, and supplements consumed by older adults place them at very high risk for adverse medication interactions. The underuse of medication for economic reasons further complicates efforts to improve medication adherence in the elderly population.

This chapter will discuss issues related to medication adherence in elderly persons and describe strategies for assessing nonadherence risk and facilitating adherence. Survey research on adherence rates in elderly persons will be reviewed, followed by a brief description of the consequences of nonadherence. A framework for idiographic assessment and treatment planning will be presented based on Lawton's conceptual model of competence/environmental press congruence (Lawton, 1982). This model provides a useful structure for identifying variables that affect the interaction between an individual patient's personal characteristics (e.g., sensory, physical, and cognitive functioning) and the environmental demands he or she encounters (e.g., number of medications, medication packaging) that might affect his or her ability to comply with a medication regimen. Finally, recommendations for additional resources will be presented.

Medication Adherence Rates in Older Adults

Accurate estimates of rates of medication adherence in older adults are difficult to obtain because of variations in the type of assessment or measurement used (e.g., self-report, interview data, pill counts, prescription claims, and electronic monitoring), differences in operational definitions of adherence, and differences in the setting (e.g., physicians' offices, general public, hospital admissions and discharges, and community-dwelling older adults) or population studied (e.g., average age of participants above 55 or over 65 years) (Lo, 2001; Vik, Maxwell, & Hogan, 2004). Studies of nonadherence have reported rates between 62% and 84% when electronic monitoring was used and between 40% and 75% when other methods of assessment were employed (Lo, 2001).

Consequences of Medication Nonadherence

Older persons are more susceptible to side effects and negative drug interactions than younger adults because of reductions in the rate at which they metabolize medications (Park & Jones, 1997). In the United States, medication nonadherence is estimated to account for $100

billion in lost productivity and extra annual medical care costs (Robbins, 1990 in Park & Jones, 1997). Hospital admissions among older adults due to noncompliance, adverse medication reactions, and inadvertent medication errors are very high (Park & Jones, 1997). In addition, medication nonadherence has been shown to have adverse consequences including (1) poor individual health, (2) need for additional diagnostic testing, (3) additional discomfort for the elderly patient, (4) increased costs to individuals and health care systems, and (5) negative impact on the doctor-patient relationship (Lo, 2001).

Predicting Nonadherence: Descriptive Versus Functional Characteristics

Several studies have attempted to develop a profile of the nonadherent elderly patient but have failed to yield consistent findings (Balkrishnan, 1998; Vik et al., 2004). The majority of studies have found that there is no consistent relationship between medication adherence and age, gender, marital status, level of education, race, socioeconomic status, or education (Balkrishnan, 1998; Carter, McKenna, Martin, & Andressen, 1989; Park & Jones, 1997; Stewart & Caranasos, 1989; Vik et al., 2004). The inconsistent outcomes are likely because demographic variables have largely been treated as proxy variables. A more useful approach for understanding the reasons nonadherence occurs and for identifying points of intervention to prevent or reduce nonadherence is to consider characteristics that can be manipulated through physical or psychological intervention (in contrast to characteristics such as age, sex, race, which cannot). Focusing on the features of an elderly person's physical and psychological functioning (e.g., sensory impairment, cognitive functioning, physical strength, problem-solving skills) that may affect their ability to manage medication and the relevant features of the medication regimen that may need to be manipulated (e.g., scheduling, organizing pills) will have the greatest prescriptive value for improving adherence.

Given the myriad of physical, psychological, financial, and environmental factors that can affect adherence, a conceptual model for organizing a patient's standing on these factors is needed. In the following sections of this chapter, Powell Lawton's (1982) model of competence/environmental press congruence will be applied to the assessment of factors relevant for identifying the types and levels of support an elderly patient needs to effectively and safely adhere to a medication regimen.

Competence/Environmental Press Congruence and Medication Adherence

Lawton's model of competence/environmental press congruence is an ecological model of aging designed to provide a predictive relation between aging and behavior (Lawton, 1982). In this model, behavior is considered to be a function of the person (competence) and environment (environmental press) (Lawton, 1977, 1982). Shown as an equation, $B = f(P, E)$, where B is behavior of the elderly person, P is the person variable, E is the environmental variable, and f represents the function of P and E on the outcome of behavior (Lawton, 1977, 1982). Competence is defined as "a characteristic of the individual, for heuristic purposes conceived of as relatively independent of factors outside the individual" (Lawton, 1982, p. 35). Examples of competence variables include (1) biological health (e.g., absence of disease state); (2) sensory and perceptual capacities (e.g., visual, auditory, olfactory, gustation, somesthesis, and kinesthesis); (3) motor skills (e.g., muscular strength and coordination); (4) cognitive capacity (e.g., intelligence tests, vocabulary tests, and matching/pairing tests); and (5) ego strength (e.g., individual differences that are not accounted for by

external events) (Lawton, 1982). Environmental press is defined as "an environmental force (physical, interpersonal, or social) that tended to activate an intrapersonal need" (Lawton, 1982, p. 39).

Competence Variables and Medication Adherence

The following sections will review the competence (person) variables associated with medication adherence in elderly persons.

Sensory and Perceptual Capacities

Declines in visual and auditory abilities related to the aging process have been hypothesized to affect medication adherence (Park & Jones, 1997). Assessment for problems with vision or hearing may indicate whether adherence to a medication regimen by an elderly patient could be difficult.

Auditory Problems. Research has found that approximately 30% of adults over the age of 85 years are unable to distinguish normal speech (Carter et al., 1989). Hearing loss of higher-pitched frequencies may also result in decreased medication adherence if the elderly patient is unable to hear the instructions related to the proper use of the medication (Lo, 2001). Assessment of hearing loss is recommended before providing instructions on medication usage.

Visual Problems. Declines in visual acuity affect approximately 85% of the population over 50 (Carter et al., 1989). Elderly patients can experience any of the following problems with vision: (1) increased sensitivity to glare, (2) difficulty with focusing on objects close to them, (3) loss of contrast sensitivity, (4) diminished color vision (e.g., differentiating between blue and green), and (5) slower dark adaptation (McElnay & McCallion, 1998; Park & Jones, 1997). Medication errors may result because the elderly patient has difficulty distinguishing between medications due to their similar appearance (e.g., color and shape) (McElany et al., 1998; Park & Jones, 1997). Elderly patients may experience problems with reading prescription container labels due to problems with glare or decreased contrast sensitivity and focus (McElnay & McCallion, 1998; Park & Jones, 1997; Vik et al., 2004). Research indicates that approximately 60% of elderly patients experience problems in reading prescription container labels (McElnay & McCallion, 1998).

Motor Variables

Motor abilities including muscular strength, coordination, and difficulty in swallowing also have been reported to contribute to medication nonadherence in elderly patients (Vik et al., 2004). Studies indicate that most elderly patients experience some degree of osteoarthritis, which may limit hand strength and the ability to manipulate their fingers (Park & Jones, 1997). Research has shown that many elderly patients experience problems opening containers with childproof lids (McElnay & McCallion, 1998; Park & Jones, 1997; Stewart & Caranasos, 1989; Vik et al., 2004) and that problems with opening container lids are a frequently reported reason for medication nonadherence (Vik et al., 2004).

Cognitive Variables

Competently adhering to a medication regimen involves comprehension (e.g., understanding what to do with a medication), working memory (e.g., the ability to store and process information), long-term memory (e.g., the ability to remember what to do with a medication plan—a temporal sequence that integrates multiple medications and doses), prospective memory (e.g., remembering to perform planned actions), and reasoning (Park, Willis, Morrow, Diehl, & Gaines, 1994). Elderly persons are at risk for age-associated declines in cognitive functioning and cognitive disorders (e.g., Alzheimer's disease or vascular dementia), which may contribute to their inability to comprehend and recall medical information (Park & Jones, 1997). Screening for cognitive impairment is important for understanding whether a patient will require additional environmental supports to safely adhere to a medication regimen. For an elderly person with cognitive disorders, proxy adherence becomes the focus. Assessment of the caregiver's status on variables that affect adherence should be conducted. For elderly couples where one spouse has dementia, the burden of managing the medication regimen for *two* persons can be overwhelming.

Providing information about cognitive supports (e.g., connecting the taking of medications with routine events such as when watching nightly news) has been shown to improve medication adherence (Park & Jones, 1997). In addition, instructing patients about the purpose of different medications in their regimen has been found to increase patients' ability to distinguish one medication from another and to compare and contrast changes in their medication regimen (Ascione, 1994). However, other research found no effect for this variable (McElnay & McCallion, 1998).

Patient Beliefs. Several patient beliefs about medication have been found to be associated with adherence: (1) that they no longer need the medication, (2) that they feel well without the medication, or (3) that the medication is ineffective or that they are taking too many medications and there is no need for any more medications (Vik et al., 2004). In other instances, the elderly patients may stop taking the medication to assess whether they still need the medication (Vik et al., 2004). Patient education regarding the inaccuracy of these beliefs may lead to higher medication adherence rates in elderly patients.

Intentional Nonadherence. Intentional nonadherence, also called rational nonadherence, occurs when the elderly patients deliberately do not follow their medication regimen based on what they perceive to be valid reasons, regardless of whether the reasons are medically sound (Lo, 2001). In this form of medication nonadherence, the elderly patients intentionally alter the prescribed medication regimen or stop taking the medication because it is perceived as ineffective or unnecessary, they dislike taking the medication, or they experience uncomfortable side effects (Lo, 2001; McElnay & McCallion, 1998).

Intelligent Nonadherence. Intelligent nonadherence occurs when patients decide not to follow medical advice based on their past experiences or information gathered from sources such as friends, family, or the Internet (Stewart & Caranasos, 1989). Basically, the elderly patient is skeptical, considers the possibility that the physician could be wrong, and decides that the instructions should not be followed (Stewart & Caranasos, 1989).

Environmental Press Variables

Regimen Complexity

Not surprisingly, the complexity of a medication regimen has consistently been found to be the primary reason for nonadherence (Ascione, 1994; McElnay & McCallion, 1998; Vik et al., 2004). Park and Jones (1997) define regimen complexity as the "number of medication events prescribed to an elderly patient in a day," which can be "either a function of taking many medications or taking only a few medications that are on a complex schedule and must be taken three or four times a day" (p. 264).

The more medication events a patient is required to organize and remember, the poorer the adherence (Park & Jones, 1997). Infrequent and irregular dosing schedules increase regimen complexity (e.g., large quantities of pills taken only once or twice a week) and decrease the likelihood of adherence (Park & Jones, 1997). With an increase in the number of medications, the number of doses per day also increases, resulting in declines in adherence (Ascione, 1994).

Adverse medication interactions are more likely to occur as the number of medications increase and may also contribute to a decrease in adherence (McElnay & McCallion, 1998). The elderly patient may actively choose not to take the medications because of negative side effects (Ascione, 1994).

Barriers to accessing medication also contribute to medication regimen complexity (Ascione, 1994). Elderly patients may not pick up a prescription medication because of the inconvenience (e.g., the long wait to obtain medication and the need to make a special trip to the pharmacy) (Ascione, 1994) or may fail to seek a new prescription when a prescription expires (Vik et al., 2004).

Physician-Patient Interactions

Research indicates that as the number of prescribing physicians and pharmacies increases, the elderly patient is less likely to adhere to a medication regimen (Vik et al., 2004). However, when a specialist, not a primary care physician, is prescribing the medications, adherence has been found to be higher among elderly patients (Vik et al., 2004). Amount of contact with a physician is also positively correlated with medication adherence (Vik et al., 2004). The elderly patients' relationship with their physician may account for the better medication adherence rates (Vik et al., 2004). In addition, higher rates of contact with the medical office staff provide more opportunities for medication management and adherence checks. Satisfaction and adherence to medical instructions increase when the physician (1) seeks and respects the elderly patients' concerns, (2) provides education about the medications, (3) provides information about their medical problem and its progress, and (4) shows concern and empathy (Stewart & Caranasos, 1989).

Economic Variables

The cost of prescription medications also contributes to medication nonadherence in older adults (Conn, Taylor, & Kelley, 1991, with patients purchasing medications they can afford and forgoing the medications they cannot (McElnay & McCallion, 1998). Elderly patients are also less likely to obtain medications not covered by their medical insurance plan (Balkrishnan, 1998; McElnay & McCallion, 1998).

Interventions

McElnay and McCallion (1998) have developed a checklist for use by health care providers in the assessment of areas that may be relevant for intervention. An adapted version incorporating additional medication adherence problem areas is presented below:

- Are all the prescribed medications necessary?
- Could the patient's regimen be simplified (e.g., using slow-release or combined dosages of prescribed medications)?
- Could the doses be administered with the regular activities of the patient (e.g., when the patient eats meals, gets the mail, or goes to bed)?
- Does the patient have cognitive, physical, or financial problems that may affect adherence?
- If the patient is prescribed a benzodiazepine, can one with a shorter half-life be prescribed?
- Does the patient know the names and understand the purpose of the medications prescribed?
- Does the patient understand the administration requirements for each medication?
- Can the patient differentiate between medications (e.g., color, shape, and size)?
- Can the patient easily read and comprehend the label and any additional written information? Is larger print needed?
- Is the patient able to open the medication containers?

- Does the patient live alone? Is someone (e.g., a family member or friends) available to assist with the patient's medication regimen?
- Would a medication memory aid help the patient?
- Has the patient voiced concerns regarding medication side effects and/or medication interactions?
- What nonprescription medications does the patient take?
- Is the patient taking any nonprescription medicines for a problem for which a prescription medication has also been prescribed?
- Is a member of the health care team available to check in with the patient regarding the medication regimen (e.g., through regular phone contact or office visits)?

Interventions associated with specific person and environmental factors are summarized in Table 24.1.

Internet Resources for Professionals

www.une.edu/uhc/bodywige/modules/harvard/index.htm

www.pueblo.gsa.gov/cic_text/health/meds4old/697_old.html

www.ascp.com/public/pr/mrps/inappropriate.shtml

www.nia.nih.gov/

Suggested Readings

Park, D. C., & Jones, T. R. (1997). Medication adherence and aging. In A. D. Fisk & W. A. Rogers (Eds.), *Handbook of human factors and the older adult* (pp. 256–287). San Diego, CA: Academic Press.

Table 24.1   Medication Adherence Difficulties and Interventions

Nonadherence Risk	Intervention
Visual problems	• Provide medication counseling, with written aids presented in large print on nonglossy paper (e.g., patient information leaflets) (Ascione, 1994; Carter et al., 1989; Lo, 2001; McElnay & McCallion, 1998) • Present instructive materials in a distraction-free environment (Carter et al., 1989) • Remind patients to ask the pharmacist to use large print on label (McGraw, 2001; Price, 2001) • Encourage patients to use clear containers when possible to help them differentiate between medications (e.g., size, color, and shape of medications) (Ascione, 1994) • Recommend using a magnifying glass to check the labels before taking medications (Price, 2001)
Auditory problems	• Provide medication counseling with written aids (Carter et al., 1989; McElnay & McCallion, 1998) • Present instructive materials in a distraction-free environment (Carter et al., 1989) • Inquire whether the patient has heard the instructions (Price, 2001) • Adjust for hearing loss of high frequencies by providing instructions clearly, concisely, and slowly in low tones rather than in a loud, high-pitched voice (Lo, 2001) • Remind patients to ask the pharmacist to write down instructions (Price, 2001) • Recommend that someone accompany the patient to the doctor's/pharmacy
Motor skills problems	• Instruct patients to patronize a pharmacy that will deliver prescriptions; inform patients that costs may be higher (Price, 2001) • Advise patients to request easy to open medication caps from the pharmacist (Ascione, 1994; Price, 2001)
Memory/cognitive problems	• Recommend that patients use memory aids and daily or weekly medication dispensers (see memory aid intervention Web sites listed below) (McElnay & McCallion, 1998; McGraw, 2001; Park & Jones, 1997; Price, 2001) • Request that patients repeat instructions regarding medications, clarify any misunderstandings, review the medications periodically (Carter et al., 1989; Lo, 2001; Stewart & Caranasos, 1989) • Perform medication counseling with written aids to promote learning (Carter et al., 1989; Stewart & Caranasos, 1989) • Recommend the use of color codes and calendar sheets for recording when each medication is taken (Lo, 2001; McElnay & McCallion, 1998; Park & Jones, 1997)

(Continued)

Table 24.1 (Continued)

Nonadherence Risk	Intervention
	• Instruct the patient to check that medications are clearly labeled and are in clear containers to make differentiation of medications easier (e.g., size, color, and shape of medications) (Ascione, 1994; McGraw, 2001)
	• Prescribe medications in a prepackaged unit whenever possible (McElnay & McCallion, 1998)
	• Advise patients to place reminder notes in clearly visible places (Price, 2001)
	• Tailor the medication regimen to increase compatibility with the patient's habits and rituals to enhance learning and memory cues (Lo, 2001; Stewart & Caranasos, 1989)
	• Inquire about social support (e.g., family or friends who can administer medication reminders) (Lo, 2001)
Regimen complexity	• Assist the patient in recording the schedule (Price, 2001)
	• Recommend using different colors on prescription containers to differentiate times of day (Price, 2001)
	• Advise patients to pair medication with specific activities (e.g., meal times, time of favorite television program, when the mail arrives) (Park & Jones, 1997; Price, 2001)
	• Prescribe medications in prepackaged units if possible (McElnay & McCallion, 1998)
Multiple medications	• Recommend that patients have their medication regimen evaluated regularly (Price, 2001)
	• Instruct the patient on the guidelines regarding polypharmacy (Williams, 2002)
	• Advise the patient to patronize a pharmacy that maintains patient profiles (Price, 2001)
	• Minimize the number of medications and doses ingested daily whenever possible (Ascione, 1994; McElnay & McCallion, 1998)
Knowledge and comprehension difficulties	• Provide complete information regarding the medications and their corresponding regimen (Stewart & Caranasos, 1989; Vik et al., 2004)
	• Complete a medication review and provide recommendations regularly (Vik et al., 2004)
	• Provide continuing feedback to the patient about the medication regimen (Ascione, 1994)
Patient-provider relationship	• Provide information about the medication regimen (Vik et al., 2004)
	• Perform follow-up calls whenever possible to ensure understanding about the medication regimen (Vik et al., 2004)
	• Invite and encourage the patient to ask questions (Stewart & Caranasos, 1989)

Nonadherence Risk	Intervention
Multiple physicians	• Instruct patients to inform all physicians of the medications they are taking (Price, 2001) • Advise the patient to limit prescription purchase to one pharmacy (Price, 2001)
Psychological problems	• Inquire about social support (e.g., family and friends) for assistance with adherence; encourage the patient to seek support from others (Carter et al., 1989; Lo, 2001; Park & Jones, 1997; Stewart & Caranasos, 1989) • Provide information about self-help groups, patient groups, and organizations that are focused on the patient's specific health problems (Lo, 2001) • Provide information about the positive impact of medication adherence (Park & Jones, 1997)
Incorrect patient beliefs	• Assess patients' beliefs about medications, reinforce accurate information, and clarify incorrect beliefs about medications (Park & Jones, 1997) • Provide information about treatment efficacy (Stewart & Caranasos, 1989) • Provide patients with information about the medication—increase their knowledge and insight regarding their medical problems (Stewart & Caranasos, 1989) • Provide information about the positive aspects of medication adherence (Park & Jones, 1997)
Economic factors	• Provide information about medication discount programs (Price, 2001) • Recommend that the patient comparison shop for lowest prescription prices (Price, 2001) • Instruct the patient to inquire whether a generic or less-costly medication is effective and available (Price, 2001) • Advise the patient to request that the physician prescribe generic medications whenever possible (Price, 2001) • Recommend that the patient ask the physician and pharmacist whether he or she qualifies for a patient assistance program through a drug company (Price, 2001)

Vik, S. A., Maxwell, C. J., & Hogan, D. B. (2004). Measurement, correlates, and health outcomes of medication adherence among seniors. *Annals of Pharmacotherapy, 38,* 303–312.

Williams, C. M. (2002). Using medications appropriately in older adults. *American Family Physician, 66,* 1917–1924.

Internet Resources for Consumers

http://nihseniorhealth.gov

www.med.unc.edu/aging/polypharmacy

www.healthsqare.com/seniorshealth.htm

www.cfhinfo.org/PDFs/MedicinesandYou

www.agingwell.state.ny.us/pharmacy/print out/index.htm

Websites Describing Memory Aids for Improving Adherence

www.forgettingthepill.com

www.eyesonelders.com/index.html

www.age-in-place.com

References

Ascione, F. (1994). Medication compliance in the elderly. *Generations, 18*(2), 28–33.

Balkrishnan, R. (1998). Predictors of medication adherence in the elderly. *Clinical Therapeutics, 20*(4), 764–771.

Carter, W. B., McKenna, M., Martin, M. L., & Andresen, E. M. (1989). Health education: Special issues for older adults. *Patient Education and Counseling, 13,* 117–131.

Conn, V. S., Taylor, S. G., & Kelley, S. (1991). Medication regimen complexity and adherence among older adults. *IMAGE: Journal of Nursing Scholarship, 23*(4), 231–235.

Lawton, M. P. (1977). The impact of the environment on aging and behavior. In J. E. Birren & K. W. Schaie (Eds.), *Handbook of the psychology of aging* (pp. 276–301). New York: Litton Educational.

Lawton, M. P. (1982). Competence, environmental press, and the adaptation of older people. In M. P. Lawton, P. G. Windley, & T. O. Byerts (Eds.), *Aging and the environment: Theoretical approaches* (pp. 33–59). New York: Springer.

Lo, R. (2001). Geriatric pharmacotherapy: Problems with adherence. *International Journal of Psychiatric Nursing Research, 7*(2), 806–814.

McElnay, J. C., & McCallion, C. R. (1998). Adherence and the elderly. In L. B. Myers & K. Midance (Eds.), *Adherence to treatment in medical conditions* (pp. 223–253). Amsterdam: Harwood Academic.

McGraw, D. V. (2001). Self-administration of medicine and older people. *Nursing Standard, 15*(18), 33–36.

Park, D. C., & Jones, T. R. (1997). Medication adherence and aging. In A. D. Fisk & W. A. Rogers (Eds.), *Handbook of human factors and the older adult* (pp. 256–287). San Diego, CA: Academic Press.

Park, D. C., Willis, S. L., Morrow, D., Diehl, M., & Gaines, C. L. (1994). Cognitive function and medication usage in older adults. *Journal of Applied Gerontology, 13,* 39–57.

Price, C. A. (2001, July). *Medication misuse among older adults.* Ohio State University Extension, The Ohio Department of Aging, Senior Series. Retrieved December 21, 2004, from http://ohio-line.osu.edu/ss-fact/0128.html

Stewart, R. B., & Caranasos, G. J. (1989). Medication compliance in the elderly. *Medical Clinics of North America, 73*(6), 1551–1563.

Vik, S. A., Maxwell, C. J., & Hogan, D. B. (2004). Measurement, correlates, and health outcomes of medication adherence among seniors. *Annals of Pharmacotherapy, 38,* 303–312.

Williams, C. M. (2002). Using medications appropriately in older adults. *American Family Physician, 66,* 1917–1924.

25

Treatment Adherence in Pregnancy

Negar Nicole Jacobs

Scott Evan Jacobs

Prenatal care ideally begins early in the first trimester of pregnancy and typically consists of 10 to 14 prenatal visits. Research consistently demonstrates that prenatal care is strongly associated with improved maternal and infant outcomes. For most women, pregnancy is a special time when they are especially motivated to care for both themselves and their developing fetus. However, it has been reported that 9.1% of American women receive inadequate prenatal care, defined as seven or fewer visits to a health care professional during pregnancy (Poland, 1985). Costs of nonadherence during pregnancy threaten both the mother and the fetus and may include the development and/or worsening of a condition, development of a collateral illness, and death. This chapter will address the importance of adherence to treatment guidelines during pregnancy, including obtaining early and adequate prenatal care, attending medical appointments early, submitting to prenatal

screens, and engaging in health behaviors to promote a healthy pregnancy, such as appropriate nutrition and cessation of the intake of harmful substances. Special adherence concerns related to high-risk populations, such as teenage pregnancy, gestational diabetes, and addiction issues, will be discussed. Particular attention will be given to common barriers to adherence in pregnancy and suggestions will be provided as to how both medical and behavioral care providers can promote treatment adherence. A case example will be provided illustrating some adherence strategies used by an innovative program.

Adherence Issues in Pregnancy

Prenatal Care

Much literature in the field emphasizes the importance of early and continued prenatal care and the favorable relationships between such care and positive clinical outcomes. In addition to lack of treatment compliance, late entry into prenatal care and failure to keep prenatal appointments are among the factors associated with poor pregnancy outcomes. Kost, Landry, and Darroch (1998) analyzed the effects of certain demographic variables and whether the pregnancy was planned on prenatal care. Researchers found that women with intended pregnancies were significantly more likely than those with unplanned pregnancies to both recognize the pregnancy in the first 6 weeks and to make an early visit for prenatal care. Results also showed that women who were Caucasian, married, college educated, and those with higher incomes were more likely than their counterparts to have recognized their pregnancy in its early stages. Women with higher incomes, those who were married, and those on some form of public assistance were most likely to get early prenatal care, whereas women younger than 20 years of age and those with three or more previous births were least likely to get such early care. The researchers further documented that the planning status of the pregnancy had no effect on whether a woman made the recommended number of visits for prenatal care. It was noted that once they had begun prenatal care, women with intended and unintended pregnancies were equally likely to adhere to the recommended number of visits.

Noting high rates of no-shows for obstetrical appointments, many investigators have focused on the reasons for failure to attend prenatal medical appointments. For example, Blankson and Goldenberg (1994) noted that 30% to 40% of their patients missed individual appointments. They examined the reasons for missed medical appointments among a sample of obstetrical patients of low socioeconomic status (SES) with medical problems deemed to necessitate regular clinic visits and monitoring. The results indicated that the four main reasons for missing appointments were transportation problems (30%), appointment time (10%), forgetting the appointment (10%), or illness (8%). These researchers also found that only 73% of the high-risk population was able to identify their medical diagnosis and only 30% considered the problem as a threat. They noted that many of the women who missed their appointments did not know why they were being seen and did not understand the importance of the visit. They concluded that (1) the system of service delivery needed to be changed such that the potential effects of the medical condition on the pregnancy outcome should be clearly explained to patients, (2) this information should be reinforced at every visit, and (3) the importance of prenatal care should be stressed. Other researchers have suggested the use of mailed appointment reminder cards and/or telephone reminders, providing transportation and/or use of taxi vouchers, use of educational materials, availability of child care, longer clinic hours, access to support groups, contracting with patients, and use of incentives such as baby clothes and supplies. However, some clinicians who have used these methods have noted no effect in reduction of the missed appointment rate (e.g., Campbell, Chez, Queen, Barcelo, & Patron, 2000).

Prenatal screens can be an especially important aspect of adherence, especially for those at risk for the screened condition. Marteau, Johnston, Kidd, Michie, and Cook (1992) found that significant predictors of uptake of a prenatal screening test for spina bifida and Down's syndrome included knowledge of the test, the subjective expected utility attached to the test, and attitudes toward doctors and medicine. Variables related to failure to use screening tests included fear about the results, worries about the screening test, and low levels of belief in the efficacy of the screenings (Maclean, Sinfield, Klein, & Harden, 1984; Nathoo, 1988).

Health Behaviors

Changes in health behaviors are suggested during pregnancy and can be an especially important part of adherence to treatment guidelines. For example, pregnant women are asked to comply with guidelines regarding nutritional supplementation, diet, weight gain, and cessation of harmful substances such as tobacco, alcohol, and drugs. Higgins and Woods (1999) found that even women receiving no prenatal care made some changes in health behaviors, including changes in nutrition, self-care activities, substance use, sleep, and exercise activities.

Vitamin supplementation is generally prescribed for pregnant women to reduce the risks of anemia during pregnancy, fetal abnormalities, and reproductive failures such as prematurity, low birth weight, and stillbirths. For example, pregnant women are particularly at risk for iron deficiency anemia. Galloway and McGuire (1994) found that compliance with iron supplementation was in part related to patient factors such as fear of having large babies, misunderstanding instructions, dosing of pills, side effects, and the doctor-patient relationship. The researchers suggested that iron supplementation could be improved by addressing personal and cultural beliefs, improving communication and providing such tools as calendars to prompt use of supplements, reducing the number and/or size of iron doses, and improving the doctor-patient relationship.

Pregnant women are also asked to take folic acid supplements. Folic acid supplementation is related to higher maternal serum folate levels, which are associated with lower incidence of fetal growth retardation. Researchers examining the role of psychological variables (including measures of depression, anxiety, stress, self-esteem, and social support) found that women with poorer psychological scores on these measures had serum folate levels compatible with poor supplementation (Goldenberg et al., 1992). Using the health beliefs model, Kloeblen and Batish (1999) found significant positive correlations between pregnant women's intentions to permanently follow a high-folate diet and perceived susceptibility, perceived severity, perceived benefits, and self-efficacy. There was a significant negative correlation between perceived barriers and intention to permanently follow a high-folate diet. The researchers concluded that a folate campaign should target these domains.

A healthy diet in pregnancy is important to both maternal and fetal health. However, such a healthy diet may be difficult to achieve, especially for certain sociocultural groups such as those living in poverty and teenage pregnant women. Research has indicated that prenatal participation in supplemental nutrition programs for pregnant women, such as the Women, Infants and Children (WIC) program, have been positively associated with birth weight (Kowaleski-Jones & Duncan, 2002) and have been found to reduce the costs of newborn medical care (Buescher, Larson, Nelson, & Lenihan, 1993). Wrieden and Symon (2003) evaluated a nutrition education program for pregnant teenage women. The program included educational strategies concerning nutrition in pregnancy, behavioral approaches regarding practical ways of incorporating nutritious foods into low-cost meals, and motivational strategies such as providing free food during the sessions and making meals as a group activity. The researchers concluded that the program was favorably received by both teachers and pregnant teens. Sultemeier (1988) developed a method of teaching nutrition skills to pregnant women. The teaching materials included a slide presentation, a teaching guide, and a pamphlet. The materials covered the importance of appropriate weight gain during pregnancy, the four basic food groups, recommendations on serving size and appropriate number of servings throughout the day, and the nutrients contained in the foods discussed. Slides were shown of typical nutritious meals, and participants were warned to avoid junk foods, alcohol, tobacco, drugs, and medications. The educational materials considered the low income and cultural concerns of the targeted population, and the reading materials were written at a third-grade level. In comparing individual and group presentation methods, researchers found that the group teaching method increased patient compliance with healthy eating skills and weight gain and was more cost-effective than the individual teaching approach. Sultemeier (1988) concluded that the group teaching method should be adapted to other prenatal topics.

Taffel, Keppel, and Jones (1993) described the change in medical opinion on optimum weight gain in the past few decades. Until 1950, the standard of practice was to hold pregnant women to a maximum weight gain of 20 pounds. In 1990 the Institute of Medicine (IOM) of the National Academy of Sciences liberalized weight gain guidelines and based them on a woman's body mass index (BMI). The standard of practice now holds women with a normal BMI to a weight gain of 25 to 35 pounds and those with a high BMI (overweight) to a weight gain of 15 to 25 pounds. Weight gains within these guidelines have been associated with healthy maternal and fetal outcomes, whereas higher weight gains have been associated with macrosomia in the neonate (Lederman, 1993; Parker & Abrams, 1992). Despite the liberalization of weight gain guidelines, a significant proportion of pregnant women exceed the weight gain goals. For example, Keppel and Taffel (1993) noted that 36% of women in the National Maternal and Infant Health Survey exceeded the IOM recommendations.

A number of clinical interventions have been created to prevent excessive weight gain in pregnant women. For example, Polley, Wing, and Sims (2002) developed a stepped-care behavioral intervention and compared it with usual care in a randomized clinical trial. The intervention included education about appropriate weight gain, exercise, and healthful eating during pregnancy. Teaching materials involved written and oral information and included biweekly newsletters and personalized graphs of weight gain. Women who exceeded recommended weight gain levels were given additional individualized nutrition and behavioral counseling. Increasingly structured behavioral goals were given at each visit to women who continued to exceed recommended weight gain levels. Results indicated that normal-weight women in the intervention group were significantly less likely than controls to exceed IOM weight gain recommendations.

The literature is full of studies that document the deleterious effects of smoking on health, especially the harmful effects of smoking on fetal birth weight (e.g., Shu, Hatch, Mills, Clemens, & Susser, 1995). Despite the known consequences of smoking during pregnancy, McFarlane, Parker, and Soeken (1996) found that 29.5% of their urban pregnant population smoked, whereas 11.9% used alcohol or illicit drugs. Women who were abused were significantly more likely to smoke, drink alcohol, or use illicit drugs than nonabused pregnant women. Lower birth weights were noted to be significantly associated with the triad of physical abuse, smoking, and alcohol or drug use (or both). Many studies have noted that pregnant women are especially motivated to quit smoking (e.g., Rodriguez, Bohlin, & Lindmark, 2000). However, the likelihood of quitting has been related to certain demographic characteristics (Kost et al., 1998). Specifically, researchers noted that women younger than 20 years or those aged 25 to 29 years were more likely to quit than those aged over 35 years, Hispanic smokers were more likely to quit than black smokers, smokers with higher levels of education were more likely to quit than those with lower levels of education, and smokers pregnant with their first child were more likely to quit than those who already had children.

Windsor et al. (1993) assessed the impact and cost-benefit of a health education smoking cessation program for pregnant smokers. The program involved teaching cessation skills, risk counseling, use of a self-directed cessation guide, and social support methods such as use of a buddy system and a newsletter with testimonials from successful quitters. The randomized clinical trial showed that pregnant smokers who received the intervention had a significantly higher quit rate (14.3%) than controls (8.5%), and that African American smokers were more likely than Caucasians to quit in both conditions. A cost-benefit analysis revealed cost-to-benefit ratios as high as $1:$17.18. The researchers concluded that their health education program was both efficacious and cost-effective for use in public health maternity clinics.

Prenatal exposure to alcohol may lead to fetal alcohol syndrome, which may involve facial malformation, intrauterine growth retardation, and mental retardation (Buka, 1991; Chasnoff, 1988). Drug use during pregnancy may also lead to serious complications for the newborn, including risk of vertical transmission of HIV, cardiac disease, hepatitis, anemia, low birth weight, and death (Chasnoff, 1988; Hanna, Faden, & Dufour, 1997). Despite the tremendous potentially harmful effects of fetal exposure to alcohol and other drugs, use of alcohol and drugs during pregnancy is a common problem. Reports from the National Pregnancy and Health Survey (1993) indicated that 19% of newborns had been exposed to alcohol and 6% to illicit drugs. Unfortunately, only 5% to 10% of pregnant substance abusers seek professional treatment for their drug abuse (Kumpfer, 1991).

Haller, Miles, and Dawson (2003) analyzed the factors influencing drug treatment enrollment by pregnant substance abusers. Compared with women who declined treatment, those who enrolled had greater drug severity, were more likely to identify crack cocaine as their drug of choice, evidenced more family and psychiatric problems, manifested greater emotional distress, showed more Axis II psychopathology, had higher rates of criminal justice system involvement, and had greater legal severity. Other barriers to drug treatment have been reported to be lack of finances to pay for treatment, transportation difficulties, lack of child care, absence of legal pressure, inadequate housing, concerns about employment, lengthy waiting lists, and absence of services sensitive to gender (Howard & Beckwith, 1996; Lewis, Haller, Branch, & Ingersoll, 1996).

Jones, Svikis, and Tran (2002) compared maternal and fetal outcomes in pregnant drug users who were either compliant or noncompliant with drug use interventions offered through their obstetrical care clinic. The drug intervention involved a combination of motivational interviewing (Miller & Rollnick, 1991) and positive behavioral incentives contingent on clean urine drug screens. The researchers found that compliant mothers had babies with significantly higher birth weights than noncompliant mothers, and that mothers who were compliant with drug treatment were more likely to be drug free at delivery than those who were not.

In a review of the literature on the effectiveness of intervention programs for pregnant substance abusers, researchers concluded that programs which included the following elements were most likely to enroll and retain pregnant drug users as well as have the best treatment outcomes: a combination of multiple services assembled into one program, individual and group therapy, involvement of social support systems in treatment, child care, multidisciplinary team approach to treatment, educational training and vocational rehabilitation, prenatal care combined with drug treatment, a focus on contraception and treatment of sexually transmitted diseases, parenting skills training, and social services such as liaisons with child welfare services and legal counseling (Freda, Chazotte, & Youchah, 1995). In addition, researchers have emphasized the importance of confidentiality, a supportive clinic atmosphere, and use of clinic staff who are nonjudgmental and who understand the unique needs and circumstances of drug-dependent pregnant women (Elk & Magnus, 1997).

Svikis et al. (1998) suggested that perinatal addiction services be offered within the prenatal clinic so that women could benefit from drug treatment when they came to the clinic for routine medical visits. This treatment approach could provide seamless integrated care and reduce barriers to treatment. Svikis and colleagues (1998) found that use of a support group for pregnant drug abusers that was located at an obstetrical clinic was associated with greater compliance with attendance at prenatal appointments and with less likelihood of low-birth-weight babies, demonstrating the positive effects of such group participation. A number of treatment programs addressing substance use in pregnant women have been found to reduce drug use and contribute to improved maternal and fetal outcomes (e.g., Elk & Magnus, 1997).

Special Populations

Teenage Pregnancy

Teenage pregnancy emerged as a national problem in the early 1970s in the United States and has received considerable attention ever since. The United States has the highest rates of teenage pregnancy, abortion, and childbirth rates among all Western countries (Hardy, 1988). Teenage pregnancy is of particular concern given the well-established fact that pregnant teenagers are less likely to seek prenatal care and have an increased risk of pregnancy complications (Stevens-Simon & McAnarney, 1992). Amini, Catalano, Dierker, and Mann (1996) analyzed the demographic characteristics of pregnant teenagers and compared the trends and obstetrical outcomes of pregnant teens to those of pregnant adult women. Researchers found that the proportion of pregnant teenagers was highest among African Americans, followed by Hispanics, Caucasians, and those of other race groups. They also noted that a significantly higher proportion of teenagers had no private health insurance compared with adults, indicating lower SES among the teenagers. Pregnant teens aged between 12 and 15 years were significantly more likely to report two or fewer prenatal care visits than were those aged 16 to 19 or adults aged 20 and above. Researchers noted a consistent pattern of less optimal obstetrical outcomes among the pregnant teens aged between 12 and 15 years, including more preterm deliveries and lower birth weights. Teenage pregnancy also brings into concern issues such as the maturity of reproductive systems, greater risk of emotional distress and poor nutrition, and frequent use of tobacco, alcohol, and drugs—all of which have been shown to be risk factors for delivering babies with low birth weight (Hoekelman, 1993).

Advanced Maternal Age

Women aged 35 and over are considered to be at an "advanced maternal age" because of the increased maternal and fetal risks involved in these later-life pregnancies. For example, some studies have shown these women to be at higher risk for pregnancy loss, gestational diabetes, and pregnancy-induced hypertension (Ales, Druzin, & Santini, 1990). In a study analyzing the health-promotion behaviors of pregnant women over the age of 35, Viau, Padula, and Eddy (2002) found that 86% of their sample reported engaging in several health-promoting behaviors on a daily basis, such as eliminating alcohol and smoking, decreasing caffeine consumption, increasing water intake, monitoring weight gain, exercising, taking vitamin supplements, and avoiding junk foods. The researchers noted that the higher developmental level and SES of the older women in their sample may have contributed to their health promotion activities.

Sociodemographic Factors

Dutton (1986) noted the existence of interrelationships between SES factors and disproportionate levels of infant morbidity and mortality, as well as maternal death and general illness. Low-income pregnant women tend to have less access to prenatal care, exhibit lower use of prenatal care, perceive more barriers to care, have less social reinforcement for receiving care, have lower education levels, engage in fewer behaviors of a healthy lifestyle, and have lower levels of compliance with treatment recommendations (Henderson, 1994; Koska, 1990; Lia-Hoagberg et al., 1990; Miller, Magolis, Schwethelm, & Smith, 1989). These factors put low-income pregnant women at greater risk for delivering preterm and low-birth-weight babies (e.g., Lia-Hoagberg et al., 1990).

Stout (1997) described a set of structural, psychosocial, and sociodemographic factors that tend to serve as barriers to prenatal care for low-income women. Structural barriers may include access to care, lack of transportation or child care, inadequate finances, and poor organization of services (Lia-Hoagberg et al., 1990). Psychosocial variables included failure to detect the signs of pregnancy, lack of awareness of the need for care, ambivalence toward the pregnancy, lack of social support, negative or ambivalent beliefs about the importance of prenatal care, depression, denial of pregnancy, and inadequate support from the biological father (Young, McMahon, Bowman, & Thompson, 1990). Lia-Hoagberg et al. (1990) also noted factors such as lack of maternal knowledge, fear of medical procedures, and personal family problems as psychosocial barriers. Sociodemographic variables included maternal age, marital status, education, and financial status (Lia-Hoagberg et al., 1990). However, these sociodemographic variables were considered to be less important when compared with structural and psychosocial barriers (Lia-Hoagberg et al., 1990).

A great deal of literature exists on the relationship between religiosity and health. Treatment adherence in pregnancy may be mediated by religious variables such as healthier lifestyles of religious people (e.g., less tobacco use, alcohol consumption, drug use) and increased social support through religious affiliations, all of which have been correlated with better health outcomes. Najman, Williams, Keeping, Morrison, and Anderson (1988) compared pregnancy outcomes of three groups of Christians: members of Christian sects (such as Jehovah's Witnesses and Mormons), Christians who frequently attend church, and Christians who infrequently attend church. Results indicated that the members of Christian sects had the healthiest babies at delivery, followed by the frequent churchgoers, then the infrequent churchgoers. The researchers attributed this finding to specific characteristics of the mother and her lifestyle required by many of the Christian sects, such as abstention from alcohol and drugs and social ties provided by religious affiliation.

Diabetes in Pregnancy

Diabetes occurring during pregnancy, or gestational diabetes, affects more than 90,000 pregnancies per year in the United States (Sepe, Connell, Geiss, & Teutsch, 1985). Diabetes is associated with an increased risk of maternal and fetal complications of pregnancy. Such pregnancy complications include fetal prematurity, delivery by cesarean section, pregnancy-induced hypertension, and preeclampsia. Diabetic pregnancies have a significantly higher rate of congenital abnormalities and perinatal morbidities than nondiabetic pregnancies (American Diabetes Association, 2002). Thus, uncontrolled levels of blood glucose, inadequate fetal surveillance, or failure to adhere to treatment guidelines for gestational diabetes can place both the mother and fetus at considerable risk.

Adherence to treatment in gestational diabetes involves a variety of behaviors, including attending appointments, taking medications as prescribed, making lifestyle changes (dietary and exercise regimens), self-monitoring of blood glucose levels throughout the day, and avoidance of risk behaviors such as using drugs or alcohol. Besides the rigorous behavioral and self-care requirements of complying with treatment guidelines in gestational diabetes, what further complicates treatment adherence is that gestational diabetes is asymptomatic. Adherence rates have been found to be lowest when there is no discomfort or immediate risk noted by the patient, when lifestyle changes are recommended, and when the desired outcome is prevention rather than relief of symptoms, all of which are the case in gestational diabetes.

Investigators have found varying self-reported compliance rates across different regimen tasks among pregnant women with preexisting diabetes. For example, 74% to 79% of women reported being always compliant with dietary guidelines, 86% to 88% reported being compliant with insulin administration, 85% to 89% were in compliance with managing insulin reactions, and 94% to 96% reported adherence to glucose testing guidelines (Ruggiero, Spirito, Coustan, McGarvey, & Low, 1993). The lower rate of compliance with dietary guidelines was explained by the greater change in lifestyle required by this regimen in comparison with the others involved in diabetic self-care.

The variance in rates of compliance with treatment guidelines for gestational diabetes has been linked to various factors. For example, Ruggiero et al. (1993) noted that adherence to dietary recommendations was mediated by stress and social support and thus emphasized the importance of teaching patients stress management techniques and finding ways to increase social support. Persily (1995) analyzed the relationship between the perceived impact of gestational diabetes and adherence to treatment. Results indicated that women who perceived gestational diabetes to have a greater impact on their lives were less adherent in the self-monitoring of blood glucose and had higher rates of hypoglycemia than were those women who felt that the gestational diabetes had less of an impact on their lives. Racial differences were found to have no connection with compliance rates in a study comparing African American, Mexican American, and Caucasian populations (Langer, Langer, Piper, Elliott, & Anyaegbunam, 1995).

Affective states have been shown to influence complications and outcomes in diabetic pregnancies. Studying the relationship between depression and complications of diabetic pregnancy, researchers (Singh et al., 2004) noted that patients with depression were significantly more likely than those with no history of depression to experience pregnancy complications, including preterm labor, preeclampsia, and fetal prematurity. Depressed patients were also more likely to require cesarean section. Based on these results, the researchers emphasized the need to recognize and treat depression among pregnant women with diabetes to maximize pregnancy outcomes. Furthermore, Cabalum, Robbins, and Rojas (1987) found that psychological stress correlated highly with increased levels of blood glucose, a risk factor associated with poor maternal and fetal outcomes. Researchers also found that women with lower anxiety scores were more compliant with diet and exercise guidelines. The investigators concluded that stress exerts a strong influence on glycemic control in women with gestational diabetes, and they suggested that providers implement interventions for stress reduction.

Treatment targeting diabetic pregnancy has been shown to improve outcomes. For example, researchers found that a multidisciplinary program emphasizing preconceptual care, strict control of blood sugars both before and throughout gestation, and the use of antepartum fetal surveillance was associated with a significant decrease in rates of perinatal mortality and congenital malformations in infants of women with Type 1 diabetes (McElvy et al., 2000). Researchers emphasized the importance of preconceptual enrollment for women with Type 1 diabetes, followed by intense multidisciplinary gestational care.

HIV and AIDS

Epidemiological data (Centers for Disease Control, 1997) indicate that the number of children with AIDS acquired perinatally increased annually between 1984 and 1992 then decreased 43% between 1992 and 1996, due to an increase in the proportion of HIV-infected pregnant women being prescribed AZT during that period. One study documented a decrease from 19.5% before 1994 to 6% since 1994 in the annual perinatal transmission rate of HIV infection (Cooper, Charurat, Burns, Blattner, & Hoff, 2000). Researchers have estimated that without treatment, 15% to 30% of infants born to mothers infected with HIV will become infected (Anastos, Denenberg, & Solomon, 1998). Despite the risks of transmission, many women with HIV do not seek or adhere to treatment during pregnancy. Focus groups have revealed the following barriers to treatment: lack of information about therapy, misinformation about therapy, lack of belief in the efficacy of treatment, concerns about side effects or harm to the fetus, insufficient peer support for the treatment, and provider factors such as perceived unwillingness to provide education about treatment and insensitivity (Sowell et al., 1996). A comprehensive literature search revealed no information on specific programs to promote adherence to antiretrovirals during pregnancy. However, existing programs such as Levensky and O'Donohue's (2002) Prescriptive Adherence and Counseling Education (PACE) intervention could be easily adapted to this population.

Bed Rest

Bed rest is sometimes recommended for women with preterm labor, hypertension, bleeding, fetal growth retardation, and multiple gestation. To investigate the degree of compliance with bed rest and to examine the reasons for noncompliance, researchers questioned 326 high-risk obstetrical patients who had been asked to go on bed rest (Josten, Savik, Mullett, Campbell, & Vincent, 1995). Results indicated that 30% of the population did not comply with the bed rest recommendation. Compared with the women who complied, those in noncompliance were single, were not trying to get pregnant, had more children, had higher levels of stress, continued to drink during the pregnancy, and did not attend prenatal classes. Reasons given for noncompliance included the need to take care of other children, the need to work, lack of partner or family support, domestic demands, not feeling sick, and discomfort. However, the researchers noted no difference in pregnancy outcomes for those in compliance versus those who did not comply. To improve compliance, the researchers suggested that health care professionals should help women to deal with child care problems, stress, and alcohol consumption. They noted that social service agencies could help with this. They also recommended talking with the woman's family about the importance of bed rest to increase family support and reduce domestic demands. Finally, they stressed the need to clearly explain the importance of bed rest, even if the woman was feeling well.

Addressing Common Barriers to Adherence

Some of the barriers to adherence have been touched on above, in addition to researchers' suggestions to overcome these barriers. In this section, common barriers to treatment adherence in pregnancy will be more fully discussed. These barriers include improper or inadequate knowledge regarding adherence guidelines, cultural issues, personality variables of the patient, mental illness factors, lack of social support, inadequate resources, lack of adherence-related skills, and characteristics related to the delivery of care. In addition, empirically supported techniques from the literature will be applied to address these adherence barriers.

Inadequate or Improper Knowledge

Lack of awareness of the importance of prenatal care and adherence to prenatal guidelines has been identified as a reason given by pregnant women for not obtaining adequate prenatal care (Leatherman, Blackburn, & Davidhizar, 1990). To address this barrier, Leatherman et al. (1990) concluded that the use of prenatal care could be improved by providing communitywide education regarding the importance of adequate prenatal care and the consequences of inadequate care. They suggested that this information be incorporated into current sex education classes. Taking this one step further, Bryne, Allensworth, and Prince (1981) suggested that pregnancy testing kits and positive pregnancy results from laboratories or physicians' offices should be accompanied by written prenatal information to improve knowledge about the importance of prenatal care. In a review of the literature, Reid and Garcia (1989) noted that women wanted more information about such procedures as routine prenatal screens, but there was a tendency for providers to give them general reassurances instead of explanations. However, they also noted that despite a lack of comprehension about the reasons for engaging in compliance behaviors, the women had high rates of compliance.

Studies have demonstrated that a person's reference group may influence health behavior and acceptance of medical advice (e.g., Suchman, 1965). St. Clair and Anderson (1989) found that pregnant women received a median of 20 pieces of advice related to pregnancy health from people in their social support networks. Most of this advice was found to be sound. Three quarters of respondents in the study reported hearing old wives' tales concerning the etiology of complications of pregnancy. Most respondents dismissed the advice, but for some the beliefs were a significant source of anxiety. The researchers also noted that 11% of women received advice that, if followed, could have been harmful. Given the prevalence and potentially powerful influence of advice given during pregnancy, the researchers concluded that health care providers need to be aware that adherence to medical recommendations may be affected by the patient's reference group.

In addition, problematic beliefs may affect treatment adherence. These beliefs may involve erroneous thinking around the need for treatment, the seriousness of the problem, the potential efficacy of the treatment, possible side effects, the importance of adherence, the relative costs and benefits of adhering to the treatment, and perceptions of the ability to adhere to treatment. For example, Galloway and McGuire (1994) noted that beliefs about iron supplementation causing large babies interfered with patients' adherence to nutritional supplementation. Such problematic beliefs may be assessed using the health beliefs model (Janz & Becker, 1984). Belief domains include the following: (1) the likelihood of the disease worsening if gone untreated, (2) the seriousness and threat of the disease to the patient's health, (3) the patient's ability to adhere to the treatment, (4) the effectiveness of the treatment in treating the disease, (5) the relative costs

and benefits of the treatment, and (6) the necessity of taking the medication as prescribed for the treatment to be effective. Problematic beliefs and deficits in knowledge can be addressed by properly educating the patient about the need for adherence to treatment guidelines in pregnancy and by discussing the pros and cons of adherence and nonadherence.

Cultural Issues

Although many studies have failed to document racial differences in rates of treatment adherence in pregnancy (e.g., Amini et al., 1996), various cultural issues such as communication styles and language deficits may affect adherence (Alcalay, Ghee, & Scrimshaw, 1993). Adherence may be promoted by providing culturally sensitive treatment and by providing either translators or services in the patient's native language. One example of such culturally sensitive treatment has been provided by Moore, Hopper, and Dip (1995). These researchers found that the use of patient-driven birth plans allowed for cultural values and customs to be incorporated into the labor and delivery process. They also noted that such birth plans empowered women by increasing their knowledge of birth practices and by helping them to make informed decisions about their labor and delivery.

Personality Variables

Personality variables such as locus of control and motivation have been associated with adherence to treatment in pregnancy. Tinsley, Trupin, Owens, and Boyum (1993) modified other health locus of control scales to develop the Pregnancy Beliefs Scales. This questionnaire was designed to assess the extent to which pregnant women endorsed internality, chance externality, and powerful others externality with respect to pregnancy and perinatal outcomes. Internality refers to the belief that factors that determine health are due to one's own behavior, whereas externality refers to the belief that health is due to forces beyond one's own control such as either chance/luck/fate or to powerful others. They found that women's perceptions of their control over perinatal outcomes were related to compliance with prenatal care guidelines, which was in turn related to actual pregnancy and birth outcomes. Specifically, middle-class women who had an internal locus of control with respect to pregnancy were less likely to use street drugs, smoke cigarettes, or use nonprescription drugs during pregnancy, and were more likely to comply with prenatal and well-baby visits than were women with an external locus of control. However, in another study using an ethnically diverse, low SES sample, results indicated that women with an internal locus of control were *less* likely than those with an external locus of control to receive adequate prenatal care (Reisch & Tinsley, 1994). The authors explained this discrepancy by noting that an internal locus of control makes more sense for an educated, middle-class sample given an environment of potential for personal control. However, disadvantaged groups must often deal with an inability to execute control over their environment, such that an external locus of control is more consistent with the reality of their environment. Researchers comparing maternal and fetal locus of control between women with gestational diabetes, pregestational diabetes, and nondiabetic pregnant controls found that women with pregestational diabetes obtained higher scores on the Powerful Others subscale than nondiabetic controls, and that women with gestational diabetes obtained higher scores on the Chance subscale than women in the other two groups (Spirito, Ruggiero, McGarvey, Coustan, & Low, 1990).

Low levels of motivation were cited by 45% of women in explaining their lack of obtaining adequate prenatal care (Leatherman et al., 1990). A variety of techniques have been shown to improve motivation, including use of patient-driven birth plans (Moore et al., 1995), motivational interviewing strategies (Miller & Rollnick, 1991), and offering incentives. For example, Stevens-Simon, O'Connor, and Bassford (1994) demonstrated the effectiveness of using an incentive (Gerry "Cuddler") in improving rates of compliance with the postpartum visit in an adolescent population. Lumley (1990) reported on a number of studies indicating that prenatal ultrasound scans could enable mothers to hasten the development of maternal-fetal attachment, and that use of ultrasounds were related to short-term effects on maternal health behaviors such as decreased tobacco use and decreased consumption of alcohol. Other incentives could include financial discounts, free baby supplies, and maternity clothes. Based on a thorough review of the literature, Levensky (2004) has suggested the following techniques to increase motivation and treatment adherence: simplifying the treatment regimen, tailoring the regimen to fit the patient's lifestyle, fitting the regimen to the patient's daily routine, addressing problematic beliefs about the health condition and the treatment, education on the benefits of adherence and the costs of nonadherence, providing information on the impact of adherence and nonadherence on clinical outcomes, minimizing barriers related to the treatment, using commitment strategies (Linehan, 1994), obtaining commitments from the patient regarding adherence behaviors, enhancing the patient's self-efficacy, treating mental health problems, establishing a system of reinforcement for adherence, and treating side effects.

Mental Illness

Depression and anxiety have been associated with adherence to health guidelines in pregnancy and to maternal and fetal outcomes (e.g., Schoenback, Garrison, & Kaplan, 1984). For example, Zuckerman, Amaro, Bauchner, and Cabral (1989) analyzed the relationships between depression, demographic variables, and health behaviors. They found that depressive symptoms were significantly correlated with the following demographic factors in the pregnant women under study: being single, older, unemployed, and having a lower income. There was no relationship between depressive symptoms and race, education, or health problems during pregnancy (such as hypertension). Furthermore, the researchers found a significant association between depressive symptoms and health behaviors such as low weight gain and frequency of the use of tobacco, alcohol, and cocaine. With the exception of cocaine, these relationships remained even when the effects of income were statistically controlled. The researchers hypothesized that depressed women may be self-medicating with use of substances, which they warned could in turn result in poor infant outcomes. Depressive symptoms were also associated with social support. Women reporting more depressive symptoms were also likely to report lower levels of social support and perceptions that their partner or family was unhappy about the pregnancy. Based on these results, the researchers encouraged clinicians to consider the affective state, mental health, and socioeconomic situation of pregnant women and to implement interventions to help women cope with depressive symptomatology. Given the lack of proven safety of pharmacological treatment of depression and the mounting evidence of the effectiveness of psychotherapy in treating depression (e.g., Burns, 1980; Lewinshohn, Munoz, Youngren, & Zeiss, 1992), medical providers should introduce pregnant women to a psychotherapist as soon as the depression becomes identified.

Pregnancy can be very stressful and ranks 12th on a list of stressful life events by Holmes and Rahe (1967). The literature is rich with studies documenting the relationship between stress and health-damaging behavior. For example, perceived stress has been associated with an increase in smoking (Epstein & Perkins, 1988) and a decrease in exercise (Rodriguez et al., 2000). Reading (1983) developed a model to explain the influence of maternal anxiety on the course and outcome of pregnancy. The model suggested that pregnancy may be a time of vulnerability to anxiety given the concomitant concerns produced by the pregnancy and the biological changes associated with the pregnancy. Reading noted that the impact of stress may be moderated by factors such as state and trait anxiety, attitudes toward the pregnancy, perceptions and appraisals of the stress, social support, and coping mechanisms available. However, this model was not empirically supported. To treat anxiety and thus promote treatment adherence, a variety of empirically supported cognitive and behavioral strategies could be implemented (e.g., Bernstein & Borkovec, 1973; Meichenbaum, 1985).

Social Support

Social support has been found to have an indirect effect on treatment adherence and pregnancy outcomes via its effect on promoting positive health behaviors. For example, Rodriguez et al. (2000) found that social support had a positive effect on exercise and predicted less smoking. Furthermore, Aaronson (1989) noted that perceived and received social support were significant and independent predictors of abstention from alcohol, cigarettes, and caffeine during pregnancy. Lack of social support has been correlated with increased state and trait anxiety levels, as well as with the consumption of alcohol. The social support system may also operate in instrumental ways, such as by providing babysitting or rides so that the pregnant woman may attend obstetrical appointments, by helping with medication taking, and by encouraging adherence to treatment guidelines. Given the relevance of social support to treatment adherence, researchers have highlighted the importance of actively including family members in prenatal care and have suggested that health care providers encourage women to increase their social support.

Social support may also be increased by encouraging the pregnant woman to attend support groups and prenatal classes, having providers conduct telephone check-ins, implementing a home visitation program (e.g., Navaie-Waliser & Martin, 2000), and providing health care in a group format. In addition to the potential for improving social support, the literature has demonstrated that group teaching is as effective, if not more, as individual teaching and is cost-effective with respect to staff time and money. For example, the superior outcome benefits and/or cost-effectiveness of group methods in comparison with individual teaching have been demonstrated in the areas of teaching mothers to care for newborn infants (McNeil & Holland, 1972) and teaching pregnant women about proper nutrition (Sultemeier, 1988). Recently, group medical appointments in primary and specialty care have been implemented by Sutter Medical Foundation in Sacramento, California (Schmucker, 2004). The format of group appointments not only allows patients to increase social support but also instills a positive and hopeful attitude in patients, helps patients to find that they have much in common with one another, allows patients to share information with one another about methods of successful adherence, and benefits from peer pressure promoting a culture of adherence (Schmucker, 2004).

Lack of Resources

Lack of resources, such as finances, insurance, child care, and transportation, have been cited as reasons for failure to receive adequate prenatal care (e.g., Leatherman et al., 1990). In fact, insufficient money to pay for services was cited as the primary reason for not obtaining adequate prenatal care (Leatherman et al., 1990). It was also noted by these researchers that almost 90% of those who started early prenatal care and subsequently dropped out did so due to lack of money to pay for the prenatal care. The researchers suggested implementation of subsidized prenatal care to address financial barriers. In addition, other researchers have suggested the use of transportation vouchers and availability of child care services on site (e.g., Campbell et al., 2000).

Lack of Skills

Treatment adherence may be impeded by a lack of adherence-related skills, by cognitive deficits,

or by a lack of communication skills (Levensky, 2004). Adherence-related skills may involve abilities related to organization and problem solving. Strategies such as skills training (O'Donohue & Krasner, 1995) and problem solving (D'Zurilla, 1986) may be used to address these deficits. Cognitive deficits may include memory problems such as forgetfulness. Memory aids such as pill boxes, calendars, and self-monitoring may help to address such deficits (Levensky, 2004). A lack of communication skills could interfere with the patient's ability to communicate questions, concerns, and potential problems with treatment. Thus, treatment adherence could be improved by teaching the patient communication and assertiveness skills (e.g., O'Donohue & Krasner, 1995).

Characteristics of Prenatal Care

A variety of factors related to the delivery of care, including characteristics of the provider or clinic, a poor patient-provider relationship, and problematic models of delivery of care, may serve as barriers to treatment adherence in pregnancy. For example, concerns about being judged as selfish or irresponsible by clinical staff have been noted to impede pregnant drug users from seeking treatment (Lewis, Klee, & Jackson, 1995). Other clinic barriers have been noted to be fears about confidentiality (Elk & Magnus, 1997), and poor accessibility of services, including insufficient hours of operation and long waits for services (Howard & Beckwith, 1996).

Problems in communication between the patient and the provider can lead to disruptions in adherence. The provider may not adequately communicate the importance of adherence to various treatment guidelines and may not explain the potential benefits and costs of adherence versus non-adherence (e.g., Reid & Garcia, 1989). The importance of properly educating the patient about the importance of adherence, as well as the pros and cons of adherence, has been emphasized above (e.g., Blankson & Goldberg, 1994). However, such education may not necessarily lead to improved outcomes. Brustman, Langer, Anyaegbunam, Belle, and Merkatz (1990) noted that an intensive nursing service intervention instructing women about the early signs and symptoms of preterm labor did not improve the patients' perceptions of preterm uterine contractility, which, if successful, could have contributed to a decrease in the rate of premature labor.

In addition, characteristics of the delivery of care may be a barrier to treatment adherence in pregnancy. For example, Olds, Henderson, Tatelbaum, and Chamberline (1986) noted that office-based visits may not be feasible for socially disadvantaged populations due to interference of difficult life circumstances. A nurse home visitation program was evaluated and compared in a randomized clinical trial with other models of prenatal care delivery. Specifically, disadvantaged pregnant women were visited in their homes by nurses who provided education, enhancement of social support systems, and linkage with community services. Researchers found that compared with control samples, the women in the nurse home visitation program engaged in a greater number of health behaviors (e.g., making dietary improvements), reported greater social support (e.g., more pregnancy interest among biological fathers and presence of support people at the delivery), use of community services (e.g., awareness of community services and use of nutritional supplementation programs), and better pregnancy outcomes (e.g., greater birth weight and length of gestation).

As noted above, the format of group medical appointments has recently been implemented in primary care (Schmucker, 2004) and could easily be adapted to prenatal care. In addition to improving the patient's social support network, group medical appointments have been noted to improve both patient and provider satisfaction, improve patient access to medical care, improve quality of care, increase the amount of time patients have with their providers, make better use of existing resources, and improve provider productivity (Schmucker, 2004). The effectiveness of group formats for teaching nutrition skills (Sultemeier, 1988) and addressing addiction issues in prenatal settings (Svikis et al., 1998) has been discussed above.

Assessment Issues

A comprehensive literature search revealed no standardized self-report measures of treatment adherence in pregnancy. Instead, most researchers either created their own measures for the purposes of the study, or they relied on objective measures such as attendance (at prenatal care appointments and substance abuse treatment sessions), pill counts (prenatal vitamins and supplements), biological markers (e.g., weight gain, blood pressure, glucose levels, urine drug tests), and fetal outcomes (e.g., fetal growth/weight, gestational age at delivery, Apgar scores). However, pregnant patients have been noted to overreport their compliance with medications using pill counts (DuBard, Goldenberg, Copper, & Hauth, 1993) and to omit or fabricate glucose levels in glucose monitoring (Langer & Mazze, 1986). Researchers found that compliance rates and accuracy in reporting of self-monitored blood glucose values could be improved when patients with gestational diabetes were aware of the memory function in the glucose reflectance meter (Langer et al., 1995).

Case Study

As previously noted (Kumpfer, 1991), pregnant substance abusers present a particular challenge with respect to treatment adherence. The Center for Perinatal Addiction (CPA; Haller et al., 2003) is a treatment program for pregnant substance abusers that combines many of the elements of successful treatment adherence that have been suggested above. The CPA was funded by National Institute on Drug Abuse (NIDA) as a treatment demonstration project in the first half of the 1990s. The program offered comprehensive services to substance abusing mothers and their infants, as well as their older children. A multidisciplinary team approach was used, with obstetrical, psychiatric, general medical, and dental care provided. Therapeutic modalities included individual therapy, group therapy, and case management. Psychoeducation was provided through manualized treatments in a weekly group format and included the following topics: substance abuse education, relapse prevention, skills building, prenatal education, parenting, mother-infant interaction, home management, nutrition, vocational counseling, spirituality, and a trauma focused group. The program also offered methadone maintenance for opioid-dependent mothers. In an attempt to eliminate barriers often cited by this population, drug-free housing, child care, and transportation were provided. All services were free to participants and their children.

References

Aaronson, L. S. (1989). Perceived and received support: Effects on health behavior during pregnancy. *Nursing Research, 38*(1), 4–9.

Alcalay, R., Ghee, A., & Scrimshaw, S. (1993). Designing prenatal care messages for low-income Mexican women. *Public Health Reports, 108*(3), 354–362.

Ales, K. L., Druzin, M. L., & Santini, D. L. (1990). Impact of advanced maternal age on the outcome of pregnancy. *Surgery, Gynecology and Obstetrics, 171,* 209–216.

American Diabetes Association. (2002). Preconception care of women with diabetes. *Diabetes Care, 25,* S82–S84.

Amini, S. B., Catalano, P. M., Dierker, L. J., & Mann, L. I. (1996). Birth to teenagers: Trends and obstetric outcomes. *Obstetrics and Gynecology, 87,* 668–674.

Anastos, K., Denenberg, R., & Solomon, L. (1998). Clinical management of HIV-infected women. In G. P. Wormser (Ed.), *AIDS and other manifestations of HIV infection* (pp. 339–348). Philadelphia: J. B. Lippincott.

Bernstein, D. A., & Borkovec, T. D. (1973). *Progressive relaxation training: A manual for the helping professions.* Champaign, IL: Research Press.

Blankson, M. L., & Goldenberg, R. L. (1994). Noncompliance of high-risk pregnant women in keeping appointments at an obstetric complications clinic. *Southern Medical Journal, 87*(6), 634–638.

Brustman, L. E., Langer, O., Anyaegbunam, A., Belle, C., & Merkatz, I. R. (1990). Education does not improve patient perception of preterm uterine contractility. *Obstetrics and Gynecology, 76*(1), 97S–101S.

Bryne, I., Allensworth, D., & Price, J. (1981). *Preparenting and prenatal care: First steps to high level wellness.* White Plains, NY: March of Dimes.

Buescher, P. A., Larson, L. C., Nelson, M. D., Jr., & Lenihan, A. J. (1993). Prenatal WIC participation can reduce low birth weight and newborn medical costs: A cost-benefit analysis of WIC participation in North Carolina. *Journal of the American Dietetic Association, 93,* 163–166.

Buka, S. (1991). Clipped wings: The fullest look yet at how prenatal exposure to drugs, alcohol, and nicotine hobbles children's learning. *American Education, 15*(1), 27–30.

Burns, D. D. (1980). *Feeling good: The new mood therapy.* New York: Avon Books.

Cabalum, T., Robbins, N., & Rojas, E. (1987). Psychological stress and glycemic control in the gestational diabetic. In *Proceedings of the 7th Annual Meeting of the Society of Perinatal Obstetricians, Lake Buena Vista.*

Campbell, J. D., Chez, R. A., Queen, T., Barcelo, A., & Patron, E. (2000). The no-show rate in a high-risk obstetric clinic. *Journal of Women's Health and Gender-Based Medicine, 9*(8), 891–895.

Centers for Disease Control. (1997). Update: Perinatally acquired HIV/AIDS–United States. *Morbidity and Mortality Weekly Report, 46,* 1086–1092.

Chasnoff, I. J. (1988). Drug use in pregnancy: Parameters of risk. *Pediatric Clinicians of North America, 35*(6), 1403–1412.

Cooper, E. R., Charurat, M., Burns, D. N., Blattner, W., & Hoff, R. (2000). Trends in antiretroviral therapy and mother-infant transmission of HIV. *Journal of Acquired Immune Deficiency Syndrome, 24,* 45–47.

DuBard, M. B., Goldenberg, R. L., Coppel, R. L., & Hauth, J. C. (1993). Are pill counts valid measures of compliance in clinical obstetric trials? *American Journal of Obstetrics and Gynecology, 169,* 1181–1182.

Dutton, D. (1986). Social class, health and illness. In L. Aiken & D. Mechanic (Eds.), *Applications of social science to clinical medicine and health policy.* Newark, NJ: Rutgers University.

D'Zurilla, T. J. (1986). *Problem solving therapy.* New York: Springer.

Elk, R., & Magnus, L. G. (1997). Behavioral intervention: Effective and adaptable for the treatment of pregnant cocaine-dependent women. *Journal of Drug Issues, 27*(3), 1–33.

Epstein, L. H., & Perkins, K. (1988). Smoking, stress and coronary heart disease. *Journal of Consulting and Clinical Psychology, 56,* 342–349.

Freda, M. C., Chazotte, C., & Youchah, J. (1995). What do we know about how to enroll and retain pregnant drug users in prenatal car? *Journal of Women's Health, 4*(1), 55–63.

Galloway, R., & McGuire, J. (1994). Determinants of compliance with iron supplementation: Supplies, side effects, or psychology? *Social Science Medicine, 39*(3), 381–390.

Goldenberg, R. L., Tamura, T., Cliver, S. P., Cutter, G. R., Hoffman, H. J., & Copper, R. L. (1992). Serum folate and fetal growth retardation: A matter of compliance? *Obstetrics and Gynecology, 79*(5), 719–722.

Haller, D. L., Miles, D. R., & Dawson, K. S. (2003). Factors influencing treatment enrollment by pregnant substance abusers. *American Journal of Drug and Alcohol Abuse, 29*(1), 117–131.

Hanna, E. Z., Faden, V. B., & Dufour, M. C. (1997). The effects of substance use during gestation on birth outcome, infant and maternal health. *Journal of Substance Abuse, 9,* 111–125.

Hardy, J. B. (1988). Premature sexual activity, pregnancy, and sexually transmitted disease: The pediatrician's role as counselor. *Pediatrics Review, 10,* 69–76.

Henderson, J. (1994). The cost effectiveness of prenatal care. *Health Care Financing Review, 15*(4), 21–31.

Higgins, P. G., & Woods, P. J. (1999). Reasons, health behaviors, and outcomes of no prenatal care: Research that changed practice. *Health Care for Women International, 20*(2), 127–136.

Hoekelman, R. A. (1993). A pediatrician's review: Teenage pregnancy one of our nation's most challenging dilemmas. *Pediatrics Annals, 22,* 81–82.

Holmes, T., & Rahe, R. (1967). The social readjustment rating scale. *Journal of Psychosomatic Research, 11,* 213–218.

Howard, J., & Beckwith, L. (1996). Issues in subject recruitment and retention with pregnant and parenting substance abusing women. In E. Rahdert (Ed.), *Treatment for drug exposed women and children: Advancements in research methodologies* (NIDA Research Monographs No. 166, pp. 68–86). Washington, DC: National Institute of Drug Abuse.

Janz, N., & Becker, M. (1984). The health belief model: A decade later. *Health Education Quarterly, 11,* 1–47.

Jones, H. E., Svikis, D. S., & Tran, G. (2002). Patient compliance and maternal/infant outcomes in pregnant drug-using women. *Substance Use and Misuse, 37*(11), 1411–1422.

Josten, L. E., Savik, K., Mullett, S. E., Campbell, R., & Vincent, P. (1995). Bedrest compliance for women with pregnancy problems. *Birth, 22*(1), 1–14.

Keppel, K. G., & Taffel, S. M. (1993). Pregnancy-related weight gain and retention: Implications of the 1990 Institute of Medicine Guidelines. *American Journal of Public Health, 83,* 1100–1103.

Kloeblen, A. S., & Batish, S. S. (1999). Understanding the intention to permanently follow a high folate diet among a sample of low-income pregnant women according to the Health Belief Model. *Health Education Research, 14*(3), 327–338.

Koska, M. (1990). Prototype women's health center eliminates barriers to care. *Hospitals, 64,* 57–59.

Kost, K., Landry, D. J., & Darroch, J. E. (1998). Predicting maternal behaviors during pregnancy: Does intention status matter? *Family Planning Perspectives, 30*(2), 79–88.

Kowaleski-Jones, L., & Duncan, G. J. (2002). Effects of participation in the WIC program on birth weight: Evidence from the National Longitudinal Survey of Youth, Special Supplemental Nutrition Program for Women, Infants, and Children. *American Journal of Public Health, 92,* 799–804.

Kumpfer, K. L. (1991). Treatment programs for drug-abusing women. *Future of Our Children: Drug Exposed Infants, 1*(1), 50–60.

Langer, O., Langer, N., Piper, J. M., Elliott, B., & Anyaegbunam, A. (1995). Cultural diversity as a factor in self-monitoring blood glucose in gestational diabetes. *Journal of the Association for Academic Minority Physicians, 6*(2), 73–77.

Langer, O., & Mazze, R. S. (1986). Diabetes in pregnancy: Evaluating self-monitoring performance and glycemic control with memory-based reflectance meters. *American Journal of Obstetrics and Gynecology, 155*(3), 635–638.

Leatherman, J., Blackburn, D., & Davidhizar, R. (1990). How postpartum women explain their lack of obtaining adequate prenatal care. *Journal of Advanced Nursing, 15,* 256–267.

Lederman, S. A. (1993). Recent issues related to nutrition during pregnancy. *Journal of the American College of Nutrition, 12,* 91–100.

Levensky, E. R. (2004). Increasing medication adherence in chronic illnesses: Guidelines for behavioral healthcare clinicians working in primary care settings. In W. O'Donohue, D. Henderson, M. Byrd, & N. Cummings (Eds.), *Behavioral integrative care: Treatments that work in the primary care setting* (pp. 347–366). New York: Brunner-Routledge.

Levensky, E., & O'Donohue, W. (2002). *The prescriptive adherence counseling and education (PACE) intervention for increasing adherence to HIV medications.* Unpublished manuscript, University of Nevada, Reno.

Lewinshohn, P. M., Munoz, R. F., Youngren, M. A., & Zeiss, A. M. (1992). *Control your depression.* New York: Simon & Schuster.

Lewis, R. A., Haller, D. L., Branch, D., & Ingersoll, K. S. (1996). Retention issues in the treatment of drug abusing women. In E. Rahdert (Ed.), *Treatment for drug exposed women and children: Advancements in research methodologies* (NIDA Research Monographs No. 166, pp. 110–122). Washington, DC: National Institute of Drug Abuse.

Lewis, S., Klee, H., & Jackson, M. (1995). Illicit drug users' experiences of pregnancy: An exploratory study. *Journal of Reproductive and Infant Psychology, 13,* 219–227.

Lia-Hoagberg, B., Rode, P., Skovhold, C., Oberg, C., Berg, C., Mullett, S., et al. (1990). Barriers and motivators to prenatal care among low income women. *Social Science and Medicine, 30,* 487–495.

Linehan, M. (1994). *Cognitive behavioral therapy for borderline personality disorder.* New York: Guilford Press.

Lumley, J. (1990). Through a glass darkly: Ultrasound and prenatal bonding. *Birth, 17,* 214–217.

Maclean, U., Sinfield, D., Klein, S., & Harden, B. (1984). Women who decline breast screening. *Journal of Epidemiology and Community Health, 24,* 278–283.

Marteau, T. M., Johnston, M., Kidd, J., Michie, S., & Cook, R. (1992). Psychological models in predicting uptake of prenatal screening. *Psychology and Health, 6,* 13–22.

McElvy, S. S., Miodovnik, M., Rosenn, B., Khoury, J. C., Siddiqi, T., St. John Dignan, P., et al. (2000). A focused preconceptional and early pregnancy program in women with Type 1 diabetes reduces perinatal mortality and malformation rates to general population levels. *Journal of Maternal-Fetal Medicine, 9,* 14–20.

McFarlane, J., Parker, B., & Soeken, K. (1996). Physical abuse, smoking and substance use during pregnancy: Prevalence, interrelationships, and effects on birth weight. *Journal of Gynecological and Neonatal Nursing, 25,* 313–320.

McNeil, H., & Holland, S. (1972). A comparative study of public health nurse teaching in groups and in home visits. *American Journal of Public Health, 62,* 1629–1637.

Meichenbaum, D. (1985). *Stress inoculation training.* New York: Pergamon Press.

Miller, C., Magolis, L., Schwethelm, B., & Smith, S. (1989). Barriers to implementation of a prenatal care program for low income women. *American Journal of Public Health, 79,* 62–64.

Miller, B., & Rollnick, S. (1991). *Motivational interviewing: Preparing people to change addictive behavior.* New York: Guilford Press.

Moore, M., Hopper, U., & Dip, G. (1995). Do birth plans empower women? Evaluation of a hospital birth plan. *Birth, 22*(1), 29–36.

Najman, J. M., Williams, G. M., Keeping, J. D., Morrison, J., & Anderson, M. J. (1988). Religious values, practices and pregnancy outcomes: A comparison of the impact of sect and mainstream Christian affiliation. *Social Science and Medicine, 26*(4), 401–407.

Nathoo, V. (1988). Investigation of non-responders at a cervical cancer screening clinic in Manchester. *British Medical Journal, 296,* 1041–1042.

National Pregnancy and Health Survey. (1993). *Pregnancy and drug use trends.* Washington, DC: National Institute on Drug Abuse.

Navaie-Waliser, M., & Martin, S. L. (2000). Factors predicting completion of a home visitation program by high-risk pregnant women: The North Carolina maternal outreach worker program. *American Journal of Public Health, 90*(1), 121–124.

O'Donohue, W. T., & Krasner, L. (1995). *Handbook of psychological skills training: Clinical techniques and applications.* Boston: Allyn & Bacon.

Olds, D. L., Henderson, C. R., Tatelbaum, R., & Chamberline, R. (1986). Improving the delivery of prenatal care and outcomes of pregnancy: A randomized trial of nurse home visitation. *Pediatrics, 77*(1), 16–28.

Parker, J. D., & Abrams, B. (1992). Prenatal weight gain advice: An examination of the recent prenatal weight gain recommendations of the Institute of Medicine. *Obstetrics and Gynecology, 79,* 664–669.

Persily, C. A. (1995). Relationships between the perceived impact of gestational diabetes mellitus and treatment adherence. *Journal of Gynecological and Neonatal Nursing, 25,* 601–607.

Poland, M. (1985). *Ethical issues surrounding prenatal care.* Unpublished manuscript, Wayne State University.

Polley, B. A., Wing, R. R., & Sims, C. J. (2002). Randomized controlled trial to prevent excessive weight gain in pregnant women. *International Journal of Obesity, 26,* 1494–1502.

Reading, A. E. (1983). The influence of maternal anxiety on the course and outcome of pregnancy: A review. *Health Psychology, 2*(2), 187–202.

Reid, M., & Garcia, J. (1989). Women's views of care during pregnancy and childbirth. In I. Chalmers, M. Enkin, & M. Keirse (Eds.), *Effective care in pregnancy and childbirth* (pp. 131–142). New York: Oxford University Press.

Reisch, L. M., & Tinsley, B. J. (1994). Impoverished women's health locus of control and utilization of prenatal services. *Journal of Reproductive and Infant Psychology, 12,* 223–232.

Rodriguez, A., Bohlin, G., & Lindmark, G. (2000). Psychosocial predictors of smoking and exercise during pregnancy. *Journal of Reproductive and Infant Psychology, 18*(3), 203–226.

Ruggiero, L., Spirito, A., Coustan, D., McGarvey, S. T., & Low, K. G. (1993). Self-reported compliance with diabetes self-management during pregnancy. *International Journal of Psychiatry in Medicine, 23*(2), 195–207.

Schmucker, D. (2004). *The changing landscape of healthcare makes room for the group medical appointment.* Unpublished manuscript, Sutter Medical Foundation, Sacramento, CA.

Schoenback, V., Garrison, C., & Kaplan, B. (1984). Epidemiology of adolescent depression. *Public Health Review, 12,* 159–189.

Sepe, S., Connell, F., Geiss, S., & Teutsch, S. (1985). Gestational diabetes: Incidence, maternal characteristics and perinatal outcome. *Diabetes, 34,* 13–16.

Shu, X., Hatch, M., Mills, J., Clemens, J., & Susser, M. (1995). Maternal smoking, alcohol drinking, caffeine consumption, and fetal growth: Results from a prospective study. *Epidemiology, 6,* 115–120.

Singh, P. K., Lustman, P. J., Clouse, R. E., Freedland, K. E., Perez, M., Anderson, R. J., et al. (2004). Association of depression with complications of diabetic pregnancy: A retrospective analysis. *Journal of Clinical Psychology in Medical Settings, 11*(1), 49–54.

Sowell, R. L., Seals, B., Moneyham, L., Guillory, J., Demi, A., & Cohen, L. (1996). Barriers to health-seeking behaviors for women infected with HIV. *Nursing Connections, 9,* 5–17.

Spirito, A., Ruggiero, L., McGarvey, S. T., Coustan, D. R., & Low, K. G. (1990). Maternal and fetal health locus of control during pregnancy: A comparison of women with diabetes and nondiabetic women. *Journal of Reproductive and Infant Psychology, 8,* 195–206.

St. Clair, P. A., & Anderson, N. A. (1989). Social network advice during pregnancy: Myths, misinformation, and sound counsel. *Birth, 16*(3), 103–108.

Stevens-Simon, C., & McAnarney, E. R. (1992). Adolescent pregnancy. In E. R. McAnarney, R. E. Kriepe, D. P. Orr, & G. D. Comerci (Eds.), *Textbook of adolescent medicine.* Philadelphia: W. B. Saunders.

Stevens-Simon, C., O'Connor, P., & Bassford, K. (1994). Incentives enhance postpartum compliance among adolescent prenatal patients. *Journal of Adolescent Health, 15,* 396–399.

Stout, A. E. (1997). Prenatal care for low-income women and the health belief model: A new beginning. *Journal of Community Health Nursing, 14*(3), 169–180.

Suchman, E. (1965). Social patterns of illness and medical care. *Journal of Health and Human Behavior, 6,* 2–16.

Sultemeier, A. (1988). An innovative approach to teaching prenatal nutrition. *Journal of Community Health Nursing, 5*(4), 247–254.

Svikis, D. S., McCaul, M. E., Feng, T., Stuart, M., Fox, M., & Stokes, E. (1998). Drug dependence during pregnancy: Effect of an on-site support group. *Journal of Reproductive Health, 43,* 799–803.

Taffel, S. M., Keppel, K. G., & Jones, G. K. (1993).). Medical advice on maternal weight gain and actual weight gain. Results from the 1988 National Maternal and Infant Health Survey. *Annals of the New York Academy of Sciences, 678,* 293–305.

Tinsley, B. J., Trupin. S. R., Owens, L., & Boyum, L. A. (1993). The significance of women's pregnancy-related locus of control beliefs for adherence to recommended prenatal health regimes and pregnancy outcomes. *Journal of Reproductive and Infant Psychology, 11*(2), 97–102.

Viau, P. A., Padula, C. A., Eddy, B. (2002). An exploration of health concerns and health-promotion behaviors in pregnant women over age 35. *American Journal of Maternal/Child Nursing, 27*(6), 328–334.

Windsor, R. A., Lowe, J. B., Perkins, L. L., Smith-Yoder, D., Artz, L., Crawford, M., et al. (1993). Health education for pregnant smokers: Its behavioral impact and cost benefit. *American Journal of Public Health, 83*(2), 201–206.

Wrieden, W. L., & Symon, A. (2003). The development and pilot evaluation of a nutrition education intervention programme for pregnant teenage women (food for life). *Journal of Human Nutrition and Dietetics, 16*(2), 67–71.

Young, C., McMahon, J., Bowman, V., & Thompson, D. (1990). Psychosocial concerns of women who delay prenatal care. *Families in Society: The Journal of Contemporary Human Services, 71,* 408–414.

Zuckerman, B., Amaro, H., Bauchner, H., & Cabral, H. (1989). Depressive symptoms during pregnancy: Relationship to poor health behaviors. *American Journal of Obstetrics and Gynecology, 160*(5), 1107–1111.

26

Treatment Adherence in People With Psychiatric Disabilities

Patrick W. Corrigan

Amy Watson

Some people struggle with mental illness for a brief span and recover either as a result of treatment or spontaneously. Others become disabled by the illness. A "disorder" becomes a "disability" when it is chronic and blocks the person from achieving goals in such important life domains as competitive employment, intimate relationships, and independent housing. Epidemiological research suggests from half to two thirds of people with psychiatric disabilities who might benefit from services either opt to not participate in treatment or fail to fully adhere to regimens as prescribed (Kessler et al., 2001; Regier et al., 1993). Barriers to adherence parallel the processes that generally seem to impede participation in health care services including aversive side effects and overly complex treatment protocols (Corrigan, Liberman, & Engel, 1990). In addition, cognitive deficits common to many serious mental illnesses interfere with persons fully understanding their illness and services needed to treat the illness. The impact of cognitive deficits on treatment adherence is developed more fully in this chapter.

Mental illness strikes with a double-edged sword. On one side are the symptoms and disabilities that prevent the person from achieving life goals and fully participating in available services. On the other is the public's reaction to these symptoms, more commonly known as stigma. Some people with psychiatric disabilities do not pursue treatment to avoid the *stigma*. This chapter includes a section that reviews how stigma impedes treatment adherence. We first provide a brief definition of psychiatric disability before discussing how these factors obstruct treatment participation.

What Is a Psychiatric Disability?

Disorders that typically cause psychiatric disabilities include those in the schizophrenia and affective disorder spectra. Many people with schizophrenia, major depression, bipolar disorders, and other psychotic disorders are challenged by significant psychological distress and/or psychiatric symptoms that prevent them from achieving work and independent living goals. Diagnosis of these disorders is not, however, synonymous with disability. There are significant numbers of people diagnosed with these illnesses who are able to work, live independently, and otherwise experience a full life (DeSisto, Harding, McCormick, Ashikaga, & Brooks, 1999). Moreover, there are other, what have been traditionally construed as less serious, disorders that may yield psychiatric disability. People with anxiety and some Axis II disorders are frequently unable to attain work and independent living goals. Other disorders, although disabling, are not typically included under the rubric of psychiatric disability (e.g., the developmental disabilities). Disabilities due solely to substance abuse disorders are not included either, although it is important to note that from one to two thirds of people with disabling mental illnesses may be struggling with comorbid substance use disorders (Cuffel, 1996). In the latter case, rehabilitation programs need to reflect the special needs of those with dual disabilities (Mueser, Noordsy, Drake, & Fox, 2003).

The psychological distress, other symptoms, and specific dysfunctions of disabling psychiatric disorders undermine treatment adherence in several ways. Perhaps the most prominent is the impact of cognitive deficits that might result from psychosis, mania, lowered intelligence, or negative syndrome. Before discussing the impact of cognitive deficits on adherence, we briefly review the menu of evidence-based services to which people with psychiatric disabilities might consider adhering.

Evidence-Based Practices

Developing treatments for people with psychiatric disabilities has been a public health priority for more than two decades. In the past couple of years, government groups like the U.S. Substance Abuse and Mental Health Administration and the National Institute of Mental Health have partnered with individual researchers and professional associations to define evidence-based practices that meet the needs of psychiatric disabilities (Lehman et al., 1998; Torrey et al., 2001; U.S. Surgeon General, 2001). These practices might simply be divided into two categories.

1. *Psychotropic Medication*: A variety of antipsychotic and other psychiatric medications have demonstrated efficacy in diminishing many of the symptoms and dysfunctions of disabling psychiatric disorders (Mellman et al., 2001). The past 15 years, in particular, have witnessed a veritable explosion of innovative pharmacology for people with psychiatric disorders (Miller, Dassori, Ereshefsky, & Crismon, 2001). Practice guidelines for psychotropic medication often include specific strategies for monitoring medication effects and institutional concerns related to disease management.

2. *Psychosocial Interventions*: Training and support strategies have been developed and tested that help people attain regular work (Bond et al., 2001), independent living (Phillips et al., 2001), and family goals (Dixon et al., 2001). Program development in this domain has evolved from the traditional train-place philosophy (train people with psychiatric disabilities to live successfully outside a mental institution before placing them in the community where everyday stress might cause a relapse) to a place-train approach (rapid placement in real-world settings followed up by intensive training and support to help people attain goals in these settings) (Corrigan, 2001; Corrigan & McCracken, 2005).

How Do Cognitive Deficits Impede Adherence to Psychopharmacological and Psychosocial Treatments?

The cognitive deficits that often accompany schizophrenia and other disabling psychiatric illnesses interfere with adaptive functioning (Green, 1996; Velligan & Bow Thomas, 1999), which, in turn, may present significant barriers to adherence to treatment. Specific areas of impairment include attention, memory, and executive function. These deficits have been found to be more predictive of poor ability to adhere to medication than demographics, severity of psychopathology, and attitudes about taking medications (Jeste et al., 2003; Robinson et al., 2002). For persons with schizophrenia, these deficits are present not only during acute phases of illness but also during periods of relative remission of positive symptoms (Gold & Harvey, 1993).

Cognitive deficits create barriers to adherence at a number of levels. Impairments in the ability to selectively attend to relevant information and screen out unimportant information (Gold & Harvey, 1993) may prevent persons with schizophrenia from fully understanding instructions from mental health professionals about how and when to take medications. In a study of adherence to atypical antipsychotic medications, Velligan and colleagues (2003) noted that discharge instructions were routinely misunderstood or forgotten, with some patients incorrectly ingesting their previously prescribed *and* more recently prescribed medications.

Even when treatment instructions are understood, memory impairments and deficits in executive functioning can prevent individuals from remembering and organizing complex medication regimens and adhering to treatment (Robinson et al., 2002). Combined with the often unstructured and chaotic nature of many individuals' lives, these deficits can undermine initiating and sustaining routines that promote regular adherence to medication and participation in psychosocial treatments. For example, many of the participants in one study did not maintain regular meal, sleep, or hygiene routines that could be linked to taking medication. Many slept through regular dosing times, and even those living in group homes often did not appear at medication distribution times, thus missing doses (Velligan et al., 2003).

Rather than refusing to adhere, many treatment nonadhering individuals may simply lack the skills necessary for following a treatment regimen. This suggests that interventions aimed at improving adherence need to move beyond education about the importance of medication to teaching persons with schizophrenia the skills that will enable them to adhere to treatment regimens (Jeste et al., 2003). Velligan and colleagues (2000, 2002) have examined the use of cognitive adaptation training (CAT) to improve multiple domains of adaptive functioning, including treatment adherence. CAT is a manualized program of environmental supports designed to compensate for cognitive deficits. Depending on specific types and levels of impairment, compensatory strategies may include removing distractions and organizing medications to minimize errors (e.g., labeled pillbox). Prompts and cues to help the individual initiate each step of a sequenced task (alarms, checklists, brightly colored signs) are also used in CAT. Studies of CAT have noted improvements in symptoms and adaptive functioning and lower relapse rates compared with standard medication follow-up (Velligan et al., 2000, 2002).

In a similar manner, changing the person's environment can greatly enhance adherence (Heinssen, 1996). This might include prominently displaying the person's appointments with the doctor so that he or she can remember upcoming meetings. In addition, pills can be sorted into a weekly pillbox so that the correct dose is taken. These kinds of cognitive prostheses help people better adhere to treatment prescriptions.

How Does Stigma Impede Adherence?

Two levels of stigma are prominent among the reasons why some people with psychiatric disabilities might not adhere to treatments: person-level stigma—social psychological processes that undermine an individual's comprehension of mental health and that motivate people to avoid the label of mental illness—and structural stigma—sociological processes that impede the mental health system's ability to respond to mental illness. This chapter specifically focuses on person-level stigma and how it discourages people from seeking mental health care. Two reasons are examined for why the person-level stigma of mental illness is perceived as harmful such that people avoid treatment where the label or stigma of "mental illness" is acquired: the threat of diminished self-esteem and of public identification.

Self-Stigma: Harm to Self-Esteem

Living in a culture steeped in stigmatizing images, persons with psychiatric disabilities may accept these notions and suffer diminished self-esteem, self-efficacy, and confidence in one's future (Corrigan, 1998; Holmes & River, 1998). Research shows that people with a need for mental health care often internalize stigmatizing ideas that are widely endorsed within society and believe that they are less valued because of their psychiatric disorder (Link, 1987; Link & Phelan, 2001). Persons who agree with prejudice concur with the stereotype; "That's right; I am weak and unable to care for myself!" Self-prejudice leads to negative emotional reactions; prominent among these is low self-esteem and self-efficacy (Link, Struening, Neese-Todd, Asmussen, Phelan, 2001; Markowitz, 1998). Obviously, this kind of self-prejudice and self-discrimination will significantly interfere with a person's life goals and quality of life.

Fundamental suppositions of social psychological research on prejudice suggest why self-stigma would dissuade people from being labeled when they seek treatment (Jost & Banaji, 1994). People in general are motivated to stigmatize others because of ego (Adorno, Frenkel-Brunswik, Levinson, & Sanford, 1950; Katz & Braly, 1935; Lippmann, 1922) or group enhancement (Tajfel, 1981). Instead of thinking "I am not competent," individuals buffer their self or group's image against interpersonal failings by viewing others as incompetent; in this case, people with mental illness (among the many possible stigmatized groups) as deficient. Hence, people do not want to be labeled mentally ill—and do not want to participate in the treatments where these labels originate—to escape the negative statements that lessen self-esteem and self-efficacy.

Public Stigma: Harm to Social Opportunities

Society harms people who are publicly labeled as mentally ill in several ways. Stereotype, prejudice, and discrimination can rob people labeled mentally ill of important life opportunities that are essential for achieving life goals. Two goals, in particular, are central to the concerns of people with serious mental illness (Corrigan, 2004a): (1) obtaining competitive employment and (2) living independently in a safe and comfortable home. Research suggests stigmatizing attitudes may have a deleterious impact on obtaining and keeping good jobs (Bordieri & Drehmer, 1986; Farina & Felner, 1973; Farina, Felner, & Bourdreau, 1973; Link, 1982, 1987; Olshansky, Grab, & Ekdahl, 1960; Wahl, 1999; Webber & Orcutt, 1984) and leasing safe housing (Aviram & Segal, 1973; Farina, Thaw, Lovern, & Mangone, 1974; Hogan, 1985a, 1985b; Page, 1983, 1995; Wahl, 1999). Stigma also muddies the interface between mental illness and the criminal justice system. Criminalizing mental illness occurs when police, rather than the mental health system, respond to mental health crises, thereby contributing to the increasing proportion of serious mental illness in jail (Watson, Corrigan, & Ottati, 2004). Finally, public stigma may negatively affect participation in the general health care system; people labeled mentally ill are less likely to benefit from the depth and breadth of the American health care system than people without these illnesses. Druss and colleagues completed two studies on archival data that suggested people with mental illness receive fewer medical services than those not labeled in this manner (Desai, Rosenheck, Druss, & Perlin, 2002; Druss & Rosenheck, 1997).

Combined, this evidence suggests that public identification as "mentally ill" can yield significant harm. Research has suggested that people with concealable stigmas (like people who are gay/lesbians/bisexual/transgender, of minority faith-based communities, or with mental illness) decide to avoid this harm by hiding their stigma and staying in the closet (Corrigan & Matthews, 2003). Alternatively, they may opt to avoid the stigma altogether by denying their group status and by not seeking the institutions that mark them (i.e., mental health care). This kind of label avoidance can undermine adherence to treatment programs.

Strategies for Overcoming Stigma

Explaining the relationship between stigma and care provides necessary information for antistigma programs. Both professional disciplines and advocacy groups have called for antistigma programs to increase care seeking for people in need of mental health services; prominent among the advocacy groups is National Alliance on Mental Illness (NAMI), the Mental Health Association, the Center to Address Discrimination and Stigma, and the Eliminate the Barriers Initiative (the last two represent Substance Abuse and Mental Services Administration (SAMHSA)

funded national projects with eliminating stigma as the primary goal). Research has identified and evaluated basic processes for challenging public and self-stigma (Corrigan et al., 2000, 2002). Integrating research with practical lessons learned by advocates will provide a framework for best challenging the stigma that prevents care seeking.

Challenging Public Stigma

Decreased public stigma will reduce the attitudes and behaviors, which may act as barriers to care seeking for people who need services. Corrigan and Penn (1999) identified three approaches that may diminish aspects of the public stigma experienced by people with mental illness. Groups protest inaccurate and hostile representations of mental illness as a way to challenge the stigmas they represent. These efforts send two messages: (1) to the media: STOP reporting inaccurate representations of mental illness and (2) to the public: STOP believing negative views about mental illness. Largely anecdotal evidence suggests that protest campaigns have been effective in getting stigmatizing images of mental illness withdrawn (Wahl, 1995). There is, however, little empirical research on the psychological impact of protest campaigns on stigma and discrimination of care providers suggesting an important direction for future research.

Protest is a reactive strategy; it attempts to diminish negative attitudes about mental illness but fails to promote more positive attitudes that are supported by facts. Education provides information so that the public can make more informed decisions about mental illness. The latter approach to changing stigma has been most thoroughly examined by investigators. Research, for example, has suggested that participation in education programs on mental illness led to improved attitudes about persons with these problems (Corrigan, River et al., 2001;

Holmes, Corrigan, Williams, Canar, & Kubiak, 1999; Keane, 1990; Penn et al., 1994). Given research that suggests having confidence in treatment diminishes the negative impact of stigma on treatment seeking (Corrigan, 2004b), education programs should also reflect evidence about the success of treatment participation.

Stigma is further diminished when members of the general public have contact with people with mental illness who are able to hold down jobs or live as good neighbors in the community. Research has shown an inverse relationship between having contact with a person with mental illness and endorsing psychiatric stigma (Corrigan et al., 2002; Corrigan, Edwards, Green, Diwan, & Penn, 2001; Pinfold et al., 2003; Schulze, Richter-Werling, Matschinger, & Angermeyer, 2003). Hence, opportunities for the public to meet persons with severe mental illness may discount stigma. The research question of particular interest here is how attitudes that may change as a result of these antistigma programs increase care seeking for persons in need.

Diminishing Self-Stigma

Consumer advocates (Chamberlin, 1978; Deegan, 1990) have argued, and research (McCubbin & Cohen, 1996; Rappaport, 1987) seems to support the idea, that many psychosocial and medical treatments disempower people; as a result, people in need decide not to fully participate in services. People with mental illness who self-stigmatize tend to report little personal empowerment in terms of treatment so that participation in services is diminished. Hence, interventions that challenge self-stigma and facilitate empowerment are likely to improve adherence (Corrigan & Calabrese, 2004; Speer, Jackson, & Peterson, 2001). Professionals must be able to recognize what adherence means in this context—not blind compliance with whatever the therapist prescribes but active participation and engagement in *all* aspects of care. Consumer-operated self-help services are among the best examples of practices that facilitate empowerment (Davidson et al., 1999).

Case Example

Sarah Jones was a 32-year-old single black female who had been diagnosed with schizophrenia 10 years earlier. Since then, she has been hospitalized about a dozen times, often being readmitted shortly after periods when she stopped taking her antipsychotic medication. One reason Sarah was unable to stay on her medication is that she could not recall the amounts of and times of the day for her meds. To overcome this problem, she bought a 7-day pill container and counted out the appropriate number of pills in each day's box at the beginning of each week. She also put a big sign up next to her bathroom mirror regimen; "Don't forget to take your meds before bedtime."

Sarah came from a family that believed mental illness was a sign of weakness. People should be able to rely on themselves to accomplish life goals. Whenever she saw her uncle Henry, he would urge her to toughen up and quit relying on a crutch like meds. Sarah realized that statements like these were not helping her deal with mental illness. So she joined a self-help group made up of people who were also struggling with schizophrenia called Schizophrenia Anonymous. This group was developed by people with mental illness for people with mental illness. By interacting with peers who were seemingly in control of their illness, Sarah realized that she did not have to be a victim to schizophrenia or to the stigma it entails. She was able to counter hurtful statements such as "You must be weak if you have to take mind altering drugs" with statements like, "My meds are just like taking insulin; no one would call a diabetic weak or bad."

Summary

Failure to adhere to regimens for psychiatric disability is multiply influenced. There are both personal and environmental barriers that can undermine a person from fully participating in care. Personal barriers may include cognitive deficits that interfere with fully understanding a treatment regimen. Environmental barriers may include stigmatizing messages from family and peers that make the person want to hide from treatment in shame. Helping the person get back on his or her treatment track requires a careful assessment of both personal and environmental barriers. With this information, the treatment provider can join the person in crafting an intervention that tears down barriers to adherence.

References

Adorno, T. W., Frenkel-Brunswik, E., Levinson, D. J., & Sanford, R. N. (1950). *The authoritarian personality*. New York: Harper & Row.

Aviram, U., & Segal, S. P. (1973). Exclusion of the mentally ill: Reflection on an old problem in a new context. *Archives of General Psychiatry, 29*, 126–131.

Bond, G. R., Becker, D. R., Drake, R. E., Rapp, C. A., Meisler, N., Lehman, A. F., et al. (2001). Implementing supported employment as an evidence-based practice. *Psychiatric Services, 52*, 313–322.

Bordieri, J. E., & Drehmer, D. E. (1986). Hiring decisions for disabled workers: Looking at the cause. *Journal of Applied Social Psychology, 16*, 197–208.

Chamberlin, J. (1978). *On our own: Patient-controlled alternatives to the mental health system*. New York: McGraw-Hill.

Corrigan, P. W. (1998). The impact of stigma on severe mental illness. *Cognitive & Behavioral Practice, 5*, 201–222.

Corrigan, P. W. (2001). Place-then-train: An alternative service paradigm for persons with psychiatric disabilities. *Clinical Psychology-Science & Practice, 8*, 334–349.

Corrigan, P. W. (2004a). How stigma interferes with mental health care. *American Psychologist, 59*, 614–625.

Corrigan, P. W. (2004b). Guidelines for enhancing personal empowerment of people with psychiatric disabilities. *American Rehabilitation, Autumn*, 10–21.

Corrigan, P. W., & Calabrese, J. D. (2004). Cognitive therapy and schizophrenia. In M. A. Reinecke & D. A. Clark (Eds.), *Cognitive therapy over the lifespan: Theory, research and practice* (pp. 315–322). Cambridge, UK: Cambridge University Press.

Corrigan, P. W., Edwards, A. B., Green, A., Diwan, S. L., & Penn, D. L. (2001). Prejudice, social distance, and familiarity with mental illness. *Schizophrenia Bulletin, 27*, 219–225.

Corrigan, P. W., Liberman, R. P., & Engel, J. D. (1990). From noncompliance to collaboration in the treatment of schizophrenia. *Hospital & Community Psychiatry, 41*, 1203–1211.

Corrigan, P. W., & Matthews, A. K. (2003). Stigma and disclosure: Implications for coming out of the closet. *Journal of Mental Health, 12*, 235–248.

Corrigan, P. W., & McCracken, S. G. (2005). Place first, then train: A substitute for a medical model of psychiatric rehabilitation. *Social Work, 50*, 31–39.

Corrigan, P. W., & Penn, D. L. (1999). Lessons from social psychology on discrediting psychiatric stigma. *American Psychologist, 54*, 765–776.

Corrigan, P. W., River, L., Lundin, R. K., Penn, D. L., Uphoff-Wasowski, K., Campion, J., et al. (2001). Three strategies for changing attributions about severe mental illness. *Schizophrenia Bulletin, 27*, 187–195.

Corrigan, P. W., River, L., Lundin, R. K., Uphoff-Wasowski, K., Campion, J., Mathisen, J., et al. (2000). Stigmatizing attributions about mental illness. *Journal of Community Psychology, 28*, 91–102.

Corrigan, P. W., Rowan, D., Green, A., Lundin, R., River, L., Uphoff-Wasowski, K., et al. (2002). Challenging two mental illness stigmas: Personal responsibility and dangerousness. *Schizophrenia Bulletin, 28*, 293–310.

Cuffel, B. J. (1996). Comorbid substance use disorder: Prevalence, patterns of use, and course. In R. E. Drake & K. T. Mueser (Eds.), *Dual diagnosis of major mental illness and substance disorder: Recent research and clinical implications* (pp. 93–105). San Francisco: Jossey-Bass.

Davidson, L., Chinman, M., Kloos, B., Weingarten, R., Stayner, D., & Tebes, J. K. (1999). Peer support among individuals with severe mental illness: A review of the evidence. *Clinical Psychology-Science & Practice, 6*, 165–187.

Deegan, P. E. (1990). Spirit breaking: When the helping professions hurt. *Humanistic Psychologist, 18*, 301–313.

Desai, M. M., Rosenheck, R. A., Druss, B. G., & Perlin, J. B. (2002). Mental disorders and quality of diabetes care in the Veterans Health Administration. *American Journal of Psychiatry, 159*, 1584–1590.

DeSisto, M. J., Harding, C. M., McCormick, R. J., Ashikaga, T., & Brooks, G. W. (1999). The Maine and Vermont three decade studies of serious mental illness: Longitudinal visual course comparisons. In P. Cohen, C. Slomkowski, & L. N. Robins (Eds.), *Historical and geographical influences on psychopathology* (pp. 135–173). Mahwah, NJ: Erlbaum.

Dixon, L., McFarlane, W., Lefley, H., Lucksted, A., Cohen, M., Falloon, I., et al. (2001). Evidence-based practices for services to families of people with psychiatric disabilities. *Psychiatric Services, 52*, 903–910.

Druss, B. G., & Rosenheck, R. A. (1997). Use of medical services by veterans with mental disorders. *Psychosomatics, 38*, 451–458.

Farina, A., & Felner, R.D. (1973). Employment interviewer reactions to former mental patients. *Journal of Abnormal Psychology, 82*, 268–272.

Farina, A., Felner, R. D., & Bourdreau, L. A. (1973). Reactions of workers to male and female mental patient job applicants. *Journal of Consulting and Clinical Psychology, 41*, 363–372.

Farina, A., Thaw, J., Lovern, J. D., & Mangone, D. (1974). People's reactions to a former mental patient moving to their neighborhood. *Journal of Community Psychology, 2*, 108–112.

Gold, J. M., & Harvey, P. D. (1993). Cognitive deficits in schizophrenia. *Psychiatric Clinics of North America, 16*, 295–312.

Green, M. F. (1996). What are the functional consequences of neurocognitive deficits in schizophrenia? *American Journal of Psychiatry, 153*, 321–330.

Heinssen, R. K. (1996). The cognitive exoskeleton: Environmental interventions in cognitive rehabilitation. In P. W. Corrigan & S. C. Yudofsky (Eds.), *Rehabilitation for neuropsychiatric disorders* (pp. 395–425). Washington, DC: American Psychiatric Press.

Hogan, R. (1985a). *Not in my town: Local government in opposition to group homes.* Unpublished manuscript.

Hogan, R. (1985b). *Gaining community support for group homes.* Unpublished manuscript.

Holmes, E. P., Corrigan, P. W., Williams, P., Canar, J., & Kubiak, M. (1999). Changing public attitudes about schizophrenia. *Schizophrenia Bulletin, 25*, 447–456.

Holmes, P., & River, L. P. (1998). Individual strategies for coping with the stigma of severe mental illness. *Cognitive & Behavioral Practice, 5*, 231–239.

Jeste, S. D., Patterson, T. L., Palmer, B. W., Dolder, C. R., Goldman, S., & Jeste, D. V. (2003). Cognitive predictors of medication adherence among middle-aged and older outpatients with schizophrenia. *Schizophrenia Research, 63*, 49–58.

Jost, J. T., & Banaji, M. R. (1994). The role of stereotyping in system-justification and the production of false consciousness. *British Journal of Social Psychology, 33*, 1–27.

Katz, D., & Braly, K. (1935). Racial prejudice and racial stereotypes. *Journal of Abnormal & Social Psychology, 30*, 175–193.

Keane, M. (1990). Contemporary beliefs about mental illness among medical students: Implications for education and practice. *Academic Psychiatry, 14*, 172–177.

Kessler, R. C., Berglund, P. A., Bruce, M. L., Koch, J. R., Laska, E. M., Leaf, P. J., et al. (2001). The prevalence and correlates of untreated serious mental illness. *Health Services Research, 36*, 987–1007.

Lehman, A. F., Steinwachs, D. M., Dixon, L. B., Goldman, H. H., Osher, F., Postrado, L., et al. (1998). Translating research into practice: The schizophrenia patient outcomes research team (PORT) treatment recommendations. *Schizophrenia Bulletin, 24*, 1–10.

Link, B. G. (1982). Mental patient status, work and income: An examination of the effects of a psychiatric label. *American Sociological Review, 47*, 202–215.

Link, B. G. (1987). Understanding labeling effects in the area of mental disorders: An assessment of the effects of expectations of rejection. *American Sociological Review, 52*, 96–112.

Link, B. G., & Phelan, J. C. (2001). Conceptualizing stigma. *Annual Review of Sociology, 27*, 363–385.

Link, B., Struening, E., Neese-Todd, S., Asmussen, S., & Phelan, J. (2001). Stigma as a barrier to recovery: The consequences of stigma for the self-esteem of people with mental illnesses. *Psychiatric Services, 52,* 1621–1626.

Lippmann, W. (1922). *Public opinion.* New York: Macmillan.

Markowitz, F. E. (1998). The effects of stigma on the psychological well-being and life satisfaction of persons with mental illness. *Journal of Health & Social Behavior, 39,* 335–347.

McCubbin, M., & Cohen, D. (1996). Extremely unbalanced: Interest divergence and power disparities between clients and psychiatry. *International Journal of Law & Psychiatry, 19,* 1–25.

Mellman, T. A., Miller, A. L., Weissman, E. M., Crismon, M., Essock, S. M., & Marder, S. R. (2001). Evidence-based pharmacologic treatment for people with severe mental illness: A focus on guidelines and algorithms. *Psychiatric Services, 52,* 619–625.

Miller, A. L., Dassori, A., Ereshefsky, L., & Crismon, M. L. (2001). Recent issues and developments in antipsychotic use. In D. L. Dunner & J. F. Rosenbaum (Eds.), *Psychiatric clinics of North America annual review of drug therapy 2001* (pp. 209–236). Philadelphia: W. B. Saunders.

Mueser, K. T., Noordsy, D. L., Drake, R. E., & Fox, M. (2003). *Integrated treatment for dual disorders: A guide to effective practice.* New York: Guilford.

Olshansky, S., Grab, S., & Ekdahl, M. (1960). Survey of employment experiences of patients discharged from three state mental hospitals during period 1951–1953. *Mental Hygiene New York, 44,* 510–522.

Page, S. (1983). Psychiatric stigma: Two studies of behaviour when the chips are down. *Canadian Journal of Community Mental Health, 2,* 13–19.

Page, S. (1995). Effects of the mental illness label in 1993: Acceptance and rejection in the community. *Journal of Health and Social Policy, 7,* 61–68.

Penn, D. L., Guynan, K., Daily, T., Spaulding, W. D., Garbin, C., & Sullivan, M. (1994). Dispelling the stigma of schizophrenia: What sort of information is best? *Schizophrenia Bulletin, 20,* 567–578.

Phillips, S. D., Burns, B. J., Edgar, E. R., Mueser, K. T., Linkins, K. W., Rosenheck, R. A., et al. (2001). Moving assertive community treatment into standard practice. *Psychiatric Services, 52,* 771–779.

Pinfold, V., Toulmin, H., Thornicroft, G., Huxley, P., Farmer, P., & Graham, T. (2003). Reducing psychiatric stigma and discrimination: Evaluation of educational interventions in UK secondary schools. *British Journal of Psychiatry, 182,* 342–346.

Rappaport, J. (1987). Terms of empowerment/exemplars of prevention: Toward a theory for community psychology. *American Journal of Community Psychology, 15,* 121–148.

Regier, D. A., Narrow, W. E., Rae, D. S., Manderscheid, R. W., Locke, B.Z., & Goodwin, F. K. (1993). The de facto US mental and addictive disorders service system: Epidemiologic catchment area prospective 1-year prevalence rates of disorders and services. *Archives of General Psychiatry, 50,* 85–94.

Robinson, D. G., Woerner, M. G., Alvir, J. M. J., Bilder, R. M., Hinrichsen, G. A., & Lieberman, J. A. (2002). Predictors of medication discontinuation by patients with first-episode schizophrenia and schizoaffective disorder. *Schizophrenia Research, 57,* 209–219.

Schulze, B., Richter-Werling, M., Matschinger, H., & Angermeyer, M. C. (2003). Crazy? So what! Effects of a school project on students' attitudes towards people with schizophrenia. *Acta Psychiatrica Scandinavica, 107,* 142–150.

Speer, P. W., Jackson, C. B., & Peterson, N. (2001). The relationship between social cohesion and empowerment: Support and new implications for theory. *Health Education & Behavior, 28,* 716–732.

Tajfel, H. (1981). *Human groups and social categories.* Cambridge, UK: Cambridge University Press.

Torrey, W. C., Drake, R. E., Dixon, L., Burns, B. J., Flynn, L., Rush, A. J., et al. (2001). Implementing evidence-based practices for persons with severe mental illnesses. *Psychiatric Services, 52,* 45–50.

U.S. Surgeon General. (2001). *Report of the Surgeon General's conference on children's mental health: A national action agenda.* Washington, DC: Author.

Velligan, D. I., & Bow-Thomas, C. C. (1999). Executive function in schizophrenia. *Seminars in Clinical Neuropsychiatry, 4,* 24–33.

Velligan, D. I., Bow-Thomas, C. C., Huntzinger, C., Ritch, J. L., Ledbetter, N., Prihoda, T. J., et al. (2000). Randomized controlled trial of the use of compensatory strategies to enhance adaptive functioning in outpatients with schizophrenia. *American Journal of Psychiatry, 157,* 1317–1323.

Velligan, D. I., Lam, F., Ereshefsky, L., & Miller, A. L. (2003). Perspectives on medication adherence and atypical antipsychotic medications. *Psychiatric Services, 54,* 665–667.

Velligan, D. I., Prihoda, T. J., Ritch, J. L., Maples, N., Bow-Thomas, C. C., & Dassori, A. (2002). A randomized single-blind pilot study of compensatory strategies in schizophrenia outpatients. *Schizophrenia Bulletin, 28,* 283–292.

Wahl, O. F. (1995). *Media madness: Public images of mental illness.* New Brunswick, NJ: Rutgers University Press.

Wahl, O. F. (1999). Mental health consumers' experience of stigma. *Schizophrenia Bulletin, 25,* 467–478.

Watson, A., Corrigan, P., & Ottati, V. (2004). Police officer attitudes and decisions regarding persons with mental illness. *Psychiatric Services, 55,* 49–53.

Webber, A., & Orcutt, J. D. (1984). Employers' reactions to racial and psychiatric stigmata: A field experiment. *Deviant Behavior, 5,* 327–336.

27

Treatment Adherence in Ethnic Minorities

Particularities and Alternatives

José R. Rodríguez-Gómez

Carmen C. Salas-Serrano

Ethnic minority populations are at higher risk for health problems that might affect their quality of life. Inadequate adherence may result in greater severity of illnesses and other health complications. Adherence is the degree to which patients follow advice, treatments, or recommendations made by health care providers as directed. The degree of adherence in the client will undoubtedly determine the results, with increased adherence resulting in better outcomes at the individual and the societal levels. Nonadherence has been considered a major public health problem. It also causes a financial burden to the health care system and can be a source of frustration to health care professionals. It has been associated with increased clinical, social, and economic costs, and it is closely linked to relapse, hospitalizations, and poor outcome among patients with a major illness (Centorrino et al., 2001).

It is well known that how people use health care and how patients make decisions about whether to follow medical advice is influenced by individual beliefs and perceptions in combination with environmental resources or barriers. The U.S. Department of Health and Human Services (U.S. DHHS, 2001a) has established that there are key elements of therapeutic success that depend on rapport and on the clinicians' understanding of patients' cultural identity, which may affect the outcome of the patient. Given that there are major disparities in ethnic group and socioeconomic status, ethnic minorities can present challenges in these areas that make them more likely to have poor adherence to treatment. Thus, ethnic minority populations are particularly affected by nonadherence issues.

Increased understanding of the mechanisms and processes underlying the individual's decision to adhere or not to adhere to treatment will undoubtedly enhance the ability to develop models of interventions with the purpose of modifying those mechanisms and processes to increase adherence. This chapter will introduce you to the particularities that characterize adherence in ethnic minority populations and will provide you with specific suggestions to improve adherence.

Particularities

According to the Census 2000, the total population of the United States is 281 million people, of which 13% is Latino/Hispanic, 12% is African American, 4% is Asian, and 1% is American Indian or Alaska Native. Between 1990 and 2000, the foreign-born population increased by 57%. By 2035, the minority population is expected to constitute more than 40% of the U.S. population (Day, 1996). These data demonstrate the marked growth in ethnic minority populations in the United States. Thus, the understanding of the particularities that characterize these groups is essential for the delivery of services to these populations. These differences are present not only between ethnic groups but also within the same group, given that various countries and languages are represented within each (Meyerowitz, Richardson, Hudson, & Leedham, 1998). It is well established in the literature that there are ethnic differences in adherence. Possible mediating variables for these differences include socioeconomic status, knowledge and attitudes, and access to services.

For example, Latinos, as well as other minority populations, have been adversely affected by undereducation, underemployment, inadequate housing, and insufficient access to health care insurance. Thus, they may not view health

services as a priority given their other significant daily needs, resulting in the underutilization of health services. All these socioeconomic barriers, together with a lack of proficiency in English, are the major obstacles to the use of health services for this population (Zambrana, Dorrington, & Hayes-Bautista, 1995).

Latinos also have disproportionately low rates of outpatient mental health service use and rates of admission for care. Latinos often perceive mental health models as unnecessary, unwelcoming, or not useful (U.S. DHHS, 2001a). Although affected by numerous socioeconomic stressors, they remain likely to use mental health services primarily in crisis circumstances, drop out of services sooner, and have undesirable treatment outcomes (U.S. DHHS, 2001a). The lack of insurance coverage can also contribute to underutilization of services (Iniguez & Palinkas, 2003).

Although African Americans tend to show poorer health than white Americans, they tend to underutilize services or drop out of services at a significantly higher rate than white populations (Kar, Kramer, Skinner, & Zambrana, 1995). They also use fewer treatment sessions for their mental health problems than white populations, are more often misdiagnosed by mental health practitioners than white populations, and are more often diagnosed as having a severe mental illness than whites (U.S. DHHS, 2001). Given that African Americans and other minorities appear to experience a higher proportion of misdiagnosis and inappropriate services, this may lead them to perceive treatment as ineffective.

In 1990 it was estimated that two thirds of the reported Asian American population is foreign born (U.S. Bureau of the Census, 1990). Given this, the current probability is that their knowledge about the U.S. health system may be limited, even if they have begun to acculturate, especially if they retain their traditional customs, which may affect the process of integration with the host society. Also, Asian American immigrants, as a group, have an increased probability of suffering from health risks and diseases that are uncommon in the United States, and many of them have been victims of war and violence in their countries of origin (Kar, Kramer, Skinner, & Zambrana, 1995; Yu, 1991). They tend to give low priority to their health care needs because they are more concerned with socioeconomic adaptation, meeting basic needs, and learning English (Chin, 1999). On the other hand, the more established Asian Americans tend to give higher priority to improved social standing and interracial relationships than to health care needs (Kar, Kramer, Skinner, & Zambrana, 1995).

To promote adherence in ethnic minority populations, the clinician has to achieve cultural competence. Cultural competence does not necessarily result from being born in, or spending significant amounts of time in, a particular culture but can be attained through systematic development of a sociocultural consciousness. Campinha-Bacote, Yahle, and Langenkamp (1996) define cultural competence as a process in which the health care professional continuously strives to achieve the ability to work effectively within the cultural context of an individual, family, or community with a diverse cultural and ethnic background and provides or facilitates care that respects the values, beliefs, and practices of the client and addresses the disadvantages arising from the client's position in relation to networks of power.

Case Presentation Illustrating Barriers to Adherence in Minorities

Mrs. Melendez, a 48-year-old migrant Latino/Hispanic female who spoke little English, had been experiencing diminished enjoyment in her work and was worried that her supervisor would address her because she was "not giving her full commitment and offering the best of her capacity." Mrs. Melendez worked as a cook for a small restaurant in the city where she lived. At home, she was quiet and had a very low level of energy. She complained of always feeling tired and sleepy. Mrs. Melendez had been married for 23 years and lived with her husband, also Latino/Hispanic, and two daughters who where born in the United States.

One of the daughters had approached her a couple of times to try to convince her that she should visit the doctor to find out why she was feeling "sad and low." Mrs. Melendez had answered that there was nothing wrong with her and that it had to do with excess work. Some weeks later, while cooking at work, Mrs. Melendez started crying uncontrollably. A Latino/Hispanic coworker recommended some "herbal tea" to help her with her "nervous breakdown," and her boss gave her the afternoon off.

When Mrs. Melendez got home, her family was very concerned because a coworker had called to see if she was doing OK. They took her to a multidisciplinary medical facility near their home. Once there, Mrs. Melendez was examined by a physician who had limited proficiency in the Spanish language. Mrs. Melendez tried to explain her feelings, but the physician did not understand her. The physician then called the husband to serve as an interpreter, and he told her that his wife was trying to communicate that she was only tired and needed to rest. He also told her that when they got home, he would give her a "herbal tea" to help her feel better. The physical examination and blood test performed were negative, and it was concluded that Mrs. Melendez was working too much and that she needed some rest. The family went home, and during the night Mrs. Melendez got worse; she was taken back to the health facility, where she was received by a Latino/Hispanic physician, who interviewed her and suggested that she could be experiencing a mood disorder and referred her to a mental health facility that catered to Latino/Hispanics. He also gave her a Spanish handout that oriented her about depression and included the address and phone number of the mental health facility. Mrs. Melendez left feeling better because she "had the opportunity to speak to the doctor in Spanish and receive the attention she needed."

Assessment Issues and Strategies for Promoting Adherence in Ethnic Minorities

An adequate assessment that is culturally sensitive is the basis for promotion of adherence in ethnic minorities. Adherence should always be evaluated by taking into account the behavioral, cultural, and environmental factors that affect it. People bring into the consultation their own beliefs and perceptions about the illness, and this may have consequences in the promotion or failure of adherence to treatment, which may affect the prolongation of life. It was found that exploring these beliefs about the illness and the benefits and barriers to taking medication and working with the patient to come up with some sort of solution led to better patient outcomes (Aarnold, 1998). Moreover, it will be necessary to study the positive short-, middle-, and long-term effects that culture-sensitive adherence strategies (CSAS) may have for the survival of minorities in order to diminish physical and mental health disparities. CSAS could be one of the first initial factors that need to be investigated and taken into consideration in order to maximize the life expectancy of minorities. Examples of CSAS include, but are not limited to, the following:

1. The therapist should understand the cultural milieu of the patient, the history of the country of origin, the main problems related to the process of migration and acculturation, and how the process affects his or her life. Thus, it is important that the clinician be familiarized with these topics and give importance to them.

2. The patient should be given enough time and attention to discuss the main concerns, life problems, false expectancies, and symptoms he or she suffers from within his or her own perception and understanding in order to avoid demoralization and social stigmatization.

3. It will be wise if the therapist knows not only the language of the minority patient but also the real meaning of the message. This means that the therapist needs to be trained not only to understand and speak the language but also to understand the idiosyncratic linguistic meanings and ideas attached to specific words, which may confuse the clinician, affecting his or her perception of the medical problem and thus its evaluation and the treatment prescribed (Rodriguez & Caban, 1992).

4. Many times the focus of health care professionals is on sick behaviors instead of healthy ones. For improvement in overall functioning, the minority patient needs people who really care for him or her without any prejudice. A CSAS should include a reasonable introspective vision of what a therapist thinks about minority groups and an evaluation of the therapist's own prejudices and biases relative to the minority population he or she is dealing with. The literature demonstrated that when a clinician shows empathy toward the patient and his or her personal support group, the adherence to treatment improves, representing substantial progress in the patient's functional status and quality of life (Clay & Hopps, 2003; Rodriguez & Caban, 1992).

Ensuring patients' adherence to treatment and to clinical appointment schedules can be a major challenge. This is particularly true in ethnic minority populations. Thus, health care professionals should work toward developing and implementing a service delivery system that provides culturally and linguistically appropriate services to meet the needs of culturally and racially diverse groups (Pasick, D'Onofrio, & Otero-Sabogal, 1996; Thompson, Rudolph, & Henderson, 2004). The aim is to tailor service provision to adapt the intervention to best fit the needs and characteristics of the specific population.

This will greatly enhance service delivery and improve patient compliance. To achieve this, a sensitive process of communication is necessary. In addition, it will be essential to train mental health professionals in multicultural awareness processes and health disparity issues, including not only the knowledge obtained from formal professional training but also an awareness of their own preconceptions about minorities' issues. It is imperative that the clinicians respect the client's culturally based perceptions, fears, and expectations. It is also important to recognize that alternative health resources may influence the course of treatment. For instance, folk healers, together with other cultural elements, may affect patient treatment adherence and outcome (Chavira & Trotter, 1981; Eisenberg et al., 1993). To take into account the impact of alternative health resources on the therapeutic process, open and trusting communication between the clinician and the patient is necessary. An example of this would be to ask questions about lifestyle, family, and spirituality issues that may affect the patient's treatment management (Thoreson, 1999).

One of the most influencing factors on adherence is communication. Patients who do not speak the same language as their clinicians rate their visits with physicians as less participatory than whites (Cooper-Patrick et al., 1999) and are more likely to miss appointments or drop out of treatment (Brach and Fraser, 2000). The U.S. DHHS (2001a) reports that the emphasis on verbal communication yields greater potential for miscommunication when clinician and patient come from different cultural backgrounds, even if they speak the same language. Overt and subtle forms of miscommunication and misunderstanding can lead to misdiagnosis, conflicts over treatment, and poor adherence to the treatment plan (U.S. DHHS, 2001b). For example, in the previous case presentation, there was no true communication between Mrs. Melendez and the physician due to a language barrier. This led to a problem with identifying the real clinical issue of the client. When client and clinician do not speak the same language, these problems intensify. In the case of Mrs. Melendez, this was resolved when a Latino/ Hispanic physician intervened.

The health care professional must promote effective communication with the client. He or she must strive to understand the patient's viewpoint about the illness, its causes, as well as its possible treatments and implications. The use of sensitive and nonjudgmental questioning and the assessment of the client's ability to adhere to the recommended treatments will help achieve this goal. Interpretation and translation services should also be provided. This can result in more accurate medical histories and lead to a reduction in diagnostic errors and unnecessary diagnostic testing. These services must be provided by a professional interpreter to ensure that the interpretation provided is adequate given that inadequate interpretation can be viewed as a form of discrimination and can lead to misdiagnosis and misinformation, resulting in inadequate treatment (Woloshin, Bicknell, Schwartz, Gany, & Welch, 1995). In Mrs. Melendez's case, the husband did not want to disclose the true reasons for her crisis because he feared she would lose her job and the implications that this might have for the family. The use of a professional interpreter would have allowed Mrs. Melendez to express her true feelings, and a valid diagnosis could have been reached sooner. Other strategies include having available translated written materials such as forms and educational material, telephone interpreter access, and audiovisual presentations in the dominant language of the client.

It is imperative to take into consideration culturally sensitive elements such as the use of folk or home remedies that may have an effect on treatment adherence. Harmful interactions between prescribed drugs and folk or home remedies can be prevented by training clinicians to ask patients whether they are using such remedies. Given that the husband informed the clinician that he would prepare a "herbal tea" for Mrs. Melendez "so that she would feel better," it is important that when she receives treatment for her mood disorder, folk remedies (i.e., herbal teas, prayers) be considered in order to assess possible interactions.

Health promotion and education materials that reflect culture-specific attitudes and values could result in more successful patient education and increased adherence to treatment regimens. In Mrs. Melendez's case, the physician gave her printed material in Spanish including the address and phone number of the place where she could find help for her condition. This, together with demonstrating an open, sensitive, and positive attitude toward her, motivated Mrs. Melendez to obtain the treatment she needed.

In addition, there are some issues that need to be taken into consideration, especially with the prescription of medications and compliance to them. For instance, Tseng and Streltzer (2001) mention the following as important factors in adherence to prescriptions:

1. The patient's concept of the illness, as well as the symbolic meaning of the illness in the patient's culture

2. Medication characteristics, which may be important to the patient

3. The symbolic power and value of the medication in the patient's culture

4. Dietary habits and nutritional interactions with alternative treatments used by the patient

5. The doctor-patient relationship, including expectations and symbolic meaning of giving and receiving medication, as well as other transferential aspects of the relationship

Health care professionals need to be adequately trained in aspects concerning ethnic and cultural diversity, spirituality issues, language barriers, and other variables affecting treatment adherence during their academic preparation and also as part of the in-service. Annual reviews of cultural competence and limitations in achieving it need to be addressed in order to administratively plan formal training in the identified areas of weakness. Moreover, it is necessary to train health care professionals in the use of interpreter and translation services, organize multidisciplinary outreach programs, and form focus groups to identify the needs of the ethnic groups.

According to Antshell (2002), several variables are extremely important to adherence to treatment:

1. Having a multicultural and multilingual staff

2. Using trained interpreters and receiving training on how to integrate an interpreter into clinical practice

3. Providing written instructions in the language spoken by the particular client

4. Training professionals in multicultural awareness

5. Using decor from different cultures in the clinical setting

6. Including relevant cultural components in treatment

7. Consulting, collaborating with, and involving folk healers in treatment

8. Respecting the client's culturally based explanations

9. Increasing participation by extended family members

We suggest that all these factors be considered to develop more successful and effective interventions with minority populations. Because the minority population is continuously increasing, it is imperative to take into consideration adherence issues in order to provide culturally appropriate and quality services to a population that is at higher risk of developing mental and physical health problems due to their socioeconomic disadvantage. Health disparities need to be diminished in minorities, and the adherence factor is essential to improve their quality of life. Lack of adherence represents danger to the health of minorities as well as to the whole collective health of any nation. Public policy makers need to address these issues in order to develop strategies that may help reduce the mortality and morbidity of minorities. This should be the goal.

Suggested Readings

Falicov, C. J. (1995). Training to think culturally: A multidimensional comparative framework. *Family Process, 34*(4), 373–388.

Fisher, B., & Hartman, D. J. (1995). The impact of race on the social experience of college students at a predominantly white university. *Journal of Black Studies, 26,* 117–133.

Huff, R. M., & Kline, M. V. (1999). *Promoting health in multicultural populations: A handbook for practitioners.* Thousand Oaks, CA: Sage.

Montague, J. (1996). Counseling families from diverse cultures: A nondeficit approach. *Journal of Multicultural Counseling and Development, 24,* 37–41.

Santiago, E. (1993). *When I was Puerto Rican.* New York: Addison-Wesley.

The provider's guide to quality and culture. http://erc.msh.org/quality&culture

Resources for cross-cultural health care. www.diversityrx.org Vargas, L. A. (1991). Evaluating outcome in a multicultural inpatient. In R. L. Hendren & I. Berlin (Eds.), *Psychiatric inpatient care of children and adolescents: A multicultural approach* (pp. 112–129). New York: Wiley.

References

Aarnold, J. (1998). *Health promotion: Handbook.* Boston: Mosby.

Antshell, K. M. (2002). Integrating culture as a means of improving treatment adherence in the Latino population. *Psychology, Health, & Medicine, 7,* 435.

Brach, C., & Fraser, I. (2000). Can cultural competency reduce ethnic and racial health disparities? A review and conceptual model. *Medical Care Research and Review, 57*(Suppl. 1), 181–217.

Campinha-Bacote, J., Yahle, T., & Langenkamp, M. (1996). The challenges of cultural diversity for nurse educators. *Journal of Continuing Education for Nurses, 27,* 59–64.

Centorrino, F., Hernan, M., Drago-Ferrante, G., Rendall, M., Apicella, A., Langar, G., et al. (2001). Factors associated with noncompliance with psychiatric outpatient visits. *Psychiatric Services, 52,* 378–380.

Chavira, J. A., & Trotter, R. T. (1981). *Curanderismo.* Athens: University of Georgia Press.

Chin, J. L. (1999). Asian American health in Massachusetts: Myths and facts. *Asian American and Pacific Islanders Journal of Health, 7,* 150–164.

Clay, D. L., & Hopps, J. A. (2003). Treatment adherence in rehabilitation: The role of treatment accommodation. *Rehabilitation Psychology, 48,* 215–219.

Cooper-Patrick, L., Gallo, J. J., Gonzalez, J. J., Vu Hong, T. P., Neil, R., Nelson, C. F., et al. (1999). Race, gender, and partnership in the patient-physician relationship. *Journal of the American Medical Association, 282,* 583.

Day, J. C. (1996). *Population projections of the United States by age, sex, and Hispanic origin: 1995 to 2050* (U.S. Bureau of the Census Publication No. P25-1130). Washington, DC: Government Printing Office.

Eisenberg, D. M., Kessler, R. C., Foster, C. Norlock, F. E., Calkins, D. R., & Delbanco, T. L. (1993). Unconventional medicine in the United States: Prevalence, costs and patterns of use. *New England Journal of Medicine, 328,* 246–252.

Iniguez, E., & Palinkas, L. (2003). Varieties of health services utilization by underserved Mexican American women. *Journal of Health Care for the Poor and Underserved, 14,* 52–69.

Kar, S., Kramer, J., Skinner, J., & Zambrana, R. E. (1995). Panel VI: Ethnic minorities, health care systems, and behavior. *Health Psychology, 14,* 641–646.

Meyerowitz, B. E., Richardson, J., Hudson. S., & Leedham, B. (1998). Ethnicity and cancer outcomes: Behavioral and psychosocial considerations. *Psychological Bulletin, 123,* 47–70.

Pasick, R. J., D'Onofrio, C. N., & Otero-Sabogal, R. (1996). Similarities and differences across cultures: Questions to inform a third generation of health promotion research. *Health Education Quarterly, 23,* 142–161.

Rodriguez, J. R., & Caban, M. (1992). The problem of bilingualism in psychiatric diagnoses of Hispanic patients. *Cross Cultural Psychology Bulletin, 26,* 2–5.

Thompson, C. L., Rudolph, L. B., & Henderson, D. A. (2004). *Counseling children.* Belmont, CA: Brooks/Cole.

Thoreson, C. E. (1999). Spirituality and health: Is there a relationship? *Journal of Health Psychology, 4,* 291–300.

Tseng, W., & Streltzer, J. (Eds.). (2001). *Culture and psychotherapy.* Washington, DC: American Psychiatric Press.

U.S. Bureau of the Census. (1990). *Census 1990, population by race: Major statistical areas, subregional areas, jurisdictions.* Washington, DC: Government Printing Office.

U.S. Department of Health and Human Services, Substance Abuse and Mental Health Services Administration. (2001a). *Cultural competence standards in managed care mental health services: Four underserved/underrepresented racial/ethnic groups.* Retrieved February 15, 2004, from www.mentalhealth.org/publications/allpubs/SMA00-3457/intro.asp

U.S. Department of Health and Human Services. (2001b). *Mental health: Culture, race, and ethnicity: A supplement to mental health.* A report of the Surgeon General. Retrieved March 1, 2004, from www.surgeongeneral.gov/library/mentalhealth

Woloshin, S., Bicknell, N. A., Schwartz, L. M., Gany, F., & Welch, H. G. (1995). Language barriers in medicine in the United States. *Journal of the American Medical Association, 273,* 724–728.

Yu, E. S. (1991). The health risk of Asian Americans. *American Journal of Public Health, 81,* 1391–1392.

Zambrana, R. E., Dorrington, C., & Hayes-Bautista, D. (1995). Family and child health: A neglected vision. In R. E. Zambrana (Ed.), *Understanding Latino families: Scholarship, policy and practice* (pp. 157–176). Thousand Oaks, CA: Sage.

28

Treatment Adherence in Difficult (Personality Disordered) Patients

Kendra Beitz

Mandra L. Rasmussen Hall

The term *difficult patient* can mean very different things to different clinicians. Depending on the level of experience and personality styles, clinicians may have diverse levels of tolerance for extreme client characteristics and behaviors. In this chapter, we use the term difficult patient to refer to individuals who are demanding, unpleasant to work with, hard to manage, and/or tax clinician resources. Our conceptualization of the difficult patient does not include egregious behaviors that threaten clinician boundaries or safety. Nor does it include the typical range of patient skills deficits that can make therapy challenging, such as interpersonal difficulties or minimal expressions of emotion. In our view, difficult patients are those who behave in ways that (a) interfere with their active participation in treatment (i.e., resistance), and/or (b) reduce the therapist's ability to deliver treatment effectively or the therapist's willingness to treat the patient (i.e., anger, lying, and manipulation). Although difficult patient behaviors are often synonymous with personality disorders, behaviors that interfere with treatment delivery occur across diagnostic categories. The mismanagement of these behaviors can lead to patient escalation, clinician burnout, and poor treatment prognosis. On the other hand, knowing how to respond effectively to "difficult patients" can have a dramatic impact on the course of treatment.

Differing Perspectives on the Difficult Patient

The Patient Is "Difficult"

One view is that some form of psychopathology within the patient causes him or her to be difficult. In other words, difficulty is a unilateral patient problem. The therapeutic community tends to associate certain psychiatric disorders with difficulty—particularly personality disorders. Patients with borderline personality disorder are often considered most difficult and tend to be written about most frequently (Brandchaft & Stolorow, 1988). Difficult patients are also identified in terms of unpleasant personality styles or characteristics and may be labeled passive-aggressive, uncooperative, threatening, or manipulative. These characteristics present particular challenges for therapists (Wessler, Hankin, & Stern, 2001) and are exhibited by patients across diagnostic categories.

One of the dangers of this point of view is the tendency to blame patients for their difficulties. According to social psychology research, people are more likely to blame the victim in situations where they feel helpless. Some difficult patients do not improve, despite therapists' intense and repeated efforts to help them. When a clinician cares about a patient yet is unable to reduce a patient's suffering, clinicians have a tendency to blame the patient for that suffering (Linehan, 1993a). Therapists may believe that patients are playing games, aren't trying hard enough, or don't want to get better. Linehan (1993a) notes that this fundamental cognitive error of attributing lack of progress to patients' internal motives has iatrogenic consequences. She warns that blaming patients can invalidate their own experience of their problems, whereby they learn to mistrust themselves. Blaming can also lead patients to feel misunderstood. When a patient feels forced to see something from the therapist's viewpoint instead of the therapist understanding the patient's point of view, he or she may experience rage, behave destructively, or

mistrust the therapist (Brandchaft & Stolorow, 1988). In addition, blaming may cause the therapist to become emotionally distant from the patient, to direct negative emotion toward the patient, to be less patient and willing to help, and to be more punitive (Linehan, 1993a).

The Therapist Has "Difficulties"

An alternative view is that difficult patients do not exist. Instead, therapists have "difficulties" working with particular patients for a variety of reasons. For example, clinicians will likely face new challenges when working with a particular type of patient to whom they have had no previous exposure. A therapist may lack the requisite experience needed to work with a particular patient population (Wessler et al., 2001). In addition, a clinician may label a patient as difficult when the patient evokes negative emotions in the therapist such as frustration or confusion. Similarly, a patient's behaviors may elicit personal issues for a therapist such as fear of failure.

From this point of view, therapists are seen as the unilateral source of the problem, which can result in a tendency for therapists to blame themselves for difficulties in therapy. Several factors feed this tendency to self-blame when difficulties are encountered in treatment. One example is the well-known "file drawer" problem, where only successful results from treatment studies are published (Bradley & Gupta, 1997; Rosenthal, 1979; Shadish, Doherty, & Montgomery, 1989). Hiding therapeutic failures may contribute to unrealistic views of the effectiveness of psychotherapy. In addition, some therapists may have colleagues who do not report experiencing difficulties with their caseloads. Depending on their area of expertise or type of employment, some therapists can be more selective about the patients they see and may rarely treat difficult patients (Kottler, 1992). Lastly, the therapist's reputation, theoretical orientation, and age can differentially affect how patients perceive and behave toward therapists (Kottler, 1992). Thus, difficulties will vary according to the patient-therapist dyad. Without recognizing these factors, therapists may be under the illusion that they are less equipped to handle difficult patients. Self-judgment and blame can lead to feelings of hopelessness and lack of motivation on the part of the therapist.

"Difficulty" Is a Transaction

We do not completely adopt or reject either of the above views. Difficulties do not arise solely from within the patient or the therapist but rather are bilateral and in the "patient-therapist system" (Brandchaft & Stolorow, 1988). Some patients are more difficult than others by virtue of their histories and current abilities to function. And some therapists are more or less equipped to treat certain patients, given their personal issues, experiences, and skill level. Difficulties arise via a transaction between the patient and the therapist. This helps explain why some therapists find particular patients more or less difficult, and why some patients seem more or less responsive to particular therapists. We argue that neither party is the sole contributor to the problem and neither party is to be blamed. We assert that viewing difficult patient behavior as the result of a transaction between patient and therapist is a more effective perspective from which to address the problem because it minimizes the tendency to blame either the patient or the therapist. By doing so, therapists and patients are less likely to encounter the adverse consequences of blaming discussed above, such as self-judgment, negative emotions, and lack of motivation.

This chapter outlines several strategies for managing difficult patient behaviors. Our suggestions are not intended to be a panacea for all patient-therapist difficulties that arise in treatment. Instead, we will outline, conceptualize, and offer techniques that can be used to manage several common difficult patient behaviors that occur in treatment. Although we acknowledge that there are many ways to conceptualize difficulties, our conceptualizations will be behaviorally

informed. Thus, we will discuss specific difficult behaviors as opposed to difficult psychiatric disorders or personality characteristics.

General Strategies for Treating Difficult Patients

In later sections, we will discuss specific strategies for addressing the common difficult patient behaviors of resistance, anger/hostility, lying, and manipulation. However, we believe there are important general strategies for dealing with difficult behavior in any form. These strategies can help reduce therapist frustration, clarify avenues for solving the problem, and increase patients' willingness to discuss the difficult behavior. We recommend adopting these strategies as tools to use in any difficult situation with a patient.

Nonjudgmental Stance

From our transactional perspective, we encourage therapists to develop and model a nonjudgmental stance toward difficult patient behavior as well as their own responses to that behavior. In other words, we recommend that therapists acknowledge and describe the problematic behavior and their responses to it, generate hypotheses about the cause of the behavior, and address it openly and directly with patients, all without judging the behavior as good or bad. For example, taking a nonjudgmental stance toward a "willful" or "lazy" patient would involve describing the problematic behaviors (and the therapist's reactions) objectively. "The client is lazy" becomes "the patient misses scheduled appointments, does not complete homework assignments, and appears apathetic in session; the clinician feels frustrated and less motivated to see the client." Describing the behaviors that interfere with therapy, rather than applying a short-hand label to the patient, provides an unambiguous foundation from which to make guesses about the cause of the behavior and present the problem clearly to the patient. Modeling a nonjudgmental stance can assist the patient in accepting and tolerating his or her own imperfections as well as those of others (Schwartz & Smith, 2002). Also, maintaining a nonjudgmental stance throughout this process can reduce feelings of frustration and hopelessness for both the therapist and patient.

Validation

A powerful tool in the face of any difficult patient behavior is *validation,* or communicating understanding. According to Linehan (1993a), validation occurs when "the therapist communicates to the patient that [his or her] responses make sense and are understandable within [his or her] *current* life context or situation" (pp. 222–223). There are a number of negative effects when therapists do not communicate that they understand their patients (Brandchaft & Stolorow, 1988). A patient may not feel cared about or listened to, which may cause the patient to disengage from the therapist and therapy. A patient may also feel that there is something wrong with him or her or his or her experience, which can engender feelings of shame. A basic way therapists fail to demonstrate understanding is by ignoring or disregarding patients' feelings, thoughts, experiences, and views. Failure to validate distress, in particular, can cause the patient to emotionally escalate and can lead to therapeutic impasses (Angus & Gillies, 1994). Even when therapists are well versed in validation, difficult patient behaviors can elicit emotional reactions in therapists that make validation difficult. In situations of ongoing difficult patient behavior, therapists may miss multiple opportunities to validate the patient. This can lead to more problematic behavior as the patient feels increasingly misunderstood by the therapist. Similarly, clinicians who push for change without balancing acceptance and validation of patients' current struggles can contribute to escalation of difficult patient behaviors (Linehan, 1993a).

Therapists can communicate understanding to their patients by using very basic reflective listening skills or describing aloud what they observe about the patient during the session (including their own responses to the patients' behavior). A higher-order form of validation involves directly communicating that a patient's behavior or emotional responses are understandable given his or her current situation or context (Linehan, 1993a). For example, in the therapist's mind, it may be unjustified for the patient to fear an abrupt, premature termination of treatment. However, the therapist can communicate that the patient's reaction is understandable given that several of his or her important relationships have ended in this way in the past. Or, the therapist can communicate that it makes sense why the patient is having difficulties expressing emotion in session, given his or her current level of skill. Validation in all its forms conveys to patients that the therapist is invested in understanding them. From this common ground, therapists and patients are able to both accept the problem *and* make necessary changes. For example, a therapist can understand the specific barriers to a patient completing homework assignments *while at the same time* expecting the patient to participate in generating solutions to those barriers. Sometimes, the simple act of communicating understanding can spark willingness and collaboration in a patient who has otherwise exhibited resistance.

It is important to note that validation does not imply agreement. A therapist can appreciate or understand a patient's point of view *and* disagree with it. Communicating disagreement effectively to a patient, rather than judging the patient's viewpoint as wrong or pathological, can also be a powerful form of validation. When patients feel listened to and respected by their therapist, they are more likely to collaborate in generating solutions to treatment barriers. Another key issue is the importance of therapists self-validating their own experiences and reactions to the patient. Therapists' reactions to their patients provide essential clinical information about the way patients affect others in their lives. In addition, therapists will be less effective at managing difficult patient behaviors if they minimize or ignore their own reactions to the patient.

Understanding Behavior in Its Clinical Context

Many types of difficulties that arise in treatment can be anticipated beforehand given the patient's presenting complaints, diagnoses, and/or personality characteristics. For instance, if a patient has pervasive problems establishing and maintaining relationships, he or she may also have difficulties forming a therapeutic alliance and/or may experience similar conflicts with the therapist. A patient who is generally avoidant is likely to have difficulties openly sharing painful emotions in treatment. With any difficulty in therapy, it is important for the therapist to understand the controlling variables for the problem and how the problems fit into the therapist's overall conceptualization of the case (Beck, 1997). That is, therapists must understand the historical experiences and current contingencies, skill sets, or beliefs that drive and maintain the problem behavior, as well as how these problems contribute to the patient's overall functioning in daily life. As therapists begin to understand the patient's problems, they gain empathy increasingly (Jones, 1987) and are more likely to stay nonjudgmental when describing and intervening on difficult patient behaviors. Through collaborative case formulation, the patient and therapist can agree on goals and targets for treatment. When difficulties arise, the patient and therapist can address the problem as it occurs, within the framework of the case formulation. In other words, when difficult patient behaviors are conceptualized as part of the client's clinical difficulties, they are less likely to derail the therapy process when they occur. Instead of viewing the problem as one that must be overcome to continue with

treatment, addressing the difficult behavior *is* the treatment. For example, when an avoidant patient exhibits little affect during a conversation about an emotional topic, it provides the therapist an opportunity to help the patient work on experiencing, expressing, and tolerating painful emotions.

We recommend that therapists and patients generate the case conceptualization collaboratively. Doing so allows patients to provide additional information about themselves that may alter the case conceptualization. This process can also foster greater commitment to treatment in the patient and may prevent some resistant behavior later in treatment. However, the direction of therapy depends on the case conceptualization; therefore, any disagreement at this stage in treatment is likely to contribute to a number of problems. For example, a patient may believe that others are the cause of his or her interpersonal problems (and that processing the wrongdoings of others will solve these issues), whereas the therapist believes that the patient is an active contributor to these interpersonal difficulties. If treatment continues without resolving these differences, the patient may become resistant or the patient and therapist may be in constant conflict over how to address the patient's daily life problems. Thus, developing a mutually agreed-on case formulation can, in some cases, prevent difficult patient behavior.

Developing a case conceptualization collaboratively can also be extremely validating for some patients (i.e., "Someone finally understands me!"). During these discussions, therapists will have multiple opportunities to validate patients' daily struggles. For example, a therapist can highlight that it makes sense why a patient is feeling depressed given the degree of chaos in his or her life. On the other hand, some patients may feel overwhelmed by this process as their problems are laid out before them. Patients may have judgmental thoughts, such as "I'm really screwed up," and feel shameful or embarrassed. Some patients may also become defensive and reject the therapist's interpretation of their problems. Orienting the patient to the nature and purpose of developing a case conceptualization together will help reduce negative interpretations of the process. For example, therapists can explain to patients that both points of view are important parts of the conceptualization. Describing patients' problems nonjudgmentally will also model this important stance for patients and reduce defensiveness. In addition, therapists can anticipate feelings of fear, shame, and hopelessness during this process and look for opportunities to validate the patient's experience.

Treating Specific Difficult Behaviors

Resistance

One of the most common problems in treatment is resistance. Resistance occurs in many forms, including restricting or omitting important information, violating rules of therapy (Kottler, 1992), refusing to talk about agreed-on treatment targets, questioning the treatment rationale or therapist's expertise, failing to complete assignments, missing appointments, and in-session passivity. Therapists contribute to resistance by responding ineffectively to patient resistance and failing to recognize their role in the transaction (Hanna, 2002). For example, a therapist may not have communicated clearly how to complete (or the importance of completing) a homework assignment. Blaming the patient for failing to do the assignment, without acknowledging the therapist's error may lead to the patient's defensiveness or frustration. In general, resistant behavior can occur when the patient does not understand the therapist's expectations, the patient lacks the knowledge or skills to comply, or the patient lacks motivation (Kottler, 1992). Resistance can also arise when the patient feels misunderstood.

Clarifying Expectations

It is extremely important that therapists discuss with patients what is expected of them before committing to treatment. Patients who have previous experience in therapy may have misconceptions about treatment that are based on those experiences. Patients with no prior history of therapy may have expectations that have been influenced by other sources of information such as popular culture, friends, or family. Therapists also have expectations about patients, including their ability to communicate effectively, express gratitude, and recognize the limits of treatment and the role of clinicians in delivering therapy (Kottler, 1992). The degree to which therapists endorse these expectations affects whether or not they will become frustrated when patients do not behave as expected (Kottler, 1992). Therapists should also be aware of the clinical expectations they have of themselves, such as "I should have endless patience." In general, when expectations are unmet, both therapists and patients may become disappointed in each other or in themselves.

Prior to beginning treatment, it is recommended that therapists carefully explain the nature of treatment, including therapist-patient roles, treatment time commitment, consequences for missed appointments or incomplete homework, anticipated course and outcomes of therapy, and therapist-treatment limitations and boundaries. The patient should also have an opportunity to discuss his or her expectations, limits, concerns, and goals. During this pretreatment orientation and commitment phase, the patient and therapist should discuss the pros and cons of participating in treatment, identify the patient's capability to engage in treatment, select treatment targets, determine how treatment targets will be addressed, identify and problem solve barriers to treatment, and obtain a verbal or written commitment. This process should be collaborative, so that the patient does not feel punished or manipulated (Fine, 1997). Compromise may be necessary; however, it is recommended that neither party compromise personal limits or boundaries (Linehan, 1993a). At the conclusion of this phase, the patient and therapist should develop a mutually agreed-on treatment contract that outlines goals, expectations, and contingencies for treatment. The treatment contract may be reviewed and revised during treatment as needed and can function as common ground from which to problem solve any difficulties that arise in treatment. This process should assist both patients and therapists in understanding and clarifying expectations to minimize disappointments later in treatment.

Assessing and Teaching Skills

Therapists should assess patients' abilities at the beginning and throughout treatment. For example, therapists must determine whether or not patients have skills for labeling emotions, tolerating distress, or asserting needs. Assessment of skill can be tricky, especially because patients may exhibit "apparent competence." Apparent competence occurs when a patient appears to be able to cope in some situations and in other situations behaves as if these competences did not exist (Linehan, 1993a). For example, a patient may be able to express needs in therapy because he or she feels safe with the therapist; however, he or she cannot be assertive in other relationships. The appearance of competence can lead the therapist to ask more of the patient than he or she is able to do, which can cause patients to feel misunderstood. Another issue to consider when assessing the patient's skill level is whether or not passivity is a clinically relevant behavior. Linehan (1993a) describes the concept of "active passivity" as "the tendency to approached problems passively and helplessly, rather than actively and determinedly, as well as a corresponding tendency under extreme distress to demand from the environment (and often the therapist) solutions to life's problems" (p. 78). A patient may truly have the skills but

lacks motivation or has been reinforced in the past for not using the skills. This sets the stage for others, including the therapist, to do things for the patient that the patient is actually capable of doing for himself or herself, which enables passivity further.

When therapists identify patients' skill deficits, it is important that therapists ask patients to do only what they are capable of doing (Kottler, 1992). This will help facilitate patients feeling understood and help therapists adjust their expectations. In addition, it is important to target deficits as part of treatment before moving on with other issues that require such capabilities. When provided skill training, patients are likely to feel that they are receiving help and the therapist is likely to feel that treatment is progressing. The balancing act is to ask patients to do only what they are capable of doing while not enabling passivity by treating patients as fragile.

Enhancing Motivation

Many factors can interfere with motivation. The patient may have a history of several failed treatment experiences (Kottler, 1992), or there may be secondary gain for failing to improve, such as financial or social benefits. Poor motivation can also be a symptom of certain psychological problems, such as depression, or patients may have a negative attribution style that affects how they view the world. In addition, the therapist may have a history of aversive therapy experiences with similar clients. The therapist may also feel overextended or burned out. It is important to assess the etiology of the motivational problems of both the patient and the therapist and problem solve accordingly. Linehan (1993a) encourages therapists to adopt the perspective that, at all times, *patients are doing the best they can and they want to do better*. However, patients' efforts and motivations are often insufficient; therefore, the therapist's task is to identify the factors interfering with motivation and help the patient problem solve these barriers.

For example, the patient may feel hopeless about his or her ability to change or may not see the benefits of change. Linehan (1993a) outlines specific strategies that are helpful for overcoming these barriers, including evaluating pros and cons, playing the devil's advocate, or highlighting the freedom to choose and the absence of alternatives (pp. 284–291). Motivational interviewing techniques may also be useful for enhancing motivation and strengthening commitment. We recommend Miller and Rollnick (2002), who provide effective, evidence-based strategies for overcoming the ambivalence that keeps many people from making desired changes in their lives.

Anger and Hostility

Patients can become angry or hostile in therapy for a number of reasons. Management of patients' anger will depend on the etiology and function of the anger. Anger and hostility are often secondary emotions. In other words, unpleasant emotions such as fear, shame, or sadness often underlie feelings of anger. For example, a patient might feel shameful about his or her life situation and instead of expressing shame in session, the patient may become angry with the therapist for "not helping," "pushing too hard for change," or "not understanding." Patients may lack the skills to appropriately identify and label these emotions. Additionally, patients may have been punished in the past for expressing certain emotions. Patients may explode at the therapist to avoid feeling other painful emotions, such as shame (Wessler et al., 2001). Angry or gruff presentations may keep people at a distance, including the therapist, which may be important for the patient who has fears about intimacy or being "found out." As Hanna (2002) noted, anger can be conceptualized as a form of self-protection when the patient is asked to change. Sometimes change can represent the onset of a crisis. This is particularly true when a patient is asked to give up ineffective coping strategies when he or she does not have effective replacement strategies. Finally, patients may become angry or hostile when their needs are not being met. Sometimes patients may lack skills to identify or ask for what they need and want and instead exhibit an angry emotional response.

Assessing the Etiology and Function of Anger

It is essential that therapists conceptualize patient anger from a nonjudgmental stance. This may be difficult, especially early in treatment, because the patient may lack insight into his or her own emotional responses, and the therapist may have limited access to the patient's history and in-session behavior. Nonetheless, the therapist is encouraged to generate and evaluate hypotheses about what might be eliciting patient anger and hostility, as well as how that anger might be functioning in treatment. For instance, a therapist might notice that a patient raises his voice and makes threatening remarks when questioned about the dissolution of his marriage. It may be that the patient is experiencing intense feelings of sadness but has difficulties expressing these feelings due to fears of losing emotional control, a history of punishment for crying, or beliefs about what it means for a man to express these feelings. The patient's angry presentation may function to stop the therapist's line of inquiry, which allows the patient to escape feelings of discomfort. Therapists may lose empathy if they fail to understand factors that might evoke feelings of anger or how anger may serve as an adaptive coping strategy for patients. Therefore, understanding patient anger and hostility is important for helping therapists respond less judgmentally and more empathically to patients. The therapist should keep in mind that anger is not generally a unilateral patient problem; therapists also contribute to patient anger. For instance, anger and hostility are common reactions when patients feel invalidated by their therapists. Therapists can further invalidate patients by responding defensively or punitively, which is likely to elicit more feelings of anger on the part of the patient.

Identifying Primary Emotions

It is important for the therapist and patient to explore any primary emotions the patient is experiencing that might underlie his or her anger. Therapists should keep in mind that patients may not have the skills to identify and express emotions. Failing to acknowledge this may lead to patient resistance as described above. Linehan (1993b) provides several handouts that therapists can use with patients to teach them how to identify and label emotions. By using these handouts, patients learn to identify antecedents, physiological sensations, urges, and labels associated with different emotions. In addition to identifying primary emotions, it is important for the therapist to help the patient make the link between primary emotions and secondary feelings of anger. For instance, when patients become judgmental of their own primary emotional responses (e.g., feeling shameful about being fearful, believing that feeling fearful is weak, or believing that feelings are unjustified), patients are more likely to experience anger as a secondary reaction. Helping the patient understand his or her emotional reactions is an important skill that is necessary for patients to learn to respond more effectively to daily life and in-session problems, without anger and hostility.

Responding to Anger and Hostility Effectively

Sitting with an angry, hostile patient can be an aversive experience for many therapists. It is important for the therapist to be aware of his or her own reaction to the patient's anger and regulate that reaction prior to responding. Failure to do so may lead the therapist to respond with anger, fear, or shut down emotionally, none of which are useful in treatment. It is a natural tendency to respond defensively, punitively, or in some other way to protect oneself when *feeling*

under attack. However, these types of responses are likely to escalate the hostility and conflict between the patient and therapist. Generally speaking, patients are not trying to deliberately attack the therapist but rather are responding in the only way they know how or in a way that has been reinforced in the past. Therapists are encouraged to monitor their own responses and at times act opposite to what may be an initial knee-jerk reaction to counterattack. Hanna (2002) suggests that patients respect therapists who do not respond fearfully to hostility. On the other hand, it is important for therapists to communicate fear if they genuinely feel threatened. Failing to establish and maintain boundaries may give the patient the message that these behaviors are acceptable. As previously mentioned, understanding is not synonymous with acceptance. Therefore, the therapist can communicate that he or she understands the patient's behavior and at the same time expects the patient to aim for reducing hostility. In general, effectively responding to anger serves as a powerful model for patients (Hanna, 2002).

In addition to effectively responding to emotion, it is important for therapists to set the stage for patients to express emotions. Although it may go without saying, patients should feel safe to openly display emotions. Therapists may be operating under the false assumption that patients are aware that therapy is a safe context. Therapists may need to explicitly explore and address patients' beliefs about and histories with expressing emotions. For instance, a patient may have been rejected in the past for being too emotional. Similarly, a patient may believe that the therapist will not respect him if he cries. Therefore, it may be necessary to revisit and clarify patient and therapist expectations throughout treatment.

Teaching Skills

Simply commenting on anger does not mean that more appropriate behavior will emerge in its place. In addition to modeling effective responses to hostility and anger, the therapist may need to teach patients skills for communicating and managing anger effectively. Because anger is often a secondary response to other emotions, the patient may also need to acquire skills for managing other emotions. We recommend Linehan's (1993b) skill-training handouts for teaching patients how to regulate a variety of emotions, including anger. If anger emerges when the patient is not getting his or her needs met, yet the patient does not know how to assert his or her needs, assertiveness or interpersonal effectiveness training may be required. As in the case of resistance, the therapist must balance asking the patient to do only what he or she is capable of doing while at the same time not treating the person as fragile.

Lying

We use the term *lying* to refer to a continuum of behaviors ranging from acts of omission (i.e., hidden agendas) and minor misrepresentations to blatant acts of deceit and gross distortions of fact. It has been suggested that conscious awareness of falsities distinguishes a lie from a delusion (Ford, King, & Hollender, 1988). Nonetheless, unconscious or deliberate, these behaviors are frustrating for therapists. Some therapists may believe that certain types of lies preclude treatment. For instance, a patient who lies about dangerous behaviors is a liability risk, or a patient who distorts factual information is wasting the therapist's time. In our view, lying is just like any other problematic behavior and accordingly needs to be targeted as part of the treatment. As with other difficulties that arise in therapy, therapists can contribute to the problem of lying through invalidating or punitive responses to patient disclosures.

Understanding Lying

It is important for the therapist and patient to recognize that everyone lies. Although there is variability with which people misrepresent, embellish, distort, or falsify facts, the tendency

to do so is rather normal (Ford et al., 1988). The therapist should communicate this to the patient. As with all other behaviors discussed thus far, both patients and therapist will be better equipped to address the problem of lying by first understanding it. Perhaps the most obvious reason for lying is to impact the environment by influencing others (Ford et al., 1988). Patients may deliberately lie to protect self-esteem (Ford et al., 1998), avoid being punished, or to seek admiration. Lying is not necessarily antisocial, in the case of being deceitful for personal profit or pleasure (American Psychiatric Association, *Diagnostic and Statistical Manual of Mental Disorders*, 2000). Lying may simply be the only way patients are able to get their needs met. They may possess little or no skills for effectively identifying and asking for what they need. Other lies may be more unconscious or delusional in nature. When untruths are repeated over the course of time they may become increasingly believable to both the patient telling the untruth and the person hearing it (Ford et al., 1988).

Addressing Lying

If patients report problems with lying or admit they have lied to the therapist, lying can be explicitly targeted as part of the treatment plan. Several techniques may be helpful, including self-monitoring. The patient can track lying between sessions, including triggers for and consequences of lying. The patient can also practice lying to the therapist and admitting the lie in session. The therapist is encouraged to respond nonjudgmentally and discuss the issue of lying as he or she would any other type of ineffective behavior. The therapist and the patient can work to identify the function that lying serves for the patient and how to respond more effectively in the future without lying. For example, if a patient admits to lying about homework completion, the therapist and patient can discuss what triggered the patient to lie, such as fear of rejection, shame, or disappointing the therapist. The therapist can help the patient practice being honest about not completing homework and observe that the therapist responds nonjudgmentally without condemning the behavior. Although the therapist might feel disappointed that the patient did not complete his or her homework or lied about completing homework, the therapist is not disappointed *in* the patient, does not reject the patient, and is willing to work with the patient to overcome urges to lie.

Some lies do not need to be directly addressed as a therapeutic issue and can simply be ignored (Ford et al., 1988). For example, consider a patient who brags about accomplishments which the therapist believes are exaggerations of facts. In the past, the patient's exaggerations may have been reinforced by the admiration of others. Ignoring the exaggerations while differentially reinforcing alternative behaviors (e.g., increasing warmth and interest when the client displays sincere expressions of feelings or admissions of shortcomings) may be enough to eliminate the problem.

Manipulation

The term *manipulation* is commonly used to describe patients who use threats, intimidation, appeal to the emotional and personal characteristics of the therapist, cajole, seduce, or in some way coerce the therapist to meet some need. Other pejorative terms, such as *splitting* and *triangulation* are also associated with manipulation. We view the term manipulation as a judgmental evaluation of behaviors that, although unpleasant to therapists and others in the patient's life, have been adopted by the patient over time to meet his or her basic needs. When patients have histories and fears of abandonment, for example, they often have urges to control the behavior of others to reassure themselves that they are less vulnerable (Gabbard, 1989); patients may harm themselves when they fear their partners may leave them, which results in greater support and caring from the partners and subsequent feelings of reassurance and relief in the patients. The term manipulation implies

that the client is intentionally trying to hurt the therapist or others. On the other hand, when viewed from a nonjudgmental stance, these behaviors become understandable as strategies that have worked for patients over time to meet their needs outside of therapy. A nonjudgmental stance toward these behaviors also reduces therapists' reactivity, thereby increasing therapists' ability to respond effectively to the behavior.

Conceptualizing Manipulative Behaviors

It is important to keep in mind that all human beings must learn how to affect their environment to meet their needs. Some patients may have been reared in environments where caregivers were not responsive to their normative attempts to meet their needs. In the most extreme cases, patients may have been virtually ignored except when in crisis. As a learned response, patients with this type of history may escalate in treatment when needs go unmet. Manipulation can be used as a strategy to meet instrumental needs (e.g., providing documentation for the court or employers, admission to a psychiatric hospital) or emotional needs (e.g., obtaining increased support, warmth, or reassurance). It is helpful if the therapist and patient identify the consequences, both instrumental and emotional, when the patient engages in manipulative behaviors, such as "acting out," suicidal gestures, threats, and the like. This will help generate hypotheses about what triggers and maintains these behaviors and how to change them.

Addressing Manipulation

The goal in addressing manipulation is to help the patient identify what he or she needs and learn how to meet that need in ways that preserve relationships and self-respect. Responding punitively to manipulation is not effective because punishment alone will not produce more effective alternative responses. Two unfortunate consequences may result from punitive therapist responses. First, patients may escalate even further when their needs go unmet and they feel invalidated. Second, the therapist may shape the patient to engage in more subtle or subversive forms of manipulation as a way to avoid aversive consequences in the future. As an alternative, we encourage therapists to remain nonjudgmental and help the patient use more effective strategies for meeting needs, such as asking for help, seeking support and validation, or expressing discontent. Like other difficulties discussed thus far, the therapist should not assume that patients have the requisite skills for identifying needs and operating effectively on the environment to get their needs met. Therefore, an assessment of patient abilities is important. We recommend assertiveness or interpersonal effectiveness skills training (Linehan, 1993b) if and when these deficits are identified.

As a general principle, it is important that the therapist addresses self-destructive behaviors (i.e., suicide attempts and self-harm) without reinforcing them (Fine, 1997). Often patients have obtained increased support and care from others when they escalate, because these types of extreme behaviors are difficult if not impossible to ignore. Maintaining an emotionally neutral stance toward the patient is helpful when addressing problem behaviors. The therapist neither provides warmth or soothing, which may function to reinforce the behavior, nor becomes angry, which may function punitively and cause further escalation. As the patient works to generate a plan for reducing self-destructive acts and increasing adaptive coping strategies, the therapist can increase his or her warmth as a way to reinforce more effective, proactive behaviors. How to respond more specifically to self-destructive behavior depends on the context in which the patient is receiving treatment (i.e., an inpatient psychiatric ward or an outpatient mental health provider); the provider and the provider's comfort level, experience, and personal limits; and the patient's history (e.g., frequency and lethality of behaviors in the past, how these behaviors were handled by providers, family, and friends). A discussion of comprehensive protocols for responding to self-destructive behaviors is beyond the scope of this chapter. Detailed guidelines in this area are discussed elsewhere (see Fine, 1997; Linehan, 1993a).

Some patients "polarize" the behaviors and intentions of others by shifting rapidly between the two extremes of idealization and devaluation (Angus & Gillies, 1994). One moment the therapist is a brilliant, wonderful clinician and the next moment he or she is uncaring and incompetent. This is a frustrating pattern for most therapists. It is helpful if therapists can recognize that the patient likely interacts with others in a similar manner in daily life. And, like all other difficult behaviors, it is simply another problem to be targeted. A similar problem that occurs is "staff splitting." Here, the patient may idealize one provider and devalue another. When providers disagree about the patient's care, providers often blame the patient for the dissention, who is said to have "split" the provider (Linehan, 1993a). From this standpoint, the providers are freed of responsibility and do not have to resolve their differences (Gabbard, 1989). When this occurs, therapists are encouraged to recognize that a polarity in viewpoints has arisen, to accept their role in the transaction, and to use their interpersonal skills to resolve the problem (Linehan, 1993a). Additionally, it is important to monitor these types of disagreements so that providers do not exploit the situation by accepting idealization and colluding with the devaluation of another provider (Gabbard, 1989). Again, remaining descriptive and nonjudgmental in such situations, as well as validating therapists' frustrations, can help all parties involved respond and problem solve effectively.

Conclusion

In our view difficult patient behaviors are caused by a transaction between the patient and therapist. Adopting this point of view minimizes the tendency to blame either the patient or therapist for the problem, which can lead to self-judgment, negative emotions, and lack of motivation from both parties. We have recommended three general tools to use in any difficult situation with a patient: (1) maintain a nonjudgmental stance; (2) validate both patient and therapist actions, thoughts, and feelings; and (3) understand difficult behaviors in the context of the patient's case conceptualization. We have also conceptualized and made recommendations for managing resistance, anger/hostility, lying, and manipulation, which are common, yet difficult issues that arise in treatment.

There are several benefits to managing difficult patient behaviors effectively. Patients are likely to feel understood by providers, develop a more hopeful outlook, engage more collaboratively in treatment, feel more positively about their experience in treatment, and feel better about themselves. Therapists are likely to feel more competent, less burned out, more motivated, and less fearful about treating difficult patients. As a result, both patients and therapists are better equipped to work effectively with one another to assist patients in solving their problems. Thus, effective management of difficulties benefits the patient-therapist transaction and leads to better treatment prognosis. We acknowledge that the recommendations in this chapter are not universal remedies for addressing all difficulties that arise in treatment. However, we hope that the guidelines presented here will help therapists feel less judgmental about their difficult patients and their therapeutic abilities and provide some useful strategies for managing therapeutic challenges.

References

American Psychiatric Association. (2000). *Diagnostic and statistical manual of mental disorders* (4th ed., text revision). Washington, DC: Author.

Angus, L., & Gillies, L. A. (1994). Counselling the borderline client: An interpersonal approach. *Canadian Journal of Counselling, 28, 1,* 69–82.

Beck, J. S. (1997). Cognitive approaches to personality disorders. In *Review of psychiatry* (Vol. 16, pp. I-73–I-106). Washington, DC: American Psychiatric Press.

Bradley, M. T., & Gupta, R. D. (1997). Estimating the effect of the file drawer problem in meta-analysis. *Perceptual and Motor Skills, 85, 2,* 719–722.

Brandchaft, B., & Stolorow, R. D. (1988). *The difficult patient: An intersubjective perspective.* In N. Slavinska-Holy (Ed.), *Borderline and narcissistic patients in therapy.* Madison, CT: International Universities Press.

Fine, M. A. (1997). Treatment of self-destructive behavior in patients with borderline personality disorder. *Innovations in Clinical Practice, 15,* 59–70.

Ford, C. V., King, B. A., & Hollender, M. H. (1988). Lies and liars: Psychiatric aspects of prevarication. *American Journal of Psychiatry, 145, 5,* 554–562.

Gabbard, G. O. (1989). Splitting in hospital treatment. *American Journal of Psychiatry, 146, 4,* 444–451.

Hanna, F. J. (2002). *Therapy with difficult clients: Using the precursors model to awaken change.* Washington, DC: American Psychological Association.

Jones, S. A. (1987). Family therapy with borderline and narcissistic patients. *Bulletin of the Menninger Clinic, 51, 3,* I285–I295.

Kottler, J. A. (1992). *Compassionate therapy: Working with difficult clients.* San Francisco: Jossey-Bass.

Linehan, M. M. (1993a). *Cognitive-behavioral treatment of borderline personality disorder.* New York: Guilford Press.

Linehan, M. M. (1993b). *Skills training manual for treating borderline personality disorder.* New York: Guilford Press.

Miller, W. R., & Rollnick, S. (2002). *Motivational interviewing: Preparing people for change* (2nd ed.). New York: Guilford Press.

Rosenthal, R. (1979). The file drawer problem and tolerance for null results. *Psychological Bulletin, 86, 3,* 638–641.

Schwartz, R. C., & Smith, S. D. (2002). Psychotherapeutic assessment and treatment of narcissistic personality disorder. *Annals of the American Psychotherapy Association, 5, 4,* 20–21.

Shadish, W. R., Doherty, M., & Montgomery, L. M. (1989). How many studies are in the file drawer? An estimate from the family/marital psychotherapy literature. *Clinical Psychology Review, 9, 5,* 589–603.

Wessler, R., Hankin, S., & Stern, J. (2001). *Succeeding with difficult clients.* San Diego, CA: Academic Press.

29

Treatment Adherence in Developmental Disabilities/ Cognitively Impaired Patients

Michele D. Wallace

Edwin J. Dyer

Becky Penrod

A dherence to treatment regimens for patients with developmental disabilities or cognitive impairments is a complex problem faced by the medical community. Various types of adherence problems occur with this population, including failure or refusal to take prescribed medication, such as taking medication at incorrect times or incorrect medication consumption; failure to comply with medical regimens (e.g., wearing corrective devices, following special diets); and interference with or resistance to medical procedures (e.g., resistance during physical examinations, routine health care procedures). Another type of adherence problem occurs when patients contaminate

sterile equipment (e.g., touching intravenous lines with nonsterile hands; McComas, Wacker, & Cooper, 1998). In any event, these adherence failures can result in the current condition worsening, relapse of a previous condition, development of additional medical concerns, and loss of preventive care.

A number of variables can contribute to the lack of treatment adherence within this population. For example, given the impaired cognitive state of the individual, he or she may not fully understand the treatment regimen. In fact, the probability of adherence is positively correlated with the simplicity of the prescribed regimen (Perkins, 2002). Moreover, there may be events that occur that influence patients' nonadherence (e.g., they may receive a lot of attention by way of having to go to the emergency room because of their lack of treatment adherence, or they may avoid aversive side effects of the regimen). In fact, the greater the severity of aversive side effects produced from adherence to a specific medical intervention, the higher the likelihood that adherence problems will occur (Diamond, 1983). In addition, individuals who stray from their regimens are oftentimes not under sufficient control of the consequences of doing so. That is, stimuli that signal adherence (i.e., instructions), as well as outcomes of adherence (i.e., benefits) or nonadherence (i.e., detriments), may be weak. Essentially, if a given individual does not perceive the benefits of compliance and the subsequent risks involved with noncompliance, adherence is not likely to be maintained (Adams & Scott, 2000).

Irrespective of an individual's probability of adherence or lack thereof, due to the reliance on other people to provide prompts and support for medical adherence in this population, individuals who do not have a supportive residential environment are more likely to have adherence problems than those who live in a structured and supportive environment (Perkins, 2002). Individuals with nonattentive, untrained, or apathetic caregivers are likely to have adherence problems, as the necessary support is not available or is not provided. As such, maintaining trained and supportive caregiver services is often of the utmost importance.

Adherence-Related Assessment

The first line of attack when faced with adherence problems should be the identification of the reasons for the lack of adherence. For example, does the individual understand the instructions? If the answer is no, then one should look for ways to make the medical regimen easier or provide supports to help facilitate understanding. If the answer is yes, the next question is whether the individual has a sufficient repertoire to engage in the desired behavior. It may be necessary to shape the desired behavior before adherence can be obtained. After ruling out understanding and sufficient behavioral repertoires, one should then assess whether noncompliance with the treatment regimen is the individual's way of getting one-on-one attention, access to some preferred activity, or is a means of avoiding some aversive properties or side effects of the regimen (i.e., conduct a functional behavioral assessment; Iwata, Kahng, Wallace, & Lindberg, 2000).

Approaches to Facilitating Treatment Adherence

Approaches to facilitating adherence to medical recommendations are directed at changing either the patient's behavior or the caregiver's behavior. Changing the patient's behavior is usually accomplished by implementing one or more of the following categories of adherence procedures: antecedent control manipulations, reinforcement procedures, and/or extinction. A number of techniques fall within these three categories. For example, under antecedent control manipulations one could provide additional cues to obtain adherence, arrange or enhance motivational conditions for adherence, reduce the response effort associated with adherence, or eliminate motivational conditions for nonadherence. With respect to reinforcement procedures, one could apply reinforcement contingencies to establish the desirable behavior or to eliminate the noncompliant behavior, with either specific reinforcers (e.g., access to attention or a preferred item) or more general reinforcers (e.g., tokens or money). Finally, one could eliminate the noncompliant behavior by eliminating the reinforcement contingency currently maintaining the behavior (e.g., eliminate attention or aversive side effects). Regarding the caregiver's behavior, training with respect to the importance of the regimen and the actual procedures involved, as well as training on the possible approaches one could use to facilitate treatment adherence, may be beneficial. Moreover, competency training as well as having a way of holding the caregivers accountable may lead to better service delivery (Luiselli, Putnam, & Sunderland, 2002; Sheras, Cornell, & Bostain, 1996). A number of training procedures have been empirically investigated over the years, as well as the development of a number of training programs; however, a review of such procedures and training programs is beyond the scope of this chapter (see Frazier, 1972; Reid & Green, 1990; Reid & Parsons, 1995; Reid, Parsons, & Green, 1989, for more information on staff training).

Examples of Antecedent Control Manipulations

Provide Additional Cues to Obtain Adherence

If an individual is required to take two different medications at different times throughout the day and the individual is not adhering to the prescription regimen appropriately, a picture schedule or prompt could be added to aid correct adherence. In other words, a picture schedule depicting each medication with the correct time to take the medication could be developed and either posted where the individual takes his or her medications or posted under the lid of a pillbox. This way the individual could match the pill depicted in the picture with the actual pill and match the time depicted with the time on a clock to ensure correct medication consumption.

Arrange or Enhance Motivational Conditions

If an individual is required to wear corrective leg braces for 8 hours a day but does not wear them because they are uncomfortable, a *behavioral contract* (Miltenberger, 2000) could be established

whereby it is agreed on by the individual and his or her caregiver that wearing the braces for 8 hours a day would allow the individual access to a preferred activity (e.g., going to the arcade, watching a movie, or playing on the computer). The contract makes wearing the braces more reinforcing by arranging for the caregiver's approval as well as by providing access to a desirable activity, thus enhancing the motivation for adherence. It should be noted that the activities should not be accessible unless the criteria listed in the contract are accomplished. In other words, if the individual wore the leg braces for only 7 hours, he or she should not be allowed access to the specified activity for that day. Moreover, to ensure success, it may be necessary to set the criterion low at first and then slowly increase it across successive weeks. For example, during the first week of intervention, the individual may be required to wear the braces for only 2 hours a day and then 3 hours a day the next week until the goal of 8 hours a day is achieved.

Reduce Response Effort

If an individual is on a special diet, whereby foods containing sugars are to be avoided, having healthy snacks (i.e., foods without sugar) readily available will reduce the response effort in eating healthy snacks and thus increase adherence to the special diet. It would also be a good idea to increase the response effort associated with nonadherence by having foods containing sugar not readily available.

Eliminate Motivational Conditions for Nonadherence

If an individual is resistant to physical exams because by engaging in such behavior he or she receives a lot of attention from nurses and caregivers, in the form of coaxing, then making sure that attention is provided in abundance right before the scheduled physical exam will reduce the individual's motivation for engaging in noncompliant behaviors. In essence, giving the individual a lot of one-on-one attention prior to the start of the physical exam reduces the individual's motivation to engage in the noncompliant behavior because he or she is already receiving attention. Another procedure that could be implemented to eliminate the motivation for nonadherence is called *behavioral momentum* (e.g., see Harchik & Putzier, 1990, for an example). In this procedure, prior to presenting a demand which the individual is unlikely to comply with (i.e., letting the doctor look into his or her ears), the individual is first presented with a number of demands which he or she is likely to comply with (e.g., requesting the individual to blow kisses, touch his or her nose, clap his or her hands) as well as receive praise for doing so, allowing the individual to be successful prior to presenting the troublesome demand.

Examples of Reinforcement Manipulations

Application of Reinforcement Contingency to Establish Desirable Behavior

If it is necessary for an individual to sit still and not touch sterile equipment so that a pic-line can be cleaned or replaced, but he or she routinely touches his or her nonsterile hands to the pic-line as well as trying to pull out the pic-line, one could provide a highly reinforcing item to the individual contingent on him or her holding still and not touching the pic-line. For example, the individual could earn access to a preferred activity or his or her favorite snack contingent on sitting still and not touching the pic-line. It would be a good idea to provide praise as a means of reinforcement throughout the process as well as providing a larger reinforcer after the completion of the process. Moreover, if the process is conducted every day, one could have the individual earn tokens for sitting still and not touching the pic-line, which he or she could bank for the opportunity to buy

something at the end of a week (e.g., buy a new toy from the toy store). This could then be faded to where the individual spends his or her earned tokens every other week and then once a month.

Application of Reinforcement Contingency to Eliminate Noncompliance

If an individual refuses to take his or her medication, when it is presented by a caregiver, because the act of taking the medication may be aversive (e.g., either it tastes bad or produces aversive side effects), one could potentially overcome the aversive nature of taking the medication by providing additional reinforcement for the actual act of taking the medication. This could be done by either writing a *task analysis* of taking medication (see Miltenberger, 2000, for how to do this) and providing verbal praise for completion or compliance with each step and then a preferred food item for actually swallowing the medication or by just providing a preferred food item or access to a preferred activity for compliance with the medication consumption regimen.

Examples of Extinction

Eliminating the Reinforcement Contingency Maintaining Nonadherence

Nonadherence can be caused by the individual obtaining something that he or she wants or avoiding or terminating an aversive event; in either case, one way to eliminate nonadherence is to no longer provide the individual with what he or she wants or to no longer allow the individual to avoid or terminate the aversive event (i.e., extinction). If an individual engages in refusal behavior (e.g., hitting the caretaker) when asked to take his or her blood glucose level because he or she then receives a lot of attention from the caretaker, in the form of reprimands and being held down so that another caretaker can take the blood glucose level, one could stop reprimanding the individual and just take the glucose level without any further attention being provided for the problem behavior (i.e., not saying anything to the individual about the problem behavior). If indeed the problem behavior is maintained by the attention provided, then eliminating the attention will stop the problem behavior (Iwata, Pace, Cowdery, & Milternberger, 1994). A better idea would be to add a reinforcement procedure to the extinction procedure. For example, one could actually provide praise for compliance with the procedure (i.e., taking the blood glucose level) as well as ignore the problem behavior.

If, on the other hand, the individual engages in problem behavior (e.g., self-injurious behavior) to terminate a medical procedure (e.g., physical examination), one could implement extinction by not allowing the examination to be terminated but actually continuing the examination until the individual stops engaging in the problem behavior (see Iwata, Pace, Dorsey, et al., 1994, for an example). Not terminating the examination will demonstrate to the individual that engaging in the problem behavior does not eliminate the aversive event (physical exam), thus he or she will stop engaging in the problem behavior. Again, combining this procedure with a reinforcement procedure would be ideal.

Summary

The purpose of this chapter was to alert readers to various types of adherence problems faced by individuals with developmental disabilities and to provide suggestions regarding ways in which these adherence problems can be circumvented. When attempting to improve treatment adherence, one should first assess what variables may be contributing to nonadherence. Potential variables that may contribute to nonadherence include (1) lack of understanding; (2) insufficient repertoires; (3) contingencies that promote nonadherence, such as attention or escape (provided contingent on nonadherent behaviors);

(4) failure of individuals with developmental disabilities to perceive the benefits and risks associated with adherence and nonadherence, respectively; and (5) lack of support from caregivers. Once the variables contributing to nonadherence have been identified, these variables can then be manipulated in such a way that treatment adherence is facilitated. This chapter has discussed interventions designed to change the behavior of both the patient and the caregiver. Interventions designed to change the patient's behavior include various antecedent manipulations and reinforcement procedures, as well as the use of extinction, and interventions designed to change the caregiver's behavior are focused on training, with respect to both the medical procedures to be employed and the various approaches one can take to facilitate treatment adherence. In summary, this chapter has illustrated how employing strategies that address variables related to nonadherence can improve, and subsequently maintain, the health of individuals with developmental disabilities.

Suggested Readings

Bouras, N. (1999). *Psychiatric and behavioral disorders in developmental disabilities and mental retardation.* Cambridge, UK: Cambridge University Press.

Bradley, V. J., & Kimmich, M. H. (2003). *Quality enhancement in developmental disabilities: Challenges and opportunities in a changing world.* Baltimore, MD: Paul H. Brookes.

Fox, J. A. (1997). *Primary health care of children.* St. Louis, MO: Mosby.

Hitchcock, J. E., Schubert, P. E., & Thomas, S. A. (1999). *Community health nursing: Caring in action.* Albany, NY: Delmar.

Iwata, B. A., Vollmer, T. R., & Zarcone, J. R. (1990). The experimental (functional) analysis of behavior disorders: Methodology, applications, and limitations. In A. C. Repp & N. N. Singh (Eds.), *Perspectives on the use of nonaversive and aversive interventions for persons with developmental disabilities* (pp. 301–330). Sycamore, IL: Sycamore Publishing.

Iwata, B. A., Vollmer, T. R., Zarcone, J. R., & Rodgers, T. A. (1993). Treatment classification and selection based on behavioral function. In R. V. Houten & S. Axelrod (Eds.), *Behavior analysis and treatment* (pp. 101–125). New York: Plenum Press.

Luiselli, J. D. (1989). *Behavioral medicine and developmental disabilities.* New York: Springer-Verlag.

Queen, P. M., & Lang, C. E. (1993). *Handbook of pediatric nutrition.* Gaithersburg, MD: Aspen.

Russo, D. C., & Kedesdy, J. H. (1988). *Behavioral medicine with the developmentally disabled.* New York: Plenum.

Singh, N. N. (Ed.). (1997). *Prevention and treatment of severe behavior problems: Models and methods in developmental disabilities.* Pacific Grove, CA: Brooks/Cole.

Sutton, E., Factor, A. R., Hawkins, B. A., Heller, T., & Seltzer, G. B. (1993). Older adults with developmental disabilities: Optimizing choice and change. Baltimore, MD: Paul H. Brookes.

References

Adams, J., & Scott, J. (2000). Predicting medication adherence in severe mental disorders. *Acta Psychiatrica Scandinavica, 101,* 119–124.

Diamond, R. J. (1983). Enhancing medication use in schizophrenic patients. *Journal of Clinical Psychiatry, 44,* 7–14.

Frazier, T. W. (1972). Training institutional staff in behavior modification principles and techniques. In R. D. Ruben, H. Fensterheim, J. D., Henderson, & L. P. Ullmann (Eds.), *Advances in behavior therapy: Proceedings of the fourth conference of the Association for Advancement of Behavior Therapy* (pp. 171–178). New York: Academic Press.

Harchik, A., & Putzier, V. S. (1990). The use of high-probability requests to increase compliance with instructions to take medication. *Journal of the Association for Persons With Severe Handicaps, 15,* 40–43.

Iwata, B. A., Kahng, S., Wallace, M. D., & Lindberg, J. S. (2000). The functional analysis model of behavioral assessment. In J. Austin & J. Carr (Eds.), *Handbook of applied behavior analysis,* Reno, NV: Context Press.

Iwata, B. A., Pace, G. M., Cowdery, G. E., & Milternberger, R. G. (1994). What makes extinction work: An analysis of procedural form and function. *Journal of Applied Behavior Analysis, 27,* 131–144.

Iwata, B. A., Pace, G. M., Dorsey, M. F., Zarcone, J. R., Vollmer, T. R., Smith, R. G., et al. (1994). The functions of self-injurious behavior: An experimental-epidemiological analysis. *Journal of Applied Behavior Analysis, 27,* 215–240.

Luiselli, J. K., Putnam, R. F., & Sunderland, M. (2002). Longitudinal evaluation of behavior support intervention in a public middle school. *Journal of Positive Behavior Interventions, 4,* 182–188.

McComas, J. J., Wacker, D. P., & Cooper, L. J. (1998). Increasing compliance with medical procedures: Application of the high-probability request procedure to a toddler. *Journal of Applied Behavior Analysis, 31,* 287–290.

Miltenberger, R. G. (2000). *Behavior modification: Principles and procedures* (2nd ed.). Belmont, CA: Wadsworth/Thomson Learning.

Perkins, D. O. (2002). Predictors of noncompliance in patients with schizophrenia. *Journal of Clinical Psychiatry, 63,* 1121–1128.

Reid, D. H., & Green, C. W. (1990). Staff training. In J. L. Matson (Ed.), *Handbook of behavior modification with the mentally retarded* (2nd ed., pp. 71–90). New York: Plenum Press.

Reid, D. H., & Parsons, M. B. (1995). *Motivating human service staff: Supervisory strategies for maximizing work effort and work enjoyment.* Morganton, NC: Habilitative Management Consultants.

Reid, D. H., Parsons, M. B., & Green, C. W. (1989). *Staff management in human services: Behavioral research and application.* Springfield, IL: Charles C Thomas.

Sheras, P. L., Cornell, D. G., & Bostain, D. S. (1996). The Virginia Youth Violence Project: Transmitting psychological knowledge on youth violence to schools and communities. *Professional Psychology: Research and Practice, 27,* 401–406.

Appendix

Patient Resources
Books on Understanding the Health Care System and When and How to Access Services

Koop, C. E. (1996). *Dr. Koop's self-care advisor: The essential home health guide for you and your family.* Washington, DC: Time Inc. Health.

Wurman, R. S. (2004). *Understanding health care.* Newport, RI: TOP.

General Web Search Engines

www.google.com

www.altavista.com

www.alltheweb.com

General Health and Medication Information

www.eatright.org/Public/

www.mayoclinic.org/healthinfo/

www.nlm.nih.gov/medlineplus/druginformation.html (information on thousands of prescription and over-the-counter medications)

http://familydoctor.org/x2544.xml (body mass index calculator)

For More Educated Patients

www.ncbi.nlm.nih.gov/entrez/query.fcgi

www.cdc.gov

Cancer

www.cancer.org

www.cancerlinks.org

www.cancersupportivecare.com

www.ivf.com/womhtml.html#oncology

www.breastdiseases.com/pemenu.htm

Pulmonary conditions

www.lungusa.org/site/pp.asp?c=dvLUK9O0E&b=22542

www.aaaai.org/aadmc/currentliterature/asthmaguidelines.html

www.acaai.org

www.nlm.nih.gov/hmd/breath/breathhome.html

www.lung.ca/asthma/exercise

www.nutramed.com/asthma/anaphylaxis.htm

www.agius.com/hew/resource/ocasthma.htm

Diabetes

www.diabetes.org

www.diabetes4patients.com

www.diabetesaction.org

http://ndep.nih.gov

www.jdrf.org/ (juvenile diabetes)

Persons With Disabilities

http://rtc.ruralinstitute.umt.edu/health/RuH
Outreach.htm

www.healthwellness.org

www.ncpad.org

www.deltasociety.org (animal assistance for the
blind)

Disabled Veterans

www1.va.gov/vha_oi

Cardiovascular Conditions

www.americanheart.org/presenter.jhtml?
identifier=3053

www.ash-us.org

www.stroke.org

www.amhrt.org

www.seals.com

http://merck.micromedex.com/index.asp?
page=bhg_report&article_id=BHG01CA19
&section=report

Elderly

www.aoa.gov/naic/Notes/alzheimerdisease
.html

www.aoa.gov/naic

www.caregiver.org

www.alfa.org

www.evercareonline.com

About the Contributors

Victoria V. Anwuri, MPH, serves as the Program Coordinator for the Robert Wood Johnson Foundation Diabetes Initiative National Program Office at Washington University School of Medicine in St. Louis, Missouri. Prior to serving as Program Coordinator, she was a public health Fellow in the Cardiovascular Health Branch of the National Center for Chronic Disease Prevention and Health Promotion at the Centers for Disease Control and Prevention (CDC). Her research, interest, and experience include understanding how to leverage health care organizations and business sectors for chronic disease prevention and control, working with state health departments funded by CDC's National Heart Disease and Stroke Prevention Program, cataract management and related quality-of-life issues, development of health communication and education materials and curriculum for diverse populations, eliminating health disparities, and policy.

Kendra Beitz is currently Project Coordinator for Care Integra, where she develops and evaluates behavioral health care programs. Her professional interests include the conceptualization and treatment of personality disorders and integrated behavioral health care. She obtained her doctorate in Clinical Psychology from the University of Nevada, Reno, in 2005.

Ana M. Bisonó is a graduate student in the clinical psychology doctoral program at the University of New Mexico (UNM). Her research interests include substance abuse, religion and spirituality, domestic violence, as well as cross-cultural issues in research. She has worked on several projects at the UNM Center on Alcoholism, Substance Abuse, and Addictions, including a Clinical Trials Network project that uses motivational enhancement therapy to treat Spanish-speaking substance abusers. She is a motivational interviewing trainer in both English and Spanish.

Arthur W. Blume is Associate Professor of Psychology at the University of North Carolina at Charlotte. His research focuses on addictive behavior change among ethnic minority populations, college students, and patients with co-occurring disorders. In addition to numerous research publications, he is author of the book *Treating Drug Problems.* He was awarded the 2003 Early Career Contribution Award in Addictive Behaviors Research from the Association for Advancement of Behavior Therapy. A former student of G. Alan Marlatt, PhD, who pioneered relapse prevention research and therapy, he received his PhD in clinical psychology from the University of Washington, Seattle.

Carol A. Brownson, MSPH, serves as Deputy Director for the Diabetes Initiative National Program Office at the Washington University School of Medicine in St. Louis. She has experience in community health, health education, program development, and capacity building. Prior to assuming her current role, she worked for 16 years in chronic disease prevention and health promotion programs at the Missouri

Department of Health and for 5 years developing the community practice program for the Program in Occupational Therapy at Washington University School of Medicine. During that time, she also directed health promotion curriculum development for OASIS, a national education program for older adults.

Jennifer L. Burden, PhD, is a clinical psychologist and the program coordinator for the Community Residential Program at the Veterans Affairs Medical Center in Salem, Virginia. She has a joint appointment as an Assistant Professor of Clinical Psychiatric Medicine at the University of Virginia. Her primary clinical and research interests are in the areas of treatment motivation, cognitive processes related to substance use, and treatment adherence and outcome. She earned her PhD in clinical psychology from Syracuse University.

Barry L. Carter is currently a Professor in the Division of Clinical and Administrative Pharmacy and a Professor in the Department of Family Medicine. He is a Fellow in the American Heart Association Council on High Blood Pressure Research (FAHA), a Fellow in the American College of Clinical Pharmacy (FCCP), and a board certified pharmacotherapy specialist (BCPS). He is a member of the National Heart, Lung, and Blood Institute's National High Blood Pressure Education Program Committee. He was also a member of the Fifth, Sixth, and Seventh Joint National Committees on Prevention, Detection, Evaluation and Treatment of High Blood Pressure (JNC-V, JNC-VI, and JNC-VII). He received his BS in pharmacy from the University of Iowa (1978) and his Pharm.D. from the Medical College of Virginia (1980). He completed a postdoctoral fellowship in Family Practice at the University of Iowa (1981).

Alan J. Christensen, PhD, is currently serving a 5-year term as Editor-in-Chief of the *Annals of Behavioral Medicine.* He is a clinical health psychologist and is Professor of Psychology and of Internal Medicine at the University of Iowa. He is best known for his work proposing and delineating an "interactive framework" for testing the

joint effects of psychosocial variables and medical treatment-related variables on patient outcomes. His work in this area has demonstrated that the "match" or degree of symmetry between health-related beliefs, preferences, and attitudes held by patients and the role that patients are asked to play with regard to their own treatment delivery is an important determinant of patient outcomes. He has received numerous awards for his scholarship, including the Award for Outstanding Early Career Contributions to Health Psychology from Division 38 of the American Psychological Association in 1999, the American Psychological Association Distinguished Scientific Award for Early Career Contribution to Psychology (in the area of Health Psychology) in 2000, the Early Career Award for Contributions to Psychosomatic Medicine awarded by the American Psychosomatic Society in 1999, and the Early Career Award for Contributions to Behavioral Medicine Research from the Society of Behavioral Medicine in 2000. He received his PhD in clinical psychology from the University of Utah in 1993.

Paul F. Cook, PhD, is a clinical psychologist who conducts research on medication adherence and health behavior change. He developed the clinical model for the ScriptAssist treatment adherence program, which is a product of Centene Corporation. He has published empirical work on treatment outcomes and theoretical work on psychotherapy techniques, and his clinical experience includes work in several public-sector mental health care settings. He is now at the University of Colorado at Denver and Health Sciences Center, where he serves as Director of the Center for Nursing Research.

Patrick W. Corrigan is Professor of Psychology at the Illinois Institute of Technology and Executive Director of the Joint Reserach Programs for Psychiatric Rehabilitation at IIT. The Joint Research Programs are services, research, and training efforts dedicated to the needs of people with psychiatric disability and their families. He has been principal investigator of federally funded studies on rehabilitation, team leadership, and consumer-operated services. Four years ago, he became principal investigator of the Chicago Consortium for Stigma Research (CCSR), the only NIMH-funded research center examining the stigma of mental illness. He is a prolific researcher having published 10 books and more than 200 papers.

Jamie A. Cvengros, MA, is graduate Fellow at the University of Iowa in the Department of Psychology. Her doctoral research broadly examines the patient-provider relationship. Specifically, she is investigating how the match between patient and provider characteristics affect important patient outcomes such as patient satisfaction and adherence to treatment regimens. She received the prestigious University of Iowa Presidential Fellowship in 2001. Her research has been published in several prominent journals including *Health Psychology* and *Annals of Behavioral Medicine.* In addition, she has presented her work at major conferences such as the annual meeting for the *Society of Behavioral Medicine.*

Edwin J. Dyer is currently interning at the Center for Autism and Related Disorders (CARD) in Tarzana, California. He is working toward a master's in behavior analysis from the University of Nevada, Reno, and holds a bachelor of arts in English from the same university. His interests include severe problem behavior, social skills acquisition, and the Beatles.

Kyle E. Ferguson is pursuing a PhD in clinical psychology at the University of Nevada, Reno. He received a master's degree in applied behavior analysis with an emphasis on behavioral medicine from Southern Illinois University. He has authored or coauthored over 40 articles, book chapters, and books.

Edwin B. Fisher, PhD, is now Professor and Chair of the Department of Health Behavior and Health Education in the School of Public Health at the University of North Carolina at Chapel Hill. He also serves as National Program Director of the Diabetes Initiative of the Robert Wood Johnson Foundation and is President-Elect of the Society of Behavioral Medicine. His research has examined community, peer, and social support aspects of self-management, quality of life, emotional well-being, and health promotion in asthma, cancer, diabetes, cardiovascular disease, and smoking cessation. Until 2005, he was Professor of Psychology, Medicine and Pediatrics at Washington University in St. Louis. He received his doctorate in clinical psychology at Stony Brook State University in New York.

Jane E. Fisher, PhD, is Associate Professor of Psychology and former Director of Clinical Training at the University of Nevada, Reno. She is a member of the Workgroup on Evidence Based Practice at the Positive Aging Resource Center, a national technical assistance center on aging and mental health. Her research interests include clinical gerontology, applied behavior analysis, and the integration of evidence-based behavioral health care in primary and extended-care settings. Her research on the development of restraint-free interventions for elderly persons with cognitive disorders is funded by the National Institute on Aging.

Alyssa A. Forcehimes is a third-year clinical psychology graduate student at the University of New Mexico. Her primary research interest is in the area of addictions, focusing on its interface with spirituality. Related interests include mutual help research, including studying spiritual transformations in members of Alcoholics Anonymous and understanding how behavior change is mobilized and sustained in Alcoholics Anonymous. She is currently working with the COMBINE study, a multisite trial studying the efficacy of combining pharmacotherapy and psychotherapy interventions for alcohol problems.

Nancy Foster is currently employed at Girls and Boys Town in Omaha, Nebraska. Her research interests include examining the effects of behavioral function on compliance training, escape-motivated time-out procedures, and behavioral pediatrics. She received her PhD in school psychology from Mississippi State University in 2004.

Patrick C. Friman, PhD, ABPP, is the Director of Outpatient Behavioral Pediatrics and Family Services at Father Flanagan's Boys' Home and Adjunct Professor of Pediatrics at the University of Nebraska School of Medicine. His research and clinical interests include habit disorders, incontinence, child behavior problems at home and school, and a broad range of topics organized under the general category known as behavioral pediatrics. He is the author or coauthor of more than 140 journal articles and book chapters.

Brian Giddens, LICSW, ACSW, is Associate Director of Social Work at University of Washington Medical Center and Clinical Assistant Professor with the University of Washington School of Social Work, where he has taught courses integrating organizational practice, leadership, and ethics. His professional background has focused on physical and mental health in community-based organizations, long-term care, acute care, and outpatient programs. In addition to roles as manager, trainer, and clinical consultant, he is committed to issues of health policy and was named a DHHS Primary Health Care Policy Fellow in 2004. He serves as President for NASW Washington State Chapter, and is a past President of the Washington State Chapter of the Society for Social Work Leadership in Health Care. From 1995 to 2004, he served on the Advisory Committee of the NASW HIV/AIDS Spectrum: Mental Health Training and Education of Social Workers Project, collaborating on creating curriculum and conducting training for social workers nationwide.

Elizabeth V. Gifford is a Health Sciences Researcher at the Center for Health Care Evaluation. She was cofounder and director of the UNR Smoking Cessation Clinic, the largest smoking cessation clinic in the State of Nevada, for which she received the David Award of Excellence for Contribution to Tobacco Control from the State of Nevada. Her current areas of interest include smoking cessation, coping with HIV/AIDS, theories of change and mechanisms of action in health-related behavior, treatment access and retention, and health-related public policy. She received her PhD in 2003 from the University of Nevada, Reno.

Elaine M. Heiby is Professor in the Department of Psychology at the University of Hawaii at Manoa where she formerly served as Director of Clinical Studies and Chair of Graduate Studies. Her research interests include integrated assessment, mood disorders, compliance to health regimens, self-control skills, psychological behaviorism, and chaos theory. She obtained her PhD in clinical and behavioral psychology from the University of Illinois at Chicago.

Marcia Herivel, LICSW, has worked as a psychotherapist at the Harborview Center for Sexual Assault and Traumatic Stress in Seattle since 1992, where she coordinates the group therapy program. She has done extensive training on topics related to sexual assault and trauma, most recently at the 2003 Annual Conference of the National Center for Child Abuse and Neglect, in St. Louis. Prior to employment at HCSATS, she was Lead Social Worker in the emergency room at Children's Hospital and Regional Medical Center, also in Seattle. She has a special interest in the treatment of trauma in adolescents.

Negar Nicole Jacobs is currently working in the Mental Health Service at the Veterans Administration Sierra Nevada Health Care System. Her clinical interests include adapting evidence-based psychological treatments to primary care settings, including addressing emotional aspects of medical problems, adherence/compliance problems, and treatment of addictive disorders. Her research interests include addressing the emotional aspects of infertility and fertility treatments and evaluating the effectiveness of self-help treatments for infertility. She and William O'Donohue have recently demonstrated the effectiveness of a bibliotherapy approach they developed for addressing the emotional aspects of infertility. She received her PhD in psychology from the University of Nevada, Reno, in 2003.

Scott Evan Jacobs is an Obstetrician/ Gynecologist in private practice in Reno, Nevada, and he serves as Assistant Professor for the Department of Family and Community Medicine at the University of Nevada School of Medicine. He received his MD from Albany Medical College in 1988.

Sara S. Johnson, PhD, is Director of Health Behavior Change Projects at Pro-Change Behavior Systems, Inc., and Adjunct Professor in the Department of Psychology at the University of Rhode Island. She led efforts in Pro-Change to receive funding from the National Heart, Lung and Blood Institute to examine the efficacy of population-based medication adherence interventions.

Preety Kalra is Study Director at the Veterans Administration Palo Alto Health Care System on a multisite smoking cessation intervention trial. Her work is focused on the social and behavioral factors associated with chronic disease, particularly cardiovascular disease. She is interested in examining the social determinants of health and the role of behavior change in outcomes. She received her master's degree in epidemiology from Stanford University.

Lana Sue I. Ka'opua, PhD, ACSW, LSW, is Associate Professor (Researcher) at the University of Hawai'i, School of Social Work and the Cancer Research Center of Hawai'i. Trained at the UH School of Social Welfare, she has two decades of clinical mental health practice. As a researcher, she is committed to the elimination of cancer and other health disparities and is involved in the implementation of a culturally tailored intervention to increase Native Hawaiian women's adherence to routine breast cancer screening, provides mental health consultation to a writing intervention study for cancer patients, evaluates breast and cervical cancer control programs, and offers technical assistance to six U.S.-associated Pacific Island nations. Active with the National Association of Social Workers, she has served on the advisory boards of the HIV Spectrum Committee and

Mental Health Specialty Practice Section. She and Brian Giddens have developed adherence curricula used across the United States. Contact may be made at lskaopua@hawaii.edu.

Steven J. Lash, PhD, is Clinical Psychologist at the Veterans Affairs Medical Center in Salem, Virginia. He has a joint appointment as Assistant Professor of Clinical Psychiatric Medicine at the University of Virginia. His primary clinical and research interests are in promoting adherence to treatment among individuals with substance use disorders. He is currently completing a large-scale clinical trial of contracting, prompting, and reinforcing substance abuse continuing care participation, funded by the VA's department of Health Services Research and Development (IIR 99–282–2). He earned his PhD in clinical psychology from Virginia Polytechnic Institute and State University in 1992.

Hillary LeRoux is currently earning her PhD in Clinical Psychology at the University of Nevada, Reno. She completed her undergraduate work at the University of Southern California in Los Angeles. As an undergraduate, her research experiences led to two publications on generalized anxiety disorder in older adults. Her research experiences facilitated an extensive interest in geriatrics, which has continued with her graduate training. For her master's thesis, she is researching how physicians' interview style affects their diagnostic judgments of older adults. Her other interests in aging include anxiety, depression, elder abuse, dementia, and caregiver burden.

Eric R. Levensky is currently serving as coordinator of the Southwest Node of the Clinical Trials Network (CTN), a NIDA-funded multisite project evaluating the effectiveness of known efficacious behavioral, pharmacological, and integrated interventions across a broad range of community-based treatment settings and diverse patient populations. A secondary goal of the CTN is to disseminate effective interventions to physicians, providers, and their patients to improve the quality of treatment throughout the country. His primary area of research interest is in the development, evaluation, and dissemination of treatment adherence interventions for patients with chronic illness, as well as examining psychosocial aspects of chronic illness management. His current work centers primarily on understanding and promoting treatment adherence in HIV patients, and he recently received a grant from the National Institutes of Health to conduct research in this area. He has clinical interest in forensic psychology, as well as the practice, application, and supervision of motivational interviewing and dialectical behavior therapy. He has coedited one book and authored 11 papers and book chapters on these topics. He recently completed his PhD in clinical psychology at the University of Nevada, Reno.

Carrie Lukens is a graduate student working toward her PhD in clinical psychology at the University of Hawaii at Manoa. Her research interests include compliance to health regimens, mood disorders, psychological behaviorism, and psychosocial treatment for severe mental illness. She received her undergraduate degree at the University of Wisconsin–Stevens Point.

Jennifer Knapp Manuel is a graduate student in clinical psychology studying coping among family members of individuals with alcohol and drug problems. Her related interests include substance abuse prevention programs in health care settings. She is currently in the third year of the doctoral program at the University of New Mexico, completing work toward her master's degree.

Bess H. Marcus, PhD, is Professor of Psychiatry and Human Behavior at the Brown University Medical School and Interim Director at the Center for Behavioral and Preventive Medicine at the Miriam Hospital and Brown Medical School. She has published over 100 papers and book chapters as well as three books on physical activity behavior. She has participated in American Heart Association, American College of Sports Medicine, Centers for Disease Control and Prevention, and National Institutes of Health panels that have created new recommendations regarding the quantity and intensity of physical activity necessary for health benefits. She is currently Principal Investigator or Co-Investigator on eight National Institutes of Health grants on physical activity behavior.

G. Alan Marlatt is Professor of Psychology and Director of the Addictive Behaviors Research Center at the University of Washington. After serving on the faculties of the University of British Columbia (1968–1969) and the University of Wisconsin (1969–1972), he joined the University of Washington as faculty in the fall of 1972. His major focus in both research and clinical work is the field of addictive behaviors. In addition to over 200 journal articles and book chapters, he has published several books in the addictions field, including *Relapse Prevention* (1985, 2005), *Assessment of Addictive Behaviors* (1988, 2005), *Harm Reduction* (1998), and *Brief Alcohol Screening and Intervention for College Students (BASICS): A Harm Reduction Approach* (1999). Over the course of the past 30 years, he has received continuous funding for his research from a variety of agencies, including the National Institute on Alcohol Abuse and Alcoholism, the National Institute on Drug Abuse, the Alcoholic Beverage Medical Research Foundation, and the Robert Wood Johnson Foundation. In 1990, he was awarded the Jellinek Memorial Award for outstanding contributions to knowledge in the field of alcohol studies; in 2001, he was given the Innovators in Combating Substance Abuse Award by the Robert Wood Johnson Foundation; and in 2004, he received the Distinguished Researcher Award from the Research Society on Alcoholism. He received his PhD in clinical psychology from Indiana University in 1968.

Barbara S. McCann, PhD, is Professor of Psychiatry and Behavioral Sciences at the University of Washington in Seattle. She is both a clinical psychologist and researcher. She has participated in numerous large-scale clinical trials of dietary interventions in diabetes and hyperlipidemia. In her clinical practice, she specializes in patients with eating disorders and obesity, including patients who are pre- and postsurgery for weight loss.

Arthur M. Nezu, PhD, ABPP, Professor of Psychology, Medicine, and Public Health, is codirector of the Center for Behavioral Medicine and Mind/Body Studies at Drexel University. He is Past President of both the Association for Advancement of Behavior Therapy and the American Board of Behavioral and Cognitive Psychology. He is a Fellow of the American Psychological Association, the American Psychological Society, the Society for Behavioral Medicine, the American Academy of Behavioral Psychology, and the Academy of Cognitive Therapy.

Christine Maguth Nezu, PhD, ABPP, Professor of Psychology and Associate Professor of Medicine, is codirector of the Center for Behavioral Medicine and Mind/Body Studies at Drexel University. She is currently President-Elect of the American Board of Professional Psychology, and a member of the American Board of Cognitive and Behavioral Psychology. She is a Fellow of the American Academy of Behavioral Psychology and the Academy of Cognitive Therapy.

William T. O'Donohue is a licensed clinical psychologist and is widely recognized in the field for his proposed innovations in mental health service delivery, in treatment design and evaluation, and in knowledge of empirically supported cognitive behavioral therapies. He is a member of the Association for the Advancement for Behavior Therapy and served on the board of directors of this organization. He has an exemplary history of successful grant funding and government contracts. Since 1996, he has received over $1,500,000 in federal grant monies from sources including the National Institute of Mental Health and the National Institute of Justice. In addition, he has published his work prolifically. He has edited over

20 books and written 35 book chapters on various topics and published reviews for seven books. In addition, he has published more than 75 articles in scholarly journals. He is currently directing a major grant funded project involving integrated care. This project is a treatment development/outcome evaluation project. Specially trained psychologists are placed into primary care, and five sets of variables are examined: (1) patient satisfaction, (2) provider satisfaction, (3) clinical change, (4) functional change, and (5) medical utilization change. He is a national expert in training clinicians in integrated care and developing quality improvement projects in integrated care.

Megan L. Oser is currently in the PhD clinical psychology program at the University of Nevada, Reno. She is developing a brief empirically based bibliotherapy intervention for improving medication adherence among patients with chronic conditions. She was co-investigator on a recently completed grant funded by the National Institutes of Health to investigate a manualized clinician-delivered intervention to increase medication adherence among HIV patients. Her current professional pursuits focus on treatment development of health behavior change interventions.

Mary L. O'Toole is currently Deputy Director at the National Program Office of the Robert Wood Johnson Foundation Diabetes Initiative located at Washington University in St. Louis. Previously, she had held faculty positions in the departments of Preventive Medicine, Orthopedics, and Physical Therapy at the University of Tennessee Health Science Center and in the Department of Obstetrics and Gynecology at Saint Louis University. She is a Fellow of the American College of Sports Medicine. She has extensive experience with large-scale physical activity and lifestyle clinical trials, including the Diabetes Prevention Program and the Activity Counseling Trial. She received her PhD in exercise physiology from Temple University.

Becky Penrod is currently pursuing her doctorate in behavior analysis. She has worked in a number of different clinical positions, serving adults and children with developmental disabilities, as well as children with severe behavior problems. She works as a behavioral consultant for Washoe County Social Services. Her current research interests are focused on the evaluation of treatments for children with feeding disorders. Following graduation, she hopes to pursue a career in pediatric behavioral health care. She received her master's degree in behavior analysis from the University of Nevada, Reno.

Michael G. Perri, PhD, ABPP, is Professor of Clinical and Health Psychology and Associate Dean for Research of the University of Florida's College of Public Health and Health Professions. He is a Diplomate of the American Board of Profession Psychology and a Fellow of the American Psychological Association, the Society of Behavioral Medicine, and the North American Association for the Study of Obesity. He has contributed to more than 100 professional and scientific publications.

Amy Peterman, PhD, is an Associate Professor of Psychology at the University of North Carolina in Charlotte. Her primary research interests lie with the development of individually meaningful measures of disease impact, and she has extensive experience in instrument development and validation. For 11 years, she was a clinical research scientist and Director of Research with the Center on Outcomes, Research and Education, the group responsible for the FACIT Measurement System. She played a key role in the development and validation of many of those quality of life scales, most particularly the FACIT-Spiritual Well-being Scale. Additionally, she is the Principal Investigator of a recently completed study funded by the National Cancer Institute, which evaluated the psychometric properties and clinical utility of a measure assessing the extent to which cancer treatment interferes with important life plans and

goals. Finally, Dr. Peterman is a licensed clinical psychologist with a specialty in health psychology and psychosocial oncology.

James O. Prochaska, PhD, is the Director of the Cancer Prevention Research Center and Professor of Psychology at the University of Rhode Island. He is one of the originators of the transtheoretical model of change and the author of more than 200 papers on health promotion and disease prevention.

Janice M. Prochaska, MSW, PhD, is President and CEO of Pro-Change Behavior Systems, Inc. and Adjunct Professor in the Department of Human Development and Family Studies at the University of Rhode Island. She leads a small business with 20 staff members dedicated to the scientific development and dissemination of transtheoretical model-based change management programs.

Mandra L. Rasmussen Hall is a graduate student at the University of Nevada, Reno, and a psychology intern at the Reno Veterans Association Sierra Nevada Health Care System. Her clinical and research interests focus on treatment strategies for individuals with histories of trauma who exhibit multiple problems, including substance abuse, self-harm, posttraumatic symptoms, relationship problems, and general difficulties identifying and regulating emotions. She will receive her PhD in clinical psychology in August 2006.

Kristin A. Riekert, PhD, is currently Assistant Professor of Medicine in the Division of Pulmonary and Critical Care Medicine, Johns Hopkins University, Baltimore, Maryland. Her research interests include developing (1) research and clinical strategies to improve patient-reported regimen adherence and (2) educational, behavioral, and motivational interventions to improve adherence and health outcomes among children and adolescents with chronic illnesses. She received her PhD in clinical psychology from Case Western Reserve University in 2000 with a specialization in pediatric psychology.

José R. Rodríguez-Gómez is Professor at the Carlos Albizu University, Puerto Rico, in the Clinical Psychology PhD Program, where he teaches social psychology and gerontology graduate courses. He is a Fellow of the American Academy of Experts in Traumatic Stress and Diplomate of the American Board of Psychological Specialties. He is the author or coauthor of over 60 peer-reviewed articles in the topics of gerontology and Hispanic minorities. He has an MD and MPH in epidemiology, a PhD in sociology, and a postgraduate certification in gerontology. His PhD training was at Fordham University as a Fellow of a program sponsored by the National Institute of Mental Health. He is available to share new research projects ideas at jrrodz@coqui.net.

Richard R. Rubin, PhD, CDE, is Associate Professor in Medicine and in Pediatrics at the Johns Hopkins University School of Medicine. He has been involved as a principal investigator and co-investigator in several long-term studies of psychosocial and lifestyle issues in the management of diabetes, including the National Institutes of Health-funded Diabetes Prevention Program (DPP) and Look AHEAD trials. Among his publications are more than 100 papers, book chapters, abstracts, and articles on the effects of diabetes education, psychological problems associated with diabetes, and techniques for counseling people with diabetes. He is also coauthor of eight books, including *101 Tips for Coping With Diabetes, Psyching Out Diabetes* (three editions), *Sweet Kids* (two editions), *Optimal Pumping, The Johns Hopkins Guide to Diabetes*, and he is coeditor of *Practical Psychology for Diabetes Clinicians* (two editions) and of *The Core Curriculum for Diabetes Education* (3rd edition). He is an active member of the American Diabetes Association (ADA) and the American Association of Diabetes Educators (AADE), holding a number of leadership positions in both organizations. He was also a member (1988–1991) and Chairman (1990–1991) of the National Certification Board for Diabetes Educators.

Carmen C. Salas-Serrano is Professor at the University of Puerto Rico, Rio Piedras Campus, where she supervises internships and works with students in training. She has been author and coauthor of various articles on attention deficit hyperactivity disorder (ADHD) in Hispanic populations. Another important activity in her work is the translation of numerous fact sheets, articles, and books about ADHD to Spanish so that the Spanish-speaking minority can have access to this important information. She has a master's degree in speech-language pathology, a postgraduate certification in gerontology, and a PhD in clinical psychology.

Heather Scarlett-Ferguson is a Clinical Pharmacist at Alberta Hospital Ponoka in Alberta, Canada, and an instructor in the Health and Community Studies Program at Grant MacEwan College in Edmonton, Canada. She specializes in mental health pharmacy and patient education. Her research focus is in distance education. She has written numerous articles and is currently revising a pharmacology textbook.

Susan D. Schaffer is Clinical Assistant Professor at the University of Florida College of Nursing. She is involved in graduate teaching and in clinical practice at the College of Nursing's Family Practice in Archer, Florida. Her research interests include asthma medication adherence and measuring asthma knowledge. She earned a PhD from George Mason University, Fairfax, Virginia, and an MS in Nursing from Old Dominion University, Norfolk, Virginia. She is certified as a family nurse practitioner.

Robin Shapiro, LICSW, is a psychotherapist, teacher, and consultant in Seattle, Washington. As a faculty member of Seattle Institute of Oriental Medicine (1999–2004), she taught "Counseling Issues in Health Care." She teaches EMDR basic courses and has presented at several regional and international psychotherapy conferences. She is the editor and a contributor to *EMDR Solutions: Pathways to Healing*, a book of EMDR strategies for special treatment populations. In the 2003 issue of *Seattle Magazine,* her peers voted her one of Seattle's "Top Doctors for Women." Her next book is about psychological issues for health care professionals.

Gowri Shetty, MS, MPH, serves as the Evaluation Coordinator for the Diabetes Initiative National Program Office. She is currently completing a PhD in epidemiology from Saint Louis University School of Public Health. She brings over 6 years of program evaluation experience and has done a considerable amount of evaluation work for the Missouri Department of Health and Senior Services including writing the Diabetes State Plan for the State of Missouri. Her experience includes design and assessment of tools to measure effectiveness of community-based interventions, conducting needs assessment of communities, and quantitative and qualitative evaluation of community-based interventions. She teaches courses in community nutrition and research methodology at Saint Louis University School of Allied Health. She has a master of science degree in medical dietetics and a master of public health degree from Saint Louis University School of Public Health.

David Victorson, PhD, is a Research Associate at the Center on Outcomes, Research and Education at Evanston Northwestern Healthcare. He is an Assistant Professor in the Department of Psychiatry and Behavioral Sciences as well as the Institute for Healthcare Studies at Northwestern University Feinberg School of Medicine. His research focuses on the development of patient-reported outcomes that measure health-related quality of life and symptom status in chronically ill populations. He also has clinical and research interests in psychosocial adjustment to acute and chronic health problems, psychosocial oncology, and integrative medicine.

Whitney M. Waldroup is currently a medical student at the University of Nevada School of Medicine and will obtain her MD in May, 2008.

She holds an MPH from Dartmouth College and BA in psychology from the University of Nevada, Reno.

Michele D. Wallace is Program Director of the Center for Severe Behavior Problems and a Senior Behavioral Consultant for multiple school districts, as well as local service agencies. She is on the board of editors for the *Journal of Applied Behavior Analysis* and is a current member of the American Psychological Association, the Association for Behavior Analysis, the California Association for Behavior Analysis (board member), and the Nevada Association for Behavior Analysis (President-Elect). She has been a Board Certified Behavior Analyst in the State of Florida since 1993 and a National Board Certified Behavior Analyst since 2000. She has over 10 first-authored publications and 17 coauthored publications; she has presented over 140 presentations. Her current research interest are related to the refinement of assessment and treatment methodologies with respect to behavior problems, parent and staff training, the acquisition of verbal behavior, and the interaction between stimulant medication and behavior in children with ADHD. She graduated from the University of Florida in 2000 with her doctorate in the experimental analysis of behavior under the guidance of Dr. Brian Iwata.

Amy Watson is Assistant Professor of Social Work at the Jane Addams School of Social Work, University of Illinois, Chicago. She was the Project Director for the Chicago Consortium for Stigma Research. A social worker by training, her research interests include mental illness stigma and issues related to persons with mental illness who become involved in the criminal justice system.

Tonya S. Watson is currently employed at Girls and Boys Town in Omaha, Nebraska. Her research interests include behavioral pediatrics, relationship between olfaction stimuli and memory/learning, and teacher resistance during behavioral consultation. She received her PhD in school psychology from Mississippi State University in 2004.

Jessica A. Whiteley, PhD, is Assistant Professor of Psychiatry and Human Behavior at the Miriam Hospital and Brown Medical School. Her research interests are in the areas of women's health, physical activity promotion and adherence, smoking cessation, Internet technology, dissemination of interventions, and gynecological cancers. She is a principal investigator on one National Institutes of Health (NIH) study and a co-investigator on one Robert Wood Johnson Foundation study and two NIH studies investigating physical activity behavior. She received her PhD in clinical psychology from Virginia Tech in 2001 and completed her clinical psychology internship at the Medical University of South Carolina in 2001.

David M. Williams, PhD, is currently a postdoctoral Fellow in clinical psychology at the Centers for Behavioral and Preventive Medicine at the Miriam Hospital and Brown Medical School. He has experience in developing and implementing physical activity interventions. He has expertise in critical analysis and integration of theoretical variables from various health behavior models that are particularly relevant to physical activity adherence. He received his PhD in clinical psychology from Virginia Tech in 2004.

Index